THE CENTENARY

OF

THE METHODIST CHURCH IN SOUTHERN ASIA

THE CENTENARY
OF
THE METHODIST CHURCH
IN
SOUTHERN ASIA

BY

JOHN N. HOLLISTER, Ph. D.
John N. Hollister.

THE LUCKNOW PUBLISHING HOUSE
OF
THE METHODIST CHURCH IN SOUTHERN ASIA
LUCKNOW, INDIA
1956

First Printing 1956

SET UP, PRINTED AND BOUND BY THE LUCKNOW PUBLISHING HOUSE OF THE METHODIST CHURCH IN SOUTHERN ASIA, AT LUCKNOW, U. P. INDIA.

To

My Father and Mother

who laboured with boys

in the

South India Conference

1888-1920

in training

the heart, the head and the hands.

Foreword

Not all books on art are works of art; many books on literature re not literary productions; and much writing on history lacks historic alue. But here is an historic book on church history. We commend it o all who are interested in the Church of Christ or the Kingdom of God r the welfare of humankind.

Readers of this volume will quickly discover reasons for the selection f John Norman Hollister to write it. The broad sympathy, penetrating nsights, capacity for understanding appraisals and lucid style which are evealed on every page were well known to those who invited him to ndertake the project. But there were other reasons for his choice vhich the author's modesty has kept him from revealing. For 44 of the 00 years of history of which he writes, Dr. Hollister has been an inside bserver and a participant in many of the important developments which e records. Moreover, his parents had fruitful experience in Methodist istory-making for 24 years before he himself joined the missionary ranks, nd for some years thereafter. To whatever extent the distilled wisdom nd understandings of experience can be imparted as a legacy by wise arents in that greatest of school rooms, the dedicated Christian home, o that extent Dr. Hollister's understandings have profited by parental e-enforcement. The combined services of members of the Hollister family s Methodist missionaries in Southern Asia have exeeded 140 years.

Church history is an inexhaustible mine. Dr. Hollister's studies have rovided him with more wealth than he can share with us in a single olume. A dozen books this size would not provide space enough to set ut for examination and appraisal all that he has learned about personal, nstitutional, congregational and connectional achievements in the glorious ine of splendor that unites the Methodist Church in Southern Asia today vith its beginnings in 1856. Marvel not, then, that the names of many otables of this and earlier generations and exploits of which you may now are not to be found in the pages of this book. But join with me n appreciation of the skills that have enabled the author to include o much.

Without the protection of factual knowledge the human mind tends o erroneous assumptions about history. Of no realm of knowledge can it be so well said that the average person knows so much that isn't tru In the Church as in all other areas of his thought and activity, man suffe because he does not know the lessons that God has tried to teach hi and his fellows. Mistakes that others have committed before him a repeated because he has not learned from their experience. Every d all over the world pastors and church committees are repeating the mi takes of their predecessors because they are ignorant of the lessons the predecessors learned through painful experience. The more churc history we study with understanding, the more likely we are to avoi vain repetition of error. We hope this book will prove a guide away fro defeat and to victory for many readers.

J. Waskom Pickett

Preface

The writing of this History was not self-assumed. Rather we and our children had expected that our missionary years would terminate with our furlough in 1954. But when, after the Central Conference in 1953 the Interim Committee invited me to undertake this task I could not refuse for I had felt that India should have a history of its Centenary as China did. I hoped some one would do it.

In the fall of 1889 Bishop Thoburn was on an extended tour of the southern portion of the India field. Under date of September 16 at Nagpur, he wrote in his Journal: "Have been visiting pleasantly at the Hollisters." For them also the visit was pleasant but for another reason it was never forgotten. Their eldest son had been long and seriously ill, and the best available doctor at Nagpur and Kamptee held out little hope of his recovery. At family prayers Bishop Thoburn prayed that the boy might be restored to health, and from that hour anxiety was lifted and the parents felt assured that he would recover.

For that boy the writing of the history has been both a task and a trust. It has also been a rewarding experience in bringing to life names of people and places that I often heard in our home in Kolar. Few, if any, survive, who attended the first session of the South India Conference to be held at Kolar when the Hollister brothers, wearing turbans, helped serve meals to the Conference guests.

During the period of this study my wife, who as Ruth Larson was a missionary of the Woman's Foreign Missionary Society, has by her encouragement and help been my Editorial Associate. She has helped me in gathering material, in criticism of rough drafts, and by assuming most of the responsibility for checking references and proof.

MORADABAD — JOHN N. HOLLISTER

September 1956

Acknowledgments

With their request to me to write the History, the Interim Committee helpfully named an Advisory Editorial Committee, including: M. H. Harper, W. R. Hogg, R. J. Macwan, G. S. Sahai, Miss M. Dimmitt, G. B. Garden and C. B. Stuntz. They met in Jabalpur in 1954 and decided some preliminary matters. Each, in different ways, has since helped: some have kept me from errors in judgment; others have made suggestions in regard to form, and several have sent material. To each I express my gratitude.

Our furlough in America gave me the opportunity to gather material not available in India, and made me debtor to several Librarians: to Miss Dorothy Woodruff, Research Librarian of the Board of Missions and Church Extension who has also sent me needed data since returning to India; to the Librarian in the Missionary Research Library of the Union Theological Seminary who kindly loaned copies of the Bombay Guardian to the Board of Missions Library for my convenience; to Albert W. Cliffe, Pastor of St. George's Church, Philadelphia, who made available material from their select Historical Library; to the Librarians at Baldwin Wallace College, Berea, Ohio, who kindly secured the biographies referred to by A. C. Boggess; and to Philip M. Benjamin, Librarian of the Reis Library, Allegheny College, who graciously adjusted his two days' holiday program that we might delve into Bishop Thoburn's Journals.

I have also to thank J. K. Mathews, Executive Secretary of the Board of Missions, who arranged financial help toward expenses in research; and Karl T. Waugh, son of J. W. Waugh, who in Los Angeles gave me correspondence of his parents that has added materially to the record of the early years.

In India also, I am greatly indebted to very many. From the beginning Bishop Pickett has encouraged me in this work and I am grateful that he consented to write the Foreword. Two old comrades in the North India Conference have given special help: Elbert Moffatt early made available a most useful selection of books on Methodist work in India, and later sent me typescript accounts related to the starting of the Bombay Office and Provident Fund; Murray Titus, for years a student of Islam in India, sent me an account of the opening of the Henry Martyn School of Islamic Studies.

From the Leonard Theological College I have received much: R. D. Immanuel, Mrs. M. H. Harper and C. S. Thoburn who introduced me to the growing Missionary Library, and left me free to browse; H. H. Presler, Director of the Department of Organized Research, for the preparation of all the Line Graphs and Pictographs made by Samuel Cariappa, Samuel Sabana and Sunder Lal Soni (Drawings); J. E. McEldowney for preparing photostatic copies of difficult-to-get material in his Audio-Visual workshop. To all these at Leonard I record my hearty thanks.

H. Ross Bunce, Jr., accepted my request to be responsible for the lay-out of pictures, and also gathered those for the modern period. Miss E. I. Bradley prepared the block graphs representing the growth of the Church in the Episcopal Areas. D. F. Ebright, Audio Visual Aids Director for the North India Conference and a Secretary of the National Christian Council, contributed the cost of the Line Graphs and the Pictographs prepared in Jabalpur. All readers will appreciate the added interest which these friends have contributed. I am particularly grateful to Mrs. Rowena Dique, the typist, for her personal interest and cooperation.

The Lucknow Publishing House where the History has been printed is in the direct succession of the first little hand press in the Mission. W. W. Bell, the Agent, has been indefatigable in personal attention to the production of this History. Its whole make-up is evidence of his care and interest amid difficulties that few can realize. Mrs. Bell has read all of the Proof once and some of it many times. Messrs. E. M. Roberts and M. M. Philip have been diligent in supervision of printing. To these and all who have worked with them I express appreciation.

Lastly, to the many who have encouraged me with their confidence and helped me with material of any kind—thank you.

John N. Hollister

The Growth Of The Missionary Concept

I. IMPOSSIBLE

II. IMPROBABLE

III. IMPERATIVE

IV. INDISPENSABLE

V. INEVITABLE

Attributed to
Dr. J. F. Goucher.

Table of Contents

SECTION III. THE IMPERATIVE

SECTION IV. THE INDISPENSABLE

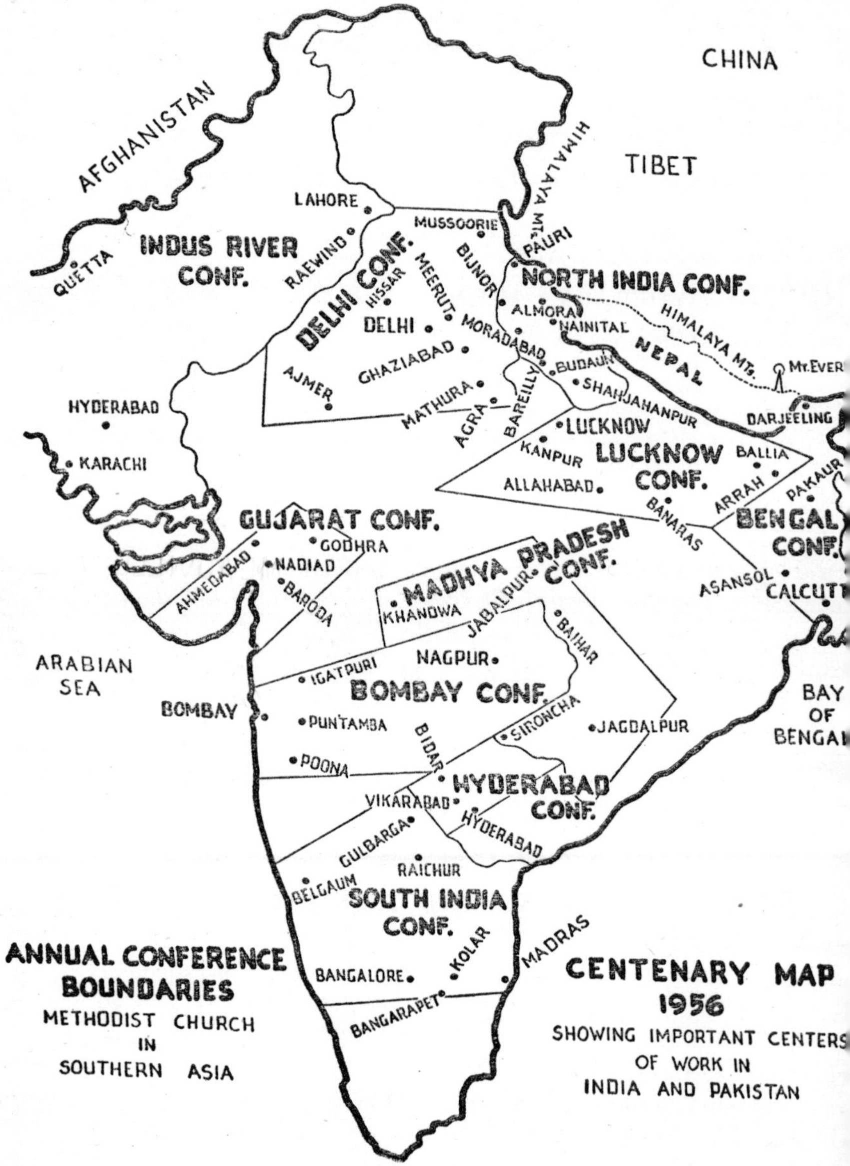
CHINA
AFGHANISTAN
TIBET
HIMALAYA MTS.
LAHORE
MUSSOORIE
PAURI
INDUS RIVER CONF.
QUETTA
RAEWIND
DELHI CONF.
HISSAR
MEERUT
BIJNOR
NORTH INDIA CONF.
ALMORA
NAINITAL
HIMALAYA MTS.
NEPAL
MT. EVER
DELHI
MORADABAD
GHAZIABAD
BUDAUN
AJMER
SHAHJAHANPUR
MATHURA
AGRA
BAREILLY
HYDERABAD
DARJEELING
LUCKNOW
KARACHI
KANPUR
LUCKNOW CONF.
BALLIA
ALLAHABAD
ARRAH
PAKAUR
BANARAS
GUJARAT CONF.
BENGAL CONF.
GODHRA
MADHYA PRADESH CONF.
NADIAD
AHMEDABAD
BARODA
ASANSOL
CALCUTT
KHANDWA
JABALPUR
BAIHAR
ARABIAN SEA
NAGPUR
IGATPURI
BOMBAY CONF.
BAY OF BENGAL
BOMBAY
PUNTAMBA
SIRONCHA
JAGDALPUR
BIDAR
POONA
HYDERABAD CONF.
VIKARABAD
HYDERABAD
GULBARGA
RAICHUR
BELGAUM
SOUTH INDIA CONF.
MADRAS
KOLAR
BANGALORE
BANGARAPET
ANNUAL CONFERENCE BOUNDARIES
METHODIST CHURCH IN SOUTHERN ASIA
CENTENARY MAP 1956
SHOWING IMPORTANT CENTERS OF WORK IN INDIA AND PAKISTAN

Introduction

In India's long history of over four thousand years, a century is ery brief. Through much of that period India received a steady flow f immigration from the northeast with the varied influences that they rought in. From the northwest came both invasions and immigrations vith influences of deeper consequence. There was much intermingling, ut racial differences still characterize large sections of the population. 'et, pervading the country there is a nexus that makes it one. A highly eveloped culture, deep rooted and dominantly religious, marks the early istory. It has become known to modern scholarship through the sacred iterature of the Hindus, and more recently it has been corroborated by rchaeological discoveries.

No other hundred years in this history has been so fraught with reative influences for India as that which culminated in 1947 in her inlependence, and launched her as a Republic into the international position hat she now holds. It was early in this teeming centenary that the first Mission of the Methodist Episcopal Church in India was launched. That Mission has witnessed many of the changes that produced today's India. A few of these we briefly recount.

Background

All ocean travel then was by sailing ships. From America two routes o India were used. The more direct and less expensive was from Boston round the Cape of Good Hope to Calcutta. The ship *Boston* which arried nine missionaries, known afterwards as the *Bostonians*, in 1859, vas a ship of 650 tons. Her cargo was ice from Wenham Lake. T. S. Johnson gives glimpses of the journey of their party in 1862. They ook 141 days, no stop at ports. Near the equator the sea was so calm they vere nine days in practically one spot. "In the tropics the drinking water vent bad—smelled like rotten eggs." The casks were cleaned and refilled vith rain water from the deck.[1]

The second route was taken by the Butlers, as he needed to consult vith representatives of Churches which had missionaries in India. This ay to England, thence to Alexandria, Egypt, by boat; then overland to Suez where they embarked again by ship to Calcutta. The company of missionaries travelling with the E. W. Parkers who were returning fron furlough, in November, 1870, was the first of any of the missions of ou Church to pass through the Suez Canal.[2] With the opening of that rout the port of Bombay became increasingly important.

The East India Company

For 250 years the East India Company had been a rising power i India. Its Charter issued by Queen Elizabeth I on December 31, 1600 was subject to review by Parliament at intervals of twenty years with suc revision as it deemed necessary. The Company was primarily for tradin and it remained such until 1757. It acquired no territory and built n forts until 1688. As the Mughal power weakened, the Company began t employ troops for its own preservation, and later made alliances wit Native States. On June 17, 1757, Clive, who was a young but brillian officer in the Company, defeated the forces of Siraj ud Daula, the Nawa of Bengal, in the Battle of Plassey. This date is usually taken for th beginning of the British Empire in India. In 1764 British supremac was acknowledged by the Mughal Emperor. In 1826 Lord Amhers announced in Delhi that thereafter the Company would be the paramoun power in India. Its monopoly in trade was abolished in 1813, and twent years later it ceased as a trading company and had to confine itself solel to administering its vast territory under rules framed by Parliament.[3]

From 1828 to 1835 the chief officer of the Company, known as th Governor General, was Lord William Bentinck. He instituted certai memorable reforms: (1) The practice of inhuman rites and *thagi* wa suppressed. (2) In December, 1829, it was made an offence to aid or abe a *sati*, the burning of a widow on the funeral pyre of her husband (3) Infanticide was forbidden.[4] This practice was especially commo among the Rajputs and Jats. "In Oudh, just before the Mutiny. . . amon nearly all the Rajput tribes, the great majority of female babies wer murdered."[5] According to reports for the year ending March, 1894, th evil practice had been crushed out in most places, but continued in reduce degree in the western part of the United Provinces and the Punjab.

The East India Company And Missions

The Company gave no help to missionary work. On the othe hand Richter says, "Every foot of broad land which the cause of Mission gained, had to be wrung from it by main force."[6]

> The Company which on many occasions had supporte missionary labor in the South of India . . . changed its religious policy and adopted definitely and resolutely, an inimical attitude toward missionary work. No preaching of the Gospel was to be permitte

in the Company's territories. . . . Every attempt on the part of soldiers to embrace Christianity was suppressed in the Bengal army, though not in the armies of Madras and Bombay which still remained independent.[7]

As late as 1819 a sepoy was expelled from the army for the crime of becoming a Christian, and the Commander in Chief of the Madras army resigned rather than submit to the degradation of saluting idols.[8]

[In 1830] an order was issued to all Chaplains forbidding them to speak to the Sepoys about religion under any circumstances whatever.

When the Charter came up for renewal in 1813, Parliament, in response to 900 petitions, provided that Christian teachers might reside in any part of the Company's territories. The first missionaries of the American Board who had been prevented from landing in Calcutta and had returned to Bombay, remained virtual prisoners under sentence of transportation from India until word of this action was officially received. This policy was further liberalized in the Revision of the Charter in 1833, at which time missionaries of the American Board from Ceylon crossed over and opened the work of this mission in Madura.

Richter gives the following statistics for the Protestant Christian community of all Societies in 1851: Total in India 91,092 distributed as follows: Madras Presidency 74,176; Bengal 14,177; scattered 2,739. "In all other provinces and states of India, nothing but modest beginnings of missionary work could be discovered."[9]

Education

In a careful study of indigenous education in India at the beginning of the nineteenth century, Syed Nurullah and J. P. Naik find that by schools or by private tuition there was considerable opportunity for education. In general, however, they appear to accept two facts: (1) that there was almost no education of females, (2) the educational opportunity that did exist was for all except "those who belong to the low castes or depressed castes"; or "The Pupils of the elementary schools came from all Hindu castes, except the Harijans."[10] The figures for literacy according to a Bombay Census in 1875 were as follows: Bombay Presidency 1 in 20 (19.72); Madras Presidency 1 in 21; Northwest Provinces 1 in 58; Central Province 1 in 67.[11] The figures probably understate the truth, but they do suggest how inadequate the facilities for education had been.

The Decade Of The Fifties

The decade in which Butler reached India was marked with events and developments fraught with great consequence for India and for Missions. As an outcome of a parliamentary investigation prior to the renewal of the Company's charter in 1853, there was issued "The Despatc of the Court of Directors of 1854" also sometimes called "The Magna Chart of English Education in India." It gave an impetus to secondary edu cation and indirectly to primary education. It led to the establishmen of Universities, first in the Presidency cities of Bombay, Calcutta an Madras, all on the model of London University which was then an examin ing body; the grant-in-aid system, and provincial departments of educatior Under the terms of this Despatch the new Mission was able to establis its extensive educational program.

COMMUNICATIONS

In 1851 the telegraph was introduced and rapidly extended over th country connecting its main cities.

Postage rates from Boston to Bareilly were thirty-eight cents fo letters and ten for a newspaper, until India joined the Latin Union, whic was the first to fix international rates.

Railroad construction commenced in 1853. A chart put out by th Government in a centenary celebration showed twenty miles had bee constructed in the first year. In 1856 the Butlers could travel only seventy six miles by rail from Calcutta to Raniganj. In 1859 there was a secon stretch from Allahabad to Kanpur. Miss Butler tells how her parent travelled beyond the railway in small carriages drawn by men.[12] Th *Bostonians* were in carriages drawn by horses, and it took them from Augus 26 to September 3 to reach Lucknow.[13] With the railways came bridge across the great rivers. Prior to that, crossings were by small boats, or o the backs of men in the dry season, or over pontoon bridges which wer removed during the monsoon.

IRRIGATION

Dr. Humphrey narrates an incident which shows how great a chang has come about in the thinking of the people. The Government ha completed work on a section of the Ganges Canal near Hardwar, and ha set April 8, 1854 for its opening.

> The Hindus all around, were greatly excited. They could no believe that the Mata Ganga would allow any portion of her sacred wate to flow in this channel made by the hated Faringhis. The Priest assured the people that Ganga would utterly refuse to flow in this alie channel.[14]

Over a half million people had gathered, anxiously watching Officials and engineers stood near the gates. When they were opene water flowed in!

> Amazement and anguish transfixed the people. . . . They straine their eyes, then turned to tell the breathless crowd to reproach th

> priests. . . . Then one terrible despairing groan burst from their lips, and with bowed heads and sinking hearts they slowly dispersed.[14]

AN AMERICAN?

Butler tells how an Indian gentleman came to his house to tell him that his coming to Bareilly had brought anxiety to the people. They felt he was involved in a plot with Government to change their religion. Butler told them he was not connected with the Government; he was not an Englishman. The caller exclaimed, "Why, Sahib, your face is white, you talk the English language, and are by religion a Christian; what else can you be but an Englishman?" Butler told him he was an American. More confused still, he asked, "A what?" He had never heard the word before, "nor perhaps one in 10,000 of his race." The name became familiar when during the American Civil War the cotton famine raised the price of Indian cotton.[15]

THE NATIONAL UPRISING OF 1857

The causes of the Uprising, now known as the First War of Independence, were many. The people had been stirred to believe that a great plot was afoot to break their caste and then make them Christians. There was a prophecy, heard very soon after Plassey, 1757, that British rule would not last more than one hundred years. The end of that period was near. This conflict had a benign result, for it put an end to government by the East India Company.

GOVERNMENT

On November 1, 1858, by proclamation of Queen Victoria, the Crown through a Secretary of State for India, became directly responsible for the Government of the Country. To the people, this assurance was given:

> Firmly relying ourselves on the truth of Christianity and acknowledging with gratitude the solace of religion, we disclaim alike the right and the desire to impose our convictions on any of our subjects. We declare it to be our royal will and pleasure that none be in any way favored by their religion, faith or observances, but that all shall enjoy the equal and impartial protection of the laws; and we do strictly charge and enjoin those who may be in authority under us that they abstain from all interference with the religious belief or worship of any of our subjects on pain of our highest displeasure.[16a]

Preparing For The Mission

> God, as in former ages, still prepares special leaders for special emergencies in the onward march of His Church for the saving of the nations.
>
> Frank W. Warne.

If the "decade of the fifties" seemed an opportune time for opening a Mission in India, events in American Methodism moved toward the same end. Dr. Durbin who had become Corresponding Secretary of the Missionary Society in 1850, brought to his task an "intense earnestness" for the missionary enterprise. Under his leadership the General Missionary Committee in 1852 set aside $7,000 for the commencement of a Mission in India in 1853. Bishops and Secretary began the search for a Superintendent. Failing to find the needed person the Committee continued the appropriation for the next year. In 1854 Alexander Duff, veteran of many years in India, visited America. His messages stirred the Churches, but in this year, too, no Superintendent was found, and the Committee for a third time appropriated money for an India Mission. The search for a Superintendent continued, for to Secretary Durbin and his Missionary Committee the call of India—steady, oft-repeated, as of God—continued to bring its challenge to their Church.

In the spring of 1855 Dr. Durbin, stirred by apparent defeat, wrote an article in the *Christian Advocate and Journal* entitled "The Crisis"in which he indicated his deep concern that the Bishops had "not been able to obtain a minister. . . as founder and superintendent of the Mission," although "this is the third year. . . [that] the money for the commencement of a Mission in India has been provided."[16]

We date Methodism's First Century for Christ in India, 1856 to 1956. Yet, years before the Missionary Committee made its first appropriation for the Mission in India, God had started—across the Atlantic, in hidden corners of the United States, and in India—to prepare the men who would be leaders in that Mission. The Methodist Church did well to plan from 1852. Her long search and anxiety created the interest needed to sustain the enterprise after it could be commenced.

William Butler

In the city of Dublin, Ireland, in 1836, William Butler was a young man in his nineteenth year, a member of the established Church, an attendant on its services and Sunday Schools and diligent in all his duties. He had won prizes for Scripture knowledge. He had never doubted that he was a Christian; he had been baptized and confirmed.

One of Her Majesty's Judges moved to a manor not far from William's residence. His wife was a religious person, regular in attendance at church services, but "she loved worldly splendor and the gaiety of fashionable life." She also loved music and had hired a Welsh harpist, who was wholly blind, to teach her. On a Monday morning she told him what a fine sermon she had heard the day before and asked him whom he had heard. With trepidation he replied: "I went to the Methodist Chapel and heard a Methodist preacher." Pressed as to why he had been with that "fanatical and ignorant" group, he bore witness of what God had done for his soul. She then resolved that she, too, would find out for herself if there was reasonable and scriptural justification for such confidence as the harpist had shown. Was it true? She went the next Sunday. The preacher's sermon went to her soul. Soon she, too, knew it was true.

She became anxious for others, her husband and her servants. From her home she daily walked out, tracts in hand, and talked with people about religion. Butler determined to avoid her but one day he could not dodge. In reply to her question, "Young man, do you pray?" he said, after thought, "No, madam, I don't," for he knew that she did not mean formal prayers. "Well, if you do not pray, what is to become of your soul? . . . Young man, God is not only able and willing to save your soul, but He is also willing to make you the means of the salvation of other people." William Butler attended the Methodist chapel with her.

> The hearty singing, the extemporary prayers, the experimental preaching, [preached, not read], all delighted me. . . . I concluded at once that these people should be my people for life. One Sunday afternoon while in a [class] meeting for Christian fellowship, . . I felt and knew that I was saved. . . . I felt a new zeal to do anything that my blessed Master might require of me.[17]

Some time later Dr. Durbin, then President of Dickinson College, preached in a Dublin Church. Butler heard him with delight and that night a special interest in America sprang up in his mind. Then he attended the Centenary of Wesleyan Methodism at Liverpool. He developed "an enlarged appreciation of the work of God being accomplished throughout the world" by the Wesleyan movement. In Liverpool he preached his first sermon. He had been announced without being asked and when he remonstrated, his friend replied, "My Brother, you must preach the Gospel or you will lose your religion." So nervous was Butler, that after he had announced his text "Ye must be born again," he said, "I immediately closed my eyes and dared not open them again until my poor little sermon was ended." Forty-four years later he heard of a man who was converted under that sermon.

He went to Didsbury College for a course in Theology. "When God saved my soul," wrote Butler, "he imbued me with the missionary spirit." In England he met missionaries: he heard missionary addresses; he read missionary literature, "the grandest of all literature"; he started a missionary library.

> In the meantime, I had been brought into intimate relations with Rev. James Lynch, who on the death of Dr. Coke [when on his way to start a mission in India] had become Superintendent of the

> Wesleyan Mission in the East. He had now returned home and was in the last years of his ministerial service, and being feeble, I was sent to assist him. From this venerable man, I learned much that was calculated to enlarge my views, and deepen my interest in missionary work, especially in India. The theme became familiar to my thoughts and sympathies.[18]

In 1844, Butler joined the Irish Conference and in 1848 was ordained. In 1850 he went to America where he joined the New York Conference and two days later was transferred to the New England Conference. He used his pen to stimulate zeal for Missions in the Methodist Church. In 1852 he published a *Compendium for Missions*, and contributed articles on British and American Missions to Newcomb's *Cyclopaedia of Missions*. He had known of the Call for a Superintendent for a Mission in India, but he had so recently come to America he felt that a younger man and one more fully in touch with American Methodism should be sent. More than anything he did want that the India Mission should not be abandoned. In October, 1855, he went to New York, "to ascertain quietly whether the way was open for me to offer myself." Learning that still no Superintendent had been found, he consulted his Presiding Elder and then, on October 10, with his wife's full consent, offered to go to India.

The long search for a Superintendent had at last succeeded. William Butler was ready. The Irishman who at his conversion was imbued with the missionary spirit, who was trained at Didsbury and there found his enthusiasm deepened and enriched, and who had so recently crossed the Atlantic was accepted to be Superintendent of the India Mission. He combined the early zeal of Dr. Coke for evangelizing India, with the tremendous energy and faith that marked growing Methodism in America. Looking back he never doubted that he had been "divinely controlled as well as guided" to this task.

James Mills Thoburn

James Thoburn's parents, like William Butler, were from Ireland. In their youth both were fruits of the preaching of itinerant Methodist preachers who found their way into Ireland in the early years of the nineteenth century. Owing to difficulties of getting a start in life in Ireland the Thoburns went to the United States. With their two children they crossed the Atlantic to Quebec, and through the Lakes to Erie, then in a wagon drawn by a pair of horses they wended their way to St. Clairsville, Ohio, where they finally settled. Here James was born on March 7, 1836. His father died when he was a youth, leaving the mother with ten children and a mortgaged farm. Every child had to help.

In 1851 James enrolled at Allegheny, but his schooling was seasonal because of the necessity of earning his way. In his eighteenth year, while a acher in a country school, during a recess period out in the sunshine, he s reading a book on *Early Piety*. This passage arrested his attention:

> 'The middle aged pastor will generally be found unfit for the new duties and ideas of missionary life. The young man on the other hand, has nothing to unlearn. He is pliable and plastic, ready to be molded into any form of physical and mental activity which exigencies of the times may demand. . . . Several of our great benevolent enterprises which are rapidly extending their influence to the remotest nations of the earth were projected by young men while they were still undergraduates.'
>
> Up to this hour, [writes Thoburn], I had never thought of being a missionary or felt interest in mission work. But as I read the above words there flashed upon my mind and heart a clear impression that my life work would be in the missionary field . . . simply there came to me an indefinable and yet clear conviction that this was God's choice concerning me. . . . At this time, I was not enjoying the witness of the Spirit's communion or the Spirit's guidance. . . . Eighteen months later I found Christ and began to live the life of Christian discipleship.[19]

Two years later he had "reached a settled conviction" that he must a preacher. The thought of a mission field "recurred frequently," but other year passed with nothing more definite. One day in the fall of 58 he read in *The Christian Advocate and Journal* that "six young men were gently needed for India." That sentence went home. He dropped the per and fell on his knees and promised God that he would accept the call He would make it clear that He sent him. Thoburn went to his Presiding der for advice. It so happened that the Presiding Elder was to preach at nearby church in that circuit and there they met. The Presiding Elder ened the conversation.

> "I met Bishop Janes on the train this morning."
>
> "Bishop Janes," I replied. "What can he be doing out here?"
>
> "He is on his way West looking for missionaries for India. He wants six immediately." My heart leaped into my throat, but before I could say anything the Elder continued:
>
> "James, how would you like to go?"
>
> "It is very singular," I said, "but I have come here with the special purpose of asking your advice about going to India."
>
> "Well, I must tell you that you have been in my mind all morning. I incline to think you ought to go. I have felt so ever since the Bishop told me his errand."

hoburn went to a little room upstairs to pray. He received such an outuring of God's Spirit that he could not pray. "It was not so much a ll to India that I received as an acceptance for India."[20] Although at hour stood out as his burning bush, yet he "did not feel that the matter was forever settled." Entries in his Journal show how the struggle co tinued.

> December 23rd. I cannot think of much else than Indi Almost fear to meet my mother.
>
> December 28th. . . . Spent the day at home. My mind is muc troubled about going to India. I have little peace except when I co sent in my own heart to go.
>
> December 31st. India engrosses most of my thoughts. "Th will be done, O God."
>
> January 1, 1859. Beautiful morning. Walked out to th woods and alone with God gave up myself finally, for India. M mind is more peaceful since. The matter is now in the hands Providence. I am ready to go to India or anywhere.

Years later Bishop Luccock said of Thoburn:

> His consecration, his zeal, his statesmanship and his resourcefu ness are alike wonderful; but the vital secret of Thoburn's life is thi he lived so close to God he could hear Him whisper, and always kne the way, and what Israel ought to do.[21]

Edwin Wallace Parker

E. W. Parker grew up on a Vermont farm. His mother died when h was nine years old. Shortly before her death she made him "promi to try to be a good boy." The usual religious influences of a home we maintained: the family altar, attendance at Church and Sunday Schoo

As the oldest boy in the family he learned to work when he was ver young. He was given, and very much liked the care of the horses, but h did much else besides. It was the custom in that section to recognize th father's right to the service of his sons until they were of age. If they le home earlier they were expected "to buy their time," that is to pay for substitute. Edwin's father insisted on this right. Between the ages eight and seventeen he never went to school more than three months i any year, when, usually, he attended the winter session in the district schoo In the autumn after he was twenty years of age, he left home to atten Newbury Seminary, "having bought my time, or rather having it give me; for my father gave me $100 and I gave back $25 for time. From th time I was my own 'boy'."

In his teens he was often convicted of sin and as often resisted. I his twentieth year he was especially helped by his pastor, Rev. W. D Malcolm. He writes of a Sunday experience:

> I returned home feeling deeply, yet undecided, until towar evening as I was taking care of the horses at the barn, while I stoo waiting for one to drink, I resolved to become a Christian. I resolve

> to go back to the meeting that evening and arise for prayers . . . that night I gave myself to God. As I entered the Church I went and took a seat with the Christians instead of sitting down with my young associates, and thus evaded what was to me a great obstacle.
>
> That night I believe I gave myself up, to a large degree, but I had not yet learned that I must follow the dictates of the Spirit. That night at family prayers I felt I ought to pray, but neglecting to do so I was kept longer from entering into salvation's stream and being healed, . . . [on the next Wednesday] I attended [meeting] and received a great blessing. . . . A few of us remained with the pastor, and in that little prayer meeting I offered my first prayer in the hearing of others and was greatly blessed; and in the evening meeting I was able to testify that my sins were forgiven and that my soul was happy in God.[22]

Almost as soon as he had this experience he felt that he must "preach ıe Gospel of the Son of God and try to call men to repentance," and he could not drive the impression away." He felt his inability and inexperi-ıce. He loved farming and "had no higher ambition than to be a ›od farmer."

> There was a long and severe struggle in my mind, which I kept mostly to myself. At last I yielded to the convictions of duty, which I could not and dared not resist, and promised "for God to live and die."

It was then that he "bought his time" that he might prepare for the ıinistry, and went to Newbury Seminary. In winter he taught school so ıat he earned enough to return for the spring term. He began to feel the importance of being wholly sanctified to God." Back in Lyndon "while raying alone in the woods, I felt that I was wholly the Lord's; that I loved Iim with all my heart."

In 1856 he married Lois Lee. Before that he told her that he had a onviction that he must be a missionary. She replied that from a child she ad felt she might be a missionary, so both were agreed on this. In May, 857, two months before the Seminary term closed, he accepted an appoint-ıent in the Vermont Conference at Lunenburg. Here in their second ear they read the call of Dr. Durbin for six married missionaries for India Irs. Parker writes:

> At that time we were both teaching in the village school in order to eke out the small allowance that the Church was able to pay us. Family circumstances were such that it seemed out of the question for us to leave America at that time. . . . Still that call from India did not leave us though for some days we did not even speak to each other about it. At last Mr. Parker asked me if I had noticed the call, and did I think we could respond to it. After much prayer and much opposition from friends we decided to offer ourselves and abide by the decision of the Missionary Society. . . . But in December, 1858 the appointment came, and early in March we left our Vermont home.[23]

George Bowen

Most Methodists have long been familiar with the names of Butle Thoburn and Parker. Fewer know "the saintly and venerable" Georg Bowen who definitely aligned himself with the Methodists in 1872, soo after William Taylor opened his campaign in Bombay.

> His praises were in all the churches of the East, and [he] brough with him a commanding influence in the city of Bombay itself. . . He continued the work which he was doing and in this way it may b said that we have always had a vernacular work in Bombay.[24]

George Bowen was born in Vermont on April 30, 1816. His parent were of Welsh descent and were connected with the Protestant Episcopa Church. His father was a business man and hoped that the son would fol low in that line. Instead he developed a strong dislike for a commercia life and early cultivated a taste for literature. Until he was twenty-eigh years of age he openly avowed his disbelief in Christianity. He accepte deism, denying the possibility of the Creator revealing Himself to man kind.

In 1843, at the wedding of a friend, he met a young lady of fin Christian spirit and charm "who was destined to change my life for tim and eternity."[25] She was even then in the grip of consumption but knew it not. She died the next year. She left to Bowen her Bible with the reques that he read it daily. This out of regard for her, he did.

Two months later at a public library he asked for Paley's *Natura Theology*. By mistake the Librarian took down Paley's *Evidences of Chris tianity*. Picking it up Bowen carried it to his room without looking at it title. When he found the mistake he was disgusted, but having time he opened the book and was struck by the opening paragraph and read on He became convinced that the Bible was a revelation from God. Having accepted the possibility of revelation he also accepted Christ.

Shortly thereafter, he decided to become a foreign missionary. On the advice of friends he went to Union Theological Seminary. He was accepted as a missionary of the American Board of Commissioners for Foreign Missions, and in 1847 sailed for India, arriving there on January 19. At Ahmednagar he applied himself to the study of the Marathi language and tried to get into missionary work. He came to feel that "missionaries should study more simplicity, live more economically, do away as far as possible with the social gap that separates them from the body of the Natives; and, in a word, be more apostolic than they are."[26] He gave up his salary from the Board in 1849 but continued his connection as a missionary. By 1855 he had accepted a position on infant baptism which he felt might lead his colleagues to question his continuance in the ıission, and resigned as a missionary of the Board. Ten years later the ıissionaries, with the approval of the Board, invited him to accept again is former relation. This he did and continued in that connection until e joined the Methodist Church in Taylor's movement, but he did not gain accept a salary from any missionary society.

Before he came to India George Bowen had written much. As a hristian, and a missionary, he continued to write. His *Life of Mohammed*, *'he Amens of Christ*, *Daily Meditations*, *Friendly Words to Educated Natives*, *riendly Words to Romanists*, and other works were well known. So greatly id Queen Victoria appreciate his devotional books that when the Prince f Wales, later Edward VII, visited India, she charged him to call on eorge Bowen in Bombay and thank him on her behalf for his books. This e did. His carriage came to a stop in front of the missionary's single room ı the bazaar, and George Bowen went out to receive the royal message.[27]

Bowen was one of five members of the Bombay Missionary Conference who felt the need of a weekly Christian Journal in India, and started *The Bombay Guardian* on March 7, 1851. In a short time one, then another, eft Bombay. With only a brief interruption Bowen continued to edit t until his death. He made it a power for good as an evangelical organ. At his death J. E. Robinson wrote:

> The loss which religious journalism has sustained cannot be estimated, neither can it ever be fully repaired. Few, if indeed any, editors known to India have approached George Bowen in facility of incisive comment on current topics; in masterly analysis of measures, methods, and men's characters; in thorough grasp of all religious, social and political subjects; in intelligent acquaintance with, and insight into, the great modern movements; in power to penetrate the core of a proposition, expose the fallacy of an argument, and pierce the vulnerable point in an antagonist's armour, or in general breadth of literary culture and philosophical attainment.[28]

For eighteen years Bowen served as the Honorary Secretary of the Bombay Tract and Book Society, much of the time living in a small room n the back of the building. His usual abode was a single room in the bazaar, vith the simplest of furnishings. More than once friends in the Church, aking advantage of his absence, would refurnish the room in an effort to nake Bowen more comfortable. In a brief time, he found others who, he hought, needed the things more than he did, and gave them away. If ıe had guests they shared what he had. To his sisters he wrote frequently. The letters give glimpses of his life:

> I get fifty rupees from Mr. Vishnu Pant for editing the *Guardian* he taking all the pecuniary responsibility. Now as to my expenses I am getting very extravagant. I pay Rs. 10/- a month for my house rent; Rs. 6/- to my moonshi, (Hindustani teacher); Rs. 1/4- to my

> dhobi; Rs. 1/10/- to my baker; plantains etc. 1/-; tram etc. Rs. 4/1 send Sister Row Rs. 10/- a month. She opposes this but they a dependent on the Church .... Wearing apparel averages I suppc Rs. 2/- a month or possibly 2/8/-. I subscribe to certain chariti and have applications from the poor which generally make away wi the remainder of the money ....I was weighed about a year ago ar my weight was 92 lbs., a good weight for a jockey. Perhaps I shou have been one.[29]
>
> I am studying Hindustani with the hope of preaching in it, ar when I get that I may take up another language. Besides Marathi have not learned any Indian language well.[30] [Written in his sixt fourth year.]
>
> As a missionary his career was altogether unique. While a admired the spirit that animated him in adopting the style of livir which he clung to, and had the profoundest confidence in the puri and sincerity of his motives, few regarded his course as wise. Th apparent lack of success that followed his labours among the native strengthened the conviction of many that his example in this part cular respect was not one that commended itself to missionaries i general for widespread imitation.
>
> It was as a pastor and teacher, a shepherd, a feeder of the Lord flock, that Mr. Bowen excelled, and that the Lord specially used hin He himself said: 'My passion is for winning souls, but it does not plea the Lord to use me that way.' The Lord did use him 'for the perfectir of the saints, unto the working of ministering unto the building up of th body of Christ.'[31]

Joel Thomas Janvier

About 1830 a boy was born to Rajput parents in Banda, Bundelkhan When eight years of age he reached the American Presbyterian Missic in Allahabad. There he was given a Christian training and an educatic that included "a fair knowledge of English with something of Greek an Hebrew." He then became a teacher in that school. He was name Joel Janvier after one of the pioneer missionaries who had been kille by a Muslim fanatic. Butler writes how on their arrival in Bareilly h commenced

> a little class meeting but soon found that Joel did not seem quite a home, and had but little to say in the exercises. So I drew him int private conversation, explained to him what we meant by the witne of the Holy Spirit, and put into his hands the 'Memoir of Williar Carvosso'. ... Before he finished the second reading he told me there wa something described there which he had not experienced. ... H saw the necessity and began to seek it with all earnestness. ... Befor long he found it.[32]
>
> First my heart was against class meeting but thank God tha enmity has gone away entirely, and now I love it very much. I ca

say with David, 'Come and hear, all ye that fear God, and I will declare what he hath done for my soul.'[33]

> As a lad he excelled in athletics. He was a man of ample proportions and muscular frame. There was a charm about his spirit that won and retained acquaintances. . . . He was prudent in council and wise in decision. As an eloquent preacher he had but few equals in any land. . . . His forte was preaching, whether to Christians or non-Christians. It was not so much his powerful exegesis as his beautiful use of Scripture, and the felicities and spirit of the true orator.[34]

> He is well informed, and speaks with dignity, fluency and force, and the missionaries add with unction.[35]

Only five months after he joined Butler, on the outbreak of ghting, Joel had to flee Bareilly, taking the *chaukidar* with him

> and passed, with his little family through its terrible scenes unscathed, though sorely pressed, amid danger on every hand. With his young wife by his side, and carrying his infant girl in his arms, he walked mostly by night, through fields and forests along bypaths, and through jungles, over 300 miles, from Bareilly to Allahabad, much of the time in the very thick of the enemy. . . . But the Lord brought him safely through, for He had a work for Him to do.[36]

After receiving a letter from Joel from Allahabad, Butler wrote to im offering financial assistance if needed. To this letter Joel replied to y that he was not in need:

> As I am at present working on the railway here and earn something to support myself and family, I do not see any necessity of your taking any further trouble about me in regard to money, until such time as I shall be with you again. . . . I am not at all discouraged by this trouble; on the contrary, I hope it has been sanctified to my good. God forbid that I may be discouraged! But may He grant me that grace which may make my hope strong, and my faith firm.[37]

Section I

THE IMPOSSIBLE

Many here in India have a sort of compassionate feeling towards missionaries and the Church of Christ, such as we feel when we see a little child undertaking to roll an immense rock uphill.

George Bowen (1850).

I remember hearing Mrs. Parker tell of the early days on their arrival when they met everywhere angry faces and fierce opposition and not a Christian anywhere. She said, "It was so discouraging and so hard to keep one's faith up to believing that even God could do anything in India".

Frank W. Warne.

India shall yet be one of the brightest gems in the diadem of Christ.

William Butler.

I

Mission to India Commenced

In the above words Church papers proclaimed the glad tidings. "Yes, our projected Mission was begun in good earnest" in a farewell neeting at the Lynn Common Church, Lynn, Massachusetts on April 8, 1856. On Wednesday, many friends were at the steamer *Canada* to bid a last farewell to the Butlers. They had the two youngest boys with them but left two in New England. They stopped in England for consultations on the location of the Mission, and on September 23 reached Calcutta. They tarried here, too, for further consultations with nissionaries and officials of the Government. By all they were cordially received. The Commissioner at Benares, H. C. Tucker, Esq., was eager for Butler to open the Mission in his area. The Butlers left their children n Benares while they continued their journey to Lucknow, which they reached on November 29, where they were entertained in the Residency for a week.[1]

The Oudh Government had recently been taken over by the "Company". Feelings of the people as well as of their former rulers, were bitter. The English officials of the new regime were sorely tried and vould give no help or encouragement for a Mission. Butler tried to find a residence thinking he would stay on in spite of official discouragement, but he was unsuccessful. They then proceeded to Bareilly where they arrived at the home of Judge Robertson, after three o'clock in the morning of December 7, having had "forty-two hours continued traveling from Futtyghur, completely exhausted. . . . Mr. Robertson is very kind to us."[2]

Butler had expected that he would need to build a residence in Bareilly and had so written to Dr. Durbin but on December 9 he wrote again :

> I find that I can obtain a house to rent here, not such a one as we could wish, but still it will do. It is very desirable not to build too soon. Time alone can tell us where and how to expend money in that way. I leave here next week *enroute* for the General Missionary Conference in Benares, and to fetch my little ones up.[2]

On the way back to Benares they went aside to see Delhi and Agra. n the latter place they spent Christmas. While in Benares for the Missionary Conference, the Butlers also had the experience and privilege, as the guests of the Governor, of attending the last durbar of the East India Company, which was held there in the end of December.

On the return journey from this visit, the Butlers stopped at the American Presbyterian Mission at Allahabad. He told them of his need of a young man whom he could trust, and who would be a help to him in opening work before the arrival of two other missionaries whom he was expecting. In the circumstances they spared Joel Janvier. To Butler "he was just the person I needed". He was now married and had a little babe. They had been living with Mrs. Janvier's mother, and there was doubt that she would let her daughter leave. But she did, saying "I give her up to the Saviour". At the time of parting she broke down and said to Mrs. Butler, "She has no mother now but you".[4] The party arrived in Bareilly on January 7, 1857. The Butlers again stayed with Judge Robertson, until they could settle in their rented house, close to the Public Gardens near the Cantonment. This site was marked during the seventy-fifth session of the North India Conference of 1939, when in a service conducted by Bishop J. R. Chitambar, Miss L. W. Sullivan unveiled a tablet on which is inscribed,

> Twenty yards North of this spot stood the house in which Rev. and Mrs. Butler lived and assembled the first congregation in beginning the work of the Methodist Episcopal Church in India, in 1856. To God be the Glory.[5]

On February 20, Butler circulated to the residents of the station, an announcement of religious services to be held at his residence at the following times :

> Every Sunday forenoon at 11 o'clock in the Hindustani language.
> Every Sunday afternoon at 4 : 30 o'clock in the English language.
> On each Tuesday evening at 6:30 o'clock in Hindustani, and
> On each Thursday evening at 7:30 o'clock in English.[6]

The circular also expressed the interest of the Mission in the religious welfare of the Hindu and Mohammedan population and requested the Christian residents not only to give their "countenance and sympathy" but to extend an invitation to their servants to attend one or the other of the Hindustani services, as might be most convenient.

On March 10, one year after he had received his commission, Butler submitted his recommendations for a field to Bishop Simpson and the Board of Managers. The choice was approved. The reasons for it were, (1) it was unoccupied, (2) it was a field of one language, (3) it was compact and well defined.

Butler's plan for occupying the field was to have twenty-five missionaries in six central and a few outlying stations. He felt that acceptance of the field implied commitment to supply the missionaries requested. He ad proclaimed "not only in India but to Christendom" the fixed intent f the Methodist Church, and to fail to meet the promise would be only public dishonour". However, the Society did not find it possible to do so uch, so soon.[7]

FIRST REPORT AND DISRUPTION

On April 1, Butler made a statistical report showing eight persons onnected with the Methodist Church: Butler and his wife, Joel Janvier nd his wife, Ann Hodgkinson, Maria Bolst, Isaac and Palwan. Ann was heir maid; of Isaac's identity we are uncertain. At the outbreak of the Jprising in Bareilly, he escaped toward Budaon and Joel heard that he ad been killed. Joel's letter says that Isaac with Palwan Singh had tried o escape in the guise of gardeners.

Maria Bolst was an Anglo-Indian girl, her father a German. They ived in a small home near the site of the present residence of the District Superintendent. In front of it was a hedge of roses. Maria had been sent o the Baptist Mission School in Calcutta where she was converted and inpired to help her mother's people. Three years earlier she had returned o her home and from that time, prayed most earnestly for missionaries to come to Bareilly. Gladly, she welcomed the Butlers. Her prayers had been answered, and now she would help in any way she could. Often did she and Mrs. Butler sit near that hedge of fragrant roses and talk and plan. They ried a school at home, but no girls came. Then they rented a room in the bazaar and paid an old woman to collect girls, but none came. Butler asked help of an Indian gentleman who knew English, and he replied, "You are going to teach women to read? You will teach the cows next." Then he women visited homes in the mohullas. Here, too, they were refused. Maria has been called "the first indigenous member of the Methodist Church, the young woman who prayed us into Bareilly".[8]

Rumours had been rife for some weeks that Indian soldiers in the Bengal Army, scattered through Bengal and North India, were preparing to mutiny. Most British officers would not believe that the rumours could be true. On May 10, 1857, three regiments in Meerut mutinied, killing their English officers. On the fourteenth, Col. Troup, commanding in Bareilly, sent a personal messenger to Butler urging him to take his family to Naini Tal. They prayed over the matter and they both felt that they should not leave. Twice again before Saturday, Col. Troup pressed his warning and advice. New rumours spread. Sunday was a solemn day. "We had but ten persons at the native service and less at the English one. People seemed afraid to come out. . . . Our class meeting was a solemn but profitable one."[9] After further consultations, it was settled that the Butlers should go. Monday was used in preparations for leaving that evening.

> We were ready when our bearers came at nine o'clock, and I went into my study once more. I looked at my books, etc., and the thought flashed across my mind that perhaps . . . I should never see them again. I took up my Hindustani grammar, two volumes of my Theological lectures, a couple of works on India, my passport, my commission and letter of instructions, with my Bible, Hymn Book and a copy of the Scripture, and woefully turned away, leaving the remainder to their fate.[10]

Butler's was a library of almost 1000 volumes. It had been gathered through sacrifice and was highly valued by him.

By morning they reached Baheri and rested there all day. Setting out again in the evening, all went well until they came to the second stage where they entered the Tarai, which was unsettled jungle. Here only nine of twenty-nine coolies asked for had turned up! Butler knew that there was a bullock cart a quarter of a mile ahead. Desperately, he ran and "by main force drove around the four bullocks, and led them back sorely against the will of the five men in charge of it". He insisted that they take him, Ann the servant, and the luggage in the cart. Two doolies would be left behind. But the men would not move. No persuasion was effective. At his wit's end, Butler stepped aside into the jungle and prayed. He writes :

> If ever I prayed, I prayed then. I besought God, in His mercy to influence the hearts of these men, and decide for me in that solemn hour . . . . And implored His interference in this emergency. My prayer did not last two minutes, but how much I prayed in that time. I put on my hat, returned to the light, and looked. I spoke not. I saw my men at once bend to the dooly; it rose and they went instantly and they never stopped a moment except kindly to push little Eddie in when in his sleep he rolled so that his feet hung out.[11]

Col. Troup's brother had made arrangements for the journey from Kathgodam to Naini Tal and it was accomplished without incident.

The first word about Joel came in a letter dated February 4, 1858 that told how the war broke in Bareilly on Sunday, May 31. At 11 o'clock sepoys commenced shooting their officers. The Emperor of Delhi had been proclaimed and Muslim rule established under Khan Bahadur Khan in Bareilly. Judge Robertson and other officers were condemned to death. Joel had just preached to his small congregation on the text "Fear not little flock".

> About the middle of the closing prayer I was informed about the outbreak. I instantly closed and began to look out for my wife and child. The chowkidar [watchman] aided me in getting the Christian women concealed. I then returned to the bungalow [where the service had been held]. By this time, it was partly looted and in flames.

> Seeing it on fire, I threw down the keys, thinking, "No use to keep them now". He went again to see if the women were safe. He saw Isaac escape from an attack and then flee toward Budaon. 'I heard he was killed on the road. I saw Maria coming, running through the trees, but before any of us could reach her a *sowar* [mounted soldier] caught sight of her and turned, and with his *talwar* [sword] he struck her head off'. The Butler's *dhobin* [washerwoman] buried Maria under the rose hedge where often she had sat with Mrs. Butler.[12]

Naini Tal proved to be a refuge for the Butlers not only from the fighting, but from the summer's heat. Until recent years, it has continued to be the summer sanitarium for North India missionaries and their families. On May 31, Butler preached twice, "the first Methodist sermons ever uttered on the Himalaya Mountains",[13] the morning service at the same hour that Joel had preached in Bareilly. All summer, Butler with other men, had to serve in an armed guard to defend the women and children. The passes for entry were continually watched. On August 4 when a large force was reported to be moving for Naini Tal, the Commander in Naini Tal ordered the women and children to be moved to Almora, and Butler was designated to accompany them. The refugees could not be starved out although they did have severe privations, for Sir Henry Ramsay, the Commissioner, had the complete confidence of the hill people who "accepted his notes as money to be redeemed when England should re-establish her authority".

Planning Anew

Butler had become acquainted with two Englishmen who had decided to join him in the work. They were delayed until early in 1858 when they reached Naini Tal. One was Josiah Parsons, a son of British Methodist parents, who had been in India for five years and who was proficient in the language. He had been "received on trial in the Northwest Indiana Conference and appointed to India".[14]

The other was Samuel Knowles who had come to India in the army in 1852 and in 1854 had transferred to the Educational Department. He was in Meerut when the fighting began and immediately enlisted in the Meerut Light Horse. He describes his new allegiance in words that reveal his spirit:

> When the Great Captain lifted us out of the military saddle, after the stress and danger of the sepoy war were over, and gave us a better warfare to accomplish, even the 'Good fight of faith' in mission work, He enlisted us in this work for life, so we intend by the grace and strength of God, to fight on till we fall into an Indian grave. Our motto here on Indian soil is that of the Roman general, '*aut vincere aut mori*'.[15]

The Quarterly Conference at Lucknow had cordially recommended him for admission on trial in the New England Conference.[16]

On the very day, May 31, that war broke in Bareilly, when Joel was speaking to his "Little Flock", there gathered in Boston, another group to bid farewell to Rev. and Mrs. J. L. Humphrey and Rev. and Mrs. Ralph Pierce. They sailed the next day and landed in Calcutta on September 22, 1857. Butler had arranged for a house to be rented for them until they could travel up country, and they improved their time in language study.

In the fall Butler needed money. He had "exhausted every resource and to borrow any more was impracticable". He held a bill of exchange which could now be cashed in Delhi, that city having been relieved in September. After receiving a letter, dated September 30, from Pierce and Humphrey, he started for Delhi with Mrs. Butler and the baby girl who had been born in Naini Tal on June 30, — the Mutiny baby they called her — leaving the two boys behind; they took the route through Garhwal and on December 5, reached Dehra Dun. After a halt there they proceeded to Delhi *via* Saharanpur and Kurnal and arrived there Christmas week.[17] They were present at a Christmas service held in the Diwan-i-Khas, within the fort at Delhi; and the next day, in the same place, Butler witnessed the trial of the Nawab of Ballabhgarh. Weary of standing, and looking for a seat Butler's eye caught " the crystal seat, no more to be occupied by its imperial master"[18] and sank down upon it. Looks of surprise he saw, but none forbade, and there he sat, and watched, and thought, "What does this mean for the Mission?" Always that question was on his mind, and the words "foundations broad and deep". From that seat he wrote to Dr. Durbin of the revelation then vouchsafed to him. He describes the experience as "one of the most exalted occasions" in his life. Clearly he saw that the new Mission must be prepared to care for orphans, boys and girls, who would be left desolate because of the uprising and the famine that would assuredly result from the disorganization. No less clearly he saw "the brightest feature as the opportunity which was involved *for woman*," by the family strength which would inhere in the Church when these trained *girls* would become the cultured wives of future teachers and preachers and with this the need of a Woman's Society in the Church. "They had no merely human authorship. They were originated by the divine suggestion."[19] In his letter he made his first move for both.

Arrival of Missionary Recruits

From Delhi the Butlers returned to Meerut, where they stayed for two months. He wrote to Pierce and Humphrey in Calcutta, asking them to meet him in Agra at the Taj Mahal. They traveled up country with Mr. Parry, brother-in-law of Parsons, and on March 11, arrived at Agra.

> Some well-furnished rooms in a building . . . called the Jawab, had been vacated for us by Rev. M. Evans and lady, who had meanwhile gone to stay with some friends in the fort. They left their servants and a nice dinner cooking for us. How we ate, rested and refreshed ourselves ![20]

At night, the attendants lighted the central room with candles. "The blaze of light from the walls was magnificent. We gathered around the tombs of the Moghal king and queen and sang the Doxology."

Butler wrote to the Missionary Secretary an expression of his great joy on the arrival of these recruits.

> I have them at last ! Glory to God ! Here they are safe and well. They have just come in, Oh, how I longed to see them after my privation of 22 months; what a joy it was to grasp their hands, and kneel down together to offer up our grateful thanks to God that I was once more among my own brethren and sisters ! And, oh Doctor, they are evidently the right manner of missionaries. It is manifest enough what kind of spirit they have.[21]

They left Agra on the next day and on the thirteenth Joel Janvier overtook them. He had left his wife and child in Allahabad to join him later.[22] They tarried until March in Meerut. Besides the missionaries the travelers included Marilla, the Pierces' daughter, Joel, Samuel and Bella. These last were a married couple picked up in Saharanpur, and now going to Naini Tal in the hope that in the new mission they might "turn over a new leaf".[23] The party arrived in Naini Tal on Saturday, April 17, about midnight. For the Pierces and Humphreys, it was almost eleven months from the date of leaving Boston. They were met by Mr. Parsons at the top of the hill and led to their new homes.

> The day after our arrival was Sunday, and we intensely enjoyed its rest and quiet. In the afternoon a service was held in the parlor of Mr. Butler's residence, and a good number of prominent people were present, especially ladies. The gentlemen were mostly in the plains on duty with the army. . . . Mr. Butler preached a delightful sermon, and it was a treat to hear a sermon again. A little later our superintendent was honored with the title of Doctor of Divinity from one of our home colleges, an honor most worthily bestowed in this instance. He was a very superior preacher. The service begun that afternoon has been continued ever since. For more than a score of years it was conducted as an evening service only; in the morning a Hindustani service was held. Our English Church in Naini Tal has been a power for good in all these years. [1905] [24]

Beginning Again

The "war" over, and a group of workers ready, work was opened in Naini Tal, where India Methodism has had its longest continuous service. Butler had purchased a property of over six acres known as "The Ruins" in a most favourable location for $1650.[25] A school for boys was started at once in the bazaar, and a building to accommodate it on our first property in India was completed before the end of the year. A school for girls was opened at Pierces' residence. Butler describes the first place of worship:

> The sheep-house [on the new property] was transformed in three days. We cleared it out, a quantity of clay was thrown in and leveled which beaten down made a good floor. I whitewashed it; Brother Pierce and Humphrey made the benches; Joel saw to the leveling of the grounds outside. When it was finished and swept out, though too humble to have a formal, public dedication awarded it, yet I was resolved that a hearty consecration to God's service it should not lack, so I shut the door and all alone knelt and offered to the condescending God of mercy, this humblest of all places where He records His name.
>
> On the following Sabbath morning, the unpretentious little church was opened for service.[26]

Here Humphrey preached his first sermon in Hindustani in September, 1858. In October, Sir Henry Ramsay laid the corner stone of a new Chapel (the present "Hindustani" Church), the first Methodist place of worship erected in India.[27] Its cost, $2500, was subscribed by Sir Henry and his acquaintances in Almora and Naini Tal.[28] Its completion was delayed by the opening of new stations. It was dedicated on the first Sunday in May, 1860.[29] From the time of the completion of the school building until dedication, the school was used for worship services.

On July 10, 1857, Butler wrote to Durbin: "We have lost neither heart nor hope. This country has a bright future before it, and our mission will live, and 'triumph in Christ'."[30] The Mission indeed had passed through "a fiery trial" but with peace re-established the team now gathered around Butler rejoiced greatly at the prospects opening before them. They met in council in "The First Annual Meeting", at Naini Tal on August 20, 1858: three ordained missionaries; Preacher on trial: J. Parsons; European Assistants: S. Knowles, Wesley Maxwell; Native Preachers: Joel Janvier, Azim Ali; School teachers: Samuel, Meabrit. Their reports showed:

> Hindustani Class: 1 member, 4 Probationers, 6 Catechumens [orphans].
>
> Mission Class: 12 members.
>
> Soldiers' Class: 6 Probationers. Total membership 29.
>
> The Hindustani congregation averaged 35 ; the English, 90.
>
> Boys in school, 25; Girls, 16.

Plans for "stations for the coming year", with appointments, were: *Bareilly*, J. L. Humphrey, J. Parsons, Azim Ali, Samuel. *Lucknow*, R. Pierce,

Vesley Maxwell, Joel Janvier. *Naini Tal,* S. Knowles and a Native teacher.[31] change made in these plans a few weeks later provided for Parsons to open ork in Moradabad.

On March 21, 1859 Butler, Pierce and Humphrey jointly signed a Statement and Appeal" as "Missionaries of the Methodist Episcopal Church India" for Rs. 60,000, to be raised in India for residences for twenty new iissionaries. The statement set forth a plan for occupying some stations strength, and reaching "the smaller places around them by a regular ystem of itinerancy and the establishment of schools". The first uarterly reports from missionaries-in-charge were made to the Superntendent for the period April to June, 1859.

Naini Tal

For Naini Tal Station, S. Knowles reported that preaching services were held in the completed school building and that a good number from he bazaars attended. Teaching in the school precluded village work. Regular English services were held on Sunday "for the dissenters" with as nany as 100 present. An English service was also held in the hot months or miners working the nearby mines.[32]

Lucknow

Butler and Pierce availed themselves of the earliest permission to leave Naini Tal, and on August 28, reached Bareilly.[33] Butler's bungalow was charred ruins; he saw where Maria was buried and where Joel used to ive. Judge Robertson and others of his friends, civilian and military, had been hanged or shot. "We were to begin again", Butler declared, "and that, too, under brighter prospects." Butler held services on Sunday for the troops and promised as soon as the Mission in Lucknow had been organized that they would return to begin work in Bareilly. Before they had been in Bareilly twenty-four hours a subscription was started to help re-open the work.

They continued their journey to Lucknow by way of Kanpur, being given an escort of native cavalry as far as Fatehgarh. Tradition has it that among the last utterances of Sir Henry Lawrence, leader and hero of the besieged community in the Residency, was, "Let a Christian Mission be established in Lucknow". Soon after the relief of the city, Mr. Montgomery, Commissioner, wrote to Butler advising immediate occupancy by the Mission. And now Butler was back! What a contrast with the city he first visited in November, 1856! Within three weeks after his arrival, "as the result of diligent search", they found premises in Husainabad for sale. Butler paid the price and the purchase was duly recorded. Mr. Montgomery and other gentlemen contributed Rs. 2000 for repairs, and the former supervised their doing.[34]

Leaving Pierce in Lucknow, where he was soon joined by Azim Al Butler returned to Naini Tal. When, in October, ladies were permitte to leave Naini Tal, he with his and Pierce's family, and Joel Janvier, move to Lucknow. An active program including bazaar preaching, English ser vices for British soldiers in the cantonments, class-meetings in English an vernacular, two schools in the compound and another in Saadatganj, wa started. A few orphans were early put in charge of the Mission.

James A. Cawdell, an English Scripture Reader of the Calcutta Cit Mission, joined the Mission on April 1 and worked among the British troop at the Machchi Bhawan Fort.[35] Ralph Pierce prepared the quarterly repor for Lucknow, which as the capital of Oudh, came to be considered the princi pal station of the Mission :

		Members	*Probationers*	*Baptized childre*
English Class ...	...	6	9	5
Hindustani Class	...	6	9	14
Total 49	...	12	18	19

> Early in April, at our Friday evening meeting, while Joel wa preaching, Hoosin Beg, an inquirer, was smitten with conviction an that night found peace. . . . On Sunday, June 12, he with his wife an daughter, was baptized. This Mohammedan family are *our first convert in Lucknow*. . . . At the same time nine orphan children were baptized. . . On Sunday, June 19, our little Hindustani Church was organized.[36]

This report from Lucknow is substantiated by a letter written by Butle from Lucknow, under date of June 13, 1859:

> Yesterday was a blessed day at this station. We dedicated the first party of our orphans to the service of the Holy Trinity . . . and when they had been dedicated to God, came forth from the congregation a Mohamedan and his wife, whom we have had under instruction for several months, and they too were baptized. . . . We had on this occasion the largest congregation in our little chapel that I have seen in it—between eighty and ninety persons, being present. Praise God, we were a joyful band; so the foundation of a Methodist Church is laid in Lucknow.[37]

Moradabad

Mr. and Mrs. Parsons went to Moradabad in late December, 1858. Houses for Europeans had been destroyed during the Uprising and the Parsons had perforce to live in a tent. To help find a residence for him the Humphreys came to Moradabad, January 26, 1859. After much searching they found a house which was scarcely habitable, for "there was neither a glass window nor door in the house".[38] Repairs were begun at once.

Early in February, while Parsons and Humphrey were engaged with .ese repairs, a man from near Garhmuktesar, representing the Mazhabi ikhs, came to them. Their Guru had heard missionaries from Fatehgarh reach and these people wanted to become Christians. The missionaries ad said, "Some day before long, missionaries will come to Moradabad id when you hear that they have come, go to them and do what they tell ou".[39] Thus soon were Methodists brought in touch with the people of eir first Mass Movement. The Mazhabi Sikhs seem never to have been a rge community. They had developed in the Punjab, where a regiment as recruited from among them during the Uprising,

> in which they proved themselves brave and faithful soldiers. An out-caste tribe, they no sooner found their position in society changed by their daring gallantry and their sudden acquisition of wealth, than they evinced a desire to shake off their present religious bonds which associate them with the very lowest class of Sikhs and Hindus.[40]

A move by this group in the Punjab in favour of Christianity had led the opening of a branch of the Church Missionary Society, Peshawar lission at Khairabad, in July, 1860. The Mazhabi Sikhs in Rohilkhand, ere now moved by the same urge to "shake off their religious bonds". 'hoburn defined the group as "Sikhs by religion, if not by race".[41] The ensus report for 1881 describes them as

> good Sikhs who take the *pahul*, wear their hair long, and abstain from tobacco. In spite, however, of these facts, the taint of hereditary pollution is upon them, and Sikhs of other castes refuse to associate with them even in religious ceremonies.[42]

In Rohilkhand "they occupied a very low social position, and large umbers of them had been professional thieves, and were known as such t the time our work commenced among them".[43] E. W. Parker, than whom o other missionary worked harder or longer for their uplift, described them t the time of becoming Christians as "fearfully depraved and altogether neducated".[44]

Parsons' report for Moradabad, divides work in two parts: (a) City: azaar preaching; a city reading room (*ziyat*) open four hours every morng, where "the Scriptures are perused by members"; Hindustani services wice on Sunday, prayer meeting, class meeting; English services Sundays nd Thursdays. (*b*) District: "The number of candidates for Christian aptism among these people (the Sikhs) now exceeds five hundred." Inuirers lived in forty-six villages. "At a village near Joah we have a native hristian and his wife stationed in charge of the work." He was assisted y the Sikh guru who had been recently baptized. "Two Sikh inquirers re stationed in villages nearby" as school teachers and Scripture teachers.

In each of these three villages rooms were rented for use as schools, or fo worship.

> Samuel, the native Christian, spends two days in each of thes three places, instructing the children, catechising the adults, and preach ing the Gospel to as many as he can reach in each neighbourhoo Every Sabbath they meet from all quarters at the little Chapels an spend something like a Christian Sabbath. These are humble begin nings.[45]

The first baptisms in Moradabad were given by William Butler o May 29, 1859. One was an Afghan soldier, "formerly a bigoted Muslim" the other "a guru of the Mazhabi Sikhs". This report of baptisms is sup ported by a letter on June 2, 1859, by Butler from Bareilly which reads "Last Sabbath I baptized our *first two converts at Moradabad*, a Mohammeda Sepoy and a Hindu priest. Both promising cases, and we believe converte in our sense of the term."[46]

Bareilly

In accordance with an arrangement made by Butler as he and Pierc passed through the city, Humphrey spent a month in Bareilly to reliev the military Chaplain. He used the opportunity to open negotiations fo renting Kashmiri Kothi as Mission headquarters. He then returned t Naini Tal until he and Mrs. Humphrey went to Moradabad, and o February 26, arrived in Bareilly to open the work there. A little late Joseph Fieldbrave and Azim Ali arrived, the latter proceeding t Moradabad. Three orphan boys received in Naini Tal, the beginning o the boys' orphanage, were now moved to Bareilly.[47] The Kashmir Kothi was a large building with numerous outhouses, giving ampl accommodation, but it was far from the city.

Humphrey's report is dated June 28, 1859: a usual Sunday congre gation of about 20; a Sunday School of 16; a small day school of 8 scholars; class meetings and prayer meetings every week; no English services. Mrs. Humphrey adds about the school:

> We organized a school in a spare room of the kotee compound of our three orphan boys, Joseph's boy and girl, Masih Baksh and 2 young men who came to us from the Sikh villages of Moradabad.[48]

In closing his report Humphrey writes of "a very intelligent Moham medan . . . who seemed deeply in earnest about his soul. He came again . . . I think him a fit subject for Christian baptism. Pray for Zhoo-al-haq."[49] This seeker was baptized, as India Methodism knows, "the first convert in Bareilly" as described by E. W. Parker in 1882,[50] won in bazaar-preaching shared by Humphrey and Fieldbrave, and described by the former as "un- furling the banner of Christ in the heart of the city of Bareilly."[51]

It is noteworthy that of the first five converts reported at this time four had been Muslims. Not less noteworthy is Butler's comment: "How remarkable it is that with few exceptions every convert God has given us has more or less adaptation to become assistants in the great work".[52] Among these Zahur al Haqq was outstanding.

ZAHUR AL HAQQ

He wrote his own account of his life. He was born a Sunni in 1834 at Tilhar. From the age of twelve he studied Persian, Arabic and some Hindi, and was carefully instructed in his own religion. But he had no spiritual satisfaction. At the age of twenty he inquired into other religions, and to this end he joined the Parnamis, a Hindu sect. With them he got some comfort, but "of their religious experience I had not a particle". At this time, he first heard the Gospel preached on the streets of Bareilly, when the preachers told of the birth of Christ as given in Luke. At his home Zahur al Haqq compared what he heard with the Quran, and "from that day my heart turned toward the Christian religion".

He was then a teacher in a small school. One day he closed his school early so that he might hear the preachers again. As they returned home he followed them. Realizing that some one was following they turned and asked what he wanted. Hesitatingly he asked for a Gospel. He was invited to Kashmiri Kothi. He spent the night in Fieldbrave's home and met the family. He was deeply impressed by their kind treatment. The following Sunday he was present at the worship service. The next week he visited the Mission and studied the Christian doctrines. On Sunday, again, he was at service and also Sunday School. He asked for baptism but Humphrey put him off for another week, when the baptismal service was held. It was previously announced and English and Hindustani friends were present. His father and others tried to make him recant. He spent a day in his home but was unable to persuade his wife to join him. She would not, and prevented the son, Fazl Haqq, from doing so, until he reached his majority when he did join the father, and later entered the ministry.[53]

On two things the records seem clear : (1) there had been no rivalry between stations for "the first convert" or the facts would have been early established and Humphrey's inquiries as to who was first in the Mission, needless;[54] (2) the date of Zahur al Haqq's baptism is uncertain. Humphrey's report of June 28 describes him as "a fit subject for baptism" —not then baptized, and later records his date of baptism as July 24, Sunday.[54] The convert's own account gives June 15 as the date. This was not a Sunday. This date is also used in his Memoir.[55]

In an article about Joseph Fieldbrave, published in 1875, Humphre refers to Zahur al Haqq as "our first convert, and was baptized *in June, think, of* 1859".[56] Mrs. Humphrey collected her letters to her mother i a little volume entitled *Six Years in India.* In a letter dated June 10, 1859 her narrative agrees in its sequence of steps leading to baptism on "Sabbath morning," and then she adds, "Zahur al Haqq's daily life *sinc that time* has been all we could wish. We have engaged him as a teacher i our school."[57] Whether the letter was completed on the day it was dated we have no way of knowing.

AMBICA CHARAN PAUL

He was born in 1843 in Bengal. At the age of seven he attended a Mission School and his heart was touched by the prayer of a Christian teacher on the first day. At the age of twelve a friend gave him a Bible which he read with interest. The seed of the Gospel found good soil.[58] His desire to be a Christian had met with opposition among his relatives. As a youth he moved with his young wife to Bareilly where he lived with his father-in-law who was the local Post Master. He had "watched the course of Zahur al Haqq with great interest," and was again attracted when he heard the bazaar preaching of Humphrey and his associate in 1861. He did not conceal his interest in the Christian religion. He frequently visited the Mission and "attended our Hindustani services as steadily as he could". He arranged with Humphrey a date for his baptism, expecting that his wife would also be baptized with him. On the date fixed Ambica Charan came, but much later than the hour set, and alone. The wife had been prevented by her father. Another date was fixed. The relatives made every effort to dissuade him. At Humphrey's request Butler baptized him on October 8, 1861.

Shortly after, the father-in-law went to Humphrey's house to see his son-in-law. Not expecting trouble Humphrey left the two in a room alone. Watching for his opportunity the visitor "dealt Ambica a murderous blow, saying as he did so, 'I am ready to be hanged for you' ". The blow did not inflict serious injury. Ambica Charan remained faithful. He never did get his wife and child back.[59]

The Period of Annual Meetings

Butler spoke of a meeting in Naini Tal in 1858 as "The First Annual Meeting". Since all members were then resident in the only station with work, we follow Reid and Gracey's account in considering the meeting of 1859 as the First in a series when members gathered annually from scattered stations to plan together.

The date of this meeting, Monday September 5, 1859, was set to nake it possible for the *Bostonians* to reach Lucknow. They arrived Saturday night: Rev. and Mrs. J. R. Downey, Rev. and Mrs. C. W. Judd, Rev. and Mrs. E. W. Parker, Rev. and Mrs. J. W. Waugh and Rev. J. M. Thoburn. Rev. and Mrs. James Baume had arrived in July.[60] The group that gathered now included nine American men, three English nen and Joel Janvier. The Americans were all members of Annual Conferences in the States, where rules of procedure were known, where ssues were decided as well as discussed and where decisions could be effected. Here responsibility was so completely vested in the Superintendent that there was nothing for the other men to do but obey directions and thankfully receive such funds as he thought proper for carrying on heir work. The situation was an unfortunate one, and in time grew to be intolerable.[61] Thoburn describes more fully the bewilderment felt by the newcomers.

> We had not sat in council an hour before perplexities began to meet us. The first question raised was a most important one, but we had no answer ready at hand. Young men were present to be received among us, but *how* were they to be received? The conference membership was to be held on the other side of the globe. We had no legal right to touch them, and yet we could not but see that we as a body were expected to do something in the premises, and if not expected, we saw at a glance that it was of the most vital importance to the future harmony and efficiency of the mission that we should have something to say in the matter. Then a most important school had been offered to the mission, and we were suddenly called upon to discuss the question of education as a missionary agency, and teaching as a legitimate part of a missionary's duty. We had first to decide whether we had any right to discuss the question at all, whether the authorities at New York, through the Superintendent, should fix our policy, or whether it should be done by formal action of the missionaries as a body. Next we had to decide whether we should establish schools or confine our work to preaching alone. Next, if schools were to be maintained, what kind of schools were to be established—vernacular, or Anglo-vernacular? And if all these questions could be settled, then who were to be the teachers? Was every missionary to be subject to an appointment to the work of teaching? Was a man who had consecrated all his days to the work of preaching the Gospel to find himself most unexpectedly transformed into a school teacher?[62]

The meeting adopted a memorial to the General Conference of 1860 asking for the status of an Annual Conference. That body

> authorized the Board of Bishops to constitute our Missions in India a Mission Annual Conference at any time before the next General Conference, if in their judgment, it will promote the interests of our Missions in India.[63]

Added to the bewilderment over procedure were apprehensions concerning J. R. Downey's health. He had become ill almost immediately on reaching Lucknow. He died on September 16, only twenty-three years of age. The spirit and consecration of the first Methodist missionary to die on this field, is revealed in the following lines taken from a letter written January 29, 1859 to J. W. Waugh. Both had been students together at Garrett Theological School.

> How much we should strive to become as holy as it is possible for mortals to be . . . Our God demands it. What physical or moral obstacle is there to prevent our becoming burning or shining lights in the Church of God ? Why may we not be as holy as a "Wesley" or as "sanctified" as any other human being that has stood out in bold relief as monuments of the power of Divine grace to save the soul from sin or uncleanness? . . . I have felt a growing desire to become as faultless as grace can make the human soul.

Mrs. Downey asked, and was given, the privilege of taking the work he would have had, which was the care of the Boys' Orphanage. Thoburn writes of Sunday, September 11: "A beautiful Sabbath. Attended love feast at 11 a. m. in the Mission Chapel. This was the first love feast ever held in Northern India and of course was a time of interest. It lasted two hours."[64] The appointments were: *Lucknow:* William Butler, R. Pierce, J. Baume, J. A. Cawdell, Joel Janvier; *Shahjahanpur:* J. W. Waugh; *Bareilly:* J. L. Humphrey; Mrs. J. R. Downey; *Moradabad:* C. W. Judd, J. Parsons; *Bijnor:* E. W. Parker; *Naini Tal:* J. M. Thoburn, S. Knowles.[65]

Before January major changes were made in the appointments. Butlers moved to Bareilly, Humphrey to Budaon, Waugh to Bareilly and Baume to Shahjahanpur. Parsons' health broke and he withdrew from the Mission before the end of the year.

The Second Annual Meeting

This was convened in Bareilly on February 1, 1861. "The first to arrive were Pierce and Joel from Lucknow, on horseback. Then Mrs. Pierce and Mrs. Baume in a *shigram* drawn by two bullocks, with luggage on three camels . . . a march of 150 miles." Seven Indian helpers were present: William Plumer, Exhorter, *Bijnor;* Stephen, Exhorter, *Shahjahanpur;* George, Exhorter, *Budaon;* Zahur al Haqq, Exhorter, *Moradabad;* Enoch Burge, Assistant in the Press; Joel Janvier and Joseph Fieldbrave. These, together with the ladies present, took part in discussions. On this Sunday, Butler baptized Tara Parshad Sarkar, who was educated under Duff in Calcutta, and a long-time seeker; also Ramzan, "the first inquirer that ever came to the mission". Humphrey and Waugh baptized seventeen orphans before a congregation of a hundred. Business followed lines of

Annual Conference. Questions discussed were: a fund for super-annuated nen; scales of salary for Indian workers; committee for the Press; a request or $4000 for a school for missionary children and the salary for its principal, other expenses to be met locally. A severe famine prevailed over most of he Conference at this time.[66]

Four new missionaries were expected in April who received appointnents at this time: Henry Jackson, I. L. Hauser, J. H. Messmore, and Miss Libbie A. Husk, the first single lady missionary sent to India by the Missionary Society, (later Mrs. Messmore). Hauser replaced Parker at Bijnor, Jackson went to Lakhimpur, Messmore to Lucknow and Miss Husk o assist Mrs. Pierce. When J. T. Gracey arrived in October work was opened in Sitapur.

The Third Annual Meeting

No meeting was called in 1862. New missionaries arrived in January, 1862: J. D. Brown, D. W. Thomas and W. W. Hicks, with their wives. A year later, T. S. Johnson, T. J. Scott, Henry Mansell, with their wives, and P. T. Wilson, arrived. Americans in this meeting were 20 men, 16 adies and 15 children.[67] Other circumstances cast a gloom over the essions of this Third Meeting convened on February 5, 1863. A few nonths before the meeting three wives of missionaries had died: Mrs. Jackson (September), Mrs. Thoburn (October) and Mrs. Pierce (November).

The work of the wives of missionaries, "assistant missionaries," as ome called them, cannot be too highly praised. They, too, shared the call and the dedication of their husbands. They were quick to recognize hat only women could enter the zenanas and learn to know and to help women and girls; they were no less quick to try to give that help. That hey had home responsibilities did not deter them. They did what they could,—*a great deal.* The three just named had been active to the limit of their strength.

Owing to Mr. Hick's ill health they had to leave at the time of meeting. An unpleasant element was friction between the missionaries and the Superintendent. The fact that the holding of the Annual Meeting was at the option of the Superintendent, and that he had not called the meeting in 1862, marred "the harmony and cordial co-operation" on which the development of the work depended.

> Owing to absence of method and fixed procedure in administration, particularly in regard to finance, . . . a number of missionaries . . . thought of declining to meet the Superintendent in Annual Meeting until the Mission was organized as an Annual Conference or some radical changes were introduced into the methods of administration.[68]

On the first day Butler read a conciliatory statement to the member which, he reported to the Corresponding Secretary,

> terminated the uncertainty and cordially invited the members of th mission to assume and exercise henceforth all the powers and dutie which belonged to them as his associates in the work of God, and whil resigning to them the extra power he had hitherto necessarily held he stated his resolve to confine himself in future to those duties whic more especially belong to his peculiar office . . . .
>
> An annual conference organization will add legality and disci plinary form to our work and then the M. E. Church of India will b fully equipped for her career of usefulness . . . . The proposed arrange ments of the Superintendent were accepted by the members of the mis sion in the same frank and brotherly spirit in which they were tendered and the entire business of the annual meeting was conducted in con formity with them.[69]

Bishop Thomson had noted "the spirit of obedience and respect fo official superiors which was both a sentiment and a habit"[70] with Butler Thoburn's *Journal* and the correspondence of missionaries show that it wa "too late" for him to yield the authority he had been accustomed to exer cise. The harmony expected was not realized. On September 1, 1863 the missionaries received copies of his resignation as Superintendent whic he had sent to New York.[71] During that winter, on the advice of hi physician, Butler took a sea voyage to Burma, returning in January.

The Fourth Annual Meeting

This opened on February 5, 1864, and continued for a week. It wa "harmonious and profitable". Butler gave a comprehensive report o the work of the Mission which was well received and which Gracey des cribed as being "like stirring notes of triumph from a warrior's bugle":

> Nine of the most important cities of North India occupied; nineteen mission houses built or purchased; sixteen school houses erected; ten chapels erected; two orphanages established; one publishing house; twelve Congregations had been gathered; ten small churches organized; 1,322 youths under instruction; 161 persons had attained a Christian experience; four of these became preachers and eleven became exhorters. $55,186.50 had been contributed in India for the work of the Mission, and $73,188.56 worth of property had been accumulated.[72]

The Meeting again sent a memorial to General Conference asking for the status of an Annual Conference. J. M. Thoburn had returned to the United States in the fall of 1863 to leave his son with relatives. He took advantage of his presence in America to attend the General Conference and represent the views of the Mission. The following action was taken:

There shall be an Annual Conference in the northwest provinces of India to be denominated the INDIA MISSION ANNUAL CONFERENCE embracing the ancient kingdom of Oudh, and the country of Rohilkhand on the west of Oudh, and lying between the river Ganges on the South and the Himalaya mountains on the north, which conference shall, with the concurrence of the presiding Bishop, possess all the rights, powers and privileges of the Annual Conferences, excepting that of sending delegates to General Conference, and of drawing its Annual dividend from the avails of the Book Concern and Chartered Fund, and of voting on Constitutional changes proposed in the Discipline.[73]

Thoburn knew that the missionaries would not be pleased with these restrictions, and so told Dr. Durbin. The debate was brief but this, as well as the conversation of delegates, showed very clearly "that the object of tne proviso was to guard against the irregularities which might be expected to arise in a Conference composed in a large measure of converts from heathenism".[74]

Bijnor

The Parkers reached Bijnor on October 14, 1859. They found a small house of four rooms. With two helpers, William Plumer and Samuel Bhagarath, work started—worship services, bazaar preaching, class meetings. The first Sunday service was held under a mango tree; later, in the sitting room. Occasional English services were held and this group contributed funds for houses, for workers, and for a Chapel, dedicated on November 18, 1860. Parker completed the mission house [75] which is still in use. They made early contact with the Mazhabi Sikh movement in Bashta. Parker baptized his first convert, Gurdayal, in June, 1860. He was a young man, "now a real Christian". He was given a Hindi Bible purchased with money given to Parker in Concord for a Bible for his first convert. In Wesleypur Gurdayal's house was burned but the Bible was saved. "I have my Bible," he said, "let the rest go." He was a day labourer but he learned to read his Bible.[76]

Both Mr. and Mrs. Parker suffered much from malaria at Bijnor. He was convalescing at Naini Tal in 1861 when the Superintendent appointed him to the Lakhimpur circuit.

Shahjahanpur

Work was formally opened here October 1, 1859. Mr. and Mrs. Waugh could find only a one-room building in the heart of the city for a residence. They had one helper whose one qualification was that he knew a little English. "He might have been useful," wrote Waugh, "but for three or four slight drawbacks, to wit, he was unconverted, ignorant, covetous, discontented, dishonest and very wicked withal."[77] When Butler learned that Waugh had been a practical printer he appointed him to Bareilly. Before going, Waugh was able to buy a mission house, and to find another helper, Stephen, who worked faithfully with Baume who succeeded him. In October Baume returned to Lucknow and Cawdell came here.

A chapel was dedicated in January, 1861, paid for by local contributions. The next year Humphrey moved the school from the mission compound to the city. Messmore and Brown followed Humphrey, the former in charge of the orphanage which had been moved here from Bareilly at the close of 1862. T. S. Johnson arrived that year and in 1864 took over from Messmore who returned to Lucknow.

Budaon

The first Methodist service in Budaon was conducted by William Butler in 1857 when Judge Edwards of the station invited him to hold divine service for his family.[78] Humphrey had made a tour into Budaon from Bareilly, and was transferred there in 1860 when Waugh took his place. A family of Indian Christians welcomed the Humphreys warmly. A small group of European civil and military officers subscribed Rs. 900 which enabled Humphrey to buy a very desirable property of five acres on which was an unfinished house for two families. This was completed during the year as also a church, a residence for the pastor, Joseph Angelo, and a *ziyat*. The church was dedicated by Butler after a service in which he preached in English and Fieldbrave in Hindustani, on July 29, 1860.[79] A school was opened in the bazaar and another school for Christian children and boys from the city who wanted to learn English, was opened near the bungalow on August 1, with nine boys present—the beginning of the A. V. School there.[80]

Work among the sweepers commenced this year with the opening of a school for their children. On a district tour a young man, Chimman Lal, who read well and knew arithmetic, went to Humphrey's tent for tracts. Later he sought the missionary in Budaon and as a teacher was needed for this new school, Chimman Lal was employed. He soon became a Christian. Of him Gracey wrote: "His conversion was so clear that the struggle was soon turned into victory." He became an excellent evangelist, a member of conference and a writer of *bhajans*.[81]

Naini Tal

Thoburn, alone of the *Bostonians*, was privileged to spend four years in one station, Naini Tal. At first he was with Knowles who was soon transferred and Zahur al Haqq was sent to Naini Tal to teach in the school, to act as language tutor for Thoburn and also for opportunity to grow in his own Christian life. Thoburn "learned to esteem and love him". More than other stations Naini Tal had an established program of work when Thoburn arrived: two English services every Sunday, one in the barracks, the other at the school; a Hindustani service in the morning; bazaar preaching two or three times a week; daily teaching in the school for two hours; completing the unfinished chapel, and besides all this he was expected to "vigorously prosecute the study of at least one Indian language".

> As I had been sent to preach the Gospel to the heathen it seemed wrong to let anything interfere with that great work. It was not so easy, however, to turn aside from this work . . . . God blessed the work, and the way never seemed open to give it up . . . . God was leading me in a way that I knew not. [The next year he wrote] I enjoyed the work exceedingly, and yet it seemed very clear that, soon or later it must draw me off from my mission to the heathen.[82]

Work in Naini Tal was seasonal. In the winter Thoburn moved to the Bhabar and Tarai, where the hills slope into the plains. He had opened a school in Haldwani; and the supervision of five others was given him by Government. With Samuel he made a tour to the *mela* on the Sarda river which separates Nepal from India, where no missionary had been before. The opportunities for evangelistic work were unlimited.

On November 3, 1861, Thoburn baptized his first convert, a young man who had been in a Mission school. He was given the name John Barker. The occasion "was an era in a life time" for Thoburn. In the same month he married Mrs. Downey. A girls' school was now opened in Naini Tal and also work among women. For a short time even the daughters of well-to-do families attended the school. An orphan boy, Harkua, and two young women were the next baptisms. A son was born to the Thoburns, and soon after, the mother took ill. "While trying to urge her Mohammedan cook to give his heart to Christ" she passed away. In the summer of 1863 Thoburn was again in Naini Tal but in October he left for America with his child, taking Harkua with him.

And now Methodism is to organize her first Mission Conference on the soil of India,—the continent on which paradise bloomed, the ark rested, the law thundered, and the cross warmed with atoning blood; the land of prophets and apostles, of martyrs and mysteries, of the arts of man and the revelations of God. We bring back to her a Bible all of whose pages were written on her soil, and are so illustrated in her living customs that they may be read by the road side without a commentator. We bring to her a religion whose first and fullest enjoyments were felt in the hearts of her noblest sons.

I stood upon the top of Cheena and looked over a field of mountains...I walked a few places and looked down upon the plain of the Ganges.... I knew that in the mountains on the one side there beat six hundred thousand hearts and in the plains on the other, fifty millions; and I said 'These all belong to Christ.' The voice of the Prophet came over me, 'The idols shall he utterly abolish'; and the voice of the Father, 'Ask of me and I shall give thee the nations for an inheritance'...and that other voice, 'A nation shall be born in a day,' a prophecy to be realized in the crystallized civilizations of the East. We have had the planting, and it has been long; the harvest may come soon. There is a plant which it requires a century to mature, but it blossoms in a day. God has great and precious promises that have not yet been fulfilled.

Bishop Edward Thomson,
Lucknow, Dec. 8th, 1864.

II

Foundations Broad and Deep

Butler received from Dr. Durbin a letter of appointment and from ishop Simpson a commission giving him "the public authority of the :hurch to establish and superintend the said mission". After dealing with ıatters of administration, organization and correspondence, he added, Brother Butler, lay broad and deep foundations for Methodism in India". 'he "commission" also included one basic direction; its repetition gave it he desired emphasis.

> We send you to preach the Gospel to those who have not heard, and do not hear it . . . . Regard the preaching of the word to the people as the principal efficient means of their awakening and conversion. . . The great design of the mission is to preach the word to the people by the living minister.[1]

The Annual Meetings provided inspiration and coordination in a ommon task, but no program for work was set for missionaries when they vent to their appointments. Under the guidance of the Holy Spirit they vent out to preach, to make disciples and to build a Christian Society—he Church. In every station evangelism was first. If in its develop-nent in the separate stations, tried methods proved their usefulness, and erved the "great design," they were adopted. Like a banyan tree vhose branches send out aerial "roots," which, reaching downward "take :oot," and growing strong, contribute their strength to the spread of the ›arent tree, so each activity or department of work, and in turn each 'center" or institution, was expected to contribute its strength to the Church—its life, evangelism.

Evangelism

Preaching under a tree, on the roadside, in the bazaar, in the village, and at *melas*—wherever people would listen—the preacher expected some seed to fall in good ground. Zahur al Haqq and Ambica Charan were men from cultured families; they stopped to listen, became interested; they were followed up, befriended, instructed, and brought into Christian worship. Then, in spite of threats and bribes, they left their families to accept baptism. The original urge for the quest of the Mazhabi Sikhs came as a result of preaching at a *mela*.

In the printed page the Methodists received a heritage throug missions and missionaries who had preceded them. The Scriptures ha been translated; tracts and song books were available, through the Britis and Foreign Bible Society, or the Tract Society, and were widely usec Almost from the beginning the Bible Society gave grants for colportage

Ziyats were small halls or reading rooms located in the city easil accessible to people. The verandah provided a platform for street preach ing; the room, a quiet place for discussion with inquirers and for readin and distribution of literature.

Gathering together in worship was from the beginning recognized a a means of spiritual growth. For this reason a chapel or church wa early provided in growing centers. The estimates for 1864 carried a asking of $200 to build a place of worship and a native preacher's hous at Babukhera, an equal amount to be raised on the field. The Supern tendent comented: "It is in my view one of the most commendabl enterprises for which aid is asked this year."[2]

Building The Church

"When the missionaries come to Moradabad, go to them and do what they tell you." This friendly advice proved for evangelists an exceedingly difficult task. From one standpoint it was welcome to the missionaries, for they realized that the larger the number that joined the Christians the fewer would be the ties with kindred and social customs to draw them back. "Those difficulties are greatly mitigated", wrote Butler, "when the people are disposed to move, as it were, *en masse*."[3] But the missionaries were also aware of the additional responsibility devolving on them and the preachers in "the daily care of all the churches", not more than a handful in any one village. Although the Mazhabi Sikhs in Rohilkhand numbered only about 5,000, their accession to the Christian Church spread over a number of years. Those who held back greatly hindered those who had been baptized from making a clear cut stand in their religion.

A second "movement", that among the Chamars, had also manifested itself in the same district in 1859. These people were leather workers and cultivators. Parsons reported that some two hundred of them had then

> openly renounced idolatry, risen superior to all the prejudices of caste, and professed their faith in the Gospel of Jesus Christ . . . . They are now being regularly instructed . . . . At the head of this list figure three of their gurus [spiritual teachers] . . . . The principal guru is a man of very great influence among them, and was considered so holy that he was regularly worshipped by 2000 "*nij chelas*". That man now bows at the foot of Jesus Christ, and declares that he will have no other Saviour . . . . The Spirit of God is moving on the hearts of many of these idolaters.[4]

This movement did not come to fruition so rapidly as did that among he Mazhabi Sikhs. Mrs. Parker wrote in 1864: "There are hundreds f *Chamars* who seem just ready to become Christians. We feel the burden f these souls and are led to agonise with God in prayer for them."[5]

By The Living Minister

Successful evangelism multiplies evangelists. From the beginning it vas very clear to Butler and his associates that even a limited field could ot be evangelised by foreign missionaries alone. Butler sought Joel anvier, and from the time of the first Annual Meeting every missionary ad at least one Indian associated with him as "helpers". In 1861 they had ot only shared in the discussions in the Annual Meeting but shared the reaching of those days.[6] The appointments following the Fourth Annual Aeeting showed the number of "Native Preachers" (Local Preachers) o be 9, Exhorters 11, and teachers 48; while missionaries were 17. The ine were: Joel T. Janvier, William Plumer, Yaqub, Zahur al Haqq, Thomas Cullen, H. M. Daniel, Samuel, James David and Joseph ieldbrave.

JOSEPH FIELDBRAVE

During the Uprising Joseph Fieldbrave had been in the police department. He had earlier been in another mission which was discontinued. Ie applied to Butler who gladly employed him, and sent him to Bareilly. There Fieldbrave eagerly joined Humphrey in opening street preaching. Ie "loved to preach and was always ready whenever, or wheresoever, the pportunity presented.... He was a powerful speaker in Hindustani.... Iis manner was very winning and pleasing."[7] Zahur al Haqq remembered vith what kindness he had been received in Fieldbrave's home and ntroduced to the family. Fieldbrave was described as "a man of childike simplicity, and John-like love".[8]

HENRY MARTYN DANIEL

As a boy Daniel was converted and educated in the Sikandra Orphanage. He entered Government service in the Punjab but, after the ccupation of Oudh by the British became Head Clerk of the Civil Court of ucknow. From there he was transferred, at his request, to Head Clerk n the office of the Deputy Commissioner, Sitapur, where, through J. T. Gracey, "he became acquainted with Methodist doctrines and discipline" nd joined the Methodist Church. The Boys' Orphanage needed a eadmaster. Daniel was approached, and at great sacrifice accepted the ost.

> By great diligence and with credit to himself he had acquire a knowledge of English, Persian, Arabic, Greek and Hebrew, a fami liarity with Hinduism and Islam, and an acquaintance with Christia doctrines and his Bible, which so eminently made him a preacher "tha needeth not to be ashamed".[9]

ORPHANAGES

On that memorable day in December, 1857, when William Butle sat on the throne of the last Mughal Emperor in the Fort at Delhi anc wrote to Dr. Durbin of orphanages, he appealed for gifts—the first designatec gifts—for the support of orphans. He estimated the cost at $25 each and solicited patrons for each scholarship, allowing them to select a boy or a girl and to name the child who would be assigned. He wrote:

> Brethren and Sisters, help us to save these poor little ones. I you *take* them, you will think about them; if you pay for them you will certainly pray for them. God will own and honour your deec of Christian mercy, and, at a future day, in many a delightful instance, when they are converted and happy, will "the blessing of those now ready to perish come upon you".[10]

The Missionary Society accepted the projects on the understanding that the members of the Mission *together* approved the plan, and that the Mission be given a legal guardianship for each orphan. They insured funds by advancing $1,000 for the first year. The Church was informed of the appeal and arrangements made to receive the designated gifts.

Early in 1858 three orphan boys were gathered in Naini Tal—the beginning of the Boys' Orphanage. The first of these was given to Butler in January, at Meerut, by his friend Major Gowan, who assumed responsibility for his support and gave to him his own name, James Gowan. He was the son of a sepoy and was found on the back of an elephant, where he had been left by his father, who presumably had been killed in an engagement of the Uprising. With the other two, Thomas Gowan and William Wheeler, James was taken to Bareilly in 1859 when Humphrey moved there. In the fall a few boys who had been received in Lucknow were added to the growing number in Bareilly under Mrs. Downey. In 1860 there were twenty-five and two years later, eighty-two boys.[11]

A large sum of money was received from England for famine relief in 1860-61. It was disbursed by the Government and a portion invested for orphan children. The Mission drew against this fund for several years.[12] Mrs. Downey, with the orphan boys and the whole staff of teachers and servants, moved from Kashmiri Kothi to the site of the present girls' school in buildings then just completed.[13] In the fall of 1862 the Orphanage was moved again to a location in the Shahjahanpur Cantonment.

The Girls' Orphanage was opened in Lucknow in the fall of 1858 under the care of Mrs. Pierce. During 1861-62 she was assisted by Miss Husk. The first girl given to Mrs. Butler was blind in one eye and pock-marked—given because such a girl was considered useless. She received the name Elmira Blake. She was one of the first to unite with the Church and was a member of the first medical class, and when the Pauri hostel was opened in 1874 she was its matron and teacher. In 1883 when the Butlers returned to visit India and a formal reception was given to them in Bareilly, the nine-year-old daughter of Elmira Blake presented the love gifts to the guests.[14]

After the death of Mrs. Pierce, in November, 1862, the Girls' Orphanage was moved from Lucknow to Bareilly, to the buildings vacated by the boys when they went to Shahjahanpur. For a year Mr. Pierce served as Principal of "the Seminary and Female Orphanage" (the next year it was called the Girls' Orphanage), assisted by Mrs. Thomas, Miss Porter and Miss White. The last two named were missionaries of the Board but in 1864, returned to America.[15]

Schools

In the First Annual Meeting, 1859, doubts and opposition to schools had been expressed. The missionaries were new, but in their several stations where those same missionaries faced the deep darkness of illiteracy and poverty, of ignorance and superstition, they opened schools. Then, schools seemed to them like windows to let in LIGHT; schools would open minds and hearts to a better WAY; schools offered an opportunity to proclaim the TRUTH that makes free, and to offer LIFE, which like leaven, could permeate the whole community.

In most cities boys' schools met with an eager response from many. In Naini Tal, Moradabad, Shahjahanpur, and Budaon, schools begun in this period have lived through the years. Their development will be treated elsewhere. Except where there were Christian girls to attend primary classes, little could be done in the way of girls' education against the vigorous opposition to such a program. In 1862 the little school in Naini Tal was discontinued after a report had spread that girls were being kidnapped; even the effort to win attendance by offering pice for each day had failed.

The girls' school in connection with the orphanage in Lucknow was discontinued on the removal of the orphanage to Bareilly, but four little schools were continued at nearby centers with a total enrolment as high as 148. Of them we read:

> 'The attendance is very regular ... the progress of the scholars has been quite rapid ... they are now commencing the regular course of vernacular education. ... In two of these schools the scriptures are

read and it is hoped that they will soon be introduced in all.' In all of these a gratuity of one pice a day to each girl attending was followed.

The ladies in Lucknow had tried for more than two years to get an opening among the Hindustani women in Lucknow, when in 1864 they heard through a Mohammedan gentleman "of a woman who would teach, and a few girls who were willing to learn". A day was fixed for making arrangements. On February 16 Mrs. Judd, Mrs. Knowles and Mrs. Messmore

> started out on our new mission. We found the teacher, a bright, intelligent Mohammedan woman, surrounded by 14 or 15 little girls who were to be her pupils. Now, to open the school, meant to hire a house; pay the teacher; pay men to find the girls; furnish books; and hire a man to bring water to drink. This we saw would make quite a large bill for every month, and was not at all according to our ideas as to how that thing should be done; but . . . considering background, environment, etc., and our hopes . . . school was opened, and in less than six months, the number of girls increased to thirty.
>
> Three months after this a Mohammedan lady . . . asked to be employed as a teacher, promising to gather her own pupils ; we accepted her proposals ; and the Naubasta Zenana school was commenced . . . . Some of the pupils were of high caste families.[16]

This was the first introduction of the missionaries to Jaffri Begum, who with two daughters five years later became a Christian. After a hard-fought court case in which they gave clear-cut Christian testimony, they disappeared. The Elich Khan Zenana school was commenced in October following and the Rustum Nagar school at the same time, but it continued only for four years, then closed. There was no success yet in opening schools among Hindu women.[17] These five schools unitedly (including the "Ragged" school) received a monthly grant-in-aid of Rs. 75 in 1865.

Mrs. Humphrey opened a class for girls in Bareilly in 1861. There were twelve pupils including three or four young women from the Mazhabi Sikhs. "Mainphul Singh's young wife excelled the others . . . . She was an ignorant young girl when brought to the Mission the previous winter." She also opened the first school for Christian girls in Moradabad in 1863. It met for three hours daily—the first given to Scripture, singing, prayers, hymns and catechism; the second to reading and writing in English and in Roman Urdu, and reading in Hindi; the third hour for knitting and crocheting in wools. She

> taught them to crochet children's socks, mittens, neckties, hoods, etc., and when a dozen or so articles were completed, I sent them to the ladies of the station for sale. In this way I paid for the wool and also gave the girls a fair price for their work.[18]

From the first Annual Meeting until the organization of the India Mission Conference was a period of five years and three months. One n realize the meaning for the Church in the changing attitude of people ward schools shown in reports:

> As the way is now open in the city among Hindus and Mohammedans, the design is to open more schools . . . as through these schools the way is opened for the missionary's wife to gain access to the women of the city.[19]

> We continue to recognize in education one of our most important agents in paving the way for the spread of Christ's kingdom among this people.[20]

The Printing Press

> It is evident that we must give not only Education but also *Employment* to our Orphan boys (now 25 in number). No other employment seems within our reach except Printing. It is the desire of our Missionary Board . . . that we should have a Printing Press; and there is no doubt but that they will give us the means of establishing one. For this purpose Bro. Waugh's experience as a practical printer seems providentially to supply the very help we need for the management of such an enterprise .... We greatly need some Hymns, our first Catechism and some Tracts.[21]

So read a circular sent by the Superintendent on January 16, 1860 members of the Mission, inviting them to loan what they could spare, ayable within four months, to be repaid within two years without interest. even persons responded with Rs. 100 each: Butler, Humphrey, Irs. Downey, Judd, Parker, Waugh and Thoburn.

On the same date that Butler wrote his appeal, including the suggestion f Waugh's new work and consequent transfer before they had been four onths in Shahjahanpur, Mrs. Waugh wrote to their families in America:

> This change so sudden, so unexpected, coming Jan. 1st just as we were about to move to our new home, has, as you may imagine, quite unsettled us. We think it for the best. The design is to have a printing establishment in Bareilly, the headquarters of the Mission, and Walter will have the charge of it. Thus employment will be furnished to our orphanage boys as they are growing up.[22]

The Press was purchased at Roorkee. A tradition says it was made f cannon used in the war and cast by trained native labourers. Waugh rove from Bareilly to Roorkee in his *tum-tum* to get it. The inking rollers ere broken in transit and Waugh made new ones, boiling the glue and olasses himself. On April 28, 1861 he wrote, "Oh, I have such a beauty f a roller, cast in the new mould. Am going to use it this evening. I have one some Rs. 20 or 25 worth of work."[22]

The Press was first established in Kashmiri *kothi*, then in a new uilding near the present girls' school, which collapsed in the first monoon. When the Girls' Orphanage came to Bareilly it moved again. "I had spent several years in America in connection with the Press, preparin copy, etc.," Waugh wrote, "but I find it quite a different matter to plung into an unknown tongue—seems strange at first—but the more I have t do the better I love the work."[23] The larger and more advanced boy worked daily, learning, and earning against the cost of their support.

The first production was a Roman-Urdu translation of *Catechism No.* 1. An early traction the *Witness of the Holy Spirit* had been written b J. Parsons. On July 9 a copy was sent to Dr. Durbin. Another earl publication was a little book of fifty hymns. Mrs. Humphrey had ac quired a facility in the use of the language, yet her frail body often defeat ed her eagerness to serve India's people. She loved music. Lying in be she would try to translate hymns. Seeing her thus engaged one da Mrs. Butler exclaimed, "Oh, it may be you can do what no one else i our missionary family can do. You can set India Methodism singing." After she had "succeeded in changing the dress of 16 of our standar hymns" Mrs. Humphrey sent them to Mr. Ullmann of the A. P. Missio for criticism. She took courage from his criticism and commendation and in the fall of 1863 wrote:

> I exerted myself to revise my latest hymns as Mr. Waugh wishe to get out a small mission hymn book. I succeeded in getting 33 ready for the press, which, with 17 selections (by permission) from the Pres byterian Mission Hymn Book made us a little book of 50 hymns.[24]

At the Conference of 1864 the Press was a vigorous sapling. Waugh reported the aggregate monthly salary of sixteen compositors, printers binders, etc., as Rs. 150. It had a new office building recently completed Commercial job work was increasing, as was work for the Church. The American Bible Society and the M. E. Tract and Sunday School Societies had given it grants. Already the suggestion had been made that it should be transplanted to Lucknow and the Mission Board was asked to consider favorably the propriety of appointing a layman to superintend the Press.[25]

The Conference recognized that "the regular distribution of the Holy Scriptures, with religious tracts and books" was one of the surest means of "diffusing the Gospel's leavening light" among India's people. The difficulties in this task were: (1) a want of reliable Christian men for colporteurs; (2) the lack of funds; (3) the illiteracy of the people. Nevertheless, it was resolved during the ensuing year to get these books into "every town and village in the bounds of our work, where there are people who can read".[26] That goal was not reached but the founders realized that the art of Printing had given to modern missionary work a multiplied power unknown in Apostolic Days.

An Experiment in Uplift

An early result of the conversion of Mazhabi Sikhs was persecution. For the many who were tenant cultivators their tenancy was terminated; labourers were no longer given work. Butler thought of a "Christian Village" where the Mission would be the land owner, and dispossessed tenants would find a place to settle. Such a village would become also a center of good influence for the region around. With this in mind Butler secured from the Government a lease of 5,000 acres on the border of the Tarai—a region which in the monsoon inclined to be marshy or very damp, and very malarious. He selected Parker, "the Vermont farmer", as the superintendent of the enterprise and transferred him to Lakhimpur some 200 miles from Bijnor, and about 20 miles east of the estate.

Parker "had his doubts" but with Mrs. Parker loyally accepted the orders. Mrs. Parker went to Bijnor, packed their goods and loaded them in oxcarts. She collected a group of Christians to join the colony, then returned to Naini Tal to get her husband. In the fifteen months that they were at Wesleypore Parker was never free for any month from attacks of disease. Difficulties mounted: many Sikhs were unwilling to move that far; many who went got sick and returned; others just criticized and did little. They merely remembered "the leeks and onions of Egypt." Some thirty of the Christians did die. One day flames consumed the grass huts in which the people lived—when Gurdayal saved his Bible. At the Annual Meeting in 1863 the experiment was closed and the Parkers appointed to Moradabad.

They had entered upon the enterprise in the hope that it might succeed and tried to make it so. They had hoped that the village would be like a "city set on a hill" with its houses, chapel and school house; that "the morality of the people, their equity in dealing, their independent, cheerful bearing" would attract attention. It closed, "the missionary, broken in health, the remnants of his colony dispersed and discouraged."[27]

English Work

Butler's arrangements in the Annual Meetings of 1858 and 1859 included provision for English services for Europeans in Naini Tal and in Lucknow. One of the instructions given to him by Bishop Simpson had read as follows:

> If there be an European population present in the country or city in which you establish your Mission, and the missionary can be made to serve their spiritual interests, we shall consent and be glad; provided such service does not interfere with the execution of your mission among the heathen.[28]

With unusual persistence, and often in direct opposition to the opinion of missionaries on the field, the Missionary Society has refused to support "English Work". The term European included not only those who had come from Europe but also the Eurasian community, widely scattered in India, and forming a large proportion of the English-speaking population. These were assumed to be Christians in accordance with the teaching of the established Church of England and the Roman Catholic Church, which regard children baptized in families of communicants as members, however nominal their relation may be.

Harper considers that it was the provision made for English services that led the Missionary Society to repeat their position on November 5, 1858, that

> it is understood that in the quality and location of the buildings [residences for missionaries] reference shall be had chiefly to the main intent of the Mission, *viz.*, the conversion of the natives of the country, and only incidentally to the European population in India.[29]

Except for the winter months, English services have continued in Naini Tal from early 1858 until now. It was an English community that built the first little chapel there, and so liberally supported Mission work that Thoburn proposed to the Superintendent in 1862 that he relinquish all claim on the Board for the work in his circuit, excepting only his own salary, "provided that the station be made financially independent, and the missionary be allowed to disburse all the funds collected by him".[30] All the work of the circuit was carried and a "large surplus of Rs. 3,000 a year paid into the Mission treasury".[31]

The earliest reports of almost every station speak of Europeans who appreciated English services. In Lucknow, Baume's ministry produced "among the soldiers a continuous revival," and in 1861 a small chapel, 40' × 26', was completed on land donated by Nawab Moin-ud-daulah.[32]

In Gonda, Mr. and Mrs. Knowles were "hospitably entertained", on their arrival to open work in 1865, by the Deputy Commissioner. The Assistant Commissioner "gave a room in his house for English service every Sunday". Soon money was collected in the station for "a convenient and substantial chapel," and the "whole station used to attend the Sabbath afternoon service held therein." There, too, Dr. J. H. Condon helped to open a vernacular school, from which two brothers, Bihari Lal and Kanhai Lal, both of whom became preachers, were early converts. Of Dr. Condon Knowles wrote:

> During the five years we had charge of the work in the station our respected friend was more to us than an Assistant Missionary; for his earnest piety and consistent example before the natives, and in the position he had, were worth more to us in our work than a clerical

co-adjutor . . . . He is now the most intelligent, hard-working, unpaid local preacher of our church in India [1889].[33]

In Rae Bareli, 1865, English residents greatly helped P. T. Wilson renovating the bungalow, and in 1871, when J. T. McMahon went there, ey contributed liberally to the erection of a little chapel.[34]

It was "at the earnest request" of a number of Civil and Military ficers in Sitapur that an English service was started in 1868; and a week-y prayer meeting was well attended. The genuine conversion of several sulted. These services forged a link between the missionary and the ople of the station which not only added materially to Mission funds, but oduced practical cooperation in evangelistic efforts :

> The wives of officers in high position have not thought it beneath them to purchase portions of Scripture in considerable numbers, and distribute them among the Natives with their own hands ; and . . . they have employed an old Native Christian to read the Word of God daily to their servants.[35]

The India Mission Conference

Bishop Edward Thomson was designated by the Bishops to visit India d to organize the India Mission Conference. He was met at Calcutta Dr. Butler, who accompanied him throughout his tour, travelling ough Benares, Allahabad, Agra and Delhi to Meerut, thence to Bijnor. this, as at other Mission stations, the Bishop examined schools, attended etings, preached and administered the Sacraments. By way of Najibabad d Nagina they went to the Garhmuktesar *mela* where missionaries and ers of the Conference were engaged in preaching. All the occupied tions of the Mission were visited in turn ; also Gonda, where it was agreed t a new station should be opened. Lastly they reached Lucknow, ere the Conference was to convene.[36]

After a memorable service in Naini Tal, when the Bishop preached l conducted the communion service in which the Governor and his staff k part, they also met and dined with Sir Henry Ramsay. Always ply interested in Mission work, Sir Henry urged the Bishop and the erintendent to open work at Pauri, Garhwal, and to re-open Pilibhit. begin the former he offered a contribution of $1500 and a recurring tribution of $25 monthly, to sustain the proposed mission.[37]

On December 8, 1864, Bishop Thomson organized the India Mission nference in the little chapel in the school at Husainabad. He read the nty-third Psalm and a portion from the fourteenth Chapter of St. John. n, following a hymn, the Sacrament of the Lord's Supper was adminis-d. The number of Indian preachers and catechists who partook, along n the foreigners, made this service "most interesting and impressive".

Quoting the action of the General Conference authorizing
Annual Conference, the Bishop referred at once to the restrictions wh
had been made, saying:

> Some of the privileges withheld were probably deemed impr ticable, one unnecessary, while the veto of the Presiding Bishop m have been thought both safe and useful.
>
> In considering these restrictions you will not impute a bad mot while you can find a good one. Certain it is that your benefit a not your embarrassment was intended.
>
> The India Mission cannot complain that it has not b favoured, or fear that it will not be hereafter, either by the Gene Conference, so devoted to the Missionary cause, the able Board which our Missions are directed, or the Missionary Secretary, wh rare eloquence, great executive ability and zeal in Missionary work eminently fit him for his position, or his worthy associates.
>
> Of the India Mission Conference I recognize the follow brethren as members, *viz.*: WILLIAM BUTLER, JAMES BAUME, CHAR W. JUDD, EDWIN W. PARKER, JAMES W. WAUGH, JAMES M. THOBU HENRY JACKSON, ISAIAH L. HAUSER, JAMES H. MESSMORE, JOHN T. GRAC DAVID W. THOMAS, JOHN D. BROWN, THOMAS J. SCOTT, THOMAS S. JOHNS HENRY MANSELL, T. STANLEY STIVERS, AND SAMUEL KNOWLES.[38]

Then, asking the privilege of submitting "a few remarks which unusual circumstances suggest" he delivered an address which in its hist cal connections possessed rare interest, and with his consent was printe full in the Minutes.

All members were present except J. M. Thoburn, then absent leave in America; and T. S. Stivers who was under appointm P. T. Wilson, who had arrived in January, 1863, was admitted into connection on the second day.

J. T. Gracey was elected Secretary and T. J. Scott, his assist The committees appointed at the last Annual Meeting of the Mission v constituted the committees of the Conference and requested to pre their reports accordingly, and the Rules of Order of the Mission v accepted for the Conference.

The restrictions placed upon the Conference had been deeply rese by its members. A committee was appointed to prepare a report on subject. It was presented, adopted and filed. To a large extent Bis Thomson's wise and conciliatory attitude had removed most of the fea The Conference elected the Committee on Missions to handle all finan matters, on the understanding that they would become the Presi Elders. E. W. Parker, C. W. Judd and J. W. Waugh, were elected.

This Conference was memorable in several respects:

1. It was the first Methodist Conference to be organized in Asia, :hat continent", as Bishop Thomson described it, "which bore up the foot-eps and echoed to the voice of the Son of Man".

2. Following a full discussion in which a strong difference of opinion as evident, the Conference, with the concurrence of Bishop Thomson, oted to receive Indians into its membership, and proceeded at once to ect four Indians and one Englishman on Trial, the first step to member-ip in any Methodist Conference. In anticipation of this action quarterly onferences had made their recommendations: From Bareilly, Joel Thomas anvier; from Shahjahanpur, Henry Martyn Daniel; from Moradabad, ahur al Haqq and J. A. Cawdell and from Lucknow, Joseph Fieldbrave.

3. Three of these men, Janvier, Cawdell and Daniel were elected Deacons' orders and ordained by Bishop Thomson.

Samuel Knowles had previously been elected to Deacon's orders and :cently had been elected to Elder's orders by the Erie Conference. He as now ordained both Deacon and Elder. His position indicates a ajor facility gained by the India field through the change from a Mission a Conference—the right to elect to ordination, and to have ordination ompleted through closer episcopal supervision. In China, the first Mission as opened in 1847; the first Conference in 1877. Chinese desiring embership in an Annual Conference applied for it in the United States. he first Chinese to be ordained in the China Mission was ordained in 369 when Bishop Kingsley was

> duly assigned by his Brother Bishops to ordain into the Ministry of the Methodist Episcopal Church those Chinese who had served acceptably as ministers in Absentia of several conferences in the United States.[40]

4. It took the first step toward a Theological School for Indian ninisterial leadership, by recommending that a Training Department for :achers and preachers be opened in connection with the Boys' Orphanage.

5. On the earnest advice of Bishop Thomson the Conference voted enlarge its boundaries by including Garhwal with a mission at Pauri.

The appointments for 1865 were

MORADABAD DISTRICT: E. W. Parker, *Presiding Elder*; *Moradabad:* I. Mansell; Ummed Singh, John Judd, *Exhorters. Moradabad* Circuit: E. W. 'arker; Zahur-al-Haqq, *Native Preacher:* Calvin Kingsley, Andrias, Gurdayal Singh, Bulloo Singh, *Exhorters. Sambhal:* J. A. Cawdell; Ambica Charan, *Native Preacher;* John Cawood, *Exhorter. Bijnor:* I. L. Hauser; 'homas Cullen, *Native Preacher;* Prem Das, Benjamin Luke, *Exhorters.* Garhwal: J. M. Thoburn,

BAREILLY DISTRICT: J. M. Waugh, *Presiding Elder. Bareilly a Khera Bajera :* J. T. Gracey; D. W. Thomas, *Principal of Girls' Orphanag* Wm. Plumer, *Native Preacher;* James Gowan, *Exhorter* ; Peggy, *Orphana Matron. Naini Tal* : J. Baume ; John Barker, *Exhorter. Budaon* T. J. Scott; Yaqub and Joseph, *Native Preachers. Pilibhit:* J. T. Janvie *Native Preacher. Shahjahanpur :* T. S. Johnson, *Principal of Boys' Orphanag* T. S. Stivers; H. M. Daniel, *Head Master in Boys' Orphanage:* Sundur La *Native Preacher ;* Thomas Gowan, *Exhorter.*

LUCKNOW DISTRICT: C. W. Judd, *Presiding Elder; Lucknow (North* H. Jackson; J. H. Messmore, *Principal of Husainabad School;* Abdullah an Joseph R. Downey, *Exhorters; Lucknow (South):* C. W. Judd; Josep Fieldbrave, *Native Preacher;* Bakhtawar Singh, *Exhorter. Gonda* S. Knowles; Thomas Scott, *Native Preacher. Rae Bareli*: P. T. Wilso James David, *Native Preacher;* Amos, *Exhorter.* Wm. Butler transferred t the New England Conference, U. S. A.

The continued growth in the number of preachers since the Fourt Annual Meeting only ten months before is significant: Native Preachers— then nine, now twelve, of whom four had been admitted to membershi in the Annual Conference. Exhorters—then eleven, now sixteen, of who four who had just received their first appointments had come from th Boys' Orphanage: Calvin Kingsley, J. R. Downey, James Gowan an Thomas Gowan.

The India Mission Conference was fortunate, indeed, in havin Bishop Thomson present for its organization. It was the first Conferenc to which he was assigned following his election to the Episcopacy in 186 A resolution by the India Mission Conference adopted after Bisho Thomson's death, in 1870, says in part:

> We all gratefully remember the manner in which he performe the difficult and delicate task which was laid on him at that time, an we have reason to believe that not a few privileges which we no greatly prize, and much of the efficiency which we now possess, ar owing to his wise administration at our first Conference session. W believe, too, that the policy initiated by him here, of organizing mixe Conferences in which race or color were ignored, exerted a most impor tant influence on our church at home, and we feel thankful that to ou little conference was accorded the signal honour of pioneering the wa in this advance movement.

Bishop Thomson, in his report to the General Conference in 1868 said:

> The India Mission Annual Conference was remarkable for th dignity of its bearing, the spiritual character of its religious exercises and the harmonious and devotional spirit of its social meetings. Neve did I attend such a conference before, never may I hope to attend suc

> again; it will be [like a thing of beauty] a joy for ever. The interest was heightened by considering it was the first Conference [in Asia].... It gave us an opportunity of striking at caste—the curse of India—by ordaining white and black, Americans and Hindus, on the same platform. The candidates admitted into the body on trial were worthy, and might have passed in any of our Conferences.[41]

William Butler

The organization of the India Mission Conference marked the close f the period of Butler's superintendency. He was "transferred to the New England Conference," and early in 1865 he left India, but he never ost an interest in the Church which he had helped to plant. Gracey calls he achievements Butler listed in his report to the Fourth Annual Meeting s "truly amazing to have been effected in so short a time". Like Coke, Butler was dominated by a "consuming missionary passion". Temperamentally he seemed unable to forget position and authority to work with is colleagues. This was true before the First Annual Meeting when ew members were "much grieved to find that there is and has been a reat want of harmony among the members of the mission .... He had cted too much on his own responsibility and ignored the opinion of his rethren in the mission."[42]

In general his plans were well conceived; in the selection of a field nd in the designation of its stations; in the securing of properties and in heir development; in his dealings with officials in Government and his ourageous stand for high principles, he was an able Superintendent. In is ability to envision large results from small beginnings, little congreations, orphanages, a hand press, primary schools,—he was a Seer. Butler had been selected to establish and superintend the new Mission. This he undertook to do when no others were ready, and he did it with ourage, confidence and vision in circumstances that were most difficult. Bishop Thomson paid him this tribute:

> He was the man for the work—prudent, pious, sagacious, with a courteous bearing, a just self-respect, an enterprising spirit, and a profound regard to the authorities by whom he was commissioned.[43]

Forty years after William Butler could "begin anew" Bishop Foss isited India. He wrote:

> The foundations of our work in India have been broadly and solidly laid in both the great departments of missionary labour, the educational and the evangelistic....Our church does both strongly and well, and makes the two cooperate with and re-enforce each other.[44]

Section II

THE IMPROBABLE

We have been trying to get a site for a hospital for women ever since Miss Swain came out. The estate adjoining the mission premises here was just the place and the only eligible place for the hospital. We had little hope of getting it as His Highness was a Mohammedan, and utterly opposed to Christianity. But Mr. Drummond, the Commissioner, advised us to go ourselves and ask for it, and got His Highness' Prime Minister to send out his horses for us.

Rampore is 40 miles from here. The Nawab sent out 24 horses for us, so that at each of the six stages of the route we had four fresh horses, and drove in a grand old carriage, with coachman, two grooms, and an outrider. At the last stage we had three cavalry men to escort us into the city. We were driven to a house that is kept up for European travelers—everything on the most magnificent scale for our entertainment. Twenty-four different dishes were served up for breakfast, of fish, flesh, fowl, eggs, vegetables, etc. . . . At dinner we left off counting, and eating too.

The next morning we were up bright and early. Brother and Sister Parker, Miss Swain, husband and I were taken to several palaces and gardens. As we entered the gateway five royal elephants made their *salaams* to us. We went up the steps into the *presence* with trepidation. He gave us a seat at his right hand in a gorgeously embroidered chair, Dr. Swain next, then Mrs. Parker and the gentlemen, then the Prime Minister and his chief magistrate. We talked a little about things generally, while His Highness smoked his *hookah* . . . . The Minister told Mr. Thomas to make his request. He said he wanted to procure, upon some terms, the estate for the purpose of building a hospital for women. He had proceeded only so far when His Highness graciously smiled, and said, 'Take it, take it: I give it to you with much pleasure for that purpose.' The gift came so freely there was nothing to say, except to express our thanks. All Mr. Thomas' fine speech and arguments, which he had been getting up in his best Hindustanee, for a week, were of no use.

We silently thanked the Lord, and said, 'He has given it in answer to prayer.' We have prayed for it these many years but never absolutely needed it as now; but now we have it. There are forty-two acres of land, an immense brick house, two fine old wells, and a garden. So we are to have a woman's hospital in India!

Mrs. Thomas,

Medical Work of the W.F.M.S.

III

Strengthening Stakes

The care of the growing Church in the India Mission was daily a burden upon the hearts of the preachers and their helpers. Oft-times they "agonized in prayer" for individuals and groups, for they wrestled against "the rulers of darkness of this world". New converts often went back before they made much progress. There was much to discourage, as also to encourage. All methods were made to contribute to the strength of the growing community.

Evangelistic Work

Bazaar preaching which was essentially the method of open-air preaching of Wesley, often yielded no apparent results but through the years was never given up and in most stations was regularly maintained. It was

> at once the most difficult and the most interesting department of Missionary labour. . . . To be able to catch the attention of men who are passing by, intent on business and 'Pleasure'; to inspire them with an increasing desire to hear what is to be said, however unpleasant or condemnatory; to induce a promiscuous company entirely unaccustomed to literary exercises; to stand amid the turmoil and distraction of the bazaar and listen while the preacher talks of spiritual things; to do all this successfully demands a combination of talent really possessed by a few.[1]

The Conference had come to recognize that quiet preaching in selected mohallas, or personal work by Hindustani preachers in families among friendly people, was a more effective means of winning men to Christ.

A Committee, on Churches in 1872 urged that the time had come for more than Bazaar preaching, which could not accomplish the whole object of the Mission. They urged the need of churches where people could assemble "for more careful and continued instruction [through] protracted efforts, prayer and social meetings".[2] The Bareilly church was opened in 1872 at a cost of Rs. 16,000 but a church "right in the city was still a necessity where Christian worship could be kept up before the people".[3] In Moradabad this need was met by the opening of the new building on July 4, 1875, for both church and school.

> After the Sunday morning service the house was dedicated to the Worship of Almighty God; Divine service was held in the afternoon, followed in the evening by a lecture on the improvement of Society, which was largely attended by non-Christian Indians of the city.[4]

"Formerly", wrote Parker, "no outsiders attended our Sunday services, now as many as two-thirds of the audience may be outsiders, and in the Sunday School many more from young and old." The evening service was regularly followed by a lecture-service on religious topics. Thus, "all classes" had been drawn under Christian influence. "If any kind of work pays," wrote Parker, "such meetings as we had for 17 days, pay"—seven days of regular religious services, followed by lectures on Christian doctrines.

In Shahjahanpur, also, in the newly built school hall a series of meetings was held in 1877.

> Each of the six meetings held was a grand success . . . the hall was closely packed, the audience crowding on the forms, thronging around the doors, and occupying every inch of available room either in the building itself or behind the door posts.[5]

The subjects treated were: God, The Word of God, Sin, The Christian Plan of Salvation, The Future State. Addresses were "attentively and even respectfully listened to".

For several years Babu Ram Chandra Bose as a Local Preacher was set apart for work among the educated and high classes. He travelled extensively in North India and the Punjab and sometimes to the South. The Lucknow report for 1877 includes this reference :

> The Babu resigned a salary about double what he now receives in order to preach Christ to his educated fellow-countrymen. For some months he delivered weekly lectures in English at the Mission Chapel on Saturday evenings. About 100 Native gentlemen attended. The lectures were well received and have been published. Bible classes and house visitation accompanied this work.[6]

Immediate Baptisms

Samuel Knowles, while in charge of the Gonda Circuit, emphasized district tours and work at melas more than some of his colleagues. One year a team on such a tour preached Christ 194 times to a total of over 27,000 people. With him was Rajab Ali, a Muslim convert of Gonda, who had relinquished a government post with a salary of Rs. 350 for one very much smaller. These were able to preach to large groups of Muslims even when they were led by Maulvis brought from Lucknow.

Before such tours Knowles gathered a group of his preachers at Gonda, where they spent a week in prayer and study. These preachers learned to use and to play together the tunes of popular *bhajans*. To collect a crowd they used a big English drum, a cornet and a large pair of cymbals ; in worship they used two sitars, two dhols and a triangle.

> They waited upon the Lord until one and all had the faith of expectation, the assurance that God would work with them; refusing to go forth so long as any one of their members had any doubt about it . . . . Few Christians sufficiently realize the power of united faith . . . that we *unite in* believing the same word of promise.[7]

For twenty-five years Knowles had believed it impossible to reach the minds of Hindus and Muslims without a course of previous instruction, but he was wonderfully taught by God to see and grasp the truth that the Word of God "was the only real medium of the Spirit of God to convince the heart of sin and of righteousness".

> I took it for granted that my work must be in the plowed fields, always sowing in hope of some future indefinite results. I never for a moment supposed it was my privilege to be sent by the Lord of the harvest into the ripe fields and with the reaper's sickle and song, to gather in the sheaves for the Master's harvest-home . . . . The mistake is to suppose that God has no other way of working.[8]

Knowles' experience and practice aroused both interest and criticism. Thoburn wrote of North India Conference feeling :

> A general conviction seemed to prevail that the dawning of a better day was at hand, and that a more vigorous evangelistic effort should be organized without delay . . . not a few of our Hindustani brethren are deeply moved.[9]

To such as would come from the crowd, facing its opposition and ridicule, baptism was at once openly given, and immediately afterwards the convert partook of the *parshad*, or food with the preachers. Knowles' experience was that such converts were "as firm in their attachment to Christianity . . . as those who had been tested for a time before receiving the rite."[10]

"Camp Meetings" Or "Christian Melas"

The earliest of these was held in Amroha in November, 1865. About 110, nearly all of the Christians, had met there with the missionaries of the Moradabad District for a week of religious services. The object of the gathering was to lead the nominal Christians to Christ, and to unite all the churches in a bond of love. It was also designed by preaching two hours daily at six different points in the city to awaken an interest among the people generally. The Meeting was a success and was held annually for several years.[11]

It was of such meetings that F. M. Wheeler wrote:

> The preceding year closed with an event both wonderful and rare in the history of our India Mission: there had been a *Revival*, or rather the *commencement* of a living spiritual faith in the hearts of the native Christians. About a dozen of them began to receive the *power* who had

before the *form* of godliness . . . . The soundness and blessedness of this work has been manifested throughout the year.[12]

In 1870 Zahur al Haqq experienced his "*new birth*" at such a camp meeting. A similar camp meeting for quickening the spiritual life within the Bareilly District was held at Tilhar, in 1868. About a hundred Christians gathered—boys from the orphanage, sweepers and others ; Judd, Johnson and Scott, with their families. "These meetings carried us back to revival scenes at home. Twenty souls found peace. Thank God, experimental Christianity is securing a well attested basis among our people.[13] Of this gathering Buck wrote:

> There was a great outpouring of the Holy Spirit for the first time among our Indian Christians. Our Indian helpers now acknowledge that up to that time they were sceptical of the new birth as taught by the missionaries. But one day Rev. T. J. Scott took for his text 'Have ye received the Holy Ghost since ye believed? ' And the word was accompanied with such unction that many were cut to the heart and began to seek the baptism of the Spirit. And they did not seek in vain. The power of God came down, and the helpers were all, or nearly all, blessed and many others too. Since then no camp meeting has passed without souls finding Christ.[14]

In the Amroha District under Zahur al Haqq an annual gathering was held at a village, Rajabpur, which was a central point for 146 villages with 1500 Christians.[15]

By The Living Minister

Peter Merrill never reached membership in the Annual Conference but for over thirty years he laboured faithfully in the circuits of the Bijnor District as an ordained Local Preacher.

His wife, Josephine, in 1858, was an orphan girl living with her aunt who lost her in the market at Najibabad. She was found by a man who sold her to a sweet-meat dealer. A year later she was put in the Bareilly Orphanage. There, Josephine grew to Christian womanhood and married Peter Merrill, a preacher.[16] On their appointment to Bijnor, about 1876, she wished to locate her relatives for she remembered the names of her father and a brother. The latter was traced. Josephine

> seemed only to live for them. When scarcely able to stand, [for she is a confirmed invalid and often near to death,] she has gone to visit them and with a zeal my heart assures me they cannot long resist. She taught them about the Saviour. 'I must bring them to Christ before I die,' she says . . . . At her first visit they were filled with awe as she knelt and prayed after she had sung and explained the way of salvation to them . . . . She made repeated visits, staying at one time for 15 days with her brother.

The next year "her brother and family, six persons in all," were baptized.[17]

MAHBUB KHAN

He was a teacher in a Government school in the Budaon District who a boy had attended a Mission School in Sialkot, and became interested in e search for truth. He read such books on Islam as came to hand, but as unsatisfied.[18] Restless in heart, he strayed into another school and sked for a book to read. There was "only the New Testament left by a issionary". Taking it home he read a little, put it aside and then took up again. The Sermon on the Mount interested him, and he read on:

> While reading the account of the Saviour's suffering as narrated in the 27th Chapter of Matthew, a profound conviction of the truth of the narrative and of the Divinity of Christ came like a flash to his soul. Without speaking to a single Christian, he had been awakened to a knowledge of his own lost condition and from reading the Word had been led to a definite acceptance of Christ....He returned to his school but could not repress the desire to tell of his new-found joy....it soon became evident to all that he was no longer a Musalman in belief, although he had taken no outward step toward the profession of Christianity.[19]

)nly after he had reached this conclusion did he go to the missionary. He old his wife of his new joy. She replied: "I am your wife and will never ave you; if you become one of the outcastes, so will I." People tried dissuade her, offering her an allowance but she refused all. Both were aptized with their children. He became a Presiding Elder.

Mass Movements

The movement among the Mazhabi Sikhs continued to progress. In e census of 1881 we read that this community "had virtually disappeared om Rohilkhand". The census official could give no explanation for is, "but in the same report", says Thoburn, "the increase of Native Christians, chanced to be about the same number as the decrease in the number Mazhabi Sikhs".[20]

In its development this movement brought its discouragements. f Babukhera, a main center of the movement, Parker writes:

> It now appears as though we had commenced wrong. A few years ago we built them a little chapel costing Rs. 400. This chapel is now a hindrance to us as it belongs to the Mission, and is not of the form that they can keep in repair. If it were not that it would seem to be going backward, it would be the very best thing for our work there to level that chapel to the ground, and then let the people provide such a house as they themselves can build and keep in repair as their own.[21]
> [In Joa] Although the work seemed to be improving more than it had done for years previously, . . . the lack of spiritual knowledge and life among the Christians hinders so....Much injury has been done to the

> people by the aid given them in secular matters. Instead of now fee ing that they must support the Gospel, they think that the Gospel shoul support them, and hence great dissatisfaction is at times manifeste towards the Mission. [22]

H. A. Cutting, who succeeded Zahur al Haqq as preacher-in-charg at Amroha in 1874, reported that there were Christians and inquirers i 120 villages, with eight exhorters or local preachers having oversight the churches and "year by year this work grows in numbers and in spiritua ity,"[23] *but* in the next report, the evil of child marriage had divided th community. Every possible effort was made to overcome the practice, eve to removing some from Church membership. As hope grew that the cu tom would soon disappear, other persons in whom there had been comple confidence, "had the heathen ceremony performed for their children' The conflict continued through years. Cutting tells of two girls who ha been married as children and later sent to the Moradabad school by the parents. Here they grew up and married men of their own choice. Th father of one of these went to the courts to secure an annulment of h daughter's recent marriage, so that she might be compelled to accept th man she had married in childhood. Since the law did not recogniz child marriage for Christians, he lost his case.[24]

Thoburn and Zahur al Haqq opened the work in Bashta, now in th Bijnor District. They were prepared for a "vigorous campaign". In few days he baptized twenty-seven adults, but—

> When I thought of those raw converts my heart almost sar within me. How could they be expected to hold together, adop Christian habits, and develop the life for a genuine Christian Church What would other missionaries think of this wholesale baptizing of igno ant men whom I had never seen before, and whose antecedents an even names I knew little or nothing of whatever?[25]

Some two years later that group bought a plot of ground and the next yea "a cheap chapel and native preacher's house" were built on it by the Chri tians in that community. The little Church grew. In 1872 there wer nine full members in the villages about Bashta, and a number of enquirer Prem Das and his wife had been faithful labourers and the Christians ha become more independent than those of any other part of the distric Their chapel and pastor's house were built by subscriptions and belonge to the people, and would be kept in repair by them.

Bashta also had its struggles and weaknesses in spirituality and i brotherhood, or *biradari*. It is significant that M. T. Titus as D. S. i Moradabad District in 1949, in a backward look over ninety years, wro of Babukhera, where the work of the District started that "there wa not now a single Christian". At the same time the Bashta circuit wa leading the village churches of the Bijnor District in what it paid its pasto

Today in the Moradabad and Bijnor Districts there are thousands who trace their ancestry to the early converts of this first mass movement.

THE CHAMARS

The indications of a movement among the *Chamars* in and around Moradabad reported in 1864 continued to develop in centres like Sambhal, Kundarki, Chandausi and in Moradabad city itself. The name of Andrias recurs in reference to the work with this group. He was probably one of the three gurus to whom Parsons made reference in his mid-year report in 1859. After his baptism he continued to move as a teacher among his own followers. One day, near Kundarki, he was asked by the missionary to take a turn in speaking to the people. He climbed on the cart which became the rostrum; people around him pressed to hear: "He spoke like a master. He parried blows from opponents with great readiness, and gave thrusts like a master of his art. From that day Andrias was numbered among our preachers."[26] His method of evangelizing was described, as more than preaching.

> Taking his Testament, Catechism and Hymn Book, he goes from village to village, and from house to house, teaching the people *by rote*, the Lord's Prayer, Apostle's Creed, Ten Commandments and Catechism, as he used to teach them *slokhs*, and he scarcely ever fails to pray with his company before leaving them.[27]

When George Bailey, who had been converted under Taylor, was pastor in Sambhal he reported that although *Chamars* had not, as a group, professed to be Christians, they allowed their children to be taught, and the adults joined freely in the services. Small numbers were baptized, but others maintained aloofness.

THE SWEEPERS

The movement among the sweepers was next. Among India's outcastes these were near the bottom. A few in each village, more in the cities, they were found everywhere. They were hungry for respect, for freedom from the darkness and limitations in their lives. Like the common people of Jesus' day, they heard the Gospel gladly. The conversion of Chimman Lal and the opening of the little school for the sweeper children in Budaon under Humphrey, in 1860, was a forecast of this turning. J. C. Butcher gives the following account of its development:

> The sweepers were from the beginning readily accessible, but for many years our missionaries did not know this, and when they did learn it many of them were undecided as to whether they wanted them. The first man to recognize them was T. J. Scott in Budaon and during the years 1863-66 he baptized quite a number into the Christian community. In the meantime Robert Hoskins had arrived in India, and

> during 1868-69 was stationed in Bijnor. He was the first man among us to really believe in these people, and during his first year baptized 53 and in the second year 40....His confidence in his people explains something of his success in winning them for Christ.[28]

About the baptisms in 1868 Hoskins says, "most of them are from the lower classes, but they already evidence the Gospel's power to elevate". The Church membership had "been under constant daily instruction; most of those received on probation have begun to learn to read, and all have been thoroughly drilled in the catechism and parables of the New Testament". Full members had increased one hundred percent; several openings had been made in "villages which give promise of a much greater work next year .... We have sought to give every Christian child the very best facility for education."[29] He describes the churches as

> greatly improved in every quality that makes up a triumphing Church militant. An effort has been made to promote indigenous Christianity; and though it has been a year of great financial depression and starvation yet nearly half enough to support a Native Missionary to be sent to a new field has been collected . . . every man gives most satisfactory proof of having been converted, and of enjoying intimate communion with God.[30]

But, writes Butcher of Hoskins:

> His missionary brethren did not all believe in him. They were alarmed at his recklessness, and were sure it meant ruin and disgrace to the infant Church in India. So he had to leave Bijnor. However, Scott had become Presiding Elder of the Bareilly District, and recognising something of the worth of Robert Hoskins was glad to welcome him to the Budaon Circuit. Here Hoskins had a free hand and in his first year baptised 215 persons. But he was really a conservative man, and after admitting so many in one year, never repeated the experiment but contented himself with a moderate yearly increase, and laid himself out to develop his converts into workers.[28]

Schools Win Their Way

The reports from 1865 show schools winning their way as an approved agency for building the Church. There was opposition. And yet the most ardent advocates for schools could not have anticipated the gigantic educational work which grew up in the Conference.

Bishop Thomson had encouraged the program when he said:

> We must teach the young both because of the ease with which impressions are made upon their minds, and because of the durability of such impressions which are interwoven with the very texture of the soul. If you would write your words in a book, if you would cut them on the lead with stillett of iron; if you would send them down the ages, and centuries and milleniums, aye, into eternity, write upon the *young* soul.[31]

The stimulus to education received from the Despatch of 1854, with the policy of grants-in-aid, produced an intellectual revival in which "western thought and culture gradually undermined systems of philosophy and religion older than civilization itself". In view of this, the Committee on Education, in 1869, pronounced the development of schools as a legitimate branch of mission work, second only to the proclamation of the Word. There were then 3906 pupils in the mission schools of whom 616 were girls. Twenty pupils were reported to have been converted during that year.[32] A most encouraging feature in the Orphanage in 1866 was the spiritual birth in the lives of forty of the oldest girls.[33] However, enough opposition to schools continued so that Messmore in his report was constrained to say

> a word or two in defense of our school work. It is expensive; much of it is in the hands of Hindus and Mohammedans; it is most exhaustive of the Missionaries' time and strength; yet we cannot do without it. Our schools give us a local habitation and a name. They are the avenue of approach to important and influential classes of community, otherwise unapproachable. They firmly impress Christian ideas upon the minds of those who in a few years will be the leaders of native society and thought. Our scholars are led almost imperceptibly to examine everything from the standpoint of Christian philosophy, and even when attempting to defend their own religion, they do it, not with the old time syllogisms based on essential error, but with the weapons which we have given them; and in such a conflict the result is inevitable. The converts from our schools are as yet few in number; but we are not labouring for today. The presumption is that more converts will appear from among our scholars after they leave our schools than while with us.[34]

Orphanages

The Annual Conference gave a great deal of attention to the careful administration of its orphanages. They represented both an opportunity for and responsibility on the Church. Certain principles were accepted for the accomplishing of the specific purposes of the orphanages: (1) in the beginning only orphans were admitted; (2) the main effort was to prepare them for the ordinary duties of life when they should leave; (3) as a part of this preparation their religious training was carefully supervised; (4) every orphan, boy or girl, was expected by some type of work to contribute to the cost of his or her maintenance; (5) all orphans attended some classes. The amount of education they could receive was adjusted to the age, ability and prospect for the individual pupil.

GIRLS' ORPHANAGES

(1) In keeping with the purposes of an orphanage, the girls in Bareilly were taught "needlework, plain sewing, making and mending their own clothes, and the various kinds of knitting and crochet". During

1865, net profit totaled Rs. 146 and in 1867, this increased to Rs. 196. I addition to making all their own clothing all girls were taught to cook, sweep their own rooms, to grind their own wheat, and required "to pum and carry all the water used in the compound, for cooking, drinkin bathing, watering the shade trees, etc.".[35]

The report for this Orphanage for the year 1865 shows that four boarde had been received.[36] This step had been taken by the Principal withou authorization, perhaps to draw attention to a growing sentiment or need In 1867 there was only one *boarding* pupil, *i.e.,* a child not an orphan, fo whom the parent paid fees.

In 1867 the Principal urged upon the Conference Visitors that " a few rooms could be provided for the purpose, a number of other gir would be sent as boarders, and in time, the orphanage might become girls' boarding school of high grade".[37] The Visitors heartily agreed an in 1868 advised "that special efforts be made to disabuse the minds of ou Christians, of the erroneous idea that there is anything degrading to hav their children educated at the Orphans' School".[38] In 1869 there wer 150 orphans when a boarding department with five girls was opened.[3 They studied in the same classes but were not required to do the work th orphans did.

A normal class was opened in 1868 for training some of the orphan as teachers; in fact, some were already teaching classes in school. Thi forward step was highly approved as a demand for women teachers wa growing rapidly. Another sphere of usefulness for the orphan girls wa suggested by Humphrey's medical class in Naini Tal. In fact Mrs. Thoma had commenced preparing a class in English, looking toward such an oppor- tunity. With such initiative it is not surprising to know that the Govern- ment Inspector wrote in the Visitors' Book: "I consider this school on of the best of its kind in the North-western Provinces, and well deserv- ing of the grant-in-aid".[40]

In the fall of 1870 Miss Fannie Sparkes reached India and was ap- pointed to the Orphanage. She worked in association with Mr. and Mrs. Thomas for a year and then assumed full responsibility. The years in which the Thomases were in charge had been years of wise planning. The Woman's Foreign Missionary Society took over support of the or- phanage in 1870 making an appropriation of $3000 for the year.

(2) A second orphanage for girls was opened in Pauri. Mrs. Mansell gathered a few orphan girls in 1869-70. They were orphans, o girls with one parent who could not care for the children and so gave them to the missionary. Of the first girl, Julia Thorn, Mrs. Mansell wrote : "One day I saw an old woman peeping in at every door and window

watching me". She wished to leave her little girl. Two years later the record reads ; "Julia is a smart little girl". The second girl, Annie Judson, "was living with her brother who hoped to sell her for a large sum of money". She would not return to him. Phulmani had been sold to a man when she was a babe. Her mother, anxious to redeem the child, asked the missionary for the amount of money she had received to get her back; she was released. Little Sundari had had her hands burned by her husband—three fingers on the right hand, two on the left. "She has surprised us by learning to sew and knit, besides cooking."[41]

In 1870 the Mansells had eight girls and twelve boys. She gives a lovely glimpse into the life of the orphans, when their daughter was nine years old : "Hettie Mansell collects the little girls for prayer meeting every Sunday after service, and the way they sing the hymns, and the intelligence of their prayers, is quite remarkable". The W. F. M. S., in 1871, agreed to support as many orphan girls as they received, [42] and the next year a suitable building had been erected for "the little girls' Orphanage". Mrs. P. T. Wilson, in charge of the Woman's Work after Mrs. Mansell, proposed to open a "boarding department for girls who were not orphans". From August, 1873, Mrs. Gill took over the orphanage with ten girls, and continued in charge until 1880, with the exception of 1876 when Miss Blackmar was its Superintendent. When the Gills left there were forty-two girls in the institution which is now known as the Mary Ensign Gill Girls' School. In 1874 the institution was called the "Girls' Orphanage and Boarding School", and Elmira Blake was the matron and teacher.[43] A building grant of Rs. 1000 was received from the Government in 1874.

BOYS' ORPHANAGES

The Boys' Orphanage moved from the cantonments of Shahjahanpur to its permanent location at East Shahjahanpur, or Lodhipur, in 1865. Here T. S. Johnson had purchased twenty acres of arable land, which a few years later was largely increased in area.[44] A year after moving, the school house and chapel, boys' and teachers' dwellings, store room, wall of enclosure and "pakka well" were completed at a cost of Rs. 13,000 of which the Mission Board had paid less than one-fourth.[45] To the Conference of 1868 the Visitors were happy to report that manual labour had become "quite popular, and many volunteers are found in the workshop from among those who are foremost in their studies". But, often, too, the older and more sombre note recurred:

> The experiment of teaching trades is not a marked success, because the boys can usually secure employment as Teachers, Colporteurs, etc., which is more profitable and congenial. We recommend that the workshops be so arranged as to become self-supporting.[46]

That report of the Board of Education brings out the triple problem tha every Principal has known to whom has been committeed the task o teaching trades: (1) the ill-repute of manual labour, (2) the attractio of more congenial lines, (3) the insistence that workshops must be self supporting although any other teaching program may be financed. Faith fully T. S. Johnson and his successors contended with these problems. Th institution at Lodhipur has never, or only recently, overcome the stigm attached to the word Orphanage,—though the name has long sinc changed—where the requirement of work in some form continues, while i "boarding schools" neither the learning of a trade nor productive work i expected of students.

> In 1869 a boarding department was opened with five boys It is quite separate from the Orphanage. It is for those who ar able to pay their own expense, both Native and East Indiar Three of the present number are very respectable boys of the latte class. The cost for board, clothing and books, is from six to te rupees each [per month].[47]

In 1872 the number of boarding boys had reached nine, and twenty fron the city were attending as day scholars.[48]

The part that the Boys' Orphanage played in opening the first classe in Theology is told elsewhere; the whole story of the contributio to the Church no one will ever know. By 1872 when the Seminary opened it had already sent out twenty-six young men as Mission helpers, preacher and teachers.[49] In 1874 the Conference authorized the Superinten dent "to gather *into the school of that institution* promising but poor Chris tian boys as circumstances may permit, to be educated and supported b scholarships".[50] The result of such a mixing of standards—orphan paying nothing, but required to work; boarders paying "fees"; and third group on scholarships—in an institution is graphically reported b the Educational Committee to the Conference in 1878 :

> The tendency of the institution is to become rather an asylun for the children of indigent Christian parents than to remain an Or phanage. In fact, it can only by a very liberal construction of language be called an Orphanage at all. The policy of the Mission should be a once decided, whether this is to become a real Orphanage or whether i is to remain what has become an Asylum for the support and educatio of indigent Native Christian parents. Such an Asylum is wanted by the Native people, circumstances seem to demand it, we have it in fac under another name. It is recommended that the Conference tak measures to change the original policy to suit the policy actually in use.[51]
>
> As a result of the famine, the number of boys in the Orphanag has been greatly increased. We shrank from the additional responsi bility, but when starving children were thrust upon us, for whom there

was no other possible hope, we could not refuse them. The strictest economy was adopted . . . an appeal to the good people at home brought Rs. 1,135 to the Orphanage, which afforded great relief, so that the year will close without debt. [T. S. Johnson][52]

A project offering hope for many was launched in 1881, by an arrangement with cloth and leather manufactories in Kanpur. Ninety boys from the Orphanage and twenty-six Christians from Rohilkhand were engaged in work, of whom eight were women; seventy-eight were in the Cotton Mills, and thirty-eight in the Leather Factory. The next year eleven families, eight boys and two widows were earning their own livelihood.[53]

THE BABUKHERA "BRANCH ORPHANAGE"

The Boys' Orphanage was connected with a very important development in the work among the Mazhabi Sikhs in 1865. The report for the Orphanage that year gives the number of boys as ninety-five, "including twelve boys in the Babukhera School who are supported from Orphanage funds. They are to enter the Orphanage school whenever it seems best."[54] The Visitors' report for 1866 gives the number at Babukhera as fourteen,

> under the charge of Rev. E. W. Parker, [they] were not examined by the Committee. They are under the immediate care of W. Plumer, and are in all respects favourably spoken of by members of the Mission who have seen them.[55]

This school at Babukhera was the first non-orphanage boarding school established in the Conference. T. S. Johnson tells of this school at the centre of the Sikh work where there was a little chapel and native church.[56]

> The opening in the Moradabad District promises much for the future of this institution. There are a large number of boys there whose parents desire they may receive a Christian education, but are not able to give them over to the mission to be educated. . . . An arrangement between Bro. Parker and myself, whereby he is furnished with money for the support and education of eight boys, who, after remaining in the village a year or two, are to come to the orphanage to complete their education. . . . The number will be increased as soon as the funds of the institution justify it.
>
> . . . 'Though these boys may not be orphans there is the same need for them being educated, and quite as much promise in them as though they were.'[57]

Just how long this arrangement lasted is not certain, nor do we know how many of these boys came to the Orphanage to finish school. A number of boys from this community were in the orphanage before 1865 including: Horace J. Adams, William R. Bowen, Benjamin F. Barnes, Lucius A. Cutter, Hiram A. Cutting, Wilbur Fisk, Seneca Falls.[58] In

1872 there was a good village school at Darapur near Babukhera which was "attended by the Christian boys of Babukhera and by the eight boys in the boarding department there". In 1873, when the girls' boarding was taken to Moradabad, this boarding was moved to Amroha where H. A. Cutting had succeeded Zahur al Haqq. He describes the purpose of the school :

> The object of teaching the young men at Amroha is to take one young man from each village where no one can read, and keep him in Amroha for one or two years until he can read, write and sing well, and also secure correct instruction in spiritual things. Then he will return to his home to support himself just as formerly and at the same time be an intelligent leader and teacher there. I know of nothing so promising to this work as this plan, especially as the wives of these young men are also being taught in the same way.[59]

Others of this community were also learning, for exhorters in their circuits were teaching about fifty boys and a number of bright boys from this community were in the Moradabad school.

School Administration

With growing approval for schools the Conference took a stronger hold on their administration and control. In 1869 responsibility for uniformity and efficiency was placed on the Presiding Elders with specific instructions to care for the religious teaching. They were also "requested to examine annually each school in his district, either orally or by written questions".[60]

Further restrictions were imposed in 1870. High schools were limited to Lucknow, Shahjahanpur and Moradabad, for "nothing but injury can result from an attempt to maintain more High Schools than are actually demanded by the state of our work". A Board of Education was constituted, composed of the three elected members of the Board of Trustees of the proposed College to provide uniformity in courses of study, in salaries of teachers, grading of pupils, etc., and to promote efficiency. The necessity of the College itself, it was felt, would "depend upon our success in maintaining these superior schools, and its success when established will be equally dependent upon them".[61]

With this emphasis on a program of coordinated Christian schools from primary to college level there followed a demand for increased attention to the education of Christian children. The Rohilkhand District Conference in 1874 urged "that we should increase the facilities for the education of Christian children, even if we were compelled to do less for other classes.[62]

Boys' Schools

A boys' school started in Husainabad, Lucknow, grew under Messmore to be known as the Central School. Four branch schools developed around it. A fine building started in 1862, was completed in 1866. It was expected that the first high school class would appear in 1867, but all the boys had been employed as teachers, while they continued studies. They were thus delayed a year. The new building was destroyed by a flood in 1870. With difficulty the school was continued, until, by a friendly adjustment, the Church Missionary Society gave their school in Naokhas, near Husainabad, to the Methodists and took the Methodist schol in Hasanganj. The Central and Nakhas schools were then united, and in a new building continued to do good work. In 1873 the enrolment reached three hundred.

The City School in Bareilly grew slowly until a new building was provided in 1866.[62] The introduction of the Bible as a text and religious instruction, brought "the usual reverses and difficulties". A fine tribute is paid to the Hindu Pandit in the school, who is described as "remarkably sincere and upright—setting in several respects, a good example for the Christians".[63]

The importance of the Shahjahanpur school was always overshadowed by the greater attention given to the orphanage. It was started in the little chapel Cawdell had built.[64] Humphrey moved it to a site in the city, and members of the English congregation helped to support it. Early missionaries gave much time to it. The student body from an early date was entirely non-Christian. A Christian headmaster was secured in 1868 who assumed responsibility for religious teaching. In 1875 it was recognized as one of three high schools in the Conference. This status was changed soon after unless it could carry high school classes without added expense to the Mission.

As in other stations a small boys' school was early started in the mission compound in Moradabad. In 1863 Humphrey moved it to a place in the city, reorganized it and with financial help received from English friends in the city, established it.[65] There were many difficulties through the years. In 1870 when the Headmaster left abruptly, a young American, Melville Cox Elliot, who had traveled to India in search of health, and had found improvement, was persuaded to take the position. With his talent for organizing he brought the school to a state of efficiency. In 1871 he joined the Annual Conference and was appointed to Bahraich. There health failed again; he went to Almora and died in August. Immediately after Parker's return from furlough and reappointment to Moradabad in 1872, he gave attention to the school and built it up. A limited number of boys from the district were brought into a boarding that year.

Parker set himself to providing a better building for the school. It was a most difficult task involving the raising of funds, buying land in several plots to get a large site in the bazaar, and finally in supervising the construction. All was accomplished and the new building, to serve also as a church, was opened on July 4, 1875.

In 1882 Dr. J. F. Goucher undertook to support 100 primary schools, sixty for boys and forty for girls, in the Rohilkhand district. He prescribed that every school should be taught by teachers who were members of the Methodist Church; every days' sessions were to be opened with Bible lesson, singing of a hymn, and prayer, all in the vernacular; and the whole plan to be under a committee of which he named several. From these schools he would support 100 boys "who evidence the greatest aptitude, application and acquirements," in a hostel to attend the Moradabad Central School. Provision was made also for eighty girls, similarly selected and supported, to attend the girls' boarding school, Moradabad. Later the same benefactor contributed to the cost of the hostel buildings for the accommodation of these scholars. A second donor, Mr. Frey, contributed for schools in Oudh, on much the same basis. His death in 1884 cut short his share in the enterprise, except for advanced students for whom provision was continued. During the period of these scholarships the Central School came to be known as the Goucher Central School. This help continued through 1900. Many a young Christian man passed from Moradabad to the Theological Seminary or the College after the start given by these scholarships.

Parker looked upon the Central School as a Christian Training School. In 1886 there were 136 Christian boys and 117 non-Christian boys in the school. He wrote:

> Our Theological School, our Normal School and all of our higher institutions are failing of doing the work they should do for want of pupils that are well trained before they reach these higher schools. We cannot begin at the top to educate. This school, therefore, is a training school for Christian boys. These boys are selected from Goucher schools all over Rohilkhand and hence we shall have choice lads in our own boarding department.[66]

The little school started by Humphrey, in Budaon, grew slowly, yet it struggled on. The needed building was completed in 1871[67] under Hoskins, who also opened a Christian hostel in 1875 when twenty promising boys were brought in from village schools.[68] Ten of the more advanced of these were taking English; all were doing well in the vernacular. Both Hoskins and Neeld who followed him considered the schools a valuable branch of the work, real training centres in which to prepare Christian young men to serve later in building the Church.

> There are 27 pupils, 23 boys and 4 men; of these men one was a Chamar *bairagi*, one a Thakur, one a Musalman and one a Chamar; I hope soon to have these men ready to take up some form of Christian work. The Musalman and the wife of the *bairagi* are both from the Etah [trans Ganges] district. Most of the boys are from the Chamars and higher castes.[69]

Thoburn reached his appointment in Pauri in April, 1866. Mr. and Mrs. Mansell had spent the summer of 1865 there and had then organized a small boys' school under a Brahmin, Pandit Purshottam, who was on hand to welcome Thoburn. In a trip which Thoburn made to Badrinath that first year he heard how Shankar Acharya had founded the temple of Kedarnath and established there the college of priests which continues in connection with that temple, and how the founder had died near the temple at the age of thirty-two. Thoburn wished he could do something "to plant a vine, or lay a foundation which might endure after I was gone". Then was born the desire to plant a Christian institution in Garhwal

> confronting the great temples, and destined to live on and bless the province for long centuries after the temple should be forgotten.... A central missionary institution [which] would become a nucleus of Christian influence around which all manner of agencies would gather, and from which streams of blessing would flow out among the people for ages to come.[70]

The little school which Mansell opened was now for Thoburn a *trust.* It was continued and in 1867 he wrote of "arrangements made for enlarging it and making it a high school for the district". The first boarding connected with a central school was opened by him on April 1, 1867, to "assist meritorious boys from village schools" to come to Pauri to continue their studies. Thirty boys came to that first hostel from the district, eighteen of whom were aided by scholarships. None of these was a Christian. "There was not a Christian in the district." He describes himself as "taking lessons in what some people call 'faith work'".[70] Help was also given to two promising girls who applied for admission on the same terms as the boys. One of these was baptized during the year and married; the other was withdrawn.

In planning rooms for the boys whom he expected, he planned each room with a window and a chimney.

> I took great credit to myself for this last innovation.... I was to teach them a more excellent way. I superintended the chimney building with great care, doing part of the work with my own hands, and felt confident that when the boys once learned how to keep a fire in a smokeless room they would go home and teach their fathers how to build chimneys. But I was doomed to disappointment. When... the

> boys began to live in them, they could not be persuaded to build a fire in a little hole at one side, but placed it in the middle of the room where they could get the largest amount possible of benefit from it when the smoke became too stifling to be endured, they would go ou of doors.[70]

Thoburn had also accepted ten orphan boys, and at the next Conference he urged that an "Orphanage" be established at Pauri for these.

> After carefully weighing all the facts in the case, and especially considering how utterly dissimilar the hill and plains people are, and how imperatively necessary it is that we secure a corps of helpers for our hill work, who have been educated in the hills, speak the hill dialects, and are strong enough for the rough work which a successful Evangelist must endure, we, the Committee on Orphanages, have no hesitation in recommending that *such a School* be established at Pauri, provided that the number of pupils be limited to thirty.[71]

"Such a school" meant "Industrial School". The Conference "urgently requested" the Missionary Society for its sanction and support for the enterprise. But no aid was included in the annual appropriation, and Mansell, who followed Thoburn in 1869, was instructed to incorporate *the children of the "orphanage" in the boarding school*, since "means had been found for maintaining them without expense to the Board".[72] But while living in the boarding these orphans continued to learn trades. In 1870 there were sixteen orphan boys and six orphan girls. Of the boys five were making good progress in English, six were "learning to work", two as tailors, three as masons and one as a cook. A beginning had also been made in fruit raising and gardening. In 1871 the number of orphans was reduced "for want of funds . . . four are now earning their own living . . . they should have had more time in school".[73] The orphan girls, still under the care of the missionary's wife, had increaased to eight.

Year by year the school grew; in 1871 the enrolment reached 110, when S. S. Dease, formerly of the Survey Department, became the Headmaster. In 1873 two boys entered the vernacular department in engineering in Roorkee. In April, 1872 Col. H. Ramsey, the Commissioner, opened the new school building of eight rooms.[74] In 1875 two boys were admitted to the Government medical school. Two also went to Eastern Kumaon in schools under the Mission. The Pauri school became a Middle School in 1881.[75]

Girls' Schools

When the Mission was started the idea of educating girls was new ; to send them from their homes before they were married, even to a hostel, was opposed to accepted traditions. The small primary schools which had been opened had prepared the way for progress in both these lines. By 1876 boarding schools were increasingly popular.

From the days of the Parkers there had been a small day school for girls at Bijnor. The boarding school was started on July 1, 1877 by Mrs. McHenry, with four boarders, the daughters of the Indian preachers, under the charge of Mrs. Peter Merrill, the wife of the Pastor, and five day scholars. At Conference time, "under the pressure of want from famine," the number of boarders reached seventeen.[76] It received the first grant-in-aid of Rs. 30 per month, in 1880. The first missionary of the W. F. M. S. to have charge was Miss Harriet Kerr, for one year, 1884, before her furlough.[77]

The first village girls were brought into Budaon for school in 1875 by Mrs. Hoskins. In 1881 a memorial gift made the Sigler Girls' School possible. In 1883 the school was accepted by the Woman's Conference and put under the Board of Education. Four girls passed the Upper Primary standard in that year. The present site of the school was purchased in 1912.

Several of the missionary ladies had opened schools for girls in Shahjahanpur, but the school for Christian girls that became the Bidwell Memorial Girls' School was opened on July 1, 1887 under Mrs. Hoskins, and at year's end there were fifteen boarders and three day scholars.

> There was no money allowed for this school this year so that we have had to be very careful in receiving pupils: there are many more ready to come so we anticipate full classes next year. No free pupils have been received, but all are required to pay at the rates established.[78]

The Boarding School for Christian girls in Sitapur had twenty-five pupils in 1884, nine of whom belonged to that Circuit.[79] A sum of Rs. 584 was collected locally that year for its needs; and in 1885 a further sum of Rs. 543 largely from residents of the Cantonments. As the only school of its grade in the Sitapur Civil District it was expected that it "would be speedily filled".

Of the little schools that had been started in Moradabad, the one near the Mission house was for Christian girls. Under Mrs. Parker it grew to be the premier school for Christian girls in Rohilkhand and as a boarding school was the first of its kind in the Mission.[80] It would be for girls what the little boys' boarding at Babukhera was for the scattered Christian homes throughout Rohilkhand District. Parents could not read; pastors had not time to teach; the only way to a simple education was to gather children at a centre.

Early in 1868 Mrs. Parker received two girls—an unusual break in social custom. She writes:

> The first year I was in India I taught a young woman to read, and then her husband. They both realized the benefits coming from education. By the death of an aunt, two cousins, little girls

> of eight and ten, were thrown on the family of this young man for support. These two girls formed the nucleus of the school.[81]

As the Parkers were soon to leave on furlough she put them in charge of Mrs. Zahur al Haqq in Amroha. The support of the girls became one of the first projects of the W. F. M. S. When Miss McMillan (Mrs P. M. Buck) took charge of girls' schools in 1872 there were twenty- three girls in the Amroha School. In 1873 it was decided to locate the boarding school in Moradabad and a building was erected in 1875. In 1883 there were 115 in the school, of whom 100 were boarders from many villages.[82] It was a model for giving a simple education with a strong foundation in Christian living, so the girls could return to villages and establish Christian homes and give a Christian witness as Aksa did.

She was one of the first girls admitted to the Moradabad boarding. Her family lived near Amroha. She was bright in class and developed a happy Christian life, with a real Christian experience. One day a messenger brought word of sickness in the family and took her home. It was a pretext to get her to her non-Christian husband, to whom she had been married as a child. Her family was bitterly opposed to Christianity. Her books were destroyed and she was forbidden to sing or pray. Neighbour Christians were not allowed to see her, nor the pastor to visit.

For three years this seclusion was maintained. At last, a preacher was allowed to see her and brought word that she was still a Christian. Soon he was asked to visit the home and to instruct the family. Then, one day the missionary on tour in a near-by village was called in. The family asked for baptism—the husband, the mother-in-law and two children. They asked for books that they too might learn. These converts are called "the first fruits" of the Boarding School because Aksa was the first girl converted in the school.[83]

> In 1886 new buildings for the girls' boarding school were opened. The morning service was only for women and girls, and at least 500 were present. All the services, of course, were conducted by women, and Hindu women and girls took part, reading essays, giving recitations, etc. . . . Many of the women had never been in such a public assembly before, and the scene to them was wonderful; a fter the service the women went all through the rooms of the boarding house of the girls. . . . In the evening the girls' school hall was again packed at a public service, closing with a dedicatory service.[84]

Mrs. Parker had received assistance from ladies of the W. F. M. S., but continued to have responsibility for the school. In 1891 Miss Day (Mrs. D. G. Abbott) was transferred to the school from Calcutta, where she had had "two years of apprenticeship", as she says, in the Calcutta Girls' School.

At the beginning of my third year in India I attained my goal, having been entrusted with a vernacular school in North India. There were nearly 200 girls in the school. I knew the untiring worker who gave me this trust was parting with a valued treasure. She had mothered the school for 25 years; from the time the first small girl was entrusted to her. Those were the days when the common people of India knew nothing of the possibilities for education latent in their little girls. Twenty-five years had passed in the history of this school and the school had amply justified its existence, but as yet no girl had proved equal to a government Grammar school test. There were experienced missionaries to assure you that Indian girls would always fall down in a Mathematics test. Their minds were unfit for Mathematics.

Nevertheless we set our stakes high. We would prepare some for the entrance examination—the equivalent of a High School closing examination. At the end of three years we had the joy of seeing two of the three who appeared for the test pass the Entrance examination. Out of this experience came a thrill, when the fathers urged me to keep their children and make them likewise efficient.[85]

'he school was recognized as a High School in 1892 and these two girls who passed the examination in 1894 were the first Christian girls from our Rohilkhand schools to do so, and *they took Mathematics.*[85]

The Press

The Press had been established in part that large boys in the Orphanage might learn a trade, and also, that the Church might have its own establishment for its many printing needs. The removal of the Orphanage to Shahjahanpur had closed the opportunity to train boys; and the "job work" had so greatly increased that it took more time than the missionary could spare from other duties. The Conference of 1866 voted to move the Press to Lucknow in the belief that there would be (1) greater facility in securing competent workmen of every grade; (2) more work given on contract to local presses; (3) economy in procuring materials, and (4) more freedom for the missionary for other work.[86] Waugh continued as Superintendent in charge of the typographical Press, which consisted of a staff of

about six individuals, one hand-press, and a room of about 16'×20', an out-house in his compound. When he took his departure to America after the Conference of 1871 this staff and plant was moved to Inayat Bagh, and Rev. J. H. Messmore became Superintendent.[87]

A part of the premises then occupied by the Witness Press in 1871 served later as a cookhouse for the adjacent bungalow. When Messmore had to be relieved, owing to sickness, Thomas Craven became Superintendent and continued in that position until his furlough in 1882.

Notwithstanding its "subjection to the Methodist itinerancy, movin about in godowns, sheds, kitchens" as Thoburn described it, the Pre put out a great deal of work. In its first year in Husainabad, Lucknow published eleven books and tracts ranging in size from 30 to 166 page with a total of 1,148,600 pages in editions running from 500 to 2000 copies.[8] It had received contributions from the American Bible Society and th Sunday School and Tract Societies of the M. E. Church. It heartily co operated in the growing Sunday School program of the Conference. fortnightly Roman Urdu paper, the *Kaukab-i-Iswi* was started in 1869 which did good work in the Christian community of our own and othe Missions. In the same year a second paper, *Shams al Akhbar*, lithographe in Urdu, was also started as a monthly, but at mid-year it became a semi monthly. It was purchased for its news by many Hindus and Muslims Messmore helped greatly in its preparation. "In these two unpretendin little papers" the Church had a powerful adjunct to Mission operations but not a rupee of "missionary money" was expended on them.[88]

In 1874 Craven found a permanent location in Hazrat Ganj. Th building and lot cost Rs. 12,000, deed free of all encumbrances, but one-hal of the sum was borrowed for three years at 6% interest. The Conferenc requested a grant of $3000 toward this purchase but the Missionary Societ was unable to give it.[89] In the purchase of the property Craven showe sound business acumen from which the Conference and church have gaine immeasurably. The publication of *The Witness* strengthened the Press a a time of need, "enabling it to add a font of type, and two compositors to it establishment".[90]

With an abundance of room in its own property the Press now lacke funds for expanding its usefulness to meet the needs. The P. E. warne the Conference in 1876, "We fear the Press cannot increase its efficienc this year as it should for want of funds. Let all be willing to help.' In that spirit it had been built up; in that spirit it continued to grow an to serve the cause of a growing evangelistic church. One marvels at the writing and the translation work that was accomplished. To a large degree it was the missionary group, all with other appointments, that create and prepared the literature needed for Sunday Schools, the Theologica Seminary, courses of study in Conference, as well as material for inquirers from Hinduism and Islam, and for the growing Christian community. The names of Waugh, Knowles, T. J. Scott, Hoskins, Thomas, Thoburn, Messmore, Johnson, Parker and Buck recur again and again in the reports of the Press, and this in addition to the three papers so recently started.

In 1875 J. H. Gill reported the translation of the Gospel of Matthew into the Garhwali dialect. About this same time the North India Bible Society requested the Conference to name persons to assist in revising the

New Testament translation in Urdu and Hindi. J. W. Waugh and Rajab Ali were named for Urdu, and J. H. Messmore and Babu Yunas Singh for the Hindi version.

The vicissitudes of the Press were numerous ; seldom, if ever, free from debt; under necessity of replenishing stock and machinery; with as many as five changes in Superintendent in the decade of the eighties[91] it yet grew, and continued to serve.

Economic Uplift

The Christian preacher, or layman, who has caught the spirit of his Master, sympathizes at once with the poverty of others. Their needs challenge him to do something for the alleviation of such conditions. The reports of the India Mission remind us over and over again how poor most of the converts were, a poverty that those who have not seen can with difficulty imagine. Oft-times, too, it was at the point of this poverty that persecution struck, in a refusal to continue employment, or by taking from them the fields which they cultivated but did not own. "Moved with compassion", the missionaries persisted in efforts to alleviate poverty.

Wesleypore was the first plan. The second was an "Industrial Association," organized by Parker in the Moradabad District, and continued by Thoburn, who followed him in 1868 as P. E., and became *ex-officio* the Business Manager of the Association. It had a capital of Rs. 750, distributed in shares of ten rupees, about half of the shares being owned by Indian Christians. It had its constitution, and members elected by the shareholders to cooperate with the P. E. in its management. It was really a plan for natives to assist their poorer brethren by providing them with some kind of work at the places of their residences. The capital could be used to afford employment in any work that would assist the Christians and also secure some profit to the company. The variety of opportunities provided is suggested by Thoburn, who found this to be "one of the most perplexing" of his duties.

> The experiment was not successful .... Those who took advances for the purchase of seed could not resist the temptation to turn the grain into bread before the time of sowing came around. The weavers did well for a time, but the temptation to bring dainty kinds of food instead of cotton yarn overcame them, and I found that their prosperity was leading them into debt. A truckster did well for a month or two, but in spite of all warnings and injunctions he would sell on credit, and soon he had empty baskets .... Two men bought carts and oxen and were able to earn about 20 cents a day above expenses .... They would not give their oxen enough to eat, they drove them too fast and too far in a day. They cut their feet by making them

> draw carts over the rugged lumps of lime stone with which the middl of the road was macadamized, . . . in less than a month the carts an oxen had been sold and the two enterprising men were bankr upt The affairs of the Association were soon wound up without any los to the native members, and with the profit of a most valuable lesso to the missionary managers.[92]

In 1868 a similar venture in the Budaon District is described b T. J. Scott. Here a sum of Rs. 282 was collected as capital and this wa contributed to liberally by some of the Churches for the help of the poore Christians. "As the most profitable way of using this money, which the are not to sink, they have engaged in brick-making, which promises suc cess." It did not last long.[93]

Then came a famine and with it one more effort to help the me improve their position, this time in securing a contract for forty men t work in a brick yard, at wages better than they had ever had, under Christian overseer. After a few days "they became insubordinate, mad unreasonable demands and finally left in a body and went back to thei village homes".

Almost ready to give up trying, Thoburn received this suggestio from Zahur al Haqq, who had "warmly seconded all his efforts which ha ended in failure". Said Haqq:

> If we wish to do these people any good *your* hand must not b seen in what is done. They think your money can never be exhausted and that there can be no failure while you stand behind, and hence the are reckless. Whatever is done must be done through their ow brethren. Let me put a little money in the hands of the two head me in Bashta, and I will take security in our way by taking brass utensil belonging to them and keeping them until the money is repaid. The will look after it as we cannot, and no one will ever know that yo have anything to do in the matter.[94]

A small beginning was made in this way and proved entirely success ful. Some families were put in the way of helping themselves . . . th condition of the whole community was said to have improved steadily. A the time of this writing that group of Christians is still the strongest in tha district. Thoburn's conclusion was this:

> We may help these very poor village Christians in many ways and ought to do so in every possible way; but after all the only wa of lifting them up into a new social life is to put the elements of such life into them. When they begin to have the Christian life in the lo depths of their present poverty they will rise as if by the power of natural law. No artificial method will materially affect their condi tion.[95]

The Conference kept on trying; compassion is long suffering. Tw efforts, started about this time, seemed for a time to succeed. (1) O uly 16, 1868 D. W. Thomas opened an Industrial Institution or "manu-actory" in Bareilly to give employment to native Christians. There were hen three departments: Cloth, *Dari* and Furniture. By Conference ime it employed eighteen Christian men and ten Christian women. To each these and to provide good articles to the public, "thirty good heathen nechanics" were employed.

The Conference expressed its "great pleasure in the successful begin-ings" of the Institution and appropriated Rs. 500 for building houses for he Christian workmen, and included in the estimates a further sum of 500 for the same purpose. During the famine it provided employment to s many as seventy "poor native Christians", and the opportunity for reli-ious teaching was "faithfully improved". Forty "very substantial houses" vere erected, but Rs. 1000 more was needed to make them "a little more omfortable".[96]

By 1871 the Industrial School was considered to be self-supporting nd seventy men and forty women were provided with employment. A ear or two later it drops out of reports. Thoburn writes, "The Christians f mature years learned new kinds of work very slowly, and, as a onsequence, their labour did not prove very profitable." In the end it eemed to be as much as anything an agency for employing non-Christian eachers.[97]

"The necessity of providing means of livelihood and homes for ative Christian families" persisted. That one experiment had failed could ot mean that another would not succeed. On June 15, 1869 T. S. Johnson urchased a tract of 887 acres, "nearly all jungle, but in a healthy eighbourhood, and the soil is of very good quality". The purchase price vas Rs. 8,510; and it was made on the personal responsibility of the mis-ionary, "but of course the Board must be looked to for help in such an ndertaking as this".[98] The village was named Panahpur—place of efuge. By early September "twenty-five families containing ninety-ive souls" were settled there. Each had put up a grass hut and started ultivation. First crops were good.

> These families are all, or nearly all, very poor, rendering it necessary to advance them money to live on until they can support themselves from their fields. This also is a very heavy expense; but the necessity of providing a means of livelihood for the poor among our native Christians compels us to go forward in this work.

Enoch Burge was appointed pastor. A little chapel and school ouse were built in 1870. The Society did not make a grant. Thereupon). W. Thomas paid Rs. 10,000 toward a total expenditure of Rs. 13,420 lready incurred, and the Conference found the difference. He agreed to

> take over the enterprise and become responsible for all further expenditures, in bringing the land under cultivation, and will give every possible assistance to Native Christians who may desire to settle there, thus keeping up the object of the enterprise, i.e., the establishment of a Christian community.[99]

By the Conference of 1873 a decided improvement in the village was seen. "Their clean, well arranged houses are in striking contrast with villages generally." Forty families now begin to pay rent regularly. Some Hindus had become Christians as a result of the village evangelistic efforts. The year 1876 was a prosperous one. There were 250 souls living there, self-supporting and comfortable. It was expected that the village would "yield a handsome yearly profit" and afford a home and accommodate 1200 to 1500 Christian people.[100] Horace J. Adams had been pastor since 1872.

The famine of 1877 was hard on them; they were aided and relieved by the subscriptions of friends. An extract from a letter from E. Cunningham is pertinent here:

> The harvest makes people glad. There has been an untold amount of suffering and death in these Provinces. The poor Chamars have died by the hundred. It is interesting to see how much more assistance has been demanded by the Native Christians in Panahpore than for a far larger number in Amroha and Bijnor. Once begin *parwaris* and you must continue to the end.[101]

In 1879 again the crops failed. Loans were given for seed; work was provided for support of some, "but with all that has been done the people remain like most cultivators, in extreme poverty".[102] The action of the Conference in 1883, that

> No mission funds shall in the future be given to this village directly or indirectly, except for pastoral support, or for schools: and that as soon as possible the burden of supporting the pastor shall be placed on the people and the expenses of the schools be met from the profits of the village,[103]

continued until patience of Conference and Managers was exhausted and the land was sold to a non-Christian, the Mission reserving a block of land at the center for church, school and other activities. Thoburn's comment was:

> It does not seem to be God's plan to gather out the converts from among their countrymen, but rather to encourage each man to remain in the place where the Providence of God has placed him, and thus scatter the good seed of Christianity among the people.[104]

Messmore considered that it "failed because people could not c ould not understand that the Mission would enforce its financial claims gainst them".[105]

It is doubtful if any other community in North India has through many years had so much done for them by the Mission, in investment of uman effort and money, as Panahpur and its two adjacent villages, which re still improvident.

You can't keep [Missions] in fences. We had a field assigned us in Northern India. . . . You might as well assign limits to the rising tide of the Atlantic Ocean as to assign a narrow field to James M. Thoburn and his fellow missionaries and the Methodist Church anywhere on the face of the earth. John Wesley told an everlasting truth concerning it when he said, 'The World is my parish.'

Bishop C. D. Foss.

You best commend the Gospel to others by faithfulness to Christ, while retaining your former customs. . . .All Christians should ever remember the responsibility resting on each of us, that of being a witness for Christ. . . . Every one of us is a missionary for good or evil as the missionary who preaches in the bazaar. . . . Every Christian man by his life and daily walk among the natives in the discharge of his duty could exemplify the character of the true religion of the blessed Jesus.

Sir Henry Ramsay.
General Committee of the Kumaon Mission

IV

Lengthening Cords

"There are many parts, yet one body." What is true of a living body is true of a living Church, whether an independent unit, or one connected with a "Mission". With growth responsibilities increase, activities become diversified, and demands multiply. Organizations need not be "mere adjuncts" ; those described herein were formed to meet needs, to serve people, to help to build the body, the Church.

The Woman's Foreign Missionary Society

This organization had its inception in convictions born and strengthened in the work of the India Mission. As early as December 20, 1857, while sitting in the *Diwan i Khass*, Butler saw the place of a woman's society that would help educate orphan girls and take the Gospel to women secluded in India's zenanas.[1]

> It seldom happens that the Church is wise to know her day of visitation. When God would have her move forward and take up some new enterprise, it usually happens that He has to beckon often and long before He is obeyed.[2]

In 1819 He beckoned. The first Woman's Auxiliary of the Missionary Society, called the Female Missionary Society, was organized only about three months after the Parent Society, in the Wesleyan Seminary in Forsyth St., New York City. This Auxiliary gave an address to the women of the Church, a definite challenge "to carry the glad tidings of free salvation to the scattered inhabitants of the wilderness". In 1855 it "had become almost inactive" and in its meeting of 1861, it reported "almost all our founders, with the earliest donors and subscribers, have passed away ; several are still with us striving to do what they can."[3] A gift of Rs. 54 from this organization is shown in the list of subscriptions to the Moradabad District in 1865, with which two women Scripture readers were employed, and another of Rs. 8 for Bareilly District.[4]

With the opening of Mission work in China in 1847, again God beckoned and the Ladies' China Missionary Society of Baltimore was formed.[5] The Woman's Union Missionary Society representing six or more different denominations was organized in 1860. The first donation from this society made for distinctive woman's work in the India Mission was a cheque for $50 to Mrs. Gracey, soon after her arrival in Sitapur, for the employment of a Christian woman as teacher or Bible readers.[6] Other gifts were received in 1866 and 1867.

With Mrs. Parker and her associates the conviction had grown deeper each year that India could be evangelized only when Christian women accepted this special responsibility. Only women could reach women, and only when women were reached and won could India be evangelized. The Parkers had their first furlough at the end of 1868, and then for reason of failing health. In Boston they were entertained in the home of Dr. and Mrs. William Butler. Conversation centered around the work and its problems, and there developed a sense of burden for women in the zenanas. On Sunday, March 14, 1869, Butler preached a missionary sermon. Mr. and Mrs. Flanders of Tremont St. Church were present in the audience and following the service met the Parkers at the parsonage.

These three ladies determined to do something. Mrs. Flanders urged on some thirty of her friends at the regular meeting of the Ladies' Benevolent Society the need of a Woman's Missionary Society in the M. E. Church. A special meeting of women of all the Methodist churches in the Boston vicinity was called for March 23, 1869. It was a stormy day. Only eight women were present, including Mrs. Parker and Mrs. Butler. A resolution to organize was approved and the meeting adjourned until the next Tuesday. That day, too, "a furious rain fell," yet thirty women showed their interest by being present. A carefully prepared constitution drafted by Edwin Parker, was presented, and adopted, for the Woman's Foreign Missionary Society of the Methodist Episcopal Church. It included the recommendation of Dr. Durbin that:

> The ladies should raise funds for a particular portion of our work in India, perhaps also in China, and leave the administration of the work to the Board at home and the Mission authorities abroad.[7]

As God beckoned for organization His Spirit was kindling in the hearts of women an eager willingness to work for women. Dr. Durbin told Thoburn before he left for India, that if he wanted fifty young ladies for missionary work he could find them in a week, but if he wanted five young men, he had to search a year or more for them. Yet it had not occurred to the leaders of the Church that "a conviction so strong and general was an indication of the will of God".[8]

This same dullness of perception prevailed on the Mission field. A year after the Missionary Society had taken a forward step and sent Miss Husk to the India Mission, members in the Annual Meeting of 1861 discussed the advisability of having "unmarried females in the mission".

Even Thoburn, who had picked up the quill of a vulture in Kundarki in the Moradabad District, and with his knife fashioned a pen with which he wrote his sister Isabella, urging her to come for educational work for girls, was so dismayed when she accepted the idea, he did not hesitate to advise her to offer her services to the W. U. M. S. of New York, rather than be sent out by the Board of our own church.[9]

Fifty years after the first Woman's Auxiliary had been organized the new Society began to work. It grew rapidly. Following a public meeting held May, 26, 1869 the women met and voted to send out a missionary. There was very little money in the treasury. Miss Thoburn's name had been presented, and in the course of discussion Mrs. Porter said :

> Shall we lose Miss Thoburn because we have not the needed money in our hands to send her? No, rather let us walk the streets of Boston in our calico dresses and save the expense of more costly apparel. I move, then, the appointment of Miss Thoburn as our missionary to India. And they all said, 'We will send her.' Part of the money was borrowed.[10]

Before the end of the year some changes in the constitution were needed so that representatives of all sections should have a share in its control. The Parkers were again called on for help. He conceived the plan of coordinate Branches with headquarters at specified cities, legislative power being vested in a General Executive composed of representatives from each Branch, the Executive to meet annually and to have responsibility for the affairs of the Society. This plan was accepted in a meeting in December, 1869.

In response to repeated requests from the field, the Society selected a second missionary, Clara Swain, M. D. to go with Miss Thoburn. They sailed from New York, November 3, 1869, and reached Bareilly on January 20, 1870, during the session of the India Mission Conference. The Conference stood as it welcomed the "first labourers" but nowhere in the Journal are their names given. Resolutions adopted recognized the "Society as a powerful auxiliary in our difficult work", and thanked the friends who had "courageously started the enterprise". The first work adopted by the Society was the support of a Bible reader in Moradabad. Dr. Swain remained in Bareilly; Miss Thoburn went to Lucknow.

The relations of members of the new Society to the Presiding Elders or to the Conference had not been worked out. The Annual Conference as a whole voted on the estimates of the W. F. M. S.; the usual Committees for auditing accounts were instructed to audit the accounts of this new Society.

A serious menace to the existence of the Society as a separate organization reached its climax in the General Conference of 1884.

> . . . In certain influential quarters a strong purpose was formed to deprive the Woman's Society of its autonomy and reduce it to the position of a collecting agency for the General Society.[11]

Parker was a member of the committee to which this resolution was referred. Bishop Andrews explained that rules had been framed by the Delegated Conference in India governing the relations of ladies to the Annual Conference, which rules had been approved by the General Executive in 1883. The General Conferenc accepted them as the basis of cooperation in all Mission fields.[12]

Medical Work

"Heal the sick . . . and say unto them, the Kingdom of God is nigh unto you." With these words Jesus linked healing and preaching. More emphatically, He linked them in the example of His own ministry. Medical work early became a part of "missionary" work. The Board of Managers had not so intended it. In 1864 they authorized an appropriation of $100 for medicines to be used by T. S. Johnson, M. D., but at the same time cautioned that they did not intend by that action "to encourage the practice of medicine to prejudice the primary work of our Mission, the preaching of the Gospel to the heathen".[13] As evangelistic work drew missionaries to the people, so did the suffering of the people impel missionaries to give relief.

Pioneer in this was J. L. Humphrey. Travelling over the mountains to his first station in 1858, he was "much impressed with the importance of having some knowledge of medicine,"—so *many* asked for medicines. He had also seen the need while waiting in Calcutta. He learned to treat the common diseases. Compelled to go on furlough at the end of 1863 because of his wife's illness, he took a pastorate. There he started to read up on medicine. His congregation allowed him to attend classes at Albany during the week if he would return for services on Sunday. In this way he completed his medical course, and on his return to India in 1868 he was stationed in Naini Tal, where Sir Henry Ramsay requested him to take charge of three dispensaries in the Bhabar and to have charge of the Central Hospital in Naini Tal. This work continued several years, the Government providing the medicines and staff.

In December, 1868, an old friend, Pundit Nand Kishore, Deputy Commissioner in Kumaon, suggested to Humphrey that he train some native women in midwifery and diseases of women and children, and that he could get the women from the Girls' Orphanage in Bareilly. Nand Kishore assumed responsibility for such part of the expenses as did not come from grants and subscriptions. The application for a grant was made at once, but there was delay in securing its approval. Civil Surgeons advised against it. "Native women", in their opinion, "had not sufficient ability to grasp the subject—nor sufficient stamina and strength of character to enable them to practice with any degree of success."[14]

Humphrey consulted the Annual Conference, which heartily approved such a class. The Visitors to Orphanages considered the suggestion as opening a "sphere of great usefulness" for the Orphanage girls, but suggested "no girls be sent out to such situations until they have married".[15] Sir William Muir, the Governor, took the view that it was "of course, an experiment, but it is worth trying; it may prove the beginning of a great popular movement".[16] Sir Henry Ramsay assumed responsibility:

> Difficulties are overcome by attempting them. If but little is accomplished some good will be done. Who shall measure the good that may result? It may exceed the value of the whole world—the extent we cannot see. The beginning may lead to a soul's being brought to Christ and thus add a jewel to His crown, which will shine through all eternity, when all the medical halls shall cease to exist. Make your arrangements and commence at once, trusting in us.[17]

The first class was opened on May 1, 1869, with ten women and six men.[18] Mrs. Humphrey accounts for nine women; three from our orphanage; three from the Sikh community; the wife of the pastor, John Barker, a Bible reader in Naini Tal, and one from the Almora Mission.[19] The men in the class were the pastor, teachers in the boys' school and catechists, who were helped financially from special funds. The female department of the Government hospital was placed under Dr. Humphrey to make possible the medical practice needed. Nand Kishore contributed Rs. 1000 to the expenses and his friends Rs. 500 more.[20]

The course extended through two hill seasons, May to November. A second class of seven women and five men was admitted the next year. In 1870 four women and one man passed; in 1871 five women and three men.[21] The Government sent a committee of three to examine the class, one of whom was the Director General of Hospitals. The certificates given to the women rated "about the grade of fourth class government doctors".[22]

> We the undersigned, have at the request of Rev. Dr. Humphrey, examined—in Anatomy, Midwifery, Pharmacy, Practice of Medicine and the management of minor surgical cases, including the more common kinds of fractures and dislocations, and we consider her qualified to practice as a midwife, and also to undertake the treatment of all ordinary diseases. She answered the different questions put to her with remarkable quickness and precision, and in our opinion, she has acquired a practical knowledge of medicine and surgery quite equal to the generality of locally trained native doctors.[23]

The experiment demonstrated that it was possible to give a medical education to India's women. A secondary result in Naini Tal is described by Mrs. Humphrey:

> By means of a high caste woman who was cured of a most distressing illness by the women of the class, our way has been opened to commence teaching the high caste women in the place. One of the women has a school for girls in her own home, and several influential native gentlemen promise to send their children.[24]

Men and women of these classes were readily placed. One woman with her husband went to Kashipur and in two months treated 232 cases, mostly women and children. Two women went as nurses to the leper asylum at Almora. John Barker and wife went to Dwarahat in 1872, where the dispensary building was completed the next year. Isa Das and wife took the dispensary in Bhim Tal.[25] In Bijnor Salina with Mrs. Jackson opened a hospital in the city.[26] Shullock, one of the women, was employed at Amroha.[27] In 1872 the "Mission Hospital" in Naini Tal treated 2078 out-patients; Bhim Tal 2003 and Dwarahat 1292![28] Multitudes learned more of the spirit of missionary work.

The First Lady Doctor

To Mrs. D. W. Thomas belongs credit for pioneering in another plan for medical care of women by women. In 1867 she mentioned to the Civil Surgeon the need of a medical missionary lady in the Orphanage. In faith that this work would open up she organized a "medical class" among orphanage girls to familiarize them with English. In an unpublished letter to Mrs. Waugh in 1868 she described some difficulties :

> The girls haven't done anything yet in medicine, because in the first place they could not manage the English physiology with the exception of Piyari. Then we sent to Agra for some Urdu books on anatomy, but when they arrived they were such a combination of Persian, Arabic and 'high falutin' Urdu, that we couldn't manage them without a Persian teacher, and have been unsuccessful as yet in our attempts to procure one, that there is no beginning made yet.

Early in 1869 Mrs. Thomas appealed to Mrs. Gracey :

> Now I see no way of having this class of native girls properly instructed except by a lady, and you will see at once that a full fledged medical missionary lady is what we want as soon as possible....Do you think the Woman's Union Missionary Society to which you belong, would help us by sending out the Doctress if one should be found willing to come?[29]

When she returned to India after her first furlough, Clara Swain gave an account in Falkland Road Hall, Bombay, of how she was led to India. It was told by George Bowen:

> She had taught school in Canandaigua, N. Y., for seven years, and nothing was then further from her thought that she might come to India....At the close of this period it was impressed upon her that the Lord had some other work for her to do, but what it was she knew not. She gave herself to prayer that the Lord's will might be clearly revealed to her. She received a letter from a dying lady, a friend of hers, a lady physician, suggesting that she should seek to fit herself for such work as her friend was obliged to resign. Though at first staggered not a little by the thought of spending years in the study of medicine, she was at length brought to see that it was the will of the Lord, and a way was opened for the prosecution of these studies. She spent four years in medical study, and during the last year she was led to offer herself to the Lord to serve Him in any part of the world, Japan, China or India, or elsewhere.[30]

In reply to Mrs. Thomas' letter the W. U. M. S. made inquiries and Miss Swain accepted the appointment to Bareilly under its auspices. In the meantime the W. F. M. S. was organized and Miss Swain, being a Methodist, preferred to go out as its missionary, and the W. U. M. S. graciously consented. She was "the first woman physician with a diploma who ever set foot in Asia".[31] She writes:

> The next morning after my arrival in Bareilly, as I came out of my room, I found a group of native Christian women and children sitting on the verandah, anxiously awaiting my appearance. I began my work at once among the Christian women, and in the families of the household servants living in the mission compound.[32]

T. J. Scott, her P. E., reported at the end of the first year that her success had exceeded their hopes. She had treated hundreds of cases.

> She has been called to the best families in the city and surrounding country. Attention has been arrested and a very kindly feeling awakened by this form of Mission work. Zenana work for a half dozen Missionary ladies has been completely opened in the city. The work is a marked success so far.[33]

On March 1 Dr. Swain began her medical class with fourteen girls of the orphanage and three married students. First classes were in anatomy, physiology and *materia medica*. One of the girls on first seeing the skeleton that the doctor had brought with her exclaimed: "Oh, Miss Sahiba, how will this woman rise in the resurrection with her flesh in America and her bones in India ?" For practical experience girls by turn looked after the sick in the Orphanage and accompanied the doctor to the city or village.[34] A member of Humphrey's class assisted Dr. Swain.[35]

In March, 1871 Governor Muir held a durbar in Bareilly, after which he and the Nawab of Rampur, with his staff, visited the Orphanage. The Nawab was pleased with all he saw and "especially with the intelligent replies of the medical class....He did not know that girls could learn so much....He sent Rs. 1000 for the Orphanage."[36]

All too soon the living quarters of the doctor were small for the morning clinics; the homes of the sick were often destitute of the comforts needed for their recovery. A dispensary and a hospital became an urgent need. A suitable site owned by the Nawab of Rampur, adjoined the Mission. "If we could secure one acre of this land, it would meet our need", thought Dr. Swain. There were forty-two acres ! An interview was arranged for October 3, 1871 by the sympathetic Commissioner for a delegation led by D. W. Thomas. Almost before he started to speak, the Nawab said, "Take it; take it. I give it with pleasure for such a purpose."[37] Many prayers had been offered in this connection; far beyond the faith of those asking, they were answered. The whole plot with a house, was a gift !

The house was immediately repaired. Dr. Swain and Miss Sparkes occupied it January 1, 1872. A temporary dispensary was set up there and a new one was dedicated on May 10, 1873; hospital buildings were ready for use on January 1, 1874. Patients—Christian, Mohammedan and Hindu—commenced to come at once, and all could have separate apartments.[38]

The list of students in Dr. Swain's first medical class is as follows: Susan Hamilton, Harriet Richardson, Libbie Husk, Melissa Jackson, Emma Baker, Emeline Howe, Sarah Mead, Elmira Blake, Elmira Colgate, Nellie Bain, Georgia Sutton, Jane N. Paul, Mrs. M. C. Mukerjie, Mary Laura Wheeler Dunn, Payoria C. Wells and Carrie Gordon. After a two-year course, thirteen of the medical class passed their examination in the presence of two Civil Surgeons and Dr. T. S. Johnson. They received the "certificates of practice in all ordinary diseases".[39] One, with her husband, was employed in the Almora leper colony. One in Moradabad ; five had husbands in the Seminary. So, the influence of the Orphanage and of the Medical Class was scattered through the Churches. Two with Rebecca from Humphreys' class continued as assistants in the dispensary. Other classes followed. S. S. Dease, M. D., writes that while he was in Bareilly Dr. Swain asked him to teach a class of young women while she gave the necessary practical instructions. It was also examined by a board of Government doctors.[40]

Miss Swain opened an active zenana work with religious instruction in addition to her medical program. In 1874 new families asked professional services and four Bible readers and teachers were employed.

In the six years following Miss Swain's arrival three more lady doctors were sent out: Miss N. Monelle (Mrs. H. Mansell) in 1873, appointed to Lucknow; Miss Julia Lore (Mrs. McGrew) in 1875, who opened a dispensary in Moradabad; and Miss Lucille H. Green (Mrs.

Cheney), who relieved Dr. Swain in 1876, when she went on furlough, somewhat broken in health. She returned to the Bareilly hospital in 1880. In 1884, S. S. Dease, M. D., who was then in Bareilly, received an urgent request to go to Khetri, in Rajputana, to treat the Rani. He requested permission for Dr. Swain to go.[40] Her treatment of the patient was so successful that she was invited to become physician to the Rani and women of the palace, and given a dispensary in the city. Dr. Swain saw in the invitation which included freedom for her and her associate "to work among the people as Christian women" an open door and accepted the position, and spent several years there.[41] Dr. Mary F. Christiancy took her place in Bareilly.

Dr. Humphrey and Dr. Swain make reference to Lady Dufferin's efforts for medical relief for women in secluded zenanas. Dr. Swain had an hour's chat with Lady Dufferin about medical work and the National Medical Association in which both were interested. The attention of Queen Victoria was called to the suffering endured by women of India in a message from the Rani of Punna, near Lucknow, which was entrusted to Miss Beilby, an English lady who had been sent to India by the India Female Normal School Society in England. She had a hospital and dispensary in Lucknow, and was called by the Raja to treat the Rani in 1881. When the doctor called on her before going to England on furlough, the Rani said: "You are going to England and I want you to tell the Queen . . . what the women in India suffer when they are sick. Will you promise me ?" And then she dictated a message to the Queen, asking that it be written small so that it would go in a locket that the Rani held and Miss Beilby was to wear. Word reached the Queen that Miss Beilby had a message and she was summoned. The Queen had not known conditions were so bad, and expressed her sympathy "with every effort made to relieve the suffering state of the women of India". Before Lord Dufferin left for India the Queen called Lady Dufferin and requested her to do what she might find in her power to alleviate this suffering. In August, 1885, at Simla, the Viceroy organized The National Medical Association for supplying Female Medical Aid to the Women of India. Its objects were three: to promote medical tuition, medical relief, and the supply of trained female nurses and midwives.[42] The result was the opening of all medical colleges to women, the establishing of "Dufferin" hospitals for women, and a widespread effort to train nurses. Dease wrote: "When the Dufferin hospitals were opened many of our graduates proved very useful assistants."

After the Medical College in Agra had been opened to women, the Agra Medical Home was opened under the W. F. M. S. to provide a place for Christian girls to live while taking this training.

The First Christian College for Women

Miss Thoburn's appointment to Lucknow did not designate her work nor did her qualifications limit its nature. She arrived in Lucknow on February 11, 1870. First weeks were taken as she said with "awkward attempts" at housekeeping and other "awkward attempts at using the language I was trying to learn....Responsibilities had not come."[43] There were three or four mission schools for *pardah* girls in Lucknow and eight homes of Bengalis were open to zenana teaching. Isabella Thoburn decided on a school for Christian girls for

> If we do any great and good work among the women of India we must show them the superiority of Christian womanhood, and we must have trained Christian women to work with us.... Beyond [the Orphanage] range is a field that must be occupied by boarding schools.[44]

At sunrise, April 18, 1870, the Lucknow school for girls was opened in a little room in the bazaar, in sight and in the dust of all passers-by. It was opened at the request of Joel Janvier, then pastor in Lucknow, in a mission house in Aminabad. There were six girls present on that first day, two of them daughters of the pastor brought by their grandmother. An older brother stood guard outside, but neither he nor his stout stick were required to protect them. A few weeks later the school was moved into a vacant room of Dr. Waugh's bungalow and at the beginning of the rainy season to a rented house in Inayat Bagh. In two months the enrolment reached seventeen and at the end of the year, twenty-five of whom four had come from out of the city and were boarding with friends. In Inayat Bagh twelve boarders were admitted. Applications came from all over the Northwest Provinces. The need was for a school "similar to the Amroha school but of a higher grade," primarily one that would give a good English and vernacular education for those who could pay most of their expenses. Such a boarding school required large and permanent quarters.[45] In November, 1871 they moved once more to the first purchase of the W. F. M. S. *Lal Bagh*, (Ruby Garden.) The first new building here was a hostel for fifty girls. As late as 1889 only six pupils were on scholarships. Others either earned their way or were supported by relatives.

This superb property included nine acres in the centre of the city. Buildings and grounds so completely met the needs in both accommodation and location that it seemed they had been kept in order for this institution. The owner demanded payment in coin. Two missionaries went to the Treasury in a buggy and returned with fourteen bags, each containing one thousand rupees, payment being made late in the evening of a Saturday, and probably every rupee was rung on steel to test its genuineness!

William Taylor's visit to Lucknow came near the end of the first year of Miss Thoburn's service. It produced a deep influence upon the new school, and on the work among the Christian women of the city. One who now became identified with the school was Henrietta Green, a Eurasian, "a pure and guileless girl of eighteen, with a moderate education, but cherishing a noble purpose to serve God, and make herself useful in life". She became a pupil teacher, a pioneer of a large succession of valuable workers. Another was a young Bengali widow who joined the Mission as a worker. "She was a gifted speaker and writer, and her coming was the means of widening the field of usefulness of both school and zenana work."[46]

In 1872 Miss Jennie Tinsley of the W. F. M. S. joined Miss Thoburn taking charge of the boarding school, while Miss Thoburn assumed charge of the city schools and zenana work, and Mrs. Craven of the Bible women. The boarding school was established primarily for Christians, but none was to be excluded. English and Eurasian girls came from the first; no non-Christians sought admission until in the nineties.[47]

Besides the responsibilities of the school, with its religious meetings, other doors of usefulness opened to Miss Thoburn in the English Church; in the extensive Sunday School work for non-Christians, where she was singularly effective in organization; and in the Lal Bagh home, where a cordial welcome, a comfortable room and a Christian atmosphere were provided to visitors at all times, but especially to the large numbers who came to the Dasehra meetings. She wrote later that she was more grateful for the privilege of extending hospitality than for any other one thing connected with those first ten years.

In 1884 the first high school class was admitted and the name of the school changed to Lal Bagh Girls' High School. Two years later three took the entrance examination of the Calcutta University: Lilavati Singh, Shorat Chuckerbutty and Mrs. Chuckerbutty, her mother.

Shorat then wished to take the First Arts examination, two years of college, preparatory to securing a degree in medicine. Miss Thoburn tried to find an opportunity for her to do this in Calcutta, but found no college without a strong non-Christian influence. While Shorat's mother was eager for the daughter to finish her education, she, as a convert from Hinduism, was not willing to have her attend such an institution. In her letter to the mother, Miss Thoburn said, "I wish we could open a Christian Woman's College in Lucknow." At once Mrs. Chuckerbutty replied offering Rs. 500 if that could be done. Then, learning that pupils who had passed the entrance examination of the first grade could not draw scholarships unless the College which they joined was affiliated with the Calcutta University, application was made for such affiliation, together with a request for a grant-in-aid. Lord Dufferin granted the affiliation.[48]

Miss Thoburn wrote an appeal to American women in January, 1886, through the *Woman's Missionary Friend* mentioning the impetus to the study of medicine; telling of Mrs. Chuckerbutty's offer, and added:

> But we need thoroughly educated teachers as well as doctors, and we need strong-minded women at the top, in order to lift up the great mass of ignorance below, and there is not a Christian Woman's College in all the Empire. Shall we not have the first one at Lucknow? Many of you who read this can spare $5000 as easily as your Indian sister can her five hundred rupees, and I send my plea to you with strong hope that you will appreciate at its true value this new project, and send over money to help us.[49]

This want of a Christian college for women was felt so strongly in North India that it was established in the summer of 1886 and Miss Hester V. Mansell, the first in the line of second generation missionaries to return to India, was transferred from Moradabad to care for the first college class. In 1888, in Chicago, Miss Thoburn appealed again:

> Such a college was begun, insignificant in numbers and every kind of strength, but a fact nevertheless. Last week's mail brought the news that the first three students sent up for University examination had passed so creditably that they have received government scholarships to enable them to continue their studies. The question is whether we shall lead in higher education for women in India, or whether we shall follow the lead of those who will give the education without making it Christian; whether we shall go on in a natural growth from our high schools to a higher grade in this college, or, having made so much progress let others take the work out of our hands and put on the head stone where we have laid the foundation.[49]

The B. A. classes were opened in 1894; and the first candidate appeared in that examination of the Allahabad University in 1896. The Lucknow Woman's College was firmly established.

During the year 1893 two new departments were added, a teachers training class, and a kindergarten training under Miss Hoge. So great was the demand for trained teachers that they were all placed during the year of training, and two had to be released a month before the year closed. The kindergarten training was the first given in India and created great interest. Five kindergarteners were under training in the year, two of whom were sent from other schools.

One of the "boarders" who was admitted in 1878 was a little motherless girl from Gorakhpur, Lilavati Singh. She was brought to the school by her aunt, and received by Miss Thoburn. She took high rank in her classes but "her impetuous nature was constantly leading her to do daring, or forbidden things". It was not until Miss Thoburn had returned from her furlough that the girl really got acquainted with her, for Lilavati was now in some of the classes that she taught. The Sunday afternoon prayer meetings; going with Miss Thoburn to a Mohammedan Sunday School week after week, to teach little girls in the zenanas; the stories she heard from her of missionary heroes; these were some of the influences under which she grew up. She passed her entrance examination in 1886.

She had refused a scholarship in High School, preferring to work her way through. Her aunt met personal expenses, but Lilavati earned all fees by teaching. She passed her F. A. in 1888. The scholarships she won now and in later examinations paid most of her college fees. The Acting Principal did not feel she could open the B. A. class in Miss Thoburn's absence, so Lilavati Singh and Shorat Chuckerbutty went to the Bethune College in Calcutta. She passed her B. A. Course with honours and took a Government position. Although "satisfied with secular work" she wrote to Miss Thoburn that she wanted to take up some form of Christian service. She accepted Miss Thoburn's offer of a position at $25 a month. Miss Thoburn said that she would not take more herself. In July, 1892 Miss Singh returned to the College staff. "These two, at first teacher and student, later co-workers as Principal and teacher, are held together always in the love, traditions and memories of the College's past."[50]

The Lucknow Christian College

The last day of January, 1866 in Moradabad, members of India's only Annual Conference had gathered. Thoburn and Messmore,

> old school fellows . . . were lodged in a small tent, under a crooked date palm on the Mission compound . . . There was more talk than sleep in the little tent that first night; and somehow, before morning, the idea was conceived of establishing a college in Lucknow.[51]

The Centenary of Methodism in America, 1869, was soon to be celebrated and a Committee recommended

> that the infant conference undertake something worthy of such a mission as we hope to establish in India . . . to strengthen our educational interests; that we recognize the urgent want of a College of high grade in connection with our work; [and] that we attempt to raise during the coming year . . . an endowment of Rs. 10,000 as a nucleus around which other resources may gather.[52]

This was a formidable task for a Conference which then numbered its Christian community as 157 Full Members and 108 Probationers. The next year the goal was raised to Rs. 25,000, and five Trustees were appointed to hold the endowment and property for the College. By the Conference of 1868 Rs. 10,000 had been exceeded and in 1874 the total amounted to Rs. 17,753 of which Rs. 2,000 had accrued in interest in the last year.[53]

It had been assumed that the College would be at Husainabad, the crown, as it were, of the school Messmore had so carefully developed. The flood changed that; and the city's growth was moving far east of that location. "So far as the embryo College was concerned," wrote B. T. Badley, "the enterprise—except for experience gained—had to be begun *de novo*."

Messmore and Thoburn purchased a new property in Inayat Bagh, in May, 1870, borrowing the money—"we need the location and are going ahead trusting in God to help us to pay for it".[54] It was not suitable for the College, but the demand for a boarding school to serve Lucknow and its vicinity had been so general that the school was opened here on February 1, 1877 by Henry Mansell, as Principal, in the same room which earlier had been the bindery-room for the Press. It was called the Centennial School in keeping with the resolution of 1866, and was a day and boarding school for Christian boys from whom Rs. 5 per month was charged for board and lodging.

> The godowns and servants' houses [were used] for the servants and also for one master who managed the boarding department as well as part of the teaching. There was an old office close to the *kothi*, rather permanent and respectable, which we used for the school house.... Mr. Cunningham had tried two years before to start the school in Ghasiyari Mandi, but had given it up....There were two Eurasian boys.
>
> We started with five or six boys; but the numbers increased till we closed the term with 40 boys on the roll....About half of them were day pupils from Ghasiyari Mandi.[55].

In 1878 B. H. Badley became the Principal. The school had a prosperous year. A commodious and well located building was purchased; additional teachers were employed, and as the only school of its kind in the Northwest Provinces and Oudh, there was promise of a useful future—"the school is no longer an experiment".[56]

Badley went on furlough in 1883 and Principal Waugh superintended the erection of the High School. The corner stone was laid May 1, 1883. The completed building had a tower and clock. Dr. and Mrs. William Butler were visiting India and he presided at the opening ceremony in December. On his return in 1885 Badley was reappointed to the College. Affiliation with the Calcutta University was effected on July 2, 1888, but B. A. classes could not be opened before 1891. The site for the College building, the triangle across the road from the school, was a gift from Government in answer to fervent, continued prayer. The college building, known as Reid Hall, was in part the gift of Dr. J. M. Reid, and Mrs. Coxe. Its foundation stone was laid on August 6, 1891 by Bishop Thoburn, and the building formally opened on October 31, 1892, although used before then.[57] By action of the Central Conference of 1894 the Lucknow Christian College became known as the Reid Christian College, but later the first name was restored.

From early in 1878 B. H. Badley had spent himself to make the vision of a College real. He was on furlough when the Centennial School was opened; illness detained him when the corner stone of the College was laid. He returned from Almora in the fall and died on November 20, 1891. Dr. Peck, Secretary of the Board, wrote during his illness:

> You are a glorious worker, one of God's heroes; and we love you dearly for yourself and for your work's sake. Your work has enshrined you in the loving gratitude of the Missionary Society, and of a large number of the Church at home who have been kept advised of your devotion and noble service.[58]

In December, 1889 Badley was joined in the College by William A. Mansell, son of Henry Mansell. He was the first second generation missionary to join the Conference, and the first missionary Professor at the College. He succeeded Badley as Principal. The second missionary, G. C. Hewes, came in 1892 for science classes.

The first Christian student to pass a University examination was Nathaniel Jordan, son of James Jordan, an honoured member of the North India Conference. He passed the Intermediate examination 1892 and two years later the B. A. examination. He served two years as Professor of English Literature after passing his M. A. examination,[59] and for many years he served as Headmaster of the Parker High School, Moradabad.

In 1892 a Department of Commercial Education, offering courses in stenography, type-writing and general business writing and accounts, was opened by H. L. Roscoe. It was an immediate success. It was in no way limited to Christians, yet it opened the way for many Christian young men to take responsible positions in Government and public service. Roscoe was followed by J. N. West and he in turn by T. C. Badley in 1904.[60] In compliance with a commission from the Provincial Government and with its co-operation, this Department developed a system of Urdu Shorthand. To M. L. Ghose, Mirza Mohammad Hadi, and Hakim Mohammad Hussain, with T. C. Badley, belongs the credit for this advance, which held promise that the speed attainable in writing Urdu could equal that of the best English system.[61]

William Taylor in North India

During his two years of secluded life in Garhwal Thoburn had thought much of our church in India and became convinced that there was a much bigger work to be done than had been envisaged by Butler. His thoughts turned to William Taylor with whom he had become acquainted in Chicago in 1858, and he invited him to come to India. Taylor had also received an invitation from Rev. James Smith of the English Baptist Mission in Delhi.

Taylor arrived in Lucknow on Friday, November 25, 1870 and started his meetings the following Sunday. His account of his work in India is entitled, *Four Years Campaign in India.* One chapter is called "The Siege of Poona". The terms "Campaign" and "Siege" well describe his methods, which were clear-cut and strongly pressed. He favoured

> getting these Europeans and East Indians saved and incorporated into our Mission working force. In their present state the mass of them make a false showing in Christianity, and are terribly obstructive to our great work of leading the heathen and Mohammedans to Jesus.[62]

He was confident of results. Thoburn, out walking with Taylor one evening, chanced to say, "if", "If we should have a revival here,"

> In a moment my arm was in the grip of a giant; 'If? my brother, there is no if about it. We are going to have a revival. That is settled. The agreement is with the Lord Almighty, and it cannot fail.' As he thus talked to me he held me at arms length, while my arm felt as if screwed up in an iron vise.[63]

He expected his converts to be taught and shepherded. If there was no other arrangement, he made one where a fellowship could grow up. George Bailey belonged to a Roman Catholic family in Lucknow. Thoburn invited them, and George, the older son, promised to come.

> His great grandfather . . . became a general of the emperor of Delhi. His grandfather was a general of the King of Oudh, and his father a Captain in the same service. . . . The French name was dropped and the name of Bailey given them instead. In the defense of Lucknow during the Mutiny, George was but a boy of 16 years, but so distinguished himself as a soldier that the rank and pension of an ensign for life were given him.[64]

On Tuesday, December 6, 1870 George "enlisted in the army of Jesus". A few days later his wife was converted. One day George was seen to prompt the interpreter whenever he hesitated for a word, and in a meeting at their house where eighty people were assembled, Bailey interpreted well. Missionaries were surprised at his clear, terse translation of Scripture passages. It was original and forceful. Before his conversion he had never read more than two chapters from the Bible. That was when his wife was ill, and he had been told that reading the Bible would cure her. She did recover. He remained with Taylor as interpreter, then worked under Parker and was "a powerful preacher of the Gospel in Hindustani and Hindi". In 1873 he was in charge of work at Sambhal, and for many years was a Local Preacher in the Moradabad District.

As interpreter George Bailey went to Bareilly. There he learned that Walker, whom he had known in Lucknow, was the *tahsildar*. Bailey purposed at once to "get him converted to God".

> The missionaries laughed at Bailey's new born zeal, and said, 'You can do nothing with Walker. His wife is a Musalmani and he has a lot of her Mohammedan kindred in his house; he never comes to preaching.'[65]

Bailey was sure they could win him and took Taylor to his friend's office. After a visit Taylor expressed the desire to "come some morning and conduct family worship for you". Walker explained that he was busy; "could not possibly give the time". However, on Sunday morning a meeting was held at Walker's home with eighteen persons present, including his family. When Taylor wished to come again, Walker replied, 'We shall be glad to see you again tomorrow morning." Daily, a meeting was held in the Walker home from seven to eight, as many as thirty being present. On a Thursday morning Taylor and T. J. Scott had a baptismal service. Taylor prayed for Walker and his wife till they were filled with the Holy Spirit, then baptised her. She gave her testimony at the Girls' Orphanage that evening. Both Walker and his wife died within a couple of years, but both "died in the Lord".

Taylor toured through most of the stations of the Conference, a few days in each place. Much of the hot season was spent in Naini Tal where he held daily meetings for several weeks, and formed a class of about thirty members. He and Mrs. Humphery compiled *Hymns New and Old.*

It had been hoped that the results of Taylor's meetings would be a large accession from among non-Christians, and Taylor had shared this hope, but when the campaign in the Conference was completed, Taylor "was constrained to admit that there were inherent difficulties in the situation" which were not present in his South Africa campaign. In the India Mission he found

> a working agency not up to the point of effectiveness . . . the spiritual development and adjustment of agency all entirely behind that of any other mission field in which I have laboured—while the combinations of the opposing forces here in India probably exceed those of any other part of the globe.[66]
>
> We cannot expect very great results . . . in the presence of a nominal ineffective Church. If there were no such Church, we might hope for more immediate results among the non-Christians, but now our

only hope is to make the Church effective. The members of the Church, men and women, in the city centres, were unprepared to work in an evangelistic campaign.[67]

In Lucknow "a deep and powerful work of revival set in, but it was confined to Europeans and native Christians". Thoburn says:

> Had Dr. Taylor's work terminated here, he would still have done a great and most important work. He had taught valuable lessons, had elevated the spiritual tone of our little Conference, and had kindled a flame which has never since gone out,—he gave an impetus to our work which it has never lost, and he committed us to advance movements which we might have shrunk from for years had he not led the way.[68]

Taylor's last appointment in the Bareilly District was in Budaon, with Hoskins, whose work among the sweeper farmers, where converts lived at home and supported themselves, Taylor felt, gave more "promise of an indigenous permanent growth" than any other he had seen in India.[69]

Sunday Schools

"The Sunday School work *as now carried* on in Lucknow is perhaps the most powerful evangelizing agency in this city, or in the entire mission."[70] So wrote Thoburn in 1874. This change had been brought about after a meeting of William Taylor with thirty-five Hindu boys from Messmore's School. Taylor said to them, "I'll teach you to sing." He saw the missionaries start up and whisper to one another, sceptical—for this had never been done.

> I sang a verse. . . . I sang again, repeating the chorus many times, till one and then another of the boys began to repeat it after me. 'There now! I knew you could sing. You have got the song in you, and if you open your mouths it will come out!'[71]

The boys sang; they liked it; "it took". They had acquired a new interest. In that simple way, Taylor, in December, 1870, gave an impetus to Sunday School work in the Conference. Messmore's boys knew a little English; that had given Taylor his chance. Thomas Craven, who was present that day, carried the idea farther.

> Going out into the street, he began to gather a few little fellows around him wherever he could, and interested and amused them by singing couplets of Christian hymns to some of their own familiar Hindustani tunes....Little by little he induced these boys to join in singing.[72]

Then he began Sunday Schools in all the rooms where day schools were held. By the singing of the boys he secured also the attention of older people. At first these Sunday Schools were little more than

'Christian singing schools". Song was the chief thing, with prayer and a talk by the teacher. Adults were always at the windows and doors to observe the novel spectacle within. Members of the English Church in Lucknow gave eagerly of their time to help in these schools. The singing schools became well organized Sunday Schools, limited only by the number of teachers who would help. In a year enrolment in Lucknow jumped from 524 to 967 in sixteen schools, with forty-seven teachers giving regular assistance.[73]

With the Lucknow example before the Conference, Sunday Schools boomed. In Rae Bareli McMahon wrote: "We can increase Sunday Schools as fast as teachers can be found for them." From Garhwal: "The Sunday Schools are becoming more and more interesting; especially in Pauri where the Hindoo school boys appear equally interested with the Christian children."[74] When Craven arrived, 1870, there were thirty-four Sunday Schools and 116 scholars in the Conference. Eleven years later there were 344 schools and 15,397 scholars,[75]—"the most powerful evangelizing agency . . . one can get a few boys in almost every part of Lucknow, who will sing up a crowd for the missionary to preach to any day".

The Annual Conference viewed these developments as full of promise. It pushed the publication of needed literature in Hindi, Urdu, Roman and English. Its Committee on Sunday Schools reminded all that the designers of the course expected in the annual examination,

> at least all the larger scholars to repeat from memory all the selected verses of the lesson, [with the golden texts], as well as the title, topic and subdivisions. In this way a diligent child with little effort will have committed to memory the substance of the entire Bible in the space of seven years.[76]

In Lucknow and elsewhere every year there were several who passed perfect examinations. The India Sunday School Union was organized in 1876. Methodists took a large part in its work; T. J. Scott was its first President and B. H. Badley the first Secretary. Badley had earlier compiled a Sunday School Manual as an aid to conducting Sunday Schools.

It was not uncommon to have conversions through the Sunday School. In 1871 there was "*an increase* of thirty conversions."[77] Many instances were on record of deep changes in belief and in life, even where conversion was not professed.

The Indian Witness

In *My Missionary Apprenticeship* Thoburn explained the start of *The Witness* as a "need of some communication with the public". The influence of the Mission which Butler and his colleagues had started now reached afar. Attendants at the Dasehra meetings had come from distant places, and on their return had won others. The aggressive evangelism of Taylor had engendered opposition. Addressing Waugh on May 8, 1871 Thoburn wrote:

> Next Friday the first number of *The Witness* will spread its wings from our Press. It will be a fortnightly English paper. The row over the Baboo's case first put it in our heads to start it, and the more we thought of it, the more reason did we see for going on with it. It will have no *visible* editor, but will be managed by Messmore and me. Johnson of Fathighur and Morrison will write editorials, as will Scott and others. It is a private enterprise for the present, and will so remain until conference. Most of the brethren are in favour of it, but Thomas, Parker and Elliott are opposed to it. Mansell also is half opposed to it.
>
> Time must reveal its fate. I believe it will find a 'Speer' and prove a blessing.

Baboo Hem Chander was a member of the Brahmo Samaj. He was converted but soon after turned back. In the *Lucknow Times* he published a statement that he had been truly converted, but he "did not mean to be a dogmatic Christian". In the next issue he formally renounced Christianity. At the same time the new Chaplain of Lucknow, with some success, was doing all he could to upset the Lucknow converts of Taylor's meetings.

The Witness gave the Christian group a voice that could effectively present the Christian view point and reach the homes of scattered hundreds. It was more successful than its promoters had hoped. On March 15, 1872, it became a weekly and was enlarged. From May 24, 1872 it was issued as *The Lucknow Witness*, but continued under its first management. Answering a correspondent in a local paper the editor replied:

> Not a rupee of missionary money has ever been expended on any of the papers from the Methodist Press in Lucknow. The Witness was aided by a special subscription at its commencement, but it almost immediately became self supporting, and continues so to the present day.[78]

Thoburn had wanted to "get out a scholarly man, with superior linguistic abilities and tastes, who should thoroughly master the literature, current and classical, and qualify himself for vernacular editorial work". At the end of 1872 he took a step that he had long contemplated. He relinquished his salary and accepted the policy of self-support for himself as Indian preachers were urged to do. He wrote the Board Secretary of his desire to resign his "salary in favour of the Press and to get an extra man sent out as Editor of periodicals and books," and was greatly encouraged a few months later to learn that

> the Secretaries at once set about securing a man for the Press as requested. In less than ten days Bro. Mudge of New England had

been secured and is now under appointment to India. I am very greatly encouraged by this news....The Press will now have a chance to develop its power for good.[79]

Mr. and Mrs. Mudge arrived in Lucknow in October, 1873, For eight years he was Editor of *The Lucknow Witness*, and very ably he did the work, which was often combined with duties in the vernacular. The paper he edited was in English, published for English-speaking people. The notion had taken full possession of minds that missionary money expended on English work was money misspent.[80] During 1880 Parker received a letter from Secretary Reid, saying, "Our orders against paying from the Treasury for work in the English language must be obeyed." It referred to *The Lucknow Witness*. In 1882, Mudge returned to America.

Two tributes to the influence of the *Witness* in these years show how far good literature can penetrate:

> I have been nearly a constant reader of the *Lucknow Witness* since 1873. I must confess that during that time I derived a great deal of benefit through its pages in morals. It preached weekly to a large non-Christian Native community on Christian topics which a single missionary can hardly do for his congregation. It was indeed a great instructor of Christianity, and a true and faithful witness of Christian religion. [A non-Christian reader].

> I am extremely sorry to part with you. Your *Witness* has been gladdening my soul and refreshing my body every week in this Musalman State where I have no Christian company. You have done me a great service which I can never forget.

> You should not measure its influence among English speaking natives by the number of native subscribers; to my knowledge one paper taken by a native of position is read by many others in the office at the same station....*The Lucknow Witness* was an important agency in establishing Christ's Kingdom in this land. [An Indian Christian Headmaster.][81]

The Delegated Conference in 1881 authorized its Board of Publication to provide, as soon as they should find it practicable, for the publication of *The Lucknow Witness* "on an enlarged basis adapted to the wants of our church throughout India". On February 3, 1882 Thoburn resumed editorial responsibility for the paper which he and Messmore had started eleven years before. From this date it was printed in Calcutta and the name changed to *The Indian Witness*. In the first issue a new policy was announced.

> Heretofore *The Witness* has been published as an undenominational paper....It is now proposed to issue it formally under the sanction of the Executive Committee of the Delegated Conference, and in behalf of the body which it represents....There was an urgent call for a denominational paper at the present time, and the friends of *The*

> *Witness*, after mature thought and careful consultation, concluded that the best and surest way to secure its perpetuity would be to place it in the hands of Christians who would not let it die.

Thoburn continued as Editor until the summer of 1885. He was succeeded by Benjamin Aitken, 1885-1886; F. C. McCoy, 1887-89; H. C. Stuntz, 1889-91; J. H. Messmore, 1891-96 and J. E. Robinson, 1896-1904.

Theological Education

At the first session of the India Mission Conference members took the initial step for providing theological training by recommending that a department for training preachers and teachers should be opened in connection with the Boys' Orphanage "whenever it may become practicable".[82] After a class meeting early in 1865, Johnson reminded the boys that God might be desiring some of them to devote their lives to the preaching of the Gospel. In a few weeks three boys came separately to tell him that they were convinced that God was calling them. He asked them to continue to pray over the matter. Then others came; in all fourteen intimated their "call". The Committee on Visiting Orphanages found a class of eleven boys from twelve to twenty years of age engaged in studying the elements of Christian theology. "Some of them give satisfactory evidence of being the subjects of a gracious work of God."[83]

The first class was ready in 1867, the second in 1868. Some who joined the Conference with this preparation were: Sundar Lal, Thomas Gowan, Horace Adams, James Jordan, H. A. Cutting, Benjamin Cocker.[84] Others became local preachers or teachers. Grateful as the Presiding Elders were for men trained at the Orphanage they hoped for men of higher educational standards.

Rivalry between the cities was keen.[85] Advocates for Lucknow urged that the Theological Department be opened even before the organization of the College, but that endowments for the two be kept separate. They had expected classes to open in 1870 or 1871. When this plan failed, D. W. Thomas, who had favoured Bareilly, wrote to the Corresponding Secretary offering $20,000 as endowment for the Seminary if the Board would furnish $10,000 for buildings. E. Remington of Ilion, N. Y., donated $5,000 toward buildings and the Board of Missions furnished an equal amount. With this support assured the Board of Education announced Thomas' gift of the Panahpur estate, and several buildings, with land in Bareilly; and a promise to pay on demand Rs. 20,000 for endowment. The Conference requested its President to appoint Thomas as Principal, and instructed him, with the Board of Education, to prepare the course of study and organize the Theological Seminary.[86]

The Theological School was opened on April 15, 1872 with sixteen young men in attendance, of whom thirteen drew scholarships and three were in attendance for the first session only, after which they returned to their work. The course of instruction in this first year consisted of Biblical Exegesis in the Old Testament; Sacred Geography; Biblical Introduction, Systematic Theology, Homiletics, and the Persian and Arabic languages. The Principal believed the students had made satisfactory and encouraging progress.[87] It was expected that "none will be retained in the school who do not give evidence of being called by God to the work of saving souls".[88]

The first classes were largely composed of men who had been engaged in work, but needed further instruction. They could not take so thorough a course as younger men, but could gain much. Many students were comparatively new Christians. For them Wheeler said, "It was like entering on the exploration of a new world where every step introduces entirely new ideas, and taxes the mind to invent new terms and new meanings to old term."[89]

Members of the first class to graduate in 1874, with the stations from which they had been sent, were: Antone Dutt, William Peters, (Budaon); F. W. Greenwold, Peter, B. Gray, Pliny Nickerson, Joshua R. Soule (Shahjahanpur); Hussan Aly, Matthew Stephens, Kallu Singh (Moradabad); Enoch Joel, Ummed Singh (Bareilly). Antone Dutt was the first preacher sent out of the bounds of the Conference, going to Hyderabad for Hindustani work. Because of a break in health, he returned to the North where his wife died. He was then sent to the Punjab to open new work, and was doing well until he was trampled under the hoofs of a trooper's horse in the streets of Patiala, and died soon after.[90]

Thomas took furlough in 1873, acting for the time as Agent for the Seminary, and returning the next year, he brought with him a further endowment of ten scholarships of Rs. 2,000 each from a liberal layman and this sum had been duplicated by a gift of Rs. 20,000 from the Missionary Society.

During Thomas' absence Scott served as Principal of the Seminary. On Thomas' return Scott went on furlough and acted as Agent of the Seminary and also of the Memorial School, Kanpur, while Thomas resumed the Principalship. With him were J. W. Waugh, as "Senior Professor" and John Thomas. In 1878 Scott joined Thomas as "Theological Professor in Seminary," and in 1879 D. W. Thomas became President of the Seminary and Normal High School, and Scott the Principal of the Theological Seminary, a position in which he rendered a long and unique service of "*training our students in the work*".

In his first year he established the custom of a regular weekly service for the students, teaching that "a pure life and fervent love for souls are above all other attainments."[91] A second principle he aimed to establish was the uniting of evangelistic work with study, every student being expected to preach at least once a week in the city bazaar, or among the villages.

> This arrangement for preaching is not only a constant practical drilling for the men, but is the means also of systematically spreading the Gospel and has borne fruit in the conversion of souls....The religious spirit of our pupils has improved....Our most interesting questions in the class room are those that start up on the subject of conversion, holiness and the moral life generally. In an eminent and special sense this Seminary can be made a 'School of Christ'....All see more clearly that men of blameless and devoted lives are required for the ministry, and we are learning to 'lay hands suddenly on no man.'[92]

A later report confirms this emphasis with good results:

> Through this organized system of preaching connected with the school, many souls have been brought to Christ and have been baptized. Two of these have entered the Theological school, and having graduated are now among our most trusted workers.[93]

Departments

The earliest action for a training department had in view the preparation of young men as teachers *and* preachers. The Conference of 1872 renewed the emphasis for a department for teacher-training in connection with the Seminary. For this purpose a High School department was opened in 1878. From 1881-1892 it was restricted to normal or teachers' training in the vernacular for village schools.

Two years before the Seminary was opened Mrs. T. J. Scott opened a little school on her verandah for Christian women, whose children were also taught at the same time. When the Theological Seminary was opened she insisted on the wives of some of the students attending the verandah school, "and taught them to read, and read the Bible to them, and tried to show them the importance of their being able to work for the Lord with their husbands".[94] Later, attendance became a rule. The Bible Teachers' Course of Study was adopted as the minimum course for women. In 1892 the kindergarten class was opened by Mrs. Neeld in a room of the house of one of the Indian Professors. This department found a home in a building provided by the Collins family as a memorial.

"The financial foundation" of the library was laid when in 1874 a Dr. Randle contributed his gold watch and some jewelry with a total value of $350.[94] At a later date J. R. Reid, a Magistrate of the Indian Government, contributed $1,200.

Work started in a small adobe house originally built for an Indian preacher. Students lived in mud houses that had been built for workmen. Remington Hall was dedicated by Bishop Andrews. Butler Hall was built with funds received on a special appeal and was opened by Bishop Malalieu in 1891. Ernest Hall, a memorial to their son by Rev. and Mrs. E. R. Kiplinger, was buit in 1893. Bishop Thoburn laid the corner stone.

District Conference

Many have described a Mission or Church set-up in India as foreign. The Methodist Church in India has not only adopted usages from abroad, but it has contributed to the ecclesiastical structure of world Methodism. The first contribution of this kind was the District Conference, described by Bishop Foss as "a manifest necessity of our work."[95] in India. The new Church needing native helpers, teachers and preachers, had employed men and called them Exhorters and Local Preachers. Only a few could hope to qualify for membership in the Annual Conference, yet something akin to the itinerancy of that body was needed for them so that standards could be co-ordinated and a unified program of training instituted. "To let them remain as ecclesiastical non-descripts," wrote Thoburn, "was undesirable."[96]

To meet this need J. T Gracey and E. W. Parker, at Sitapur in 1862, planned a Mutual Improvement Missionary Association to include the missionaries of Oudh and Shahjahanpur and their Indian helpers.[97] Essays and addresses were given by all. By 1867 this had become the Ministerial Association of Oudh.[98] In 1864 Parker organized an Association in Moradabad for the improvement of its members in the acquisition and diffusion of scriptural knowledge. The program included preaching, discussion, reading of original essays and relating of experiences. Some of the subjects assigned for essays were: (1) Trinity in Unity. (2) God causes everything, good and bad, to be done. How then can man be responsible? (3) How shall we know which is the true religion? Show that the Bible has not been abrogated by the Koran. (4) Divinity of the Holy Ghost. (5) Divinity and Humanity of Jesus Christ. (6) The all-sufficient argument of the Hindus; "We must do as our forefathers did." Mansell wrote that Zahur al Haqq gave an account of his experiences at that time which filled all hearts with joy.[99]

The Committee on Education in 1868 was "requested to take into consideration the best means of educating and appointing local Preachers and Exhorters". They recommended "that the brethren in each district meet their Presiding Elder annually, when practicable, to make the necessary arrangements for them". As to "educating" workers not connected with the Annual Conference, the Committee recommended that one person from each district be named to prepare a course of study and report at the ensuing Conference.[100] The next year when the question of transferring helpers came up the Presiding Elders were instructed to bring to the next conference a "Plan for the better organization of our Native Helpers". Their report in part was:

> 1. There shall be an Association organized in each Presiding Elders' District which shall meet annually.
>
> 2. All members of the Annual Conference shall be *ex-officio* members in their respective districts. All local preachers and exhorters in the employ of the Mission shall be constituted members at the first organization, but subsequently members shall be received only by vote of the association, a majority of $\frac{2}{3}$ being necessary to an election. All Christian teachers and other helpers in the Mission, may become members.

The term Association was used lest the word Conference excite alarm in America. Indian members voted upon the report with "an intelligent interest and a frank independence....They did not hesitate to amend, or strike out portions....The three year limit was added by them by a large majority."[101]

The clause requiring the organization of an Association in each District appeared to be an act of legislation reserved to the General Conference. In answering a question on a point of law, Bishop Kingsley replied, "Under the Methodist Discipline, it is always right to do the best you can under the circumstances."[102]

The regularizing of procedure in all Districts proved most helpful. Each Presiding Elder *found opportunity to shape a program and build leadership.* The memorable camp meeting in Tilhar was held with the ministerial meeting. In 1871 the Oudh Association followed evangelistic services in Lucknow, when "a dozen professed conversion, nine united with the Church as probationers, and a number were led forward into a higher spiritual life".[103]

The Conference instructed H. Mansell, its delegate to General Conference, "to endeavour to secure the organization of District Conferences in connection with our Conference," not thinking of a wider usefulness. American papers had carried reports of the District Associations in India and Local Preachers' Associations had been organized in the United States. Some of these had sent memorials to General Conference for a District Conference. The opposition to such legislation was strong and stubborn but approval was given by a narrow margin, 144 to 136.[104] For the first time following its organization the M. E. Church added a Conference to the traditional three, when the Discipline of 1872 listed: General, Annual, *District* and Quarterly. The new legislation included all that India asked and more when it added authority "to hear complaints against, to license, and to recommend to the Annual Conference Local Preachers as suitable candidates for Deacons or Elders Orders and for admission On Trial in the Traveling connection".[105] As time went on the District Conference "boldly added to its functions as necessity called for action" and it became in some respects "a more important body than the Annual Conference".[106] Bishop Foss felt that work could be studied best in the District Conference.

English Work

Taylor's year in the India Mission Conference stands like a great divide: *Before* Taylor, the English-speaking congregations had been preached to, a few were baptized, but they were not asked to join us. "Visibly the work had been fruitless." *After* Taylor, English churches were organized. The new mood found expression in the first issue of *The Witness*.

> We might as well try to make the Ganges and Jumna keep their waters from mingling while following in the same channel, as to keep up a permanent distinction between 'Native' and 'English work'. Two hearts filled with love of a common Saviour will flow together as naturally as two drops of water unite.

The early program for Europeans and soldiers in Lucknow had been closed under Board insistence, and turned over to the British Wesleyans. When they established their church in the Cantonments several regular worshipers could not go, and a Sunday evening service and a week-night service were again started. The "Lucknow English Church, E. Cunningham," appear for the first time in 1875. Both congregations used the same Chapel until an "English Church" was dedicated in March, 1877. It had cost Rs. 20,000.

In 1874 the English congregation in Naini Tal asked for a full time pastor to be supported by the congregation, and two years later N. G. Cheney arrived for this pastorate. The corner stone of the English Church was laid on February 7, and the Church dedicated on October 9, 1881 when P. M. Buck preached. Its cost was Rs. 26,000.[107]

Kanpur

On a Friday Thoburn was at the railway station in Lucknow when a gentleman came to him with an open telegram, a request to get some one for a Sunday service in Kanpur. He agreed to go. The congregation had been ministered to by Presbyterians and Baptists from Allahabad on two Sundays a month. They now asked Thoburn either to open a mission there, or to arrange for vacant Sundays from Lucknow. He accepted

9

the second alternative for there were difficulties in the first: Kanpur was West of the Ganges, therefore outside of the accepted Conference bounds; other denominations were concerned and rules of comity required that they be consulted; no new station could be opened without action of the Annual Conference.

This congregation invited Taylor. He held services until Christmas week in the prayer room of Dr. Moffatt, the Civil Surgeon. Then they were continued in homes of East Indians, and in the bazaars by Myall, his interpreter. With the approval of Thoburn and Mansell, Presiding Elders, Taylor organized two classes, twenty-two names in all, and brought with him to the Annual Conference a petition that Kanpur be put in the list of Mission stations, and a pastor appointed. The Conference gave its approval provided that no American missionary be sent there.[108] P. M. Mukerji was appointed pastor and the Indian Church organized soon after. English services were provided by missionaries from Lucknow.[109]

In November following, Thoburn organized an English class of ten under Dr. Condon who had joined the Methodist Church. J. W. Gladwin reached India in December, 1871 and was appointed pastor of this growing congregation.

Allahabad

At the time of his conversion Dennis Osborne was Superintendent of the Chief Engineer's Office in Lucknow.[110] As a class leader he surprised people with his gift of exhortation. One Sunday the pastor was sick and Osborne was prevailed upon to conduct the service, from which time "he has held his place as one of our leading preachers in India". Taylor considered him "the most effective soul-saving person in the North West," while Bowen described him as "a man full of holy enthusiasm, and burning to have Christians know and enjoy the fullness of their privileges in Christ.[111] He and his friend J. F. Deatker, another convert, held meetings in Allahabad. There were conversions but the group left without a pastor, fell apart. In 1873 Osborne went again and this time continued as their pastor, leaving a salary of Rs. 450 p. m., for a salary estimated at Rs. 150, with no hope of receiving more than Rs. 100 p. m. He and his wife were as happy as birds set free from a cage. He joined the India Conference in 1874 and was appointed to Allahabad. A commodious house was remodeled for a hall and pastor's residence. On October 13, 1877 the corner stone of a Church was laid and on July 3 it was dedicated.

Dasehra Meetings

The idea of a series of open air meetings at the time of the Dasehra festival in 1871 came to Dennis Osborne in prayer.[112] With Thoburn plans were perfected for "a miniature camp meeting" in the English quarter of the city. It proved a great success. Groups as large as thirty came from Calcutta and Allahabad; individuals and smaller groups "from Naini Tal to Ceylon". The influence of the Holy Spirit was wonderfully manifest. Sometimes called the Lucknow Camp Meeting, the Dasehra meetings continued through many years, reaching all parts of the country and many missions.

English Schools for Boys

An early development of English work was the English School. The Conference of 1874 approved a Committee's report recommending that a boarding school be established for boys and girls in Kanpur, "for training not only in the ordinary branches of education, but also in the Holy Scriptures".[113] The school would be self-supporting except that the Board was requested to send out a trained teacher as Principal, and to assume his salary. It was opened by H. Jackson on February 15, 1874 and was immediately popular. The Board did not assume responsibility for the Principal. Fees could maintain the recurring expenses, but heavy debts were incurred in the provision of buildings. Students came from all parts of India, some traveling 1,000 miles or more, for members of the scattered English Churches were deeply interested in schools for their children. But in English schools, as with other English work, the Board refused to have any continuing share. If Conferences persisted in English work, they were to do so alone. Despite generous co-operation from laymen the school continued in debt.

There were other difficulties also, for the Memorial School. Most of the English churches were in the S. I. Conference. Kanpur would have been included in that Conference if it had been willing to take over the debt of that school. This it refused to do. On the other hand the N. I. Conference desired an English school where the children of the missionaries could go. For such a school they preferred one of the hill stations. They had neither the man to spare for it, nor the means to establish it. But in 1880 the Conference asked for the appointment of Waugh to Naini Tal. A school was opened on April 1, in the parsonage. Owing to the large enrolment it was soon moved to "Ivy Park". The expensive first year was made possible by the liberal assistance of H. Petman, Esq., a Kanpur layman. The next year the school moved to *Stoneleigh,* where the Ramsay Hospital now stands. It was the largest house in Naini Tal, but soon proved too small. The school perforce remained there until 1887 when it moved to the Oak Openings estate, 1,200 feet above the lake, and an altitude of 7,500 feet. The site cost Rs. 52,000. Here, under the Principalship of F. W. Foote, who seemed to be called to the task, "Oak Openings" was strongly established.

When Osborne went to the General Conference in 1884 he secured funds for a memorial to Philander Smith, and built an English school in Mussoorie. Further help was given again in 1888. The school continued until 1905, useful to a large degree, but with inadequate funds. It was then merged with Oak Openings under the name of Philander Smith College. Many sons of missionary families have been boarders at this school in preparation for High School or College in America. The Kanpur Memorial School closed in 1890, its remaining students going either to Naini Tal or to Mussoorie.

English Schools for Girls

In the beginning the Memorial School was co-educational. On February 1, 1877 the girls' department was made a separate school, the Kanpur Girls' School, on a beautiful estate of twenty acres on the Ganges banks. Before May it had thirty-nine boarders and eleven day scholars. During its first year Miss Thoburn was in charge, and she went each week from Lucknow to give the necessary supervision.[114] The next year Miss S. A. Easton, an experienced teacher, newly arrived in India, assumed the superintendency of the school. In 1879 Ellen D'Abreu passed the entrance examination for the Calcutta University—the first lady of these Provinces to do so.[115] On the closing of the Memorial School the Girls' School moved from its location near the Ganges to the property vacated by the boys' institution and a department for small boys was opened. In 1886 Miss Easton was followed by Miss Harvey.

A girls' boarding school in Naini Tal was approved by the Conference in 1881. It was opened by Mrs. Craven in a house rented by Mrs. Petman. It continued through the year "but severe sickness prevented the reception of boarders.[116]

Miss Knowles, a qualified teacher chosen for this school, reached India early in 1882, accompanied by Miss Thoburn who was returning from her furlough, who offered also to help her get started. They were on their way up the mountains from Kathgodam, the rail terminus, when they met a gentleman "on whom they were chiefly depending for assistance," who told them that they were too late. "If you had come a year ago, something might have been done." It had been expected that he and other friends would finance both girls' and boys' schools under one management.[117]

Miss Knowles was not one deterred by such disappointments. Both ladies felt the school was needed and they proceeded to plan together. Miss Knowles' only asset was her year's salary of $650. On this security she rented a furnished house, Buttress Castle, and advertised the school. It opened with nine pupils but at the end of the year there were twenty-one of whom six were boarders. The school moved to Southwood, then to Forest Lodge, and in 1884 to the Smugglers' Rock estate of twenty acres, its permanent home. Buildings on the grounds were used temporarily until 1887, when with $11,250 from the W. F. M. S. and a Government grant of $3,000, new buildings were erected costing $26,000. In August, 1893 the school was out of debt. For a new building needed later Miss Knowles put in a "mortgage of hard work and careful economy".[118]

The school was first known as the Slater High School in memory of one whose bequest was applied on the first property. Miss Knowles named it Wellesley, after her *Alma Mater*. Sixty years later coolies of the station knew it best as *Knowles Sahiba ka iskul*. She was followed in 1888 by Miss Easton who continued as Principal until 1912. She was succeeded by Miss Rue Sellers who had joined her staff in early 1890. A summer guest saw Miss Sellers carefully removing the string from a parcel and winding it on a ball. The guest protested that the Principal should not take time for such trivial tasks, to which Miss Sellers replied: "Such economies have made Wellesley possible". Wellesley also received the life long service of many talented and devoted teachers.

SELF-SUPPORT

It is an axiom that a country can only be evangelized by indigenous preachers. The Missionary Society concluded, therefore, that the proper work of the Mission was to preach the Gospel, to assist in establishing churches, and when organized to "commit the oversight of them to Native preachers who are to be *sustained by their own people*".[119] Parker's lament concerning Babukhera suggests that each church should have a large part in the erection of its own place of worship. T. J. Scott put the matter in other words: "The problem is to raise up a living, self-supporting church, spontaneously active in the surrounding non-Christian mass."[120]

From the opening of the Mission, Butler and his colleagues were mindful of the importance of financial support. In a strange land, and without a community, they accepted a method approved at the time. They circulated by a peon, subscription books to Europeans and Eurasians whom they adjudged likely to be interested. Soon such books were taken to men of good will among non-Christians also who would give as to a charity. The numbers of non-Christian donors in a station varied, but in one year, 1866, in Bijnor they contributed over Rs. 900 out of Rs. 2,511 raised.[121] Butler reported a sum of $55,186 as having been received from all sources in India during the period of his superintendency.[122] Mudge says:

> We have taken pains to add up the sums acknowledged from year to year since the beginning, as donated or collected in this country.

They amount, including grants-in-aid, to the magnificent sum of Rs. 614,172 or something over one-fourth as much as the entire sum appropriated to this field down to 1875, by the Missionary Society.[123]

That total did not include the land given for the Clara Swain Hospital, nor the gift of D. W. Thomas for the Theological Seminary. This showing of income received in India for the Mission, *was truly* "magnificent". But, however much these contributions helped in securing property, land and residences, or in establishing the orphanages and schools in a permanent way, or even in meeting the cost of preachers, they did not contribute to self-support in terms of training a pastor to expect his support from his congregation, or teaching the congregation their obligation to maintain their pastor.

The Conference was expected to raise the annual apportionment asked by the General Missionary Committee. In 1874 this was $500 for North India and $1000 for "India Beyond".[124] Ten years later the two Conferences, North and South India were each apportioned $500.[125] These sums were distributed to the Districts. Reports reveal a complete absence of the idea of self-support, as we use it:

> At the beginning of this year our Native helpers began systematic effort to collect funds from our native Christians to aid in supporting the *work of the mission* on the district. [Moradabad, 1869] [126]
>
> The native congregations have raised Rs. 121, and the English congregation in Naini Tal about Rs. 250 ; Total Rs. 371, which is at least 8 times our [District] share of the amount *assessed our Conference by the home Committee*....I trust that it may result to great good to the Church here, because is it not more blessed to give than to receive ? [Kumaon, 1873][127]
>
> The missionary collection amounted to Rs. 578 being nearly three times the amount *assessed* us. (1874)[128]
>
> D. W. Thomas was appointed to receive and transmit to America the amounts collected....It was voted that the Finance Committee be instructed to distribute among the various charges the missionary apportionment for the present year. [1880][129]

A total of Rs. 42,688 was "collected for Missions" in 1865. This included grants-in-aid, fees in schools and other monies for "Mission purposes". "Benevolent Contributions" for 1872 included (1) "For Missionary Society Churches, $27,373 (Rs. 54,747) an inclusive total; (2) "For N. India Tract Society" $71.50 (Rs. 143); (3) "For N. India Bible Society" $213.75 (Rs. 427).

The report for 1873 had for the first time a column for "ministerial support". Bareilly with $25 (Rs. 50) and Moradabad with $62.40 (Rs. 125), were the only vernacular churches to win places. In 1874 the results were better : The Lucknow Hindustani Church had raised

$90 (Rs. 180), while in the Rohilkhand District Shahjahanpur, Lodhipur, Budaon and Bijnor had *started* toward self-support. All English churches were in line. Previous to 1873 their giving, too, had been included under "Missions". Statistical columns showed income in dollars until 1881—a significant indication of the close tie the Conference had with New York !

The new interest in ministerial support developed from a resolution in 1873 introduced by W. J. Gladwin. He was working on the west side of the Ganges, which was William Taylor's preserve, where Mission appropriations were unknown:

> That, in order to encourage our people to contribute toward the support of the ministry, this Conference recommends that each congregation undertake to support its Pastor wholly, or in part, according to the disciplinary plan.[130]

Self-support in the Vernacular work, in this meaning of pastor-congregation inter-dependence, began in the India Conference with the adoption of this resolution. It affected the whole structure of the growing Church, from Seminary to farthest preacher. The Conference recognized the principle as right. Ten years later reports read:

> The 117 Native preachers and exhorters with a few exceptions, receive salaries from the Missionary Society, though several are partly supported by the Native Christians whom they serve. [Rohilkhand District. 1883][131]
>
> On the question of foreign salaries, we constantly urge on our students the propriety of being satisfied with the lowest salary consistent with moderate comfort and with efficiency in their work. We also urge on them the importance of taking support in whole or in part from the Native Church at the earliest possible moment. [T. J. Scott, 1883, Theological Seminary.][132]

The Missionary Committee expressed its approval of the policy:

> The time has come when it is important and desirable that the native helpers should be supported as far as possible by the Native Church. So only can the work be extended as it should be and so only can the Native Church rise out of the disadvantages and weaknesses of a state of dependence, and we
>
> Therefore, recommend the India Conference, in distributing this money to take into account the ability and duty of the Native Church in this respect and only appropriate such sum for the support of the native preachers asmay be necessary to supplement the contributions which ought to be expected from the Native Church.[133]

Notwithstanding its approval of self-support, the Board continued to make an assessment and to receive collections from the several circuits as a benevolence, "For Missions," "For Missionary Churches," or "For Missionary Society". Here was an opportunity for the Board to discontinue its assessment as its contribution to the better program now being started. The collection to "Missions" had been "to aid in supporting the Mission work". To that extent self-support had started, but the money raised had been sent to the country from which salaries had come. Neither the villager nor the Mission employee, understood much of the process. To them pastoral support was a second "assessment". Had the Board stopped its assessment, and reduced its appropriation by the amount it received from the India Conference, a circuits' contribution could have been conserved as the first step in a new and climbing program to full *self-support*. It began in 1873, as something new, and as something additional.

It was unfortunate also, that in the same year a new column was added under "Benevolences": "For Woman's Foreign Missionary Society." It became another channel to draw off from the only potential that existed for self-support. This "Benevolence" was not sent to the States; it was well used in India. But it drove a wedge into every congregation (auxiliary societies were both urban and rural) separating men's work from women's work, or men's responsibility from women's responsibility; when all the strength and cooperation of both men and women in the church were needed to make possible a pastor-supporting church.

The problem of self-support was further complicated by fixed salary scales for preachers of all grades. The first Conference instructed a Committee to prepare a scale of salaries for Indian preachers and exhorters, to be confirmed by the Board. The scale provided for "a single man", additional for wife, "and for each child under 8 years," and "each child between 8 years and 18 years". It recognized two grades of Exhorters, two classes of Local Preachers, Conference probationer and Conference member in rising grades, with an increase on receiving Deaon's Orders, and a further increase for Elders' Order.[134] By these scales the Conference Committee and the Board, albeit unwittingly, created a "Mission Service",— a term still constantly used with never a thought of anything untoward parallel to Government service, which with alterations, continues to this day. Nothing in the scale suggested the basic principle that "pastors are to be sustained by their own people" or that scales were for an initial period.

With the help of resident missionaries and institutions city churches could make the grade. Stimulated by this new aim the Moradabad church in a year paid one-half of its pastor's salary, and hoped to achieve full support the next year. The Hindustani Church in Lucknow was not made a separate charge until 1872. It became self-supporting in 1882.[135] In the Rohilkhand District in 1875 seven men received nearly their entire support from the churches.[136] In the Palee circuit the little churches each determined to pay from Rs. 3 to Rs. 10 a month in 1876.[137] In Balrampur and Nawabganj the members agreed to "support a Native preacher to be known as our Home Missionary,"[138] which really dodged the issue. Hoskins reported:

> Self support is gaining ground, though progress is slow. People know how to give from the motive of fear, but giving systematically for the good of others is unknown in this country.[139]

In 1886 an Indian membership (i.e., omitting English churches) of about 6000 members and probationers, raised "for pastor" Rs. 2,637.[140] And yet contributing to the support of religious teachers was indigenous in India with both Hindus and Muslims. For the *guru* to receive was just as natural.

> The Hindus are good givers. It is admitted that one-fifth of the people of India live on religion. Four-fifths of the people feed this one-fifth out of religious regard....It seems to me that God has prepared these people to be a self-supporting Church.[141]
>
> As Hindus and Muslims these Christians all gave something for their religious purposes, and gave it frequently too. They will not give less for Christ's Church unless missionaries, unintentionally lead them to do so.[142]
>
> It seems to be a very stern and severe thing to demand of our poverty stricken Christians regular contributions for the support of their minister, but in no other way can Christianity become self-propagating. They certainly are relieved of the heavy burden imposed by idolatry; and are profited by habits enforced by Christianity....As far as possible Native Pastors should be placed over these Churches who will do faithful pastoral work and *whose salary shall not be much above the average income of their people.*[143]

As for profiting by "habits enforced by Christianity", an Indian Christian sets forth the viewpoint of some:

> (1) Many, by becoming Christians, have lost employment or other privileges that had pecuniary advantages ; (2) educated and intelligent men who could have entered "walks of life, which lead to wealth and affluence," have accepted Mission service; (3) some avenues of public employment have been closed to Christians in consequence of their 'proselytizing zeal'; (4) Christian standards add to expense; for example, a man wants his wife and children to go to church or school. He cannot therefore, 'leave the former in rags and the latter thoroughly naked' as he would have done if they had not become Christians.[144]

The advantages of self-support came to be more clearly stated: (1) an increase in independence of the Indian Church. (2) An independent church more active in evangelism. (3) An increase in spirituality of the Indian Church, which means the life and power of self-propagation.[145]

Mission and Mission Conference

"As fast as circumstances have allowed," wrote Butler in 1861, "all the institutions and usages of our Church have been introduced into every mission," or station.[146] These included provision of a "pastor", whether local preacher, exhorter or pastor-teacher; arrangements for worship services; Sunday Schools, and a Quarterly Conference. Leaders had taken part in the Annual Meetings, and when the Annual Conference was organized in 1864, candidates for admission had been duly recommended by Quarterly Conferences. The Annual Conference united these scattered congregations into a legal ecclesiastical body, with authority over its members and the right to coordinate and control institutions and to legislate policies.

The restrictions upon the Conference, which had so aroused the missionaries, were removed in 1868, and the India Mission Conference was "declared to be an Annual Conference, endowed with all the rights, privileges and immunities usual to Annual Conferences of the Methodist Episcopal Church in the United States of America".[147] Anticipating this decision the India Mission Conference elected J. T. Gracey as its delegate to the General Conference of 1868. He was seated in that body immediately after the withdrawal of the restrictions had been approved. The General Conference recognized the continued status of Mission by declaring specifically "that the Missionary interests of the Conference *would be administered as before*, its relation to the Missionary Society being continued as a Foreign Mission".[148] The name, India Mission Conference was continued through 1872, (Mission denoted only that it was in a Mission field) in Conference Journals and Disciplines, after which for four years it was called the India Conference.

Until 1876 the term Mission in the Discipline referred only to work under the Missionary Society. After his experience in the Annual Meeting of 1859 Thoburn had wished for an opportunity to re-write that chapter. It came to him in the General Conference of 1876 when he became Chairman of a sub-committee to revise the chapter on Missions.

> By introducing a few slight changes into this chapter the legal status of a Foreign Mission was established, the duties of a Superintendent specified, and for the first time a legal standing given to him, while the Annual meeting was elevated to the position of a District Conference. The Committee readily adopted our report, and it passed the General Conference without a word of discussion. Had this very simple, and manifestly necessary step been taken thirty years earlier, it would have been better for the interests of more than one of our Foreign Missions, and Dr. Butler, I am sure, would have found a less perplexing problem to solve when he organized our first work in Oudh and Rohilkhand.[149]

This plan was tested when Bishop Harris organized the Bombay-Bengal Mission as a District of the India Conference.

The Finance Committee

Previous to 1864 matters of finance were in the authority of the Superintendent. The Annual Meeting had no power although members expressed opinions. Estimates sent by the Superintendent were subject to approval of the Society.

The Annual Conference in Methodism is an autonomous body subject only to the Constitution and legislation of the General Conference. The organization of the India Mission Annual Conference gave it this freedom, but its dependence on the Missionary Society for funds brought it under its rules also. These were set forth in a report given to Bishop Thomson before he came to India, among them a rule that made Presiding Elders paymasters of the preachers, a practice that has had pernicious results. Class IX included all items relating to missionaries, since removed from Conference control.

Until 1876 all business now done in the Finance Committee was done in open Conference. It was democratic; but it was time consuming, and outside of the main purpose for which the Conference convened. In 1876 the following resolutions were adopted:

> *Whereas*, It has been found in the practical work of our Conference that the business growing out of our relation to the Missionary Society imposes upon us such a vast amount of work not suitable for an annual Conference, and
>
> *Whereas*, It is highly desirable to reduce the amount of secular work to be transacted at our annual sessions, and thus confine the Conference in a large measure to its proper ecclesiastical functions, and
>
> *Whereas*, We believe it would remove from many minds a serious objection to a more general introduction of Native preachers to Conference membership in all our mission fields....
>
> Therefore, Resolved, that we respectfully request the approaching General Conference to amend the Discipline . . . by adding a provision for the appointment of a Committee . . . to which shall be entrusted all matters pertaining to the distribution of appropriations of the Missionary Society.
>
> Resolved, that we respectfully suggest that such Committee should consist of the President and Treasurer of the Conference, and Presiding Elders of the Districts receiving appropriations, and two other persons, ministers or laymen, nominated by the President of the Conference and approved by the Board.[150]

The General Conference approved the resolution but enacted that there should be five additional members who should be elected by the

Conference.[151] The first Finance Committee was formed in 1877. In 1882 Zahur al Haqq became an ex-officio member; in 1883 J. T. Janvier and T. Gowan were among elected members; and the next year, H. A. Cutting and T. Gowan.

Extending Boundaries

It had been Butler's intention, concurred in by the Missionary Society, to limit the India Mission to a field embracing the ancient Kingdom of Oudh and the Province of Rohilkhand "lying between the river Ganges on the South and the Himalaya mountains on the North".[152] Thus "man proposed, but God disposed".

The events of 1857 led to the first extension of bounds by Butler himself. During his refuge in Naini Tal, in the Kumaon Province, continuous with his selected field, he learned that a hill station would really be a necessity for the health of missionaries unaccustomed to the heat of India's plains. The Naini Tal district was also unoccupied. In 1864, presumably with Butler's approval, Garhwal, a second district in Kumaon, was occupied; and work was opened in Gonda on the plains by Knowles. At the same time P. T. Wilson was appointed to Rae Bareili. "By this action", Thoburn says, "the field first chosen by Dr. Butler was extended to include the whole of Oudh.[153]

In 1871 the boundaries were breached by crossing the Ganges—India's Rubicon, as Thoburn called it, to include Kanpur.

> I knew beyond a doubt that if we planted ourselves in Cawnpore, we would not stop there. If we crossed the Ganges at all, the same guiding hand which led us to the first city on its western bank, might assuredly be expected to lead us on to other cities.[154]

These changes in boundaries were confirmed by the General Conference of 1872: "The India Conference shall include the Provinces of Oudh and Rohilkhand and Kanpur in the North-West Provinces, and Kumaon and Garhwal in the Himalaya mountains."[155]

In 1857 the only other Christian outpost in Kumaon was at Almora where the London Missionary Society had opened work under J. H. Budden in 1850. He had been in Mirzapur from 1843 to 1848, and was acquainted with Sir Henry Ramsay, who with other Christian gentlemen of Almora agreed to pay his salary and other local expenses of a Mission if he were sent to open it. The Society later resumed responsibility for the missionary's salary, but the Kumaon Committee continued to support the vernacular work under the Mission for many years. In 1869 the L. M. S. opened work in Ranikhet under J. Kennedy,[156] which also came under the same Committee. In 1871 when Humphrey wished to send John Barker to open medical work in Dwarahat, near Ranikhet, he consulted

Kennedy who apprised the Committee. Not only was there no objection, but the Methodists were asked to form a Naini Tal Branch of the Kumaon Committee. Barker opened his work April 1, 1872. The next year, Mansell from Pauri, was invited to form the Garhwal Branch. Members of these branch organizations were Indian and British residents, many of them officials, and the resident missionaries. The object of the General Committee was

> by mutual consultation and help, to promote the one object of all the missions incorporated, *viz.*, the evangelization of all the Province, without affecting the internal affairs of each Mission by its own Committee, or its relation to its parent Society.[157]

The work of the Almora Mission spread in 1871 to Eastern Kumaon. It was hoped that the L. M. S. would provide a second missionary for supervision. When they did not the Kumaon Committee invited the India Conference to take it up. They accepted the schools in Lohaghat and Pithoragarh with one helper, Gabriel Frances; and appointed R. Gray, M. D., the first missionary in 1874. He opened dispensaries in both centres. In 1875 there were seven small schools. The Kumaon Committee contributed Rs. 600 per year towards expenses.[158] John Barker was transferred to this new field and Harkua Wilson went to Dwarahat.

The India Mission Conference in 1872 adopted a special report on extension of the work:

> Resolved, that the Presiding Elders are hereby recommended to organize in connection with our Church, any persons who may desire our pastoral oversight, whether said persons live within the present limits of our Mission field or not, provided that in so doing they assume no financial liabilities, and provided further that the persons wishing to unite with us have been converted under our ministry.
>
> That they be further recommended to watch closely for special indications of Providence, as to where our efforts should be directed, and to recognize the conversion of souls as an infallible token that God accepts our labours in any specified place.
>
> Resolved: further, that they be instructed to consider carefully the project of opening evangelistic missions in Bombay and Bengal . . .
>
> That in the judgment of this Conference such missions should be purely evangelistic, and that no native helpers should be employed in them until suitable men are raised up from among the converts and supported by their contributions.[159]

From Allahabad, Dennis Osborne established English-speaking congregations at Agra, Roorkee, Mussoorie and other points west. In contrast, unknown by name, some Mass Movement Christians from the

Budaon circuit, illiterate folk and uninformed about Conference boundaries, just visiting across the river in 1875, told of what they had learned and new experiences they had had. Others heard when they crossed to homes on the eastern side. What are boundaries when hearts have opened to a new affection ? Hoskins' report of this historic crossing reads:

> *Mahrera.* This place is across the Ganges, in the Etah District. Nine have been baptized and many more are candidates for baptism. The people of several adjacent villages have requested to be taught with the idea of becoming Christians. Munshi Tori Dutt, another Bareilly graduate, a Local Preacher, has been appointed to this charge, and the indications promise an extensive work.[160]

Workers Together

It is a significant fact that among the Indian preachers all castes and classes were represented. Zahur al Haqq and Mahbub Khan were Muslims. The first named became the first Indian Presiding Elder in 1882, and built the Amroha District to a standard of high efficiency. Ambica Charan Paul was from a Brahman family. The Gospel message reached those at the top and at the bottom; it found its way to the hearts of village dwellers and to those in the city's mart. Where hearers were found, teachers and preachers from among them came forth to lead.

Andrias

Andrias was born in 1826 in a family of Kabirpanthis, in the Moradabad District. He was baptized in Mussoorie in 1853 by Rev. Lamb of the C. M. S. He met Joseph Fieldbrave in Moradabad and at his suggestion joined the Methodist Church, his old station being discontinued after the war. His wife, Priscilla, was "an excellent young woman" and a great help in the work with women. She died in 1871.

Before becoming a Christian Andrias was a *fakeer* among the chamars. His work was not confined to them nor to the Moradabad District.

> Wherever he goes, his strange garb, his musical instrument, his clear strong voice, his popular couplets prove a great attraction and his preaching is listened to by hundreds, Christians and others.... [He is] an apostle of holiness, a preacher whose words take deep root in men's hearts. He preaches his own experiences; he uses illustrations taken from every day life, apt and powerful. Divine grace supplemented by a perfect consecration has given peace of heart and serenity of features....The converted fakeer is exerting an influence for God which cannot be estimated.[161]

> God is leading this dear brother into a richer and richer Christian experience and he is the most devout and spiritually minded among us.[162]

> [In 1884 he] voluntarily gave up his salary . . . he continues to itinerate preaching Christ crucified. . . . He took this step against the advice and without the moral support of his own brethren, but he did it beyond doubt under the quiet leading and influence of God's Good Spirit.[163]

Isaac Fieldbrave

Among members of the North India Conference Isaac Fieldbrave was the first whose father had been a member. He was born in Delhi in 1848 and was early taught to love the Lord. He joined the Conference, On Trial in 1874. He was successively pastor at Lucknow, Moradabad and Kanpur. He was among the best preachers; and was in demand for camp meetings and conferences. "His language was choice; his style pleasing, his voice musical and his numerous illustrations well chosen."[164]

He excelled as a writer of hymns, some original, but many translated from among those in Sankey's *Songs and Solos*. He also wrote gazals and bhajans. The present Hindustani *Git ki Kitab* has more hymns translated, or written by him, than by any other single person.

Abraham Solomon

He was of the house of Levi, and was born on February 11, 1836 in Jerusalem where he spent his youth. He studied under Rabbi Ezra Hasometh and received his diploma. He wished to go into business and his father gave him $15,000 capital. He went to Persia, thence to Bombay in 1857. Conditions in India being upset he went to China, Australia, Philippines, Singapore and then back to Calcutta. He had a brother in Allahabad who sent him to Bareilly to watch his interests, and there he found another Jew with whom Waugh used to read Hebrew. One day this person brought home a New Testament. Abraham read it with interest and was almost persuaded to become a Christian.

When his brother died Abraham left for Peshawar where he met a Presbyterian missionary, Isidor Lowenthal. His studies here confirmed his convictions, but he left for business in Balkh and Bokhara. In 1864 he returned to India and in Moradabad he met Parker, who urged him to accept Christ at once, and on June 3, 1864 he was baptized in the chapel at Moradabad. He was employed as a teacher and later sent to be with Zahur al Haqq, and at a Camp Meeting in 1866 was soundly converted.

In 1879 Solomon was admitted to the Annual Conference, and the next January he was put in charge of a new circuit, Fatehganj West. There were twenty-three members, two day schools and three Sunday Schools. Baptisms increased from five in 1880 to 105 in 1887, giving a total for eight years of 518.[165] In 1890 he was made P. E. of the Pilibhit District which included Fatehganj West, and so continued until in 1900 he was superannuated. The Pilibhit District then had: 2229 Full members; 1954 Probationers and 1708 baptized children.[166] His successor, H. A. Cutting said that Solomon knew the District like a farmer knows his fields, or a shepherd his flocks.

Horace J. Adams

Horace J. Adams and his wife were among the finest products of the early orphanages. He was admitted as a youth of thirteen from the Mazhabi Sikh community in January, 1860 and was baptized the next year.[167] He joined Johnson's class in Theology and in the beginning of 1867 was sent as a preacher to Tilhar and in 1871 to Panahpur where he continued for twenty-six years. He joined the Annual Conference in 1874 and in the same session was ordained Deacon by Bishop Harris. Three years later he was ordained Elder by Bishop Andrews.

His wife, Minerva, was rescued as a famine waif and was educated in the girls' orphanage. Of her it was written: "We think her one of the brightest ornaments of the church in India. She is a woman of wonderful faith in prayer, (and) is very energetic....She prays with and instructs (the women) daily."[168] There are many descendants of the twelve daughters and their children rise up and call them blessed.

THE FIRST METHODIST CHURCH IN CALCUTTA—built by William Taylor in 1873 to house, temporarily, the many people who wanted to join him in worship.

JOEL JANVIER—First preacher

WILLIAM BUTLER—Founder of Methodism's India Mission

These were the beginnings—the first leaders of Methodism's India Mission. The call to enter India, long prepared for, long unheeded, was answered when, on October 10, 1855, Butler and his wife offered themselves as Superintendent. All of them, like Butler, combined English zeal and American energy, never doubting their divine guidance to succeed. Many of them, like Janvier, were eloquent and wise, ready to do the work God had for them to do.

MRS. WILLIAM BUTLER—From the first the Church grew strong by the readiness of wives to share in the work.

ISABELLA THOBURN—First Woman's Society educator

E. W. PARKER—Vermont farmer's son and village teacher who left New England for India in 1859.

LOIS LEE PARKER—From childhood she felt "she might be a missionary." She served in India more than 60 years.

ZAHUR-AL-HAQQ—One of the first converts and first National to become District Superintendent.

In the year after Butler's arrival came the Humphreys and the Pierces. Then, through the persuasion of Dr. Durbin came more. To his work as Mission Secretary in 1850 he brought an intense earnestness and the conviction that God wanted Methodists in India.

His article "The Crisis" asked for six young missionaries. In response came the Parkers, the Downeys, the Waughs, Judds, and Thoburn. Now the Asian continent was irrevocably a part of the Wesleyan world parish...These were the beginnings.

The JOSEPH R. DOWNEYS—He was the first to die on the field.

ANNUAL MEETING OF THE METHODIST CHURCH IN INDIA—1863—BAREILLY

WILLIAM TAYLOR—The meaning of Christ and the dignity of Christian worship came alive in his words.

JAMES THOBURN—No village too far away, no man or woman exempt from the glory of God in Christ.

ANNUAL MEETING—1863

L.-R. (upper row) Lawyer, Janvier, Judd, Jackson, Caleb. (far right) Thoburn, Joseph.

L.-R. (middle row) Gracey, Wilson, Baume, Hauser, Scott, Mansell, Mrs. Messmore, Thomas, Humphrey, Butler, Pierce, Brown, Hicks, Waugh, Cawdell, Parker, Johnson.

L.-R. (bottom row) Mrs. Gracey, Miss White, Miss Porter, Mrs. Hauser, Scott, Mansell, Thomas, Humphrey, Butler, Brown, Hicks, Waugh, Cawdell Parker, Johnson.

ROBERT HOSKINS—Maker of preachers, whose efforts gave the church the men it needed and the men the spirit they needed.

THE NAINI TAL CHURCH—First Methodist Sanctuary in India.

The clear conviction that this was God's choice for me...... And the life of Christian discipleship was incomplete unless it touched the far-off corners of the world with the demand to join Christ's followers.

WOMAN'S FOREIGN MISSIONARY SOCIETY IN 1876
Standing: Misses Tinsley, Sparkes, Thoburn, Lore. Sitting: Misses Pultz, Swain, Blackmar.

Unique the opportunity for Christian service by single women in the younger churches. Unique the response of these women to that opportunity. With a single eye, through the annals of missionary history, they have searched for Christ and found him in showing others the hidden wealth of education, the healing touch of hospitals, the love of God in self-giving care for his children.

PHOEBE ROW—First woman evangelist in North India—1887.

NURSAMMA—"Soul-Winner" in South India

CLARA SWAIN—First woman M. D. in all India—1870.

With purposeful confidence Methodist women have pierced the veil of strange customs and alien thought. In India centuries of misunderstanding have quietly fallen to the self-less dedication which they could make.

(left) MARY REED—For 50 years she served the helpless need of lepers in the hills behind Pithoragarh.

The Nawab of Rampur gave this land and buildings for the first medical work among India's women. That gift is now the sprawling campus of Clara Swain Hospital in Bareilly. The far building still stands as the administration center of the hospital.

Those of India who listened to the zealous and energetic Americans stepped up to match their new understanding with equally devoted work.

ABRAHAM SOLOMON—One of the first Presiding Elders.

HASAN RAZA KHAN—Able early organizer and administrator.

W. P. BOWEN, H. A. CUTTING, H. J. ADAMS—Their combined years of service in North India were more than 150.

GANGA NATH SHUKLA—long associate Agent of the Lucknow Publishing House.

ANDRIAS—CONVERTED "fakir" of Moradabad and staunch evangelist.

I left Bangalore next morning reluctantly. An open door seemed to stand before us, but it is thus all over India. It is an empire of open doors. May God raise up men and women from near and far to enter into and possess every one of them.

J. M. Thoburn. The "Indian Witness" Feb. 15, 1890

It is practically a law of life that where one door closes to us another opens. The trouble is that we often look with so much regret and longing upon the closed door that we do not see the one which has opened.

Quoted in "Reader's Digest" Aug. 1948.

Behold, I have set before you an open door, which no one is able to shut.

Revelation 3:8 (R. S. V.)

V

Doors Wide Open

New life was pulsing through the India sub-continent when Taylor came to India. Its cities were throbbing with activity. Railways, telegraph, a better postal system, bridges across great rivers—all were creating a unity in the country which before had not been possible. The Suez Canal and steam ships brought other countries nearer. The heartbeats of One World were being felt.

Taylor had not chosen his time; he felt that his times were God-chosen. Nor did Taylor work by fixed program; he constantly sought God's direction. His methods were suited to the opportunities that quick communications were providing, and to that other opportunity, which he found in the Anglo-Saxon Dispersion, an English-speaking people throughout the country.

> Revivals and all forms of revival work, were unknown in India. The great cities were well supplied with Christian Churches, but nothing like a revival had ever been witnessed in any city of the empire. A growing feeling of despondency had taken possession of many missionaries, and not a few of those who had witnessed revivals at home were inclined to think it would be too much to expect a time of refreshing in India.[1]

Taylor Leads The Way

After his year in the India Mission Conference and a short period in Delhi, Taylor accepted the invitation of the American Marathi and the Free Church Marathi Missions in Ahmednagar and Bombay. He reached the latter city on November 10, 1871, and for most of a month he held meetings, speaking through interpreters. He found it necessary "to preach very cautiously for a week or two to allay prejudices" and to get cooperation. "The ministers are most learned in their efforts to promote God's work; but as for lay-workers—I have yet to see them."[2]

Bombay

On December 8 he started an independent program with English meetings in the Institution Hall. Audiences increased and after the first night seekers came forward after each meeting. Taylor doubted that pastors who would not let him speak from their pulpits would take much interest in his converts. He, therefore, organized them into Fellowship Bands on the lines of Class Meetings, so that he might get "an organized, witnessing, working Church".

Early in the campaign George Bowen joined Taylor. Differing in many ways they were yet kindred spirits. Bowen threw the full support of the Bombay Guardian to Taylor, defending him against attacks by correspondents in other papers, and consistently reporting and supporting, and sharing in his meetings. The first Fellowship Band was organized in the home of Mrs. Miles on December 30. Bowen was appointed its leader. In the first meeting "28 persons told their Christian experience, most of them young converts. In circumstancial detail, variety, simplicity and point," Taylor had never heard better testimony for Christ.

As interest grew Bowen rented Framji Cowasji Hall belonging to the Parsees. Regular services were held there, also at Dhobi Talao and in the P. and O. Theatre at Mazagaon Docks. By January 23, eight bands had been formed, the last, in the sitting room of Mrs. Miles' home—a spacious room accommodating over one hundred, "which became known as the Falkland Road Hall, the predecessor of Grant Road Church".

In other countries Taylor had not organized churches. His effort had been to help churches to develop their own organizations for receiving members. His Bands were training classes; he hoped that members would find their places in the churches where most of them had belonged. But he came to realize that the Fellowship Bands needed connection with each other. In February, eighty-three members of the several Bands made a written request that he organize them into a Methodist Church. He replied:

> I now see with you the guiding hand of God by which you have been led to your present conclusion; and I am bound by my loyalty to Christ to concur with you in this movement. After I received your letter I read to the 'fellowship bands' the 'General Rules of our Societies' that all might know from the start the self-denying, crossbearing life necessary to constitute a true Methodist.[3]

On February 14, 1872 the Methodist Episcopal Church was organized in Bombay by receiving members on probation, and on June 30 Falkland Hall was opened with the reception of twenty-one full members; James and Julia Morris, Major and Roseline C. Raitt, W.A.E. Boyd, William and Eliza Ashdown, George Miles, Matilda Miles, Dorothea, Emily and Alice Miles, Mary and Julia Cassidy, C.W. Christian, Capt. Joseph and Eliza Winckler and the following on their previous standing in other churches: William J. Coen, James Shaw, Joseph and Mrs. Powell. The next day the first Quarterly Conference was held when James Shaw was recommended for a Local Preacher's license. At the love feast held in connection with the Sacrament, Trimbak Canaren and his brother Asa were converted.[4]

It was from the start distinctly stated and unanimously concurred in by all our members, that ours should be purely a missionary Church, for the conversion of the Native nations of India, as fast and as far as the Lord should lead us; . . . it should neither ask nor receive any funds from the Missionary Society beyond the passage of missionaries to India; . . . but be led directly by the Holy Spirit of God, and supported by Him from Indian resources.[5]

The writer [Bowen] has been preaching for 24 years in the vernacular in the open air in Bombay; but it is a new thing to preach with a body of Christians, ladies and gentlemen, European and Native, giving the moral force of their presence and prayers, uniting occasionally in singing, and ready to bear their personal testimony to the value of true faith in Christ. It is not easy to over-rate the importance of this kind of testimony. Many of the Natives . . . are much impressed by the evidence now furnished that there are many who profess to know Christ as their personal Saviour, and under the influence of their faith in Him, have a desire to welcome them, the people of this country, as brethren and sisters in Christ.[6]

Taylor wrote to the Missionary Committee asking that they send two missionaries to work with the Church just organized, providing their passage out, but without responsibility for their salaries. He also sent a petition to General Conference, through Bishop Janes, asking for the organization of an Annual Conference. This petition was read in the Committee and "laid on the table". God raised up many in the local and itinerant ministry in Bombay:

James Shaw, an Irish army scripture-reader; Manekji Mody, the Parsee; W. Curties and G. K. Gilder, of the government telegraph department; Charles Christian of the Bank of Bombay; such outstanding Local Preachers as James Morris, the architect; George Miles; William Boyd; George Ainsworth; Sydenham Smith, the lawyer; Thomas Glover, a municipal official; William Badfork; Trimbak Canaren and Krishna Chovi, Malayalam Hindus; William Wright, railway official; Samuel Page, police officer; William Ashdown; Namaji Powar and Rava Shankar, Marathi Hindus; and Ruttonji Mehta, the Parsee.[7]

As the work in the city grew it soon extended beyond Bombay An Inspector of Police, Henry Bailey, a convert, invited Taylor to go with him to Poona for a rest, where Taylor laid plans for special services and wrote to the pastor of the Free Church of Scotland that he would help his people all he could, but others would be free to join a Methodist Church if they liked. He replied: "If I can see people brought to repentance they may become Methodists or whatever they like."[8]

On August 14, with James Morris, Taylor opened the "Siege of Poona". When Morris had to leave, James Shaw, Krishna Chovi and Jurian reinforced Taylor. On alternate Sundays Bowen went to Poona and Taylor returned to Bombay, so the "siege was steadily kept up". On

September 28, a fellowship meeting was held at the home of Angelo deSouza. The names of thirty-seven were written down who chose to join the Methodist Church. Dr. Fraser was the first to give his name. A place of worship was secured for the members. The first Communion service was held October 12, 1872 when sixty-four communed and 130 were hearers. "A living, working, growing Church" sprang up at Lanowli. Dr. Fraser and Col. Everzard became "clean, powerful, local preachers . . . Seale, a young officer in the army, also became a successful local preacher."[9]

Two recruits asked from the Missionary Committee, D. O. Fox and Albert Norton, reached Bombay on December 1, 1872. A third recruit, W. E. Robbins, had seen Taylor's call for preachers. Not being accepted by the Committee, but eager to come, he paid his own way, deck passage, and arrived before the other two. He learned to preach in the Marathi language within the first year. It was arranged that these new missionaries should be boarded at such places as offered on the circuits and have all necessary expenses met. They received no salary and the Rs. 30 a month pocket money offered each of them by the stewards was declined with one accord, that they might say they got no stated allowance. On November 15 James Shaw resigned his appointment in the Army to become a full-time itinerant preacher.

With these reinforcements in Bombay and with the concurrence of his colleagues, Taylor left Bombay for Calcutta in January, 1873. George Bowen expressed the thought of all: "We can't wait to see the full growth and fruit bearing of one tree, before we plant another, but must go on planting."[10]

Calcutta

Taylor went to Calcutta with a conviction that God would raise up an evangelistic church in that city as in Bombay. He had offered the Wesleyan missionary there "a week of special services" after which he would be free, if so led, to organize a Methodist Church. The missionary, John Richards, promised full co-operation.

Taylor commenced his services in the Wesleyan Chapel on Sunday, January 12, 1873. Then for a few days he held services in the home of the American Zenana Mission and some morning prayer meetings at Jeffries' home. Later, public meetings were held at the Baptist Union Chapel where some converts were won. Among the earliest who expressed a wish to join the new church were Mr. and Mrs. Harris who gave their home for a Fellowship Band, and Miss Purchase.[11] Capt. Jones, who had been converted in San Francisco under Taylor, helped him greatly. Besides preaching services with a seekers meeting following, Taylor held weekly meetings in forty homes. Of this period he wrote:

> The hardest work of my life, I believe, was here in the streets of Calcutta, under the greatest discouragements. For months it seemed very doubtful, by all outward indications, whether we could raise a working force at all. I became more and more convinced that a great work of God was what Calcutta least desired and most needed... so I determined, as the Lord should lead, to push the battle and win, or die at the guns.[12]

About April 9, Taylor gave the first opportunity for converts who had been in fellowship meetings to enrol as member of the Methodist Church. Thirteen gave their names. "A very small beginning after two months of so hard work; but thank God! it is a germ of His planting, and will become a banyan, with branches and trunks innumerable."[12] From Fellowship Bands other names were added, yet of the first twenty names recorded by Taylor not one was connected with the Dharamtala Street congregation. However, a number were in Christian work and two were pastors in India.

Two months of meetings in a room at the Y.M.C.A. in Bow Bazaar followed on Sunday mornings and two nights weekly. There were some forty converts and a Fellowship Band organized with Frederick Curties as leader; the beginning of a church. Taylor wrote to Bowen concerning plans for a building:

> We are going to build with Calcutta funds a cheap preaching bungalow near Bow Bazar. We have rented a lot for Rs. 100 a year and will put up a bungalow 36′×48′ to cost with sittings about Rs. 1,000. It will last at least for 5 years. It is possible the Lord will have me buy several good sites, suitable for both English and Native work as we shall progress and need them and put up cheap bungalows [Hall with pastor's residence, attached] .... The building I shall begin with I copied from a Native theatre now nearly completed in the city .... This we can build in a few weeks, and we can go on then rapidly, economically and not get stuck in the mud—bricks, mortar, church debts, etc.[13]

This "preaching bungalow" on Ziz Zag Lane was opened on November 9, 1873. "Taylor lived at this place and received his food from a godly sister, Mother Freude."[14] The "little hut", as C.J.A. Pritchard, a Calcutta layman, called it, held 150-200 people; but it was as Thoburn said, the first Methodist Episcopal Church in Calcutta.[15] It was built "in a most primitive style, bamboo being freely used in its constructing," with roof of tile.

As a result of the letter to Bowen plans for a more permanent building got under way. The change in plans came through a gift of Rs. 10,000 from Bombay. It was money that had been put to George Bowen's account by a friend for his private use—a furlough to America was suggested. Bowen would not use it and had offered it for a church in Bombay, but when members heard of Calcutta's need "all parties with one consent said that as the Calcutta brethren were few and poor, the money should go to them".[16] With this gift, and some raised in Calcutta, a lot was purchased in Dharamtala Street near Wellington Square, for Rs. 4,600 and a contract let for a permanent brick hall forty by eighty feet.[17]

Taylor was joined by C. W. Christian from Bombay. He had recently resigned his position as head of the Correspondence Department in the Bombay Bank, "under a sense of a divine call to devote himself entirely to the Lord's work".[18] E. Jeffries was licensed as a Local Preacher by the Calcutta Quarterly Conference.

In December, 1873 M.C. Harris arrived in Calcutta having been assigned to the presidency of the India Conference. In answer to a cable Thoburn was there to meet him. There had been misgivings in New York with regard to Taylor's work for these churches that he had organized had no relation to the Missionary Society, and yet he had asked for an Annual Conference. Bishop Harris had been instructed to bring plans into harmony with established Methodist practice. This was not difficult for fears had been exaggerated. The agreed program included the following: (1) A Bombay and Bengal Mission to include all that part of India outside the bounds of the India Conference; (2) William Taylor to be the Superintendent of this Mission; (3) until the work of this new Mission was organized as an Annual Conference, the Superintendent and his ministers should hold their membership in the India Conference; (4) The India Conference would sustain no administrative responsibility to the work of the Mission.[19]

The Bombay and Bengal Mission

These arrangements were consummated at the regular session of the India Conference which convened in Lucknow on January 7, 1874, under Bishop Harris. D.O. Fox, W.E. Robbins, and Albert Norton, probationer in the second year, were admitted by transfer from Conferences in America and Robbins was elected to Elder's orders. On the second day Taylor was introduced, and on the third day "J. M. Thoburn presented the certificate of location of William Taylor, formerly of the California Conference, and moved that he be admitted to the India Conference."[20] This was done; Norton was also admitted into full connection.

> Rev. George Bowen, an ordained minister of the Presbyterian Church, having become a minister in the Methodist Episcopal Church, submitted his credentials of ordination to the Conference, when on motion, the Conference recognized him as an ordained Elder of our Church, on condition that he take on him the ordination vows of our ministers, and on further motion he was admitted to membership in the Conference.[21]

Members of the India Conference ordained as Deacons were: Richardson Gray, A. D. McHenry, J. E. Scott, Dennis Osborne, John Thomas, H. J. Adams, Isaac Fieldbrave, H. A. Cutting and Prem Das, and as Elders:[22] Gray, McHenry, J. E. Scott, D. Osborne, Sundar Lal and Ambica Charan Paul.

Several members of the Bombay and Bengal Mission were not present. James Shaw and G. K. Gilder, on recommendation of the Bombay Quarterly Conference, and C. W. Christian and C. R. Jeffries, on recommendation of the Calcutta Quarterly Conference, were admitted On Trial. Shaw was elected to both Deacon's and Elder's orders under the Missionary rule; and under the same rule Christian, Jeffries and Gilder were elected to Deacon's orders. Local Preachers, Frank Pearcy and Joseph Powell from the Bombay and Bhusawal Quarterly Conferences, respectively, were elected to Deacon's orders. On January 25, 1874, Christian, Jeffries and Gilder were ordained in Allahabad, and on January 30, Shaw, Pearcy and Robbins were ordained in Bombay.[23]

The appointment of "Missionaries to Bombay and Bengal Mission" with William Taylor as Superintendent officially constituted the Mission. Only one name not mentioned above was included that of James M. Thoburn. The appointments within the Mission were:

William Taylor, Superintendent

BOMBAY PRESIDENCY

Bombay, Callian, Egutpoora, etc. George Bowen, William E. Robbins, James Shaw.

The Deccan: Poona, Lanowlee, Dexale, etc., Daniel O. Fox.

CENTRAL INDIA

Bhosawal, Nagpore, Jubbulpore, etc., Albert Norton, George K. Gilder.

BENGAL PRESIDENCY

Calcutta, Dinapore, etc., James M. Thoburn, Christopher W. Christian, Charles R. Jeffries.

All of India excluding the India Conference, like Caesar's Gaul, was divided into three parts. The three letters "etc." in each circuit express the wideness and the indefiniteness, of the field.

MADRAS

With the appointment of Thoburn to Calcutta, Taylor was "foot loose". In Kanpur he visited Dr. James Condon who had received a letter from his brother, E. H. Condon in Madras, asking that Taylor go there. Col. Goddard, Dr. Van Someren, and Mr. Bowden joined him in the invitation, but Dr. E. H. Condon expressed the hope that Taylor would not organize a church there. To this Taylor replied: "I will leave that entirely to the Lord's leading; as He may manifest it clearly, not only to me but to you and your friends."[24] They made arrangements for all services.[25]

Taylor found his way to Dr. Condon's home on February 4, 1874. The campaign opened on the tenth in the Evangelistic Hall of the Free Church of Scotland, which was "packed with attentive hearers of all sorts, including twenty or thirty Hindus". On the second night "some thirty" seekers came forward. The first Fellowship Band was formed on February 22. A month after Taylor's arrival there were eight. For four months Taylor led these bands himself trying to develop leaders from among the converts. In June, George Bowen, Mrs. Miles and Mrs. Raitt from Bombay, gave valuable assistance. With extending work, churches were organized at Perambore, the centre of railway work shops; Salem, 207 miles distant; and Palaveram, a colony of retired people. Bowen wrote: "We are not aware that there has ever before been in India so powerful a work of grace as that which has attended the labours of this evangelist in Madras."[26]

At hours when meetings were not held, teachers voluntarily conducted schools for Indian children for two hours daily and a half hour longer for those who wanted to sing Tamil lyrics. Other societies were organized in Arkonam, Jalarpet and Salem. Philip Gordon, a successful lawyer who was converted in July, devoted all his leisure to preaching "with marvellous power in Tamil, Telugu, Kanarese, Hindustani and English". Taylor baptized six Hindus who had made public profession of conversion.[27] The first quarterly Conference with twenty-one present early in July, 1874 was organized in the first week.

> At a love feast the chapel was crowded, 250 took the Sacrament; 106 bore clear testimony for Jesus. There are 335 members, most of them are still probationers—only 5 months since meetings started! There were 18 classes, ten being in Madras. One of these was a Tamil class. All have their leaders now.[28]

Grace Stephens became the best-known convert from the Madras campaign. Her account, "How I became a Methodist", describes both Taylor's methods and her experiences. Her family were faithful members of the Church of England. At sixteen she was confirmed but did not know much of the Spirit's inward work. Then Taylor came.

> His teaching, his doctrine and his preaching were all so new to me. Never till then had I heard of 'seekers', of 'penitents at the altar',

and 'testimony'. When the people went forward and professed conversion, I often felt inclined to kneel there too, but the thought always came, 'I have sought and found.' . . . Nevertheless I enjoyed the meetings and received much good.

Her father gave the use of their home for a Fellowship Band. At the close of a meeting Taylor invited her to another Band on a Sunday. She went in her carriage. The hall was full of people. Taylor met her and showed her a seat.

> Oh how the people testified! I did not think of taking part in this meeting . . . . Several times he beckoned me to speak, but I could not. Whenever he turned toward me I turned my face away. To my horror, he left his place, came and sat next to me and gently asked me to speak . . . . I was so frightened and nervous for I had never, spoken a word in public . . . . 'Tell me and I shall tell the people.' So in his ear I whispered my testimony, and he then in a loud voice repeated what I had told him. This was my first work in the Methodist Episcopal Church.

That evening she received a full-membership ticket in an envelope. She was uncertain whether to destroy or return it. She did neither. It was that way with the meetings also. She thought she would not go, but she did. The meetings "held a fascination for me which I could not resist". To decide whether to keep the ticket or not she asked her father. He replied: "You must join a church where you can do the most good." So Grace Stephens joined the Methodist Church; what more needy place than this?

> The struggle was over. I accepted the much despised and slandered name of Methodist. I came out from my companions; no more did I sit in the old family pew. I was missed; my parents felt the separation keenly; my brothers did not understand, and my minister scolded. But a Methodist I was, and I was led to take upon myself all the duties the new church imposed from its earliest days when the people learned to give and to support the work.[29]

Bangalore

Putting Madras under the general oversight of Mrs. Raitt, whom Condon described as "worth her weight in diamonds", Taylor went to Bangalore taking Gordon and Jordan with him. Gordon procured a lot for a chapel in Richmond Town and Jordan at St. John's Hill. Because of a very heavy monsoon Taylor returned to Madras for a time but again went to Bangalore at the close of September and "pushed the battle for five weeks".[30] Arrangements were made for the use of Clarendon Hall which seated 300. Converts numbered 140, and a hundred united in church fellowship. They were organized in four Fellowship Bands.

A contract was let for "a cheap chapel" on the St. John's Hill lot. James Shaw of Bombay was appointed as pastor "and initiated into the work" when Taylor left him in charge, while he himself went to Madras, Secunderabad and Bombay. This "chapel" was dedicated on February 28, 1875 by C.P. Hard and E. Jeffries.[31] It was renovated and re-furnished at a cost of Rs. 7,000 under W.E. Newlon, pastor, and on June 19, 1879 was dedicated as the Memorial Church "in commemoration of the bountiful harvest after the great famine".[32] The Richmond Town Church was built in 1875-76.

In Bombay Taylor held a District Conference of churches in Western and Central India. The licenses of local preachers were renewed, and six new licenses were granted, most of them to men with qualifications for vernacular work. On Friday, December 19, 1874 Taylor welcomed three recruits from America: Clark P. Hard; John E. Robinson, and Frank A. Goodwin.[33] Work was awaiting them. They left on Monday for their first appointments: Hard to the Madras circuit where there were 350 church members and probationers; Robinson to Secunderabad, and Goodwin to Karachi. Extracts from letters show their calibre:

> Safe arrival, after joyous journey; crowds of friends—full salvation—good health—plenty to do—I need not complete the sentence which started to tell you I am very happy. [Hard to Taylor, December 28, 1874].
>
> Memorial Hall was full last evening, the Methodists being there .... Licenses were granted to three; Bros. Haudin, Gordon and Peters, as I said you had proposed their names. Brother Peters is to teach me Tamil three times per week from twelve to two p.m. Brothers Haudin and Peters are to be students in my theological seminary. [Hard to Taylor, January 5, 1875].
>
> These ten days have been delightful. Never has work for the Master been so blessed. Like you I have had plenty of it, but strength and grace have been vouchsafed me .... Never have I had a deeper sense of the Father's love and care than since I arrived .... For the first time I administered the Holy Communion, and for the first time I welcomed members, my members, into the fold .... I am getting a hold on some of the natives. There were four, (one a Mohammedan) at our Monday evening prayer meeting, ... the Lord wonderfully supplied me with thoughts and utterance. The whole four rose to publicly testify their belief that Jesus Christ was the Son of God .... I wouldn't exchange my humble appointment for any American pastorate. I wouldn't care if I didn't receive a rupee salary. I have asked not a single question in answer to it; the Lord will provide.[34] [Robinson to Clark, January 2, 1875]

Bombay, Bengal and Madras Mission

William Taylor attended the Conference session in January, 1875, stopping *en route* at Agra with a church newly established there. He was made a member of the Committee on Missions with other Presiding

Elders, and in his turn "represented his large and growing work". Hard, Goodwin and Robinson were admitted to the Conference on transfer, and Curties from Bombay, was admitted On Trial. Piyare Mohun Mukerji, minister of the Congregational Church, was received on the same condition as was made for George Bowen.

Albert Norton refused to "submit to the authority of the Conference", and was suspended from the ministry of the M. E. Church for one year. In 1876 he withdrew from the connection.[35]

The Mission now became the Bombay, Bengal and Madras Mission. In the expectation that it would have the oversight of William Taylor, Conference members were appointed to charges, or circuits in three major divisions: Bombay, Baroda and Central India; Bengal Presidency and the Madras Presidency.

After the Conference Taylor went to Lahore for services with the Presbyterians, expecting to go from there to Sindh. In Lahore he received an invitation to go to England to assist Moody in his campaign in that country. He left from Bombay early in March with every intention of returning to India. To the next Conference he wrote:

> I long to be with you to drive into the Native lines. As certainly as that the Bible is the Book of God, the soul-saving resources in Christ through the Holy Spirit are amply adequate and gloriously available for the conversion of India to God. We must get at the masses of Natives as fast as we can, but must ever keep in mind, that soul-saving is a hand-to-hand personal business.[36]

At this Conference five new missionaries for this Mission were admitted to Conference by transfer and appointed as indicated: M. H. Nichols, (Nagpur); John Blackstock, (Bombay); F. G. Davis, (Madras); W. E. Newlon, (Bangalore); D. H. Lee, (Agra). T. H. Oakes was admitted On Trial and appointed to the Seaman's Church, Calcutta.

George Bowen was present for the first time. The Conference, by a rising vote, adopted the following resolutions:

1. That we hereby express the heartfelt satisfaction which it gives us to welcome among us, for the first time, our beloved and revered brother, Rev. George Bowen.
2. That we assure him that we have appreciated more fully than we can express in words, the service which he has rendered us, by casting in his lot among us, bringing with him a ripe experience in missionary work, and a rare reputation as a Christian minister and a devout believer.[37]

Bowen wrote his impressions of the India Conference:

> Every morning during the sessions of the Conference there was a prayer meeting; every evening a preaching service, followed by an

after meeting. The presence of the Spirit of God was very marked in these meetings, not so much in the conversion of sinners, as in the blessings bestowed upon believers. There was much hunger and thirsting after righteousness, and the unsearchable riches of Christ were realized by many. Nothing could be more edifying and quickening than some of the accounts given of personal experience. At the Love Feast on Sunday morning 63 persons gave some account of the way in which the Lord was leading them. From day to day the presence of the Spirit of God was more and more blessedly manifest and we felt it a great privilege to have been present.[38]

The appointments for 1876 show William Taylor as Superintendent, but work was organized into three Districts, Bombay, Calcutta and Madras, with Presiding Elders Bowen, Thoburn and Hard, respectively. William Taylor never did return. He wrote in 1882, "I am longing to be with you and go campaigning . . . . The Lord will let me do it by and by." He never lost his interest in the work he had opened. In 1884 while attending the General Conference as a lay delegate from the South India Conference, he was elected Missionary Bishop for Africa. He died in 1902.

What a flame of revival power he had become. The Living God was with him and pentecostal fire fell upon the people wherever he went. He was a great religious pioneer. He blazed pathways through unknown moral wilds, and left the organization mainly to those who might follow after.[39]

Wherever churches have been planted by Mr. Taylor the older organizations have been strengthened, there is more life in the members, more zeal, more prayerfulness, a better attendance upon the services.[40]

The South India Conference

A memorial to General Conference adopted by the India Conference in 1876 asked for a second Annual Conference. Approval was given for a Conference, including Allahabad and all those parts of India not embraced in the North India Conference, to be called the South India Conference.

It met for its First Annual Session, Thursday, November 9, 1876, at Falkland Road Hall, Bombay, Bishop E. G. Andrews, presiding . . . . The Bishop, E. W. Parker and George Bowen led in prayer after which Bishop Andrews read the following paper:

'In accordance with the action of the General Conference of the Methodist Episcopal Church held in Baltimore, U. S. A., May 1, 1876, whereby the South India Conference was constituted of all those parts of India not included in the North India Conference, I hereby recognize the following brethren as members of said Conference, namely: William Taylor, George Bowen, J. M. Thoburn, W. E. Robbins, C. P. Hard, D. O. Fox, P. M. Mukerji, D. Osborne, M. H. Nichols, J. Blackstock, G. K. Gilder and C. W. Christian. And the following brethren as probationers in the said Conference, namely: F. G. Davis, F. A. Goodwin, J. Shaw, D. H. Lee, J. E. Robinson, W. E. Newlon,

W. T. G. Curties, and T. H. Oakes. I also announce the transfer of W. J. Gladwin, an elder from the North India Conference; I. F. Row, an elder from the New England Conference, and of Levan R. Janney, a probationer, from the Central Ohio Conference, as by the accompanying certificates.

'And on this first session of the South India Conference I invoke the special blessing of the great Head of the Church. May love, faith and wisdom, attend its deliberations; and prepare the way of a long history of distinguished usefulness in this Indian Empire.'

Mansell, Cunningham, and Wheeler of the North India Conference, were invited to partake in the proceedings of the Conference. Revival services had been conducted by J. M. Thoburn for a week before Conference.

A delightful spiritual feeling pervaded the whole session. The Conference love feast continued more than two hours, which were filled with personal testimonies . . . . Bishop Andrews won all hearts by his kindly interest in both the ministers and their work.[41]

Oaks and Curties were ordained Deacons in the morning at Falkland Road Hall, and Christian, Gilder, Oakes and Curties as Elders, in the evening at Framjee Cowasjee Hall.[42] At that time there were 1,596 members and probationers; thirteen churches with a value of Rs. 115,391; collections for ministerial support were Rs. 14,250; for general expenses, Rs. 13,117 and for transit fund, Rs. 4,814. The appointments of the Conference for 1877 were:

BOMBAY DISTRICT: George Bowen, P.E.; Conference Evangelist, William Taylor; *Bombay*, George Bowen, Isaac Row; *Poona*, John Blackstock; *Tanna*, W.E. Robbins; *Egatpura*, to be supplied; *Mhow*, M.H. Nichols; *Nagpur*, Wallace J. Gladwin; *Karachi*, D. O. Fox.

CALCUTTA DISTRICT: James M. Thoburn, P.E.: *Calcutta*, J.M. Thoburn, F.A. Goodwin, *Seaman's Church*. T.H. Oakes; *Darjeeling*, to be supplied; *Rajmahal*, P.M. Mukerji; *Allahabad*, Dennis Osborne, L.R. Janney; *Jabalpur*, to be supplied; *Agra*, C.W. Christian; *Meerut*, G.K. Gilder; *Roorkee*, D.H. Lee.

MADRAS DISTRICT: Clark P. Hard, P.E.; *Madras*, C. P. Hard; F.G. Davis, Benjamin Peters; *Bangalore*, James Shaw, W.E. Newlon; *Bellary*, to be supplied; *Hyderabad* and *Secunderabad*, J.E. Robinson, W.T.G. Curties.

The Conference had its weaknesses. First, was its tremendous size, roughly equivalent to the United States east of the Mississippi. The transfer of Goodwin from Karachi to Calcutta at the first session represented a journey of nearly 2,500 miles. To attend sessions of the Annual Conference several members had to travel from 500 to 1,500 miles. The time consumed in such travel, as well as in the administration of districts, was a serious handicap when it is remembered that the Presiding Elders were also pastors of churches. The expense was a heavy personal burden.

Another weakness was the inexperience of Conference members. Twenty-four men received appointments. Only three of these had been in the ministry before 1872; Bowen, Thoburn and Taylor. Three others were recruited in 1872: Gladwin, Fox and Robbins; nine were added in 1874; six in 1875, and three in 1876. Of the total, eight had been recruited in India, of whom only Mukerji had earlier ministerial experience. Those from America were in a foreign country with the adjustment that that implied, even in English work. Those recruited in India faced adjustments no less serious, in relinquishing salaries for insecurity and in adapting to ministerial work for which they had no special training.

While all accepted the aim of the churches to be "the conversion of the Indian people", few if any, had grasped the meaning of that task, for to receive their support each had his own supporting English congregation to which he ministered. Also, there was involved the need of proficiency in an Indian language; of going to people in their villages as well as in the city; of providing for worship, for teaching and for nurturing converts in the faith. In this far-flung field it was well that they did not comprehend, lest they might have been deterred.

What the Conference did have was of immeasurable value: two dozen leaders with deep Christian experience, a call, dedication, enthusiasm and a sense of urgency. Behind these were as many churches, whose members had come into a Christian experience and were irrepressible in sharing it in grateful allegiance to their Saviour. The fields all around seemed "white already to harvest". In the churches and in all efforts to win the Indian people, self-support was a cardinal principle. This

> was not clearly defined at first and has been a shifting term all along. . . . We adopted this principle for several reasons. Some of us had been distinctly called to this type of work. It was considered very desirable to try, at least, to develop a self supporting work among the Indians; and it was believed that such a work, commenced among English-speaking people, would propagate itself among the Indians.[43]

Right bravely did the churches move toward their task. Although the Conference was united on the principle they never devised a constructive program for vernacular work. Congregations and individuals were left to initiate what they could. About Bombay, Bowen wrote:

> Many English members of the Church are endeavouring to improve their knowledge of the vernacular and to use what they have of it. Some go about the Native *chauls*, from door to door, telling the people of the Native services and inviting them to come with them and hear the Gospel preached, and they generally return with a goodly number thus gathered. Others gather the Native children of the neighbourhood together for an hour or two's instruction daily. Some that can play

on instruments bring these with them to the vernacular meetings, t add to their attractiveness. All these tokens of interest have this valu because they are voluntary.[44]

Numerous laymen employed in the railway, or other services, gav time and private means that the Gospel message might reach Indian: Some English congregations employed catechists, preachers or teachers, t work among the Indians. Much good was done through all of these effort: but the great rural population in the hinterland remained almost ur touched.

In 1882 the Missionary Board, through Bishop Foster, offered som aid to the Conference for vernacular work on a grant-in-aid basis. It wa rejected; only five men argued in favour of accepting such help. In 188 Bishop Hurst being present, the question was again raised—and this tim debated, and a committee appointed to study its implications. It reporte at the session in January, 1886 :

> After a careful consideration of the entire work of the conference i all its details that the outlay on Indian work from Indian resources i our various charges would be in 1886 Rs. 25,000, the equivalent c $10,000; and . . . this sum was allotted to the different points accordin to the exigencies of the native work.
>
> This principle it was believed would relieve none of our Englis charges of the burdens assumed by them for the prosecution of Nativ work, but would simply supplement what they are doing and give ther the means for enlarging their work.[45]

The years 1876-1888 were rugged times for both pastors and peopl but they bred rugged Christians.

> Eternity alone will reveal the results, but a few facts are eloquen We had become two Conferences with 29 churches worth Rs. 300,000 14 parsonages worth Rs. 80,000; and Rs. 16,000 indebtedness. Th Church was raising annually over Rs. 50,000 for pastoral support, an Rs. 17,000 for local Mission work. That money was almost entirel given by Europeans and Anglo-Indians who had been won to Chris That young Church was full of vitality . . . .
>
> God honoured our faith . . . . In our gathering today [Jubilee 1906 there are bishops whose salaries were then less than Rs. 100 a month Conference journeys sometimes a round trip of 3,000 miles . . . an often required a year to save enough for the purpose. Those days sel support gave us a strong grip on the European community.[46]

When in January, 1886 the S. I. Conference voted to accept a gran for vernacular work equal to the sum the Conference raised for the sam cause, the Committee distributed Rs. 25,423 ($10,000), to districts as follows Allahabad 2,624; Bombay 3,420; Burma 7,350, of which 7,050 was fo Singapore; Calcutta 4,614; Central India 4,090; Madras 3,325. Som figures used in apportioning were : Missionaries 720 or 480; Indian preache apparently varying with stations, 72, 54, 150 or 75; Helpers, 48; Bangalore and Vepery Tamil Missions 240 each. To Igatpuri "to extend native work, Rs. 300". The Report concluded: "All apportionments shall be strictly applied to the specific purposes for which given, failing which the amount must be refunded to the Treasurer."

This Conference took a further significant step. It organized a Church Aid Society whose purpose was to strengthen English work by supplementing the meagre salaries of preachers in remote places, and along the railway lines where groups were too small to maintain a pastor.[47]

When the General Conference defined the boundaries of the South India Conference to include all India outside of the North India Conference, literally, "all India became our field".[48] "Perhaps . . . the special service for which God raised it up, [was] that it led the Church forward to a work which otherwise never would have been assumed".[49] That judgment, written eighty years ago, stands confirmed at this Centennial.

"GET ME THAT BOOK"

Let me tell you a story. I was sent to survey the desert of Rajputana. When night came on I would send a message to the little oases; my servants would go and say, 'Our master will be here and after the evening meal he wants to see you.'

When the time came I stepped out of the tent, and there were the people. I stood and looked out on that company and was strangely moved. I was six weeks out in desert, 180 miles from any town in any direction. Those who were listening to me had probably never once heard the name of Jesus Christ.

I talked to those men that night. At the close this happened: An old man came forward. He was the son of a king, his long beard flowing down to his waist. He came up to me, leaning on his staff. The young men courteously made way for him. He stood there looking up at me, his strong face alert in that bright moonlight. He said: 'How do you know these things? How do you know them?'

I answered, 'These questions which have troubled your heart and all human hearts . . . our Great Father has written down the answers in a Book. And the answers to these questions were written in a Book.'

'Do you mean there is a book with all these things you have been telling us about . . . about a love that is good, and all the rest of it?'

Then I said, 'There IS a Book. It is God's Book, and the answers are in it.'

'Young man', said he, 'is that book in my language? Did you read it in my tongue?'

'Yes, I have the Book.'

I wish you could have seen that old man. He straightened up, and pointing his finger at me, I shall never forget it as he said:

'Get me that book!'

I ran back to my tent and brought back two copies of the Bible in their language. Forty brown hands were stretched out for them as I returned. I put one into his hand, and when I told him that the answers to the questions were in that Book, the old man looked up and said, 'Sir, how long has this book been in the world?'

'It has been here for hundreds of years; for hundreds of years.'

'Did your people have it?'

'Yes'

'And I am an old man. All my friends have died hopeless. I am nearly gone myself. And all this time the book was here and nobody brought it to me. *Why didn't someone bring us this book long ago*?'

William F. Oldham,

Bible Society Record, Sept. '47

VI

Conferences Foreshadowed

In Bombay, Calcutta and Madras, the great Presidency cities of India, Taylor established churches, each church an island, almost 1,000 miles from the others. A local Quarterly Conference sufficed for organization. From these centres by transfer, or design to give their witness, men moved out like kindled sparks. New churches formed their Quarterly Conferences which grouped with others became circuits, still so remote from others as to need no boundaries. Then came districts, still called Bombay, Calcutta and Madras, in territory immense, in activity spontaneous, in fervour intense, each the harbinger of an Annual Conference.

Bombay District

Under Bowen's inspiring leadership the Bombay church of 1873 became a hive of activity with an ever widening influence. The city

> was divided into eight pastoral districts so that each pastor by devoting the forenoon of Tuesdays and Thursdays, every family could be visited weekly . . . . The evenings of the four days in the week were taken up in street preaching in different places, both in the English and the Vernacular . . . . The outdoor preaching at Falkland Road Fountain and on the Esplanade were well supported by lay brethren and sisters, not only by their help in singing but by their testimony, so that there was much enquiry and the whole community was stirred as never before . . . . Not a few came out boldly as Christians and were baptized . . . . The excitement among the Parsis reached its climax. Merwanji Mehta and other Parsis had been baptized early in the year; and in September these were followed by Maneckji Mody, who was not only a member of a high Parsi family, but was from the very first bold in his testimony for Christ, indoors and out.[1]

Maneckji's conversion was the occasion for the most serious opposition the missionaries had had.

By the construction of the Suez canal Bombay had become the premier port of India, and the city's development challenged the growing Methodist Church. There was still only one Quarterly Conference when in January, 1878 under W. B. Osborn, it was decided to build a church on Grant Road. Funds were raised locally and on Tuesday, November 26, 1878, the corner stone of the first Methodist Church in Bombay was laid by Bishop Bowman. The building cost Rs. 33,000 and except for the

"McAllister legacy" of Rs. 6,000 the money was raised in India.[2] In 1908 this congregation sold the building to the Bombay Financial Board and erected a new church named the Taylor Memorial Church in Byculla where many members had moved. The original Grant Road Church is still used by the Malayalam, Gujarati and Hindustani congregations.[3]

Separate Quarterly Conferences were organized for the Grant Road, Dean Lane or Fort, and Mazagon Churches in 1886, whose pastors were respectively, G. I. Stone; Crawford R. Thoburn, son of J. M. Thoburn born in Naini Tal in 1863; and Ira Richards. This reorganization caused some friction in the work although made in accordance with the desire of the people and church officers,

> who did not perhaps perceive that it would tend to displace the local preachers and exhorters from the sphere in which they had been trained and their gifts exercised. [also] Bombay had been relieved of supplying Lanouli and Eguptpoora occasionally, . . . the new arrangement involved to some extent a diminishing need for the ministry of lay brethren . . . . If the result will be that these brethren are led forth in evangelistic efforts in the surrounding communities, it may tend to the advancement of the cause of the Master.[4]

The second building enterprise was for a church at Mazagon which had paid out about Rs. 6,000 in rent.[5] A meeting was convened at Grant Road Church in 1886 when Rs. 2,000 was subscribed. A site was secured which was large enough for church, parsonage and school. In time all were built. The school for six years was an English school; it became a vernacular school, and after that an orphanage. Years later this property was sold and the proceeds reinvested in that at Grant Road.[6]

Early reports make frequent mention of Dean Lane Hall in the Fort. An appeal introduced by Oldham, was made by the Conference in 1887.

> In the interests of the Methodism of India it is necessary that a suitable church building should be erected in the Fort, Bombay . . . the point of debarkation of thousands of strangers . . . . The Fort Church, representing our Church at large, should be housed in a manner worthy of its representative character.[7]

The appeal was made while George Bowen lived. After his death it seemed appropriate to perpetuate his name in the city where he had rendered such useful service to the Christian cause and to Methodism. The church was, therefore, named the Bowen Memorial Church. A grant of $5,000 toward its erection is said to be the only amount ever given by the Board for an English Church, and the only contribution from it for any building in Bombay until the Centenary of the Missionary Society in 1918.[6] It still provides services in English, and a small Hindi congregation also worships there.

Frederick Wood says that a Marathi branch of the Methodist Church was organized in 1874 because of the ever increasing number of Marathi converts who did not understand English. For the first quarter of 1875 Taylor lists seven Local Preachers and two prayer leaders for the Marathi work, and the number of converts at "about sixty – mostly from Hindusim".[8] The total number of Indian converts when the South India Conference was organized was eighty-six. In 1880 there was preaching in Tamil, Malayalam and Marathi with a Fellowship Band at Grant Road; preaching in Marathi at Dean Hall; pushing of vernacular work by Gladwin at Colaba, and a day school and open air preaching at Khetwady.[9]

The Conference appointments show an increasing provision for vernacular work before any grant-in-aid was considered: a Marathi circuit under Bowen in 1880; a Marathi and Hindustani Mission under Bowen and Hard in 1884, continued in 1886 under Bowen and Bruere; an East Bombay Mission under Bowen and Prautch in 1887. The next year a Marathi Mission under Bruere; a Mission to Educated Natives under Bowen (interrupted by his death), and the Umarkhadi Marathi Mission under Prautch. Stephens at Mazagon was directing vernacular schools and preaching; Gyanoba Khundaji who joined the Conference in 1882, and was ordained in 1884, worked at Igatpuri. Gungadhar Bhaskar Kale, another Marathi convert, who joined the Conference in 1888, was ordained in 1891, after years of working as a school teacher and local preacher. The first District Conference for the Bombay District was held by J. E. Robinson in August, 1899 in Poona.

These were only beginnings. Stephens says, "The large work in the Pantamba District (1927), was born in our Poona English Church." He would not be eager to separate the Poona and Bombay influences. The following incident occurred in Bombay; its results shook Gujarat.

> In 1889, a work of grace commenced among the Gujarati speaking people, members of the reformed Hindu sect, the Kabir Pant. On one Sunday the first four converts were baptized by Homer C. Stuntz the pastor of the Grant Road English Church. The leader of this band was a bhagat or 'elder' in the Pant, named Kershan Ranchhod, a municipal contractor, who, filled with an over-flowing love for the Saviour who had found him, returned to his native village in Gujarat and witnessed for Christ.[10]

Of this work George Bowen wrote that only Dr. Stone, Pastor of Grant Road Church, had thought such a work could be self-supporting, but "the mustard seed has become a large tree without adding anything to the financial burdens of the Bombay churches".[11]

> [Stone] first furnished tea to some of the neglected sailors in port. The work so enlarged that a call was made for more space. A small room was rented for Rs. 40 p.m.; a revival broke out, and then they

had to go to a still larger hall costing Rs. 110 a month. Up to this time the expenses had all been paid by private subscriptions. A. W. Prautch was put in charge of it and during the first full year nearly 300 sailors were converted. The city government now gave a grant of Rs.200 per month seeing the good done by the mission in restoring and keeping order along the extended quays, before unsafe to orderly people from rowdyism and drunkenness.

At once an American coloured man offered to build a commodious house for this amount and receive his pay for it in monthly instalments; so they have just completed on the main street at Prince's Dock a house worth Rs. 20,000 with chapel, refreshment rooms, reading room, home for the superintendent and his assistants, besides several rooms to rent. The present superintendent, Rev. B. Mitchell, a Scotchman who four years ago was penniless—and almost in despair, was found on the streets of Bombay by Rev. J. A. Stone, and led to Christ. During the present year 280 have been converted or reclaimed here, including four captains of ships, besides other officers. Meetings are held every night except Wednesday and Saturday. On Thursday there is free tea and after that preaching with as many as 150 present. It is supported by private subscription. These are solicited from every ship that comes in as well as from individuals in the city. The sailors reached here, and helped, go all over the world.[12]

Work for women and girls by wives of missionaries and ladies in the church had started before Miss Sarah De Line, the first representative of the W. F. M. S. in Bombay, arrived in 1884. Among these were Misses Shewanti and Sundar Bai Powar, Marathi ladies of fine family, who had won access to some zenanas. Another was Miss Sarah Cassidy who had come from N. India and with Mrs. Hard had opened schools. Miss De Line organized a more extensive zenana work. Miss Elliott (Mrs. W. H. Stephens) who came in 1885, Miss F. Abrams in 1887, and Miss Carrol in 1888, opened schools of which a boarding and orphanage combined with day school became the largest of its kind in the city.

Poona

The start made in Poona by Taylor continued to develop under Fox. In the fall of 1873, Lanowli and Deksal were regular outstations for preaching from Poona, and by year's end the "word was preached" as far as Sholapur and even to Shahabad, 250 miles from Poona.[13] A neat chapel was dedicated at Lonowli on December 4, 1874.[14]

Among the first converts of Taylor in Poona were the Mulligan sisters, of whom Marie became Mrs. William F. Oldham. Oldham's conversion came under Fox, when with some friends, he attended services "just to see". He was the son of an officer in the Indian Army, born in Bangalore in December, 1854. At a testimonial dinner on his seventy-fifth anniversary he told this experience:

> God came to the thoughtless young man who was fast going to the bad, and saved him by His grace. He was just a young surveyor under the Indian Government and was fast learning evil ways. But God converted him. Soon after, he stepped outside his tent in the moonlight, sat down on a little rock, and God talked to him. It is wonderful how we can talk to God in the quiet of the night. 'You are called to be a missionary', said the voice and the man consented.
>
> Leaving this little lady, (with pride he so spoke of Mrs. Oldham) I found my way to Allegheny College. From that hour to this, up and up, God has opened doors, this way and that, through it all and I have felt God's presence . . . the God consciousness has been with me.

Frazer and Evezard were active Local Preachers in Poona. A well worked-out plan to build a church in 1877, was delayed by the transfer of active members. By 1885, thirteen years after the church was organized, it had paid out more than Rs. 12,000 in rent. The Official Board and members decided during the pastorate of Blackstock that the time had come to stop such outgo of funds. The church was dedicated on June 19, 1886.[15]

A Methodist High School was opened in January, 1879 for boys and girls of the English Churches to the entrance examinations of Bombay University. It started with forty-nine pupils of whom sixteen were boarders. In 1890 it was named the Bishop Taylor High School.

In 1878 the first camp-meeting was held in a grove nearby, and for many years it continued to meet at Easter holidays.

> There were wonderful meetings in that old grove. It attracted a class of people who are not commonly found in our churches today. Officials, military and civil, . . . and many of high position were greatly attracted . . . and would come and spend days with us . . . . They did not come from mere curiosity, but came to take part in the meetings.[16]

Vernacular services were held regularly from 1873 in Poona when four Indians were baptized, two farmers and two Brahmins.[17] In 1886, Mrs. Blackstock and Miss Small, daughter of one of the Free Church missionaries, opened schools and zenana work in the city.[18]

Karachi

The work started in Poona in 1872 spread to Karachi when the 56th Regiment, in which were thirty-six who had been converted there was transferred the next year. Fox went with them, and in January organized a church there. He appointed Sergeant Seale, a convert and a very earnest Local Preacher, as their pastor. In a short time as many as 115 had joined the church.[19]

On his arrival from America Goodwin was sent to Karachi. He "laboured with untiring energy and perseverance, and his people heartily and nobly sustained him".[20] On May 27, 1876, "a beautiful house for the worship of God" and a small parsonage on the same lot were dedicated by Fox, free of debt. Excepting Rs. 100/-, the cost, Rs. 5,159 was raised in Sindh.

Fox followed Goodwin as pastor for three years. A church trial broke the spirit of the Church for a period,[21] but in 1887 J. E. Robinson, P. E., reported, "Time and patience and conciliation have healed old sores. There have been not a few conversions especially among the soldiers." Laymen in the military were most helpful. Work among the seamen was opened in 1885.[22] Vernacular work was begun by Plomer in 1882.[23] Five years later Gilder urged the need of medical work; "there's not a lady doctor to be found through the length and breadth of Sindh".[24]

Calcutta District

Thoburn had had "an impression" as early as 1869 that he might some day be working in Bengal. He then procured a Bengali grammar. Four years later, Mrs. May, who was attending the Dasehra meetings, following an evening service invited Thoburn to Calcutta. "You will find more work than you can possibly do", she said, "and there will not be a place in the city that will hold the congregation."[25] He was appointed to Calcutta in 1874 and his Journal says, "I go very cheerfully."[26]

The spiritual life of the evangelical churches in Calcutta had reached a low level by 1873. A leading non-Christian paper had affirmed that there had not been a single baptism in the city for a year. Hindus and Mohammedans had both come to think it was impossible for Christians to make converts.

> All this, . . . was changed in 1874 . . . the evangelical pastors of Calcutta were moved to unite in a series of revival meetings, which God richly blessed. A deep and powerful impression was made upon the whole city, and a new faith and courage took possession of Christians of all names and denominations.[27]

Thoburn opened his work on January 25 in the Entally Baptist Chapel. The preaching hall toward whose cost Bombay had helped, was dedicated on February 23.[28] Its cost was Rs. 16,000. The hall was crowded for every regular service; it was a continuous revival. In the first year 300 persons were converted. "The work of revival then commenced has never wholly ceased. Every Sunday service during the past ten years has been conducted as a revival service."[29]

After the hot season a theatre was rented for Sundays. It, too, was inadequate. A new Church building was a necessity. On the anniversary of his first Sunday in Calcutta, Thoburn was sitting in his room thinking of the prospect before him, when a messenger brought him a letter from a poor widow, not a member of his church, asking him to accept Rs. 63 from her sister and herself toward the cost of a larger church. This, to Thoburn, was God's token to move for a new church building. That evening he announced his purpose to plan for a building "that would hold all the people that wished to hear God's word preached".[30] The Dharamtala Street Church, known since 1906 as the Thoburn Methodist Church, was dedicated on December 31, 1876. It had a seating capacity of 1500, or with crowding, up to 2000. The debt was heavy but it was paid off in four years. Until their new church was erected, the Bengali congregation used "Taylor's preaching hall" which was later included in the Lee Memorial property.

After the organization of the South India Conference Thoburn continued as pastor of the English church and for two years was P. E. of a district including Allahabad, Agra, Meerut and Roorkee, the last named station being 1,200 miles distant. He called it "more a geographical term than a real district". For three years more he was P. E. while the church was supplied. The Allahabad district including the remote parts of the Calcutta District, under Dennis Osborne, was formed in 1880. J. M. Thoburn, Jr., nephew of Bishop Thoburn, was pastor of the Dharamtala Street Church for four years and was followed by Frank W. Warne early in 1888.

Warne describes a "Believer's Meeting" started by Taylor and continued by Thoburn and himself which met *every* Saturday morning at 7 o'clock.

> I think I may safely say that all the new movements such as founding of institutions that have taken place in and around Calcutta and eastward to Manila, have been born in prayer in that Saturday morning meeting. I did not name it . . . I inherited the name . . . . All I can claim for myself is that I had sense enough to know its value. For thirteen years, Sunday morning and evening, I announced that meeting and urged attendance.[31]

The attendance of many seamen at the services drew attention to their need. Thoburn "came to feel that seaman, as a class, are more impressible than any other men in the world". Thomas H. Oakes, son of a Madras family, felt called to this work and was the first preacher set apart for it. His support came from those to whom he ministered. In the beginning (1874) he lived on one ship a few days, then moved to another. Later a one story house was rented in Lal Bazaar easily accessible to seamen. It was made attractive, a comfortable reading room was provided with books and magazines, where coffee was available in a corner and where religious meetings were regularly held.

The Seaman's Mission Church was organized on December 5, 1875. It had a membership, provided regular services and fellowship bands, and maintained contact with those at sea by letters.[32] It directed many to services in the English Church; and converts were widely scattered, but very many remained faithful, maintaining their integrity amid temptations of a seafaring life through many years.

A second centre for Seamen's work was opened by Goodwin in April, 1880 in the suburb of Hastings. He collected Rs. 1,800 toward the purchase and enlargement of property and superintended much of the work. "He had a genius for work and was never happy unless engaged in some form of intense activity. His face was familiar on every street and on every ship. His health broke and he died in America in 1881."

In the winter of 1890-91 when F. H. Northrop, from Agra, was supplying at revival services in Dharamtala St. Church, G. F. Grundy, a seaman, was converted, and from that time he felt he must be a missionary to India. He came out under the Salvation Army, but later established an independent work at Berenag, in the Kumaon hills in North India, where at each decennial census, his little flock recorded themselves as Methodists.

"The Woman's Crusade" patterned after a similar organization in America, was organized near the close of 1874. On their first Sunday four ladies moved out on Flag Street "which is principally devoted to grog shops with men more or less intoxicated filling them and rambling all about". A gentleman who accompanied them asked admittance for them to a hall. When they were refused, they sang the Gospel at the door. In other places when the ladies themselves asked permission to enter, they were allowed. After the first Sunday they not only sang, but exhorted and prayed.

> Thus from Sunday to Sunday [Mrs. May writes] our work progresses. During the cold season as many as 50 of an evening, are induced by us to go to God's House, and during the last 4 weeks, twelve have remained after the service to be instructed in the way of salvation . . . as a whole it is a work of faith.[33]

In April, 1877 a Roman Catholic gentleman asked Thoburn why he kept aloof from schools. "Lack of money", was the reply. "If that is the trouble", he said, "I am willing to help you", and he promised one hundred rupees a month. Thoburn opened a day school at once in the little Church they had just left, for both boys and girls.[34] Having no other accommodation for boarders half a dozen children were cared for in the parsonage. This school was soon combined with the Calcutta Girls' School which had earlier been organized under a committee and was now offered to be put under Thoburn's charge.

In 1878 Miss Layton came out as the first representative of the W. F. M. S. in the S. I. Conference, to take charge of the school on the basis of support from the institution, as in all the Conference. Soon after her arrival she wrote, "Never have I seen so much to do, and so little to do with."[35] But under her direction standards and discipline improved rapidly. In 1882 we read, "This long established and well known institution offers superior advantages to pupils, whether boarders or day scholars."[36] Attendance for the previous year had been two hundred.

Mr. and Mrs. Inskip collected $10,000 for a new building for the girls' school which was completed by 1887, at a cost of $60,000, most of it debt. Miss Hedrick joined Miss Layton in 1885 and relieved her the next year to proceed on furlough. The W. F. M. S. granted nineteen scholarships to the Calcutta Girls' School in 1898.

The Calcutta Boys' School started in 1882 in a "commodious three-storeyed house" which was leased. The management promised that "Added teachers will be employed and no pains spared to make the school thoroughly efficient in every respect".[36]

Madras District

The first Methodist Church in the Madras District which included both the Madras Presidency and the Deccan, was gathered in Secunderabad by a layman, Walter Winckler. He was a nephew of Mrs. George Miles and was in England when he heard of the conversion of his relatives in Bombay. The news made him angry. When he returned to Bombay he resisted, then softened, then became an ardent Christian himself. Four months later he helped Taylor in the Poona siege. The next year he was transferred as a Civil Engineer in charge of railway construction to Secunderabad. He arrived there a complete stranger. His duties and position soon made him acquainted and with acquaintance he gave his Christian witness, first to soldiers whom he gathered in a cowshed, then to civilians. One of these was Dr. Trimnell, the Civil Surgeon, who answered Winckler's call in illness. Through the sick man's testimony the surgeon becam a live Christian.[37]

As preacher-in-charge of Bombay Circuit Bowen visited this new church from February 20 to March 2, 1874, sixteen days after Taylor arrived in Madras. He held daily meetings, twice led the Fellowship Bands and had four morning prayer meetings. There were thirteen seekers. He organized a church with fifty members, eleven full and thirty-nine probationers, and on February 28 organized the first Quarterly Conference. Winckler and George U'ale were licensed as Local Preachers; Trimnell as an Exhorter.[38] Winckler and his associates opened a series of prayer services at various centres attended by 200 people. Many were converted. When the second Quarterly Conference was held, April 27, 1874, there were 100 church members and they requested a pastor. James Shaw went temporarily until the arrival in December of J. E. Robinson. After completing his work in Madras, Taylor visited this "healthy, growing, working church of God" for a few days. There were 120 communicants at the sacramental service which he held.[39]

Seven years passed before the congregation gave up hired halls. Had F. G. Davis not volunteered to go to the Secunderabad Church at a critical period, the name "would have been stricken from the list of appointments in 1880. The Church . . . owes its existence to him."[49] The corner stone of the church was laid by Fox and Davis on November 19, 1881 and the "beautiful church building" to seat 170 persons was dedicated on June 8, 1882. It cost Rs. 4,700.[41] Secunderabad was a "boom" town. Railway construction and military Cantonment gave it temporary prominence. Nearby was the great city of Hyderabad, capital of the Nizam's Dominions. Conference appointments show the trend; "1876, Secunderabad—J. E. Robinson and W. T. G. Curties"; "1877, Hyderabad and Secunderabad—J. E. Robinson and W. T. G. Curties"; "1878, Chadarghat, James Shaw; Secunderabad—W. J. Gladwin". Chadarghat was the European settlement just outside of Hyderabad. Secunderabad gave Methodism its entrance to its large opportunities in Hyderabad. The Church owes much to the local preachers and laymen of the Secunderabad—Hyderabad Church, many of whom remained un-named. A. C. Davis, W. A. Moore, W. Marrett are known, but there were many active, loyal Christians whose lives and devotion made the Church strong—families like the Westons, whose children imbued with their parents' faith have served the Church they loved and put their own lives into the Baldwin schools.

Madras

Marked growth and activity characterized the church Taylor organized in Madras. In 1880 a church was erected at Vepery and a Pavilion costing Rs. 2,000 was built as a preaching centre on the Esplanade. W. B. Osborne, who followed C. P. Hard as Presiding Elder, organized a Camp Meeting at Ennore, north of Madras. Methodist attendants were in the majority but ministers and laymen from the Baptists, Wesleyans and Plymouth Brethren attended, and ministers of the Church of England and the Madura Mission aided in conducting services.

In 1876 Bellary was listed "to be supplied". Work was opened here by Hard and Robinson with meetings in the Railway Reading Room. When use of this was forbidden they tried to get the school, but this was refused. Since no house was large enough the meetings were continued under the night skies. "Many whole families, unbelieving husbands, erring sons and careless daughters were gathered into the fold." Jeffries became the first pastor.

Mr. and Mrs. Rudisill who arrived in Madras in 1884, early saw the need for such work for women as was being done elsewhere. On their representation the Baltimore Branch made provision for starting such work and Miss Grace Stephens was chosen to open it. She had continued active in church work in her own community, but she had been praying for a "large field of labour". This seemed an answer to her prayer.

The work was a challenge: she was unknown; she knew no vernacular; she was not used to the mid-day sun and "hearts and homes seemed alike impenetrable". To get entrance to homes she carried an old tin box with "attractive bits of needle work, pictures and other things," but in most places she was rebuffed. Finally, she secured three pupils; one to learn Tamil, one English and one knitting. For the Tamil pupil she had herself to take lessons but she learned. Men scoffed at the idea of women learning to read; "Would women pass the B. A. and the M. A. exams.", they asked.

Eventually, Miss Stephens won an entrance to the best homes and organized many activities. Four children given her in 1887 led a few years later to a full Orphanage. Zenana work was opened in six districts of the city. Through anxiety for Miss Stephens' safety in going about the city the first Bible Woman was employed as a companion and paid by the Vepery Sunday School.[42] Miss Stephens was the first representative of the W. F. M. S. in this Presidency and was recognized as a missionary in 1891.[43] Miss Mary Hughes, their first missionary from America to Madras, arrived in 1888. Mrs. Rudisill was the first editor of the Tamil Woman's Friend, *Mathar Mithiri*, and continued as such until her death in 1889 when Miss Stephens took it over.

As a young man Rudisill had been a practical printer. He knew the great help that literature could be in evangelistic work. Now, in a conference which had work in several languages without the needed literature, his old interest in printing was awakened. He secured a boy's press which would print a leaflet four inches by six inches and a small font of Tamil type, and set up a shop in a small room near the parsonage, and started printing. This little "acorn" grew to "oak hood" as the Methodist Publishing House in Madras, doing work in Kanarese, Tamil, Telugu and English.

Bangalore

The Memorial Church had a few prosperous years, but by 1880 it languished. In 1882 the P. E. reported:

> Bro. D. H. Lee has laboured two years in St. John's Hill amid much discouragement.... This has been a barren field for three years past. There are 13 members on the Church register; six of these are absent and only 3 of the remainder are male members. There is a congregation of about 40. There is no field in India more needy than that which lies around and within the reach of this Church. This year a Christian lady ... built a commodious parsonage, entirely at her own expense, and gave it to the Church.[44]

The Development of the Richmond Town Church was stimulated by its proximity to the Baldwin School which had been started by the Oldhams when he was in the Survey of India with headquarters in Bangalore. In 1879 Mrs. Oldham opened a private school in their home and was the chief teacher. When they left for America the school was continued by J. E. Robinson in the vestry of the Church as the Methodist School. In 1880 he rented the buildings on the present site and the school was moved to its new location as a boarding school with M. B. Kirk in charge. C. B. Hill was the first boarder; his sister, one of the first teachers. Kirk was followed by I. A. Richards. John Baldwin of Berea, Ohio, gave $10,000 for the school.[45]

Benjamin Peters was thirty years of age when he was converted in March, 1874 in Madras. He was one of Hard's theological students in 1875. He joined the Conference in 1880 and was appointed to the "Tamil Circuit" at Bangalore. In June "he was lying in jail for the crime of preaching the Gospel."

His street preaching led to counter preaching by Mohammedans. Letters and articles in the papers, brought an order by the Magistrate prohibiting preaching in public places. Peters changed his place of meeting, but the police drove his audiences away. He was summoned before the Magistrate, and imprisoned but on appeal he was released on bail. The Judicial Commissioner decided that "there could not be a sweeping prohibition against all Gospel preaching in public places". Peters had challenged the order of the Magistrate because there was no way "for the order to be tested except after it had been violated and appealed". On his release from prison he returned at once to street preaching.[46]

Hyderabad

The beautiful church in Hyderabad was dedicated on January 28, 1877 by Bishop Andrews. The site and part of the building were a gift of Mrs. Walker; no aid was received from outside of India. There was a good parsonage. The report of the pastor, R. E. Carter, in 1883 is significant testimony of the inter-relations of English and vernacular work:

> What proved a great help in this work was the meetings held in the Theatre Royal rented in connection with Bro. Ward's work. The

congregations were English and Native. Addresses and testimonies were given in four languages. The laymen took an active part and were strengthened themselves. Many were converted here, and among them some who never attended the regular services of the Church.[48]

An item of unusual interest in the history of this Native State is recorded by Ward. Sir Salar Jung, Prime Minister, died in 1883. He had been Prime Minister for thirty years and had built strength into the Nizam's Dominions. He had welcomed missionaries. On February 5, 1884, the young prince and heir, having attained his majority, was installed as Nizam by the Viceroy, Lord Ripon. Intrigues to put forward rival heirs had failed; then they were attempted in the selection of the Prime Minister.

> But God made use of the instrumentality of one of our Methodist preachers to defeat those plans and secure to the prince a prime minister of liberal and enlightened mind, and, without doubt, thus securing a measure of secure and real religious freedom hitherto unknown in this Mohammedan state. We are not permitted to enter more fully into the details . . . it is the surprising answer to four years of praying for an open way for the Gospel among these people.[49]

The new Prime Minister, Sir Asman Jah, K. C. I. E., continued the liberal policies of his great predecessor.

There had been some street preaching, with selling and distributing of tracts and portions of scripture, but from 1884, under the pastor of the English church, James Lyon, who knew Hindustani, vernacular work was prosecuted more vigorously than before. Advocates of this work were greatly encouraged. They asked for a missionary who could devote full time to it, and "enter the city itself." S P. Jacobs, having had the longest experience, was appointed to the "Hindustani Mission, Hyderabad" in 1886. To break down opposition he opened two schools, one in Chadarghat, and one within the walled city, known as the Shalibunda school not far from the Char Minar.[50] The Prime Minister showed his liberal attitude by sending a personal donation and one from the government "in aid of the Methodist Mission Anglo-Vernacular School in the city of Hyderabad, started by the Rev. S. P. Jacobs, Superintendent". This not only helped in finances but also put the approval of the government of the State on the school. "In the state of public opinion in the city" it seemed unwise to open with Christian teachers, so Jacobs found a Brahman, both educated and liberal minded, and of "unusually chaste character", with whose aid the Bible was taught.[51] Mrs. Jacobs shared her husband's work by scattering the truth "in the hovel and in the princely zenana".[52]

In 1887 G. I. Stone was appointed to the "Kanarese Mission, Chadarghat" and S. P. Jacobs with Antone Dutt to the "Hyderabad Hindustani Mission." Dutt was the first native missionary sent from the N. I. Conference, and received a fraternal welcome. When Mr. and

Mrs. Jacobs returned to America the next year, Lyon with Dutt was appointed to the Hindustani Mission, and the Hyderabad schools were provided for. Ernsberger was appointed to Gulbarga and Raichur; and J. H. Garden to Telugu work in Tandur.

Rudisill as P. E. of the Madras District, urged the W. F. M. S. to open work in Hyderabad. Correspondence resulted in the transfer of Miss L. E. Blackmar from N. India to Hyderabad in 1889. By the end of the year she had secured admission to thirty-one houses within the city wall, twenty houses just outside and thirty-nine in more remote sections.

In 1880 G. W. Woodall, a Methodist teacher from America opened and English day and boarding school with some fifty pupils, at the earnest request of English-speaking people, with ten children as boarders. A few non-Christian gentlemen sent their girls. The Prime Minister received Woodall cordially and promised cooperation and financial help in the plans he had. T. R. Toussaint, who was later in the Baldwin Boys' School, was a teacher in this school for three years.[53] The school continued until 1893, when it became an English Girls' School under Miss C. Wood. In its first year forty-nine different pupils were enrolled under three teachers.[54] Some of these were from the homes of influential Muslim officers. On February 6, 1896 it became an A. V. Girls' School under Miss Alice Evans. At the close of the year thirty were enrolled of whom twenty-three were boarders.[55] The first boarders were two sisters from a village home forty miles away. Miss Evans opened the school to girls of all communities.[56] Some boarders were from Muslim homes within the walled city; Pulmani first came as the servant of two Eurasian girls and studied as she had opportunity. When she lost her place as servant she became a regular pupil in the school.[57]

Central India

"Meantime Brother Norton had opened up a new work in Bhusawal, 276 miles east of Bombay".[58] Thus Taylor describes the earliest penetration of Bombay Methodism into Central India, in September, 1873. Norton's own account to Fox is fuller:

> My plan is to spend Wednesday and Thursday at Jabalpur; preach Saturday night and Sunday morning at Nagpur; Sunday evening at Kamptee, and Monday or Tuesday evenings at some of the towns between Nagpur and Jabalpur. Last week I preached at Khandwa on Tuesday to an audience of about 20; this week at Bhosawal. This evening I've held our first Saturday evening meeting at Nagpur. I feel quite hopeful in regard to the work at all the stations which I am visiting .... God is giving me abundant strength for the work. After the preaching here in the morning I walk ten miles to Kamptee making pastoral visits, and preach at six in the evening. Then I rise at half

past four the next morning and walk back to Nagpur to take the morning train for a journey of 580 miles to Jabalpur. But I am very weak spiritually and need the constant prayers of my Christian friends.[59]

After the organization of the Bombay Bengal Mission Norton returned to Nagpur. "Conversions in Bhusawal and Kamptee," were reported in February.[60] Norton had earlier indicated his interest in independent work and soon left his appointment for residence at Ellichpur where he opened work among the Koorkoos, an aboriginal tribe. An early account of work tells of "long and faithful marches through the jungles, burning with fever and thirst".[61]

Nagpur and Kamptee

Until 1886 these two stations were under the same minister. Gilder awakened much interest by special services in the Railway Institute and in Museum Hall. Members of the United Free Church Mission, with Andrew Fraser and Mr. Jacobs of the Civil Service assisted. Fifty-four professed conversion and some joined the Methodist Church.[62] In 1876 there were seventeen full members, five probationers and a Sunday School with ninety enrolled. A year later there were twenty-three members and twenty-nine probationers.[63] In 1885 Dr. Fraser, the first to join our Church in Poona, and for some years a local preacher, became pastor. His son, Sir Andrew, later became the Chief Commissioner of the Central Provinces. The Nagpur congregation built a *pandal* for a place of worship in 1882, but in 1887 the present Church building was erected. A legacy which Hard had received met a part of the cost.

In 1882 Morton reported ten Indian members under Samuel, a Local Preacher who had good Tamil and Marathi congregations. In 1885 Dr. Fraser reported "favourably of the prospects of Native work in Nagpur, three baptisms and four seekers. Natives attend in great numbers the preaching of the Gospel".[64] Two boys' schools with an enrolment of 183 were opened in 1884. There was a Native M. E. Church building at Kamptee.

From the first grant-in-aid for vernacular work in 1887, Kamptee received Rs. 1,420 as follows: Missionary's salary 720; schools 500; rent 150; Moving expenses 50. In the same year W. H. Stephens, experienced in Marathi work in Bombay, was appointed to "Kampti Mission". In 1888 the appointments read "Kampti Marathi Mission . . . . W. H. Stephens, Gungadhar Bhaskar Kale," and also a "Nagpur Marathi Mission—to be supplied"; doubtless from Kamptee, while the English Church in Nagpur was in charge of W. H. Hollister.

Jabalpur

An early sketch of Methodist work in Jabalpur reads:

> A little band, but earnest, devoted, and determined . . . the Methodists are here. These people seem to be irrepressible . . . . Mr. Norton created quite a stir. But his stay was too short for permanent good. After him came Mr. Gilder, but his health failed and he had to leave. Then came Mr. Curties, a good man and greatly loved. The little body prospered and good work was done. But he was removed, and Mr. Nichols was sent here. His stay was only for a few months. After he left the light nearly went out . . . . Besides, the little body was torn asunder by internal strifes . . . . Rev. D. Osborne with commendable zeal visited them every two months regularly. His words of cheer were of great encouragement to the two or three families who willingly bore the despised name . . . . The sun had only passed behind a cloud. Mr. Janney came; he steadily kept on. His congregation was often two or three. He had a pretty hard time . . . . Bovard followed Janney. Several were converted under his ministry assisted by Mrs. Amanda Smith, a negro evangelist who did much good in other places.[65]

By such labours of others, has Methodism in Jabalpur entered into its present day. Changes in pastors were many, but greater changes in church membership came from the constant transfers in military, railway and other services among whose people the pastors ministered. Gilder went there in 1874.

> During the first day in his new appointment, he shared with another his board bill, consisting of a 'dry loaf of bread, two or three morsels of native sweets, some green indigestible plums, and a pint of cold milk'. His house-keeping outfit was as follows: 'An empty, rented bungalow, a *charpoy* [bed] , a small table, one knife, two forks, two spoons, two plates, and two cheap bamboo chairs'.[66]

The Bombay Quarterly Conference assumed his support while he was getting started.[67] At the first services held in the Railway waiting room a guard and his wife, Mr. and Mrs. Mitchell, were converted. In an early revival "fifty-six, young and old, were also converted, and two classes were organized. In May Gilder suffered from exposure to the sun and had to leave, but he left a small congregation." The next meeting place was a building which had been the Artillery Mess room;[68] after that, the Masonic Lodge Bungalow or the Theatre. When Bowen visited Jabalpur in 1874, he preached in a hired house on the verse, "Fear not, little flock." Nichols, from Nagpur had charge in 1876. Notwithstanding the difficulty of having frequently to vacate the Theatre in favour of theatrical companies, the church carried a program:

> We have about 13 English services (including Sunday School) weekly. In the city a native day school for boys, and a native Sunday School under a smart native Christian named Hume . . . . We are anxious to put in a native catechist for Jubbulpore . . . . We have 75 day scholars

and 65 Sunday School scholars . . . . Our most urgent need is a suitable hymn book. We need at least 100 copies . . . . You will be glad to know that our work is deepening. People who have grown cold are coming out again on the Lord's side.[69]

In 1878 Jabalpur was included in the Calcutta District with J. M. Thoburn as P. E. He held meetings in February but left with a regret that he could not do more for the soldiers and railway employees. A building fund was started in 1882. Three years later Rs. 1,400 was raised for pastoral support and an organ was purchased. Hard raised money in Australia which was distributed by the Conference. With the Jabalpur share the congregration began building. The corner stone was laid by the pastor, A. G. Creamer on May 12, 1886 and the dedication was Sunday, October 15, 1887.[70] It was enlarged in 1893 without debt. The corner stone of a large mission House was laid by Sir Alexander Mackenzie, the Chief Commissioner.[71] He closed his address with these words :

> And now friends, I proceed to lay the corner stone of your little range of prophets' chambers, and in doing so let me breathe the prayer that the sons of the Prophets may indeed dwell here, full of the Holy Ghost and of faith and that you and all this neighbourhood may receive much blessing from the counsel, admonition and the life of those who inhabit these rooms.

In 1886 Creamer reported early vernacular work:

> I visit Nasirabad weekly, on Friday, and preach to the soldiers. Four railway points are visited fortnightly. I have over 330 miles of railway under my pastoral care. While on the wing I have the privilege of speaking a word for Jesus to the natives, to whom I give religious tracts and books which they gladly receive and peruse. We have two native helpers who preach on the streets.[72]

W. D. Brown preached in the bazaar steadily.[73] A Hindustani and a Tamil Methodist Church were organized by Tindale in 1888, under Jacob Samuel. In October of that year there were thirty-four Open Air Scripture Schools attended by 1651 children and 1129 adults. Jacob also helped with fifty other schools on week days.[74] A site for a Hindustani Church was secured, a corner lot, adjoining the Mess Bungalow which had been the early preaching place.[75]

Khandwa

Norton preached at Khandwa in 1873,[54] but the organization of a church followed in 1880 when Osborne preached in a Railway Institute on his trips to and from Mhow. The little congregation gathered then collected Rs. 600 and a small church was built in 1880 costing about Rs. 2,000, W. H. Howe paying most of the difference.[76] A small parsonage was built in 1882. The church in Mhow took an interest in this new congregation. General Phayre gave Rs. 2,100 and others Rs. 900 toward the enlargement of the church.[77] Following a revival in Mhow three men and four women went to Khandwa for mission work.[78]

Webb reports "native services" being held in the English church in 1887, when there were four members and eight probationers, and also "a very interesting fellowship band in our Mission Home every Friday evening (in Hindustani)." Some were baptized that year, including Jacob, from the police. He was much persecuted and at one time was handcuffed by the chief constable. In 1889 work was opened among the Balahis, resulting in converts in several places in 1890. Govind Ram became a local preacher in 1892, and Samuel Benjamin a probationer in Annual Conference in 1894.

ALLAHABAD DISTRICT

The formation of this district under Osborne in 1880, strengthened the supervision of distant places like Agra, Roorkee and Meerut which in the beginning had been connected with the India Conference. Including Jabalpur, Mhow and Harda, it still covered a large territory. On the organization of the Bengal Conference the boundaries were altered again to include Lahore.

Vernacular work in Allahabad was opened soon after the church was organized. Indian Sunday Schools were opened and regular Hindustani preaching was conducted on most Sundays. Three native schools were carried on with marked success. John F. Deatker opened work in Chunar and as a local preacher held services in both Hindustani and English for some years. A noteworthy feature of the work in 1881 was the first camp meeting in Fatehpur; held in March.

> The attendance was entirely encouraging. The spirit of the meeting was excellent, and it is believed that those who attended were truly refreshed and blessed. The occasion proved a rare and unexpected opportunity for native work. Vast throngs of attentive hearers including many influential gentlemen of the city and District, gathered daily to hear the Gospel preached and sung, and it is certain that from this center of blessing went forth far-reaching influences for good.[82]

F. J. Blewitt was converted in 1874 and was sure he had a call to preach the Gospel. He did not consent. In 1881 he was in charge of the Lawrence school in Lahore. He attended the Fatehpur camp-meeting and received a blessing "beyond anything I had ever experienced." The spirit seemed to say, "Have you no souls to save?" This time he yielded for work with the people of India. He started work near Lahore then gave up his school and at James Shaw's advice joined C. B. Ward's work in the Nizam's Dominions. He "arrived on horseback, with fiddle and banjo and a few other traps." He had travelled 2,000 miles at his own charges to join a self-support work.[83]

Agra

In the spring of 1874 five families who had joined Taylor while employed in the Telegraph Department in Calcutta, were transferred to Agra. On their arrival they found other Christians from Allahabad and Lucknow. Bates, of the Calcutta group, gathered all these together in a fellowship. They then invited Dennis Osborne to help them. This he did, holding special services in the home of Mr. Rae, when fifty were converted. A church of forty members and probationers was organized. So far as possible pastoral care was given by W. J. Gladwin from Kanpur.

At the request of his friends William Taylor, accompanied by Dr. Fraser, stopped at Agra for a few days at the end of 1874, with Fraser's son-in-law, Capt. Angelo. Taylor writes of this time:

> We had a few persons saved; I conducted their first watch-night service and the infant church was quickened. But though my Calcutta members organized the first class, and though Agra territorially belongs to this Bombay and Bengal Mission, as the work had been developed principally by Brothers Osborne and Gladwin, I stipulated with them and with Bro. Mansell, their P. E., that for the present they might include it in their work, and supply it, provided they would conduct it on our self-supporting principles—which they promised to do . . . . Gladwin was appointed as preacher in charge of the Agra circuit.[84]

From 1876 it was regularly provided for by the South India Conference by D. H. Lee, C. W. Christian in 1877-78, followed by J. Lyon, A. C. Gilruth, W. T. G. Curties, C. H. Plomer and A. T. Leonard.

Mussoorie

Dennis Osborne tells how he was led to open work in Mussoorie.

> Declining an invitation to visit the station, made to us in June, we were two months later forced to seek a change there for the benefit of a sick child. Some meetings held in a private house grew so rapidly as to necessitate removal into the public Municipal Hall. The result was a general request for an effective church organization, and the appointment of a Pastor. Such a request, with our own conviction that there was vital need in a vast community like that of Mussoorie and Landour for an aggressive soul saving work, could not be set aside. A church organization was accordingly effected, and I moved Bro. M. Y. Bovard to take charge of the new work . . . . On the 14th August, the Quarterly Conference was organized and regular work started . . . . Our public services have been well attended, and a thriving school maintained . . . . We took early steps to secure a good building site . . . convenient both to the residents of Mussoorie and Landour.[85]

Services continued to be held in a hired place, but audiences were large, and God's presence was manifested both at special and ordinary services. In 1883, Mussoorie became the headquarters of the District. While a delegate to the General Conference in 1884, Osborne received news of the death of his daughter, Lily. Deep sympathy was expressed and gifts for a Memorial Church were received. It was dedicated on June 15, 1886.[86] In 1885 thirty Hindus were baptized and a vernacular church organized.[87] Osborne reported "a warm and active band of Christian workers" in Dehra Dun and a Rajpur Mission in 1887.[88]

Meerut and Roorkee

Meerut was first visited by Dennis Osborne in July, 1875. In a series of meetings for ten days about fifty persons publicly received Christ and "many joyfully witnessed his saving power." In 1876 the circuit was left "to be supplied," and was visited weekly by Missionary brethren from adjacent stations.[89] In 1877 G. K. Gilder was appointed to Meerut but "in consequence of broken health, was unable to join . . . . The work being unsupplied gradually decayed and died out."[90] It was re-established in 1892 but due to neglect a second time it dwindled again.

Roorkee was important as the headquarters of the Ganges Canal Works and the location of the engineering college and a small cantonment. Methodist work was opened in 1875 by Osborne. The group undertook the support of a preacher, and William Eales, who had joined the Church in Meerut, was licensed as a local preacher by the District Conference and sent to Roorkee.[82] As a result of special services held here in January, 1877, fifteen were converted.[90] D. H. Lee was here in 1877 and 1880, P. T. Wilson in 1878, then W. Bowser and DeSouza from 1884 to 1888, when the English congregation numbered twenty-four members and probationers.

W. A. Revis records a report that before "any missionary activity in the station, one Miss Jarman had been doing work among the Indians of Roorkee.[91] A local preacher began vernacular work in 1882 with a small congregation of a dozen that met regularly. Not a few of the English congregation manifested an earnest interest in the bazaar preaching."

Ajmer

In opening work at Ajmer Methodist preachers followed the opening of Rajputana by new railways. DeSouza was the first to visit the city while a Local Preacher at Bandiqui in 1881. W. F. C. May Smith went in 1882, also from Bandiqui, and held services with English speaking employees of the railway. In July, Jeffries having resigned a Government position, was appointed to Ajmer. He conducted services in the Railway Institute and in the homes of the people,[92] and was greatly encouraged in visits to this people who received him gladly.[93] The first public service was held on Sunday, July 23, 1882. On Thursday following, a week day service was held and on August 1 a church was organized by Dennis Osborne with

Jeffries as pastor, and two members, F. Welsh and W. Bird, and two probationers. Welsh was licensed as a Local Preacher. At the end of the year membership had increased to fourteen, probationers to five, and a second Local Preacher was licensed, and Rs. 402 had been raised for ministerial support.[94]

In January, 1883 Webb visited stations between Bandiqui and Abu Road. An Indian preacher opened services in the bazaar, a small school and Sunday School. The English Church was "earnest and active". Both English and vernacular work were continued through the following year and in 1885 Ajmer became a part of the Central India District with C. P. Hard, P. E. in Nagpur. A commodious hall was rented for meetings and the pastor lived in a house next to it. W. F. Oldham opened the hall with a lecture on "America". Hard followed with revival services. During the year a sum of Rs. 2,000 was raised.

In 1887 Ajmer became the centre of a district, Hard continuing as P. E. The work grew and in 1888 Jeffries returned as pastor and Blewitt was appointed to the Boys' Orphanage and the Native Circuit. Mrs. Blewitt assumed charge of a Girls' School. Zenana and village work were conducted by Jacob and his wife. The vernacular church was fully organized with a promising membership. Two local preachers were sent to the Theological Seminary in Bareilly.[95]

A fine site for a church building costing Rs. 5,000 was secured in 1887. Hard made an appeal for "the last large enterprise of the old Central District". A Mission building with twenty rooms supplied preaching hall, school room, orphanage, residence for the Indian preacher and the missionary. The building was called *Blue Castle.*[96] Ground was reserved for a Church.

The first marriage of Indian Christians in 1887 was of a Brahmin convert, Isa Das, with a zenana worker. Both were in charge of day schools and Isa Das had also a night school.[97] In 1888 Paul Singh, later a member of the Bengal Conference, opened mission work in Bharatpur and Jacob Samuel was put in charge of the school and work there.[98]

Lahore

Bombay, Calcutta, Madras—there was yet a fourth corner, if such is possible, in the triangular sub-continent called India—Lahore. Taylor had opened work in the three; he had also gone to Lahore, but he did not stay to organize a church. The leaders of the S. I. Conference had long wanted to open work there. At the conference in 1880 they got their chance: James Shaw, Taylor's first itinerant preacher, volunteered to go. He was in the midst of a successful ministry in Madras, where a church building was dedicated by Bishop Merrill on February 5, 1881. It was described as "excellent in its acoustic qualities, accommodations and appearance".[99]

> Shaw was formerly a gallant soldier of Her Majesty, . . . but he never showed a more heroic spirit than he does now as he thus volunteers as a Christian soldier to go forth to an enterprise which many are inclined to regard as extremely rash, in view of his family responsibilities.

The writer of those lines, I. F. Row, a brother minister, headed a subscription list for "the new mission at Lahore" with a contribution of one hundred rupees, as a thank offering to God for "numerous unmerited and unexpected mercies received during my four years ministry just closed in Bombay".[100]

James Shaw had a wife and six children. The journey for which he had volunteered, Madras to Lahore, was 2500 miles, *via* Bombay and Allahabad. There was neither Church nor Society to guarantee support when they arrived. The day after the dedication he preached in his new church and on the next day, February 7, they left Madras where they had been for three years. In Bombay Shaw heard Bishop Merrill and was led "to a fuller appreciation of the Redeemer's work". On the twentieth in Allahabad he heard Osborne preach on "Grace Reigning," the day memorable to him, "as the day on which God brought me out of comparative darkness into the full light and liberty of salvation . . . I had never really understood what *full salvation* was."

Leaving his family in Allahabad Shaw went with Osborne to Lahore where they arrived on the twenty-third. Osborne's eldest daughter went along to preside at the organ and to lead in the singing. They were met at the station by Bro. "B" and welcomed to the home by Sister "B" whose house was made available for religious services twice daily. "Souls were saved and believers quickened and sanctified." On Sunday a Sunday School was organized with forty children and six teachers, and a Church was organized with twenty members and probationers. The next day a visit was made to Meanmeer, the Cantonment, where they found thirty-five men who held membership in the Wesleyan Church but without pastoral visits or opportunity for worship. In less than two weeks Osborne returned home. Shaw wrote:

> Bro. Osborne will leave here tomorrow night for work in his district having seen to the question of temporal support, organization of a Quarterly Conference, and all other necessary matters. My dear wife and children will join me in a few days. The outlook is bright and hopeful; my soul is happy, jubilant, triumphant; and we are looking for a year of happy work for God.[101]

Two real needs were a church building and a school for the children. The congregation had worshipped in a tent near the railway quarters and in hot weather an adjacent house was used. In 1883 Gilder followed Shaw, and began his work with a glorious revival which drew many into the Church.[102] The American Presbyterian Mission gave a site in an excellent location near the Railway quarters and on October 27, 1883 the corner stone of a church was laid. In 1887 the church property was valued at Rs. 14,000 with a debt of Rs. 6,490. "The amalgamation of several railways" had led to the removal of many people so that only ten members were left; but, added the pastor, F. D. Newhouse, "I have recently received twelve on profession of faith".

Vernacular work was pressed in 1883 by Gilder with the cooperation of church members. Both out of door preaching and services in a building in the city were carried on with spirit and earnestness. In line with the new policy of grant-in-aid for vernacular work, the Conference appointments of 1886 separated English and Hindustani work, C. H. Plomer being named for the latter.

In the Botanical Gardens at Calcutta—which it may be noted in passing had their conception in the prolific mind of the famous pioneer missionary, William Carey—there stands a remarkable banyan tree. True to its nature, from its spreading branches it has dropped aerial roots which, taking root in the friendly soil, have each in turn developed into strong and vigorous new trunks that serve not only as pillars to support the branches from which they have dropped, but also become new channels of life. This process has gone on unceasingly through generations until the banyan tree has become a glorious ever-green canopy, three thousand feet in circumference....

After the manner of the banyan tree, Methodism of India has been dropping its roots here and yonder in the great Southern Asia field and its branches have spread....

VII

Pioneering

Concerning the work in India Thoburn said, "[it] has continued to extend its borders steadily, as if following the drift of an unknown current." But he never felt the process was adrift. He and his associates felt that a hand was on the helm, the course known to One who chose and called men and women from lands afar and raised up others in India.

The Telugu Field

Charles B. Ward was an Illinois lad, not yet seventeen, when

> I was converted to God in my father's corn field. The reading of Thomas Dick's *Christian Philosopher* had led on to deep conviction that I was in the way utterly wrong. At about the same time a German Methodist . . . began to follow me up . . . . Brother John never let me go till he saw me soundly converted.[1]

In January following, while reading an appeal to Christian young men and women in America from Dr. Baldwin, a missionary in China, he was seized with a conviction that some day he would become a missionary. He went into his father's hay loft and promised the Lord that if ever an open door presented itself, he would enter in his Master's name.

He taught school for some months to earn money to go to college, and while at college, sawed wood two hours every day and all day Saturdays to meet expenses. He entered the Preparatory School of North Western University in 1870. His church gave him an Exhorter's license, and soon after a Local Preacher's license. He was surprised, but he felt it was of God. To meet expenses he dropped out and taught school for six months. On Sundays he preached and had Sunday School in his school-house, and also in a second school. People were converted, and the two congregations joined together in one.

He completed his preparatory course with distinction in Greek. His future seemed bright. He worked in the Halsted Street Mission for a year, and then for a second. When in India, Ward considered those two years as the best preparation he had received. He met William Taylor in the latter part of 1875, and twice later. Taylor wanted a man for India at once; Ward wanted to go to college and left Taylor, but he had gone only a short distance when

> the memory of my hay loft conversation came to mind. I stopped stock still on the side walk, and a voice seemed to say to me, 'Now will you stand by your promise?' . . . It was a battle for a few moments . . . . I felt it was of God and I settled the matter right there and said, 'I will.' I was filled with peace.[1]

In three days he gave Taylor his answer. Ward sailed from New York on November 4, and reached Bombay December 24, 1876. His first appointment was Bellary. He applied himself earnestly to the work of the Church and in the first year they erected a church building. The years 1877 and 1878 were the worst of the "great famine" in which five millions are said to have perished. At the Conference in 1878 Ward asked for an appointment to Indian work, but was halted by the query, "Where will you get your support?" He returned to Bellary for a third year during which he found his answer.

On February 21, 1879 he was in Gulbarga on pastoral duty and spent that night at the home of A. C. Davis, a civil engineer, and a Local Preacher of the Hyderabad Circuit. Davis, with other gentlemen and their wives, had assumed the responsibility for the support of a number of orphans and some destitute children with their mothers, during the famine. Copious rains had now fallen and although no crops had been harvested, some of the group thought that the "poor house" could be closed. When only four children were left Davis took them, as he told Ward, "to rear for God. He meant that they should accompany him as he moved about at his work, and that they should preach the Gospel to their countrymen".[2]

This idea went through Ward's "soul as a revelation from heaven". He could not sleep. In his two years in Bellary and in his travels on the railway he had seen "the haggard, bony, starving forms of hundreds of poor children"; he had also seen "the dead and dying in and by the road with never a thought that I could do anything". In the waking hours of the night "God called me to cast in my lot with Bro. Davis and endeavour to do what could be done". He wrote an appeal to be published in the *Bombay Guardian* which he showed to Davis, and got his approval. He decided that a response would confirm the "call" to gather such little ones and "lead them to be God's children". He waited a month before the first answer came, a letter from the South, with ten rupees, which reached him March 21, at the home of P. Geering, a Loco Foreman, at Raichur. Ward wrote: "I praised God, took courage, and gathered assuredly that this was the long-looked for signal for adding to Bro. Davis' four orphans." The next day he went to a relief centre intending to bring away five children. He brought fourteen to Gulbarga! Of the eighteen now gathered together, three were Muslims, three Telugu and twelve Kanarese. During the months of gathering he had received Rs. 2,000 for support. Two things seemed clear: God would help them to raise up their own helpers; and He had shown how the Wards' support "could be gleaned", for on April 1, 1878 "C. B. W." had married Miss Eileen M. Welch, to whom he was engaged in Chicago, and she continued a partner in his labours through all his years.

Ward's appointment for 1880 read, "Telugu Mission". His request to open missionary work "in the name of the Lord and the M. E. Church in the Telugu country" had been granted. It was a rugged road they were starting on, not only in the way of finances—in the month of April, 1882 seventy people lived on sixty-six rupees—but also in endurance in many lines.

Land arrangements in the Nizam's Dominions were very unsettled, but Ward selected two sites for the orphanage, one a location at Curreemnagar, some ninety-six miles north of Hyderabad, and the other at Mylarum, twenty-two miles nearer the city. He acted on an earnest invitation from William Marrett, an Executive Engineer in the Nizam's services, and a Local Preacher in the Hyderabad circuit; and also because of the transfer of Davis, then to Marrett's division.

In Gulbarga in 1879 the orphanage had been accommodated in Mohammedan tombs. The number of orphans in 1880 was sixty-eight. The children left Gulbarga on foot on March 16 and on April 5 reached Mylarum. They were welcomed by both Davis and Marrett. When quarters were ready in Curreemnagar some moved forward. Both camps were maintained by securing contracts for work. Early in 1882 Ward had to move the whole colony to a new place which he called Premoor.

Life in the Christian Orphanage was planned at the village level—a style of life and dress that they could maintain by their own means in after life; "their food plain native food; their houses small huts of their own building with our help . . . . Indian diet for India life became a motto with us . . . we found it after all the line of health." Every child shared in maintaining the camp, in cultivation and in production.

Assisting the Wards in opening the Orphanage were Miss O'Leary and Miss Ruth Freer, Methodists from near Madras. In this new field they showed the same energy and faithfulness that had marked their years in Madras. Blewitt joined Ward here in 1882 coming at his own expense, without stipulation of salary. He became a Conference member.

From its inception Ward had thought of his institution as an agency for preparing "helpers". The spiritual nurture of the children was always the first care. Their first field training came in April, 1882 when five of the promising boys went with Ward to a *mela*. Their chief work was the selling of Scripture portions and tracts. Next came aggressive work in the villages around Mylarum. In 1883 the "Secunderabad Contingent", including the Wards, Blewitts, four boys and four girls marched sixty-six miles to Secunderabad and set up a base for evangelistic work there and in Hyderabad. With instruments and singing to draw the people and ready with personal testimony, the Contingent preached in the bazaar and other public places for "definite and direct results." In company with R. E. Carter, Pastor of the Hyderabad Church, they opened meetings in the Theatre Royal in Hyderabad on August fifth. On the ninth a *Sanyasi* showed interest, and on the eighteenth he was converted. The next day Paramanandam was baptized before a very large crowd in the Theatre, *their first* Hindu convert. In September he joined the Contingent in preaching.

In December they won a second convert, Narsiah Naidu, who was bitterly persecuted. On December 12, 1883 in a bazaar service,

> Narsiah stepped forward, gave his testimony, and kneeling down was there and then baptized. Almost breathless stillness prevailed. Many Brahmins were by to see the strange sight. The crowd was immense.

He, too, became a preacher. At a Quarterly Conference in Ward's home in Secunderabad, on October 11, 1884, Fox presiding, both Paramanandam and Narsiah Naidu were granted Local Preacher's licenses. Ward's vision of 1879 had, in part, been realized. From a group of famine waifs he had seen Christian preachers develop. Some were with Robbins in Bombay; others joined Ernsberger. The first converts had been won and they, too, had become preachers. Only God would know ultimate results.

In 1888, Ward moved his "little company of about fifty souls of all ages" to Yellandu. Here, after years of moving from one camp to another, what Bowen called a "peripatetic mission", they purchased land—land in the Telugu country and in the Nizam's Dominions as he had purposed. Here he established a "Christian colony" in a village with 2000 acres of mostly arable land, and a fine large tank with an ample supply of water for irrigation.

> The native Christians out of their tithes support an evangelist and a colporteur both of whom are constantly employed in itinerating. They have visited 70 villages during the year and have received much encouragement.[3]

Tandur And Bidar

Ward left Bellary with a vision of preparing Christian workers for Telugu fields. In 1886 other young missionaries, Joseph H. Garden and his wife, after two years of pastorate in Vepery, Madras, were appointed to English work at Bellary. While faithful in the work of his pastorate, Garden applied himself to the study of Telugu. Two years later, in 1888, his appointment read "Tandur"—a new field rich with promise, where he would use his Telugu. A quite large and important Telugu work had been developed at Tandur by Benjamin Paul, a Local Preacher, sent and supported by the Hyderabad English Church. In 1890 they were constrained to ask for financial assistance in its maintenance.[4]

To this work Mr. and Mrs. Garden came. Early in the year they were asked to move to Gulbarga while Ernsberger took his motherless son to America. But Garden did have time to go to Bidar with Paramanandam, who three years earlier had made the visit with Jacobs. They went from Tandur in an ox-cart. Again they stayed outside the city in an open *dharamshala* near the city gate called *Fateh Darwaza.* They remained two days and preached as opportunity offered. They here met a *Sanyasi,* a traveling mendicant much as Parmanandam had been. He listened with interest to this new preaching by one who had been converted. It was not possible for Garden to keep in touch with the *Sanyasi* because of the interruptions in his work already referred to; but they learned on inquiry that he had continued his search for truth. In 1920, when Garden did meet him again, he had two children in our schools in Bidar, one of whom became a teacher in the Bidar Girls' School and the boy became a preacher. The father "had been a very imperfect convert" but made a clear confession before he died and was baptized by N. E. Samson.[5]

The next year Garden was needed in Madras to help in the Press while Rudisill was on furlough. He was happy, however, that the appointment read: "Press and Telugu Mission." It was the beginning of Telugu work in Madras. He was prevented from the Tandur field for a third year by the necessity of taking Mrs. Garden to America for medical care. At the end of 1890 he was back, alone, to continue work in the Hyderabad District. A part of his time was given to pastoral duties in the Telugu church in Hyderabad whose members carried on bazaar preaching three times a week and also helped in services in the Mission Hall in Market Street. Yet 115 days of 1891 were spent in touring among Telugu villages near Singampalli, Tandur and Gangawaram, the early name for Vikarabad. He tramped several hundreds of miles on foot with one or two Indians helpers in these tours.[6] C. E. Parker tells how, in May, 1891,

> Garden with brothers Musilmani and Maigur, while touring in the vicinity of Vikarabad, came to the land on which our Mission now stands. Being wearied with their journey, they decided to camp under a large mango tree for the night. While there, the burden of prayer came upon them. Together they knelt by the side of a European grave near the tree and prayed earnestly that the Lord would give them the land on which they knelt for the Mission. Soon afterward without any other action on their part than that prayer, the plot was given to the Mission in the name of the Presiding Elder of the District.[7]

Samuel Maigur was born in an orthodox Brahmin family in the village of Maigur, near Dharwar, and received his education in the Basel Mission High School. Here he was attracted by Christian doctrines and to the

Bible. There was in Dharwar a Government officer, an Anglo-Indian who had been converted under Taylor. Maigur made his acquaintance, and through him and the Basel missionaries, Maigur received public baptism on December 27, 1886. He was at once cast out by his family.

He secured temporary employment in the city library but desired Christian work and wrote to Ernsberger. After an interview in the Dharwar railway station, Maigur gave up his eighteen rupee position for one paying ten only, in Gulbarga, the second Indian worker in that field, the first being Chinappa. After two years he was married and became headmaster of the Residency Mission School in Hyderabad. Here he was made a local preacher. In 1896 he entered the S. I. Conference and was ordained. His main appointments were Gulbarga, Shorapur and Belgaum. "He had a passion for preaching and he had rare gifts as well as great grace for that work". He died in 1913.[8]

When in 1891 Bishop Thoburn reappointed the Gardens to Gangawaram he instructed him to commence work in the Bidar area. The way was open, for the British Methodists had invited the Conference to occupy Bidar and had referred to the P. E. in Hyderabad an inquiring Madiga family since they were working chiefly among the Malas. The head of this family was Mutayya. He had been for many years a sepoy with Engineer Marrett, and first heard the Christian message from him, and had told his people. His home was at Mirampur, eight miles east of Bidar. Garden and his preachers met Mutayya and his grandson Munayya at Kandi, and they were baptized on January 1, 1892. Then together they traveled to Mirampur. A party of relatives met them at Nealkal where five more were baptized. A small school was opened in Mirampur and David Marian was put in charge. Later, C. Gnanappa, a Local Preacher, was sent to them.

> Strange to say the Lingaits, Hindus of the Veera Shaiva sect, were even then the most receptive of our teaching in Mirampur, and some caste people in other villages were then baptized. In January, 1893, Bakayya, a potter of this village was baptized, and through him several others in Mirampur and Ratnapur, which is only two miles off. In November, 1894, two were baptized in Hominabad, and four in Hussainnagar. Of these last was Naryan Rao, the eldest of three brothers, sons of the Patel, or headman of the village, a man who was intelligent and well read in his own language. He was made teacher of a school using the Marathi language.[9]

Bakayya was a zealous worker and book seller. David Marian became a Local Preacer and in 1894 moved to Bidar. The next year he joined Annual Conference and was the first Indian member to be appointed to Bidar.

BISHOPS PRESENT IN 1906

.-R *Front Row:* C. D. Foss, J. F. Fitzgerald, J. M. Thoburn

.-R *Back Row:* J. E. Robinson, F. W. Warne, W. F. Oldham

The seed was planted; the pioneers could leave the growing church to the Indian Leaders who had heard and understood.

BISHOP
J. W. ROBINSON

GANGU DHANJIBHAI—Patriarch
Schoolman of Gujarat

YUSAF DHANJIBHAI—Partriach
Theologian of Gujarat

CHARLES EDWIN PARKER—Hyderabad Evangelist in the first three decades of the twentieth century.

JOHN LAMPARD—Wide-ranging Organiser and Preacher in Gujarat and Madhya Pradesh.

Missionaries were needed also to nourish the seed. Consecrated men and women came ready to go where the problems seemed the most difficult—indifferent to the hardships of travel and the strangeness of an alien culture.

EARLY LEADERS OF TIRHUT DISTRICT—Jessie Peters, Margaret Denning, H. J. Sheets, J. O. Denning, Grace Bills Sheets, F. M. Perrill.

As the Church grew, the concept of its task widened and fertile minds were challenged to carry its leaven into all of life. God's care for all His children was manifest when Church leaders made schools and orphanages and printing presses and newspapers

THE T. S. JOHNSONS—Father and Mother to orphans.

B. H. BADLEY—Founder of Lucknow Christian College

J. W. WAUGH—Founder of Lucknow Publishing House.

Today Lucknow Christian College has over 1500 students. The Indian Witness is a religious weekly with more than 1,000 subscribers and the Publishing House is one of India's most modern religious presses grossing more than Rs. 1,93,000 per year.

J. H. MESSMORE—First Editor of the Indian Witness and well known Educator

CENTRAL CONFERENCE—1894—ALLAHABAD

CENTRAL CONFERENCE—1936—JABALPUR

In the beginning the Methodist Church in Southern Asia was constrained to lean on missionaries from other countries. There, in the older churches, came the vision of the Gospel to all the world. There, sprang forth an armoured spirit ready to explore the heights and depths which could not hide the love of God. Clearly understood, however, in the advance of the Church has been the principle that it must be a self-nourishing movement, replacing the pioneers from older churches with nationals from the ranks of Christ's conquest. That the Methodist Church in India reaped the harvest of this principle is revealed not only by the vast increase in Central Conference delegates between 1894 and 1936 but in the proportion of Indian leaders who were represented.

J. H. GARDEN—Pioneer of Telugu Work

DANIEL O. FOX—One of the First Missionaries in the new Bombay—Bengal Mission.

Almost twenty years after Butler came into the North, the early planting by William Taylor in the South of the Ganges bore fruit.

FIRST SESSION OF THE SOUTH INDIA CONFERENCE—BOMBAY
November 9, 1876

DAVID O. ERNSBERGER—Pioneer in the Kanarese field

Now the work in the South is rich with opportunity and strong with confident promise

SOUTH INDIA CONFERENCE
1876

L-R-Back Row: Thomas Oakes, Daniel O. Fox, Isaac F. Row, Milton H. Nichols, William E. Robbins, William T. G. Curties, Piyari M. Mukerji, Dennis Osborne, John E. Robinson, John Blackstock.

L-R-Centre Row: E. W. Parker, George Bowen, Bishop E. G. Andrews — presiding, J. M. Thoburn, Clark P. Hard, James Shaw.

L-R-Bottom Row: George K. Gilder, Benjamin Peters, Wallace J. Gladwin, Frank A. Goodwin, David H. Lee, Levan R. Janney, W. Christian, F. G. Davis Henry Mansell.

C. P. HARD and GEORGE BOWEN—First Presiding Elders of the Madras and Bombay Districts

L-R: N. E. SAMSON, S. NOAH, G. GERSHOM—Outstanding Early Leaders of the Church in the South

EARLY BENGAL PREACHERS

Rev. Lakshman Chandra Sircar, Rev. Sital Chandra Biswas,
Rev. Ananta Kumar Mondol, Rev. Surju Mohan Mondol.
Rev. Bono Mali Mozumdar.

In Bengal Conference is a school called "Jidato", which means "persistent advance". From the early days of Thoburn and Taylor, this spirit has marked the "growing fringe" of Methodism. That is why, In speaking about the increase in national leadership in Lucknow and Bengal, Thoburn said—" I feel exceedingly encouraged."

EARLY LUCKNOW PREACHERS

Chimman Lal, C. E. Savaille, Ram Chandra Bose, Matthew Stephens, Philip Andrew

The Kanarese Field

The opening of Kanarese work in the Nizam's Dominions harks back to a visit that Ward made to Shorapur early in 1878, at the invitation of J. J. Ottley, an engineer. The country was "full of sheep without a Gospel shepherd". In 1880 Ward was led to pray for a missionary. He mentioned this need in the *India Methodist Watchman*, and received the money for passage for a missionary, and asked William Taylor to find the man.

Taylor visited the N. Indiana Conference in April, 1882, with a big box of books to sell. He did not mention the need of men until questions were asked. Then he said he had received from India money for the passage for a man to open work in a district with "half a million souls, and that the man who undertook the work must be willing to 'rough it' ". Listening in the audience was a young man who had just been admitted On Trial in the Conference—David O. Ernsberger. Now he remembered a promise he had once made to the Lord. "Here is an opportunity, a way opened, now will you go?" came the question to his mind. When others had left the hall he went to Taylor and "offered himself." Taylor consulted his P. E., and accepted the volunteer. That was on April 8; on May 15 he bid his father farewell. On July 22 he reached Ward's Christian Orphanage.[10]

Here Ernsberger was housed in a hut of mud walls, twelve by fourteen feet with roof of palmyra leaves, just high enough for him to stand up inside. It had been made by the boys; the inside plastering was by girls. Ernsberger was happy! "He seems", wrote Ward, "to be a man God has prepared and called to be a faith missionary of a radical, faithful stamp."

The main purpose of his stay at the Orphanage was to study Kanarese, but he was happy to have a share in the work with the orphans also. He went with Ward and a group of orphans to Lingumpully, where the boys worked for six months in the construction of five miles of public roadway near the Lingumpully Railway station. The experience was good in toughening their bodies and building self-reliance.

Ernsberger had suffered from fever so in the summer of 1883 he went to the better climate of Bangalore. Here were better facilities for studying Kanarese, and also the chance to work in the language with S. P. Jacobs who was then in the Kanarese circuit. "His ripe experience and spiritual insight seem to have greatly enriched the work."[11] His emphasis on entire sanctification was seen and felt years after they left India. Of him it was said, "He was as immaculate in person as he was spotless in character." Young Ernsberger greatly esteemed the two years in which he was associated with him.

For 1884 Ernsberger was appointed to Lingasagar in the Nizam's Dominions. He was with the Secunderabad Contingent when Narsiah Naidu was converted, and when Narsiah was prevented from visiting members of the Contingent, Ernsberger sought him out. On February 27 Ernsberger took Beema, one of the orphans, and left for his Kanarese field. In this year he married Miss Dema Stone to whom he had been engaged in the States. From money raised in India they received Rs. 50 per month.

The appointments for 1885 showed "Lingasagar—S. P. Jacobs, D. O. Ernsberger". The appointment indicated a field more than a station. The two men were to open the vast Kanarese field. They essayed to enter it at Shorapur. Capt. Fallon, in charge there, had been converted in the Taylor revival, and hoped to welcome the missionaries, but while giving them permission to make the journey, the Nizam's Government issued orders that they could not enter the Cantonment. They had to stop outside "at lonely rooms once occupied by the rajas of Shorapur."

Defeated in their first plan the missionaries—their wives were with them—went to Lingasagar. After a few months they divided, the Jacobses to Gulbarga and the Ernsbergers to Raichur. Each party had two helpers from the Christian Orphanage, some of Ward's best who had volunteered for this work.[12]

It was from Gulbarga that the orphans had started their trek only five years before. English services had often been held there, but the Jacobses had come to work with Indians, and to do so in their own language, Kanarese. No house was available for them. They cleaned up a large "mausoleum-like deserted building"—perhaps one of those lived in by the orphans—and started life there. From here Jacobs and Paramanandam made a tour to Bidar, ninety odd miles distant, the first Methodists to preach there. They appeared in the Bidar market on December 22, 1885 on the day of the weekly fair and attempted to preach. "They were so beaten, . . . and threatened that they left their quarters, which were outside the city, before daylight."[13] In Gulbarga armed men, at mid-night, robbed and looted their "home" in the mausoleum. Then the Jacobses went to Hyderabad where they remained for two years.

Two months after the Jacobses had left Lingasagar the Ernsbergers went to Raichur. There was no house available for them. They accepted accommodation in a "a public place, half temple, part Caravansarai or Rest House, where there was little or no privacy, and where the people gathered in the mornings to bathe".[14] Raichur was a railway junction, with a large railway community. A Parsee kept a general store. In 1886 the Missionary Society gave $2000 to build a home in Gulbarga. The next year the Ernsbergers were alone in the "Gulbarga and Raichur Kanarese

Mission". They moved to Gulbarga where he purchased a good property and built the bungalow. For ten years this remained the head quarters of the large district. Gulbarga was a stony field; "opposition was adamant". The people welcomed a school until the missionary insisted that there would be Bible teaching also. It took years to open the first Sunday School, and three years to open a school in a village near by. At the end of 1886 Ernsberger wrote:

> We have one organized church consisting of my wife, myself and a native young man who is acting as colporteur. In all we are three. We have no church building, nor a parsonage, but God has given us faith, courage and triumph. We shall yet see these barren fields blossom as the rose. We are just beginning.[15]

The first convert was baptized in November, 1888 by J. H. Garden who had moved to Gulbarga after Mrs. Ernsberger's death. The convert was Bucchanna. He came from outside the district, but he had heard the Gospel preached by Ernsberger at the Tintani Jatra and remembering that the preacher had come from Gulbarga the convert went there. "It was a strange sight," wrote Garden, "a group of five heathen men from the interior led by a white bearded patriarchal Shastri taking a journey by common bullock cart and on foot, for one hundred miles to seek Christian baptism."[16] Six years later there was a second convert in Gulbarga as a result of street preaching.

Bidar

The first work in Bidar was chiefly east of the town, among the Telugu-speaking people; its greatest development has been in the Kanarese-speaking population. In 1895 A. E. Cook was associated with Garden in Vikarabad and the next year the Cooks moved to Bidar. They lived in a native house in the walled city. "In seven years the Christians with one worker of 1896, had increased to ninety-three with four workers. Most of them were in the village of Mirzapur".[17] The first converts from the village were Jotappa, father of J. Jacob, and Parbappa who were baptized in April, 1896. Cook secured a Telugu worker, from Medak, and a Kanarese preacher, W. Paul, from Bangalore. Mrs. Paul taught in a school near Jotappa's house. It was moved to Bidar in 1898. Cook sent some boys to Raichur, Gulbarga and Kolar for school and training. Some girls and women were also sent for training.[18] Before he left Bidar in 1903 Cook received

> a document from H. H. the Nizam's Government that settles, we trust, the question of our rights to hold land; and states in no uncertain terms the equality of the Native Christian with the Mohammedan and Hindu before the law . . . . Under the orders given in this document, the local authorities have granted to Bro. Batstone a plot of ground near five acres in extent, carrying with it the right to erect Mission buildings . . . . A

> prominent Missionary of another Society has called the document 'the Magna Charta of Christian rights in the Nizam's Dominions,' and benefits secured by these many years of effort.[19]

Cook was followed by Batstone. Work on the bungalow and a hospita kept Batstone from doing much evangelistic work. "People far and nea have been impressed by the building operations, for such a building speak of permanency."[20] The sight of 160 people in the new bungalow, Bisho Oldham among them, while curious faces filled the doors, was impressive Several Bible women and teachers were working under Mrs. Batstone.

Kolar

Miss Louisa H. Anstey had been a missionary of the London Missonar Society, working in Mysore State. In 1874 her health broke and she returned to Scotland under doctor's orders. After she regained her health she offered to return under her Society to "labour outside existing missio lines" but the Society refused her condition. She then resigned her connec tion with it to follow the "leadings of Providence". There followed a physi cal relapse. She read of faith healing, and by faith was healed. In 187 she came to Kolar Town when the State was in the grip of famine an opened orphanages for 600 boys and girls.[21] Her program grew to includ evangelistic work in the town and surrounding villages; primary schools i some villages; work for women and widows, supervision and care of littl colonies of Christians from the orphanages on land she owned in village near by; Elim, Bethany, Nazareth and Rollinspur, and others farther out At the centre tailoring, carpentry, blacksmithing, masonry and farmin were carried on, on a superb site, *Khas Bagh,* that was granted to her i town limits. As famine conditions worsened not only did she put all he own resources into relief for orphans and adults, but also received funds fro Scotland without direct solicitation. In 1878 there were "1270 childre in her charge in addition to a community of adults".[22]

Friendly relations were early established with the Methodists i Bangalore. Her report of the Faith Mission for 1880 speaks of M. B. Kir as one "long accustomed to practical mission work, and who understand farming, carpentering, etc".[23] In 1880, "Colar Orphanage" first appear in the appointments when Miss Anstey asked for Kirk's help. The nex year S. P. Jacobs was appointed, again at Miss Anstey's request. He le a deep spiritual influence. Many of the orphans were converted and fro these he formed a theological class and trained them as teachers an preachers.

In 1890 Miss Anstey felt that she could no longer continue the wor and offered it to the S. I. Conference. The work and property were fo mally taken over by J. E. Robinson and A. H. Baker on October 3, 189

At the ensuing Conference Miss Anstey was present and made a statement on the origin of the work and its transfer. A Conference resolution expressed its most hearty appreciation of her "generous confidence" in entrusting to our church "her noble work of faith and labour of love".[24]

The transfer brought to the Conference a Christian community: Married 226, (settled out are "113 pairs"), single 104, Widows 13 and Children 170; Total 513.[25] It also brought two orphanage schools with 50 boys and 60 girls, and responsibility for other work.

A. H. Baker and I. A. Richards were the first appointees to the work under the Conference. The following year, 1892, Richards and W. H. Hollister were appointed. The last named found here a task matching his convictions and native skill, with results which unfolded in the twenty odd years that he received this appointment. He developed the Industrio-Educational Department for "the training of the heart, the head and the hands" with a program in which the boys

> have a half day's training of the mind in school, a half day's training of the hand at some useful employment and whether in school, at the bench, or on the farm, we keep before them constantly the all importance of seeking first the Kingdom of Heaven.[26]

Richards continued at Kolar for five years. In addition to the pastor's work and a theological class, he was engaged in the preparation of literature for

> a whole Christian community thrown upon our hands while we had not a single line of church literature in the Kanarese language . . . . We now have our three Catechisms, a short Compendium of our Church History, Nast's First Scripture Catechism, seven of Bishop Thoburn's sermonettes, our Discipline, Wesley on Christian Perfection . . . and we have 'The Evangelist' , a live semi monthly paper.[27]

Until the W. F. M. S. provided for the Girls' School and Evangelistic work for women, the wives of the missionaries gave it the necessary supervision. Miss F. W. Maskell, a deaconess from Madras, arrived in 1893 and opened a program in evangelistic and village school work in which she continued for many years. In 1897 Miss F. F. Fisher, a missionary of the W. F. M. S. and a deaconess, came from Poona for the girls' orphanage and school. *Khas Bagh* was divided between the Board and the W. F. M. S. after the Conference of 1897 when Bishop Foss, Dr. Goucher and appointees of the Woman's Conference, went to Kolar and agreed upon its partition.[28]

Important as was this property in the development of the work, it was exceeded in its intrinsic worth by a group of men and women, trained under "Mother Anstey" as they affectionately remembered her, who through years continued in their work the contagion of spirit which she and her associates had imparted—like Suhrudia Noah, Govindaraju Gershom and Benjamin Luke and their wives. They and their children in the Conference have won other victories "by faith".

Foundations in Bastar State

Ward was by nature an evangelist and a pioneer, ready for anything that might extend the Christian Mission. Hardly had they settled at Yellandu when he became interested in the Koinoors, an aboriginal tribe, and purposed to trace them to their homeland. He went in 1892 with Narsaya and Rama and two servants in two ox-carts. In three weeks they reached the base of the mountains that form the western border of the plateau of Bastar. Climbing one of these he was moved to prayer and praise; praise for the beauty of nature that he saw on all sides; prayer for missionaries to enter this unoccupied land. After that day he wrote: "I have never had any doubt that I had business in Bastar."[29] They reached Jagdalpur on March 6 and he made large plans for its occupation. On his way back he met A. H. L. Fraser, Commissioner of the State, and was assured of his encouragement and help.

In November Ward heard by mail that Dr. and Mrs. Batstone, on their way to Bastar, had reached England. "The brethren in America had caught on to the Bastar work, and here were reinforcements coming for that work." They reached Yellandu in December. The appointments of the S. I. Conference for 1893, included for the first time "Jagdalpur—supplied by William H. Batstone, M. D." In February Ward went with the new missionary to his station. On their way they left Narsaya and Chandaya with their families in Sironcha. They were kindly received in Jagdalpur. Together they looked things over and approved a site for the Mission and land for a village for both the Parent Board and the W. F. M. S. After staying two weeks Batstone returned to get his wife and child; Ward remained to put up a temporary residence for the family, and a room for a dispensary. At first no one would help in the work. After ten days the boycott broke; "a few horse-keepers ventured to try it . . . and the way to success [was] open". With this work completed Ward started home, expecting to meet the Batstones on the way, but they arrived May 24, without having seen Ward.

> It was a heroic, long journey for Sister Batstone, just out from home, and that too knowing that she would have no society but that of her husband . . . alone among the heathen, 300 miles from the nearest Methodist brother Missionary. But they went and stuck, under much and deep trial of faith.[30]

After Ward, the Batstones laid the foundations of Bastar work. They commenced with preaching, Bible teaching and medical service. The dispensary opened on June 22. Not knowing the language their conversations were limited to the few English-speaking natives. Preaching was necessarily translated by non-Christian interpreters. To Conference Batstone reported:

> Our medical work has been a source of encouragement. In our little mud and grass dispensary during the last five months we have had 8 in-patients and 1992 out-patients. Some of them have come sixty miles for medicine . . . . If we could have two self-forgetting native brethren to follow up this hospital work many would seek the Lord.[31]

On March 1, 1894 they were burned out. The doctor was out at his work. Mrs. Batstone was unaware of the fire until the whole house was ablaze. She just escaped with their little Evangeline. All was a complete loss; clothes, except those they wore; medical and religious books, instruments, apparatus and personal effects.[32]

Ward had tried during 1893 to get the W. F. M. S. interested in Bastar work. Bishop Thoburn took up the matter with Mrs. Keen of Philadelphia, then visiting India. She authorized Miss Blackmar to draw on her for the expenses of a tour in the state and Bishop Thoburn commissioned her to go. Others in the party were Gilder, the P. E., Ward and his son Wesley, all riding horses. Ox carts took some Christian families, tents, stores, etc., for the Bastar Mission. They set out on March 8, 1894. There was an unexpected delay at Sironcha. A horse had cast its shoe. The nearest blacksmith could not come to Sironcha so the horse was sent to him. This gave the missionaries an opportunity to study the locality. All realized that it was a strategic centre for work. On Gilder's suggestion Ward gave this Sironcha field to the Missionary Board and it became a part of the Hyderabad circuit. Gilder conveyed to the W. F. M. S. thirty acres of the plot he had received and in 1896 the W. F. M. S. bungalow was begun and completed in April, 1897.[33] In Sironcha Gilder baptized Somnath, a Bastar boy who had been with Ward. He was the first fruits of the new work. The party reached Jagdalpur on April 13. They had brought a large stock of medicines, and iron and iron ware for the hospital, also a large amount of iron for a new bungalow. They visited five possible centres for work in Bastar State.

> We saw the two wings of the hospital started while there and the doctor will live in one and work in the other for the present, till a bungalow and dispensary is built. When we left Jagdalpur, the work was in a fine state of progress and our pioneers were in fine cheer at their prospects.[34]

In 1895 Ward was on furlough. The funds that had been promised for the support of the medical work were not received and during the year because of the depression the Batstones left the station. In 1897 Ward sent the Plumleys from Yellandu to hold the work.

William Ward tells of some of the early Christians: Soon after Dr. Batstone reached Jagdalpur he was visited by a lame man for whom there seemed little could be done. "He hobbled about on a crutch with one foot stuck well out behind, the lame leg forming two sides of a right angle triangle." He had lost his employment and the condition seemed hopeless. Dr. Batstone treated him and finally succeeded in getting the leg so he could again walk. The kindly treatment, the unexpected cure, and the Christian teaching touched the heart of Siva Charan and he became a disciple of Jesus Christ, "who, he often said, gave him a new leg and a new heart".

When Ward visited the station in 1894 he found Siva Charan learning the Gospel message and sharing it with others. In a little village two miles away he was *guru* to three families. "Later on these families became our first converts in Bastar after Siva Charan himself." Because he could not walk great distances he "at his own expense and of his own accord bought a small pony and on this, ranged far and wide preaching Jesus," and was much beloved by his people.

A few years later W.T. Ward baptized a group beneath a mohwa tree, the first Christians in the village, Sindhgaon, some forty miles from Jagdalpur. One of them was Prabhu Dayal. He had little education, but he studied, made progress, and was recognized as the leader of the group. Under that same tree, again and again, others were baptized as a result of Prabhu Dayal's teaching until they numbered sixty-five in nine different villages. Prabhu Dayal became the "esteemed and faithful pastor and teacher" of them all, and was held in esteem and respect by all communities because of his character.[35]

Section III

THE IMPERATIVE

THE UNFAILING PRESENCE

I dwell alone, and all I hold most dear
Are far removed beyond the trackless sea.
So very far they seem tonight from me.
Yet for a moment brief methinks I hear
The echo of loud voices in my ear;
The dear home faces seem to shine again,
Then swiftly vanish in a mist of pain.
Yet it is but a moment that I turn
And with heart longings for my loved ones yearn
For hush! I'm not alone; a Presence blest
Fills all my chamber with a sense of rest!
A moment's darkness, then a flood of light,
A moment's sadness, then a great delight;
A well known voice is whispering unto me:
'Am I not better, O Beloved, unto thee—
Am I not better far to thee than all?'
Low at His feet I then adoring fall.
Outbreathing there in speechless love and praise
The song the heart is quite too full to raise
Thou art enough, my own Beloved One,
And work with Thee is sweet till day is done,
And when at even time I close my door,
Shut in with Jesus, what do I need more?

MARY REED

VIII

Growing Together

Members of the North and South India Conferences had been brought together in the period of the Bombay, Bengal and Madras Mission. With the organization of the S. I. Conference they had parted, but at every session of either Conference in intervening years visitors from each Conference were present at the other. They were separated by distance and by financial policy, but their hearts were as one. Together they planned a reunion. Prime movers in this get-together were Parker and Thoburn.

> In 1879 I became impressed that we needed an organization in which all parts of our scattered work in India would be represented, to look after the general interests and to keep us from drifting apart. I thought this out for some time and then wrote to Brother Parker, giving an outline of what I thought seemed needed. By an extraordinary coincidence my letter on its way to him crossed one from him to me of almost practically the same import. Our minds had been running in the same channel, and the coincidence impressed us both very deeply as an evidence that God was leading us.[1]

The United Conference

Since plans had been made for the N. I. Conference to meet at Kanpur and the S. I. Conference at Allahabad in January, dates were set for a joint gathering for two days at the latter city. On January 13, 1880 they met in United Session. All the members of both conferences including most of the wives of the missionaries and the W. F. M. S. ladies from N. India were present. George Bowen was elected President of the united body. It was a Delegated Conference in the sense that both Conferences had empowered this "United Conference"

> to organize a representative assembly and provide for its perpetuation, by the election of delegates at stated times from each conference in India, provided that no action shall be taken which will in any way interfere with the rights or operations of the General Missionary Society, or contravene the organic law of the M. E. Church.[2]

The S. I. Conference added a further proviso: "to avoid any action interfering with their accepted policy of self support".[3] The Conference was acclaimed a delightful reunion and "nothing could exceed the hospitality shown by the good people of Allahabad".

> The love feast on Wednesday morning followed by the Sacrament of the Lord's Supper, was so crowded wih the presence of God, and the

hearts of those who took part were so surcharged by the emotions of the hour, that tears of joy flowed freely, shouts of praise were frequent, and it was almost impossible to bring to a close . . . one of the richest foretastes of heaven we have ever known.[4]

The decisions of most significance were that there should be a Delegated Conference to meet in July, 1881 to watch over and control the interests common to both conferences; and that the delegates to the General Conference, Thoburn from S. India, and Cunningham from N. India, should press for recognition of a Delegated Conference to which should be committed "all those interests of the Church in India which are included in Part IV of the Discipline entitled 'Educational and Benevolent Institutions' ".

"I feel", wrote Thoburn in his Journal, "that I shall have some serious work at General Conference in pushing through a measure securing recognition"[5] of a Delegated Conference. It was, indeed, a high adventure on which these delegates embarked: for "the proposal was a novel one, and . . . created serious inquiry if not positive alarm, in the minds of many of our leading men. It looked like a General Conference in embryo."[6] Thoburn's Journal best describes the result:

> May 15. Our memorial for a delegated conference has stirred up the deepest interest and was debated in Committee [on Missions] for two days. The Bishops had Cunningham and myself before them for a long time on Thursday and every phase of the subject has been canvassed. The final vote was taken this afternoon, and carried by a large majority. It must now come before the General Conference where it will encounter a still more determined opposition.
>
> May 21. Its prospects are not cheering. Nearly all the Bishops and Board are very active in their opposition, and many weak men begin to waver.
>
> May 24. We lost the order of the day on Saturday . . . . The opposition to it is intense, and the whole affair has convinced me that we have nothing to hope for from this General Conference in the way of legislation for our self-development in India. My visit to this General Conference has convinced me that I need never come back again. God must be our guide and our problems must be solved in India.

The Delegated Conference

The Delegated Conference, called in its minutes "the Second Delegated Conference of the M. E. Church in India",[7] met at Allahabad, July 14—18, 1881. The delegates were:

> North India. *Ministerial*, B. H. Badley, E. W. Parker, T. J. Scott, James Mudge, T. S. Johnson, Isaac Fieldbrave, P. M. Buck, *Lay*, J. H. Condon, Ram Chunder Bose. South India: *Ministerial*, D. O. Fox, Dennis Osborne, J. M. Thoburn, J. A. Northrup, I. F. Row, George Bowen; *Lay*, James Morris, W. A. Thomas.

Only two in the total number were Indians: Isaac Fieldbrave and R. C. Bose. The Conference elected as permanent officer: J. M. Thoburn, President; Dennis Osborne, Vice-President T. J. Scott, Secretary; T. S. Johnson, Treasurer. The Conference was convened with a view

> to have the management and control of such interests as are common to the M. E. Church in the Indian Empire, and do not legitimately belong to a single Annual Conference, and [it] may authorize such measures as are needful for promoting or conserving such interests, provided no action be taken contravening the organic law of the Methodist Episcopal Church.[8]

The Conference adopted a constitution with a ratio of representation for ministers of one delegate to five members, and Lay representation of one delegate to each Presiding Elder's District, to be chosen by District Conferences, or by Quarterly Conferences.

Assuming authority it approved: (1) A General Board of Publication and Management, which should establish a central Publishing House at Allahabad, and provide for the publication of *The Lucknow Witness* on an enlarged basis. (2) A Board of Education to present to the next meeting "an educational scheme, affecting educational institutions of all grades in connection with our Church in India". (3) A Report on the Relation of Lay Agents to our Work. (4) Instructions for the protection of Church Property by its registration and the forms to be used for each class. (5) A memorial to the Viceroy of India on the subject of laws governing Marriage and Divorce, asking for amendments needed "especially among our Native Christian communities"; and for uniform rules and equal privileges for Christian Ministers of all denominations. (6) A request that visiting Bishops remain two years, or at least through two cold seasons in India.

The Executive Committee was asked to fix the time of another meeting to be held at Allahabad and accordingly, made plans for a session of the Delegated Conference in 1884. Both Conferences elected their delegates, but an unexpected turn made the meeting unnecessary.

The Central Conference

Neither the N. I. nor the S. I. Conference sent a memorial for a Delegated Conference to the General Conference of 1884, where they were represented respectively, by E. W. Parker and R. C. Bose, Dennis Osborne and William Taylor. Nor was such memorial introduced when that body convened. "Yet", says Worley, "the influence of that memorial [of 1880] must have held over and been in the thinking of the missionary leaders of the Church."[9] If so, the patient work of Thoburn and Cunningham four years before now bore fruit.

The Committee on Missions had a new problem before it in a request from the Mission in Japan to unite with the Methodist Church of Canada. Its report expresses "great anxiety . . . to approve the same, but your Committee find insuperable difficulties in the way of its adoption".[10] While the Committee was wrestling with this problem, on May 20 Parker presented a memorial signed by himself and William Taylor, for "the organization of a subordinate General Conference in India, which was referred to the Committee on Missions".[11] The report continued:

> We have become convinced in the course of our investigation that union in many of the interests of our Missions would not only be possible, but at times greatly to the interest of the work of God on earth. This is further confirmed by the petition from the Conference in India for a Delegated Conference.
>
> With a view to provide for these needs thus made manifest, your Committee recommend that the following be inserted in the Chapter on Missions, namely:
>
> 'When in any of our Foreign Mission fields there is more than one Annual Conference or Mission, or more than one form of Methodism, it shall be lawful, either by order of the General Conference, or by a majority of all the Conferences or Missions wishing to unite, with the written call of the Bishop having Episcopal Supervision of the field, to organize a Central Conference to be composed either of all the members of these Annual Conferences or Missions, or of representatives from the same, elected according to such ratio as may be agreed upon between the constituent parties, who may also provide for the admission to such conferences of laymen, the number not to exceed that of the clerical delegates.'[12]

There followed rules for the organization and the authority of such a Conference—much as India had advocated in 1880. As soon as the report had been adopted, L. M. Vernon, Chairman of the Committee, moved: "That a Central Conference be hereby constituted in India, and one authorized for Japan, under the rules just adopted by the General Conference."[13] In the course of the debate J. M. Reid, Missionary Secretary, who had recently visited India, said, "The action was needed in India in their educational and publishing work . . . . I cannot conceive the least danger." E. W. Parker added: "It would be a great help to us, in India. We have had two meetings of this kind in that country, and a third was contemplated. An organized form would possess decided advantage over an informal meeting."[14]

A motion to lay the resolution on the table was lost. Immediately L. H. King moved the previous question. It was ordered and carried. Vernon's motion was adopted May 28, the last day of the Conference, in the afternoon session. Thoburn expressed his joy: "We have our Central Conference formally 'constituted' and can now do permanent and satisfactory work."[15] Elsewhere he wrote:

> Dr. Parker succeeded in securing the authorization of the Central Conference . . . . I have always regarded this as perhaps the greatest measure of his life. He managed the matter with great skill and good sense, and the chapter on the subject incorporated into the Discipline was substantially his own production.[16]

The Central Conference had been asked for by two Conferences in India as a co-ordinating authority. Its advocates, however, had looked down the decades yet to come. They saw that the two Conferences must soon become four; and four become eight, and so the Church continue to grow. The Delegated Conference expressed this confidence in its constitution in the words, "concurrent action of *all* the Annual Conferences in India," and the first Central Conference even more emphatically with the words, "by the *several* Annual Conferences and Missions in India".[17] Only in the use of the words "in India" did vision dim. In a brief fifteen years after it was constituted, the Central Conference *in* India welcomed among its delegates men and women from Annual Conferences and Missions in Burma, Malaysia and the Philippine Islands, and became known as the Central Conference of the Methodist Church of Southern Asia. The Central Conference for which India pleaded in vain in 1880, only six decades later, became the pattern in American Methodism for the Jurisdictional Conferences which made possible the united Methodist Church.

The first session of the Central Conference was convened by Bishop J. F. Hurst in Bareilly, on January 13, 1885. "The roll was called and fifty-one members responded to their names."[18] Of these forty-one were from North India, twenty-one of them Nationals. The N. I. Conference had adjourned in Bareilly the evening before. Many had stayed to attend this historic session and, apparently, all members of either Conference who were present, were by courtesy considered as members.

By adopting the methods of the General Conference, the Delegated Conference had acquainted members with a familiar procedure. Reports, practically the same as those approved at the Delegated Conference—On Publication, Education, Church Property, Sunday Schools and Lay Missionaries—were presented and approved; necessary Committees appointed, and the Conference adjourned after its session on the second day. After the Conference Bishop Hurst said that "his fears in relation to it were all gone, and that he had been quite converted to faith in it".[19]

The Central Conference met for its second session on February 17—19, 1887 in the Fort M. E. Church, Bombay, Bishop W. X. Ninde presiding, for the General Conference had directed that there should be two meetings in a quadrennium. Among the elected Lay Delegates three ladies were seated : Mrs. Parker, Amroha; Miss Blackmar, Oudh; and Miss Warner, Burma.

Isaac Fieldbrave in 1887 was the first Indian minister to be elected to a Central Conference. In the same year Harkua Wilson and J. Jacob, were elected from North India as Laymen and J. F. Deatker, James Morris, W. B. Wright, Peter Geering and C. S. Gordon from South India. In 1892 the North India ministerial delegation of fifteen included four Indian brethren: H. A. Cutting, William Peters, Charles Luke and Samuel Tupper. The first Indian lady to be elected was Miss Phoebe Rowe in 1894, from the Northwest India Conference.

With careful attention to many matters of Administration the Conference (1) recognized the Press in Madras as the third Publishing Agency of the Church in India; (2) approved the following as official publications of the Church: *Kaukab-i-Hind; The Indian Witness; India's Young Folks; The Woman's Friend;* (The *Bombay Guardian* and the Bengali *Christian Herald* were edited by Methodist ministers but were not official publications); (3) memorialized the General Conference to organize the work at Singapore and its vicinity as a Mission; (4) fixed the boundaries of the Bengal Conference, to which Bishop Ninde signified his concurrence; (5) adopted a report defining the official relation of lady missionaries to the Conference as it was accepted in 1883 by the General Executive; (6) adopted a memorial to the General Conference to so plan Episcopal supervision "that a Bishop may come to India as a General Superintendent residing in India".

In the third session, 1889, Parker, on a point of law, questioned the validity of ladies being seated as lay members of the Conference. Bishop Thoburn presiding, remarked:

> Bishop Ninde had allowed their admission, and in our field ladies are appointed to Conference work, as they are not in America, and thus an analogy on this subject between the two countries fails; and that if this conference sees proper to allow lady delegates to occupy places, he does not choose to object.[20]

In this, India moved ahead of the mother Church. It was not until 1900 that the right of women to sit as "laymen" in the General Conference was established. Two women were elected as lay delegates from India in 1896, Mrs. E. W. Parker and Mrs. J. C. Butcher. With three others, they took their seats but when challenged withdrew while their right to sit was being decided. After a long procedural battle they were seated without prejudice, and an amendment clarifying the issue was submitted to Annual Conferences and carried.

The Missionary Episcopacy

In 1852 the General Conference proposed and the Annual Conferences approved an amendment to the Third Restrictive Rule giving the General Conference power "to appoint a missionary bishop or Superintendent for any of our foreign missions, limiting his jurisdiction to the same respectively".[21] This was first done for Liberia. Three years later the Bishops assigned the supervision of Foreign Missions among its members so that one among them would be familiar with the work and needs of each field. Bishop Simpson was thus connected with India when Butler came out.

The India Mission Conference in 1868 expressed "the sense of the Conference that no resident Bishop should be elected for India for at least four years to come",[22] feeling that such an arrangement would weaken the connection with the church in America. Six years after Bishop Thomson visited India Bishop Kingsley made the second Episcopal visit. Such infrequent supervision crippled the young church by inadequate provision for ordinations. Kingsley's death in Beirut while returning from India drew attention afresh to the need of a better method of supervision. Those visits were appreciated; the administration provided had been helpful, but there was neither full intelligence nor continuity in administration.

A plan of biennial visits was approved by General Conference in 1876. Under this program the following Bishops came to India: E. G. Andrews 1877; Thomas Bowman 1879; S. M. Merrill 1881; R. S. Foster 1883; J. F. Hurst 1885 and W. X. Ninde 1887. None came out twice; none stayed long. Each gave help, and all were appreciated for their inspiration and encouragement, and for their representation of the work to the Home Church. But biennial visits failed to meet the needs of the work. The Delegated Conference, in 1881, asked for "a more constant and direct superintendence and leadership, such as Bishop Asbury gave to our Church in America when it was new". Bishop Ninde's recommendation to the Board after his visit in 1886-87, that the work in India should be restricted to two areas, a Hindustani field in the North, and a Kanarese field in the South,[23] showed how difficult it was for a bishop in a hasty tour to grasp the true perspective of a whole field.

The General Conference in 1884 gave earnest and protracted thought to the question of supervision of foreign missions. The Committee on Episcopacy recommended "an episcopal residence in India". The Conference asked the advice of the Bishops as to "whether the emergencies of our Mission work require that an Episcopal residence be established in Europe, India and Africa, or in either country". They answered, "It would not be wise at the present time to fix residences . . . in any one of them." Bose, Osborne and Parker were given additional time to speak on an amendment that Bishops "shall preside over two consecutive session's spending the intervening time in the supervision of our work in India". The suggestion was defeated. In a final vote on the original motion a call for vote by orders was made, and "for want of a concurrent vote the report was not adopted", although the majority of the total was in favour.[24] In

America there was dissatisfaction at the long and frequent absences of its Bishops.

MISSIONARY BISHOP

Opinion in India came to be outspoken. "If we are to have a Missionary Bishop", wrote Bowen, "Thoburn is the man. All would recognize his fitness."[25] This nomination drew a rejoinder, "To be placed under a Bishop inferior in ecclesiastical rights and privileges . . . is being reduced to a position inferior to that occupied by us before. Such action is in violation of the genius of the Methodist Episcopal Church." Bose pleaded for "a man above local traditions".[26] Meantime God had been preparing Thoburn for a "new work". His Journal gives some of the steps:

> The proposition to have a Bishop in India gave rise to a very warm discussion . . . . As my name was freely used in connection with the proposition I was placed in a delicate position, and I fear I did not act as discreetly as I should have done. [Jan. 21, 1876]
>
> My days in the pastorate are probably over. What may be done with me officially, I know not, and care but little, but I believe God is calling me to a general work among the churches all over our field. [Jan. 3, 1880]

In the summer of 1885 while supplying the Union Church at Simla, Thoburn was thrown from his horse, and when able to travel was ordered by his physician to go to America for a prolonged rest. He did not return to India before his election to the Episcopacy. A letter to J. W. Waugh is pertinent:

> Your discussion of the Bishop question naturally interests me. In 1876 I made up my mind that this question was one of a remote future, and not until 1884 did I change my mind . . . . I certainly had no ambitious design in my mind when I tumbled off my pony, and yet that fall was a turning point in my life. It sent me home, gave me sympathy at New York, and opened my way before the public. At no time in my life have I been more impressed that God was leading me, and yet I do not profess to see very far into the future.
>
> My mind is made up on a few points. First, and *always*, I don't want and cannot have such an office without the consent of my brethren in India. How they stand I am not quite sure . . . . Second, before being clothed with such immense responsibility, I want to know just what the office means. They must define the functions of a "missionary" bishop before I can assume. Third, if elected as a full "bishop" I should make it as a condition that I shall not be expected to remain in America. My work is in the Mission field. But I am not persuaded that God's plan is revealed to any one yet . . . . I do believe that God has a great work for me yet to do. I have been feeling in a

peculiar way, for two years past, that His hand is upon me, and that He will send me forth to what will probably be my real life work. I am not at all sure that official life is to be my life, and less than ever before do I desire it.[27]

Early in its session of 1888 the General Conference asked the Committee on Episcopacy for an interpretation of the term "Missionary Bishop". Their report included: "A Missionary Bishop is a Bishop elected for a specified foreign field, with full Episcopal powers" but limited to that field. He was not a General Superintendent "but is co-ordinate with them in authority in the field to which he is appointed". His election carried his assignment to his field. To be a General Superintendent would require a re-election. His support would be from the Episcopal Fund.[28]

The acceptance of this report by the General Conference cleared the way for the Committee on Missions to recommend "that a Missionary Bishop be elected and consecrated for India and Malayasia". This was approved on May 25 by a majority of 121 and immediately after, the Conference proceeded to elect a Missionary Bishop for India and Malaysia. Thoburn received 286 out of 410 votes, and was asked to join the other Bishops on the platform. Dennis Osborne was seated in his place. The consecration service was on Sunday. Thoburn wrote:

> I had no doubt in my heart that the Lord of the harvest set me apart for the work. The service of consecration had been altered somewhat by inserting the words Missionary Bishop of India and Malayasia [but] . . . God must vindicate my title, or it will at best be worth very little.[29]

The first word to reach India was a cable: "Thoburn missionary bishop for India. Status satisfies." Readers in Bombay were bewildered for India had wanted and asked for a General Superintendent, yet reactions were exuberant.

> Dr. Thoburn's election was a foregone conclusion. His wide experience, his thorough consecration to India, his loyalty to principle, his eloquence in the pulpit and on the platform, his ability as a writer, his genial disposition combined to give him peculiar fitness for the position in which he has been honoured. [H. C. Stuntz in *Bombay Guardian*][30]

Thoburn's arrival in Bombay on December 17 was marked by a reception at Grant Road Church. In his response he said that

> he felt it was a great work that he had come to superintend . . . . He shrank back from one word that had been used, the 'office' of a bishop. He felt that it was a work to be done, and not an office to be held, that had settled him in India. He had not come out there to rule over any person or be their lord; he had come out to serve . . . . The work of the villages was the easiest work, but the problem of how to win the great towns for Christ was a most important one. Bombay for Christ meant all western India for Christ in 10 years.[31]

God's best gifts to his Church are ministers and missionaries of Christlike spirit, pastors after his own heart, true under-shepherds, who feed the flock of Christ, who seek the lost, who relieve the suffering, and in purity of life and sincerity of purpose seek the advancement of the Kingdom of God.

F. W. Warne (J. G. C. 1904)

And now, Brethren, let me exhort you to put forth every effort to promote the cause of our Blessed Lord in Allahabad: . . . The Spirit of our holy Christianity, as the genius of our cherished Methodism, is 'All at it and always at it.' In prayer, in fellowship, in testimony, in the onward charge, let not the beloved pastor have to mourn the lack of cooperation on the part of any.

. . . Let each preacher take his responsibility as from and unto the Lord, thus approving his own ministry, as also relieving the Pastor of much care and labor . . . .

Above all, let me beseech you, Brethren, to consecrate yourselves to the steady prosecution of [preaching]. Here is our field; this is our mission; upon the success or failure of this depends the bright shining or the final setting aside of the Methodist Episcopal candlestick in India. If you cannot preach yourselves, see to it that your heart with all its sympathy, your purse and your prayers are consecrated to it.

Dennis Osborne to the Allahabad Quarterly Conference.

Bombay Guardian September 1, 1883

IX

The Thoburn Period—India

One of the weaknesses of the S. I. Conference was its great size. Another was the variety of people within its bounds. With the increase of vernacular work this aspect became increasingly manifest as it could not be when all work was in English. Actually there was little in common between the people of Bengal and those of Madras, between whom there were hundreds of miles and large populations speaking diverse tongues; or between the Gujaratis and the Marathis who were thrown together in the city of Bombay and close neighbours in the Presidency. The reflective in 1876 knew that new conferences must come.

The Bengal Conference

The General Conference of 1884 approved an enabling act for a third Conference in India, the boundaries to be fixed by the Central Conference with the concurrence of the presiding Bishop. This was done at the second Central Conference in 1887.

> The North India Conference shall consist of the North-West Provinces, and Oudh, excepting the Districts of Saharanpur and Dehra Dun and the Allahabad English Church.
>
> The South India Conference shall consist of Sindh, Gujarat, the Bombay Presidency and all of peninsular India South and West of a line drawn from Burhanpur, C. P., to Jabalpur, not including them; thence due East to Bengal, and along its Southwest border to the Bay of Bengal.
>
> The Bengal Conference shall consist of Bengal and the portions of India not included by the North and South India Conference, with Burma and the Straits Settlement.[1]

The Bengal Conference of the Methodist Episcopal Church met for its first session in the Dharamtala Street Church, Calcutta, on January 13, 1888 at 10-30 a.m. C. P. Hard, Secretary of the last Central Conference, called the Conference to order and requested the Rev. J. E. Scott, Ph. D. of North India and W. F. Oldham to conduct the opening religious services. C. P. Hard called the roll of Conference and the following members responded to their names: D. Osborne, C. P. Hard, T. E. F. Morton, C. W. DeSouza, J. P. Meik, A. S. E. Vardon, A. Gilruth, E. Jeffries, F. J. Blewitt, J. M. Thoburn Jr., W. F. Oldham, A. G. Creamer, C. M. Miller, F. L. McCoy, J. D. Webb—J. M. Thoburn was in America.

Probationers: C. H. Plomer, S. P. Long, W. A. Carroll, F. D. Newhouse, E. S. Busby, M. Tindale, S. N. Das. Transfers from Rock

River Conference, F. W. Warne, and from Minnesota Conference, R. H. Craig.[2]

Dennis Osborne and F. L. McCoy were elected by ballot to be President and Secretary respectively. W. P. Byers, C. G. Conklin, L. E. Koepsel, Neils Madsen, P. C. Nath and Paul Singh were received On Trial. The Conference adopted a memorial for the General Conference asking it

> to provide for a formal recognition of the office of Deaconess in the Methodist Episcopal Church [and] in connection with the said office, provision be made for the administration of the Sacraments in Zenanas.[3]

Francis Wesley Warne

The transfer to the Conference of F. W. Warne with his appointment to the Dharamtala Street Church, was the opening of a unique missionary career. Born on a farm in Ontario, Canada, he left his home for the United States in 1873 to prepare for the ministry to which he had felt a call. In 1884 he graduated from the Garrett Biblical Institute and joined the Rock River Conference. He was finishing the third year of a pastorate when he "was strangely impressed that something was going to happen that would change" his life. He had no light as to what it would be until the session of his Conference in the autumn, after Bishop Thoburn had addressed the body, and added:

> 'I call the young men of this conference to India in the name of the Master.' ...As suddenly as a flash of lightning I knew the interpretation of the abiding impression. God had called me to India. I trembled all over and shook the seat. I had thought I was ready for anything, but this was more than I expected.[4]

They had guests at their home those days At the dinner table Warne remarked to his wife: "What do you think happened at Conference?" She did not know. "I have been asked to go to India", he replied, and the friends "threw back their heads and laughed at the idea". On the morning of the third day when they had gone Mrs. Warne said:

> Frank, it is all settled .... The very moment you mentioned it I knew we were going and I had to get ready .... I began by giving up father and mother, my country, my friends, and so on until I came to the baby .... This morning I heard as it were the voice of Jesus saying, 'Give the baby to Me, and I will give her back to you,' and I answered, 'Lord Jesus, I surrender the baby; I am ready.'[4]

And so "Frank" Warne and his wife with their baby, Edith, reached India in January, 1888; their first appointment, the Dharamtala Street Church which Thoburn had built. "There is no spot on earth", said Warne, "where I feel more at home than in the pulpit of that dear old church."[5] By 1892 he had received 210 persons as probationers of whom 131 had become full members. Probably as many more had been converted who were temporarily in the city. These were not won in special evangelistic meetings but in the regular services. "They have all been known and followed up."[6] He had wanted to become an evangelist when he left Garrett, "but instead of going then into evangelistic work I went to Calcutta . . . and now I am put into the work that will give me continuous opportunity for evangelistic work."[7]

As Bishop Thoburn's burdens grew heavier his associates realized that there should be at least two bishops. What wonder that Warne's name came to mind! As with Thoburn so a revealing of future responsibilities was vouchsafed to Warne. Early in 1887 he dropped in to a preachers' meeting in Chicago when Thoburn was to speak. "Whilst listening to the address a powerful conviction took possession of [him] that he should one day occupy the position in India held by the speaker of the hour."[8] In 1895 Warne wrote in his diary:

> I have been more or less excited during the past few days over a letter from . . . in which he nominates me for Bishop . . . . I also told my Chicago experience to Miss Maxey and asked her advice. She told me that Bishop Thoburn would prefer me to anyone in India as his colleague. This is to me most wonderful . . . . I have just read an article of N. L. Hastings on Principle and Policy. Principle—'Find out what is right and do it.' Policy—'Find out what is safe, proper, politic and do that.' I want at all costs, before and after, to act on principle. When a man has fixed in his heart that he will do right, he becomes strong. One such man with God is a quorum and a majority.[9]

Calcutta Boys' School

Warne had an interest in English Schools for he realized the intimate connection they had with the community to which his church ministered. Concerning the Calcutta Boys' School he wrote:

> The heaviest burden and the most difficult task that I have had in India, has been to keep the school afloat. Dr. McCoy made the saving of the school one of the last mighty efforts of his great life, and dying, said: 'The school must live,' and when the responsibility came upon me I took it as a sacred trust . . . . I had to collect Rs. 400 a month to keep the school open . . . . Public confidence began to grow, and the sinking ship began to ride the wave, and without one anna of missionary money we came to the end of 1891 with every pice of debt and current expense paid.[10]

Soon after that Robert Laidlaw, a business man who had joined the Church under Thoburn, a leader of a Fellowship Band, and a member of the Official Board many years, bought a site for Rs. 100,000 and gave to the Pastor a note for Rs. 73,000 more toward the cost of a new building for the school. On January 14, 1893 Warne signed the contract for its construction.[11]

Queen's Hill School

In the hot season of 1875 Thoburn went to Darjeeling. There he found a building called the Union Church, intended for members of the Free Churches, which had been empty for years. Thoburn had it renovated, announced meetings and a fairly good congregation greeted him on the first Sunday afternoon. After a couple of years he discontinued all connection with the Union Church.[12]

In the nineties attention veered again to Darjeeling, this time in favour of opening a school there for non-conformist children. Miss Knowles, who had started Wellesley in Naini Tal, opened the new school in March, 1895 with thirteen pupils, "in a long, low building" called Arcadia, by which name the school also was called. In 1899 the enrolment had trebled when Miss Stahl was officiating for Miss Knowles. On a late September evening, following a deluge from continuous rain, "the ledge in front of the school became a river of water". The children were evacuated to a home higher up. Some little ones had already fallen asleep in this new refuge when a great boulder hit the corner of the room, destroying two walls. Two children just moved to "safety" were killed, all others being unhurt.

On the same night in a cottage not far from Arcadia, six children of Mr. and Mrs. Lee were living in the care of their oldest sister and trusted servants. They attended Arcadia as day-scholars. The next morning revealed "not a vestige of the cottage or of anything it held". A hand extended above the mud located the body of Lois, the second daughter. Lower down the hill a slight movement of earth led to the finding of Wilbur. He lived "a few brief days" to tell the stricken parents when they arrived from Calcutta, how they "had tried to escape to safety; how they had failed; how at last they had given themselves into the Father's care, and . . . unafraid sat waiting until the blow came".[13]

Following this disaster "Arcadia" closed, and opened again on March 1, 1900 on a site known as Queen's Hill, and under that name has continued.

Bengali Work

From a sprinkling of Indians in the English congregations there emerged a small congregation of Bengali Christians.[14] P. M. Mukerji was appointed to their care at Raj Mahal in 1876 and at Howrah in 1877. Thoburn held special meetings for them.

> The Bengali services closed last night. I preached as usual in the English Church, and then repaired to the old chapel where I addressed the people and administered the Lord's Supper. A large congregation was present. At the close 41 persons testified to having received the pardon of their sins during the meetings. I appointed

four of the villagers to act as leaders in their villages, and Prabhu Din has gone today to start the work for them. On the whole I feel exceedingly encouraged.[15]

The Bengali Circuit is first named in the appointments of 1880, and in 1882, an Indian, Prosunno Koomar Nath, was in charge. In 1883 the circuit was under J. P. Meik, "born, educated and converted in Calcutta",[14] whose name recurs frequently in connection with Bengali work. There were then thirty-three members, fifty-three probationers, one Local Preacher, two Exhorters, three class leaders and much inquiry.[16] From 1888 to 1893 S. N. Das was in charge of the circuit.

Work began in Bolpur in 1892 and in four years there were thirteen members, fourteen probationers, fourteen baptized children, ten primary schools, seven for boys with 236 enrolled, and three for girls with sixty pupils.[17]

A night Bible Training School was opened for Bengali workers under Meik in 1884. First enrolled were: Lakhon C. Sarcar, C. Das, Sana C. Sircar, Surju M. Mondol, K. C. Mullick and S. C. Baswas. In 1892 a "Brotherhood" of four young men was organized under B. J. Chew which more definitely committed the Conference to vernacular work than before.

The Bengali community had grown to 247 in 1888, and the circuit included Dharamtala, Diamond Harbour, Kulpi, Buddipore and Jhanjra. It was divided into three circuits in 1894: Bengali Church, South Village and Beg Bagan. B. M. Mozumdar was in charge of Beg Bagan in 1899—1902, and at South Village from 1902 to 1906.[18]

The Lee Memorial

David Lee and Ada Jones were both graduates of Scio College, Ohio. Their years had overlapped, and they had met as friends. Lee had no interest in India until after graduation when he heard William Taylor and accepted his call. In her first year in college Ada had a religious experience which somehow linked her with India. Much later, Thoburn visited Scio and there heard of Ada Jones' interest and sent her name to the W. U. M. S. whose Secretary called her for an interview. She went to Calcutta for zenana work at the end of 1876. The next October she went with the Thoburns to the Dasehra meetings in Lucknow. There she again met D. H. Lee, who had come to the meetings from Roorkee. Renewed friendship was followed by engagement.

From Calcutta Miss Jones was sent to Allahabad for work among Bengali women. In the course of her duties she rescued a girl from a den of vice. The irate Eurasian proprietor threatened her life. On hearing of her plight Thoburn arranged for her to be escorted to Calcutta and from there she was sent in June, 1881 to Madras where she was married to Lee, then pastor of the Memorial Church in Bangalore.[19] In 1883 his illness took them to America where he joined the East Ohio Conference. In 1894 they returned to India, independent of any Society but Methodists still. Friends for the support of a work had been raised up. In 1895 they organized the Dennett Training School in Calcutta, a Girls' Middle Vernacular (Bengali)[20] school, under Mrs. Lee. Fifteen girls were under training to be workers, and Mrs. Lee was confident of owning property for a fully equipped training school in Calcutta.[21] The next year there were fifty bright Bengali girls in the Training School and fourteen definite conversions.

News of the Darjeeling Disaster was widely read. The courage and faith of the bereaved parents drew attention to their work and won friends for its maintenance. "The work grew; famine orphans filled their home; missionaries came out to assist them; in 1906 a mighty revival changed things."[22] After twelve years of continuous service the Lees went on furlough, but in 1907 they were back. The buildings near Wellington Square were erected in 1908, "In Answer to Prayer—Psalm 27 : 1". Regarding the name of the school Mr. Lee explained that the institution

> was not built up 'in memory of our children' . . . [in the beginning] it was always known and called the 'Bengali Mission'. All our letter-heads and calendars were in that name until recently. When we built our new plant we began to be called the 'Lee Memorial'. As the name 'Bengali Mission' in Calcutta might cause confusion, we did, as the early Methodists, take the name by which the people called us, and so about four years ago I had it put on the house and it has become our designation but not with the slightest thought of making a memorial to ourselves.[23]

Asansol

When Mr. Kendall, a Wesleyan Missionary at Raniganj, left India in 1881 he informed Thoburn that a railway community in Asansol to which he had occasionally ministered, should have care. Ever alert to such opportunities Thoburn arranged for services in the Railway Institute by laymen of his Church—Robert Laidlaw, C. J. A. Pritchard, Benjamin Aitken, W. T. Thurlow and others. In March, 1883 Thoburn, with G. I. Stone and his wife and Miss Battie held a series of meetings. W. A. Thomas, the son of an indigo planter at Giridh, who had been converted in Calcutta, joined them at Asansol. A large notice of the meetings was posted. The Loco Foreman, who was prominent in the community read the notice and tore it down and passed on. Troubled in mind at what he had done he returned, and replaced it. Then he felt that he should attend, and did, with his wife.

Conversions included the foreman. One, Andrew Cooper, continued a member for thirty years. They asked that a church be organized; twenty joined. The first Quarterly Conference was held March 15, 1883. Thomas acted as pastor, and at the next Annual Conference the appointments read, "Chord Line Circuit—W. A. Thomas". He was ready for a larger field!

A chapel fund was started at once. Thomas' father drew the plans and contributed Rs. 1,000. Thoburn wished for a site adequate "for a mission house and such other buildings as might be needed in connection with a permanent Mission". Efforts to get it were repeatedly thwarted. Finally Thoburn approached the Governor directly for a site on the Grand Trunk Road. It was granted and orders given to properly mark it. Material for building had been quietly gathered and construction started promptly.[24] The work prospered. Two years later when Thomas moved to Monghyr, W. P. Byers assumed responsibility for the circuit in addition to his work at the Seaman's Lal Bazar rooms and at the Methodist Press. Three years later he was transferred to Asansol. His first Indian convert was his language teacher, Harbhajan Lal Williams.

The Indian Church at Asansol was organized with seven members in February, 1889.[25] The first Indian preacher-in-charge was Keshub C. Mullick, in 1900. The next year there were three day schools for boys and one for girls. A boarding school for boys was opened in 1895. Mr. and Mrs. Kullman were sent in charge. They both died of cholera within the year.

A girls' boarding had been opened in 1892 in the home of Sophy Simons, the wife of a Bengali clerk. The first girls were two untainted children of lepers, a little girl sent from the railway hospital and the fourth, an orphan received from her dying father. She became a Bible reader, Mrs. Alice Samson. Miss Forster, a sister of Mrs. Byers, came with them after their furlough in 1899, and helped in the supervision of the school and other Woman's Work, as did some from the English Church, Asansol, and the Calcutta Girls' School. Miss Eugenia Norberg, the first Missionary of the W. F. M. S. for evangelistic work in Bengal, arrived in 1908; and Miss Rachel Carr in 1909, for educational work.

In 1891 Byers started a Sunday School among a group of lepers. This developed into a leper asylum which was at first supported by the English congregation and later by the Edinburgh Mission to Lepers.[26]

The vernacular work in Asansol was mostly in Bengali but some work was done in Hindustani. The Asansol District was formed from the Northern part of the Calcutta District in 1896 with J. E. Robinson, the Editor of *The Indian Witness*, as Presiding Elder.

Pakaur

In 1884 an earnest Christian, E. McLeod Smith, was Sub-Divisional Officer at Pakaur. It was his custom to gather his servants together for a religious service on Sunday. Others were welcome to attend. A Muslim clerk, Shahoo Munshi, who resided in village Sangrampur, was a regular attendant. In time he asked for baptism and Thoburn sent Thomas to administer the rite. He was a real convert and quickly brought others to Christ.[27]

For two years Meik supervised this growing group from Calcutta. S. N. Das and other workers made longer visits, and sold and distributed literature. A little school was opened, eight persons were baptized, and a small house with two rooms was built for a teacher in Sangrampur. In 1886 E. S. Busby was appointed to Pakaur; he lived in one of the teacher's rooms until other quarters were completed. Nineteen persons were baptized in this year, all Muslims. One of these was a bright young man of a good family who was persecuted by his relatives. His wife at first left him, but came later to be a Christian with him. At the end of the year two small boys' and one girls' school with daily attendance of forty were meeting regularly.

The movement at Sangrampur was significant not only in opening a new station, but because it was the largest group movement among Muslims that our history records. It continued for some years, but when the young people grew to the age of marriage there seemed to be no community from which they could make a suitable arrangement. Many of them accepted the condition for a partner which was that the whole family should revert.

When in 1888 the headquarters of the Government at Pakaur were changed, the Conference purchased the whole site, twenty-one acres with old buildings. The Bengali boys' and girls' orphanages were moved from Calcutta to this new location. In 1891 there had been gathered a community of 130, most of them from among Muslims.

Twelve miles to the west were the Santal hills, the home of an aboriginal tribe that had been driven back by the invading Aryans, the Santalis, people skilled in the use of the bow and arrow. The buildings purchased in 1888 had seemed substantial, but they were badly broken by an earthquake in 1897. J. E. Robinson wrote:

> The mission house was severely shaken by earthquake . . . (nothing available for repair) . . . . The roof of the old jail . . . was completely dislocated by the earthquake and must come down. The girls moved to the boys' dormitory and the boys to another building altogether unsuitable to them.[28]

In 1898 Miss Alma Jacobson, the first W. F. M. S. missionary to Pakaur was associated with Mrs. Meik in charge of Woman's Work. During her furlough, Miss Jacobson, who was a Swedish Methodist, visited the churches of the Swedish Conferences in the U. S. A., organized auxiliaries of the W. F. M. S. and aroused a missionary interest among the churches for the work around Pakaur. The coming to India of Misses Hilda Swan, Pauline Grandstrand and Eugenia Norberg, and also the Henry Swans, was a direct result of Miss Jacobson's visit.[29]

Hindustani Work

In 1885 a Hindustani Mission or circuit was opened in Calcutta under F. J. Blewitt. He had left the Telugu Mission to join the S. I. Conference in 1884. Calcutta was primarily a Bengali city, but Hindustani speaking people were found wherever Muslims had ruled and commerce had gone. Many thousands were in Calcutta. Benjamin Luther and J. H. Messmore followed Blewitt, and then Charles Dowring was transferred from North India and stayed until 1902.[30] The Mary C. Nind Boarding School was opened in 1897 with Misses Soderstrom and Campbell in charge. It was hoped that this would do for the Hindustani Church what the Dennett Training School sought to do for Bengali girls, seeking to provide for children where both parents were employed.

Tirhut

Bishop Hurst in 1885 came to have an eager desire to see a Mission in the Tirhut District, Bihar, a large state between the Bengal and N. I. Conferences. Gossner's Evangelical Mission had opened work in Muzaffarpur in 1840,[31] but at this time their work was remote from this growing city. Encouraged by Bishop Hurst Dr. Day of Syracuse University took an interest in sending out Rev. and Mrs. Henry Jackson, formerly in North India.[32] They were appointed to Muzaffarpur in 1888, and pioneered in this new field by preaching to English congregations in the city and in Samastipur; and by bazaar preaching and touring. Mrs. Jackson, although not a physician, opened a dispensary and with the help of an Indian assistant, was able to treat an average of more than fifty persons a day.

Jackson was P. E. from 1888-1902 when W. P. Byers took charge. He was followed by J. O. Denning in 1903. Vernacular work was chiefly in Hindi or Hindustani and the great need was for co-workers who knew those languages. Charles Dowring came from Calcutta, and was a great help. Baptisms during this period were few, but an attitude of friendliness had been won, even in some places like Bittiah, where there was at first strong opposition. In Chapra a small girls' school had been opened.

Owing to the illness of their sons the Dennings had to go to America in 1904. In their absence Mr. and Mrs. W. D. Beal (daughter of the J. E. Robinsons), had charge of this developing work.[33]

The Bombay Conference

The fourth Conference to be organized was the Bombay Conference, to include "the Bombay Presidency, the Central Provinces, Berars, that portion of the Nizam's Dominions north of the Godavary River and all of Central India south of the 25th parallel of latitude". The S. I. Conference met in Bombay, on December 22, 1892, at the call of Bishop Thoburn. After the devotional service and a brief address, the Bishop read the following statement:

> We are met here today to give effect to this action of the General Conference by formally organizing the new body. I therefore recognize the following persons as members and probationers of the Bombay Annual Conference:
>
> *Members: Elders;* Thomas S. Johnson, Daniel O. Fox, William E. Robbins, Clark P. Hard, John E. Robinson, George I. Stone, William Bruere, William H. Stephens, *Gyanoba Khnundaji,*[a] Algernon S. E. Vardon, Thomas E. F. Morton, Arthur W. Prautch, Clayton E. Delamater, Edwin F. Frease, George F. Hopkins, Fawcett E. N. Shaw, John O. Denning, *John W. McGregor,*[a] *Paul Singh,*[a] Archibald G. Gilruth. *Deacons: Gungadhar Bhasker Kale,*[b] Charles G. Elsam. *Probationer:* William H. Grenon.
>
> I also announce the transfer to this body of Horace E. Grace, an effective Elder, from the North Nebraska Conference, and William E. L. Clarke, an effective Elder, from the South India Conference.
>
> Invoking the present and abiding blessing of God upon this new body, I now declare the said Conference to be legally constituted, and ready to proceed to the election of officers and the transaction of business.[34]

Ladies of the W. F. M. S. in the Conference were: Misses Izillah Ernsberger, M. D., and Anna Thompson in Baroda; Misses Sara De Line, Mary E. Carroll and Christine Lawson in Bombay; and Miss Minnie F. Abrams on furlough. With these in the Woman's Conference were the wives of sixteen missionaries.

The Bombay Conference held its sessions in the forenoons and the S. I. Conference met in the afternoons in the Grant Road Church. The work was organized into three Districts; Bombay, Central Provinces and Sindh under Presiding Elders J. E. Robinson, T. S. Johnson and G. I. Stone, respectively.

Some early reports provide glimpses of laymen, who were then young but faithful in a very little, who rose in a few years to positions of leadership in the Conference, as for example:

> The persistent devotion and enthusiasm of one of our earnest laymen, E. W. Fritchley . . . to whom more than to anyone is due under God the newly awakened interest and hopeful aspect now apparent at Mazagon . . . .
>
> With Brother Frederick Wood, late of the Salvation Army, as local preacher, the Sabbath congregation has increased and the finances have improved.
>
> Warm praise should be given to . . . C. B. Hill, second master of the Taylor High School, who has had pastoral care for the past two years spending from Saturday evening till Monday morning with his flock at Lanowli.[35]

Quetta (Sindh District)

A new outpost of the Mission was opened in 1891 at Quetta. The city was first visited by Gilder from Karachi in 1881. The next year, when a regiment which he had served as chaplain was transferred to Quetta, he went again but he was unable to provide a pastor. In 1890, W. G. Tinckom, a clerk in a Government office in Quetta who was visiting in Karachi, was converted under Stone. On his return to Quetta he started a movement for a Methodist Church in the station. Bishop Thoburn requested Stone to organize it. The first meeting was on June 30, 1891 at J. J. Cumming's home. J. N. C. Cumming, a brother, moved the proposal to organize and W. H. Daniels, a located Elder of the Methodist Church, became pastor. The foundation stone was laid by him and James Shaw, Chaplain of the Church of Scotland, on August 19, 1891. In a few months Daniels left Quetta, J. J. Cummings died; some others removed. Tinckom and William Canall, Local Preachers, supplied until 1893 when Stone succeeded as Pastor and P. E. for two years. Following him Shaw conducted the services in addition to his other work.[36]

Gujarat

Two of Taylor's converts in Bombay, Lynn and Wilcox, were officers in the Army of the Gaekwar of Baroda. An engineer, Mr. Garmet, was also an active Christian. The three had meetings in their bungalows and in 1872 invited William Taylor to visit them. He went, and the little church was strengthened by the meetings held. "Baroda was occupied in 1875."[37] In 1880 the congregation built a small place of worship on the site of the present Methodist Church in Baroda.[38] The South India appointments for that year include: "Baroda and Ahmedabad—to be supplied"; and in 1882 A. H. Baker was appointed to "Ahmedabad and Baroda". Then followed more years when the church was supplied. The Annual Conference Journal showed Captain Edwin Lynn as a Local Preacher in Baroda for many years and doubtless he mantained services.[39]

While English work continued in Baroda a Gujarati community was developing in Bombay. Gujarati villagers had been attracted to the city by the good wages offered for scavenger work. Their families remained in their village homes. From time to time the men returned for a visit and then went back to the city. Among this lowly group Arthur Prautch began work in 1887.

The story of this missionary, only eighteen when he reached India, is interesting. Brought up in the home of German immigrants in Wisconsin, in 1882 at the age of sixteen, he found employment in a railway freight office in Chicago. Strolling on the city's streets on a Sunday evening he was invited by two young men to attend Moody's church. The singing and speaking appealed to him; he stayed for the after meeting and accepted Jesus as his Saviour. Moody took an interest in his spiritual progress. He joined a Bible class and later the Yoke Fellows Band, which met Sunday evenings and then paired off, two and two, to take printed announcements of the service on assigned routes. He was on such a route in 1884 when he met a well dressed gentleman of whom he asked:

> 'Are you a delegate?' He looked surprised and said, 'Yes.' I told my companion to finish the route alone as I was going to accompany this stranger to Chicago to our Church; that he was a delegate to the Republican Convention. I was interrupted by the 'delegate' who told me he was Rev. Dennis Osborne of the South India Conference, and a delegate, to be sure, but to the Methodist Episcopal General Conference . . . we both laughed at the error I had made. I walked with him to his appointment at the Grace M. E. Church. I told him that I thought he was a political delegate and concluded that as such he needed religion.[40]

Osborne arranged with the Mission Board to send Prautch out as a missionary apprentice. He sailed August 31, 1884. His first work was in the Seaman's Mission in Calcutta, then that in Bombay. He saw a little of the Mass Movement in the North, and joined the S. I. Conference in 1886.[41]

> By the year 1888 he had so ingratiated himself among the Gujarati sweepers . . . that he began to call in the missionaries who were ordained to baptize them in considerable numbers. Thus during his stay there a community of nearly 500 of these people had been added to the Church and were under pastoral care and supervision.[42]

> This work began with two men, one a foreman of sweepers and the other a contractor on a small scale. He was a priest in a heathen temple. About ten years ago some of his relatives were baptized; since then he has opposed the Christian religion until one of my teachers met him and presented the claims of Jesus, so that the two were converted. Then I was invited to come and see them; we held a meeting and these two stood up and gave their reasons for leaving their religion and told why Jesus is worthy of their faith and love. After they both finished I invited all others who felt thus to stand up. Two more stood up.[43] [Prautch]

The contractor and priest was Kershan Ranchhod;[44] his "contract" was to supply scavengers for the Bombay Municipality. Ranchhod was a man of influence, widely known and a money lender. On his recurring visits to his home in Kasar village he won his own family and others by his Christian witness. Vernacular work was opened in Baroda when C. E. Delamater went there in 1888. He soon opened a little school, but fell ill during the year and removed to the "Gujarati Mission" in Bombay. The next year E. F. Frease was appointed to Baroda. Miss Ernsberger and, a few months later, Miss Anna Thompson (Mrs. W. H. Stephens) opened the first work of the W. F. M. S. in Gujarat. Members of the English Church had led their servants to be Christians also. Gangu Dhanji, son of Motibai and Dhanjibhai Lalji, who were servants of Garmet, began work with Miss Thomson. He also went to the villages with Frease, for he could play the violin and sing.[45] J. E. Robinson describes these early days:

> A solitary missionary in Gujarat, with his English and vernacular courses of study on hand, besides the immediate care of an English congregation and boarding school and responsibility for indispensable translation work etc., can hardly be supposed to have much time for systematic village work . . . . Very urgent is the need of provison for a simple inexpensive training of converts for village work, and for the suitable education on similar lines of our Christian boys and girls . . . . This is the work of supreme importance.[46]

The Mission purchased a desirable property in Baroda in 1894 for Rs. 10,000.[47] In 1892 some of the workers attended the District Conference in Bombay. Two men, Elia Narottam and Shiva Tora, were given Exhorter's licenses. For joy, their missionary not only garlanded them, but "took them for a ride in a four horse carriage".[45] The first District Conference in Baroda was held in 1893, and proved a great inspiration to the workers.[48]

Frease was ever awake to the need of educating and training the growing Christian community. The little boarding school left by Delamater was never closed.[49] In 1896 there were sixty-five boys in it; thereafter it was filled to capacity, for older boys were admitted to get what they could in two years as preparation for teaching in village schools. This school, an Evangelistic Training School for men and women in separate departments opened in 1895, and the District Conference, were all made to contribute to the development of an incipient Mass Movement. Success is shown by the statement of the P. E. that whereas the majority of workers in 1896 were unable to attempt the Exhorter's Course of Study, in 1899 there were sixty-eight licensed men to thirty-eight unlicensed, and all thirty-eight were "much further advanced than any unlicensed men were in 1896". The first Local Preacher, Anandrao Shastri, was given a license in 1894. Two years later four others received theirs: Gangu Dhanji, Natha Punja,

Lakshman Dana, and Yusuf Dhanji. The last two named were in 1899 the first in the District to be admitted to the Annual Conference. In 1901 Gangu Dhanji and Henry Narottam were also admitted.[50]

Men had gone to Bombay from many villages in Gujarat. As the work of the Gujarati Mission in the city grew, the Word was literally "scattered abroad" by villagers returning for vacations at home. The Irish Presbyterian Mission and the Salvation Army had had work in some parts of this territory, but they were unable to follow up these openings. It became necessary for the Methodists to do so carefully. In 1894 a preacher was stationed at Kasar, and G. W. Park opened work north of the Mahi River. In 1895 a movement began among the Dhed caste in Kasar and Od. Before Conference, J. E. Robinson and Bishop Thoburn attended a one day *mela* at Bhalej. Over 400 Christians were present and others numbered 300 more. The Bishop baptized forty-two that day and administered the Sacrament to over 200, of whom many had never communed.[51] It was, as Robinson reported, "a glorious opportunity, but a tremendous responsibility".

A second Christian mela, was held on December 1, 1897, when Bishop Foss and Dr. Goucher were visitors and over 1,500 were present. One delegation walked a round trip of over thirty-six miles; hundreds over twenty miles: "Nothing was given free to anybody . . . and none complained."[52] The work in Gujarat was organized as a District in 1896, with four circuits; Ahmedabad, Baroda, Bombay Gujarati Mission, and Godhra. Five years later the four circuits had become nine: Ahmedabad, Baroda, Godhra, Kapadvanj, Nadiad, Od, Umreth, Vaso and Wasad. To quote Robinson, "on a field where we had but a handful of converts all told" there were at the close of the century, 4,667 Christians with 132 Christian workers.[53]

Work of the W. F. M. S.

Miss Sundarbai Powar went to Poona in 1892 to work with Pandita Ramabai. She offered to visit the mothers of girls in the Marathi school and continued that work for several years. Pandita Ramabai's daughter, Manoramabai, regularly helped in Sunday School work and in a sweeper school.

Two institutions in Poona helped to build the Church in Western India: The Anglo-India Girls' Home which was long under the care of Mrs. Hutchings, who put into it her substance and her life, and the Taylor High School which was a recognized English school for boys and girls. In 1895 an Anglo-Indian Boys' Orphanage was established and united with the Girls' Home. Its older pupils attended classes in the Taylor High School. The W. F. M. S. accepted responsibility for the girls' department of the high school in 1895.[54] The next year Misses Benthien and Fisher arrived in Poona. In June, 1897 the Taylor High School for Girls became a separate institution under Miss Benthien and moved into its new home in 1900. A graduate from the Lucknow Woman's College, Miss Elliott, became headmistress in 1899. A Teachers' Training Department was opened in 1901.[55]

Miss Thompson reached Baroda in 1890 and opened a little "Orphan" school to which both Christian and non-Christian children were admitted. She also took an active part in village work and encouraged the larger girls to share in it. She rented a building in the city for the school in 1894. Two years later Miss Spears assumed charge of the school which grew rapidly, many coming from the homes of village Christians. In 1896 three girls passed the sixth class and started as assistants in school or medical work.

Marathi Work

The Marathi Mission in Bombay opened the first vernacular work in the city. The community with which the Mission dealt was largely drawn from distant villages. The people were employed on railways, in mills and in domestic services. Besides his pastoral work the pastor shared in street preaching and edited the Marathi weekly paper, *Surya Prakash.*[56]

In 1896 the Marathi church had a membership of about one hundred. They supported both their pastor and a Bible woman. There was a Marathi Boys' Boarding School with about forty boys, and a Girls' Boarding School. There was steady growth and a widening service.

The Poona-Marathi circuit included that city and work in the valley toward Lanowli and a Marathi Christian Boys' Boarding School in Poona. The report for 1897 describes it:

> The care and education of a hundred Christian boys in Poona, and of the same number of girls in Telegaon; the management of a number of Mission schools culminating, for the present, in a middle grade school for boys; the pastoral care of 250 Christian widows supported by Pandita Ramabai, as also of our own Native Church in Poona, and important evangelistic circuits on the lines of the railway radiating from Poona . . . . The baptism of more than 200 grown converts on confession of faith . . . was an inspiring sight and the earnest of similar and increasing trophies elsewhere.[57]

A significant contribution from the English church to the Marathi work was the opening of a dispensary by Dr. Mrs. H. Stephens in 1895. She rendered this service for several years.

Troublous Times

Bishop Thoburn described the years 1898–1900 as "troublous times". There was first the bubonic plague which, starting in Bombay, spread rapidly to Poona and Karachi, then to numerous points inland, threatening all

India. While it yet raged, rains failed and famine spread, nowhere with greater intensity than in Gujarat and Rajputana. With the famine came cholera. People died in such numbers bodies were gathered in piles and burned. Panic stricken people fled their villages carrying the dread disease in all directions.

The missionaries co-operated with the Government relief agencies, but also established their own agency. Appealing to America for relief for all who were in distress, they agreed on main principles which would

> avoid that gratuitous relief which pauperizes and to provide, first work at a living wage for those who could not otherwise obtain it, and at the same time to supply food grains to be sold to them at a rate to correspond with the wage. By persistently doing this the Committee was able to use its funds over and over again.[58]

Plans included all—Christians and non-Christians. Weavers were given yarn and paid wages with which to buy from grain shops, at cost. The money was reinvested in more grain. Heavy cloth was used for shelters erected by the Public Works Department which purchased in all Rs. 65,000 worth of the blankets made by refugees. A Kaira District Committee purchased 12,000 heavy cotton blankets.

> Our Committee undertook to make up both blankets and shelter tents, thus employing a small army of tailors, who were suffering from the pinch of famine . . . these weaving operations provided regular support for 500 people . . . . Roads, wells and other earth works were taken in hand at other places giving work to many hundreds of people while the construction of orphanage buildings at Baroda, Nadiad, and Godhra gave steady employment to many hundreds more, not only in the work of actual construction but in the making of bricks and tiles needed.

When rains came cash and seed grain to the value of Rs. 75,000 were given to the distressed farmers, who were also able to continue work until their crops were ready.

With one accord the Church discontinued baptizing while the famine lasted. The normal work of providing services and teaching was badly disorganized, but it was continued wherever possible. Frease's report expresses profound gratitude to God that the losses had been unexpectedly small, and the Christian community was practically all accounted for. After the famine Fox and Robbins, old pioneers in the Conference, came to the District to help in reorganization. Some 300 had been prepared for baptism before the famine when the rite was indefinitely postponed. After full consultation and examination of the catechumens it was decided that they should no longer be kept waiting. By the end of the year a total of 6,291 were baptized. Most of these were in villages where other Christians lived. The proportion of women and girls was greater than before.

This brought more of balance into the community and made the work of the District more a work by families—a decided gain for strength and stability.

The Americo-India Relief Committee made special grants of Rs. 10,000 for industrial equipment in the Nadiad school, and Rs. 4,000 in Baroda. A large number of orphans were committed to the Mission for care and education. Most of them were illiterate and class work had to be organized anew, but their progress in schools rapidly became satisfactory.[59]

Central Provinces District

This great territory had never been organized as a unit. Divided between districts, and then between Conferences, it had lacked coherence and direction. It differed in every way from the Gujarat District; its area was more vast; its work was in two languages; its parts unrelated. With characteristic foresight Bishop Thoburn had persuaded T. S. Johnson, after twenty-nine years of service in North India, to go to Jabalpur in 1891, as P. E. of the Narbada District. The new district was formed after the Bombay Conference. Johnson's reports in his first two years show how precarious were the beginnings of Indian work:

> Our effort has been to try to conserve and establish rather than to greatly extend the work. In the West end of the District Christians stand firm .... In other parts of the district, some do not now acknowledge themselves Christians, others say that they cannot separate themselves from their castes while many others know but very little of Christian life. Under these circumstances the work of building up, though very difficult, is an imperative duty.[60]

> We grieve to hear that in some places the new converts are not sufficiently cared for after baptism . . . the converts need more instruction in doctrine . . . they ought to be better instructed. There is, however, an extenuating circumstance in this conference . . . the whole native church is new .... This throws greater responsibility on the laborers in the field.[61]

One year after its organization the C. P. District reported a total Christian community of 1089 of whom 105 adults and 83 children were baptized; 603 probationers and 298 full members. There were eighteen Local Preachers, including one Elder and two Deacons. Eight members of Conference were working in the District of whom only one, Paul Singh, was an Indian. The first missionary of the W. F. M. S., Anna Elicker, arrived in the fall of 1894. Out of the material in hand Johnson and his associates set about to train workers, the most urgent need. In 1892 Vardon selected five young men, recent converts, for training as pastor-teachers.[62] In 1893 two classes in Marathi were opened at Kamptee, one with three men, the other with four women.[63]

The Johnsons, not surprisingly in view of his North India experience, believed in schools. The Girls' Boarding School in Jabalpur was organized in 1893 by Mrs. Johnson with three girls.[64] The number soon increased to six. Two little orphans were brought in from a village where they were wandering without home or care. Christian families persuaded against the prejudice of the day, brought their children. The first teacher was a Bible woman who also mothered the little boarders in their tiny mud hut on the Mission compound. Mrs. Johnson directed the little school which met on their verandah, and also did some teaching. One of the girls became Mrs. B. R. Judah; a second, Dr. Magania Singh, and a third, a sister of A. Rahim, Mrs. Sakhawat Masih. After Miss Anna Elicker arrived in the fall of 1894 she took charge of the school which then had thirty-five girls.[65]

A very desirable property in the city, Pilikothi, was purchased in 1893 for the W. F. M. S. There were four acres of land with residence and out-houses.[66] Work on new dormitories was begun in 1896 with the permission of the Municipal Board and the foundation for the first building dug, when an order to stop work was received.[67] Correspondence was prolonged and negotiations for a new site had to be started. In December Hawa Bagh was purchased and in January the school was moved to its new home. It was a year of famine and the Orphanage received many waifs. Dormitories were built under Dr. Johnson's supervision and the new school building was completed in February, 1900.[68]

The need for trained teachers was felt immediately. In 1900 six pupil teachers and the matron were listed with the staff.[69] In 1902 five girls appeared in the Government examination for teachers certificates. The class was approved by the Educational Department.[70]

An orphanage and school was opened in Khandwa in 1885 when C. P. Hard was P. E.of the Central District and also pastor in Khandwa.[71] It was growing and prospering under the Webbs when they were reappointed there in 1886 "to take charge of this orphanage and school" in which his wife was an "invaluable help". There were then fourteen orphans. Some Anglo Indians had been received but in 1887 it was "intended for Indian girls only".[72] It was maintained by voluntary subscriptions. In 1892 it became a boarding school of the W. F. M. S. under Mrs. Vardon.[73] It continued under the wife of the pastor until 1900 when Miss Elicker (Mrs. Guse) assumed charge. Mrs. Vardon also had a training class for Bible Readers. Most of the women could not long stay away from their homes for they were married, but the aim was "to prepare them to be good workers".

Light And Shadow

Narsinghpur had been opened in 1878 by the Swedish Evangelical Lutheran Missionary Society. They had a school for boys, another for girls and some evangelistic work. Desirous of concentrating their efforts elsewhere they gave the field to the Methodists for a moderate payment on property. C. P. Hard was then in charge of the District. His first effort was to open a Training School for workers. He started with nineteen young men. Because support was received from Hardwicke College, Adelaide, Australia, the school was named the Hardwicke Christian School. Hard's efforts raised hopes for a mass movement, but its results were transitory. In 1893 a boarding school was opened by J. O. Denning as "little brother" to the Training School but it came to greater prominence in 1897 under Felt, when due to famine, the number of boys swelled to 200 and industries were added. In 1900 boys were in school six hours and at work two—about 100 boys were learning carpentry; an equal number shoe-making, and some twenty tailoring.[74] A church was erected in 1898. In 1901 Aldrich assumed responsibility for the school and Felt for medical work and evangelism.

In 1877 three ladies sent out from Boston by Dr. Cullis commenced work in Basim, Berar. One of these married W. A. Moore of the S. I. Conference and he went to them. In 1895 "at the request of the Dr. Cullis Mission Committee the Basim Mission was transferred to the Methodist Mission".[75] There was a small English congregation there.

If we received from others we sometimes gave, also. In 1896 Bhusawal, a "very important missionary field was made over to the Alliance Mission" because we could not supply it.[76] Again in 1899 steps were taken for the transfer of Harda to the Christian Mission.[77] The church in Mhow was sold to the Wesleyans for Rs. 3000 which was used in partial payment for the Narsinghpur property.[78]

In every station the missionary's wife had opened zenana work and started Bible women in it. In 1899 the first W. F. M. S. missionary for evangelistic work, Miss Louisa Heafer, was transferred from the N. I. Conference.

At the close of 1903, twelve years after the District was formed, the Christian community numbered 2,538 (1,089 in 1893) with thirty-six adult baptisms in the year and 128 registered candidates under instruction. The number of Local Preachers was twenty-seven; only five Indians were in the Annual Conference; Exhorters numbered twenty-two. The number of Board missionaries was six, and of W. F. M. S. missionaries four. The efforts put forth to train new workers was bearing some fruit.

Among converts of this period was Beemabai, of Kamptee, of whom Stephens wrote:

> I have always felt that [her] baptism . . . would have rewarded us for all the labour and expense of these years. She was a Brahmin devotee, who had spent many years in travelling from one shrine to another, looking for peace which never came, until the day when she met

the Prince of Peace. She adopted the children of her husband's second wife, and saw that they received a Christian education. The conversion of that woman started influences of lasting good.[79]

Johnson, the seer, wrote in his report in 1895; "The day may not be distant when the district will be divided into a number of districts and constitute an Annual Conference." There were already in effect two districts, for it had been necessary to hold the District Conference in two sections, owing both to distance and to language.

In July, 1898 Gilder suggested to Johnson and Denning that the Godavery District of the S. I. Conference and the C. P. District be merged into a Central India Mission Conference. They felt that it would be better to wait until such a merger could receive Annual Conference status. In 1902 the S. I. Finance Committee initiated a move to have the Godavery District become a Mission Conference. Then, in the C. P. District Conference, Felt moved that the C. P. District become a Mission Conference.[80] The Central Conference in 1904 duly memorialized the General Conference to organize both districts into a Mission Conference, to be called the C. P. Mission Conference, and also to grant an enabling act whereby the proposed Conference might be organized into an Annual Conference during the next quadrennium with the approval of the presiding Bishop.[81]

After a preliminary statement, Bishop Warne organized the central Provinces Mission Conference in Khandwa on January 27, 1905, with the following charter members: Transferred from the Bombay Conference; David A. Abbott, Samuel Benjamin, Zachariah Cornelius, Frank R. Felt, William H. Grenon, Thomas S. Johnson, William A. Moore, Paul Singh, William D. Waller. *Probationers;* Floyd C. Aldrich. Transferred from the S. I. Conference: George K. Gilder, C. F. H. Guse, Benjamin Luke, Monella Narsaya, Charles B. Ward. *Probationers:* Gathu Chandaya, William T. Ward. Transferred from the West Wisconsin Conference, Valentine G.McMurry; and from the Kansas Conference, Howard A.Musser.

Members of the Woman's Conference: Mrs. Abbott, Mrs. Aldrich, Mrs. Chandaya, Miss Elicker, Mrs. Cornelius, Mrs. Felt, Mrs. Gilder, Mrs. Grenon, Miss Harvey, Miss Heafer, Mrs. Holland, Miss Hyde, Miss Lossing, Mrs. Luke, Mrs. Moore, Mrs. Paul Singh, Mrs. Richards, Mrs. Waller, Mrs. Ward, Mrs. McMurry and Mrs. Musser.

In the same Conference the following were received On Trial: Itwari Walter, Dauli Das and Walter Ariel. The work was organized into four districts: Marathi, Godavery, Jabalpur and Raipur.[80]

The North-West India Conference (Delhi Conference)

This, the fifth Conference in India, was approved by the General Conference in 1892. It included "that part of the North-West Provinces which lies south and west of the Ganges, the Punjab, and such parts of Rajputana and Central India as lie north of the 25th parallel of latitude".[82] It was organized by Bishop Thoburn in Agra on January 18, 1893 after he had read the following statement:

> The General Conference made provision for the organization of a new Annual Conference . . . to be known as the North-West India Annual Conference. We are met here this morning to organize this new body, and I hereby recognize the following persons as members of it by the action of the General Conference:
>
> Robert Hoskins, Philo M. Buck, Jefferson E. Scott, Dennis Osborne, Mahbub Khan, Hasan Raza Khan, Charles W. DeSouza, Albert T. Leonard, Charles Luke, James Lyon, John D. Webb, Isa Das, Rockwell Clancy, Matthew Tindale, Frank J. Blewitt, Claudius H. Plomer, Edward S. Busby, John E. Newson, Edwin F. Farnon, and Chunni Lal; and the following persons as probationers:
>
> Daniel Buck, Yakub Cornelius, Joshi Sumer, Jhabbu S. Joseph, Edwin W. Gay, and Mohan Lal.
>
> I further recognize Henry Mansell, James C. Lawson, Chimman Lal and Tafazzul Haqq, (a probationer) by transfer from the North India Conference. The North-West India Conference is now therefore formally constituted, and prepared to proceed with its organization and the transaction of business. May the blessing of God descend upon its members, the Holy Spirit guide its deliberations and great prosperity attend its future progress.

Members of the Woman's Conference, other than wives of missionaries named above, were: Misses Clara Swain, M. D., Phoebe Rowe, S. McBurnie, Martha Sheldon, M. D., Ada J. Lauck and Mrs. G. F. Matthews.

The work thus organized included English Churches started by that prince of India's evangelists, Dennis Osborne; and mass movement work opened in hundreds of villages by preachers and villagers from Budaun, Moradabad and Amroha districts of the N. I. Conference for which the Ganges now again formed the western boundary.

Work was organized in seven districts with Presiding Elders as follows: *Agra*, J. E. Scott; *Ajmer*, C. W. DeSouza; *Allahabad*, D. Osborne; *Bulandshahr*, Charles Luke; *Kasganj*, Hasan Raza Khan; *Meerut*, P. M. Buck; *Mussoorie*, H. Mansell. Beside Conference members there were ninety-two Local Preachers. At the second Conference session, 1894, there were sixty circuits and a Christian community of 28,683; an increase in one year of 8,468. Two of the districts, Kasganj and Bulandshahr, were under Indian leaders and in these the Christian communities numbered 8,990 and 5,153 respectively.

Hasan Raza Khan was outstanding. Born in a respectable family in Rampur State, he hated Christians and had often taken Gospel portions and Bibles from colporteurs only to destroy them. His teacher, Mahbub

Khan, was converted in Budaun. One day in the seventies, in the Punjab, Khan heard a colporteur repeat John 3:16, and when the crowd rushed upon him he rescued him and took him to his home, where he asked him if the verse he had repeated was really true. The colporteur assured him that it was, yet for four years Khan would not yield. Then one morning in prayer, he was convicted of sin and "at last, against my inclinations I was obliged to admit the truth of Christianity". He resigned his post and went to his old teacher in the Budaun district where he also came under the influence of Hoskins, and was baptized in 1880. Four years later he was made pastor in Budaun. When Hoskins needed a man for Kasganj, Khan offered to go.[83] He found only fifteen converts in Marehra but by faithful work and his ability to organize he made the Kasganj District. He died in 1899. Thoburn described him as "a man tried and true . . . he was probably the most successful worker among Mohammedans who has yet appeared in the missionary ranks of India".[84]

Mass Movement

This Conference was pre-eminently a Mass Movement Conference. Such a movement usually included the members of a single social or caste unit, scattered in small groups village after village, through whole districts or provinces. Its strength was in the coherence that led members of the group to act together; its weakness in its scattered dispersion in hundreds or thousands of villages, only a few in each. When their true nature was understood such movements could be, and were, encouraged; new fields were opened up. In 1889 Parker and Thoburn selected "three man, gave them careful instruction as to procedure," then took them north, across the Ganges and further north, then left them where they thought they were complete strangers. They met men of their own caste, gave their witness, and after an agreed interval of time missionaries and men met at Muzaffarnagar. They were in high spirits; they had baptized fifteen in one place and twice that number in another. "The field was boundless and we had nothing to do but press forward."[85]

When Buck was appointed as P. E. of the new Meerut District, "Bishop Thoburn expressed the hope that he might have twenty years in this work. Curiously enough," wrote Mrs. Wilkie, his daughter, "it was an almost uninterrupted service of 21 years that he gave to this district."[86] The plans that he developed and proved so effectively became standard practice in Mass Movement fields. Each plan was shaped to meet the urgencies and pressures of mass movements by careful *evangelism*, *teaching* and *training*.

Evangelism was by witnessing—perhaps that of a preacher; more likely by one of the caste group who had heard a preacher, or perchance a relative come from afar who had brought "good news". The preachers gave most of their time to those who had become interested and called them, those who, therefore, seemed accessible.

> The work is growing and spreading, and the calls from new places are almost legion .... From another where fifty were wanting to be baptized a representative came to one of our ministers ... begging him to come to them .... With double our force we could scarcely answer the calls and care for the harvest before our eyes. There is a great movement in this district among the *chamars* towards Christianity .... Doors are opening in many directions.[86]

Why did they come? The motives were mixed. The common people who heard Christ gladly, did not know just why they listened. These group movements were among the "oppressed" or "depressed classes", among those who had been deprived of opportunities that others had. Somehow they felt that this new message carried hope, hope for them. They were not people lacking in capacity, either moral or mental.

> They are influenced by the hope that Christianity will improve their status. At first, some may have come with the hope of temporal help but in most places this hope has long since disappeared. For temporal assistance, under any ordinary conditions, is fatal to success in dealing with them. To support the Gospel in their humble way, is one condition of steadfastness. Just when spiritual motives begin to operate, is difficult to determine. The doctrine that all men are equal before God is certainly attractive to them. Many are influenced by the hope that their children will be taught and will enjoy improved conditions. But, they do discover that Jesus Christ is the only Saviour. They do prove that they are not anchored to their old religion. They freely permit the destruction of their symbols of idolatry. They gladly join in the Christian worship. If carefully taught, they soon respond to a living Gospel.... Some of these humble converts have borne bitter persecution, but few on this account, or when neglected, have lapsed from Christianity.[87]

Witness needed to be followed by *teaching*. What a lack of teachers there was! The enquirers were illiterate, or literature might have helped; they were labourers with little free time, and teaching by repetition, over and over to be remembered and understood, took time. Yet people were taught, but if ever labourers were lacking for a plenteous harvest, teachers were lacking for the mass movements. Usually the P. E. with his wife, made the round of Quarterly Conferences three or four times a year, holding them in centres where the largest numbers might gather, and giving two days to each Conference so as to have time for helping both enquirers and workers. Primary schools were opened wherever a teacher made it possible.

A major activity in every mass movement district was that of *training* workers. The Theological Seminary and the Boarding Schools provided the best leadership, but many more were needed and each district had to prepare its own. The most promising men from the village primary schools were gathered and taught, for two or three years, then sent out to teach. Where possible their wives were also trained. Such training schools were opened in many districts. Those who completed the course were not highly qualified, but they knew much more than the enquirers or converts whom they would teach. Such trainings were indispensable.

At a higher level, and most vital, was the monsoon school, or the Summer Bible School, held for a month or more in July or August, when the monsoon rains interrupted village work. All the workers, men and women, were brought together "for a month of solid work". In Meerut their number sometimes reached as many as 300. There the program included a devotional service each morning, followed by five hours of teaching by the preachers-in-charge. Afternoon lectures on Christian doctrines by the P. E. with other classes where workers preached, told Bible stories, or taught *bhajans*, filled the day. At the end of the month examinations were held. What wonder that a P. E. who followed such a program could see the "growth in knowledge, spirituality, and general efficiency" of his associates, and find it a "pleasant experience that workers were becoming true evangelists and gaining skill in leading souls in the spiritual life".[88]

In 1896 another forward step was taken in using voluntary village leaders, Chaudhries, with responsibility for the care of Christians in their villages. Selected by the Quarterly Conference, their duties were to get children to school, bring people to religious services; gather collections, etc. In Meerut, undergirding all efforts in evangelism, teaching and training, was the Prayer League of District Workers which Buck organized when he first went to Meerut. Members were pledged to pray daily; for fidelity to their calling; for the conversion and spiritual development of Christians; for advance toward self-support, and an opening to other castes. "Were we to start again we could not do without such a prayer league. If India is to be won it must be on our knees."[89]

Woman's Work

In 1894 missionaries of the W. F. M. S. were in only two stations of the Conference. The Woman's Conference asked for three more ladies to be sent out "in the present year". In the new Conference an old name returns in the list of appointments: "Miss Clara Swain, M. D.—Khetri", under the Meerut District. Among women recruited from English work are Mrs. Matthews, Miss M. Seymore and Mrs. Worthington, each of whom gave faithful service for many years in this and the N. I. Conference. English work in Allahabad was that year in charge of four ladies of the Friends Society.

Miss Phoebe Rowe was General Evangelist. Hers was a deeply spiritual nature. Her mother had died when she was not yet two years old; her father reared her tenderly. She "united in her character the gentleness and devotion of her Indian mother and the Scotch integrity of her father." Father and daughter were church members. One day a Baptist missionary passing their home in Allahabad, stopped to visit with her on her verandah; talked with her "of a new heart and life and conscious salvation . . . . Sitting there in the winter sunshine she received her Lord and became his disciple."

Three years later her father died. Dennis Osborne recommended her, young though she was, to Miss Thoburn, who invited her to join the staff. For ten years Lal Bagh was her happy home. "No teacher was ever more successful in molding character." There came a time when "self-sacrifice brought an inward shrinking and unwillingness". She set aside a Sabbath for prayer, locked the door of her room and expected to struggle, "but when I knelt beside my bed and looked up, I saw the face of my Heavenly Father, and the work was done". The joy of that experience never left her.

In 1882 she was recognized as a missionary of the W. F. M. S. When Miss Nickerson, in Pithoragarh, needed an associate, Phoebe Rowe was sent in the hope that her own health would benefit from the hill climate. It became necessary for Miss Nickerson to return to America in 1887, and Miss Rowe was asked to accompany her. She died *en route,* and Miss Rowe continued to America. At the anniversary of their Cincinnati Branch she was invited to speak of the life and death of Miss Nickerson who had been a missionary of the Board. At its close Miss Rowe asked if some one present would not offer to take her place in India. "This appeal was Miss L. W. Sullivan's call to the Mission field."

Phoebe Rowe's last itineracy in India was in the winter of 1897-98 when she thrilled with the victories in the Mass Movement. In Naini Tal the summer following she contracted diptheria and died. "I only wanted to live for the work; for those sheep in the wilderness; but God will raise up others to go to them."[90] Of her Thoburn said, "The most peerless saint I have ever known destined to live in our history as the Phoebe of our Indian Methodism, and to be known amongst us as the founder of our village evangelistic work".[91]

Work like Miss Rowe's revealed more clearly the backwardness of the women in the Christian communities, "more tenacious in their adherence to hurtful superstitions and unworthy customs, and . . . very much more ignorant of nearly everything which constitutes vital and spiritual Christianity". The Central Conference in 1896 urged the W. F. M. S. to send out to each Conference women who were spiritually fitted for evangelistic work.[92] Gradually the practice grew of having two ladies in a district, one in educational work, and the other supervising evangelistic work. Auxiliary Missionary Societies were urged, as far as possible, to apply their funds to this evangelistic work.

Institutions

When the Woman's Conference was organized it had the following institutions: (1) Kanpur Girls' High School. (2) Hindustani Girls' Boarding School, Kanpur. (3) Home for Medical Students at Agra. (4) The Mathura Training School. (5) Boys' and Girls' Boarding Schools, Ajmer. The Home in Agra was opened in 1888 and many girls held Dufferin scholarships. It was closed in 1907 when the girls were accommodated in dormitories at the College. A gift from W. E. Blackstone made possible the opening of the Mathura Training School in 1888. There were two departments, English and Hindustani for training European Assistants and Bible readers. In 1891 a small girls' boarding was opened with fifteen girls. Until the dormitories were completed they shared rooms with the Training School girls. Classes were held on the verandahs or out-of-doors until Gracie Hall was completed in 1892.[93] Miss M. E. Gregg, formerly of the Chicago Training School, was Principal when the Central Conference approved it as an All-India Institution with representatives from all Conferences on its Board of Trustees.[94] In 1901 it was given the name Blackstone Missionary Institute.

In 1893 three new Boarding Schools for girls were provided through gifts: The Howard Plested Memorial School in Meerut; The Avery Girls' School, Ajmer;[95] and the Louisa Soule Girls' Boarding School, Aligarh. The Bucks had gathered both boys and girls on the compound as soon as they arrived in Meerut and Mrs. Buck supervised both boardings. When the W. F. M. S. took charge of the girls in 1895 with Miss A. E. Lawson as Principal, there were sixty-eight girls in the hostel.[96] The boys' school continued under Mrs. Buck most of the time until 1905. Mrs. Lawson opened the school in Aligarh in 1893 in a rented house. The school building, made possible by the gifts of Mrs. Louisa Soule, was dedicated by Bishop Thoburn on January 15, 1896.[97] Miss L. D. Greene was the first missionary of the W. F. M. S. appointed there. After 1897, when twenty-four orphan waifs had been gathered in the Mathura hostel, they were exchanged for school girls from Aligarh, making the hostel there the orphanage for the district.[98]

Famine

The famine of 1876–78 was said to have affected an area of 225,000 square miles; that of 1899–1900, an area of 400,000 square miles. Plans for relief were as those described in the Gujarat District.

The *Christian Herald* reopened its columns for famine relief. Many connected with the Conference worked valiantly, but on those in the Ajmer District fell the heaviest responsibility. Miss Marks described the poignant conditions that led to orphanages:

> Heart rending cases have come under my own observation . . . . Families setting out to seek food, and being separated, too feeble to seek any child who might linger by the way . . . . The aged, the crippled, the blind die; of course . . . . Last night I found a boy about four years of age by the wayside. He looked so sad, and his little sunken cheeks and bright eyes told the now all too familiar story. 'Mera koi nahin hai', [I have not anyone] he wailed as he looked tearfully in my face.[99]

Gifts came from afar. From S. Africa a contribution of two pounds, of which fifteen shillings was contributed by the Kaffir servants of a Christian master who had "read to them of the famine and need." The students of our Anglo-Chinese College in Foochow sent a contribution through their President, Dr. Simester, father of Mrs. Garden of the Hyderabad Conference, "to be used among the Christians, and they be told that it represents the Christian love of their brothers in China". With their little gifts American children wrote: "I had it to buy candy with"; "I gave up my birthday party"; "Hazel sold her three chickens".[100]

In 1900, instead of two small schools, Rajputana had "nearly 800 famine waifs in the four orphanages at Ajmere and Phalera". Those in Phalera were also Industrial schools.[101] In Aligarh there were 375 in the Boys' Orphanage and Industrial School; 300 in the Girls' Orphanage and 330 in the Widow's Home.[102] Both Dennis and Rockwell Clancy lived in Allahabad. The former wrote:

> The Lord laid the care of deserted and orphan children upon our hearts, and we promised Him that we would not refuse to take any child who might be brought to us. We had no money for support of children but believing God . . . we received all who came . . . about 700 children.[103]

When Scott was searching for a store house for grain, he espied at an insignificant railway station, Tilaunia, an abandoned cotton-press, which he made a base for feeding hundreds. A few years later the site became the first Sanatorium for tuberculosis patients.[104]

Mathura

Work in Mathura was opened from the N. I. Conference by W. R. Clancy, when in charge of the Agra Mathura Circuit of the Rohilkhand district, in 1887, he sent two Indian brethren, William Plomer and Ummed Masih to the city. Their wives found entrance into several zenanas while the men preached in the city and as far as Hathras and Sikandra Rao. Plomer found an orphan lad in the city whom he took to his home for instruction. "This", wrote Clancy, "is the first fruit of the Mathura work."[105]

The next year Mathura became the centre of a circuit, under Scott. He at once took over two private schools "on favorable terms", and united them to form an A. V. Middle School, where Flora Hall was built in 1893. Other branch schools were opened, four for boys and three for girls. These were also Sunday Schools. Preaching was regularly done at *melas*, on the street, at the ghats, and in the city school and among the English soldiers.

A Sunday evening service in the city drew many. The organ playing by Mrs. Scott attracted people, and many Brahmins joined in the singing. The mission house was built in 1889, and the boarding for boys opened in 1890. Hindustani services were held in the military chapel which was also built in 1890.[106] The Agra District including Agra, Mathura, Aligarh and Etah districts, in large part, and territory around Ajmer, was formed the next year.

What was probably the first preaching by women to women at a *mela* in Vrindaban, took place in 1888. The Raja of Bharatpur had put his palace at the disposal of the missionaries for ten days. Mrs. Scott reported that the ladies had worked mornings and evenings for nine days among crowds of women. Behind the courtesy of the Maharaja were contacts and a testimony. Paul Singh, resident in Ajmer, had opened a school in Bharatpur state, and was soon appointed to reside there. He carried the Gospel within the city walls. When Hard visited the city they interviewed H. H. Maharaja Jaswant Singh. In a second interview Paul Singh continued the acquaintance, and in the conversation, was asked; "What are you doing here?" "I am preaching the Gospel of the Lord Jesus Christ," was Paul's reply. The Mahäraja's silence was his consent. The door was open; and friendly contacts continued.[107] During the year 140 homes had been opened for zenana work; four schools for girls were started, and the foundations of the Deaconess Home and Training School were laid. Its corner stone was laid in 1889 by Scott. After that service two widows who had been prepared by Mrs. Scott and Miss Sparkes, the first Superintendent of the home, were baptized. Her Assistant, Mrs. Matthews, came from Bijnor and brought the first three girls for the vernacular course. Work started before the building was ready. Three enrolled in the English, and eight in the Hindustani course.

Miss Kate McDowell M. D., opened a zenana dispensary in 1889 in Mathura, "Both office and waiting rooms were daily crowded with sick women."[108] A dispensary was opened in Vrindaban in 1897 by Miss Emma Scott, M. D. She was the first foreigner to live in the city and had only a native house in the heart of the town. She became a vegetarian out of deference to the religious scruples of the Brahmins. In 1898 a bungalow and dispensary were completed. Work expanded in town and district.[109] During the famine Dr. Scott threw herself into relief work until her own sickness took her to the hills.

The Punjab

This Province, in which Delhi was then included, was a large territory, but so pressing were the demands of the Mass Movement in the *doab*, the region between the Ganges and the Jumna, that work in the Punjab could not be pushed. From 1891 to 1902, Blewitt was the only missionary in the province, and that for a brief period in Delhi.[110] "Beginnings of work have been made across the Jumna in the Delhi and Gurgaon districts". In the middle of the year Blewitt, at his own request, was transferred to the S. I. Conference. Local Preachers continued the work. In 1893 there were in the Delhi circuit: 2 Local Preachers, 345 Probationers, and 30 members.[111] Fazl Haqq, a Conference member, was appointed to Delhi for 1894. He was the son of Zahur al Haqq by his Muslim wife. Taffazzul Haqq, a probationer in the Conference in 1893, was a son by his Christian wife. A third son, Mazhur al Haqq was a member of the N. I. Conference until his death in 1939.

In August, 1891 in Patiala, 120 were baptized.[112] Work in Multan was opened among the troops in 1888 by C. G. Conklin. He also travelled an extensive railway circuit, as a result of which many were converted. In 1893 J. F. Deatker was appointed to Lahore. English work continued to be encouraging. At the end of 1893 Hindustani work showed 485 Probationers and fifty members with three Local Preachers.

BISHOP WARNE IN BORNEO

In 1901, Warne received a letter from China:

> About 300 of our Kucheng Christians, together with 100 or more from Nirgchiang District, are just now leaving for Borneo to start a Christian colony in that part of the island which is under English rule. They are to be followed by other large companies of our Kucheng people next year. A number of our best families and workers are going, and we are sustaining a serious loss thereby. They can be easily self-supporting in any church work, for many of them have property, but they will need supervision. They should receive it from our Malaysia Mission.

Warne was in Singapore for the Malaysia Mission Conference in February, with steamer ticket for Manila, when it came to pass that one group of colonists arrived in the harbor. He found the junk Binghai. Its passengers were a discouraged lot; the seas had been rough; many wanted to return. Their leader Kong Nai Siong could not talk English, but a young man from Foochow knew a little. Sensing their discouragement, the Bishop said: "Tell them for me that if they will press forward to Borneo I will go with them." He cancelled his own sailing that he might go to Borneo to plan for their settlement and a self-support work.

> March 11. Tomorrow I go to Borneo .... It is to me most wonderful that I should be in such a work, in such a place; but God's ways are truly wonderful. 'My soul doth delight herself in God.' March 20. I have been up to Sibu .... I held a service on Sunday. Eleven adults wanted to become Christians. [Diary]

Warne asked "the several local preachers present" to explain to the inquirers the importance of the step they wanted to take. In the evening after the whole group assumed responsibility he baptized eleven men, one woman who joined them, and two children. Then followed a communion service and a love feast. "Almost naked Dyaks with their knives crowded the room and I had much sympathy with the poor Chinese." They wanted a missionary.

The next year Bishop Warne presided at the Malaysia Conference and told this story—James Hoover, one of the "twelve", was moved to volunteer, but did not, and Dr. West was appointed to Borneo. During that year Hoover read all he could find about Sarawak and Borneo; by the next Conference he was ready. For more than thirty years he and Mrs. Hoover laboured in Borneo. "Tuan" Hoover died there in 1935. So strong was their hold on the affections of the people that, flags, were flown at halfmast on the day of his funeral by Government order.

X

The Thoburn Period—Beyond India

If "great size" was deemed a weakness of the S. I. Conference, why hink "beyond India"? So thought the advocates of an intensive program vhose number was legion among nationals and missionaries. It was a ecurring conflict in approach. Was the intensive view "the measure of nan's mind"? In the three steps here narrated Thoburn was the leader. Vas he really an expansionist? Or was it true as one has said, that he ould hear "God's whisper"? Certain it is that Thoburn felt *led* to Burma, o Singapore and to the Philippines. In each case he pondered long before ie acted, and concurrent circumstances suggest that he "hit" the time when)ne unseen worked with him. The inspiration and thrill of the opening f each, and its development is a portion of the heritage of India Metho-lism and a part of its history.

Burma

Shortly after reaching Calcutta in 1874 Thoburn received an in-itation to visit Rangoon. In 1878 he definitely decided he would go and rote William Taylor to send a missionary for a church there. The Rock .iver Conference promised to pay outgoing expenses. Extracts from 'hoburn's Journal tell the story as it developed in 1879.

> *May* 5. A letter from Bro. Taylor received on Saturday informs me that a man and his wife were about to sail for Rangoon. This news was a little startling at first, but I feel more hopeful about it. We have no organization at Rangoon, and the man who had urged us to send a minister there is now at another place, and we have no place for even a single man. But God knows his own plans best, and He, no doubt, has a place for these workers.
>
> *May* 31. I hear that Bro. Carter is in Rangoon, and Bro. Goodwin [Thoburn's associate] and myself purpose leaving a week from today to hold a series of revival meetings in that place.
>
> *June 13, Friday, Rangoon.* The Yerburys, Mr. Boyd and Philip Bates met us at the wharf. Bro. Carter was too ill to come. We suffered sea-sickness all the way down and were glad of rest on Wednesday. We, however, managed to call on the Baptist missionaries, and in the

evening I attended the Baptist prayer meeting and gave a brief address. But few were present, and the outlook was not inviting. The Baptist missionaries receive us very cordially . . . .

Last night I opened our commission in the Baptist Chapel. The room holds 200 and was not full. God helped me, and the Word was with power.

June 16th We had good meetings on Friday and Saturday. Yesterday A. M. we had a fellowship meeting . . . . In the evening I preached in the Town Hall to a very large congregation. I do not suppose Rangoon ever saw as large an audience before . . . . God is working among the people.

June 18th, Wednesday. The congregation last night was larger than at any previous meeting . . . . Today . . . I preached through two interpreters, one rendering into Armenian and the other, in a lower tone, into Burmese. God is working in our midst . . . I need to stay 2 or 3 months.

June 21st, Saturday. Eighty persons have sought God, and many of these have been converted. On Thursday night 38 stood up to testify that they were saved . . . . Last night I dined at the Chief Commissioner's and received a promise . . . to aid us for getting a site for a church.

June 25th, Wednesday. The special meetings close tonight. I shall feel a measure of relief when the last service is over, for I feel very tired. We had a grand meeting at the Town Hall on Sunday night. The audience was very large, and 31 persons at the after meeting rose for prayers. I have seldom seen a meeting of greater spiritual power. We organized the church on Sunday. Twenty-nine members and probationers were received. Others have since joined, and many others will follow.

Rangoon became a station of the Calcutta District. Work prospered and conversions took place every week. By December there were nearly 120 members, and many others among soldiers and sailors were converted.[1] Government sanctioned the grant of a building site at Phayre and Fraser Streets and a Church to seat 300, and a parsonage were erected. In January, 1880 Carter was transferred to Bangalore and J. E. Robinson to Rangoon, on a salary of Rs. 100 per month. The Church was dedicated[2] on March 25. There was a debt of over Rs. 8,000 on both Church and parsonage, but the new pastor felt that

> it was of the greatest importance that we should get out of the very inconvenient, unsuitable, and expensive quarters in which the work was being carried on as soon as possible . . . . I have covenanted with the Lord to devote my time to the purely spiritual part of the work leaving to Him and His people the matter of wiping out the debt.[3]

Robinson laboured in Rangoon until 1886 when he was transferred to Simla. In the last year he was assisted by S. P. Long who succeeded him in the pastorate and district.

Institutions

Mrs. Carter had opened a flourishing day school which in September had an enrolment of twenty-six, and was much appreciated. Robinson agreed that its maintenance was necessary, but how it should be done was a problem. With Thoburn he walked the city "through cheerless, drizzling rain" to find a suitable plot for a large school building. Sources of help were few. In 1881 the W F. M. S. responded to an appeal and Miss E. H. Warner, from Berea, Ohio, was sent to establish the school. Robinson's efforts secured a building grant from the Government, and a fine large plot of ground donated by the Municipal authorities. With these and many private subscriptions, a school building was erected and the school opened in 1882.[4] The next year Miss Mary McKesson, also from Berea, joined Miss Warner. This institution grew and greatly strengthened the work of the church in Burma. It was the first in Burma to open a kindergarten, and in 1892 it "added a thoroughly organized gymnasium with American methods".[5]

An A. V. School for Burmese boys was opened in Rangoon in January, 1904 in the buildings formerly used by "The Rest". Soon after, the Burmese Girls' School was moved from the site of the English Girls' School to "Shattock Hall".[6]

The Seaman's Rest which was opened in 1882, was under an undenominational committee.[7] It soon developed to occupy two leased buildings, one for lodging, the other for refreshments, reading room, chapel, etc. The cost was met from subscriptions and a monthly grant of Rs. 90 from the city.[8]

> More hard work without adequate remuneration has been done by the superintendents and managers of this institution . . . than in any other institution I have ever known. It has secured these workers almost always from the membership of the English Church.[9]

An account of its religious work was given by Miss McKesson in 1885. She shared in it as recreation from school work.

> I have seen scores of sailors happily converted; in a few cases the captain and nearly all the crew have left our port at peace with God, blessedly saved. I remember now two cases of shipwreck in which I knew men that were lost who were prepared to meet their God [through] our little mission.
>
> There have been other sailors that have returned to us again and again who were living victorious Christian lives, and had brought their sheaves with them. On the steamer *Martaban* there are about a dozen Christians, members of the Rangoon M. E. Church, with an officially appointed class leader. They hold their class and prayer meetings regularly, and have had several conversions among the crew.[10]

Vernacular Work

True to the Taylor tradition and almost from the date of organizing the Church, volunteer workers engaged in vernacular preaching. Most of the English-speaking laymen had come from South India as had the majority of Indian immigrants who had set up business in the country. For this reason street preaching was done in Tamil and Telugu. This work continued for years with a few converts from the start. Two laymen, R.C. Cully and C. Small, who were in Government service, gave their time freely and regularly held Tamil and Telugu services on Sundays and also did much pastoral work. In 1887 there were twenty-eight members in the Native Circuit with two catechists employed for colportage work, and two Sunday Schools and a day school with twenty-five pupils.[11] Since many immigrants had come alone and returned to India in a relatively short time, the churches did not increase in numbers rapidly.

Some Burmese were baptized before 1887 when grant from the Board was received, but the demands of the English work were so heavy no missionary could be spared for Burmese work. On the occasion of a visit by Bishop Thoburn an Indian Christian told him of a Burmese neighbour on the Pegu river who wanted baptism. A party went out by boat to investigate the opening. It was genuine. The Bishop preached using a girl in the school as interpreter. "The whole village assembled in front of the house at which we stopped. Before leaving I baptized four adult Burmese, one Tamil and a Burmese child....The whole adventure showed how accessible the people are."[12] Two years later Smith went out to visit this village and others nearby. "It was a great joy to him to find converts still true to all they knew of the Gospel. One of them had a Bible and some tracts which he could read. The first considerable awakening among these people occurred later.[13]

Work in Pegu, the second station occupied, was made possible by the arrival of new missionaries, Mr. and Mrs. G. J. Schilling in 1893 and J. T. Robertson soon after. Pegu was near the plot of ground that had earlier been given for a colony of Burmese cultivators under Mission direction. That enterprise had failed because the land was poorly drained and fields were flooded. However, there had remained a feeling of friendliness toward those who had encouraged it so that converts were won in a second village colony established nearby but on higher ground.

From the beginning the Burma climate had proved to be hard on missionaries. Robertson's health failed and he had to go to the hills in India. A year later, in 1898, the Schillings returned to America. Julius Smith's service of over ten years was at that time unique, but his family had preceded him to the States.

A. T. Leonard was sent from India early in 1899 and the next year he baptized more than one hundred converts from Buddhism, of whom seventy-seven were adults. His circuit spread

> from Deiku to the North of Pegu, to Naungni, South of Rangoon where we have members, . . . from Twante where are some families of Potters . . . to the distant villages which border on the Sittang . . . over which he faithfully itinerates.[14]

A little school opened with six boys in Pegu grew steadily as a distinctly Christian institution without any grant from the Government. Buddhist parents sent their children and made no objections when they embraced the Christian faith. In 1901 there was a hope that the school might develop into the Bareilly of Burma Methodism. The need for trained workers was urgent.

Thandaung

As the school in Rangoon grew objections were made by parents who paid fees, to keeping orphans who paid nothing in the same institution. The call for a separate orphanage became insistent. It was organized in 1887 under Miss Stacey. Smith had been on the look out for a suitable location for an orphanage outside of the city, and also for a hill station where missionaries could escape the oppressive moist heat of the delta region. Thandaung, an abandoned military station, seemed to meet both needs and the Conference gave its approval in 1897.

> Temporary quarters had been prepared, in Burmese style: made of bamboo mats, and supported on bamboo poles with split bamboo used as tiles folded over each other for a roof. The floor was two feet from the ground, and consisted of split bamboos spread out flat and laid on bamboo poles. . . . The whole structure cost thirty dollars, and 35 people moved into it, Miss Perkins, the Principal of the Orphanage and the writer and his family included . . . . In this house we kept school, had our sleeping apartments, and did the cooking and baking for this large family. At first boys and girls were rebellious against assisting in household work.

But they became used to work. Boys cut wood, carried water, milked cows and cultivated vegetables, and planted over 8,000 coffee trees the first year, as one source of income. The girls

> learned to bake excellent bread, to cook and serve a variety of food in a cleanly and orderly manner, and to keep the entire house in good taste and comfort. . . . Our girls are self respecting young women, far beyond what they could have been if they had not received the advantages in character that come from self-help in ordinary daily tasks.[15]

It had been expected that permanent quarters would be ready before the rainy season, but the temporary quarters, somewhat strengthened, served throughout the monsoon. In September Bishop Thoburn telegraphed, "God has sent you a thousand dollars for a house." It was the gift of a lady from Scotland who was unacquainted with Methodists but interested in Missions. From the Thoburns she heard of several projects and chose this.

> The school has run four years without a servant, and is stronger than when it began. In this it is the only institution among Europeans in all Asia that is so managed. It is absolutely unique in this.[16]

Self-Support

Thirteen years after he had organized the church in Rangoon, Thoburn wrote: "In all the Methodist world no church of equal membership can be found which has undertaken and accomplished more than has been done by this little band of Christian believers."[17] An extract from a letter by Buck, Corresponding Secretary of the Bengal and N. W. India Conferences illuminates the Bishop's tribute with detail:

> Brother Long asks Rs. 2,000 to meet the indebtedness on the Orphanage property. Said property cost about Rs. 15,000. The local Church has paid about Rs. 13,000. Besides this they have supported 35 orphans at a cost of about Rs. 4,000 during the past twelve months; and it has met all the expenses of the local Church amounting to about Rs. 5,000. There are but about 135 members, and they are not rich by any means. . . . The Committee felt that if possible they ought to have it.[18]

Other askings by the same Correspondent, for help under the grant-in-aid system for vernacular work, evidence the sincere effort made on the field for this purpose.

Conference Organization

Starting as an appointment in the Calcutta District, Rangoon was made a District of the Bengal Conference in 1884 under J. E. Robinson. In 1885 Singapore was added as a station of this district, and the next year W. F. Oldham, still resident in Singapore, became Superintendent of the Burma District. When the Malaysia Mission was constituted Burma continued as a District in the Bengal Conference, which in 1892 became the Bengal-Burma Conference as a proper recognition of the "Burma" part.

In 1900 the Central Conference memorialized General Conference to grant an enabling act permitting the Burma District to be organized as a Mission Conference during the quadrennium. Bishop Warne constituted the Burma District into the Burma Mission Conference composed of the following members: Julius Smith, Albert Thomas Leonard and Charles Baglis Hill, on February 2, 1901 at Rangoon. The W. F. M. S. missionaries were: Misses F. A. Perkins, C. J. Illingworth, L. G. Rigby and S. S. Turrell.[19]

From 1912 to 1924 each General Conference approved an enabling act for the Burma Mission Conference to become an Annual Conference when the disciplinary conditions could be met but not until 1927 was the Burma Mission able to get the number of members necessary for the status of an Annual Conference. It was organized then by Bishop Warne.

That long wait of fifteen years was typical of the history of work in Burma—under-staffed and under-financed. A note recurs, as in the Minutes of 1913: "We have no more Burmese workers now than 10 years ago, and only one of the men and one woman who was with us then, are with us still."[20] With this lack was a further unprovided need, that of an institution for training workers. The first Burmese admitted to the Mission Conference was Maung Pe Htoon in 1904. The first Chinese, Tan King Seng, admitted in 1906 who died in the same year, was the first in the roll of Deceased Members. Julius Smith had rendered heroic service for upwards of ten years, the longest to that time, but he did not return. Mr. and Mrs. B. M. Jones reached Rangoon in October, 1903, and a week later Mr. and Mrs. C. H. Riggs arrived. Among Board missionaries they were the first to provide the leadership that comes from experience in service.

Continued advance is suggested by comparing the "circuits" in 1913: Pegu—Sittang; Rangoon; Syriam; Thongwa and Twante, with the Districts in 1926: Pegu, Rangoon, Chinese, English and Indian. A new tendency to think collectively of the growing Christian Church in Burma was indicated by the transfer of classes of Bible women to the Baptist Bible Women's Training School by Miss Stockwell and by the appointment of Jones to the Baptist Theological Seminary at Insein.[21] In 1941 the total Methodist community numbered 2,068 of whom 980 were in Burmese congregations.[22]

The Japanese invasion of Burma from 1941 to the close of the war destroyed much of the property and closed most of the work of the church. The first post-war conference convened in 1946, "found fewer than half the 1941 numbers reportable and the succeeding years have barely brought the numbers on the church rolls to 2,000".[22] Owing to the reduction in its members the Conference has held its status as an Annual Conference by special action of the General Conference. It expected to reach the required number of twenty-five members before the 1956 General Conference.

The connection of the Burma work with the Central Conference of Southern Asia had been natural because of its beginning and also from the country's political connection with India. There were conditions, however, which always set Burma apart from India— religion, language, and racial differences. When, after the war, both India and Burma had separately attained their freedom, the advantages of the attachment with India Methodism diminished. The Burma Annual Conference voted in 1950 to be linked with the Southeastern Asia Central Conference.

Malaysia

When work began among the seamen in Calcutta, Thoburn soon heard of thriving Singapore. Then occasional invitations to open work there came to him. He became assured that God was beckoning for work to be opened in Singapore and through the *Western Christian Advocate* asked for two volunteers for the task. Some twenty responded but "no two seemed quite adapted to the very peculiar service required".

On his way to India in 1884 Bishop Hurst visited the Missions in Europe. While travelling eastward, his mind was strangely drawn to Singapore by tourists on the steamer, and also by a resident of the city whom he met. He had heard nothing of Thoburn's thoughts about Singapore, nor had he heard of his call for two men to open work there. Yet, almost his first question of Thoburn when they met was, "What can we do for Singapore?"[23]

That question which had arisen in the minds of two men a world apart, was the most prominent in the session of the S. I. Conference at Hyderabad. Singapore was outside of India; who would go? After much discussion thoughts turned to the Oldhams who had gone from Bangalore to America, to prepare for service in India and were now on the way back. When the appointments were made there was a new station and the name of a new man in the Calcutta District: *Singapore*—W. F. Oldham. Thoburn met them in Bombay. Oldham had, of course, expected an appointment in India and had prayed that he might be ready for any place. A little staggered at the name Singapore—way through India, and beyond—he turned to his wife and asked, "What do you say?" Promptly she replied: "If Singapore is our appointment, we will go to Singapore."

Oldham's membership was transferred from the South India to the North India Conference where he was introduced and his transfer read. On motion, he was elected to Elder's orders under the Missionary Rule; he was ordained on Sunday, January 11, 1885, and the next day his transfer back to the South India Conference was announced.[24]

A few days later Oldham, (Mrs. Oldham had remained with her mother in Poona), Thoburn, Mrs. Thoburn, and Miss Battie of the Calcutta Girls' School were on a steamer to Singapore, but without money to return. The first stop was Rangoon, affording this group an opportunity to meet the band of workers there. They, in turn, found such inspiration in the project on which this party was embarked, that they contributed the cost of the return from Singapore. There had been no opportunity to inform anyone in Singapore of their coming, but Mr. Phillips, who had more than once invited Thoburn to the city, having seen a vision in the night of four persons on a steamer, was on the dock to meet them and to take them to his home for the period of their stay. Oldham describes the setting of meetings which were advertised:

> Sunday morning found us in the Town Hall. A little Estey organ—the gift to Mrs. Oldham of her fellow students at Mt. Holyoke—was unpacked and pressed into service. Miss Battie sat at the organ; Dr. Thoburn sat on a small improvised platform at a table; Mrs. Thoburn led the singing while I played usher and handed round the hymn books. After singing and prayer, the text was announced 'Not by might, nor by power but by my Spirit, saith the Lord,' and Dr. Thoburn proceeded to preach the first Methodist sermon in Malaysia. . . .
>
> The people returned again and again in large numbers. . . . At the end of two weeks a considerable number were converted, and their testimony was heard to the great help of the services.[25]

Seventeen joined the new church. Two of these, John Polglase and F. J. Benjafield, who had been members of the English Methodist Church, and one other, Maurice Drummond, were received as full members; others as probationers. A Quarterly Conference was organized. Only the three named seemed fitted to be office holders:

> After we had named the same men over and over again for all the offices that Methodism knows . . . we came to the question 'who shall be the Committee to estimate the pastor's salary?' . . . John Polglase was named. He saw the difficulty of the situation . . . . Dr. Thoburn looked at him with deep concern, and said 'Do you think it can be done?' . . . [Polglase] turned to Brother Oldham and said, 'If Brother Oldham can stand it, we can!' It was settled that the church now begun should be continued.[25]

After two days Oldham was left alone at his post. A Chinese gentleman who had been baptized in another Mission soon joined Oldham's church. Out walking with him one day, Oldham saw a sign, "Celestial Reading Association". It was a club where young Chinese met in debates to improve their English. Oldham could not join, but his offer to give a lecture was accepted. The lecture, on Astronomy, was given in the home of one of the leading Chinese with all the elite of Chinese society present. Such friendliness from foreigners the Chinese had not known. "That evening", wrote Oldham, "was laid the foundation of our Mission work among the Chinese." In a day or two the host of that evening wanted Oldham to tutor him in English. This Oldham did. In a speech at a public dinner his pupil did so well, others wanted to engage the missionary tutor. Oldham suggested that they open a school for their children and he would teach English in the school. The Government gave the land; the Chinese paid for the building and instruction. The extensive system of Anglo Chinese schools in the Malaysia Conference has developed from this first school which opened on March 1, 1886.

The Church also grew. After depending on the hospitality of others for a place to worship for two years, a commodious and comfortable church building was dedicated on December 15, 1886.[26] There was also a Tamil congregation of twelve members. Captain Shellabear of the Royal Engineers was cooperating in preaching to the Malays, and in printing tracts in Malay on a small hand press.

In 1886 Mrs. Oldham wrote to Mrs. Mary C. Nind, a personal friend and Corresponding Secretary of the Minneapolis Branch of the W. F. M. S., appealing for a missionary for women's work. The General Executive Committee had appropriated all funds and so could do nothing. After careful consideration and prayer, Mrs. Nind personally assumed responsibility for $3,000 for work at Singapore,[27] saying "Frozen Minnesota will plant a Mission at the Equator". Then a second difficulty arose; there was no candidate. Prayer continued in both Singapore and in Minnesota; its answer, in the words of Mark Guy Pearce, is one of "The Pretty Ways of Providence".

In distant Australia a young lady, Sophia Blackmore, an Australian Methodist, had long had the conviction that she would be a missionary among Chinese. Yet her church had no work anywhere among the Chinese. Miss Isabella Leonard, an American Evangelist who had completed a season of meetings in India, was nearing the end of a tour in Australia expecting soon to return to India for another cold season. In her itinerary she met Miss Blackmore and was used to lead her to a deeper, richer spiritual life. Friendship grew and Miss Blackmore told Miss Leonard of her call. "Come with me to India and you will find work to do", she said. They arrived in time for the session of the S. I. Conference where they met Oldham. After conversation he felt that Miss Blackmore was well-adapted to their need. Miss Leonard also knew Mrs. Nind and she and Oldham both wrote to her. There came in reply a cable: "Blackmore—Singapore." In July, 1887 the accepted young missionary entered upon her work.

At the end of her first year she reported to the Bengal Conference that homes were opening up in an encouraging manner. She had a small school for eight Chinese girls in the front room of a Chinese widow's home. Including older girls being taught at their homes, there were twenty-five Chinese girls learning to read. There was also a small Tamil girls' school of over twenty pupils, most of its expense being met by a Tamil merchant.[28]

MALAYSIA MISSION

On Central Conference recommendation "the Singapore work, with the work of that entire vicinity was organized into a Mission . . . administered directly by . . . the Missionary Society", but it was not deemed advisable "to detach Burma from the work in Peninsular India".[29]

This work was opend without reference to the Missionary Society. There was for this reason a tense debate in the General Missionary Committee of the Missionary Society in November, 1887 when its sub-committee included in the appropriation recommended for the Bengal Conference a sum for work in Singapore. "A letter from Bishop Ninde to the Board of Bishops was read [which] was calculated to do us much harm . . . . He took strong ground against our grant-in-aid...[and] also advised against our extending our missions so widely."[30] Bishop Merrill opposed the grant because it was opening new work, and saddling the Committee with increasing responsibility for men and money, when the Committee was already "crippled on every side by want of reinforcements". Bishop Hurst insisted that it was not a question of a new mission, but of giving proper efficiency to work already established and a part of the Bengal Conference, making it a separate Mission under the name of Malaysia. To this Dr. Cranston replied; "I understand we have established a Mission and did not know it. This General Missionary Committee is the only power which can properly establish a Mission."[31]

General Conference approved the report of its Committee on Missions, "that the Peninsula of Malacca, with the adjacent territory and islands, in which the Malay language is spoken, be constituted the Malaysia Mission under the administration of the Missionary Society".[32] It was organized by Bishop Thoburn on April 18, 1889 on the verandah of the Mission House in Singapore. Its members were W. F. Oldham, Superintendent; Benjamin F. West, M. D., Ralph W. Munson, members of Annual Conference; William N. Brewster, in charge of the English City Mission; M. Gnanamuthoo, of the Tamil Mission and Alexander Fox, L. P. Lady members were: Mrs. Oldham, Mrs. Munson, Mrs. West and Miss S. Blackmore. In the English Church there were 68 members, 19 probationers. There were 360 day scholars and 16 boarders. Dr. West had lived in the Chinese city and opened a dispensary where as many as 1,500 had been treated.[33] The Mission had been "formally organized", but Bishop Thoburn wrote

> It was a very informal organization. The workers were few in number, their plans had to be discussed from the very foundation, and their prospects of immediate expansion were anything but bright. If I remember correctly there were only a dozen persons on that verandah for the organization of the Mission. This year, [1890] the annual meeting convened in the Church and a goodly number of our membership in Singapore were present; not only the missionaries, but all the

> workers of both sexes connected with the Mission, were present and enrolled in the Annual Meeting. The whole number of those who received appointments was 25, and most of them were present at all the meetings. . . . A profound impression was made upon the people of our church in this place by the baptism of 13 adult converts at the closing meeting of our little Conference last evening. A large number of friends of the converts were present and looked on with sympathetic interest. . . . If ever in history God has led us into anything, it has been in coming into this remote region. Daily tokens show us that God is with us.[34]

Annual Conference members continued their connection with the Bengal Conference and newcomers sought membership there. Thus in 1890 W. N. Brewster; and in 1891, W. G. Shellabear and B. H. Balderston were received On Trial. During the year Brewster went to Foochow and was transferred to the Hingwa Conference, China. Dr. H. L. E. Leuring, a noted linguist, who arrived in 1889, was a member of the Germany Conference. Before the second meeting the Oldhams had gone to America due to ill health.

At its first session the organization of a Press for Malaysia was discussed, doubtless with Shellabear in mind. Oldham described him as an "example of how the moral earnestness and enthusiasm of Methodism kindles missionary fire in the hearts of good men the world over". Brought up strictly in the Church of England, he had been early impressed by the piety of a couple in a non-conformist group. In Singapore he had regularly attended the Methodist Church. As a brevet captain of the Royal Engineers Corps, he had to learn Malay for his duties and thus he got interested in the people. A sense of "call" grew on him. Before he returned to England on leave, he said to Oldham, "I have determined to leave the army and to give myself wholly to the Malays as a missionary among you, if you will have me."

> How my heart bounded within me [wrote Oldham]. There he stood, under 30 years of age, tall, soldierly, a pure transparent man of great mental power, well educated, speaking and writing Malay exceedingly well; tell me, was not this man's call and appointment made directly by the God of Missions?

His father cut him off, but his fiancée entered fully into his plans. To prepare himself the better, he went to Hugh Price Hughes' West End Mission and also entered a printing office to learn its management, and to familiarize himself with the details of its departments.[35] The Press was started in 1891, on his return to Singapore, and the *Malaysia Message* in the same year.

A school was opened in Penang in July, 1891 by Balderston. Moore went a little later and started English services in a rented hall. After the third meeting "he had a small and constant congregation". An Anglo-Chinese Girls' School was opened in October.

At the Central Conference of 1892 Bishop Thoburn said: "Wherever the Methodist system is found fairly at work, it seems constantly driven forward as if by the power of an invisible master wheel."[36] That spirit permeated this newest Mission. At its first meeting it approved "a commission of exploration for new and wider fields". In January, 1890 West and Leuring went on an exploring and book selling trip to the west coast of Borneo. Conditions seemed favourable but nothing could be done.[37]

A second venture was made to Borneo in 1892 by Leuring and Floyd, who was then acting as Superintendent of the Mission. They went to Gaya on the north coast within the boundaries of the British North Borneo Company. No extended trips could be made. Dr. Leuring stayed eight months and then returned, for he was needed in the rapidly developing work in the Straits Settlements. The next year West made a tour of exploration to Sumatra, then a nine days' trip to Siboga near the city of Silindong. Here was a large tract of country in which there was no missionary.

> The inhabitants were Bataks, who about 50 years before became Mohammedans, and it was among these people that Miss Medham, an English lady of means at Silindong, desired that a Methodist Mission be established. There were several large towns in the interior. There was but one missionary on the entire coast.[38]

Bishop Thoburn was unable to be present at the Malaysia Mission in 1892 and requested E. W. Parker to serve in his stead.

Conference Organization

The General Conference of 1892 approved the organization of the Malaysia Mission as a Mission Conference within the quadrennium. Bishop Thoburn thought best to do it soon, and effected the organization on April 1, 1893, with the following transfers: Ralph W. Munson, Benjamin F. West, Daniel D. Moore, William B. Urch, from the Bengal Conference; Henry L. E. Leuring from the Germany Conference. *Probationers:* Benjamin H. Balderston, William G. Shellabear, W. T. Kennett, and John Deatker, from Bengal Conference; Charles C. Kelso from the Detroit Conference. *On Trial:* William J. Wager, George F. Pykett. In the *Woman's* Conference were: Mrs. Munson, Mrs. Kelso, Mrs. Leuring, Mrs. Shellabear, Mrs. West, Misses Blackmore, Emma E. Ferris, and Josephine Hebinger.

The final step in the upward progress of Malaysia from a district of the Bengal Conference, came under Bishop Warne, when he organized it as the Malaysia Annual Conference on February 25, 1902, with twenty members, eleven probationers, and a total church membership of 3493. Among its members were two Chinese: Lau Seng Ching and Ling Ching Mi; and among the probationers Ngu Luang Sen, a Malay, and Ong Oa Lai. Four of the members and two probationers were in the Philippine Islands

District. At the time of this session Shellabear had been working for three years on the translation of the New Testament into Malay.

Because of their intimate connection with India in the beginning the Malaysia Mission Conference was associated with the Central Conference of Southern Asia. Its first delegates attended the Central Conference of 1894. They were Leuring, Ministerial Delegate, and Mrs. Munson from the Woman's Conference. The largest delegation came in 1904; W. T. Cherry, B. F. West, H. C. Stuntz, and Mrs. W. P. Rutledge and Miss Anderson. Increasingly it became evident that the differences in conditions in India and Malaysia gave them little advantage from the Central Conference connection. In 1912 the Central Conference petitioned the General Conference that Malaysia be permitted to withdraw from the jurisdiction of the Central Conference. In 1916 J. M. Hoover and W. G. Shellabear, with layman Goh Hood Keng, Miss Blackmore and Miss March were present in the Central Conference and at the Lucknow session in 1920 H. B. Mansell represented the Netherlands Indies Conference and F. H. Sullivan and Miss Dean, the Malaysia Conference. With this session Malaysia's connection with the Central Conference of Southern Asia ceased.

The flame kindled in the hearts of men and women in the meetings in the Town Hall of Singapore in the spring of 1885, did not die out. It leaped from life to life, island to island and to mainland. Today it still burns. Its growth is seen in the activities of four Annual Conferences: Malaya Annual Conference, Malaysia Chinese Annual Conference, Sarawak (Borneo) Mission Conference and Sumatra Provisional Conference.

The Philippine Islands

"The beginning of Methodism in the Philippine Islands," says Dr. Cornelio M. Ferrer, "started upon the landing in Manila, on December 17, 1898, of a Methodist Local Preacher by the name of A. W. Prautch."[39] He had withdrawn from the Bombay Conference in 1897 and returned to America. On the fall of Manila he went there to see what could be done.

Thoburn's thought had often turned to those islands. From Singapore he had looked eastward with the hope, that some day the Gospel would be preached in that closed country. When the British and Foreign Bible Society sent two colporteurs there, with a supply of New Testaments, and they were imprisoned and their books burned on the Plaza, it "stirred him to even stronger desire to preach in the Philippines".

> By action of the last General Conference those rich and beautiful islands had been included in the Malaysia Mission Conference, and accordingly as soon as they had been formally ceded to the United States, Bishop Andrews and Dr. Leonard, acting in behalf of the Missionary Society, cabled to me a request to proceed to Manila and

carefully examine the situation. For more than a dozen years God has been turning my thought in that direction and it was with a thankful heart that I set out upon that voyage.[40]

Thoburn was in Singapore for a session of the Malaysia Mission Conference when the cable arrived. He had also received a letter from Prautch, *via* Bombay on February 14. He left Singapore Saturday evening, February 18 and entered Manila Bay ten days later and went to Prautch's office. Prautch took the Bishop to one of the best hotels whose proprietor was a Bombay Gujarati who could speak Hindustani. In the evening he called on Mr. and Mrs. Owens who had been sent out by Bishop McCabe "some little time ago". Owens had preached to the soldiers but had had no regular service in the city. Thoburn arranged to rent the theater March 7 for Sunday services.[41]

In the audience was a man named Plummer, originally from Albany, New York, a sea-faring man who had been wrecked near Manila sixteen years earlier. "As he listened to the simple Gospel story, the tears ran down his cheeks and his heart warmed. He begged Bishop Thoburn to send a preacher and promised that he would do his share to support him."[42]

Bishop Thoburn's stay was brief. He had come to "examine the situation". The war was not over; Manila was under martial law; streets were cleared every evening at seven o'clock; a permanent English congregation then seemed unlikely but Chaplain Stutt of the Montana Regiment promised to maintain English services in the theatre until he was moved; Rev. J. C. Goodrich of the American Bible Society helped from October to March when Thomas H. Martin, sent by the Board, arrived. J. L. McLaughlin and wife arrived soon after. He was to be the Mission Treasurer, and P. E., for the new Mission had the status of a District in the Malaysia Mission Conference.[43]

Bishop Thoburn considered "the time as fully ripe" for a Soldiers' Institute on the pattern of the Seaman's work of Calcutta and Bombay. Prautch knew that work and accepted the responsibility. The offerings on Sunday exceeded the rent for the theatre and $50 was left for new work. It took until May to find a building for the Institute which opened on the first of June. Captain Plummer contributed $1000 toward this work in its early stages. It was largely under the management of Mrs. Prautch and provided temperance drinks, meals, games, lodging and general social enjoyments free from the temptations of drink. Two evening services and a prayer meeting were held weekly, and Sunday services from June.[44]

Bishop Thoburn's services in the theatre had been announced in the Spanish paper. The Roman Catholic Archbishop threatened the Editor and Manager with excommunication if they did not do penance for giving notice to the heretics. The Editor printed this threat with a defiant challenge and a hurrah for liberty of conscience; and this incident has given columns in *Manila El Commercio* against the intolerant spirit of Rome . . . . No Protestant has written a line. We stand by and reap the fruits.[45]

These were publicity for the Soldiers' Institute, and requests for Protestant services in Spanish made by men who had been imprisoned for having a Bible, or for being a Free Mason, and by others. Spanish services were started on Sunday afternoons. Preaching, through an interpreter, was done by Chaplains and Prautch or by friends that he was able to secure. One Sunday there was no interpreter. Senor Paulino Zamora was asked to speak. Some sixteen years before as a ship's Captain, he had received a Bible from a friend. The new ideas that came from reading it gripped him. At home he read it with the famliy. Rumors about the Bible got out; Friars made inquiries; the house was searched, the Bible found. Senor Zamora was tried by an ecclesiastical court and banished to an island in the Mediterranean for five years, and had only recently returned. He and his son Nicholas were among the first to join the Protestants. Senor Zamora spoke very briefly in this meeting, then called on his son, a graduate of the Santo Tomas University to speak, for he knew both Spanish and Tagalog. From that day the son became the accepted preacher.[45]

Bishop Thoburn visited the Philippines a second time on his way to General Conference in 1900. Owing to his poor health Warne was with him to take his place in everything except his purely official duties. There had been great progress during the year; an American church of 50 members; a Filipino church of 200 members, with a weekly attendance of about 600 at services; four representatives of the W. F. M. S. were on the field, and there were a few Chinese Christians. The Soldiers' Institute was doing valuable work.

Bishop Thoburn ordained Nicholas Zamora to the ministry to meet the urgent need of an ordained man to baptize and to solemnize marriages.[46] In order to do this he cabled A. B. Leonard of the Board, to request a Conference in the United States to receive Nicholas Zamora, On Trial, to elect him to Deacon's orders, and then transfer him to the Malaysia Mission Conference. Dr. Leonard received the telegram while in attendance at the South Kansas Conference which took the required actions and notified Bishop Thoburn in Manila by cable. Dr. Warne assisted and Paulino Zamora witnessed his own son receive ordination as the first Filipino ever received into the Christian ministry, for the Roman Catholics did not admit Filipinos to their monastic orders. Warne described it as "one of the most pathetic, inspiring and I believe will be one of the most historic scenes I have ever witnessed".[44]

Leaving Warne in Manila Thoburn left for America. At this time Warne organized the first Quarterly Conference, the first Official Board, the first class meetings, and held the first series of united evangelistic services in which some sixty conversions took place, and many professing Christians were quickened. Returning to Manila after General Conference Bishop Warne held the first District Conference when Prautch was given a Local Preacher's License and H.C. Stuntz was invited to become the Presiding Elder and pastor of the Church for Americans. He arrived in Manila in April, 1901. Bishop Warne was there to receive him and the second District Conference was held soon after.[47]

Under the leadership of Bishop Warne the Methodists united with other denominations to form the Philippine Evangelical Union. This body assigned specific areas for the several missions to occupy and evangelize, such assignments subject to revision after three years. Time has shown the wisdom of this arrangement. A similar plan operates today under auspices of the Philippine Federation of Christian Churches.

Nicholas Zamora very soon found two helpers, Jose Bantista and Victorina Gomez and services were regularly held in ten centres in and near Manila. Most of these were held in the homes of devoted people who gathered their own small congregations. The first Methodist Church in the Philippines, a one-room thatched building, was dedicated by Bishop Warne on August 12, 1900 at Pandacan.[48] When the Manila congregation bought its first site and sought to secure their title for the property they learned that there was no law by which non-Catholic bodies could secure title to real estate. Stuntz approached Governor Taft, under whom the Civil government was established on July 4, 1901.

> Without consulting a book or so much as moving his chair, [Taft] touched a bell, summoned his secretary, dictated a law in three sections covering the whole case and in 15 minutes it was in typescript before him. . . . [He said] that it was the intention of the Committee and himself to remove all disabilities from Protestants just as soon as their existence was brought to their attention.[49]

Through the Malaysia Mission Conference the Philippine Islands were at once connected with the Central Conference of Southern Asia. In 1904 that body, with Stuntz a delegate from his Conference, memorialized General Conference "to authorize the organization of the Philippine Islands District of the Malaysia Mission Conference into a Mission Conference".[50]

In 1908 D. H. Klinefelter represented the Philippine Islands Mission Conference at the Central Conference of Southern Asia, in Rangoon, which petitioned General Conference, (1) "that for administrative purposes the Philippine Islands Mission Conference remain a part of the Southern Asia Mission Field"; (2) to grant it an enabling act to be organized into an

Annual Conference, and (3) to authorize the organization of the Northern District of Philippine Islands Mission Conference into a Mission Conference.[51] In 1912 the Philippine Islands Conference was unrepresented at the Central Conference. In 1916 Bishop Eveland alone was present to represent the work of his area. The Central Conference in this year, as in others, named the Agents of the Publishing Houses and the Local Publishing Committees for Singapore and Manila. In both years, 1912 and 1916, the request of those Conferences for withdrawal from the jurisdiction of the Central Conference of Southern Asia "on account of different conditions prevailing" in those countries, was recommended to General Conference. Twice that body had agreed "but, in both instances, before final action could be taken and at the request of the delegates from the Conference concerned, the General Conference rescinded its preparatory action and continued the old relation between the two sections".[52] In 1920 the connection was terminated.

FOR THE HONOUR OF "THE SERVICE"

That "Reproach may not Fall on The Service!"
Lord! 'tis for this we gird our armour on,
Knowing the heights Thy Soldier Saints have won
Can ne'er be reached by us, if Passion swerve us
One single hair's breadth from the Right; or Self,
With baleful magic so warp Sight and Soul
That Vision fades; Ideals grow dim; the whole
Of Life low-prized, be spent in Pleasures or for Pelf.
So we our Captain's Honour guard with care,
The Shield of Faith, the Spirit's trenchant Sword,
The Armoured Mail of Righteousness, with Prayer
We gird upon ourselves, trusting that Word
And Love of Thine, vibrant with Power, may nerve us
To keep "Reproach" from falling on "The Service."

BISHOP W. P. EVELAND, December, 1916.

XI

"Fitly Joined Together"

The Central Conference was needed to conserve and to promote those interests common to all Annual Conferences in India. Its members in every quadrennium have found the field a very wide one. The national outlook engendered in coming together created an outlook unique among missionary organizations in India. Every Methodist knew there was Methodist work beyond his Conference, and many were informed on All-India interests. Of a truth the Methodist Church of Southern Asia—Mecosa in short—had been "fitly joined together". Triumph in one part became the triumph of all. The transfer of Thoburn from North India to Calcutta took him from his first field, but brought all other fields closer to North India. Mark the trail of J. E. Robinson—Secunderabad, Bangalore, Burma, Simla, Bombay, Calcutta—an all-India parish. Phoebe Rowe, pioneering as a District Evangelist in N. W. India Conference, traced a path for some one in every Conference. So Mary Reed's heroism helped the cause of lepers everywhere. Gilder, DeSouza, Frease and Ernsberger belonged to India Methodism and Oldham to Southern Asia. We are limited to a cursory glance of a few of the common interests which were advanced under a great missionary leader who thought and worked for India, and beyond India for Southern Asia.

Sunday Schools

No other department of work received such enthusiastic support as Sunday Schools. They afforded an excellent opportunity for laymen to help in a really useful way. Delighted with the progress made in this branch in the preceding biennium the Committee on Sunday Schools declared that this "alone would be sufficient reason for [the] existence" of the Central Conference.

The India Sunday School Union was organized at Allahabad in January, 1876 with eight Missionary Societies represented. Two years later there were eleven Societies and members came from all parts of India. Denominational Auxiliary Unions associated with the All-India Union were formed. T. J. Scott and B. H. Badley continued as active leaders of the

A. I. S. S. U. for many years. In no Auxiliary was more active work done than in the India Conference, where it was looked on as an opportunity, for in "getting hold of the children we have the future life of India."

At the United Conference a Methodist Auxiliary for All India was formed. This became a standing committee of Central Conference. There was no abatement in Sunday School work, nor in the effort to expand the program as the following report shows:

Conferences	No. of Sunday Schools	No. of Officers and Teachers	Christians, Males-Females		Non-Christians, Males-Females		Total Scholars
1885							
North India	479	646					18069
South India	55	319					2882
	534	965					20951
1903							
Bengal	60	167	573	679	1078	361	2691
Bombay	253	356	2739	1888	3279	1813	9719
N. India	995	1262	13170	8169	12827	6718	40884
N. W. India	1029	793	14711	7315	7595	3723	33344
S. India	107	267	939	967	1228	1027	4161
	2444	2845	32132	19018	26007	13642	90799

Epworth Leagues

Church leaders early manifested an interest in the development of the young people in the Church, beginning in the schools. One of the first auxiliaries of the W. F. M. S. in India was in the Girls' Orphanage. In 1885 Allan J. Maxwell, who had arrived in India only two years before, started *India's Young Folks*, a popular Sunday School paper in English, and continued to edit it until his death in 1890. It was continued by others, but for lack of funds was voted to be discontinued in 1892 until a grant, subsidy or other help could be obained.[2] Somehow it survived and in 1894 Miss Blair was elected its Editor.[3]

When the Oxford League was organized, Dr. and Mrs. Parker, not now young, organized the first chapter in India, at Moradabad. "As soon as its effectiveness in training and character building was proved the organization spread rapidly over the entire Mission."[4] Meanwhile, the Epworth League spread through the Church in America, and was started in the S. I. Conference.[5] An enthusiastic meeting in the interest of the Epworth League was held at the Central Conference in 1894. The Board of Epworth League was established with members from each Conference and E. W. Parker as President, and H. C. Stuntz as General Secretary. The Conference urged Presiding Elders to avail themselves of the advantages of the Epworth League as a great moral power throughout the Church.[6] A constitution was adopted to secure uniformity in program and efficiency in advancing its object. In 1896 Warne became General Secretary, with J. E. Robinson as Associate for India and B. F. West for Malaysia. At the end of the first biennium there were in the six Conferences 139 chapters with 6555 members.[7] All-India conventions were held in Lucknow in 1895, in Poona in 1897 and in Kanpur in 1899.

> The attendance of a large number of delegates and members from many chapters, the profitable discussion of the subjects of a comprehensive programme, the excellent singing and happy enthusiasm of all, left no question as to the importance and value of League Conventions.[8]

In 1896 *India's Young Folks* was placed under the management of the Board of Control of the Epworth League, and continued as the *India Epworth Herald*.[9]

Teaching Self-Support

The widest gap between the Conferences in 1876 was in financial policy. In dedication to "native work" they were agreed. Under the grant-in-aid policy initiated in 1887, and the challenge of doors swung wide open, the gap began to close. By the Central Conference of 1892, when all Board appropriations had been cut three years in succession, the Conferences suffered alike. Addressing the Central Conference, Thoburn said:

> We must give our careful, prayerful, and I had almost said our desperate attention to the necessity of teaching *even the poorest of these people* to take care of themselves. This is one of the great problems of our immediate future.[10]

Two years later he again stressed the importance of the subject in view of the great measure of independent action that had been given to the field. It was fitting that the Church should learn and practice "dependence upon our own financial resources, to a greater extent than ever before. These resources are by no means limited."[11] Again, with obvious reference to the Kasganj District where the P. E. and all his Preachers-in-charge stepped out on full support, a report stressed the importance of "regular and systematic giving for the support of the Gospel" and noticed "the growing determination to place our work as far as possible on a self-supporting basis."[12] Bishop Foss describes a self-support anniversary in 1898 where

> the intensest enthusiasm prevailed. Reports were made from all the districts in the Conference of what had been done for self-support during the year. Hymns, addresses and prayers, all relating to the same subject

were offered. . . . Hasan Raza Khan asked those of his preachers and Bible readers who were ready to stand with him to come forward. Twenty-two came, and at the close of the meeting another native Presiding Elder stepped out on the same platform. [Then he quotes H. R. Khan.] 'I made up my mind a few years ago that I would not put my faith in American rupees. While I was on the Missionary Society I never owned a cow or bison; but since I have been on self support I have three cows and a bison, and have not lacked for anything. The first two years I was on self-support there were only two of our workers that stood with me. Last year there were six, now there are twenty-two on self-support in my district; the time will come when the Church in India will do its own work.'[13]

The Central Conference again and again urged the importance of everybody giving. "The value of the money saved by the introduction of this new policy is a small matter when compared with the new energy and confidence which are thus infused into the minds and hearts of the people."[12]

Bishop Foss and Dr. Goucher had been commissioned to study the relation of self-support to the contributions from the Church in America, for "If India is ever saved, it must under God be saved by India. America can never save India, England can never save India." Memorials from the Annual Conferences approving a system of grant-in-aid toward pastoral support were before the Central Conference. It provided that each Finance Committee should annually apportion an amount to be raised by each preacher toward his expected support, the balance to be paid by the Conference Treasurer. If only a part of the apportionment was met by the circuit or station, then only a like proportion would be paid by the Treasurer.

The report of the Committee On Pastoral Support in 1904 stressed two sacred obligations: (1) the importance of giving for Christ as well as living for Him, and (2) the obligation of regular, systematic giving. Here tithing was for the first time commended by Central Conference with the expectation that faithful, conscientious pastoral work would yield a response.[14]

The Woman's Conference

While the India Mission Conference was in session in 1871 the missionary ladies, both married and single, met together. On the last day of the Conference they adopted a constitution for "The Woman's Missionary Society of the Methodist Episcopal Church in India, associated with the W. F. M. S. . . . in America". Its purpose was "to aid the Society in the United States in carrying out its plans, and also to collect funds in this country to help forward the work of educating and saving women".[15] It provided for Auxiliary Societies wherever a group could be gathered whose total dues would not be less than five rupees a year, Indian women paying eight annas and Europeans one rupee annually.

Before the Delegated Conference met in Allahabad certain usages grew up which proved useful and successful. These were embodied in a "Report on the Relation of Lay Agents to Our Work" which was then adopted. In 1887 the Central Conference approved these rules which had in the meantime been adopted by the General Executive Committee in 1883. In pursuance of this plan the ladies in each Annual Conference organized a Woman's Conference Missionary Society, with its Auxiliaries. There has been a Committee on Woman's Work in the Central Conference since 1887. In that year the Committee stressed the importance of securing

> permanent results which will aid in building up the Church. We should endeavour to secure and encourage voluntary workers, keeping in view the fact that permanent success will be secured largely in proportion as the work can become self-supporting.[16]

Looking to the achievement of these goals special efforts for training workers were encouraged and schools urged to cultivate the missionary spirit, but in 1892 the ladies established their own Mission Service, with examinations, salary scales for Assistants, Bible readers and others,[17] which at once reduced voluntary efforts. The same Committee urged that Auxiliary Societies "devote as far as possible a part or the whole of the funds raised to this work".[18]

Faced with Mass Movements in three Conferences the Central Conference in 1892 recommended the discontinuance of zenana work and day schools in cities, in order to reach women converts and inquirers.[17] Four years later the need was more urgent. More women and children, nominally Christian, were continuing the old rites and customs. The Conference approved two suggestions: (1) to organize in every district bands of three or more women from the most experienced workers, to itinerate among women, village to village, house to house; (2) to make the first effective, a request to the W. F. M. S. to send women fitted for evangelistic work, who would give their whole time to its direction among women.[18]

The Order Of Deaconesses

The Deaconess Movement started in Germany; then took root in England with headquarters in Mildmay, London. On their way to America in 1885 Dr. and Mrs. Thoburn and Miss Thoburn made a short visit at Brighton with acquaintances of Lucknow days. There they met deaconesses from Mildmay. It had already been planned to have a woman's mission in Calcutta, and this glimpse of deaconess work led to the thought that it might be conducted on similar lines. Thoburn presented the subject in an address to the Central Ohio Conference in 1886. In Chicago Mrs. Lucy Rider Meyer opened a department in her Training School for Deaconesses.[19]

The first memorial sent to General Conference in 1888 asking approval for an order of Deaconesses, was from the Bengal Conference.[20] The General Conference approved "an order of Deaconesses" whose duties

> are to minister to the poor, visit the sick, pray with the dying, care for the orphans, seek the wandering, save the sinning, and relinquishing wholly all other pursuits, devote themselves in a general way to such forms of Christian labor as may be suited to their abilities. . . . No vow shall be exacted from any deaconess, and any one of their number shall be at liberty to relinquish her position as a deaconess at any time.[21]

Within one year three Deaconess Homes were established in India: in Calcutta under Mrs. J. M. Thoburn; in Lucknow under Miss Blackmar, and in Mathura under Miss F. J. Sparkes, who had just returned from America.[22] Deaconesses lived together in these homes under a person designated as Superintendent. They accepted two principles described by Miss Thoburn:

> There is so much to be done in the world it is impossible to accomplish it all, or even a large part of it, by salaried work, and, next, that life is not long enough, to spend much of either on the clothes we wear.[23]

They received their food, their garb, which was a means of recognition, and a small allowance: in 1889 twenty-five rupees per month; in 1897, thirty; probationers, fifteen. The Central Conference established a Deaconess Board which determined rules and coordinated conditions in Conferences and fixed the course of study. In each Conference another Board passed on candidates recommended by the Quarterly Conference, arranged for their examinations and reported to the Central Board.

The first Deaconess Home was that in Calcutta. The first deaconesses, Misses Black, K. A. Blair and Maxey, reached Bombay on December 31, 1888 and Calcutta on January 5. Dr. and Mrs. Warne gave them the lower flat of their house and after their first breakfast Dr. Oldham read a Psalm and commended the Home and work to the Father in a prayer of dedication. Owing to the great heat in February, Mrs. Warne gave them a part of her drawing room enabling them to move their beds upstairs. In the same month "Miss Thaddeus and Miss Oram came to live in our house. Miss Oram came as Probation Deaconess," and in January, 1898, "Miss Louise Campbell and Miss A. Suderstrom were transferred to Muzaffarpur and Miss Oram to Pithoragarh."[24] In a few years other Homes were opened at Madras, Bangalore, Pithoragarh, Bombay, Kolar, Singapore and Jabalpur.

When Bishop Thoburn consecrated Phoebe Rowe, Lucy W. Sullivan, Gertrude F. Matthews and Martha A. Sheldon to the office of Deaconess, he explained:

> When I lay my hands upon these consecrated women, I can confer upon them no power, or functions beyond those authorized by the Church as pertaining to the office of a deaconess. Inasmuch, however, as this office is a peculiarly sacred one, authorized by the highest authority of the Church, and inasmuch as these candidates have, after due probation, been formally elected to this office by a duly appointed Annual Conference Board, I think it is in every way proper that they should be consecrated to this service by an appropriate and impressive ceremony and shall therefore introduce into the form of service prepared for the occasion, the scriptural precedent of laying on of hands.[25]

A small volume commemorating the Jubilee of work in Calcutta, 1873-1923, was dedicated to Miss Maxey who had given

> devoted service to the work she loves—a truly remarkable record. Her efforts to capture the young men of the church, in whom she was keenly interested, met with a ready response, and in this respect she has an unequalled gift. Miss Maxey has garnered in a rich harvest, and has prevented many a young man from drifting. . . . [She] was also a devoted worker among the poor and will be remembered by many for her kind sympathy and help in time of need. One of her chief delights was welcoming strangers to her Home, and visiting the sick in hospitals. [J. M. Buckley][26]

A STUDY IN GROWTH OVER 45 YEARS

	Probationers	Full members	Beptized children	Total	Missionaries	Missionary Wives	W. F. M. S. Missionaries	W. F. M. S. Assistants	Indian members of Conference	Loeal Preachers	Exhorters	Other male workers	Other Female workers	Total Christian workers
1858														
Naini Tal	10	13	6	29	5	5	...	...	...	3	...	2	...	15
1903														
Conferences														
Bengal	932	1371	1078	3381	13	7	9	9	8	14	23	52	38	173
Bombay	12185	2243	5685	20113	19	15	16	15	9	73	197	113	188	645
N. India	17330	13798	14136	45264	15	13	24	35	71	272	254	276	687	1647
N. W. India	26218	17331	20770	64319	11	11	13	34	48	213	208	263	409	1210
S. India	1605	1020	1060	3685	17	11	10	23	9	32	54	96	103	355
Totals	58270	35763	42729	136762	75	57	72	116	145	604	736	800	1425	4030

Property And Finance

Where to apply the rent from a Mission bungalow; the scale of salaries for preachers; a more simple form for keeping Mission accounts[27]—

all business touching Finance and Property came on to the floor of the Annual Conference until 1876. Only gradually had matters been referred to committees: the first Trustees were elected in 1867 to hold funds and other property for the projected college; the first report of a Committee on Endowments, covering Khera Bajerah, the management of Panahpur village, the Centenary School fund and the Press endowments was made in 1873; a Conference Board of Trustees was created in 1873; the Finance Committee, with approval of General Conference, was organized in 1877.

Much of the property purchased in Butler's time was paid for with funds raised in India. It was purchased by different people in their own names on behalf of the Board. In 1873 the Conference asked the Board in New York to give Power of Attorney to the Treasurer "enabling him to act as legal agent in the purchase and sale of endowments here and the property of the Board in this country."[28] In 1875 the Trustees enlarged their number so that they might obtain a charter from the Government of India, constituting them a legal Board of Trustees for holding and managing endowments, and the next year designated T. S. Johnson as their representative to press upon the Board in New York "the urgent necessity of their granting to this Board of Trustees the Power of Attorney to buy and sell property for them."[29]

One of the first concerns of the United Conference was property, how it should be deeded and the forms of deeds. With the extension of work to Presidencies, Provinces and Native States, each with its own laws, the problem became more intricate and much more urgent. In 1894 the Central Conference established the Financial Board of the M. E. Church in India to be registered (incorporated) in Calcutta, with nine members; the Bishop, four ministers and four laymen. A similar Board was ordered for Singapore.

These Boards would hold and control "all donations, bequests, funds and properties, the tenure of which is not otherwise provided for". Its first members were Warne, Messmore, Conklin, Chew; laymen, Thurlow, Remfrey, Pringle and Ross.[30] Two years later ministers were forbidden to hold church property in their own names and were instructed to deed such as they had to the Financial Board. All deeds were ordered to be kept in the custody of the Treasurers of the Conferences, only copies to be given to the Presiding Elders. In 1900 it became necessary to have Financial Boards at Bombay, Lucknow and Madras, each under authority of Central Conference.

The Central Conference of 1889 provided for an Executive Committee "to have cognizance of such interests as may demand attention" between the biennial sessions, and to fill vacancies which occur in other Boards.

In 1904 this was enlarged as an Executive Board of the Methodist Church of Southern Asia, to include all the Bishops of Southern Asia, the Treasurers of the Missionary Society and of the W. F. M. S. in the several Annual and Mission Conferences and the Corresponding Secretaries of the same Conferences. Its powers were to administer Special, Famine and all connectional funds; to be the official representative of all our church in Southern Asia; to fill vacancies in Central Conference boards and committees, and being registered, to hold all property of the Methodist Church not deeded to regularly constituted boards of trustees.[31]

In the early nineties the Missionary Society faced a serious crisis. By opening new Missions in other countries it had greatly increased its obligations, while a financial crisis in the United States reduced its income, and forced it to reduce its appropriations. With due recognition of the extraordinary financial stringency with which the Society was confronted in apportioning its depleted funds, Bishop Thoburn and the Central Conference in 1894, protested the method of "*a uniform* retrenchment over the entire missionary territory", for fields differed from each other. India was facing "an imminence of need, an opportunity, a door opening, inviting, and threatening to close against us if not speedily entered," and also "our estimates contained no appropriations for buildings and similar enterprises capable of postponement". The whole reduction, therefore, cut down on salaries of workers or their numbers, and "could not but lamentably cripple our work".[32]

In the N. W. I. Conference, the N. I. Conference and the Gujarat District of the Bombay Conference, mass movements were in full swing. The figures over leaf suggest the marvellous growth of the church during the eight years following 1887:

	1887	1895
Communicants	7,944	69,802
Baptisms	1,959	15,459
Christian community	11,000	97,610
Native preachers	168	1,237
Christian teachers	308	1,241
Day Schools	504	1,297
Day Scholars	16,412	30,852

In the same time the work had grown from two Conferences to five. The appropriations from the Missionary Society in 1887 were $133,490 and in 1896, $130,000.

> There was no alternative but to go forward with the work which God has placed in our hands, and this duty has placed our beloved Bishop Thoburn under obligation to attempt to supplement our diminished appropriations by personal presentation of our needs. Burdened with this duty he now proceeds to the United States.[33]

In this way the Bishop Thoburn Special Fund was started. At the beginning of the India Mission Butler solicited "designated gifts" for the support of orphans *through* the Missionary Society. Now they were solicited *directly*, by correspondence from the field and by Bishop Thoburn and others in the States. Rockwell Clancy was appointed secretary of this fund at its inception. He was followed in the middle of 1893 by N. L. Rockey. The annual reports from all districts were printed together, and appeals presenting the special needs of the work were sent to many. This program met with opposition from leaders in the Church and from the Board. Thoburn made a vigorous defense of it in General Conference in 1896. The added toil for him in campaigns in America, together with the responsibility for administering the All-India field, finally broke his health, but to a great extent it saved the work. Gifts were sent to the Secretary, assigned by him and acknowledged to the donors. This Special Fund provided support for hundreds of pastors and village teachers who lived among the people.

The Central Conference of 1896 appointed a committee to consider the provison of a Missionary (Conference) Claimants fund. It reported favourably in 1896 on establishing such a fund for Superannuated Preachers including Local Preachers and Exhorters who had given their life service to our work, and the widows and children of the same, through collections for this object and special donations; with a treasurer for its investment, distribution to be on the order of the Annual Conferences.[34]

On Publishing

No one in any Mission has valued the power of the Press more than did J. M. Thoburn. In 1890 he wrote: "More and more I am convinced that this press work is the demand of the hour. Now is the time for us to strike."[35]

The difficulty of editing *The Indian Witness* in Calcutta and printing it in Lucknow led to the founding of the Calcutta Press in 1884. It was opened in a back lane by Thomas Craven who had been Agent of the Press in Lucknow. As the Board refused funds for English work so it withheld aid to publishing concerns. All such enterprises were the responsibility of the field. This new Press was soon heavily in debt, yet, it continued and in 1892 moved into property purchased by Warne on Dharamtala, a good business street and near the Church. In 1900 the Central Conference expressed itself as gratified with the favourable condition of the Calcutta Publishing House, which in the biennium 1898-1900 had put out more than ten million pages of religious literature, in English and Bengali, including *The Indian Witness*, *Woman's Friend*, Sunday School Lessons, Tracts, etc.[36]

The Lucknow Press had continued to prosper, but not without its financial struggles also. It had by now built up an endowment of over Rs. 200,000 and in 1897 distributed over six million pages of free literature. Seven periodicals were being issued from this Press, printed in three different characters.[37]

The Madras, Press known as the Mary M. Rudisill Publishing House, continued to serve the Church with literature in the languages of the S. I. Conference; Kanarese, Telugu, Tamil and English. One service peculiar to it was printing of embossed work for the blind in four languages. It had some indebtedness in 1900.

The fourth Publishing House was at Singapore. The Committee found it to be "thoroughly organized and in a state of efficiency." It printed in Malay, Javanese, Chinese and English. The Central Conference was told this incident in its development. The type ordinarily used in printing Malay could be secured only in Beirut, Turkey. Suddenly the Turkish Government put an embargo on the export of any more type. In this emergency Shellabear, the superintendent, went to Beirut, "pulled off his coat, went to work in the type foundry, and soon mastered the art himself", then returning to Singapore made type for his press and sold it to other firms.[38]

A Publishing House was approved for Bombay, and opened in early 1896. Plague and famine in the city affected business adversely. Its field was in the literature of western India, primarily Marathi and Gujarati.

To Bhot—And Beyond

Miss Martha Sheldon came to Moradabad as a missionary of the W. F. M. S. in 1889 and in 1893 was appointed to Pithoragarh. There she heard of Bhot, and beyond was Tibet. With Miss Budden she sought an outpost among the Bhotiyas, a nomadic people engaged in trade between Tibet and India. They selected Dharchula for winter quarters, and Sirkha, twenty miles up-valley for summers. Shibdata, Santukiya and Sipahi were the first Indian associates in this field. In 1896 Miss Sheldon was joined by Miss Eva Browne, a young English woman. Their work was undergirded by prayer.

> On a steep hill side under the shelter of a great rock in Larket [above Dharchula], i· a small stone slab, known as the Prayer Rock . . . and in Chaudas, . . . at the highest point of the property, on the edge of a great precipice, is the Prayer Room, another power house of Bhot.[39]

Landor, who dined one Sunday with Miss Sheldon and her Christians, mentions "among the converts some Hindus, some Shokas, some Humlis, and a Tibetan woman . . . about twenty of them".[40] Miss Sheldon was very practical. She planted fruit trees, grew her own vegetables, planted Kentucky blue grass on the mountain slopes, and from 1900 declined salaries from the W. F. M. S. for Bible readers, saying:

> In the economics of a self-supporting Church, we do not see the possibility of supporting a large number of Bible-readers. More and more, woman's work in India must be carried on, as it is at home, by voluntary service and self-sacrifice. Our idea of self-support is except for the matter of religion, *living like other people*. We do not wish to introduce in Bhot an exotic civilization supported by foreign money.[41]

Dr. Sheldon's ambition was to work into Tibet. She had learned something of the language. Her medical work opened the way to the pass. In 1896, with Miss Browne, a couple of workers and coolies, she arrived.

> June 4th. A red letter day! 5 miles in Tibet! . . . We crossed great beds of snow which never melt. The road packs down over it 15 to 30 feet. Up, up, up again till the pass was reached. There were, two shrines to *devatas* at the top of the pass . . . . We Christians shouted our battle cry "Masih ki Jai! Masih ki Jai!" [Victory to Jesus.] From this pass we were in Tibet . . . we are here and tent up and everything settled. We are only 4 miles from [the Raja's] residence at Takalakot, and D. V. tomorrow we will go there and pay him our respects.[42]

In 1890 Dr. Harkua Wilson, with helpers was appointed to the Bhot circuit. He had been in Dwarahat from 1882, joining the Annual Conference in 1887. In the year that Dr. Sheldon entered Tibet, Dr. Wilson also entered from another direction, but these efforts did not, as hoped, open the way for developing work there.

"Cleanse Lepers"

Mary Reed was born in Ohio. At the age of sixteen she gave her heart to Christ; and soon "realized that she had been saved to serve". Reading about India's zenanas while she was a school teacher, she felt her call and came as a missionary of the W. F. M. S. in 1884, to Kanpur. Hardly had she settled there when she became ill and was sent to Pithoragarh in the Himalayas. She recovered strength, studied the language, and shared the missionary's tasks. Here she saw, and was touched by the gathering of lepers on a ridge, some two miles from the Mission. She returned to Kanpur, and in 1889, went to Gonda. In 1890 she returned to America and the next year entered Christ's Hospital, Cincinnati.

To an extent her health was restored but there still remained symptoms that baffled the doctors, a tingling sensation in the forefinger of the right hand, and later a strange scar on one cheek near the ear.[43] One day while "listlessly tapping the counterpane with her finger . . . and thinking of God's dealings with her," as clearly as if a voice had spoken she learned that her disease was leprosy, and that she should return to India to superintend the leper asylum at Pithoragarh.[44]

On the doctor's next round she confided to him what then she knew. He was not acquainted with leprosy but reference to medical books and consultations with specialists confirmed the diagnosis. Miss Reed went home for a brief visit and left for India as though in good health, having revealed her secret only to her sister, Rena. In London a specalist confi-firmed the diagnosis. From Bombay Miss Reed wrote her sister permitting her to tell their mother, then proceeded directly to Pithoragarh *via* Almora, with a song in her heart: "My Lord, Thy will be done."

While Miss Reed had been recuperating in Pithoragarh, S. S. Dease was in correspondence with The Mission to Lepers, regarding a Leper Asylum there. It was opened in 1886 on the understanding that the missionary in the station would have immediate oversight of it.[45] Dease purchased the land.[46] In 1886 M. B. Kirk, of the S. I. Conference, was appointed in charge, but died during the year. He had started a subscription list for a chapel at the Asylum, which was built in 1887 and named the Kirk Memorial Chapel.[47] On the day of its opening twelve lepers were baptized some of whom had their first Christian teaching from him.

Bishop Thoburn met Miss Reed in Almora. He and Miss Budden had arranged that Miss Reed should be the Superintendent of the Asylum. In answer to many prayers the progress of Miss Reed's leprosy was arrested; Miss Reed knew it had not been cured. She worked as a missionary of the W. F. M. S. and for the Mission to Lepers until 1898 when she asked release from work outside of the Asylum. She never lost her missionary spirit and her greatest joy was to win the lepers for Jesus Christ while she did all she could to alleviate their suffering.

Miss Reed's name continued in the N. I. Woman's Conference until her death in 1943. *Chandag Heights* was her home for over fifty years. She was alone, but never shut out. With her large library of up-to-date books and newspapers, she kept abreast of current history, local and world. During his years in the Kumaon District the writer was often in her home. Her cottage was her own; its parlour-library the place for visiting; visits to remember. Nearby was her guest house where, with every need provided by her forethought, overnight guests were accommodated. In "The Unfailing Presence" she gives the secret of how she lived alone for so long and achieved so much.

Twelve Apostles

Early in 1899 Bishop Thoburn made "A Call to Our Young Men". Financial resources were down, mission stations were being closed and missionaries of advanced years needed to be replaced and money was insufficient to send married couples. He said:

> Our plan is this: We can receive 12 unmarried men provided they are qualified for immediate work, and either by placing them two and two, or arranging for them to board in missionary families, can make it possible for them to live in comfort without much expense. They should all be able to preach, and most of them would be expected to take at least one service in English on Sunday and one meeting during the week. A few might be given work as teachers, but in no case would any of them be expected to do full work. They would receive about $300 a year each, paid by the English people to whom they preach or by the schools in which they teach. They would take about half work, the rest of their time being given to study. At the end of four years those of them who shall have proved successful in work will be received as regular missionaries.

Other conditions were: The call to preach and ability to do so without manuscript; good health; a college education if possible, or at least a high school course; experience as a Christian worker; not under twenty-five years; men of broad views and free from narrow prejudices.[48]

Secretary Leonard backed up the Bishop's appeal. "If the young men have the qualifications, we are prepared to give them a chance. I would to God that at least a dozen young men would respond at once . . . we would take double the number if we thought desirable." The Board of Managers approved the plan, outgoing expenses to be met by the Missionary Society. About twenty applications had then been received.[49] Candidates were approved at different times:[50] Lewis A. Dyer, Robert I. Fawcett, Ernest B. Lavelette, James M. Hoover, Charles E. Bowen, Mott Keislar, Herbert G. Ozanne and Karl E. Anderson on July 18; B. T. Badley on September 19 ; Homer Wroten and B. F. Van Dyke on November 28. The last of twelve was Lee Tung Hwee who had been born in Malaysia; now a graduate of Ohio Wesleyan and Yale Universities. He and James Hoover were the first of these recruits to sail, going to Penang.[51] Van Dyke also went to Malaysia. Others came to India. Fawcett, Anderson, Hoover, Keislar and Badley spent their whole lives on their fields; Ozanne, Van Dyke and Lee gave several years beyond the four expected. The rest left earlier. Thoburn asked for twelve. Who first used the term "Twelve Apostles" for this group, and when, has not been traced, but it was early applied and they have often been referred to as such.

Immediately after the General Conference of 1900 Bishops Thoburn, Parker and Warne met together to plan their work. Together they made another appeal for twelve more young men for Southern Asia on practically the same conditions as were set in 1899: half pay—$325, to be provided on the field, for half time service by the church or institution they served; other time for language. They should remain unmarried for four years, thereafter if they had proved efficient they would be put on the roll as regular missionaries.[52]

In September three names were approved: D. G. Abbott, H. R. Calkins, and W. B. Empey,[53] and in April, 1901, C. E. Parker.[54] Nine months after the appeal Bishop Warne wrote: "Qualified men have not responded; why, I do not know, but the consequences are serious indeed." He named Kolar, Yellandu, Raipur and Jagdalpur as some places where they were greatly needed. Dr. Leonard added:

> To this second call a large number responded, but upon investigation most of them were found unsatisfactory, usually because of too little educational preparation. Only two have been accepted and appointed. . . . Persons who have not had a liberal education [the equivalent of the usual college course] need not offer their services.[55]

Episcopal Supervision

After eight years under the Missionary Episcopacy the Central Conference in 1896 declared that

> the plan which provided our work with a resident Bishop of long and practical experience in Missionary work in this land was a providential one . . . it is but a clear matter of history that the occupation of many new places, the founding of various important institutions, the undertaking of not a few extensive enterprises, and the accumulation of much valuable property, would not have come to pass, but for our Missionary Bishop . . . a peculiar bond of unity characterizes our work. Our plans and methods are substantially one throughout all our borders.[56]

They also asked for the election of a second missionary Bishop "to be chosen from the missionary body of the field. This was not done, but the intention to do so was defeated only by being included in a motion that included other foreign mission fields.[57]

From 1889 to 1897 Bishop Thoburn administered the field alone. In 1896 the General Conference provided for the joint superintendency of all Missions which were under Missionary Bishops, to be by them *and* a General Superintendent once in a quadrennium. Bishop Foss was the first General Superintendent to visit the field under this plan, being present at the several conferences and the Central Conference, which expressed its deep appreciation of the visit. One phrase from his address remains in our history. "Grave problems confront us in this vast, various, intensely interesting field, which ought no longer to be spoken of as India and Malaysia, but as Southern Asia."[58] The Journals of the Central Conferences of 1898 and 1900 have the words "Southern Asia" in brackets under "India and Malaysia". After 1900 the new name became fixed by approval of General Conference.

Twelve years of unceasing labour and increasing burdens had so impaired Bishop Thoburn's health, that by 1900, he had felt unable to prepare the usual Address or discharge the duties of his office "in more than a merely nominal sense".[59] For more than forty years he had laboured in and for India and twelve of those were as Missionary Bishop. In a retrospective glance over this later period he named the following particulars in which advance ground had been taken:

> (1) in becoming better messengers of God to the poor; . . . (2) in the rapid increase of our Native Christian workers, especially from the lower ranks of society; . . . (3) in the promotion of Indian preachers to the position of presiding elders; . . . it has to a large extent inspired our preachers and people with a new sense of their personal responsibility; (4) in the enthusiasm which has in many places been developed in the hearts of the people.

The Central Conference asked for three Bishops permanently residing on the field. The General Conference in 1900 elected Francis Wesley Warne and Edwin Wallace Parker to the Missionary Episcopacy and continued Bishop Thoburn as effective. He came to India in some cold seasons and to an extent represented the needs of India to the American churches. He was present at the Jubilee in 1906. At his own request he was retired in 1908. On that occasion J. W. Robinson presented him with flowers in "token of the high appreciation in which all missionaries held him as the incarnation of the missionary spirit".[60] He died at Meadville, November 28, 1922.

Bishop Warne

Parker and Warne were elected on the first ballot for Missionary Bishops. On the evening before his consecration Bishop Warne wrote: "I greatly felt the responsibility, but at the same time had the greatest confidence that it is in accordance with the will of the Lord." In India the Church also had a profound feeling that he was God's chosen leader. None could understand how Bishop Parker, who had been in India for forty-one years should be taken from the work without his holding an Annual Conference, while Bishop Warne, only twelve years in the country should now find himself responsible for administering the entire field of India, Malaysia and the Philippine Islands. Often he leaned hard on a favourite verse, "My God shall supply all your need."

Bishop E. W. Parker

Edwin Parker had received 558 votes out of 667, "the largest numerically ever received by any episcopal candidate. He and Mrs. Parker were not elated." To them it was "*a burden of work and care to be borne*". They were aware that a group in his own conference had opposed his candidacy. In a letter following his election he wrote to them asking their help, "help us with advice and suggestions, by word or by letter, whenever and wherever you see the opportunity". The weeks in America before they left for India were filled with engagements that precluded the rest he should have had. They sailed from New York on September 19; on October 15, he wrote in his journal: "Moving on; will reach Bombay tomorrow morning." His biographer says:

> These are the last words of Bishop Parker's diary; although he knew it not, and his friends knew it not, they were written by the hand of a dying man.... What remained was little more than a brave battle for life, and death at last prevailed.

In the division of work Bishop Parker was to have had the Bombay and the two Northern Conferences. On landing in Bombay, he was confronted at once with emergencies. He and Mrs. Parker were enthusiastically received at their home in Shahjahanpur, and the next week he met with Bishop Warne and the treasurer of the Bishop Thoburn Special Fund at Allahabad. He went to a District Conference at Aligarh where he preached his last sermon in Hindustani. He rallied from death's door in Meerut. On New Year's day he arranged with Bishop Warne to take his Conferences, and Warne's last interview was after those Conferences when he went to him to report. Early in the morning he was allowed in his room. He found Parker's face aglow with a light from the Spirit World and heard from him the following experience:

> I had a vision last night; the Lord Jesus came into my room and appeared to me in all His glory, and said, 'I have two propositions to make to you.' With awe and rejoicing I replied, 'What are they?' Jesus said, 'The first is that you may continue to live, but you can never be strong.' I asked, 'Can I be of any use to any one and do any good in the world?' He said, 'No; you can never be strong enough to help any one, but will always have to be taken care of as you are now.' I said, 'Then I do not care to live; what is the second proposition?' He then took me away into a very bright and beautiful place which He called the lower department of heaven. He showed me the higher and still higher, grander and much more beautiful and wonderful departments of heaven, but asked me to look around me and see the people by whom I was then surrounded. I looked and saw great multitudes of people, and noted and rejoiced that many of them were our village Christians who had passed on before. He said, 'These are my little ones who have received me in India, but have never had the opportunity of receiving much teaching, and they are here waiting to be taught before they are promoted to the higher and highest places in heaven. If you will choose to come with Me I will appoint you to teach these little ones, and you will have the privilege of doing much good.' This was an entirely new idea of heaven to me, and when I thought that

I could do no more good on earth I at once said, 'Blessed Lord Jesus, I will go with Thee, and I rejoice in the prospect and privilege of being permitted to further teach our Indian village Christians.' All at once all anxiety about leaving the work and the world was gone, and there opened up before me a new and blessed work of which I had never thought: the blessed privilege of teaching Christ's little ones. I said to Jesus, 'I will be delighted to teach these poor people as long as you wish.'

Filled with this thought Bishop Parker patted his wasted hand upon his chest outside of the bed covering, and while tears of joy coursed down his emaciated cheeks he said: 'O, I am so happy at the prospect of teaching Christ's little ones; I have a new appointment! The future is all glorious! I long to be away to my new appointment!'[61]

For a few weeks there was hope of Bishop Parker's recovery. In April and May he was in the salubrious climate of Naini Tal. From there, on June 30, 1901, he joined his "new appointment".

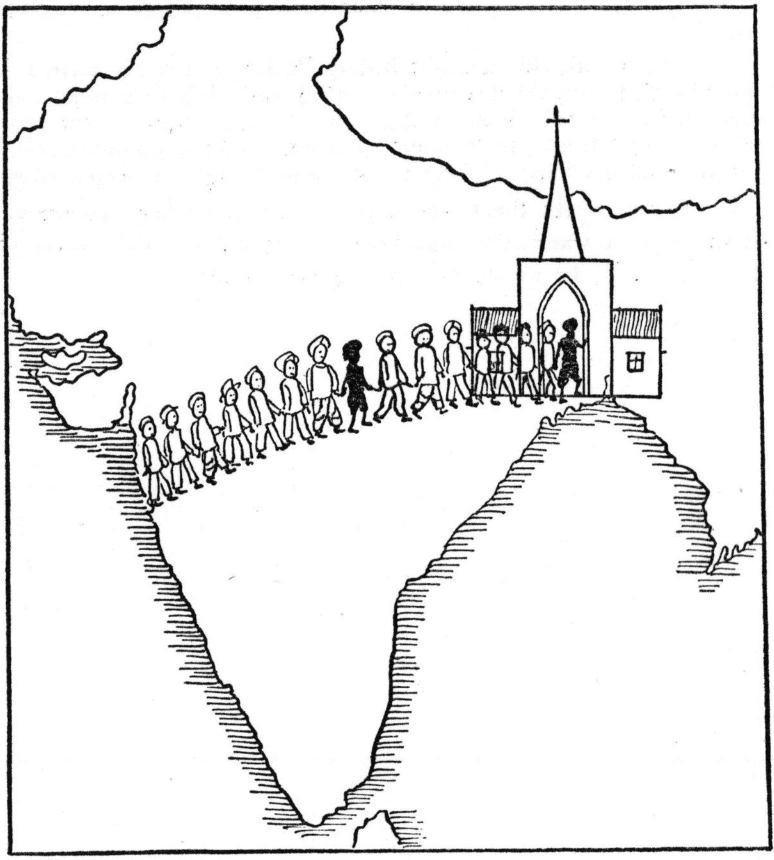

1 in 8 Indian Protestants is a
Methodist 1952 A.D.

Section IV

Indispensable

I

O Master of the ransomed life,
Give me the word to set them free;
Let thy sweet calm replace the strife,
Teach them the joy of trust in Thee.

No cost too great to make them Thine
These hungry crowds that seek in vain.
O, fill thy Church with power divine,
The clamouring millions to reclaim.

Bishop F. B. Fisher.

II

"HE SHOWED THEM HIS HANDS AND HIS FEET."

Luke 24:40.

LORD, when I am weary with toiling,
And burdensome seem Thy commands.
If my load should lead to complaining,
Lord, show me Thy hands,—
Thy nail-pierced hands, Thy cross-torn hands,—
My Saviour, show me Thy hands.

CHRIST, if ever my footsteps should falter,
And I be prepared for retreat,
If desert or thorn cause lamenting,
Lord, show me Thy feet,—
Thy bleeding feet, Thy nail-scarred feet,—
My Jesus, show me Thy feet.

O GOD, dare I show Thee—
My hands and My feet!

Bishop B. T. Badley.

XII

Entering A New Era

Strange though it may seem the occasion of the departure of a British Viceroy "was the occasion of popular demonstrations unparalleled in Indian annals". These marked

> the beginnings of a united national life, the birth of a new spirit of co-operation among Indian people . . . . It was not that Lord Ripon had been able to do much; but the purity of his intention, the loftiness of his ideals, his hatred of racial disqualifications, were an open book to the people of India. They read it and poured out their hearts in gratitude to the Englishman who . . . realized the great mission of England in India, and sought to fulfil it.[1]

Indian nationalism was not born in oppression, nor conceived in hate. It sprang from ideals of freedom and human worth that had for twenty-five years found expression in schools and colleges and intercourse with the ruling country where hundreds of its leaders were educated. Its methods were to be "constitutional agitation in India and in England". The first Indian National Conference met in Calcutta in Christmas week, 1883. A second National Conference convened in 1885, and at the same time the first session of the Indian National Congress convened in Bombay. The movements were simultaneous but the arrangements were quite independent of each other. In 1886 the two merged in the second session of the Indian National Congress at Calcutta.[2]

> The immediate effect in India was the quickening of the national spirit, and a passionate expression of the belief that India's sons were also able to direct their own affairs, or, at least, a very much larger degree of self-government.[3]

These Conferences promoted a unity throughout India. The victory of Japan over Russia in 1906, sent a thrill through all of Asia. In the first World War India's soldiers gave new dignity to their country and its people when they fought shoulder to shoulder with British and Allied troops.

The Episcopal address at the Central Conference in 1908 said: "A new East is evolving before our eyes . . . a new era in the National life of these Eastern peoples". In 1920 the Bishops urged the Christian community to overcome the mistaken impression among educated non-Christian Indians that, to become a Christian is to become de-nationalized.

The development of this new national consciousness "produced such a vigorous and vital church life" that the church machinery and authority proved inadequate for its normal expression. There was a growing desire for *swaraj* or self-determination, and for more immediate Indianization. Fortunately these advances could be met by an increase in the powers of the Central Conference. First steps were taken in 1920 on recommendation of a Commission under Bishop Berry, when authority was given:

> to arrange courses of study for its ministry subject to the approval of the Bishop; to prepare a simplified, adapted form of parts of the ritual; to extend article 23 of the Articles of Religion to recognize the Government... of countries within its jurisdiction; to make adaptations regarding membership, special advices, worship, and the local ministry, not contrary to the Discipline; to incorporate an Executive Board, subject to proper agreements with the Board of Foreign Missions, to establish rules, rites and ceremonies for the solemnization of marriage; and to make rules and regulations for the purchase, holding and transferring of property not related to the Board of Foreign Missions and the Woman's Foreign Missionary Society.[4]

In 1928 a Commission with L.O. Hartman as Chairman, and C.B. Stuntz as Secretary, recommended that Central Conferences be empowered to elect Bishops. To make this possible the General Conference submitted to the Annual Conferences an amendent to the constitution of the Church for their approval; and authorized the Central Conference of Southern Asia to elect one Bishop or General Superintendent when the amendments were approved.

Changing Episcopal Supervision

The burden of supervision had been heavy on Bishop Warne in the quadrennium 1900–1904, but he won the hearts of people in every Conference and field. To General Conference he said, "The thrilling events of the quadrennium ... fill me with gratitude and loneliness." Bishop Thoburn had made two winter visits to India "presiding at the Conferences and giving general direction to the work". Because these visits were "an inspiration to our work and workers" and because he had "an unparalleled hold upon the hearts of the home Church" the Central Cenference earnestly requested his continuance as an effective Bishop.[5] This General Conference approved, and also elected two additional Missionary Bishops, William F. Oldham and John E. Robinson, for Southern Asia.

In the election of both these men India rejoiced. Residences for four Bishops were fixed: *Bombay*, J.M. Thoburn; *Lucknow*, F.W. Warne; *Calcutta*, J.E. Robinson, and *Singapore*, W.F. Oldham.

Bishop J. E. Robinson

J.E. Robinson continued as Bishop until 1920; 1904–12 in charge of Bombay, Bengal and Burma, and after that in supervision of S. India and and Malaysia. Versatile and effective, his wide experience equipped him for this new office. At his retirement the Central Conference recorded its "appreciation of the consecration, ability and the whole-hearted loyalty to our Lord and Master Jesus Christ, which continuously characterized his lengthy period of varied service."[6] All six children of Bishop and Mrs. Robinson returned to India, five daughters as missionaries of the W.F.M.S. Fletcher, the only son, came as a doctor, but not under the Society, yet he made himself one of the group and many missionaries and Indians are grateful for the kindly, skillful service he rendered. The family gave 212 years of service under the Missionary Society, not counting the years since Muriel commenced her own Home School in Bangalore where she still labours.

Bishop Oldham

Between 1890 and 1904 Oldham had been in America as Pastor, and then as Professor of Missions and Comparative Religions at Ohio Wesleyan University. Of this last period Dr. Bashford said: "At times I have wondered whether any pastor in Methodism ever accomplished a greater work than did Dr. Oldham during this last two years."[7] From 1904 to 1912 he was Missionary Bishop for Malaysia. In 1912 he was elected as one of three Coordinate Secretaries of the Board of Missions and in 1916 as a General Superintendent assigned to South America. He retired in 1928.

Bishop J.W. Robinson

John Wesley Robinson was elected Missionary Bishop in 1912. Twenty years before, he and Mrs. Robinson came as young missionaries to the North India Conference. Few have been given such varied responsibilities as came to him: Pastor of the English Church, Agent of the Lucknow Publishing House, District Superintendent, Editor of the *Kaukab-i-Hind*, and problems galore in matters of finance and property. He demonstrated a superb mastery of details and principles. Abilities he showed in his Conference were further proved in the Central Conference for All-India situations. He was wise in administration and patient in dealing with people and their problems. His election by 686 votes out of 739 reflects the unanimity of sentiment on the field. At the time of his retirement by General Conference in 1936, he asked "that by such private efforts as I may be able to make the rest of my life, I be allowed to do what I can to further the cause of the Methodist Church that I love".[8]

With Bishop Robinson it was not a rhetorical request. He retired from the work of a Bishop and continued to live in India. He was willing to fill the vacancy of a Bishop; to be Editor of *The Indian Witness*, or to act temporarily in a District. He was always ready to be adviser and friend. He was in Naini Tal for a short vacation when he heard the summons to other service and a "Well done" for a life of service here.

General Superintendents

An unexpected situation arose in the General Conference of 1916. It had been decided to elect seven General Superintendents and one Missionary Bishop. For this latter office it was generally expected that Oldham would be elected, but he was elected fifth of seven—a General Superintendent. Three days later resolutions were presented for the discontinuance of the Missionary Episcopacy and the electing of Missionary Bishops General Superintendents. It seemed probable that this procedure would be adopted but the resolutions were referred to Committees and finally tabled. Warne commented on this: "With that the question of making Missionary Bishops General Superintendents was forever closed, or so it seems."[9]

Four years later the Episcopacy Committee reported:

> 1. The Missionary Episcopacy was designed to meet special conditions at a time when continuous supervision by the General Superintendents had not been extended to our foreign fields.
>
> 2. While the achievements and successes of the Missionary Episcopacy have amply justified its institution, none the less it is the deliberate judgment of your Committee that the point of its highest usefulness has been reached and that in the new era upon which we are now entering all our foreign fields should have the benefit of supervision by General Superintendents assigned to such fields.[10]

The Committee further recommended that the present Missionary Bishops should be elected General Superintendents. Bishops Warne and J.W. Robinson were so elected. The assignment of General Superintendents to residences for the quadrennium were: *Bangalore*, H. Lester Smith; *Bombay*, J. W. Robinson; *Calcutta*, F.B. Fisher; *Lucknow*, F.W. Warne.

Bishop Fisher

As a student in Asbury College, Fred Fisher attended the Student Volunteer Convention in Toronto, Canada, in 1900. He was thrilled by Bishop Thoburn's address and early the next morning searched out the house where he was staying. After breakfast the Bishop met him. Pointing his index finger in the lad's face, Thoburn said, "I know what brought you here . . . . I will wager you want to go to India." There, in the middle of the floor, they prayed together. "Now I am going to pray that God will take you to India, that you will love the Indians, and that you may be a great Christian worker." After that he put his hand on Fisher's head, saying, "Now remember, my lad, I have put my hand upon your head and set you apart for India . . . . Finish your college course. I will be waiting for you in India." Bishop McCabe ordained Fred Fisher as Deacon in 1904; Bishop Warne ordained him an Elder. But he counted Thoburn's dedication as his first ordination: "I set you apart for India."

Fred Fisher came to India with his bride, Edith Jackson, in July, 1904. He was pastor of the English Church in Agra, and did some village work. Within three years they had to return to America on account of Mrs. Fisher's illness. They were in India again in 1917—18 in connection with the Mass Movement work. They came again in November, 1920, on his assignment as General Superintendent, his Area including the Bengal, Burma and later, Lucknow Conferences. "He comes," wrote Warne, "with all the freshness, vigour, enthusiasm of his young manhood, and his life long training in committee work. He went into everything with holy enthusiasm. . . . It is a joy to have him".[11] Mrs. Fisher died in Darjeeling on June 5, 1921.

Fisher loved India and its people. He sought acquaintance with India's leaders in all walks of life, and tried to develop Indian leadership in the Church. "My job during recent years has been to try to prod our Indian laymen and ministers into assuming and demanding absolute control and influence." Yet in the middle of his third term he resigned his office in a letter to the Board of Bishops, giving his decision to cease from traveling at large among the people.

> The simple truth is that technical obligations, incessant travel, judicial trials, ecclesiastical umpiring, responsibility for the actual destiny of fellow ministers, financial and temporal management, with other kindred burdens, brought distress, grief and slavery. To allow my soul full play of expression in times of crises in church or state, became embarrassing to a large organism which looked upon my official self as its conservator rather than a prophetic spokesman . . . .
>
> Power is a strange thing. Those who wield it are in constant danger. It affects not only those who are ruled, but the ruler himself. Several years ago I took a personal vow that if and when I found myself taking any pride in power I would renounce it forthwith. I gradually became conscious of the almost unparalleled power of the Methodist episcopacy, not at all in prestige but in administrative fact.[12]

Fisher believed it would be "a good thing to reduce the administrative power" of a bishop by restricting his appointing power; by accepting decisions of a majority of a cabinet; by the election of District Superintendents, and by confining a Bishop's authority to his area. On the other hand a Bishop's spiritual responsibilities should be increased by making him responsible to receive all members into full membership, making it "a rich spiritual event" and giving him a personal contact with the growing church;

by making him responsible for all church dedications in his area, and for visiting institutions of the area to instruct and inspire.[13]

The Lucknow Conference, in 1930, was the first to have an all Indian Cabinet. The *Indian Witness* commented, "Bishop Fisher will be remembered long after other things are forgotten, for his stalwart insistence upon Indian shoulders being found for India's ecclesiastical responsibilities."[14]

Bishop Badley

In 1924 the General Conference made its last election for a Bishop for Southern Asia to take the place of Bishop Smith who did not return. The choice fell on Brenton Thoburn Badley, eldest son of Rev. and Mrs. B.H. Badley who had reached the North India Conference in 1872. In the assignment to areas Badley went to *Bombay;* Warne to *Bangalore*, Fisher to *Calcutta* and Robinson to *Delhi.*

"Bren"—for so his friends knew him—was the first second-generation missionary to be elected a Bishop. He grew up with Indian boys as companions; he learned stories from "Old Sirdar", the family servant; he received early years of education at Oak Openings, and when he completed his college course at Ohio Wesleyan, America could not hold him against India's pull. He was one of twelve to answer Thoburn's call. He did not need to learn the language—he polished it, so that he could use Hindustani as easily as he could English. Professor at Lucknow, General Secretary for the Epworth League, District Superintendent, keen student of Mission history, fluent writer, renowned story teller—all that he had was dedicated. Happy in the ability to do many things he was happiest preaching and presenting Christ, and in this he was at his best.

Central Conference Bishops

In keeping with the development of a National consciousness the General Conference of 1920 formed a Commission on Central Conferences to consider needed legislation which reported in 1924 regarding Memorials received concerning the nomination and election of Bishops by Central Conference. It said: "the time is ripe for the nomination or election of Bishops by the Central Conferences." The amendments submitted to Annual Conferences in 1928 were adopted. The Central Conference convened in Kanpur on December 27, 1930 had the honour of electing the first National Bishop, J.R. Chitambar on December 31. He received eighty-five of 121 votes cast on the second ballot, and was escorted to the platform by Bishop McConnell, Bishop Robinson and G. L. Lorenzo. Mrs. Chitambar was also escorted to the platform and introduced.

خدا محبت ہے

God's house is where His people worship—seated on hard earth floors beneath the sky, or gathered within the simple beauty of a campus sanctuary. There where the spirit has lived and multiplied the people are a church......

Chapel of
Isabella Thoburn College
for Women—Lucknow

District preacher on tour erects portable worship center in the midst of a village congregation

The Lord's Supper for a "Central Church" congregation.

Led into holy communion with God by pastors who know where to find Him—in large city sanctuaries and small village court-yards.

. . . . Led by pastors who are proud of their calling unafraid of the overwhelming problems their call has made them face—minority loneliness, poverty and the frustration of work that can never be called finished.

Village preachers share their problems at a District Council meeting.

In the open "sitting room" of a village the District Superintendent and circuit-in-charge lead the services.

Chitambar Chapel—Lucknow

Vikarabad District Hyderabad

On the outskirts of Delhi

SARAH CHAKKO—beloved spokesman for the church, President in the World Council of Churches until her death in 1954.

Village Woman's Society meeting.

Out of the worshipping congregations great and small came the Christian community. They sang their hymns and made their crosses—and sent their children to lead the world.

At the sign of the cross—a symbol to all that Christ is known here—

J. R. CHITAMBAR—chosen by his people to be their first Bishop—teacher and preacher whose eminence gave honour to his Church.

Village Christian home.

Youth Institute.

From the meager village come the young to find the treasure of kindred youth. Some also find in this fellowship a new purpose leading them to seminary.

Leonard Theological Seminary, Jabalpur. Advanced training center for India's Methodist pastors.

J. W. PICKETT—Delhi

S. K. MONDOL—Hyderabad.

C. D. ROCKEY—Lucknow.

J. A. SUBHAN—Bombay.

Bishops of the Methodist Church in Southern Asia—1956.

The Christian community of India needs an economic foundation which the Church has tried to establish...but the effort has brought conflict with ancient patterns of culture which gave little respect to manual labour.

Shoemaker in training.

Lampshades of grass bring creative expression.

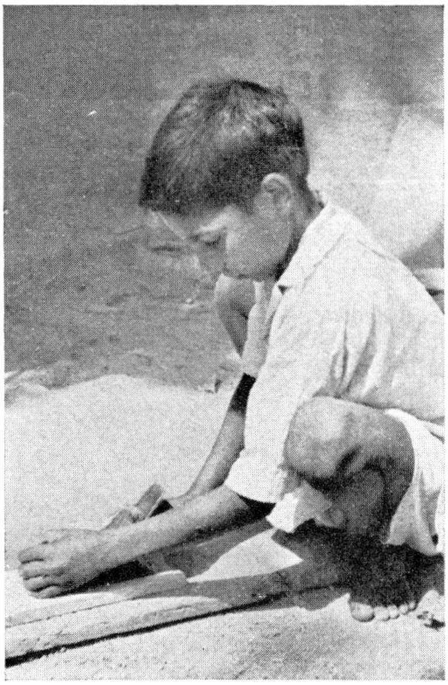

Child carpenter learns early the joy of labour.

Expert guidance prevents discouragement

Assisted by a free nation with aspirations toward an industrial place in the sun, the youth have gradually begun to unwrap their creativity and ask for the skill which will give them a new and rewarding vocation.

Bishop Chitambar

Jashwant Rao Chitambar was the second son of a Marathi family, originally from Nagpur. They were Brahmins. The father was converted through the reading of the Bible and was baptized in Allahabad by Dr. T.S. Wynkoop about 1876. For a few years Raja Ram Chitambar was pastor of the Jumna Church, Presbyterian, in Allahabad. About 1889 the family moved to Kanpur where he became the pastor of the M. E. Church and Headmaster of the Mission School. Jashwant was then ten years old. In 1893 his father died, and Jashwant and his elder brother, Parmeshwar Datt, removed to Lucknow, to the Centennial School. His brother died soon after.

Jashwant was converted in 1895–96 during meetings held for his students by W. A. Mansell. He heard his call to preach in February, 1896, during meetings held by John R. Mott. He then signed the "Student Volunteer Pledge to take up direct Christian work unless prevented by God". He was nurtured in the Sunday School where Miss Thoburn taught the college students, in the Epworth League and in the Church services. He drew great profit from the Dasehra meetings.

On completion of his Conference course his friends urged him not to join the ministry, but his earlier resolution held firm. At this time he married Miss Satyawati Singh, a student of Isabella Thoburn College, and together they went to the Theological Seminary in Bareilly—the first graduate to attend that institution. His biographer says it was the "unusual help and sustained inspiration" that he received from his wife that steadied him in these years, and later. After completing his course he taught two years in Bareilly, then went to his first pastorate in Naini Tal. After that he became Headmaster of the Centennial School until 1913, during which time he served as pastor of the Central Church, Hindustani, for a period. It was also in this period that he went as delegate to the World Student Conference in Tokyo; and to the World Sunday School Convention at Washington and then the Missionary Conference in Edinburgh.[15]

He joined the North India Conference "In Studies of the First Year" in 1905. In 1915 he became Superintendent of the Eastern Kumaon District, then followed five years as General Secretary of the Epworth League for India and Burma. In 1922 he was installed as Principal of the Lucknow Christian College, and from that position he was elected to the Episcopacy. The Chitambar home was a Christian home; a haven where the peace of Christian experience prevailed. He died at the Episcopal residence in Jabalpur, September 4, 1940. His colleagues paid this tribute:

> As valuable as were his services to the Church as an administrator, Bishop Chitambar probably achieved even more of lasting worth through

> preaching. Whether the medium was Urdu, Hindi, or English, the place in India, America or some other country, his preaching was dynamic and persuasive; he always exalted Christ and helped his hearers....[16]

Bishop Pickett

Acting on the authorization of the General Conference of 1932, the Central Conference in December, 1935, elected an additional Bishop or General Superintendent. Jarrell Waskom Pickett of the Lucknow Conference, received seventy-nine out of 107 votes cast in the first ballot and was declared elected. He was escorted to the platform by Bishop Chitambar and A. A. Parker.

Pickett came to India in 1910, joined the North India Conference on probation in 1911 and was ordained Deacon and Elder under the Missionary Rule at the same session, and appointed to the English Church, Lucknow. In 1916 he married Ruth, the daughter of Bishop and Mrs. J. W. Robinson. He was a charter member of the Lucknow Conference where he was Superintendent of the Arrah District. He was selected by the Indian National Christian Council whose Chairman was Dr. V. S. Azariah, Bishop of Dornakal, to be the the Director of a Survey of Christian Mass Movements in India. The report was read with deepest interest in India for as John R. Mott wrote, these movements had "stimulated the interest of Moslems and of high caste Hindus in the outcastes and other depressed groups of India".[17]

Bishop Pickett's residence was fixed temporarily at Lucknow and after General Conference at Bombay, with supervision of the Bombay, Gujarat and Indus River Conferences. In 1945 he was assigned to the Delhi Area, with the Delhi, North India and Indus River Conferences. The years ahead were fraught with tremendous significance and Pickett's coming seemed to be "for such a time as this". In the stormy days that followed partition his fortitude and leadership helped the Christians to organize the relief of refugees, immigrants from and emigrants to Pakistan. In this they demonstrated their innate loyalty and devotion to their India, now free and independent. Partition at once disrupted the Indus River Conference adding four big districts to the growing Delhi Conference. By his administration from Bombay Pickett was already acquainted with their work. Through twelve years his intimate contacts with Prime Minister Nehru, President Prasad, the American Ambassadors and other Statesmen, enabled him to help the Government to understand the Churches and through the National Christian Council, to help the Churches in many difficult situations. At the recent General Conference he had the honour to be the first Central Conference Bishop to preside at one of the sessions. At the Central Conference in 1956 Bishop Pickett will retire under the age limit prescribed for its Bishops.

Election Under The Methodist Church

The Uniting Conference in May, 1939, effected the union of The Methodist Episcopal Church, The Methodist Episcopal Church, South, and The Methodist Protestant Church. These "had their common origin in the organization of the Methodist Episcopal Church in America in 1784 A.D., and have . . . preserved a common belief, spirit and purpose". They adopted the name The Methodist Church for the United Church. India was represented at the Uniting Conference by four delegates elected by the Board of Bishops: Ministerial—E.M. Moffatt, E.M. Rugg; Lay—Mrs. C. Premnath Das, J.S.K. Patel.

The first General Conference of The Methodist Church met in 1940. It authorized a fourth Bishop for Southern Asia. The Central Conference which convened in Delhi, December 28, 1940 elected this bishop and also a second to fill the vacancy caused by the death of J. R. Chitambar. Shot K. Mondol was elected on the sixth ballot and Clement D. Rockey on the eleventh.

Bishop Mondol

Shot Kumar Mondol was the first son of an Indian Methodist preacher to be elected to the Episcopacy. His father, Ananta Kumar Mondol, was received into membership in the Bengal Conference as a probationer in 1903. He died in 1909. The Bishop's uncle, Surju M. Mondol, also a member of the Bengal Conference, joined in 1896 and died in 1938.

S.K. Mondol was admitted On Trial in 1921. He was for some years a District Superintendent, and early became a recognized leader in the Bengal Conference. He was a delegate to Central Conference in1928 and the leader of the Bengal delegation in 1935, 1939, and in 1940 when he was elected Bishop. He was assigned to residence in Hyderabad, and since then has held supervision of the Hyderabad, South India and Central Provinces (Madhya Pradesh) Conferences.

Bishop Rockey

Clement Daniel Rockey, a second-generation missionary, is the son of the Rev. and Mrs. N.L. Rockey who came to the N.I. Conference in December, 1884. An elder brother, Lee, joined the S.I. Conference, and a sister, Lois, after several years at Queens Hill, Darjeeling, married A.G. Atkins of the N.I. Conference. The Rockey children, as many other missionary children, had their education in Oak Openings and Wellesley in Naini Tal. Clement returned after his courses at Ohio Wesleyan and at Drew, to the N.I. Conference. He was admitted On Trial in 1914 and during his first term was appointed to the staff of the Bareilly Theological Seminary. Later years were spent as District Superintendent, Pastor of the English Church in Naini Tal and Principal of the Theological Seminary.

After his election Bishop Rockey, with his wife, Helen Cady, daughter of Methodist missionaries in China, was assigned to the Lucknow Area which included the Bengal, Burma and Lucknow Conferences, and for the quadrennium 1952–56, the Indus River Conference in Pakistan. Under the age limit for Central Conference Bishops he will retire in the fall of 1956.

Bishop Subhan

Our history has given several examples of converts from Islam who have become effective District Superintendents. In the election of John Abdus Subhan to the Methodist Episcopacy we have our first Muslim convert attaining to that office.

Subhan belonged to the Mughal race, and was born in a family that "held hereditary office in the Court of Mughal Emperors". The ancestral home was in Benares. Because of their suspected alliance with the Mughal Court in the Uprising, Hafiz Allah Baksh, Subhan's father, gave up old connections and learned the art of gold embroidery, becoming skilled therein. For the sake of trade the family moved to Calcutta. There John Subhan was born in 1897. His mother ruled the home and directed his education as a good Muslim. "Indeed," he writes, "I was growing up into a fanatic . . . . I would delight in dreaming of another *Jehad*, a holy war, and draw the sword against all unbelievers."

In his study of the Quran he was intrigued by the names of Moses, David and Jesus, and references to their books. A hunger to know more of God himself led him to books on Islamic mysticism. In this pursuit he became a Sufi. After his initiation into the Qadriya fraternity he was one day given a Gospel. On an earlier occasion he had torn one to pieces, but this time "he was prompted to read it". The result was startling. He found nothing "blasphemous and satanic". Rather he "was impressed with the high ethical teaching of the Gospel". It spoke to his soul, "every sentence touched it to its very depth". He decided to be a Christian.

There were other steps of which he writes. They included years in St. John's College, Agra, where he grew in things Christian. Other years he was a Roman Catholic. As such he visited the home of E. Millicans Khan, a Civil Surgeon and a staunch Methodist. Subhan knew the family well and had had spiritual fellowship with them. Now he refused to join in grace at meals, and absented himself from family worship. He asked a special dispensation to share in these and was refused. Because he could not believe his Protestant friends were not Christians, he left the Catholic

Church. For some time he was without a church home, and lived with his mother and brothers.[18]

Through Dr. Paton of the National Christian Council he was put in touch with M.T. Titus, who recommended him for the new Department of Islamic Studies in the Bareilly Seminary in 1925. This was work he wanted —a work to reach Muslims. He was married the next year in the Methodist Church. In his new associates—J. Devadason, H.J. Sheets, P.S. Hyde, and Albert Gulab—he found new fellowship and joined the Methodist Church.

He joined the N.I. Conference, becoming a full member in 1931. He was transferred to the Indus River Conference in 1934 where he had become a member of the staff of the Henry Martyn School of Islamic Studies. He was elected Bishop by the Central Conference in 1944, the year in which Badley retired as General Superintendent. He was assigned to the Bombay Area, including the Bombay and Gujarat Annual Conferences, and the Bhabua Mission.

A Higher Comity

A century ago there were accepted principles for the regulation of relations of missions with each other. These assumed friendly relations and a brotherly spirit, but stressed especially the rule that "when the missionaries of one society are in possession of a field of labour, other societies should not, as a general rule, enter it without their cordial consent".[19] These principles were included in the word "Comity". In the first Ecumenical Methodist Conference convened in London in 1881, to which J.W. Waugh was a delegate, complaint was made against William Taylor by the Rev. Dr. Rigg, a Wesleyan missionary.

> With the name of Dr. Butler . . . is associated the observance of the established Indian rules of missionary procedure . . . with the name of Rev. William Taylor . . . is associated, at least in the minds of many, the thought of intrusion and irregularity, and much that is more or less disturbing and perplexing . . . . [He has] set an example of uncoordinated action within the same Church which has its dangerous side.[20]

Twenty years later the Wesleyan Provincial Synod in session in Lucknow, addressed a letter to Bishop Warne and the N.W.I. Annual Conference. It was written in most friendly terms and said:

> It is a cause for gratitude that those questions which in former days have been in dispute, and, at times, have separated between friends, are now finally laid to rest, and are well nigh forgotten, and that there exists today that substantial unity of spirit which is even more valuable and desirable than external uniformity of organization and government.[21]

That change in attitude for the churches was as marked a characteristic of the period 1880 to 1930 as was Nationalism. Neither was cause, neither effect of the other; they developed side by side. Cooperation for the churches was just as indispensable as unity throughout India was essential for freedom. The roots for "Togetherness" reached back to Provincial Missionary Conferences, in Calcutta, 1885; Benares, 1857, when William Butler was present with thirty-five other members; South India, 1858; and Punjab, 1862. In 1872 the first Decennial Missionary Conference convened in Allahabad with 136 members from all parts of India. The second Decennial Conference met in Calcutta in 1882 with 475 members representing twenty-seven Societies;[22] the third in Bombay in 1893 and the fourth in Madras in 1902, December. This was a delegated Conference, and with special efforts to bring in Indians the "effective membership" was 286. Bishop Whitehead, the Lord Bishop of Madras, delivered the address of welcome. After reviewing the past, he said:

> As we look forward to the future then, what is the chief need; what is the thing most wanted to enable the Christian Church to advance by leaps and bounds and rise to a higher moral and spiritual life? I would answer without hesitation, *Unity* . . .
>
> The divisions and disunion of the Christian Church have been no doubt a source of weakness in the past, but their influence is likely to be far more disastrous in the present century . . . . The weakened life of a divided body cannot bear that moral witness to the world for which our Lord prayed.[23]

A dozen years later, John R. Mott visited India. His message too, was "Together". Province to Province he went; the Provincial Missionary Councils were formed—not union, but together, to understand each other and then to work together. Associated with the Provincial Councils, not to "tell them", but to help as might be possible, and to promote a unity in action, was the National Missionary Council, with its office in Calcutta. Its first meeting was held on February 4–5, 1914.

Into this field, prepared for harmony and cooperation, evangelists moved out. There was Jawala Singh, doughty champion of the Gospel and a keen debater with Muslims and Hindus. Many churches requested his services. In the all-India field was Stanley Jones. He speaks of 1919, as "a year of exceptional blessing and opportunity". For six months he was engaged in evangelistic work with Dr. Sherwood Eddy. Union campaigns took them to forty-three cities.

> The Christians thus began to feel their unity and learned to respect Christians of other denominations. A strong movement for the union in South India of the Mar Thoma Syrian Church, the Anglican Church and the South India United Church practically grew out of this campaign. Whether it may be consummated or not, it brought out

evidence of a very sincere desire on the part of Indian Christians for closer union.[24]

E. Stanley Jones, Evangelist

At the session of the North India Conference in January, 1908, Stanley Jones was introduced as a newly-arrived missionary. He was admitted On Trial, and ordained both Deacon and Elder under the Missionary Rule, and appointed to the English Church in Lucknow. After three years he was transferred to Sitapur circuit in charge of the Boys' Boarding School. In his report for 1912 his D.S., J.W. Robinson, reported that with the "help of Mrs. Mabel Lossing Jones, we have at last been able to inaugurate a long cherished plan. The smaller Christian boys are now under the direct control of women teachers."[25]

In 1917 Jones' appointment, with Sitapur as headquarters, read "City school and circuit", and "Conference Evangelist". Stanley had launched into the field of his life work—Evangelist. The appointment varied: "Evangelist to Educated Indians", 1926; "Evangelist at Large", 1946; "General Evangelist", 1950. He was "retired" at the Conference of 1954, but he continues active as an Evangelist.

Mrs. Jones maintained the home in Sitapur, and the little boys' hostel continued "under the direct control of women teachers". Although the advantages of such care for small boys have been stressed over and over again, few are the places where it has been arranged. Mrs. Jones has been careful to provide scholarships for Sitapur boys and for many more in other schools, and she is building an endowment fund that will continue to help deserving boys through years to come.

The General Conference Journal for 1928 carries a story that is unique in Methodist history, and in every way a credit to Jones, the Evangelist. The twentieth ballot cast for General Superintendent showed that E. Stanley Jones had been elected, receiving 560 of 778 votes cast. On motion of C.D. Rockey, Bishop-elect Jones was escorted to his place among the Bishops by the four Bishops resident in India where he was presented to the Conference by the Presiding Bishop. At the evening session the next day, Saturday, before the Sunday when the consecration service would be held, Stanley Jones got the floor on a question of privilege, and read the following:

> Dear Fathers and Brethren: On more mature deliberation, which under the circumstances was impossible last evening, I have come to the conclusion that I should continue the work I am doing, and I hereby resign as Bishop-elect of the Methodist Episcopal Church.
>
> I am grateful to those who have voted for me—grateful far more than this resignation would imply.[26]

After consultation among Officers and Chairmen of Sub-committees, the resignation was accepted, "with the greatest appreciation for the spirit and conviction which moved him to his decision".

Stanley Jones was free to continue the work he was doing. Other countries have received much of his time and his messages but he returns to India every year for three or four months as Evangelist. At Sat Tal in May and June he is Acharya to his Ashram group which includes eighty selected persons: college students, pastors, missionaries, educationists and new converts.

All-India Institutions

Miss Lilawati Singh's return to the Lucknow Woman's College in 1892, after working for two years in Dacca, was very welcome to Miss Thoburn who wanted educated Indian women for the College staff and especially desired Miss Singh's "services for Christ". She was then the first Indian member in the senior staff. In 1895 she took her M.A. from the Allahabad University. Miss Singh went to America in 1899 to help Miss Thoburn represent the needs of the institution to the Societies. Her poise and quiet manner were impressive. "The audience listened, at first with interest, but soon with undisguised amazement." In the first months she prayed and worked for money for the College. Then she felt the need of personal consecration. The burden of prayer changed to "more of Christ in my life before I go back to India". On recommendation of the Woman's Conference in 1901 she was given the status of a missionary of the Society.

Miss Thoburn died in Lucknow on September 1, 1901, of cholera. Miss F.L. Nichols succeeded her as Principal of the College, the name of which was changed in 1903 to Isabella Thoburn College. Miss Singh was appointed Vice Principal of the College from 1903 to 1907. During the next year it was decided that Miss Singh should have furlough and opportunity for study in America, and then return to be Principal of her *Alma Mater*. She spent her strength in pleading the cause of the College. She died on May 9, 1909, following an operation in a Chicago hospital. She was laid to rest in the cemetery at Elgin, Illinois. The marker on the grave reads: "The peace of God was on her face".

Miss Nichols carried the Principalship from 1902 to 1908, and then returned in 1921 for a short term. Misses Ruth and Flora Robinson, daughters of Bishop J.E. Robinson, both served as teachers and as Principal in years of great growth and development in the institution.

In 1920–21 two influences brought important changes to Lal Bagh and Isabella Thoburn College. The first was the fact that "in the old home at Lal Bagh there was not room for both college and school to grow". The other was the establishing of the Lucknow University by the Government. At this time the College moved across the Goomti River close to the University. On a new property of thirty-two acres Miss Nichols commenced building the new home for the Isabella Thoburn College—Chand Bagh. Miss Mary E. Shannon, who followed Miss Nichols in 1925, describes the first occupation:

> In 1923 the classes and residential life were moved to the new site. Nothing was finished. The bare field, boasting but one tree, had been cut up by cart tracks, strewn with brick and the remnants of mortar pits. The new white buildings stood out with never a moment's relief of green shrub or vine, and most of all, there was an utter lack of all that had made Lal Bagh a place of tradition and rich memory.[27]

Mrs. Chandrama Premnath Dass was elected to succeed Miss Shannon at the opening of the school year in July, 1939.[28] The enrolment continued to grow. In 1929 it was 121 of whom only ten were in the B.A. Class. In 1938, enrolment reached 250, and in 1940, 272. "Numbers show increase and growth," she wrote, but the real development lay in "the intangibles of education".[29] From her earlier association on the staff and more recently as Vice Principal, Mrs. Dass knew how deep and permanent the "intangibles" could become. The dedication of the Clotilda Lyon McDowell Chapel on February 24, 1939 was to her "the most vital achievement of the year".

In January, 1940 the Board of Governors selected Miss Sarah Chakko as Vice Principal, and she succeeded Mrs. Dass as Principal. Her service was suddenly cut off while on the play ground with the girls, on January 25, 1954. In the period following India's independence Dr. Chakko's fearless spirit, sound judgment and broad outlook served the College and the Churches like a bulwark. In 1951 she took leave in connection with duties she had assumed for the World Council of Churches. At the time of her death she was one of six Presidents of that Council in which her contributions had been unique.

In the emergency Miss Ava Hunt, who had more than once served the College as acting Principal or Vice Principal, and was soon to leave on furlough preliminary to retirement, accepted the request to act again as Principal with Miss Sommerville as Vice Principal. The Board of Governors selected Miss E. M. Thillayampalam, Ph. D., to be Principal. She had been a student of Isabella Thoburn College in the time of Miss Ruth Robinson; she joined its staff under Miss Flora Robinson, then after graduate study in Columbia University, returned to Isabella Thoburn College again as a member of the staff. After an absence of eighteen years during which she was principal of a college in Ceylon, then of the Lady Doak College in S. India, she returned to her *Alma Mater.* The inaugural exercises were held on August 19, 1955.

For fifty years the Isabella Thoburn College received its students from every Methodist Conference and almost every Province, in India, and also from other countries. In 1948 eighteen different languages were spoken by members of the student body. Independent India has adopted Hindi as the national language, and insists that teaching in colleges shall be increasingly done in that language. By this the College will lose something of its cosmopolitan student body, which was All-India, multi-lingual, and also included students of several religions, as in 1950 Christians numbered 155, Hindus 118, Muslims 26, Sikhs 12, Zorastrians 5, and one Buddhist.[30]

Soon after the College moved to Chand Bagh the American Presbyterian Mission commenced cooperation with Isabella Thoburn College. It now has a Board of Governors in India and a Board of Directors in America.

To meet the needs of S.I. Conferences the W.D.C.S. participates in the Woman's Christian College, Madras, and also in St. Christopher's Training College there which prepares for teaching in secondary schools with special attention to practice teaching.[31]

Lucknow Christian College

Like its sister institution the organization of the Lucknow University brought changes to the Lucknow Christian College. J.J. Cornelius left the college to join the Department of Philosophy in the University. E. M. Moffatt gave part time as Dean of the faculty of Commerce and did some teaching for two years. Moffatt's connection, although temporary, strengthened our school of Commerce.[32] The University took from the College the last two years of the College course for the B.A. and B.Sc. degrees, leaving to "L.C.C." an Intermediate College, including the first two years of college work and the two of High School—a four year course, with Province-wide examinations after each two years.

During the years 1920–22 a comprehensive reorganization of the institution was effected, involving the complete separation of the College, the School of Commerce and the High School plants. Reid Hall, the former College, was given for the exclusive use of the School of Commerce. Fairfield Hall, the Centennial School building, was taken for the College; and a new building erected for the Centennial School. A new science block was built and a new hostel. On ground newly acquired new play grounds were made.[33] The year 1922 marked the close of the Principalship of T.C. Badley, as he assumed the duties of Educational Secretary. He had come to India in 1904 and became Principal after C.L. Bare, in 1914. J.R. Chitambar, M.A., D.D., outstanding alumnus, was installed as Principal in 1922.

With the election of Chitambar to the episcopacy, Dr. R.D. Wellons, who joined the College in its English Department in 1916, was elected Principal. His report to the Annual Conference in 1934 shows the Departments of the College and gives the wide range of training offered and the large enrolment in that year: Intermediate College, 811; School of Commerce 136; Teacher Training College, 30 ; College of Physical Education, 7; Centennial School 362; University House (a residence for students attending the University) 24 ; Total 1,370.[34] Training in Physical Education was a field in which the College pioneered, even as it had earlier opened Commercial classes. The excellent work of E.W. Mumby in this Department was acknowledged by Government, and the Education Department introduced a plan to send batches of teachers for three months' intensive courses.[35] In 1954 the Principal described a plan to make this a centre for training for athletes from all over India under A.W. Howard.

In later years Religious Education had become a problem. S.W. Clemes organized an effective program in this field which is now in charge of W.K. Whetstone. A beautiful chapel erected in 1953 as a memorial to Bishop Chitambar gives a center for this work, which is reaching both Christians and non Christians.

In 1949 Dr. C.M. Thacore became the second Indian Principal. With the growing demand for College education the Lucknow Christian College was again affiliated to teach for examinations for both the B.A. and B.Sc. degrees. The Principal's report for 1954 shows the following enrolment: Degree College, 862 with 74 Christians; Teacher Training College, 75 with 20 Christians; College of Physical Education, 66 with 19 Christians; the Centennial Higher Secondary School (two years in the College course) 554 with 47 Christians; a total of 1557 with 160 Christians.

The relatively small number of Christians is accounted for in part by three facts: there is no hostel in connection with the Centennial School to care for boys from outside of Lucknow; too few scholarships to assist Christian students to get the College education, and the change in the medium of instruction from English to Hindi, which cuts off students from several Conferences. To some degree this limits the opportunity for "L.C.C." to serve as our all-India institution but it may still reach a large Methodist constituency.

The Division of World Missions has been cooperating with the Meston Training College, Madras for the training of graduate teachers since 1945.[36]

Leonard Theological College

When the Bareilly Theological Seminary opened in 1872 it was necessary to admit students with the lowest educational qualifications and improve these while training them for the work. Gradually standards were raised; but very slowly. In 1915 Principal Core wrote:

> The educational standard of the students is still very low, only four out of the seventy having read up to the entrance, [through High School] and nineteen having passed the middle examinations . . . . It would seem that the standard is going down instead of coming up as shown by the quality of the Junior class. This is very serious, for our older men are passing away rapidly, our principal Churches are clamouring for good and qualified men, but we have not got them, nor is there any prospect of improvement immediately . . . . If we are to hold to the Church the increasing number of educated laymen now found in every large city, and impress the higher classes of the Indian community among whom are found men of the highest training and finest possibilities we must make a serious effort to improve the quality of our Indian Ministry.[37]

Returning to the subject three years later Core explained "that even a middle class man can get five to six times the income that he gets *in the Seminary*".[38] This situation had created considerable discontent where stipends were small. Against this background we get a new sense of the dedication to his call, shown by J.R. Chitambar when he and his wife went to Bareilly, and a new appreciation of the interest of Mr. and Mrs. Mansell, who encouraged them and gave the time needed in special classes.

The importance of enlisting better qualified men in the ministry was of vital importance, not alone in North India, but in other Conferences also. In an attempt to get better men an English Department was opened in 1918. The staff had never been stronger, including now L.A. Core, C.L. Bare, C.D. Rockey from the missionary group and H.L. Mukerjee and J. Devadson, B.A., in the Indian staff. The year opened with five men, but two soon dropped out.[39]

To meet the need of other Conferences it became apparent that a more central location would be needed. In 1923 A.L. Shute was appointed Principal of the English Department, and a search for a permanent home resulted in the selection of Jabalpur. In July, the English Department from Bareilly opened as the India Methodist Theological College in its new home, a site of six and a half acres including two bungalows and numerous substantial smaller buildings. Its cost with alterations and furnishings was Rs. 66,336. In 1925 Dr. A.A. Parker became Principal of the College and for ten years put the impress of his gifted personality upon it, setting it upon its course. What was a three year course in Bareilly became a four year course and in 1926 Matriculation passed became the entrance requirement. "The course was arranged so as to give the student much of the cultural value of a B.A. Course [with] specific training for the Christian ministry." In this it is unique. Affiliation to Serampore College was effected in 1927 for the B.D. degree. The first class in this course graduated in April, 1930 with three men receiving the B.D. degree, others the G. Th. Diploma.[40]

The name of the College was changed to Leonard Theological College in 1931 in memory of Dr. A.B. Leonard who was for twenty-four years Secretary of the Board of Foreign Missions. His son, Bishop A.W. Leonard, was instrumental in raising funds used as an endowment and for Property Development.

Herman J. Sheets succeeded Parker as Principal in 1935. His death in August, 1936, was a distinct loss. W.G. Griffiths officiated until 1938 when Dr. Orville L. Davis was elected, and he in turn was followed by Dr. M.H. Harper in 1945, who still serves. The Leonard Theological College comprises four schools: the School of Theology, the School of Religious Education, the Post Graduate School and the Woman's School. It became a union institution in 1949 with eight Missions or Churches cooperating.

Madar Union Sanatorium

With the opening of hospitals in the several Conferences attention was drawn to the prevalence of tuberculosis. The first protection that seemed to be available was to have all school children tested and afflicted ones removed from the institution. In 1905 the Woman's Conferences of North and N.W. India constituted a Joint Committee to select a location for a Sanatorium where such patients could be sent. This committee recommended Aligarh as the location and presented plans and estimates for the plant. The Finance Committee on July 27, 1905 decided not to embark on an expensive set up, but

> to ask for Rs. 1,800 to be provided by the two Conferences for the building and running expenses for the year of one or two experimental sanatoriums, the number and place to be decided by a committee consisting of Drs. Scott and Beck . . . and Drs. Gimson and Lewis. This Joint Committee met . . . November 3, 1905. It was suggested that Superintendents be free to send girls to the Sanatorium established by the London Missionary Society, but that we do not join them as a mission, but have a separate place in the plains . . . . In Tilaunia cheap land is available . . . building material cheap and abundant; labor cheap; native pastor and his wife located in Tilaunia; climate preferable to any others on the plains.[41]

Tilaunia was agreed upon and Dr. Beck (Mrs. Keislar) was authorized to make the plans and put up the necessary buildings with the Rs. 1,800 provided. Hearty approval was given to "the proposed plan for a Tubercular Sanatorium in Almora" and it was recommended that hill girls be sent there, and girls from the plains to Tilaunia which would have medical supervision by Dr. Beck from Phalera.

The selection of Rajputana for the Tuberculosis Sanatorium was a happy one and time has vindicated the judgment. Drs. Mrs. Keislar, Baksh, Huffman, Riste and Kipp, and a succession of other doctors and nurses made the Mary Wilson Sanatorium, Tilaunia, a place for recovering health to many. Through the years the number of in-patients ran into thousands while out-patients, even though Tilaunia was a village, numbered tens of thousands.

During 1920 W.W. Ashe, M.D. returned from furlough after special training, to start a sanatorium for men in Rajputana. His first choice for location was Taragarh, near Ajmer, but 800 feet higher. It had been a cantonment for British troops. He thought that the empty barracks could be useful in this new cause and started the sanatorium there.[42] For difficulty of access and for lack of drinking water Taragarh was unsatisfactory. In February, 1923 Ashe moved to the better accommodation of Madar, five miles from Ajmer, on the railway, where a tract of forty-five acres had been purchased, and where the first buildings—administration, first ward and doctor's bungalow—were nearing completion. Servants' quarters, compounder's house and power house had been completed earlier.[43] Madar had its hard years. In the beginning of 1925 Dr. Ashe went on emergency leave. George Eldridge, the pastor in Ajmer had to carry on with the help of an Indian doctor. The next year owing to the "cut" it was necessary to carry on "with only a compounder and a nurse," but word came that Dr. and Mrs. O.G. Taylor would arrive in January. They continued until 1931.[44]

In 1938 the Mary Wilson Sanatorium moved from Tilaunia to Madar. At the same time the Scottish Presbyterian Mission in Rajputana started cooperating, since when the name has been the Madar Union Sanatorium. Soon after, the American Presbyterian Mission also voted to cooperate.[45] In this larger, united program Bishop J.W. Robinson was the "prime organizer".

In 1940 the Board of Managers of the Sanatorium sent an urgent appeal to the Board of Missions for a doctor trained in the treatment of tuberculosis to take charge. The appeal reached New York just at the time that Drs. Sherwood and Marian Hall were to leave Korea. They accepted this opportunity for service in India [45] and arrived in January, 1941. With these doctors and the dynamic leadership of Bishop Pickett, Chairman of the Medical Council, the Madar Union Sanatorium entered upon a new era and a phenomenal development. Dr. Hall introduced in India in 1941 the use of Christmas seals for promoting the fight against tuberculosis. Among Methodists Madar has been designated as an "All-India Institution". By the generous gifts of M.C.O.R. Methodist T.B. Patients are assisted in getting the best care that India affords, not alone in climate, but from experienced personnel using the best modern equipment. Not the least important is the excellent Rehabilitation Program directed by Miss Margaret Johnston, O.T.R. Its buildings include nine wards, twenty-three cottages, a new surgical block, a recreation hall, Tuberculosis Prevention Clinic, a school and Sanatorium farm.[46]

The All-India Missions Tablet Industry

This started from an experiment in 1920. Dr. H.H. Linn had returned from his first furlough and was appointed to the Crawford Memorial Hospital in Vikarabad. He had no compounder and it was difficult to prepare all the powders he needed. He secured a small hand machine for making tablets and found he could make 75 to 100 a minute. It worked very well with Cinchona Febrifuge, used for treating malaria. His friends asked for some pills for their schools or hospitals or village work. Sales increased from less than Rs. 1,000 in 1920 to over Rs. 17,000 in 1924. During his furlough Dr. Noyes and M.D. Ross kept the good work going, while Dr. Linn learned more of the pharmaceutical aspects of making tablets.

Friends of the work helped him secure a small power driven machine, and a small plant for generating electricity. For the growing business Vikarabad proved to be an unsatisfactory location. Linn moved to the bungalow in Bangarapet. It was ideal: on the railway, climate cool, electricity cheap. New machines replaced the first ones; and these in turn were replaced by a rotary tablet machine making 500 tablets a minute. In 1938 Kenneth Linn a trained Pharmacist, joined his father and today continues his work. . . .

> thirty-five and a half million tablets of our own manufacture were sent out besides many specialties made by other companies. About two tons of ointments were manufactured and distributed in one pound containers, and four hundred Bibles [Heart Tonic] were sold.[47]

H.H. Linn combined his interest in evangelism with his interest in better health, even when most of his time was taken in the business of Tablets. His letter heads with the name of the industry had in their upper corners, in red letters, the words: "Preach the Kingdom of God," and "Heal the Sick". The son continues this interest.

Vellore Christian Medical College

In 1943 Dr. J.C. McGilvrey of the Vellore Hospital Board wrote: "We have come to a stage when the future of Christ's ministry of healing in India is at stake."[48] That was a sobering thought, for the volume of work being done through Christian medical institutions was very great. At that time it included almost all homes for lepers; one-third of the beds available for tuberculosis patients; about one-eighth of the work in general hospitals; and a much higher portion for women and children.

Looking ahead, as McGilvrey did, he saw the M.B., B.S., degree as the sure-to-be requirement by the State and Central Government for all doctors. Already the L.M.P. (Licensed Medical Practitioner) was being discontinued in some States. McGilvrey estimated a need for 670 Christian doctors for existing Mission institutions, in which there were only eighty with the M.B., B.S. degree. "Unless we train Christian leadership now in an All-India Christian Medical College," McGilvrey continued, "our opportunity will be lost."[48]

The Christian Medical Association of India had been studying the same problem with Committees from the three Christian Medical Schools in India, those at Vellore in South India; Ludhiana in the Punjab and Miraj in Western India. It found that the Medical College for Women at Vellore had "by far the largest investment in suitable buildings". It was the preferred site for a Christian Medical College for men and women.[49]

The Vellore Hospital for Women was opened in 1903 by Dr. Ida Scudder of the Arcot Mission of the Reformed Church in America. It became a medical college in 1918 for training women in a four years, course leading to the L.M.P. examination. This course was superceded by a higher standard of M.B., B.S., which became effective in 1940–50 making some decision necessary even during the war years. With Vellore as the preferred place a further recommendation of the C.M.A.I. that provision be made at the same place for training men and women commended itself to the Missions which were interested. A new Governing Board was formed which convened for its first meeting on May 18, 1945, and incorporated in 1948. Both Divisions of the Methodist Board of Missions have cooperated in this Advance program which has already brought Indian leadership into some Methodist Hospitals. Highest tributes have been paid to the work being done. Rajkumari Amrit Kaur, Minister of Health in the Government of India, told Bishop Pickett that "Vellore is far ahead of any other medical college in India," and the Chief Minister of Madras is reported to have said publicly that it "is now beyond question the best medical college in Asia".[51]

Christian Medical College, Ludhiana

> Whereas the North India School of Medicine at Ludhiana has requested and urged our Mission to join them in their efforts to build up a strong inter-denominational Christian institution where girls may receive a good medical education and preparation for this form of Christian work:
>
> Resolved, that we recommend that the authorities of the Woman's Foreign Missionary Society send out a lady doctor, qualified to act on the staff of this school as soon as possible.[52]

The N.W. India Woman's Conference approved this resolution in 1906. Even before this, girls had been sent to Ludhiana for nurses' training—in 1905 Miss Beck welcomed back for her Phalera Dispensary, an Ajmer girl, Kesri Dass, who had been sent two years before for nurse's training.[53]

It was not until forty-seven years later in 1952 that a regular Methodist Missionary, Dr. Margaret E. Tucker, formerly of China, joined the staff as Radiologist. In 1953 Dr. Roland J. Garst, an Orthopedic Surgeon, also joined as a representative of the Division of World Missions.

On March 24, 1954, the Christian Medical College celebrated its Diamond Jubilee —sixty years of medical work and training, and the ninetieth birthday of Dame Edith Brown, the founder. It was the first Christian Medical School for Women in India and opened with four students and a staff including Dr. Brown, Miss Greenfield and two part time Assistants. Its aim was "to train doctors, nurses, midwives, dispensers [pharmacists], and hospital laboratory technicians."[54] In these sixty years 600 doctors, 400 nurses, 200 compounders, 1,500 midwives and nurse-dais and thirty health visitors have passed from this institution.

Recent steps in its progress have been: 1947, during the riots following partition the hospital started admitting men since when it has been a general hospital;[55] 1949, inauguration of the Health School in cooperation with the Punjab Government; 1951, the admission of men to the medical course for the first time; 1952, the licentiate course was discontinued, and in 1953 the admission of men and women to the new M.B.,B.S. course with fifty students, twenty-one men and twenty-nine women. Both the University of the Punjab and the Government of India had insisted that the Christian Medical College should either go up in grade or discontinue medical training. The last alternative was unthinkable; the former must be implemented. The Methodist Church is one of sixteen cooperating Societies that have united to maintain at Ludhiana an institution worthy of the Christian Church.

In addition to the course for doctors, there are classes for training nurses, midwives, health visitors (midwifery plus eighteen months public health instruction), laboratory technicians and prescription compounders.

Nurmanzil Psychiatric Centre

In this "small" centre in Lucknow one sees today what may well be in India's future as vital a contribution to Christian medical service as the medical work of Dr. Swain in Bareilly in 1870. Consider that beginning against today's accepted standards. The idea of a Psychiatric Centre was conceived in the mind and heart of E. Stanley Jones during his missionary years, when he

> saw large numbers whose potentialities were curbed and whose usefulness was curtailed by emotional difficulties.
>
> The Nurmanzil Psychiatric Centre is a non-profit institution which serves people regardless of caste, creed or colour. Patients are accepted for treatment on the basis of their therapeutic eligibility and fees are charged—in accordance with their ability to pay.[56]

Clinical Director is Dr. Miss Dagmar Norell, trained in Sweden and America; and Psychotherapist, K.V. Rajan, who are assisted by Nurses and others. The institution is becoming established and a policy for personnel has been worked out. Professional staff members cooperate in social welfare projects in the community; conduct a seminar at the Psychology Department of the Lucknow University; give lectures to groups of psychiatrists and ministers, or serve as part-time lecturers at the Jail Training School. Summer courses are sometimes given in Sat Tal and sometimes in Mussoorie.

Necessarily the work has been largely with out-patients. The Centre has facilities for only twelve in-patients. Provision for a larger number is in the projected plans. It is becoming increasingly apparent that the Nurmanzil Centre must become a training centre, for the demand for psychiatric help is increasing with the knowledge that it is available. A first step in this direction is to have final year nursing students attend for a period of psychiatric orientation.[57]

Henry Martyn School

The idea of the Henry Martyn School of Islamic Studies was born in Dr. Zwemer's Conference in Lucknow,[58] in January, 1911. No steps were taken to organize it for nearly fifteen years; the opportunity was awaited. The initiative was made by the Secretaries of some Mission Boards in the United Kingdom. Then the Methodist Missionary Society in London offered a contribution to cover the salary of a missionary.

About 1926–27 Dr. M.T. Titus as National Christian Council Secretary for work among Muslims, with Dr. William Paton, of the International Council and Rev. L. Bevan Jones met for discussing plans. A Committee of the N.C.C. met in Lahore in 1928 to draft a constitution and prepare a tentative budget to present to interested Mission Boards and Societies. Three lines of activity were outlined: (a) research studies by members of the staff; (b) training Christian workers for the task (c) the preparation of literature for giving the Christian message to Muslims.

The first meeting of the Committee of Management was in 1928. Representatives from six different Societies were present. L. Bevan Jones was elected Principal; L.E. Browne and J.A. Subhan as members of the staff. The school was formally opened in January, 1930, in Lahore, where the Church Missionary Society placed some rooms of St. John's Divinity College at its disposal.

For nearly fifteen years now the school has been located in Aligarh, the seat of the Muslim University. It occupies on rent, buildings owned by the Woman's Division of Christian Service, formerly used by a Vocational School. Bishop Pickett's long connection with the Indus River and

Delhi Conferences has enabled him to be of great service to the School as Chairman and otherwise. Bishop Subhan, too, since being Bishop, has been on the Committee, but Dr. Titus had the longest close connection with the School. Dr. A. Abdul Haqq, member of the Delhi Annual Conference, has recently assumed the Principalship.

Home and Foreign Missionary Society

The biennium of 1898 had been difficult. Every Conference was faced with openings for expansion but everywhere a lack of finances seemed to make the maintenance of old work impossible. It was hardly a time to expect the Episcopal address to record advance movements. Yet Thoburn reminded:

> So long as we preserve a genuine spiritual vitality among us, it will be as impossible to repress a normal expansion of work as to prevent the growth of trees or the blooming of flowers.[59]

The same Central Conference received a memorial on "an indigenous movement, deserving encouragement, called the *Desi,* or India Missionary Society," which had operated in North India and had "exhibited commendable zeal in our Mission field". It worked in close cooperation with Conference organizations but it was not authorized by the discipline to act as the approved Society.[60] The Central Conference gave its approval for such societies in Annual Conferences under the disciplinary plan where they "will not conflict with the more necessary and already existing plan of Pastoral support".[61]

The early years of the Twentieth Century were marked by a tide of spiritual life surging through Christian Churches in India. Outpourings of God's Spirit were felt in widely scattered sections of the country "on a scale and to an extent previously unknown in India". In Methodist fields the greatest evidences of the Revival were found in the N. India and N.W.I. Conferences during the year 1905 and after. Powerful touches were also felt at other scattered places in our work. Especially noteworthy were the effects "in the hearts of multitudes of boys and girls in our schools". The revival was accompanied by much deep conviction of sin, a tendency to private and public confession of wrong-doing and a willingness to make restitution. There was much intercession, personal study of the Scriptures, and a new spirit of evangelism. Large numbers of workers "attained to a definite spiritual experience never previously enjoyed". Many young people were definitely converted.

> Churches and village communities have been profoundly impressed with the reality of spiritual experience. The possibility of an Indian Church enjoying the fullness of spiritual life and living on a high plane of Christian experience has been brought more vividly nigh to us all.[62]

It was under the inspiration of this revival that the National Missionary Society was organized, an indigenous, non-denominational movement, in which Jashwant Chitambar "was one of the influential young" founders.[63] Nathaniel Jordan was another, who through a long life was active in its organization and support.

The Central Conference in 1904 appointed a Commission which, with other duties, would "devise a practical method . . . of organizing a Missionary Society of the Methodist Church in Southern Asia," with a view "to the self-propagation of the Church".[64] Four years later we read, "It is our judgment that a Missionary Society will ultimately become an essential unit of our work. The Commission . . . is, therefore, continued."[65]

This "essential unit" was born in prayer at the Central Conference, January, 1920. On Saturday the 24th a Special Committee was appointed on the formation of an India Missionary Society. Sunday was set apart for prayer and intercession under the leadership of Bishop Warne. The constitution proposed by the Committee was adopted article by article on Wednesday, after which the congregation broke into singing the Doxology. Bishop Warne then "led in prayer voicing devout thanksgiving and the dedication of the new organization to its great work".[66] J.R. Chitambar was elected Executive Officer or Corresponding Secretary.

Time was taken in organizing, in appealing for funds and in selecting a field. Mesopatamia was first suggested. Bishop Warne visited that country but because of unsettled political conditions did not recommend it. Jaisalmir was next considered. A third place, Bhabua, was selected. It was in the group movement District of Shahabad (Arrah) in Bihar. W.H. Soule, one of the fifteen original volunteers was chosen as the first missionary. He was a member of the C.P. Annual Conference. In an appropriate ceremony during its session he was set aside and officially appointed by Bishop J.W. Robinson to this new work in December, 1921. A married Local Preacher, Prem Das, was associated with him.[67] In 1924 it was constituted a Mission by the General Conference, and its boundaries were made to include the Bhabua sub-division in Bihar.[68]

The name of this Board was changed in 1935 to the India Methodist Missionary Society.[69] During the decade of the forties it supported a married missionary Rev. Kristmukti, for a few years in Umtali, East Africa. His work was chiefly among the Indians resident in that section. The work at Bhabua has continued regularly and is now under J.B. Singh.

In 1945 the name of the Society was again changed to the Missionary Society of the Methodist Church in Southern Asia.[70]

Hold high the torch!
You did not light its glow—
'Twas given you by other hands, you know.
'Tis yours to keep it burning bright,
Yours to pass on when you no more need light;
For there are other feet that we must guide,
And other forms go marching by our side;
Their eyes are watching every smile and tear
And efforts which we think are not worthwhile,
Are sometimes just the very helps they need,
Actions to which their souls would give most heed;
So that in turn they'll hold it high
And say, "I watched someone else carry it this way . . . ."
Hold high the torch!
You did not light its glow—
'Twas given you by other hands, you know.
I think it started down its pathway bright,
The day the Maker said: "Let there be light."
And He once said, who hung on Calvary's tree—
"Ye are the light of the world . . . ." Go . . . Shine for me.

From "The Open Door"

Author Unknown.

XIII

Bombay Area

With the formation of the Gujarat Conference the old Bombay Conference lost its largest district. Then to the Indus River Conference it contributed Quetta and Sindh which from the beginning had been a part of the Bombay District, and Kathiawar. To make the Bombay Conference largely a one language, Marathi, Conference, parts of the C.P. Conference were added to it. The details of the boundaries are intricate, but they include the territory contiguous to Bombay City, and a large wedge of territory reaching east for 500 miles from Bombay, to include the Southern part of the Central Provinces and the northern strip of the Hyderabad State.[1]

Bombay Conference

In Bombay itself there are more than twenty churches and circuits where services are regularly held in English, Marathi, Gujarati, Hindustani, Kanarese, Tamil and Malayalam. Outside of Bombay City work was organized in the Basim, Bombay, Nagpur, Poona and Puntamba-Igatpuri Districts. At the Conference in 1906 W.H. Stephens, gave an account of the old Marathi District, precursor of the new Conference. It was "the oldest vernacular field of Methodism in the peninsula", he wrote. "George Bowen was a Marathi scholar . . . and about him gathered our Marathi church."[2] It never had as close supervision as it needed to develop its fullest growth. The Gospel had taken deep root in Poona and its villages. Talegaon was "one of the most important points in the Marathi field". The large Orphanage and High School of the W.F.M.S. were there.

Puntamba

Igatpuri does not hold a large place in today's Methodism, but fifty years ago it was the centre of an active church. There the missionary lived and regular preaching, Sunday School, mid-week services and bazaar preaching, had their place. "The big work in the Puntamba district was greatly assisted by Igatpuri."

> Large excavating operations were being conducted by Government near Igatpuri, where thousands of people from Puntamba side were employed. Our Igatpuri workers preached the Gospel to them,

and many were baptized. When they returned to their homes, some of our preachers went with them, and we began operations in that field.[3]

The Igatpuri-Chitli circuit began at the foot of the Ghats and extended 150 miles to the Nizam's Dominions. Some of these who had gone to Igatpuri were from Chitli and there heard the Gospel from Gyanoba Khanduji. Now they cordially welcomed teachers sent to their villages. Some delegations brought a horse to take a teacher back with them; some offered a house for a teacher, and some who came asking were from the high castes.

When an issue of comity was raised the Methodists altered their boundary, surrendered a community of 150, and entered a much larger field opened to them by this transaction. It was the Puntamba field. The circuit became the "Igatpuri-Puntamba Circuit".[4]

J.C. Fisher, stationed at Puntamba in 1909, wrote that the most important outward event of the year was the coming of a Local Elder, R.N. Duthie, a supply: "He has won that section of the country to a favourable consideration of Christianity." In the same year a school building was completed, the bungalow nearly so and the church would be ready by the end of the year. Many people around there had never seen a Church and people were curious to know what kind of a god would be put into it.[5]

The Puntamba field is rural; its largest town thirty years ago was as Kopargaon, with a population of over 7000; Puntamba then had 5000. There was not one Anglo-Vernacular school in the area then. Steadman Aldis, the D.S., decided that the Mission should provide the education for its community. A beginning was made in 1924 with a dozen boys in an orphanage at Kopargaon, under the supervison of the Pastor, G.N. Divekar, and a small day school supplied by P.M. Salve.[6] In 1925 the school was moved to Puntamba where a Girls' School was begun by Miss M.E. Sutherland. Arrangements were the simplest:

> a temporary building for a dormitory and another building for a master's house and for the first class of the middle school. We decided to use the church for a school room. Miss Sutherland built a shack for a cook house and dining room, and the church was to be used as a dormitory at night for the girls, and so by June 16th we were ready for the children.[7]

At the opening there were 26 children. The number grew to 64 boys and 23 girls. Many others were turned away. A "good staff" was secured and a full Primary, I–V, with one class of the Middle, was carried on. When the Board of Education voted to close this last class, Aldis sent the most advanced boys to the vernacular school in Puntamba, to the Ahmednagar Mission High School or to the C.M.S. Mission School in Manmad.[8] The school grew, but for a few years the children lived in temporary sheds. In 1930 the enrolment was 77, including 28 girls.[9]

Something of vocational work started about 1928, gardening for the boys; rugs and fancy sewing by the girls. In a year that he held the District, when P.C.B. Balaram was away, 1940, Minnis called the school "a successful attempt at co-education," and expressed the hope that the W.F.M.S. would give a bit of grant towards teacher support. The Puntamba Rural High School today is jointly supported by the D.W.M. and W.D.C.S. It is co-educational through the middle school, training for the rural environment in which it is set.[10]

THE BOWEN BRUERE HOSPITAL

For several years medical work had been done in Puntamba. The need increased when the schools were started. In August, 1925 Aldis was able to get the services of Mrs. Bowen Bruere for this work. She was a trained nurse with much experience. She continued in this service until the end of 1927, her dispensary always "one of the bright spots in the District".[11] After she left Mrs. A.M. Wood conducted the Dispensary which received the name Bowen Bruere Memorial Dispensary when Bishop Badley unveiled a tablet in November, 1928. Dr. and Mrs. George served here for several years. The first unit of a hospital was commenced in 1954 when Dr. S. Krishnamurti, M.B.,B.S. from the Madras Medical College arrived to assume the work of Superintendent.

DHULIA

Until the union of the Methodist Churches in 1939 Dhulia was a station of the Methodist Protestant Church, their only station in India. Their missionaries were Rev. and Mrs. J.F. Minnis, Miss Edith Lacy, M.D., and Miss Mildred Miskimen. The work included two circuits, a small hospital and an orphanage.

> During the cool season in 1905–6 two consecrated young ladies landed in Bombay to do evangelistic work in this land. They went to Khedgaon and worked with Pandita Ramabai while learning the Marathi language. After language study they began to search for a field for their labors. The C.M.S. informed them that the Dhulia Taluqa was not occupied and they were given that area in which to do mission work.... They found a bungalow with a large compound for sale. This they purchased and started[13]

the work of the Methodist Protestant Church in India. The first orphan to be received by the ladies was a baby girl, a pretty child, named Suwartha. She fell ill one day and in spite of the best the ladies could do, she died. They wished much that they had had the facilities to save the little girl, and planned at once for medical work, but this took time. In 1923 the corner stone of a hospital was laid. A missionary nurse looked after the sick until in 1927 Dr. Edith Lacy arrived in Dhulia. The hospital has been enlarged since. A modern operating room was added in 1952–53 and an X-Ray plant. It can now care for fifty in-patients.[13]

During earlier years Dr. Lacy had the help of Dr. Sunderajulu who was "well trained, efficient and [of] a beautiful Christian character". She remained in charge during the furlough of Dr. Lacy. In 1954 Dr. Kali Das was in charge.[14] The hospital is now a project of the D.W.M. and W.D.C.S. jointly. The Orphanage has a capacity of fifty children.

Minnis was admitted to the Bombay Conference as a full member in 1939. They had arrived in India in 1922. The number of Christians in the circuits in 1954 was 221.

Mecosa Bagh Schools

In 1924 A.N. Warner wrote of the Nagpur District: "There are two serious weaknesses in all our educational work in the District—the lack of trained teachers, and the lack of suitable plant and equipment."[15] The Boys' School in Kampti was in buildings then decrepit. The Girls' Boarding School was at Gondia, 70 miles from Nagpur, on the outer edge of the District.

> Our educational work has always lagged behind the evangelistic in the Nagpur District . . . . It has only been since 1917 that we have had any school at all for the Christian girls of the District; and a little before that what provision we had for Christian boys, was closed and the boys sent to Basim for education.[16]

In answer to earnest prayer and cooperative effort a large property of forty-seven acres was obtained in 1923 in Nagpur.[17] The beginning of the Girls' Primary and Normal School in Nagpur was "a notable event". It was "the first piece of property secured by the W.F.M.S. in the District". At the same time there was another advance—the beginning of a plant in Nagpur to replace the Boys' School in Kampti. The first appointments in 1926, to these schools in Mecosa Bagh were: Miss J.A. Blasdell for the tuitional side of school and Normal Training, and Miss M. Corner. To the Nagpur Boys' Boarding School B.B. Samuels, and L.S. Gadeker were appointed as Headmaster and Housefather, respectively. In 1930 Miss B. Elliott and Miss M.G. Drescher succeeded Miss Corner and Miss Blasdell. In 1929 the Government of Central Provinces gave temporary recognition, later made permanent, to the Normal Training School; in 1954 there were thirty-six in the Normal Training.

The Hutchings Girls' High School

English schools inevitably grew up with the English Churches of the Taylor revival. The Churches felt the best way to insure Christian training was to have children in schools which were concerned with religious education as well as with school examinations. "If we would keep our children in the Methodist Church, we must educate them in Methodist schools."

Earlier reference has been made to the institutions in Poona. Here were: the Taylor High School for Boys, and another for Girls; the Anglo-Indian Girls' Home; and the Boys' Orphanage (Anglo-Indians). They were established for the good of the Anglo-Indian community, and financed by them with liberal grants-in-aid from the Government. First, the Taylor Boys' School was discontinued, then the Orphanage was merged with the Girls' Home. The founder, and for her life time the Superintendent of the Anglo-Indian Girls' Home, was Mrs. Hutchings, a woman of strong character and a good administrator. In 1925 she received the Kaisar-i-Hind Medal from the Government of India for her services to her community. The final merger was between her Anglo-Indian Home and the Taylor Girls' School. In naming it for Mrs. Hutchings the W.D.C.S. honoured itself as it honoured her who had so unselfishly put her life into the lives of the children that had been cared for in the Home.

The Hillman Memorial Girls' Sshool, Talegaon

"Since the rains [1896] Misses Abrams and Stirling have been itinerating through the villages between Poona and Lonauli and have met with an encouraging reception in many places."[18] Miss Abrams' appointment for 1897 was again "Talegaon—Evangelistic Work". Itinerating that year was with much encouragement. Gangadhar B. Kale was then appointed to the Talegaon circuit. Dennis Osborne, his P.E. reporting to the next Conference, wrote of Talegaon: "We have a substantial school building which serves as a church. The services have been well attended, the girls of the Orphanage forming the principal part of it."[19] Some of the orphan girls that had crowded the orphanage in the city had been provided for in Talegaon. It became "one of the most important points in the Marathi field. The large Orphanage and High School of the W.F.M.S. are here. The Parent Board own a good school building in the village."[20] Large buildings were erected for the Society for educational evangelistic work. Miss Lawson was superintendent of the educational work and Miss Durant with Bible women, devoted herself to evangelistic work. Repeated tribute was paid in the annual reports to the courage and steadfastness of the ladies in this lonely place.

A new school building, the Ordelia M. Hillman Memorial School at Talegaon, was dedicated on September 6, 1912, by Bishop J.W. Robinson. The Conference Board of Education gave its approval to a hostel for primary boys, starting with standards one and two, and gradually working up. Coeducation increased to include a middle school with a hostel for boys.[21] At the end of 1898 the Talegaon circuit had a Christian community numbering eighty-eight. In 1954 the Sangamner and Talegaon circuits, adjoining each other, had a community of 772.

Nanded And Udgir Districts

In 1930 Nanded and Purna were circuits of the old Basim District, with a Christian community of 112. Ten years later Nanded was marked off as a District, including a Marathi and Telugu circuit in Nanded itself, with Bhaisa, Purna and Udgir as outlying circuits, with a Christian community 767. In 1954 Nanded and Udgir were both centres of new Districts with Christians numbering 508 in the one, and 1579 in the other. They are centres of new group movements, still young and therefore hopeful. The D.S., Paul Wagner, asked the Conference for "specific directives to shepherd and care for the Christians of the Bhaisa area", for, said he, "we are not showing concern to feed the sheep as long as we are fed."

One of the circuits of the Udgir District, Deoni, has been set apart as a separate unit known as the Udgir (Deoni) Mission, to be "a completely indigenous evangelistic and missionary effort of the Bombay Conference".[22]

Gujarat Conference

The "troublous times" that preceded the close of the nineteenth century in Gujarat, did not come to an early end. Frease describes the monsoon of 1906 as "the first approximately normal monsoon Gujarat has had since 1898". But with the rain there was a recrudescence of plague with the consequent vacating of villages. In that year the Christian community reported 1123 deaths.

There were other troubles also. The work had grown so rapidly that in the District Conference of 1905 "forty appointments, including one hundred and forty-four villages were left to be supplied". The situation for the Christian flock was serious. At the same time the missionary force, from strain and broken health, dropped from seven to five, three of whom had been on the field less than two years.

It was about this time that the office of the Bishop Thoburn Special Fund, with its full time secretary and staff, was superceded by a plan which virtually left each missionary responsible for raising the funds for his own work. Frease well describes the situation with two examples that represent the position not only in Gujarat, *but in all India.* The burden was heaviest in mass movement districts where the need of supervision was greatest and the most urgent work was the training of workers from among new Christians, and guiding them as they entered on their duties as teachers.

> Brother Bancroft has had the oversight of six great circuits, in which there are 8000 Christians in 225 towns, and the direction of one hundred Gujarati workers.... With his six circuits to supervise,

> he must also keep in touch with one hundred donors—writing personal letters himself, securing and having translated letters to the patrons from the workers, sending reports at stated times, answering inquiries, making adjustments, seeking new supports to take the place of those lapsing.
>
> Take another case. Bro. L.E. Linzell has charge of the Baroda Boys' Orphanage, supported entirely on scholarships, and he must keep in touch with over two hundred donors. He has four great circuits besides, and must keep in correspondence with seventy more friends . . . . There is no escape from it. [Each missionary] is literally ground between the upper mill-stone of the clamouring demands of the work on his time and strength—the work for which he came to India—and the nether mill-stone of this necessary and inexorable correspondence.[23]

In the opening decade of the new century, persecution, "often cruel and persistent," became a portent of deepening and organized opposition. Only God's grace with the loyal support of thousands of donors, and the faithful labours of uncounted Indian workers, made possible the continued growth of the Gujarat District.

At Vaso the first entrance was made into the Gaikwar's state in 1900 when Fox and Robbins baptized a number of converts. Except for the difficulty of procuring permission to build there had been no hindrance to work, and in many ways "positive sympathy" was shown. From Vaso work spread from village to village until it reached the Sabarmati river, then it at once crossed over to Kathiawar. The peninsula was not occupied without the full consent of our missionaries and of the Bishop and the expressed desire of other Missions that we enter. The Kathiawar District was formed in 1905. It included the Vaso and Danduka circuits in Gujarat and was under W.E. Robbins.[24] In the appointments of 1909 the Gujarat District gives place to two Districts the Ahmedabad, under G.W. Park, and the Baroda under L.E. Linzell. In both, at the end of 1908, were 17,456 Christians.

The Gujarat workers had so often met together in District Conference that to many it seemed almost like an old Conference when it convened on December 14, 1922 at the Girls' Normal School Chapel, Godhra, under the Presidency of Bishop J.W. Robinson, to organize as the Gujarat Annual Conference. After a brief service in which J. Lampard and Gangu Dhanji assisted the Bishop in the administration of the sacrament, the roll of the members was called by R.D. Bisbee:

> *Members*—R.D. Bisbee, Punja Bhudar, Kalidas Chunilal, C.H. Conley, Nanji Deviji, Gangu Dhanji, Yakub Dhanji, Yusaf Dhanji, Musa Dahya, Laxman Dhula, Ganesh Gangaram, Dhula Govind, Asha Jeram, Whalji Kalidas, Musa Karshan, Virji Khoja, Hiralal Lalji, John Lampard, L.E. Linzell, Amarsing Meheraji, Kalidas Mulji, Chatur Nabha, Madhva Nana, Eliyah Punjah, Govind Ramji, and L. G. Templin.

Probationers—Dahya Dalpat, Lallu Dana, Somchand Dhanji, Devji Jethalal, Kisa Jetha, Ashirward Kalyan, Whalji Khandas, Ulphilas Kuber, Whalji Laxman, Manganlal Mathurdas, Khoja Mitah, Daud Morar, and Kalyan Ramdas.

The work was organized in four districts: Ahmedabad, including Nadiad, Baroda, Godhra and Kathiawar under Conley, Linzell, Bisbee and Musa Karsan, respectively, as District Superintendents. Gujarat has been fortunate in its institutions which developed in Baroda, Godhra and Nadiad.

Baroda

Where the State does not provide public education for all, the schools of a Conference become an integral part of its work, supplementing evangelistic efforts with teaching, character building and the preparation of its young people for leadership. Frease was quick to see this necessity; there was no alternative. The annual appointments for the old Gujarat District included provision for "Boys Boarding and Evangelistic Schools"—growing successors to the little school Delamater had commenced. In 1902 these became separate appointments: (1) Boys' Boarding School and Orphanage, and (2) District Evangelistic Training School under Frease and Yusaf Dhanji. Five years later the same appointments read: Boys' Orphanage and High School, under A.C. Parker and Gangu Dhanji, and Florence B. Nicholson Memorial School of Theology under A. A. Parker and Yusaf Dhanji.

Consider the harvest from Garmet's Christian witness that won his servant whose two sons now held these key positions. Yusaf was born in 1869 at Baroda Camp. He was baptized in 1881 by D.O. Fox, who with others supplied the church in Baroda and also held meetings for the Indians. Yusaf was taught first by a preacher in the Irish Presbyterian Mission and then he joined a school opened by a Mahratta named Pandurang. Here he also learned singing and playing on the violin as well as reading and writing. He was employed as a teacher at Rander by a Presbyterian missionary. He married in 1892. When a teacher was needed for our girls' school in Baroda, Gangu, Yusaf's brother, urged Frease and Miss Thompson to offer the position to Yusaf. They did, and he came. "By his hard work and enthusiasm the school prospered and was registered by the Government." His later association with Frease in the Evangelistic Training School made him the logical associate with Parker in the new School of Theology. He continued in the position of Headmaster and Vice Principal until his death in 1924.[25]

> . . . talented in singing and music, a good Christian gentleman, punctual and practical, respected and respectful, patient and persevering and a devout Indian Methodist minister. He played very melodiously on his violin at social gatherings and religious meetings. He has translated many songs from English which are found in the Gujarati Hymn Book.[26]

Florence B. Nicholson School of Theology

Frease sent a report in which he stressed the need for more advanced training for some workers, and for a "general training of the mass of our workers" to Field Secretary, W.F. Oldham, who presented this need to George E. Nicholson of Iola, Kansas. He decided to establish such an institution at Baroda as a memorial to his wife. He provided $13,800 for new buildings and the support of a missionary principal for five years. The main building was opened on March 9, 1906 by Bishop J.E. Robinson.[27] The Theological School opened its first class on November 26, with fourteen men students and two women admitted with their husbands. I.B. Bawa then became a teacher. Departments opened were: (1) The regular School of Theology with a three-year course; (2) The Evangelistic Training School, a course for one year as individual cases required; (3) The District Workers' Training Department in place of the summer school, with groups of workers for two months at a time; (4) A Woman's Department or School, under Mrs. Parker, to train women along lines that would answer their needs. A Normal School Department for training teachers was projected.

During its first year the School of Theology had an enrolment of 247 in all departments. The first class of thirteen was graduated November 30, 1909, "a real commencement day—the commencement of a new era for Methodism in Gujarat."[28] By 1910 the District Superintendent reported that the influence of the institution had been felt from one end of Gujarat to the other. The caliber of the men entering the Theological School improved steadily. In 1913 three had passed the High School stage. That year A.A. Parker, on furlough, was succeeded by R.D. Bisbee.[29]

Events in the mid-twenties changed the program of the School of Theology. With the opening of the India Methodist Theological College at Jabalpur, advanced students went there. Owing to the "cut" in appropriations in 1925 the Evangelistic Training Department was closed. On the death of Yusaf Dhanjibhai, Ishwardas Narsingh became Vice-Principal. Tulsi Govindbhai, a graduate from Jabalpur, and Lalbhai Amtabhai, a graduate from the Teacher Training School, Moga, joined the staff. The course of study was extended from three to four years to include a full year's work in Teacher Training. An English class enabled students to know English equivalent to class five. Practice in bazaar preaching and in teaching village Sunday Schools was steadily maintained.

In a recent adjustment to changing conditions the Gujarat United School of Theology is run in cooperation with the Irish Presbyterian Church and the Church of the Brethren.[30]

Baroda Schools

Following the famine in 1899–1900 the schools in Baroda and Nadiad were more than full. So urgent did it seem that the young men should receive a thorough training in some trade that industrial classes were opened in both schools. But in 1905 it was decided to concentrate in Nadiad on the Industrial training and in Baroda on other education. Some adjustment of boys from each school to the other was made in line with this decision.[31]

In the year 1907 the Girls' and Boys' High Schools were united in an experiment in coeducation with the approval of the Education Department under one supervisor.[32] This continued until 1914 when the venture closed. It was "a question whether the girls do their best work before the boys or the boys make the advance they would were they alone."[33] It was decided to return to separate schools.

The Boys' High School lacked an adequate building. In 1927 they moved into rented quarters in the city for the Mission was unable to buy land. It was felt that the school in the city had a real Christian influence there. In a total enrolment of 285 there were 199 Christians, of whom 185 were in the hostel.[34]

In 1954 a Committee was appointed to make a study of the schools of the Gujarat Conference with a view to raising their standards. It recommended that coeducation should be started in the Baroda High Schools "to save both high schools from the present deplorable condition." The Board of Education reaffirmed the policy of coeducation in these schools to start from June, 1955. Classes VIII–XI meet in the Hill Memorial High School, and other classes in the Webb Memorial School.[35]

Nadiad

The Industrial School at Nadiad came to be considered as the largest and best equipped under our Church in India.[36] For many years it was under G.W. Park. It was held in high esteem by the Educational Department and received liberal grants, recurring and special. It was the first such school to which the Board sent out a technically trained lay missionary, Howard F. Bishop, in 1906.[37] Three years later the majority of its staff were Christians, men trained in the institution. Under Bishop's care it achieved the name "Nadiad Industrial and Engineering Institute." A pump manufactured there had a good reputation. Work of the boys in iron and wood was good.

On June 2, 1910 Bishop lost his life by drowning in a rough sea off the Tithal Coast in an effort to save Miss Williams, a W.F.M.S. missionary. He was followed in the Institute by Carl Conley, then a lay-missionary, A.P. Young, and others. But the Nadiad Institute passed its zenith under

Bishop. By death, transfers, cuts in Mission appropriations and other exigencies, the industrial emphasis dropped out entirely years ago.

Godhra Normal Training School

When the relief work of 1898–1900 closed the Government gave the missionaries the support and care of some four or five hundred women and girls. This was the beginning of the present Girls' School in Godhra. *Christian Herald* funds helped build permanent dormitories.

In 1902 the W.F.M.S. took a share in this work when Miss Anna A. Abbott was transferred from Mathura and with Miss Muriel Bailey, a graduate from the Mathura Bible Training School, took charge. There were then 187 girls attending school whether old enough or not, none beyond the first standard. The late monsoon that year added to the famine suffering and the number of girls increased to over 300. Another 100 were sent from Baroda as they could not be cared for there. The staff in Godhra was limited: one old Christian man who had studied to sixth; another to fourth; three Hindu men untrained, and a deaf Muslim *darzi* who taught sewing to the older girls. The staff improved gradually and with difficulty as there were very few educated girls anywhere who could be sent for teachers' training. The lack of a Christian community in Godhra made Christian men unwilling to accept work there. The new school building was completed in early 1908, at which time the staff included one trained teacher, with a second joining at the end of the year.

The Normal Training Class opened in April, 1909, with a preparatory class of sixteen girls, the majority of whom had no other recommendation than that "They are too old for the A.V. School and unequal to the study of English." The three trained teachers then in all of our Gujarati Methodist work were from the Irish Presbyterian Mission. The first year class of the Normal Training College was started in 1910 and registered in 1911. There was no building for this so the Primary School building accommodated the training classes until 1921 when the new College building was ready.

The first Vernacular Final Examination for girls was held in Gujarat when this school sent up 26 candidates of whom 24 passed. Dhanbhai, the first student trained in the Methodist Teacher's Training College for Women, was made Headmistress of the Practising School in 1937.

The new Practising School, the McCabe Memorial, was dedicated in 1940. It was made possible by a teacher in the public schools of Portland, Oregon, who left her estate to the W.F.M.S. revealing then that it had been her heart's desire to become a foreign missionary but the care of an aged mother made that impossible. The Secretary wrote: "It seems fitting to us that the bequest left by a school teacher should go into a building used for training other teachers."[38]

The Boys' School is a part of the Practising School. A boys' hostel is maintained.

Village Education Service

The Gujarat Conference placed strong emphasis on village education. In 1922 there were 212 village schools in which it was expected that the number of Christian children should be at least twenty-five per cent. It was felt that village schools "should be as expertly staffed, as efficiently managed, as systematically organized, and as educationally effective as any other branch of our educational program". To make it possible to maintain a teaching staff free from transfer by a District Superintendent; uniformly paid and equipped for work district by district, a Committee met in August, 1937, to plan a Village Educational Service. Plans that had been worked out were unanimously adopted and a Board set up to administer the Service.

Every effort was made to meet all standards fixed in the Presidency for such schools and their teachers. To this end some schools were closed; some older teachers pensioned; qualified teachers brought into the Service. At the same time each member of the service was urged "not as a teacher, but as a Christian," to participate in the work of the village circuit.[39] In 1940 there were in the service 100 schools, 176 teachers and 2810 pupils. All but three schools taught only classes kindergarten to four.[40] As the State put increased emphasis on compulsory primary education, and gave more detailed attention to the conditions in schools, the need of the Village Educational Service decreased. In 1953 only forty-seven schools were being conducted by the Service. Of these seventeen were closed in 1954.[41]

Medical Work

It was Gujarat's good fortune that medical and evangelistic work opened together, Miss Izillah Ernsberger, M.D., the Freases and Miss Thompson arriving together in 1889. In the first year the doctor treated 3,800 patients and visited over 350 in their homes. In the second year she opened a dispensary in Camp and one in the city; and in the third year treated 6,800 patients.[42] When Dr. Ernsberger returned to India after furlough in 1895 she went to Sironcha, and Emma Hodge, M.D., who came with her, went to Baroda. Her appointment linked "Medical and Evangelistic work", so that while the sick were helped, evangelism was able to effectually reach the family as a whole.[43] Dr. Hodge welcomed this double task.

In 1903 Miss Tuttle, M.D., reached Baroda and after a year for language study worked in the District from dispensaries at Baroda and Umreth. It became evident, however, that cases most requiring treatment could not be reached in this way; there was need for a central hospital. In recognition of the Jubilee it was decided in 1906 to erect a hospital for women and girls at Baroda as a memorial to Mrs. William Butler.[44] The Conference appointments made that year included this Memorial Hospital under Belle J. Allen, M.D. Three years later the hospital was still "far from finished . . . there not being funds on hand for its completion". During this period Dr. Allen worked chiefly with the Women's Department of the Theological School and in the Girl's Schools at Baroda and Godhra.[45]

About this same time Eldridge was transferred to Baroda for educational work. He had a knack for medical work. Without nurses or hospital or proper appliances he rendered helpful medical service.[46]

The buildings for the Mrs. William Butler Memorial were opened in July, 1910. Dr. Allen was assisted by a European nurse, Miss Law, and a qualified Indian nurse. They at once opened a nurses' training class with six young women.[47] In 1913 Dr. Laybourne followed Dr. Allen and in turn was followed by Drs. Huffman and Ferris.

Nadiad

The earliest reference to a dispensary in Nadiad is in 1908 and reads: "Bro. Eldridge has had his hands full. A dispensary has been opened in the town in addition to one at the orphanage. He had also visited Godhra several times a week."[49] The need had long been felt. Eldridge was a layman, untrained as a doctor, but he opened the way for something better.

The Conference appointments for 1911 included, "Thoburn Memorial Hospital—to be supplied". Early in that year Dr. Alexander Corpron was transferred from Pithoragarh in North India to Nadiad. We read of his second year: "He has done wonders in spite of poor equipment and no assistance from mission funds." Corpron was supported by two kind friends, but his work had to meet its running expenses. He regretted that he so often had to take the paying patient to the neglect of others who were needy. Even so, he had

> created for himself a reputation as a skillful surgeon, and patients have visited him from all points of the province and beyond. The number of tuberculosis cases he has treated have been very many; and his successful treatment of cataract has brought large numbers to his operating room. Some cases of healing have seemed little less than miraculous.[50]

For the year 1912 he had In-patients, 237; Out-patients, 15,935; and 214 operations requiring anaesthetics. Twelve years later the Superintendent wrote: "He operates most of the day and sees the out-patients in the evening and the night."

In 1915 Miss W. Cracknell, an English nurse joined Dr. Corpron in his work and later became a missionary of the Board of Foreign Missions.

Later Miss Steepee, Miss Boggs and Miss Florence Taylor rendered fine service here. Last year Miss Taylor was one of two nurses in India awarded the Florence Nightingale Medal by the International Committee of the Red Cross for "exceptional devotion to duty" and "outstanding role" in raising the standard of nursing in India. Since 1946 she has served as Dean of the School of Nursing in the Christian Medical College in Vellore.

Dr. Herschel C. Aldrich joined Corpron in 1930. The hospital closed during 1935 when both doctors were in America owing to ill-health. Corpron did not return. In 1936 Aldrich returned and remained until 1947. Dr. Staley officiated for a year and Aldrich resumed the Superintendency in 1948. The School of Nursing received official recognition in 1953, its first students passing the next year.[52]

In 1952 through the week of Dedication and local gifts a new surgical ward was completed.[53] The Methodist Hospital is now supported jointly by the two Divisions of the Board. Its present efficient Superintendent is Dr. Isaac A. Chitambar, M.B.B.S., M.S., son of Bishop and Mrs. J.R. Chitambar; Miss Theresa Lorenz is Superintendent of Nurses and Director of the School of Nursing; Miss M.L. Precise, Associate, School of Nursing and Miss Gallagher, Director of the School of Laboratory Technicians. Mr. Nilajagi, trained in the U.S.A., is the Business Manager.

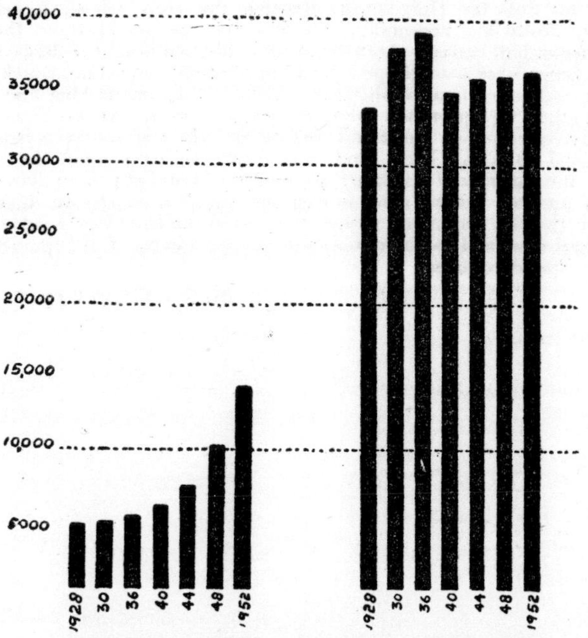

GROWTH OF THE CHRISTIAN COMMUNITY
BOMBAY CONFERENCE GUJARAT CONFERENCE [53]

A mighty work is going on among the workers also. For many years, we have felt that until our band of workers received in reality the baptism with the Holy Ghost, there was little use of talking about a great spiritual movement, self-support, self-management or any such thing. We have felt that the whole future of the Church depended upon this baptism coming upon our Indian Church. This burden was pressed so heavily upon the hearts of Brothers Seamands and Ross that they, not wishing to be disobedient to the Heavenly Vision, planned for a Holiness Camp Meeting in a jungle, far off from any village, out between Vikarabad and Bidar. Select workers were invited to the meeting. On arrival they were surprised to find that the meetings were to be held in this solitary jungle place. They said "Here *we* are, but where are the people? How are we to have revival meetings here, far away from the village, where there are no people to listen to our preaching?" They were told that they were not there to preach to others but to receive a special baptism from the Lord. . . ."All were encouraged to look for the extraordinary, to pray and search the Scriptures, seeking constantly that Holiness might become a personal and definite experience in every heart." The purpose of the meeting was kept constantly before them. They were exhorted to "Seek the Holy Ghost, Receive the Holy Ghost, Receive him Definitely, Positively, Personally," in fact no one should leave the place until Pentecost had certainly been repeated in his own heart. A large number in the audience were soon gripped by an unrelenting conviction, which caused them to spend hours beneath the trees, fasting, praying, seeking and faithful was our Father who promised who also began to do it. At the close of the second day, one brother came and requested help, stating 'It is time I am getting fixed up with God.' And out under the trees amid the evening shadows, the darkness of his heart gave way to the light from above. The next day, another brother came in from the jungle with request that he be allowed to give his testimony, saying 'I received the Holy Ghost today noon!' With these new and positive testimonies, new visions of the possibility in Christian experience arose.

M. S. I. C. 1923 pp. 449-50.

XIV

The Hyderabad Area

A plan for "districting of Bishops" was new in Methodism when in 1908 the General Conference requested the Bishops, "if they shall find it practicable, (1) to arrange the Annual Conferences into groups covering contiguous territory; (2) to form several groups of Conferences into districts; (3) to assign the individual Bishops within said districts".[1] In 1916 the General Conference confirmed the "Conferences related to the several Episcopal residences". In 1920, and since Episcopal "Areas" have been established by the Committee on Episcopacy with the approval of General Conference.[2]

The Central Conference asked General Conference for authority to fix the Episcopal Residences.[3] The request was approved and used the first time by Central Conference in 1912, when Lucknow, Bombay and Singapore were designated. With the election of Bishops by the Central Conference that body received the authority also to assign its Bishops to their residences.

The South India Conference

Repeatedly made smaller by the formation of other Conferences, the S.I. Conference never ceased to grow, first, as an innate expression of spiritual vitality, and second, by incorporating in itself contiguous territory and work. Belgaum was such a unit.

In 1820 the Commanding officer of Belgaum applied to the London Missionary Society missionaries in Bellary for one to be chaplain of his troops, promising his support. In answer to this call Joseph Taylor opened work in Belgaum on September first. A church was soon organized. In 1830 W. Beynon also went from Bellary. Public preaching was done in Belgaum and Shahpur. Over 400 Indians had been baptized. About a third of these were Kanarese, a few were Muslims, but the majority were Tamil speaking. The first Kanarese converts, Dhondappa and Devappa, were much persecuted, and their property taken from them, but they were steadfast. Taylor died in Bombay in 1859. Beynon retired in 1870, never having revisited England in his forty-five years as a missionary. The farewell address he received describes the public appreciation for the English School which he and Taylor opened in February, 1832 which became a high school in 1873.

> This school has the credit of being the first English school in Belgaum; there was no Government school here until twenty years later. It has supplied the various branches of the public service with competent young men and to this day they are holding responsible posts . . . . You and Rev. J. Taylor have been the first to open vernacular schools for boys and girls in this place. Hundreds of children, who would have been otherwise the source of misery to their parents and of mischief to the public, have been thus brought under restraint and regularity, and fitted for higher branches of learning. Female education in this part of the country owes its origin to you.[4]

James Smith reached Belgaum in 1867 and J.G. Hawker in 1871.

Belgaum

In 1903 the London Missionary Society found it necessary to discontinue the Mission in Belgaum and offered it, with the property valued at Rs. 55,000 to the Methodist Board in New York. The offer was accepted. On June 1, 1904 Mr. and Mrs. Ernsberger took over the Mission as a part of the Raichur District.

> Mrs. Ernsberger took up the Principalship of the High School and the Superintendence of the Girls' Schools and Bible women, while I became the business manager of all the schools, Wesleyan Chaplain and Preacher in charge of the Circuit . . . . a Christian community of about 200 of whom six are catechists, two colporteurs and two Bible women; an Anglo-Vernacular High School, seven Vernacular schools.[5]

The Christian community was small but all converts were from the high castes. When in 1910 Ernsberger reported three schools in the Bail Hongal circuit under S.L. Aralikatti, a Local Preacher who had been in the Belgaum Mission, and that "two [were] for caste people and one for outcastes . . . . The former we inherited and the latter we established", he announced a major change in policy.[6] The new program included an opportunity for the depressed groups. The first break among these people came in 1907 in this circuit when there were 410 baptisms bringing the total number of Christians to 880. The Belgaum District was formed in 1909 with the Bail Hongal, an English and the Belgaum Kanarese circuits,[7] this last under S. Maigur. In addition to pastoral duties he spent much time in street preaching and serving as "working Editor" of the *Suvarta Patrika.* Some responsibility for the chaplaincy with troops continued as a part of the English circuit. The C.W. Scharers joined the Ernsbergers in the fall of 1904. They continued in the district for nearly twenty years.

A girls' boarding school was opened in 1907 when Bishop Oldham divided the girls' boarding school in Raichur and Miss Grace Woods took one group to Belgaum. When on furlough she secured $10,000 for a new school which was built in 1910 under Miss Ericson.[8] It was known as The Sherman Girls' School. When, as a High School it needed larger quarters, the W.F.M.S. purchased the former Beynon-Smith Boy's School building and that institution moved into a new plant on land purchased from the military authorities. A boys' hostel was opened in 1904. G.N. Prakash and A. Barnabas were the first two boarders. A "splendid hostel building" was provided after the visit of Dr. A.B. Leonard in 1906, when Mrs. W.D. Beal became "the first hostel mother".[9] The name of the school was changed to Beynon-Smith during the time that E.L. King was Principal. He helped several teachers to secure their training, and encouraged boys in extra-curricular activities in a group known as "Knights of Service". This school has for years been the largest boys' school in India Methodism.

E.C. Reddy became the first Indian Principal in 1933. The school has had unusual growth in this period. He showed initiative in improving and enlarging the school, and in winning the cooperation of the public. With a larger enrolment the stability of the staff was increased. New departments were added: agriculture, commercial, vocational, physical education. He has been succeeded by Smith Gershom in 1956.[10]

The Raichur District.

The "Kanarese Mission" of 1885 in which Jacobs and Ernsberger pioneered, became the Gulbarga and Raichur circuit of the Madras District. It included a territory about 200 miles long with an average width of sixty miles and a population of two million. In 1890 it became a circuit of the Hyderabad District. By 1900 the Christian community numbered over 500.[11] The report for 1892 briefly describes the preliminary work that had been done.

> In Raichur there are two Sunday Schools with fifty scholars. Preaching has been carried on both in town and villages. In Shorapur, there is a flourishing Sunday School of 100 scholars; and in the vicinity there are numerous honest inquirers who do not hesitate to avow openly their faith in our Lord, and who would willingly receive baptism, if they could do so without publicly breaking caste.
>
> In Gulbarga in addition to street preaching and Day and Sunday Schools, a Book Depot and Reading Room have been opened, proving very helpful to the work.
>
> Mrs. Ernsberger has opened a Girls' School in Gulbarga that promises well.[12]

In its five stations in 1900 there was a total of twenty-six workers; including the missionaries. Its connection with the Hyderabad District gave to these workers an inspiration and fellowship that meant much to them. Gilder describes the District Conference of 1895 as more than any other to have brought "clear and indisputable manifestations of the Divine power".[13] These initial contacts made later contacts possible. In 1924 thirteen women and twenty-one men and boys attended the camp meeting in the Vikarabad District.

In 1900 this circuit became the Raichur District. There were four main centres for work: Raichur, Gulbarga, Shorapur and Yadgiri. Today each of those is the centre of a District. In 1904 Belgaum was added to the Raichur District under Ernsberger. This greatly increased its area and population. It was not long before another circuit was cut out from the Belgaum rural section to be a district on its own in the S.I. Conference.

Gulbarga

As the oldest centre and the longest occupied, Gulbarga continued as the headquarters for the Presiding Elder. It was Ernsberger who purchased the spacious site; seven acres near the old Treasury in 1888.[14] From 1886 to 1894 he was the only Conference member appointed to the circuit; and from 1884 to 1910 he was always in some way connected with it.

The year 1893, a good year, was marked by several baptisms and many inquirers. A Christian boarding school was started with five boys and by year's end the number grew to fifteen. Several of these were converted. "In this circuit . . . our greatest need is native workers trained by us and for us." This group of boys, the P.E. thought, would be the nucleus of a training school for men for this part of the field.[15] That was hope; set with it the pangs of heart behind his report in 1901:

> A serious lapse into heathenism of a community of baptized persons in one section of the District, bring us face to face with one of the terrible results of our inability to supply and support sufficient and duly qualified helpers for evangelistic work.[16]

Yet the Gulbarga work grew, not only at the centre but within its vast circumference. In 1893 the W.F.M.S. financed the opening of a Christian boarding and day school. Miss Izillah Ernsberger, M. D. opened medical work in the city and assisted with the boarding schools after the death of Mrs. Ernsberger. Work was somewhat interrupted by frequent changes until J.H. Garden took over from 1907 to 1913.[17] From 1922 to 1925 Nanappa Desai was Superintendent of the Gulbarga District. As Preacher-in-charge at Shorapur, and District Evangelist, he had worked in and near that circuit for nearly thirty years. He had been converted on the Poona Race Course under the preaching of Prautch; he was baptized by W.W. Bruere in Grant Road Church and Garden brought him to this large district.[18]

Miss J.E. Morrow, the first W.F.M.S. missionary after Dr. Ernsberger, came to Gulbarga in 1921 for supervision of Evangelistic work and the Boys' Boarding School. In 1911 Garden opened an Elementary Training School for men and their wives. Besides learning the three "R's" they committeed to memory passages of Scripture, the Catechism, Christian Hymns and for practical training taught Sunday Schools and preached in villages.[19] In 1925 the number of Christians in Gulbarga District, after Raichur had been formed as a separate district, was 5692 and in Gulbarga circuit 405. In 1954 in the co-educational High School in Gulbarga there were 203 Christian boys and 131 Christian girls. The Shanti Sadan Girls' Hostel and a Boys' Hostel gave homes for Christian children.

Raichur

Ernsberger was here for a short time in 1885 but early work was supervised from Gulbarga. Raichur work was carried on in both Kanarese and Telugu. When the large Raichur District was formed there was a small Christian community. For three years the Mission had been trying to buy land and build here for the W.F.M.S. without success.[20] When A.E.Cook was in charge of the District from 1904 to 1912 he succeeded in buying the land so long needed. Garden found that Joseph Buchanna, "the first indigenous convert of the Raichur District," was still working on the District.[21] In 1907 most of the girls from the Raichur Girls' School were taken to Belgaum. The small number of girls left behind were cared for by Mrs. Cook in the old dormitory near the bungalow and others added. Soon after the removal of the girls, permission to purchase the land was received from the Government. But the immediate need having been cared for and other funds not available, the new school plant was not erected until 1923-24 when it was completed under Miss Ericson, who wrote:

> We began the year in the small cramped rooms of the General Missionary Society quarters, and now . . . find ourselves in our spacious compound with room enough to run and play and sing . . . without . . . being a nuisance to anyone.[22]

This school had an enrolment then of 169 of whom thirty-four were boys. It continued to serve both the Raichur and Gulbarga districts and numbers came from both.[23] The boys' boarding was opened on August 1, 1925. The school is still co-educational under both Divisions, with Miss E. S. Edwards in charge. The enrolment in 1954 was about 300.

The Crawford Memorial Hospital, Vikarabad, had a Branch Dispensary at Raichur which proved very helpful both for the schools and others for some years. In one year they treated 6768 out-patients.[24]

An institution of great promise to the district is the Village Leadership Training School sponsored jointly by the two Divisions of the Missionary Society. It was started in 1938, a two-year course open to middle school graduates for work in villages. Miss Ollie Leavitt is the Principal.[25]

The Christian community in the District at the close of 1925 was 3,553. In 1954 it numbered 14,418. The Raichur District at the close of 1954 was under the efficient care of Rev. E. Gershom. In 1950 his son Benjamin Smith, a graduate of the Lucknow University, was admitted to the Conference, a third generation member.

Shorapur

Shorapur—the town where Jacobs and Ernsberger essayed to open the "Kanarese Mission"—early became a circuit of the Raichur District. Ernsberger describes the people in 1893 as those "who are seeking the truth". and commends them for largely supporting the schools which had been opened among them. In this circuit the W.F.M.S. had perhaps their first day school for non-Christians in the District.[26]

The first "break" that Gilder reported in this territory was "near Shorapur, the old capital of the Beyder Rajas".

> One of this tribe, Hanumaya . . . in quest of truth, a few years ago, abandoned his fields and family and became a Sadhu donning the tawny coloured garb peculiar to Hindu sainthood, taking up his abode in a cave.

He heard the Gospel message of God's love from one of our preachers, was baptized and declared his faith to his followers. Two of them were baptized; one a leader in Hanumaya's village, the other a widow "whose one end and aim now" was to tell others.[27] In 1895 several were baptized who continued faithful.[28] Enquirers among the low castes were numerous. Later a boarding school was opened for boys, some three miles from town. There were "forty pupils in the midst of a large and growing community".[29]

When Shorapur was constituted a District the Conference had wisely approved a policy of central, co-educational schools at Gulbarga and Raichur. Shorapur had a school for Lombardi children, an enterprise of both Divisions, "doing pioneer work amongst children from Lombardi families, setting their as yet unwritten language to Kanarese script".[30] In 1951 it was under Miss Leavitt. The District Superintendent was H.G. Mitra, a product of the Middle School in Gulbarga, the Beynon-Smith High School and Leonard Theological College.[31] In 1954 the Christian community numbered 6,815.

Yadgiri

"In the month of February, 1884, two missionaries with two native orphan boys set out from Yadgiri station by bullock cart for Shorapur."[32] This account, by Ernsberger tells Yadgiri's first connection with Methodist history. The connection has grown both strong and deep in the seventy-two years since that little expedition set out.

The year 1910 under Malappa Lewis had been "a good year" in the circuit.[33] The preacher had been "diligent in touring and preaching the Gospel and in pastoral work". There were sixty-three baptisms that year making a total of 127 Christians in his circuit. Only fifteen years later this number had increased to 1,563 which was more than one-fourth of the total in the Gulbarga District. In 1954 the total reached 6,717, and the Yadgiri District was described as "the fastest growing section of the Conference".[34] Its Superintendent is John Paul Karodi, a graduate from Beynon-Smith and Leonard. It has not built up schools. After the first standard the children are sent to Gulbarga, but the latest report speaks of the need of a hostel to be "run on indigenous methods"; the parents to provide the food grains and clothing, and the church the accommodation and books. "Later on this too must be found from local resources." The District has two institutions:

The Linn Dispensary and Health Centre at Yellari, opened about 1943, was "an outgrowth from Kolar opened by Dr. Deena Sonna, after five years on the Kolar staff and Eva Logue, Public Health Nurse". In this project both Divisions of the Missionary Society have equal share. An important part of the program is health education. The medical needs they could not meet emphasized the need of the Holston Hospital, only recently completed in Yadgiri. R.H. Pickard, M.D. is the Director.[35]

Kolar

Medical. The Ellen Cowen Thoburn Memorial Hospital is named for a sister of Bishop Thoburn. The site of eight acres on which it was built adjoins the town and was obtained after two years of negotiation. Permission to build was received during the mid-year Finance Committee meetings and plans were immediately made for a sod breaking ceremony. Bishop J.E. Robinson conducted the service before a large and select gathering, on July 3, 1909. The students of the masonry and carpentry departments of the Industrio-Educational School erected the building.[36]

Dr. M.D. Lewis was transferred from North India to Kolar and she opened a dispensary immediately after her arrival, in a small room back of the Post Office.[37] Her knowledge of Hindustani was invaluable since nearly half of the patients were Muslims. More than 6,000 patients were cared for during the first three months. The first ward was opened in January, 1910. The arrival of Miss Griffin, R.N., in the end of 1913 added effectiveness to the work.

The foundation stone of the Wilbur Paul Graff Baby Fold was laid in 1922. Its first Superintendent was Miss Griffin.[39] She was followed by Miss E. Wheelock. Miss Griffin started the Nurses' Training School in 1911. Its new building was dedicated by Bishop Badley in September, 1928.[40] Dr. Lewis retired in 1927. For a short interval Miss Walker, M.D., was in charge until Dr. E. Shoemaker arrived in October. A public health service was opened by Miss Saunby after 1935. Gradually the educational standards for nurses have been raised to high school pass.

The first Indian Medical Assistant, a graduate of the Ludhiana Medical School was Dr. Elizabeth Peters. In 1923 Dr. Achy Ooman, "the first Vellore graduate" joined the staff.[41] Dr. Maria Selvanayagam joined about 1933, remaining until 1951 when she went to Yellari. The hospital is now a 150 bed hospital. Dr. Corpron served here 1937-41 since when it has been a General Hospital. X-ray work was started in 1936. In 1952 Dr. R.H. Pickard was Superintendent of the Men's Department, and Dr. Huitema of Holland and Indonesia was Medical Superintendent, with Dr. E. Shoemaker as Hospital Superintendent.

> From 165 in-patients in 1911 we have grown to 3,400 in the past year. Out-patients have grown from 4,000 to more than 50,C00. There were 3 graduate nurses in 1927; now in 1954 there are 30 graduate nurses and 44 student nurses. Since 1934 compounders have been trained, and from July 1954 laboratory technicians have been in training.[42]

Education. Miss F. F. Fisher was the first W.F.M.S. missionary sent to Kolar for educational work in 1897. From kindergarten through middle classes there is coeducation. The W.D.C.S. maintains high school classes for girls. The total school enrolment in 1954 was 682. The school is maintained in three units: Primary, total enrolment (1954) of 272, Christian boys and girls 55 and 42; Middle, with 245, Christian 32 and 38. High School classes for girls only, enrolment 145 of whom 23 are Christians. The middle school is now accommodated in a building of its own, the remodeled workshop.

Industry and *Agriculture.* The Industrio-Educational school started by W.H. Hollister in 1893 and with which he spent twenty-seven of his thirty-two years as a missionary, continued to the thirties. Farms in the "Christian" villages, as well as the large compound in Kolar itself gave opportunities to teach agriculture. Miss Anstey had teachers for carpentry, but the new missionary found that "the teachers could not saw the end of a board true to line; that all work was done sitting on the ground and toes and hands were both used to hold pieces of wood in position. Teachers and students both, sat on the board being planed and moved the plane before them." He believed there were better ways and that by working two hours a day and Saturdays, all day, that boys could earn their clothing and bedding. His hope was realized. In his first furlough he bought some plow shares from John Deere in Moline, to bring back to India. In five years he sold seven. Then a man wo had bought one came forty miles in an ox cart to get seven. Another returned for five.

> In the past ten years the school has sold three thousand six hundred plows. A plow a day for ten years, and the supply has been far below the demand. Are the ploughs used? The sale of 5,750 extra shares to replace those worn out is a sufficient answer.
>
> The school has widely influenced the standards, the styles and quality of household furniture. It has also been the pioneer . . . of the use of machinery in vocational education and the making of furniture.[43]

All Missions buildings for a period of twenty-five years were put up by the Industrio-Educational Department. An unusual situation prevails near Bidar, Deccan. The building and carpentry trades there are largely in the hands of Christians. Students who learned in Kolar by what is today called the "dirty hand" method, opened the way to that progress.

Madras

Of the cities opened by Taylor Madras had the largest immediate results. It lacked for its follow-up leadership the acquaintance with, and experience in India that Bowen had for Bombay and Thoburn for Calcutta. As a port Madras was much smaller than the other cities. In consequence it lacked the financial strength they possessed. In 1892 the Presiding Elder lived in Bangalore as being more central since his District included Madras and Kolar. Madras appointments included Blacktown Tamil and Telugu circuit, the Vepery English church and Vepery Tamil and Telugu circuit.[44] Miss Stephens had, indeed, developed a work among Indian women unequalled in any other place. "This", said Rudisill, "would be a sufficient representation of our Mission in this city, and that of which the church at home might justly be proud."[45]

A Tamil work had been developed to the south and west of the city by the W.F.M.S., with which Kingham and Gopalah were actively associated, but the intensity of caste prejudice hindered its progress. In 1906 J. H. Garden was appointed to the Pondicherry Circuit and two extra workers were appointed where only one man and his wife had been working. Some had been baptized but the need and opportunity were great. Early in 1907 the first man, who had come from near Pondicherry, was transferred to Malaysia and no responsible leader was left in the circuit.[46]

A second Tamil field had been opened near Tuticorin where three circuits centered. A plot of ground had been purchased and a church building erected. The congregation started from a group in the Church of England which objected to the increasing ritualism that was being introduced. They asked to join the Methodists. Bishop J.E. Robinson held out against our accepting the responsibility, but in 1910 he, with Gopalah, Kingham and Baker, the P.E., visited the people. Then the Bishop said to Baker: "You better go ahead and receive them. I believe God is leading us."[47]

The Church had an honorary pastor, Rajappan, a Local Preacher. It supported a teacher and a Bible woman and contributed toward the salary of a preacher in Tinnevelly. Kingham was appointed in charge in 1911.[48] The work spread so that there was a Christian community of 1,500 in Tinnevelly in 1912. Batstone pleaded for schools and more men. The Conference did not have the resources to maintain the work, and after several years, withdrew from that southern field.

Lack of men and lack of funds prevented a Tamil District and a Tamil Conference; or had those men who went to Tuticorin misread God's leading? In 1913 the Tamil Boys' Boarding School and Orphanage was in rented premises. There were twenty-four boys in residence. A Boarding School for girls that year had 160 girls in it.[49] In 1926 there was a Boys' Boarding in Madras with seventy-one boys and a Girls' with 139 girls. There seemed to be promise. The Superintendent wrote: "We have more High School boys than last year. Eight manly, fine looking young Indian men live with us on the compound and attend High School in a city institution." There were high school students among the girls, also. The W.F.M.S. ladies had assisted the boys school with fifteen scholarships for orphan boys and the support of a lady teacher.[50]

With field gone the schools lost their reason for being. Edwin Gershom, D.S., in 1940, wrote: "The Girls' Middle School will close next year." The Boys' School had closed earlier. In 1955, Madras, in the Bangalore District, had two conference appointments: an English Church and a Tamil Church; in the Woman's appointments: the Balar Kalvi Nilayam (Vepery Nursery School and Teacher Training Center) under superintendency of Miss J. Comstock, and the Vepery children's school.

The Baldwin Schools, Bangalore

The Bangalore Methodist School, long since known as the Baldwin Schools, and fostered by J.E. Robinson was in the beginning a school for both boys and girls. In 1883 the schools were divided but remained under one Principal. They so continued until 1902 when the Girls' School was moved to its present site on Richmond Road.

T.R. Toussaint was the first non-missionary Principal of the school, 1891 to 1898. After a short interval he was succeeded by P.V. Roberts, who served until 1910. Mr. and Mrs. C.N. Weston and R.A.B. Andersons have faced many difficulties, financial and other, in the years since 1927 when they came to Bangalore from Naini Tal. The school has not only rendered a service to the Anglo-Indian community , but it has also had an open door for very many Indians who have sought an English Education.

The Baldwin Girls' School came under the W.F.M.S. in 1903. Early Principals were Misses U. Montgomery, Holland, Benthien and Fisher. They ınd their successors—Miss M.E. Robinson's term was the longest, 1917 o 1930—have made for the school a splendid record. It is located on a roperty of eight acres, in a most desirable section of Bangalore. The Society xpected that the school would be self-supporting, except for salaries of missionaries and the upkeep of the property.

Hyderabad Conference

The General Conference approved an enabling act for the S.I. Confer-nce to divide during the quadrennium "by a majority vote of members resent and voting and with the concurrence of the Bishop presiding."[51] s its session in 1924 the Conference appointed a "Committee representa-ive of all the Conference interests" to report the next year. At the next ession in 1925 the Conference voted to divide, "the Madras, Bangalore, Belgaum, Gokak, Raichur and Gulbarga districts to be in one Conference ınd the Bidar, Hyderabad, Vikarabad, Yellandu and Sironcha districts in he other". On the last day of the session, December 15, 1925,

> The Hyderabad and South India Conferences have assembled each in its place on respective sides of the Hyderabad English Church, J.J. Kingham moved that the South India Conference be now organised as a separate Conference and C.E. Parker moved that the Hyderabad Conference now be organized with Bishop Warne in the chair for each.[52]

Thereupon Bishop Warne declared both Conferences to be properly con-tituted. Each Conference then elected its officers.

The first session of the Hyderabad Conference met on December 16, 926 in the Mary A. Knotts Girls' School Hall, Vikarabad, under Bishop Badley. The following were present:

> Kondru Ambiah, A.S. Abraham, K.E. Anderson, Mariappa David, Ongole David, Thomas Devapriam, George Garden, G.H. Job, Garnipudi Joseph, J.R. Luke, Manipalli Luke, B.J. Lyman, S. Noah, J.T. Perkins, T.A. Peter, B.N. Rajah, G.N. Ratnam, M.D. Ross, N.E. Samson, Gabriel Sundaram and Jotappa Jacob. A.E. Cook, C.E. Parker, John Patterson were On Leave in America; H.H. Linn was absent.

Besides the wives of missionaries named above the following were charter nembers of the Woman's Conference: Misses S.L. Dodd, M.D., A. Harrod, K. Metzker, Margaret Morgan, Mabel Morgan, N.F. Naylor, M. Older, V. Otts, R. Partridge, C. Smith, M. Smith, E.J. Wells, N. Low, M. Simonds, M. Simpson, Mrs. Hanock and Mrs. D.O. Ernsberger. Misses Chinniah, C. DeLima and Mrs. R. David were admitted at this session.[53]

Fifteen years before all the territory of this new Conference excepting Sironcha and Yellandu was included in the Hyderabad District of which W.L. King was the P.E. from 1896 to 1912. At the end of 1895, when the Society did not own "a single square inch of property" in this the fourth city in India, George Gilder, the rugged pioneer who had given charge to King, recorded his hopes for the future: "There is no reason why Hyderabad from a Methodist point of view should not, in relation to the Dekkan and Telengana territory, be what Lucknow is . . . . in our North India field."[54] Yet ten years later the Society owned no property. King fretted at the "exorbitant rents" being paid annually, and at the "rising prices of property". In 1906 "the property occupied the last four years" by the W.F.M.S. was purchased "a result of very great moment at this present time".[55] Two "eligible properties" for the General Society were purchased in 1907, but this they were not permitted to hold. However in 1909 they secured a "property better located and with better buildings for the Hyderabad Bible Institute" within the Residency limits.[56] In retrospect we see the Providence that directed the opening of work in Secunderabad and Hyderabad in the Cantonment and Residency, so that when the city "opened" the Church could move forward with an established and growing work. A few small properties for workers in outlying stations had been earlier secured. Many more were needed.

The work of the new Conference was organized in six Districts,—Bidar, under Anderson; Hyderabad, under J.T. Perkins; Sironcha, under Ongole David; Tandur, under N.E. Samson; Vikarabad under M.D. Ross, and Yellandu under Mannapalli Luke. In 1956 there were eight Districts, all under Indian Superintendents.

Hyderabad Schools

The little school that Miss Evans opened on February 6, 1896 had prospered. Rathna Abana won a government scholarship for Madras University in 1915.[57] In 1921 there were nine graduates of Stanley Girls' High School in other schools: three in the F.A. Class at Isabella Thoburn, two in the Woman's Christian College in Madras; five were attending the Vellore Medical College and one working for a Medical degree at Ludhiana. Miss Evans continued as Principal, except for furlough, until 1921. Miss Margaret Morgan and Miss Wells succeeded her until in 1936 Miss DeLima became Principal. She was followed recently by Miss Chandra Christdas. The enrolment in 1955-56 was 1652, with a staff of seventy-four. The boarders number two hundred.

As Miss Evans had welcomed all girls to the opportunity that "Stanley" gave, so she felt for the boys without a school. In 1919 she opened her classes to them. The first she received were for a time housed in a stable; in 1921 there were eighty-two in all classes. They became the foundation for the Methodist Boys' School which was opened in July, 1921 by Mr. Patterson. At the end of the year there were eighty enrolled. Upper classes were held in the missionary's bungalow.[58] The next year the enrolment climbed to

153 of whom thirty-four were in High School classes. George Garden, son of J.H. Garden, followed Patterson as Principal.[59] The present Principal is Challagali Luke. The school has a greatly enlarged plant and an increased enrolment.

Group Movements

C.E. Parker, known to some as "Parker of Vikarabad" was the leading human agency in the Group Movement of this Conference. In 1902 J.H. Garden wrote: "We see reasons to expect . . . a true revival that will bring thousands of these people to Christ. It seems to be upon us." Parker says: "It began in the Shankarapally circuit, a part of the Vikarabad field in 1905, when the people began to come by communities." It was Parker's first year in charge of that circuit of the Hyderabad District.

> In 1905, 54 were baptized; and two years later, 294. About the same time a movement broke out in the Hyderabad circuit, under Rev. A.H. Baker and 306 were baptized . . . . In 1908 our first evangelistic campaign was held. We prayed until God gave us His plan. He laid it upon our hearts to go into every village in which there was a single Christian and not to preach, but just to testify what Christ had done for us. From 1903 to 1913 our Christian community increased to 17,391 . . . in the Hyderabad - Vikarabad district only.

It was chiefly a movement among the Malas and Madigas (horse-keepers and leather workers). But there were a few from several of the higher castes also. When the Christian community numbered 30,000 Parker noted that the missionary personnel included only two W.F.M.S. missionaries more than it did when there were only 532 Christians.[60] Parker's faith and zeal were contagious; with the workers it "took". He was "the only man we have been able to set free for this work in the entire district". With this plaint, King added, "Give Bidar another man, and to one of the two an evangelistic commission". "Brother Schermerhorn must give much and ought to give all of his time to . . . the Bible Institute"[61]—such was the challenge of the opportunity, and such its regrets. In 1923 when M.D. Ross was in Bidar and E.A. Seamands in Vikarabad a Jungle Camp Meeting was held at Bandla Bavi. It was continued annually at Dharur and brought a deeper spirituality to the workers. "Through it," we read, "a mighty work is going on among the workers also."

An outstanding convert in this Movement was Nursamma, described by Mrs. Parker as "Soul Winner". She was a priestess, called to perform *puja* wherever epidemics broke out. She had often opposed preachers. Her home was in Kohir Village, where one night she attended a meeting under an evangelistic band, and heard John 3:16, and the testimonies of village Christians. As Merghanna spoke, "Light came to Nursamma and she was gloriously converted". Miss Partridge tells how at that meeting,

Nursamma went forward for baptism. The preacher recognized her, hesitated, then consulted. "Why do you not baptize me?" she inquired. "Your message is for sinners and I am the chief." She was known to be a fighter, so they decided to baptize her and make no record. Miss Partridge did not recognize her when next they met in Kohir. " I am Nursamma," she said, "what can I do for Jesus?" "What has Jesus done for you?" inquired the missionary. "He has washed away my sins; He has made me a new woman." Then "you can tell this story for Jesus." To learn more she purchased a Bible. She could not read, but others would read to her, and she remembered well and amazed preachers with her knowledge. Her secret was her constant communion with God. One day she was overheard while praying: "Oh, Yesu Swami, why could I not have heard about you earlier. Here I am an old woman; I could have done so much more for You. Oh, Yesu Swami, why could I have not heard earlier?"[62]

Outside of Divine grace the most important need in every Group Movement centre was that of trained workers. The Hyderabad Bible School was born of this need. During 1909 it had thirty students of whom ten were women preparing for woman's work.[63]

Vikarabad Schools

In May, 1906 the C.E. Parkers visited Vikarabad to escape the heat of Hyderabad. He found "on every hand evidence of the earnest, self-denying fifteen years of Bro. and Sister Garden:" a wide-spread evangelistic work, a Christian community of 455 and a little school with thirty-one boys and girls, the beginnings of the influential schools in Vikarabad today. During that visit the Parkers were burdened for a group of boys that they had gathered in Hyderabad, and spent much time in prayer under the Prayer Tree for a building for them. At the next Conference the Parkers were transferred to Vikarabad and their boys went with them. The need for a building was now more urgent. There was more praying and even "while they prayed a cablegram brought word of $3,000" for a building. It was from Mrs. J.L. Crawford. A second sum of equal amount came a little later.[64] The school became a memorial to her husband. About the same time George O. Holbrook, of Sorrento, Italy, sent $1,300 above the amount he had been giving for scholarships, for a building in memory of his mother. In 1907 Bishop J.E. Robinson laid the corner stones of the Crawford Boys' School, the Marion Marshall Holbrook Home, built on the site of the little school Garden had, and the Mary A. Knott's Girls' school.[65] In January, 1910 during the session of the Annual Conference, Bishop Warne dedicated the Crawford School building.

At the end of 1908 there were 90 boys in the boarding and three appeared that year in the Middle School examinations. New missionaries, the Hottons, were appointed that year for full time for school and hostel work.

The Crawford Boys' School and the Mary Knott's Girls' School work together as a coeducational Middle School. The Board of Education approved the policy of a High School in Vikarabad as soon as conditions are favourable. The enrolment in 1949 was 415. Of this number 232 were boys and 183 girls. Non-Christians students numbered thirty-four boys and seven girls.[66]

Bidar Schools

The P.E.'s report for 1905 first mentions boarding schools for boys and girls as one of "the special needs of Bidar". Another was a W.F.M.S. missionary "to take in hand much needed work for the women and girls".[67] Two years later the boys' boarding school was opened, and the W.F.M.S. was supporting "several day schools . . . and a considerable force of Bible women". A site for the W.F.M.S. was secured in 1906 and the Girls' School was opened by Miss N. Fenderich, the first missionary of the Society in Bidar, in 1908. Of the ten girls enrolled five were orphans.[68] The year 1912 was a splendid year in the Bidar Girls' School in charge of Miss Biehl. Four corner stones of buildings in connection with the school and W.F.M.S. were laid. Miss Fenderich was supervising the work herself. In 1927 the number of boarders was fifty-four of whom twenty-six were in the Middle section. There were seventy-seven boys enrolled in the Boys' Middle School in that same year, but because of the "cuts" in appropriations the number in the hostel was limited to fifty boys. As in Vikarabad these two schools were organized as a coeducational Middle School. In 1949 the Conference Board of Education approved a Coeducational High School.[69] Miss Ada Luke, daughter of Benjamin Luke of the S.I. Conference, became its Principal.

Zaheerabad

In Zaheerabad in the Ekele District the Conference has a coeducational, Rural Vocational School under Mr. and Mrs. George Garden. Students and staff live in simple, neat buildings, largely constructed by the students. The farm connected with the school gives scope for learning by doing in experiments in drainage, irrigation and soil improvement for vegetables and field crops. Villagers have been keen observers of experiments and their results. Larger boys share in the evangelistic opportunities in the countryside.

Medical Work

Bidar. Except for the simple remedies given by individual missionaries the first medical work in the Conference was opened by Dr. Batstone at

Bidar.[70] In 1904 the All Nations Missionary Union of London began its support of a medical program. In the first year 6,500 people were treated and a number of operations performed. People came from all directions within a radius of thirty miles. The next year a dispensary was opened and in 1908 two wards of a hospital were provided by the ANMU and "a devoted friend in America"; an operating room was added in 1911.[71]

When Dr. Batstone left in 1909 medical work was in the care of Dr. Mrs. J. Little, a graduate of the Agra Medical School. Dr. Linn was in charge from 1910 to 1916. Dr. Pinckney, Capt. H.W. Knight, M.D., and Dr. Lewis also had charge of medical work in Bidar. After serving together for a year in Kolar, Dr. Obed Shantappa and Mrs. Shantappa, nee Peters, also a doctor, assumed charge of the hospital at Bidar on an independent basis, giving twenty-five years of devoted service to the work. It is now supported jointly by the two Divisions. Miss F. Wright is the Superintendent of Nurses.

The following item from the Journal of 1910 enables us to rejoice in the progress medical science has made in half a century, albeit there is so much more to be done.

> All children seeking entrance to our Boarding Schools [were ordered to] undergo a medical examination and any one found suffering from tubercular disease should be refused, and all tuberculous children at present in our institution should either be isolated or dismissed forthwith.[72]

Vikarabad. C.E. Parker considered the site on which the Hulda A. Crawford Hospital stands as the "choicest in Vikarabad", and it was a "glad day" when, in 1913, they gathered on that hill-top to turn the first sod. Mrs. J.L. Crawford had given $10,000 for the hospital in memory of an only daughter who died in childhood. W.H. Hollister had just been transferred from Kolar to superintend the building operations in Vikarabad and in Bidar. While the hospital walls were rising news came from Mrs. Gisriel of Baltimore that the support of a doctor, O.G. Taylor and his wife, a trained nurse, was guaranteed for three years. The Conference appointments for 1914 show: "Vikarabad Medical work—Missionary Doctor to be supplied". Mrs. Crawford later gave an endowment of $100,000 to maintain a Doctor at the hospital and a Principal at the school.[73]

Dr. and Mrs. Taylor organized a class of young men in First Aid, Nursing and in Rural Work. These went to the villages on cycles. In 1923, work for women was strengthened by the employment of an Indian lady doctor.[74] A branch dispensary was opened at Raichur. H.H. Linn was Superintendent from 1921 to 1924. It was in these years that he started his tablet industry.

Dr. B.V. Canaran was employed during 1924. He had two ambitions: First, to secure local aid for the support of the hospital and he succeeded in getting five wards built by Hindu and Muslim patients, and other contributions; Second, to make real John Patterson's hope "to project the work of the Christian Hospital to the villages". In medical set-ups at several centres a good beginning has been made on this. Since 1927 Dr. B.V. Canaran has been "Physician in charge".[75] He writes: "The Hospital spreads the Gospel of love, of cleanliness, of the brotherhood of man and the Fatherhood of God," and thus fulfills Mrs. Crawford's purpose.[76] Miss Eunice La Rue has recently joined the hospital as a representative of the W.D.C.S. for a Public Health Program.

Sironcha

The chance "discovery" of Sironcha by Gilder and Miss Blackmar in 1894, has been recounted. He transferred to the W.F.M.S. thirty acres of land he had secured from Government, and through Mrs. Keen's reports the Society became interested in the new outpost. Miss Blackmar visited the station in 1895 and with the wives of two workers whom Ward had placed there started village work. A bungalow with kitchen and outhouses was completed in 1897, and Miss Blackmar and Miss I. Ernsberger, M.D. were appointed to Sironcha—a journey of "eighty miles of rough cart tracks through the jungles, with their belongings and some missionary helpers, in forty-two small country carts"—to their new home. A Government school had been opened in Sironcha and some girls from the high caste homes had enrolled. No one believed girls of the low castes could learn from books. In April a school for village girls was opened on the verandah of the ladies' bungalow. When cholera spread, and famine started, Miss Blackmar opened relief work. In May a woman and her daughter were baptized. Miss Ernsbergers' health failed and she had to leave. Miss Partridge then went to Sironcha. Dormitories and school were built with relief funds. In 1900 Miss Blackmar was transferred to Raipur. Miss Fuller went to Sironcha but died there the next year. Sheet anchor of the Mission for several years was Benjamin Luke and his wife, who with indomitable courage supervised the work of both Societies.[77]

C.B. Ward reported that thirty-seven were baptized in 1905 bringing to 144 the number of Christians. There were twenty-two girls in the Orphanage and ten women in the Widows' Home. Bible Women worked in the villages but not in the city. The day school was kept up as also the orphanage. New missionaries, Mrs. Turner 1905-1908 and Miss Galbraith 1907-1908, came, worked and broke in health.[78] Miss Ada Lauck followed in 1908 at which time the girls' school had classes through VI and thirty five girls in the hostel, and twelve widows in the Home. Luke had a group of boys by 1908.[79] In 1910 Miss Lauck rejoiced to have two bright, happy girls who had passed High School and one who had the full Mathura training. Her own duties were numerous. She "was so tired with the strain of being architect, overseer, doctor and nurse all in one," that she found it a good change even though it took seven days to go a distance usually covered in two, to attend the mid-year Finance Committee with its opportunity for fellowship.[80]

Many attempts to get a doctor had been made without success. Yet people continued to come in increasing numbers, and she did what she could. "Imagine", she says, "our classes from the kindergarten up to the seventh grade meeting in one room and the verandah around." The Government had given a grant of Rs. 2,000 but the new building was not ready. Village schools also were doing good work. Evangelistic work was done regularly in villages during the cold season. The Widows' Home also took time; of this Miss Lauck wrote:

> [The widows] came first of all for the sake of their little ones, and for their own sakes as well as the children's we kept them. We expect to build hopes on CHILDREN, but I say to you, if you want to see modern miracles observe the refining and developing process go on in the women . . . . Give them a home.[81]

Forty-four children had come into the schools with these women, some of whom were still there, while others had gone out as workers.

The Clayson Memorial Hospital was built in 1912. From the few simple remedies that Miss Lauck had dispensed "in love and faith from the back verandah of the bungalow," she had become known as the "big doctor". A baby born with two teeth was, for this misfortune, to be destroyed. Saving this child started the Baby Fold in 1911. The next year a school building and a new hostel were completed. Luke's "boys" did much of the carpenter work. In 1915 Miss Blanche Moore, nurse-missionary, took the hospital work and opened a class for nurses with two pupils who had completed the course in the girls' school. In the same year Luke, with his school boys, built the boys' dormitory. They dug the stone, burned the lime and made the tile and brick. Some special gifts completed what they could not do. A class for teachers was added to the Girls' School in 1916.[82]

Sironcha had been a part of the Nagpur or other Districts. As Superintendents Mussa, Guse and Felt had visited it. In 1917 it was made a District under Luke. The work grew; "advances were made along the line of self-support." Hope rose for a group movement, but the workers were too few to meet the opportunity. On October 6, 1918, the Superintendent started on a tour to the South. In its course he was seized with influenza and died before he could reach home.[83]

Benjamin Luke was born in a Hindu home in Bangalore about 1863. As an illiterate famine waif he reached Miss Anstey's orphanage. Mrs. S.P. Jacobs taught him English. He soon evinced a love for Bible study and became a close student of its truths. He was licensed as an Exhorter in 1890; as a Local Preacher in 1891 and the next year, joined S.I. Conference on probation. When the Godavary District was formed "two workers with their families constituted the entire staff and Christian community".

> His absolute *fearlessness* in the cause of right, his great *humility* of spirit and his burning *desire* to *spend and be spent* in the service of his Master [marked his life]. He had . . . a love that constrained all to honour his Christ.[84]

He left his widow and four children. C. Chandaya took the District for two years, followed by Scholberg, Perkins and O. David. The original circuit became too large for efficient supervision. In the early forties a part of the territory and community was given to the Wesleyan Church. A little later the Vinkatapur section was made a district.[85]

The Girls' School, now known as the Francis C. Davis School, continues as a primary and middle school seeking to train for Christian homes in village life. The hostel is like a practice school. The Clayson Memorial Hospital received its first doctor, Miss S.L. Dodd, M.D., in 1922. She served until 1931. In 1925 she was joined by Dr. Jaya Luke, who with short interruptions, has administered the medical work in this secluded station,[86] so that her name and the hospital's are synonymous. Miss Ada Luke, for a period had the educational work, and a brother, Jeeva Ratnam Luke, after his theological training in Bareilly, worked in Sironcha for eight years. How better could the children call their parents blessed!

The Central Provinces
(The Madhya Pradesh Conference)

The first Mission Conference to be formed in India was the Central Provinces Mission Conference. Its organization in 1905 united its territory into one administrative unit for the first time. Its status as an Annual Conference was delayed for want of the requisite number of full members. On February 27, 1913, the second day of the Conference session, the names of S.L. Mathew and F.D. Campbell were called and they, having met all conditions, were admitted into full membership. Bishop J.W. Robinson then read the disciplinary provision approved by the General Conference in 1912, which constituted the enabling act for the formation of the Central Provinces Annual Conference, and declared the conditions fulfilled. Thereupon George K. Gilder, thirty-nine years after he had first been appointed to Jabalpur, moved the resolution "that we hereby form ourselves into what shall be known as the Central Provinces Annual Conference, and request the

Bishop to give his consent to the same."[87] After its adoption the Doxology was sung, and India's sixth Annual Conference was on its course. It has adopted the name Madhya Pradesh, now used instead of Central Provinces.

The experiences of this conference were not unlike those of others. In the nineties and later, it had incipient Group Movements, but nowhere so strong as in Gujarat and in north India. The financial difficulties of this period restricted work. The famine and plague spread through these Provinces, as in many others, leaving in the institutions numbers of orphans whose care and education became both responsibility and glad service.

Then followed a short period of calm before the World War which brought much discouragement. The observance of the centenary of the Missionary Society in 1919 aroused hopes for more adequate financial support and added missionary personnel. More men put on in the India field, and Training Schools for village workers were opened in Khandwa and elsewhere. But the centenary was followed by "cuts" continued, severe and repeated. Discontinued workers became disgruntled and dissatisfaction spread. Writing in 1929 Auner said: "The last few years have been a struggle to hold our own, yet they have not been without victories."[88]

First of these victories was a continued growth in numbers of the Christian community, as these figures of the C.P. Conference show: 1913, 5,566; 1926, 10,020; 1930, 9,562; and 1940, 11,481. The drop in 1930 was not due to difficulties but to the transfer of the Marathi section of the Conference to the Bombay Conference. Second, there was growth in Christian life. Group Movements revealed an amazing courage in converts, an ability to withstand severe persecution and a strong purpose to choose their own course. Third, was a growth in the number and size of our institutions. There were more pupils in our schools; many more served in dispensaries and hospitals, and in a general way the whole Central Provinces gained by the service they rendered.

Boys' Schools

In 1912 there were in the C.P. Conference the following schools for boys: A High School at Narsinghpur; Middle (Grade) Schools at Basim, Burhanpur, Khandwa, and Raipur and a Primary School at Baihar.[89] Forty years later the Boys' Schools were coeducational Middle Schools at Baihar and Jagdalpur; Middle Schools at Khandwa and Narsinghpur, and the Christian High School and Boys' Hostel, a Union Institution, in Jabalpur.[90] The two Coeducational Schools are Girls' Schools, under the W.D.C.S. in which boys from hostels whose supervision is arranged by the Annual Conference enroll. They provide the best opportunity for the boys. The Baihar hostel for boys serves the Balaghat, Jabalpur and Narsinghpur Districts, for the hostel in Narsinghpur due to lack of funds was closed at the end of 1954. The Middle Schools are Mission Schools of the Parent Board, open to all communities. Christian students are largely out-numbered by non-Christians, and the Christian influences are therefore limited to what the boys receive in their hostels. For further education the boys may go to local High Schools or to the Christian High School in Jabalpur. For many boys the distance and expense are hurdles that prevent; the enrolment in the High School rose to 571 in 1954 in the Middle and High sections, with a total of 215 Christians. It has ten Christian teachers in a staff of twenty. The C.P. Conference has approved a resolution looking to the possibility of continuing cooperation with the Disciples Church on the basis of the Methodists "taking over the permanent responsibility of the actual management of the school."[91]

Khandwa

The Girls' School of which Miss Elicker assumed charge in 1900 has played a significant part in the educational program of the Conference. An early report, 1905, by Miss Lossing, when they had just entered a "fine new school house with its black boards and class rooms," showed 126 girls, six classes and three certificated teachers. Their work was supplemented by pupil teachers, "the most capable girls to teach one or two hours each day." Two other changes were the opening of classes in English for girls who might go on to High School in Jabalpur, and a weekly teachers' meeting which proved most helpful.[92]

A Teachers' Training Class of seven girls, recognized by the Government, was opened in 1907. The popularity of this class among all Missions, brought an enlarged enrolment in the school the next year. Girls in the Khandwa school had an enviable record in Bible knowledge. Two years in succession the girls won the silver medal in the All India Sunday School Examination.

In 1909 Miss Lossing was moved to Lucknow for four months and then to Jabalpur to open a Teachers' Christian Training School which offered an opportunity for Hindi speaking girls to get vernacular training. Twenty years later, when the English Training class was opened in Jabalpur, this Training at the Vernacular level was moved to Khandwa where the Girls' Middle School serves as the practice school for the Normal Department. The D.S. called this one of the most important events of the year. Work began on July 1, under Miss Banerji with two other teachers.[93] The missionary in the school wrote:

> The conviction grows that nothing can be more important than the training and developing of these children upon whose shoulders will and should fall great responsibility in winning this land for the Master.[94]

Jagdalpur

The real beginning of the Church in Jagdalpur was the organization of the Quarterly Conference on May 11, 1893, by Gilder. Four converts were baptized, the fruit of Batstone's work, at that time. Later—

> A number of village enquirers were baptized in Dasapal, some ten miles north of Jagdalpur. Bin Bhagat, one of the number, had been a religious teacher among these . . . . He became a Christian leader to these very ones and is still a worker in our midst. More than 30 members were present at our Fourth Quarterly Conference recently.

C.B. Ward continued to take an active part in the Bastar work until his death in 1908. For some years his son, William, worked with him and continued until 1910. Mr and Mrs. Plumley, lay missionaries until 1905, were strong supporters, the former superintended the industrial and construction work and shared in preaching.[96] The first W.F.M.S. missionary to Jagdalpur was Miss S. Stumpf. She arrived in Calcutta early in 1902, and was appointed to work in that city. During her first year there she "received a distinct call to Jagdalpur" and pleaded for her transfer. This was granted in December, 1905. She died at Jabalpur on January 21, 1907 after a visit to Calcutta. She opened medical work for women and children, for although a Government hospital was in the city, they had no woman assistant and women would not go there. Her report mentions Miss Ruggles whose work for 1906 was interrupted by illness, but she continued to labour in that State until 1910.[97]

In his report for 1905 Ward expresses his amazement at the expansion of the work to sixty-five villages, as far as thirty or forty miles to the north and south. Gattu Chandaya was the Indian leader—one of Ward's "orphan rescues". Twenty-four workers, more than half of the total, had been in Ward's orphanage. They were the most efficient.[98] After Miss Stumpf's death Mrs. C. E. Williams had the care of the boys' and girls' orphanages with eleven and twenty-two residents respectively, and the medical work. Miss Ruggles supervised the Bible women and schools. The next year Mrs. Felt and Miss Ruggles shared the work.[99] The heavy financial responsibility resting on Ward in these years is suggested by his statement that the Board's appropriation for Sironcha in 1906 was "only one-fiftieth of the whole amount the work of the District calls for".[100] When he died the work which he had so long sustained by correspondence and a small paper, "The Watchman", had to be reduced.

The F.D. Campbells followed as resident missionaries in Jagdalpur for some years. He reports that he received "gifts for a number of buildings vital to our work," by selling the skins of tigers he had shot.[101] Bishop J.W. Robinson in 1913, was the first Bishop to make a visit to the Bastar field. It was a visit full of encouragement and inspiration to the Churches.

The work then was a part of the Raipur District under the veteran G.K. Gilder. In 1915 there were 19 Sunday Schools with 347 scholars. That in Jagdalpur met in the Christian Herald School chapel. There was a complete plant for the Girls' Orphanage and School. Christian families were encouraged to settle on plots of land and to cultivate them. A few boys worked in carpentry—"simple work rather neatly done".[102]

Gattu Chandaya became a full member of Conference in 1905 and with the exception of the time in Sironcha his whole ministry was in Jagdalpur, where he was first appointed in 1897. Born of Hindu parents in Raichur in 1866, his father died when he was ten years of age. Life became difficult for the lad and his mother in the famine of 1877-1879. For a period she gathered famine children and sold them in Hyderabad. Somehow mother and son got separated; neither could trace the other. One day Gattu saw two men going toward the railway station with a group of children. Near the station he slipped into the group. One of the men was C.B. Ward; the children's destination was Gulbarga, in care of A.C. Davis. Chandaya belonged to the Sudras. He was baptized on September 14, 1880. He says that

> In 1884, in Secunderabad I truly repented, believed on the Lord Jesus Christ and received a new heart. I forsook sin with all my heart.... Either in 1886 or 1887, I received what I conceived to be the baptism of the Holy Spirit.

His native tongue was Kanarese. In the Orphanage he had learned Telugu and English. In Bastar he had to learn Hindi and Oriya. For twenty-five years he was a good minister of Jesus Christ.[103] He died in 1921.

By 1916 most of the village schools were closed. The E.B. Alderman Girls' School became a coeducational school in 1931, with Miss Bose as Principal. The enrolment of 159 included forty-eight boys. Seventeen boys from the hostel under Mrs. Lanham attended the State Middle School.[104] A few years later the number of boys in the coeducational school was nearly equal to the number of girls.

An outstanding program for the developing of village centres has been worked out by Miss Helen Fehr. In this the District Superintendent and the District Evangelist work together in close association for building up a group of worshipping Christians responsive to efforts in their behalf. Each village leader is both a religious and a secular leader. The program is led by trained helpers from the Agricultural Institute, Allahabad, and from the Religious Education Department at "Leonard". Each worker in a circuit or school, each *nayak* or *payak* in the village, is trained to work in the program.

> A ten-acre farm serves as an experimental and demonstration centre in animal husbandry, poultry raising and home improvement.

A "movable school," an ox-cart, is taken from one village to another for a week of teaching and demonstration.[105]

Baihar-Balaghat

The Baihar-Balaghat Mission became an integral part of the Methodist Church in 1906. It was pioneered by John Lampard who had once been with the Salvation Army, then started his independent work among the Gonds 100 miles south of Jabalpur, at Balaghat. Mrs. T. Williams writes of its beginning:

> Operations were commenced on very simple lines. The missionary wore the dress of a humble Indian peasant, ate the simple food of the people, travelled everywhere in a small ox-cart which contained all his worldly possessions. After many months touring . . . he selected a Gond village in the . . . Satpura Hills and there built his house. This was constructed of the same materials as the other houses in the village, viz., poles, bamboos and grass, but was better and more airy. It consisted of two fair sized rooms with a bath and store rooms . . . . One room was the missionary's living room, and the other the church; the whole structure cost Rs. 110 . . . and the missionary spent four very happy years with this as headquarters.[106]

In months a group of converts was worshipping daily in the church. In the famine of 1897 some wandering orphans were collected and the first school was commenced. Lampard married at this time and his wife threw herself into the work with these children. Headquarters were moved to Baihar where another famine added more orphans to care for. At the first station, Nikkum, a farm was started, which gave work to a few families and to some boys. The Mission soon had nine European missionaries in four stations. Only the Lampards and the Williamses joined the Methodists. The work was included in the Jabalpur District under Johnson.

The first grant from the W.F.M.S. for this new work was received in 1908 and used for Bible women.[107] The Lampards believed in coeducation and their school in Baihar was opened on this line. Most of the children were in school four hours daily and in the fields the rest of the day. Miss Keyhoe reported that the coeducational school in Baihar was the centre of many activities in the community. The eighth class of the middle school was opened in 1930; its teacher, Miss Johnson, who had just finished her High School in Jabalpur. Full of promise was the knowledge that Baihar girls were in other schools; one in High School in Jabalpur; two in the Khandwa Normal School and two taking Nurses' training.[108] There were about forty boys in the hostel under supervision of Mrs. Williams. Ten years later when the school was under Miss M. Warner she reported all seven teachers in the school as trained, and four of them were from the Baihar school. All the students in class seven had passed and most had gone for further training.[109]

Due to the opening of a Government school near our coeducational training school, it was feared that the attendance might be reduced and the school lose its recognition. The Conference Board of Education in 1954 voted that the Baihar school should be recognized as the Coeducational Middle School for Balaghat, Jabalpur and Narsinghpur Districts.[110]

The Johnson Girls' High School

In 1907 the school which Mrs. Johnson started was named the Johnson Girls' School in her honour and that of Dr. Johnson who was its loyal friend. Fourteen years later Miss Holland wrote that "one of the growing problems" was the placing of girls who were old enough to leave its shelter. Two, Dhangi bai and Radha bai had answered Ward's call for Jagdalpur. Taramani was teaching in Muzaffarpur; six were teaching in Hawa Bagh. Magania, "the last of the original number left in the school" entered the Medical School for Christian Women at Ludhiana and passed from there creditably after a two-year course in 1909."

The supply of "trained" teachers made it possible to discontinue the use of pupil-teachers in 1907. In that year American desks were provided for the English and Teacher Training classes, but the idea of desks was so new that on the first day after they were put in most of the girls were found sitting on the floor in the aisles. Another innovation was the introduction of "gymnasium classes for fifteen or twenty minutes of vigorous systematic physical culture". The Nursery Education Department of today is the outgrowth of the children's department of forty years ago, when there were fourteen children too young to attend kindergarten. They lived in the hospital compound and were cared for by the larger girls.[112]

The early course of Teacher Training was superceded in 1909 by a Government recognized vernacular course in the Teachers' Christian Training School opened by Miss Lossing. In the first class were twenty-five girls from eight institutions and several different Missions. Miss L.S. Pool, who was connected with the institution many years, describes the course: "It means an eighth grade girl who has spent one or two years in reviewing her work and has taken School management and some practice in teaching."[113] Miss Beno Banerji first came to the Training School as Headmistress in 1911 and on November 28, 1922 was appointed Principal. "She has the distinction of being the first Indian lady to be placed in full charge of a school in the Methodist Episcopal Church in India."[114] When this Training School was moved to Khandwa, Miss Banerji went with it to develop that work in its new location.

A new High School plant was completed in 1928 and opened by the Minister of Education of the Central Provinces. Much of the credit for the development of the High School and its improved accommodations belongs to Miss E.L. Clinton who served for so many years in this school. She saw the need for English Teachers' Training and arranged for this in 1928 with Miss Hildegarde Schlemmer as the first principal. She was followed the next year by Miss Lucile Colony who remained in charge for the next thirteen years. "Miss Colony put in her best self to build it up. Much of the progress made here is due to her efforts."[115] Previously, girls who had passed the High School and wished to take this training had gone to Lucknow, but admission of girls from another Province was at this time not permitted. The opening of B.T. Classes in the Hawa Bagh Training Institute for Women was approved by the Board of Christian Education in 1954 and classes were opened in 1955. Its Principal is Miss Zilla Soule who in 1922 was the first girl to pass the Matriculation Examination in the Johnson Girls' High School.[116] Miss A.N. Gadre is Principal of the High School which, in 1954, had an enrolment of 684 and a staff of twenty-six teachers excluding the Nursery and Kindergarten. The Training Institute had a staff of eight.

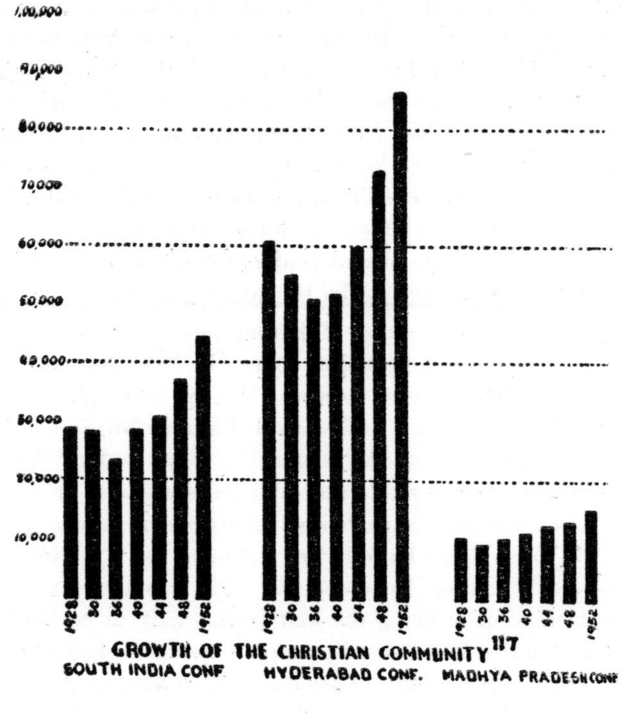

GROWTH OF THE CHRISTIAN COMMUNITY[117]

When we had come through Bombay on our arrival in India, we had met the pastor of the Hindustani work in that city, whose wife was a physician. It occured to our minds later, when we were casting about for a worker for this district work, that if we could get our friend Mr. Ilahi Baksh and his gifted wife we could ask for nothing better. . . .As our own guests for several weeks they brought us a wealth of understanding of the people. . . .

My object in writing this is to tell of . . . Dr. Esther Ilahi Baksh. . . .I remember how a mud house was finally rented in a place called Rasra. . . .They had lived in America, had been entertained in homes of luxury, had dwelt in comfortable quarters in Bombay. . . .Without a word of protest, even gladly, they moved out into that almost hostile village, took up their abode in those unpromising surroundings, and proceeded to make of them a Christian home and centre of Christian influence. One of the indelible memories is a visit I made to this home. I saw what must often have met the eyes of our Christ in his busy, crowded, ministering life—the sick, the lame, the poor, the blind, sitting on their haunches around the house, crowding the small verandah, lining the walls of the diminutive operating room and consulting room all in one. Many of them were blind, for the doctor's fame had spread with her success in cataract cases. . . .

Dr. Esther moved calmly and serenely among them, speaking a word of cheer here, lifting a bandage there, giving a word of advice, warning or reproof, every face lighting a bit at her approach. . . .

But the story is not complete without telling how the opposition was broken down among the village headman and the apostate Christians. . . .One day the village headman fell from his horse and his thigh was badly injured. A servant, in haste to help him, by mistake rubbed on an acid instead of a soothing lotion with the result that the skin was dreadfully burned and became most painful. Various remedies were obtained from the government dispensary but nothing availed and the servant timidly suggested the mission doctor as a last resort. Frantic with pain the man agreed to anything. Mrs. Baksh got down beside him and in her own kindly, skilful way brought soothing and blessed relief and final healing. I scarcely need to tell the rest of the story. As the headman himself said, "How could I resist such kindness? As if she were my own mother, the Doctor Mem Sahib got down on her knees beside me and brought me help that I needed, even though I had been her enemy."

Bessie Robinson Beal,

The Indian Witness April, 1931.

XV

The Lucknow Area

In recent years this Area has included the Bengal, Lucknow and Burma Conferences. After Burma's connection with the S.E. Asia Central Conference was established, the Area included only two Conferences, until the quadrennium 1952–1956 when the Indus River Conference was added. Although the Tirhut District was included in the North India Conference from 1913 to 1921 the account of its development is included here.

Bengal Conference

The call of Districts brings to mind the early days of the Conference, and new names give proof of continued growth and expansion into present day India—1914: Asansol, Calcutta, Vernacular, Diamond Harbour and Pakaur; 1926: Asansol, Birbhum, Calcutta Bengali, English and Hindustani, Pakaur and Tamluk; 1954: Asansol, Birbhum, Calcutta Bengali, English and Hindustani, Dhanbad and Pakaur.

Asansol District

Reporting for this District for 1926 the P. E., James Lyon, veteran of forty-six years, wrote:

> Asansol District has had a very hard and trying year. We have had very hard Financial pressure arising from the great Cut, then we have had too few workers for the great work in hand and in addition we have suffered very much from sickness among our workers and their families. However, in spite of all the drawbacks and the hinderances we have kept looking up and going forward and God has blessed us.[1]

The District had grown: In 1913 English members were 120; and Indian members 1,003; in 1926 a total of 2,893 in the District of whom 225 were in the English Circuit in Asansol and 476 in the Indian circuit. To Lyon "the Head Quarters of our Great District with the Railway Chaplaincy and a beautiful English Church and Parsonage" were happy reminders of foundations laid more than forty years before. Then he turned to institutions no one had dreamed of in the early days when the English Church was built.

Quarterly Conference on the verandah of a circuit headquarters.

The Methodist Church has penetrated to the heart of village India. In the beginning Janvier preached; "...fear not little flock..." and in the humblest places the Church is conquering fear.

Village baptismal service.

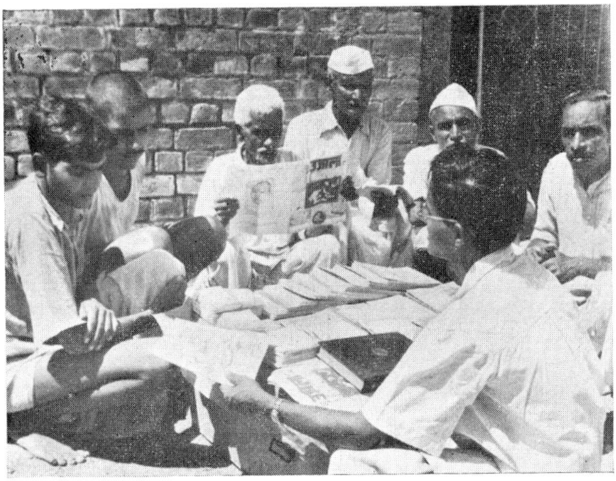

The Church must touch the "whole of life". Not only must eyes see, they must know what it is they are seeing. Literacy increases as the Church brings to its people the treasure of language's printed symbols.

In a corner of the market . . . . .

At an outdoor village school . . . .

In the seclusion of the woman's court yard . . . .

Old and young alike . . . . . share in the discovery . . . and new readers are eagerly invading the world of books which is no longer a strange land.

EDUCATION—the key to abundant life. But in India, still, a key offered to a fortunate few. The Church was one of the first custodians of that key and now the village kitchen is often deserted by the hard-working mother to gather her brood for the simple instructions which the Church has shown her how to give. In another place the evangelist faces her curious students to begin with them the golden journey.

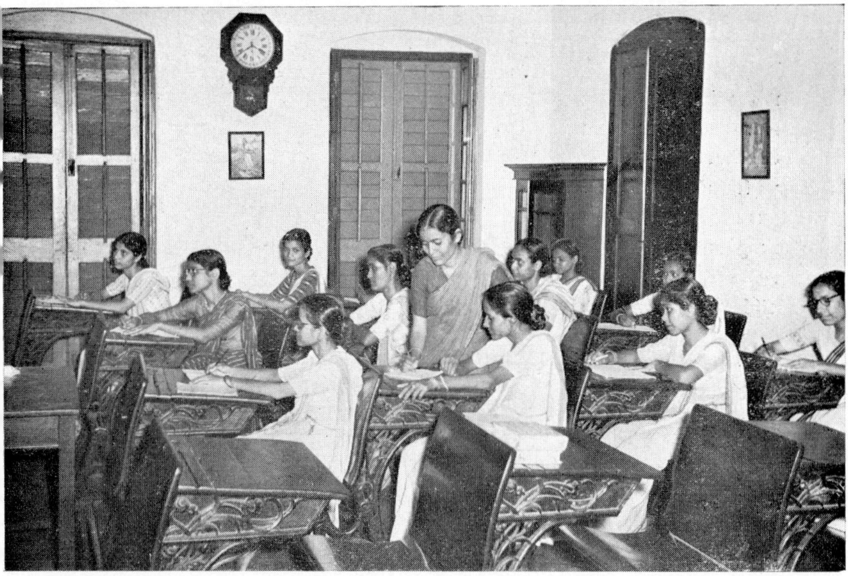

Wherever possible the Woman's Society continues its teacher training courses to supply vast vacancies in Christian schools.

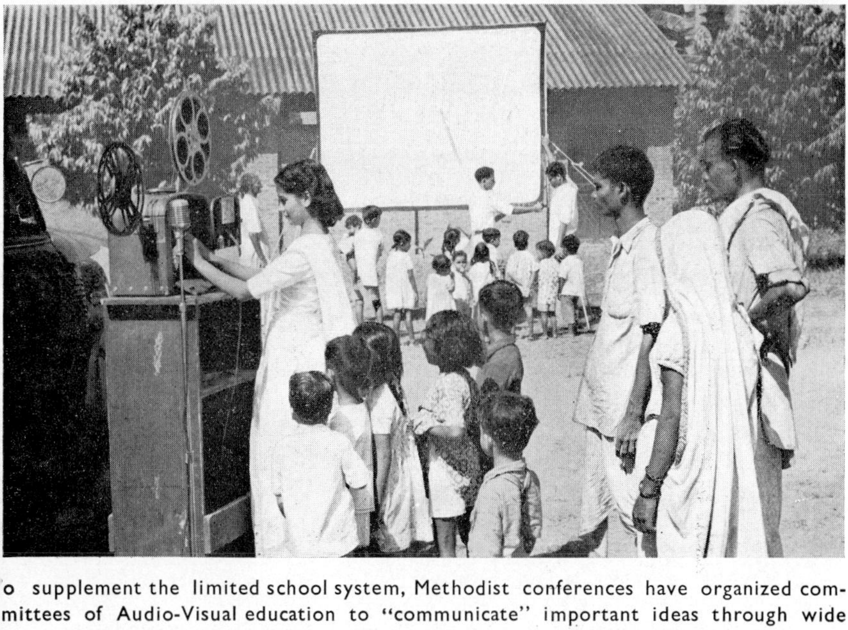

o supplement the limited school system, Methodist conferences have organized committees of Audio-Visual education to "communicate" important ideas through wide areas for masses of people who would otherwise remain untouched.

In the world of youth, values are unstable and ambitions wax and wane. The firm foundation of the Church is urgently needed. The young of the younger churches are even more susceptible to the currents of restlessness......

College choirs become proficient in both English an Indian music.

"Senior Brotherhood"—dormitory student government meets for worship and discussion.

Student "shramdan"—manual labor for the good of the country.

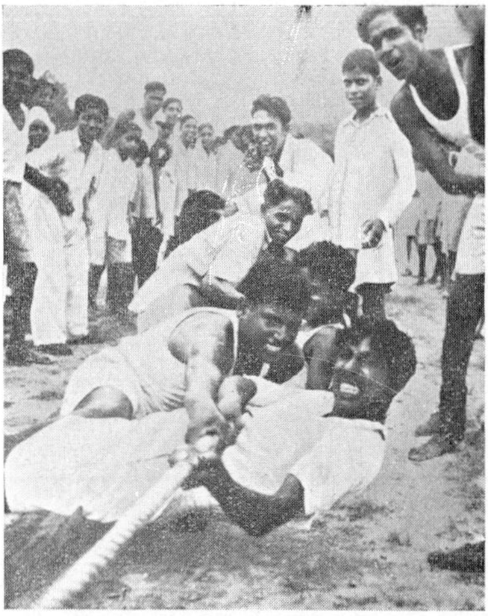

High school boys compete in inter-mural tug-of-war.

Church school class on the campus of a North India hostel.

...but in dormitories built by the Church for students who must leave their homes to go to school, they find security as they sing, worship, play, work, and study together.

Hostel residents help each other in the study-hall.

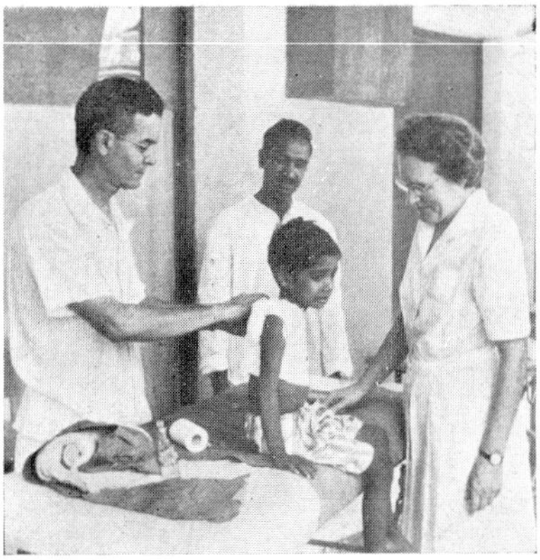

A broken bone is mended.

Christian girls make excellent nurses.

Medicine will always be one of the most impressive symbols of the Christian faith...... "those who are well have no need of a physician......" The doctors' care, the nurses sympathy, the miracles of the hospital......these all speak of the kind of God that can be found in the Christian Church.

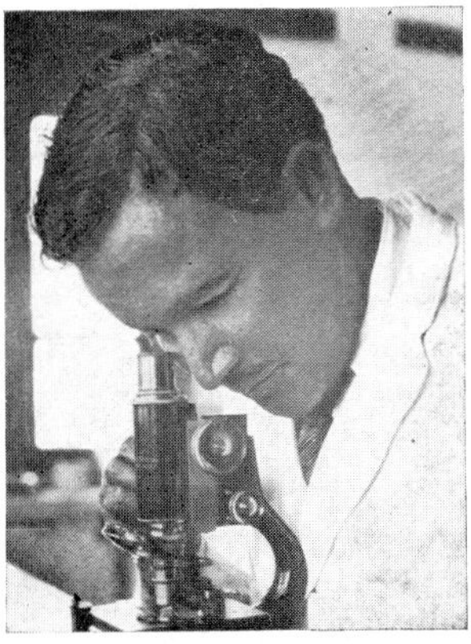

Doctor to lepers—a life of revealing dedication.

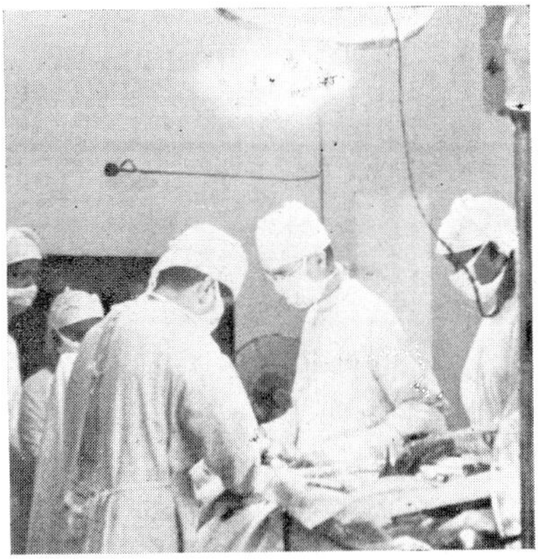

A broken body is healed.

In Asansol these were a Community School under Dr. and Mrs. Fred Williams, a large Bengali Girls' School, under Miss Carpenter, and a Hindi school and a Bengali school for girls in the Compound of the English Church under Miss Boles and Mrs. D'Crutz. The last two schools survive in a city day school which is maintained by the W.D.C.S. and for which a new building was erected in 1952.

The Community School carried a new idea; it was different. It was outside of the city with extensive grounds. While the school was open to all communities the grounds and small cottages were primarily for Christians with a rural back-ground. For these special courses, beyond those in the government prescribed curriculum, were offered in agriculture, irrigation, carpentry, care of cattle, building adobe houses, etc. Newly broken land became the laboratory for useful study and experiments. The school was called Ushagram, "Village of the New Day". Shortly after it started the large Bengali Girls' School at Ashabaree moved to an adjacent site and shared the name. Together they organized a cooperative and sought to learn by doing and sharing as village folk, the important tasks in daily living. An Ushagram Council served as a planning body for the colony. It had its own place of worship. The girls were divided into groups taking turns in cooking, gardening, weaving, arts and music, and village work. Miss Horshabala Biswas was the first Bengali woman in our church to become Principal of the school.[2]

Ushagram was completely disrupted during the war. The Army requisitioned the grounds and buildings. The girls' section moved to Pakaur for the duration and the boys' school continued at Asansol with half the enrolment of 1942. Before the war the high school had largely passed from the hands of the Mission and negotiations for a new arrangement in which the staff and students should be predominantly Christian were difficult. Both boys' and girls' sections returned in 1947 with H.E. Dewey as Ushagram Director. The school has continued to pioneer in lines of education leading to trade and home industry.

Pakaur District

The Bengali Boys' and Girls' Orphanages in Calcutta were the first vernacular institutions in the Bengal Conference. After the purchase of the property in Pakaur in 1888 the orphanages were moved there. Santals, Muslims, Bengalis studied together. From this school as early as 1891 two boys became members of the District Conference.[3]

By 1916 the numbers of Santal converts increased so as to outnumber the others. Their tribal and social customs differed and Hindi had been recognized as their official language. So, perforce, the time came when it must be the language of their schools. In the year 1924–1925 the Santal children were removed from the Bengali schools and put in their own.[4] Miss Mildred Pierce felt the need of a separate school for the Santals where their school life would be linked with their simple village life and she laid the foundations for it. Ultimately the W.F.M.S. purchased the main portion of the Pakaur Mission property from the Board of Missions and there established the Santal School plant. In four years the number of girls doubled and that of the boys trebled.[5]

The Santals have come to appreciate an education. Built much like a village, the school has for twenty-five years been known as "Jidato" which means "Village of Persistent Advance". Their church is also known by that name. The school now ranks as a High School.[6] With "book learning" they also have opportunity for doing, especially in gardening and field crops. Since its separation from the Bengali school it has been coeducational. Its Principal, Miss Premi Lee, was one of two students in the first class of the Johnson Girls' Training Institute.[7]

A small school had been maintained at Sangrampur for many years. The church there had suffered much from persecution, but in 1941 it was showing signs of steady growth. A very commodious school building, simply built, was dedicated at the time of District Conference by Bishop Rockey in 1941.[8] Its walls were of mud; the tile roof rested on heavy timbers that would stand for years, and it gave tone and stability to the community. When the Santal children were taken from the Bengali school, the older Bengali students were sent to Asansol but the younger ones attended the Sangrampur school.[9]

The W.F.M.S. retained "the property of the Bengali Girls' Boarding School, the so-called Alma Jacobson—Keventer School." This is now a coeducational middle school under both Divisions of the Board of Missions in the Birbhum District. The Principals are Rev. and Mrs. M.K. Das.

Henry Swan tells us that a dispensary was opened in Pakaur some time before 1898. In 1913 the work was "carried on by Miss Hilda Swan assisted by a nurse and a retired assistant-surgeon. On her arrival from America Miss Marnie Reilley was able to expand the work.[10] Each year the deepening appreciation of the people for the service rendered by the dispensary only revealed more clearly the need of a hospital. The record of the Dispensary alone showed in 1919 that there had been 235 in-patients and 13,825 out-patients. A gift of $150 was received for a contagious ward which was much needed. Miss Alley, "a most faithful worker and a splendid physician is in charge.... She wins the confidence and the hearts of the people."[11]

The next report opens with a note of joy "in the prospect of having a sick ward in which to care for our patients". There was the case of a sweeper woman who was finally persuaded to come to the dispensary for confinement.

> Her mother and mother-in-law went with her. The latter told Miss Alley that the woman had an evil spirit and until this was driven out the child could not be born. She wanted to go and call someone else she knew to come and drive out the evil spirit . . . . When the baby was born the mother-in-law was greatly surprised.[12]

In the summer of 1923 Bishop Fisher transferred the Edith Jackson Memorial Dispensary from Calcutta to Pakaur, and donated the sum needed to pay off the building debt on the sick ward.[13] Through the years since the Memorial Hospital has continued to render much needed service. In recent years it has been under Dr. Mrs. R.N. Peters.

Calcutta District

The Collins Institute, first known as the American Methodist Institution, opened as the "Native Department" of the Calcutta Boys' School in 1893, when G. S. Bomwetch was Principal. He was followed by B. J. Chew, J. E. Robinson and others. Lolit B. Chatterji was the first Indian Principal of the School and S. K. Mondol of the Boarding and Training School. Both "appointments were made in recognition of long and very efficient service",[14] and were an early expression of Bishop Fisher's purpose to give "our Indian Brethren the fullest possible recognition and opportunity". In 1921 of 175 candidates sent up for the Matriculation examination 136 passed, the best record in the Province. Chatterji died during 1925. S. K. Mondol became Assistant Superintendent of the Calcutta Bengali District and shortly after the District Superintendent. The present Principal is A. B. Singh.

The Institute was established to develop Indian leadership in the Conference. In 1926 Bishop Warne felt that the school had its special advantages as an evangelistic agency, but it seemed doubtful that the purpose of the founders had been achieved.[15] In 1954 the total enrolment was 780 of whom there were ninety-seven Christian boys and thirty-eight Christian girls. The Principal has fixed his sight on the original purpose of the school to supply the Conference with leaders—preachers and others.

> We have noticed with concern that there has been a gap . . . when no recruit for our work has been enlisted from this source. We have a long-range program to meet this need and have made a beginning . . . . Today four are in college, . . . we hope in the course of a few years to supply the Conference with a number of graduates and trained young men.[16]

The Lee Memorial has always been an integral part of the Calcutta Bengali District. Dr. Lee died in 1924. Mrs. Lee carried the responsibility of the work until 1940, then because of failing health gave charge to

Dr. Walter and Mabelle Griffiths. They had spent their first two years in India with the Lees and knew the work from that experience. Mrs. Lee survived until June, 1948.

In addition to the school and training centre at Wellington Square, the Lee Memorial Mission owned other property and had small orphanages and schools, and some work at Beliaghata and other centres. Some of this scattered work has been closed; but the Mission still supports boys in other schools, and assists girls to get higher education. It has representatives in evangelistic work and directs the church at Beliaghata.

Desirous of perpetuating the work which they had initiated and protecting the properties from being alienated from the causes for which they were secured, and also providing some control and direction for the work, Mr. and Mrs. Lee in 1906, deeded the property to Trustees representing the Methodist Church of Southern Asia, the Divisions of the Board of Missions, and the Bengal Conference.

Mr. H. C. Fritchley completed thirty-one years of service as Principal of the Calcutta Boys' School in 1951 and was succeeded by Clifford Hicks. The School has entered into the new life of free India. It finds that all the communities it serves feel that Christian, English-speaking schools, are doing a service that no others can do and they appreciate it. The school celebrated its seventy-fifth anniversary in March, 1952. It seeks to keep alive the visions of its founders. In 1954 there was an enrolment of 404 of whom 104 were Christians.[17]

Through the years the Calcutta Girls' School has maintained high standards in character and scholarship. Its enrolment in 1954 was 529, divided as follows: Primary, 405, Christians 118; Middle sixty-four, Christians eleven; High School sixty, Christian seventeen. Of the total number only sixteen are boys, and they are in the primary section. In March, 1942, the boarding department was evacuated to Kanpur. It was not reopened when the pupils returned in May, 1947. "Communal trouble has not entered our school. We continue as a united group in all activities and phases of school life."[18] A Nursery class was opened during the war.

Dhanbad District

In 1926 Dhanbad was a circuit in the Asansol District. The number of Methodists in Dhanbad, "Jherria and all the coal fields" was 564.[19] The five year plans of the India Government include emphasis on industrialization. In making Dhanbad a District the Conference is keeping step with the Government, confident that where industry is there the Church needs to be. The Dhanbad-Katras field seems certain to have such a destiny.[20]

For long this coal-field circuit was under the able ministry of Benjamin A. Mott, with a strong Quarterly Conference to back him. He was the the only Hindi preacher left in the District in 1948 when there were several centres for worship. The Superintendent of this new District is J. E. Titus, formerly a member of the Delhi Conference.

The District includes Gomoh which for a short time was a district headquarters. B. A. Mott is the resident pastor. In 1954 the Bishop Rockey High School in Gomoh had a total enrolment of 384, including eighty-nine Christian children. It is coeducational through the middle section with fifty-five girls enrolled.

Lucknow Conference

By an enabling act of the General Conference of 1920, the North and Northwest India Conferences were authorized "to divide their territory and adjust their boundaries".[21] By their action the N. I. Conference agreed to divide so that the Lucknow and Barabanki Civil Districts of the Lucknow ecclesiastical district, with the Gonda, Rae Bareli, Ballia, Arrah and Tirhut Districts, be placed in the new Conference.[22] The N. W. I. Conference gave its territory from the Kanpur District southward.

The new Conference met under the presidency of Bishop Warne in the Lal Bagh Church on Tuesday, Friday 1, 1921, in a service of intercession, and at eleven o'clock when Bishop Warne assisted by Bishop H. Lester Smith and Elders conducted the Sacrament of the Lord's Supper.

R. D. Wellons read the names of forty-one members and probationers from the North India Conference, of whom thirty-one answered present. The names of thirty-one members of the Woman's Conference were read and fifteen were present. G. W. Briggs likewise called the names of sixteen members from the Northwest India Conference, of whom fifteen were present, and eight members of the Woman's Conference, with six present.

Eight districts were formed with Superintendents as follows: Allahabad, J. H. Wilkie; Arrah, J. W. Pickett; Ballia, F. M. Perrill; Kanpur, G. W. Briggs; Gonda, J. O. Denning; Lucknow J. R. Chitambar; Rae Bareli, S. B. Finch, and Tirhut, R. I. Faucett. It is noteworthy that only two of the eight Superintendents, Chitambar and Finch, were Indians. The question of the name for the Conference led to a great debate of which Bishop Warne writes:

> The missionaries, including the W. F. M. S. wanted it called the "Ganges Conference" and after 4 ballots by a majority of one, for 35 against 34, it was given the name of the Ganges Conference. The next day the question of "naming the baby" was reconsidered. The Indians did not want the name Ganges. They said it was the name of a Hindu god, and they did not want their conference to be named after a Hindu god, though the missionaries thought it would be understood in America as being at the very heart of the job in India.

Tirhut District

When the Dennings returned from America in 1906 they brought with them to the District two young missionaries, Herman J. Schutz (Sheets), Fred M. Perrill, and for the W. F. M. S. Miss Grace Bills, later (Mrs. Sheets). A large house and five acres of land had been purchased in Muzaffarnagar in 1904, and the boys' school was moved there. That year the W. F. M. S. began to support work at this centre and a bungalow and girls' dormitories were erected and Miss J. I. Peters put in charge.

An independent work had been opened at Ballia by a Committee in Canada, but in 1905 they requested Bishop J. E. Robinson to take the work under the Methodist Church. This he did by first transferring Rev. J. A. Ilahi Baksh and Mrs. Esther Baksh M. D., to Rasra, twenty miles from Ballia where some work had been done. Together they won the confidence of the Christians they found, then the work spread to Dumraon where a preacher was stationed. Ilahi Baksh took some of his Christians from Rasra to Dumraon. Denning relates an incident of a widow convert who did servant's chores for Mrs. Baksh who took two days off to see relatives eight miles distant.

> While there she said: 'I've changed my religion. I don't worship your idols any more.' Then she sang a couple of hymns she had learned, and told what she could about this religion. An old man, Ramu, heard her and said, 'That is a true word. I heard it in South America many years ago. It's the good word.'[23]

Several men, at her suggestion, went to see Ilahi Baksh. He sent a worker to instruct them. After some months fifty-three persons were baptized in that *mohulla*. J. A. Ilahi Baksh died during 1909 from cholera. H. J. Sheets then took charge of the Ballia circuit.

In October, 1907 the Arrah circuit was added to the Tirhut District. A. L. Grey, an independent missionary, had opened work there in 1904. When financial suport fell off, Grey, asked Bishop J. E. Robinson to include their work in that of the Methodist Church. Adjustments were mutually agreed to. Mr. and Mrs. Grey were "two devoted servants of God whose hearts [were] aflame with zeal for the Kingdom and for the salvation of souls."[24] They brought with them property, a small orphanage and a small band of workers. At Denning's suggestion they worked in Dumraon among the chamars with encouraging success. At the end of 1911 there had been 1200 conversions. Grey was transferred to Ajmer at this time and F. M. Perrill was put in charge of the Arrah circuit. Converts in this area were very severely persecuted.

> From the inception of the Mass Movement in Ballia, the Christians have suffered bitter persecution. They were flogged, they were incarcerated unjustly, their crops were destroyed, their houses burned, their rights taken from them.[25]

The Ballia-Arrah District was formed in 1917 with Sheets as Superintendent. Of the preceding year he had written: "The most severe persecution was in 1916," but "in no year were greater triumphs won". He praised the medical work done by Dr., Mrs. Ilahi Baksh at Rasra and by Dr., Mrs. E. Sukh in Raghunathpur as "tremendous auxiliaries to the evangelistic work". The Arrah District was formed in 1919 and placed under J. W. Pickett. Miss Hyneman was the first District Evangelist. M. C. Singh followed as D. S. in 1926 and was succeeded by G. M. Massey.

The Buxar District was next formed, in 1923, by Bishop Fisher, and placed under Emanuel Sukh, M. L. C., (Member of the Legislative Council) as District Superintendent. In his reports recurred "a phrase something like this: 'the baptisms this year might easily have been doubled or trebled, or quadrupled, but we put the emphasis . . . on more instruction and pastoral oversight'."[26] Sheets added, ten years later:

> Incredible as it may seem today, it is only the naked truth to say that again and again we might have baptized thousands instead of hundreds, but with no means of doing the follow-up work, we lacked the faith to go ahead. Whether we erred by being over cautious it is now hard to say.

Institutions

The girls' school was opened in Arrah in 1918. A gift to Pickett of Rs. 500 by a visiting missionary lady helped to start it. Its future seemed very uncertain until 1921 when the W. F. M. S. adopted it. Pickett purchased the Solano Estate, one third for the W. F. M. S. and two thirds for the Board. Here the Sawtelle Memorial Girls' School was opened by Miss Edna Abbott, its first Principal.[27] In 1926 the school was "making great strides forward" under Miss Hyneman and Miss Tirsgaard.[28]

A boys' school was started from the little orphanage opened by the Greys. Many of the boys were from village homes, the result of group movements. Here they were growing up together with sons of pastors—a good way of diffusing culture. In 1926 there were fifty-four boys in the hostel under the superintendency of Miss Richmond.[29] Today the Sawtelle Memorial School is coeducational through the Middle section. The boys' hostels are supervised also by the ladies of the W. D. C. S. The enrolment of the school in 1954 was 249, with 107 Christian boys.

A new form of village service was imagined and implemented in Buxar—a Brides' School. Its success is due to Miss Mabel Sheldon and to Miss Frances Paul. The early marriage of children still troubles the rural Church as well as society in general. Many village boys have had a taste for better homes by seeing more of city culture. But custom has created ties of early marriage that hold them back and many have broken with their families.

> Why not train the young brides? . . . It has proved its value from the very beginning. It has saved homes from disruption . . . . It has trained the wife, preparing her to establish a Christian home, clean, neat, tidy, to be a real helpmeet to her husband . . . . The brides are enthusiastic and do their best for their own sakes as well as for the sake of the husband they expect to join . . . . Each husband is overjoyed to know that as he completes his own education his wife is being trained to be a real partner.[30]

Although there has been a girls' boarding school in Gonda since about 1890, it was not until 1916-17 that it became known as the Chambers Memorial School and was built up and put on a sound foundation.[31] The present Principal is Miss Martha Sahai. The Hudson Memorial School in Kanpur "was started in 1892 by Miss Downie with the help of Mrs. Worthington who took over charge the following year and looked after the school for the next thirteen years".[32] The school grew rapidly. It is now coeducational through the primary classes. Miss Gladys Walters has been in charge for the past several years. The Kanpur Girls' High School had an enrolment in 1954 of 234 distributed as follows: Primary 50 boys and 78 girls; Middle, 39 boys and 40 girls; High School, 12 boys and 15 girls.

LAL BAGH

Until 1923 the story of Lal Bagh and Isabella Thoburn College were one. When the College moved to its new home the High School classes were also transferred as a part of the Intermediate unit. However, with the increase in the number of students in the four college classes and graduate students, the High School classes were returned to Lal Bagh, where all classes were growing rapidly.[33]

In 1939 buildings adjacent to Lal Bagh which had belonged to the Christ Church School were purchased and dedicated to "the service of little children." This department at once filled, and "classes once admitted have a way of moving up," and gradually the enrolment in classes VII-X grew in four years: 157, 190, 204 and 220. In 1947 Miss Grace Davis completed thirty-eight years at Lal Bagh. Appreciation of her long service was shown in a pageant entitled "Launch Out Into the Deep." At this time the new Primary School Building was named for her. Miss E. Williams, the Assistant Director of Public Instruction sent a letter in which was this tribute to Miss Davis' school:

> There may be other local institutions with as large an enrolment, but there is no other institution that has the same orderliness, internal organization, and personal influence in spite of its overwhelming numbers. If only there were just one girls' school in every town in the Province like this school we would be making strides forward.[34]

Miss Edna Hutchens, who at different times has had many years of service with Miss Davis, followed her as Principal.

In 1951 Lal Bagh became a Higher Secondary School,[35] including the first two years of the College course. Lal Bagh's total enrolment for 1951 was 811, with 476 from the kindergarten through the fifth; and 335 from the sixth through the eleventh. In its enlarged program Lal Bagh has added Departments in General Science, Home Economics and Nursery School with Nursery Teachers' Training.

THE ALLAHABAD AGRICULTURAL INSTITUTE

In 1944 a proposal was made by the Allahabad Agricultural Institute to some Boards in America that the Institute should be reorganized on a union basis. This important institution had been started by Sam Higginbottom who went to India in 1903 to teach Economics in the Ewing Christian College. There he realized that the basic economic problems in India were agricultural, and that the Christian message and spirit should be brought to bear on those problems also. During his furlough he completed a course in Agriculture and in 1911 returned to India with $30,000 he had secured to found this institution.

Dr. Higginbottom's dream was first to develop a college of Agriculture that would be recognized by the Government, and then to "add a thorough department of extension to the work of Allahabad". By 1944 this first stage was accomplished.

After mature deliberation and consultation with the field, the Inter-Division Committee approved cooperation and contributes finances and personnel.[36]

THE LUCKNOW PUBLISHING HOUSE

This was the first and is now the only Publishing House of the Methodist Church in India, those in Madras, Bombay and Calcutta having been long since closed. It is equipped for work in English, Urdu and Hindi, but only in the first of these can it now serve the All-India field. To the degree that Hindi, now designated as the National language, comes to be used throughout India, the Lucknow Press may extend its service to all Conferences. Today, however, the differences in Hindi in Uttar Pradesh, the North, and Madhya Pradesh, Central India, are so marked as to make separate editions of our hymnal necessary. *The Indian Witness*, now edited by A. J. Shaw in Lucknow, is not only printed by the Publishing House but it is heavily subsidized by it to enable many preachers to receive it.

Agents of the Publishing House have from the beginning been missionaries. Of these a few had some practical training for such work, others had not. One of the stated purposes for starting the Press was to teach young men a trade, yet in the years we have dismally failed to produce practical printers or men to head up the several departments of a Publishing House, or to serve as Agent. Rev. Ganga Nath Shukla of the North India Conference, for many years supervised the Book Room, and more than once served as Acting Agent either for a furlough or other temporary period, and none could have proved more faithful.

In 1947 Henry Wilson, B. A., L. T., having shown practical common sense in many business lines was the first national to be elected Agent of the Press and served faithfully for over four years. He was followed by E. M. Moffatt. The Hazratganj buildings so adequate at one time could not serve the needs of today. Moffatt sold the old property and erected a modern plant on a new site. W. W. Bell has been Agent since January 1954. Known for his business and technical skill, he has brought the Publishing House to a state of efficiency in production and in financial stability that is not exceeded in all its years of service.

Indus River Conference

The Indus River Mission Conference was formed from Patiala and the Rajputana, Punjab and South Punjab Districts of the Northwest India Conference, and Baluchistan and Sindh of the Bombay Conference. At 7:30 a.m. the Conference met for the Sacrament of the Lord's Supper which was administered after a message from Bishop J.W. Robinson. The first session was convened on November 1, 1922 in Marks Hall at Ajmer, Bishop Robinson presiding. The Secretary, W. C. Fawell, elected at the preliminary organization on January 24, 1922, at the seat of the Northwest India Conference, called the roll. On the call of Question two, Bishop Robinson announced the transfer of the following:

> From the Bombay Conference . . . . W.L. Clarke, George Eldridge, Philemon Navalkar, H.R. Walter, Bunsaram Barjivan, Devji Karshan; From North-west India Conference. . . . Asgar Ali, W.W. Ashe, Umar Baksh, Chatur Bhuj, K.K. Chakervatty, Lakshmi Chand, Joseph Cornelius, Henry Daniel, I.U. Daniel, M.L. Davis, W.C. Fawell, A.L. Grey, J.M. James, Emmanuel Joseph, L.S. Joseph, Mott Keislar, I.B. Khan, Zahur Khan, Alfred Luke, Khushiya Mall, Gauhar Masih, Madho Parshad, L.R. Paul, I.D. Revis, E.M. Rugg, N.P. Sampson, James Shaw, Arjun Singh, C.B. Stuntz, James Lyon and K.B. Khan.[37]

Early in the third annual session of the Indus River Mission Conference, on November 19, 1924 Mott Keislar introduced a resolution:

> whereas, all conditions have been met in regard to number of members, and other requirements . . . we request the presiding Bishop of the Conference to declare the body an annual conference. . . . This resolution was

carried with enthusiasm. Bishop Robinson declared the existence of the Indus River Annual Conference and the Conference joined heartily in singing the Doxology.[38]

This newest among Conferences in India had in Karachi one of the oldest stations of the original S. I. Conference. In area it exceeded other conferences. In the Punjab it shared in full the thrill and the responsibility of a Group Movement; in vast areas there was no other Christian group at work.

The Annual Conference organized its work in eight Districts, with Superintendents and Christian community for 1924, as follows: Ajmer, E. M. Rugg, 3,693; Baluchistan (Quetta), A. L. Grey, 525; Batala, I. U. Daniel, 11,282; Bikaner, Mott Keislar, 1,517; Bhatinda, Alfred Luke, 13,812; Hissar, I. D. Revis, 7,015; Lahore, Mott Keislar, 20,770; Sindh, G. B. Thompson, 1,812. Among the Superintendents Daniel, Luke and Revis were Indians.

The institutions of the Conference tell something of its history. Some have local significance; others bind all as a unit. The history of thirty-two years, 1924-1956, was tragically broken in August 1947, by the partition of India, when Pakistan was formed and both became independent.

Raiwind

To get its workers the new Punjab District had to train them from the raw material of new converts. A school was essential, but they had none. On an extremely hot summer day three strangers in a carriage drove up to the Thomas' residence in Lahore and inquired for the Methodist missionary. Cordially Thomas invited them in under the *punkah* and listened to the story of the elder lady, a widow. Her husband, an engineer, had died in India. She and her children had come to mark his grave and to establish a memorial. The missionary's need of a boarding school for boys appealed to her. Months passed; almost two years, before a letter came to Butcher enclosing a cheque for $5,000. The Johnston Memorial Boys' School was opened. In 1908 Butcher "had in all 35 boys and young men studying in our Boarding and Training School."[39] The rooms in the "school" served for classes by day, and "as living rooms for the Boarding Department." After the "third class, students were sent to the Government or Municipal High School located in Mozang" where there was a Christian Headmaster, H. D. Burke. This was the condition when the F. M. Wilsons took charge of the District at the end of 1915.[40]

In January, 1916 Clyde B. Stuntz was appointed to this school. He set himself to providing for more boys, a larger staff and a location outside of the city. Raiwind, a railway junction twenty-five miles from Lahore, was chosen and in 1920 twelve acres were purchased. In 1922.

when W. C. Fawell was in charge, the Johnston Memorial Boys' School moved to Raiwind. The enrolment was 124 of whom 114 were Christian boys through Class VI; Class VII and VIII were added in 1923. Three men were taking teacher-training. All work was done by the boys for whom scouting made "play of every task that fits us to care for ourselves and to serve others".[41]

> We want every boy by the time he has finished his 8th standard to know how to make first class brick, how to weave cloth on an Indian loom, and how to direct simple agriculture. Then. . . one year's Normal Training, which will put him in touch with the best methods of teaching and entitle him to a Government Certificate. A boy with such training will be capable of real village leadership.[42]

There was a department of Normal and Bible Training for couples and single men preparing for village work. In 1928 the school received permanent recognition for the A. V. Middle standard and a grant. Rugg was in charge of the institution from 1926 for some years. In 1936 the school was recognized for High School classes.[43]

The American Presbyterian Church and Methodists effected a union at Raiwind in 1952 under the name Raiwind Christian Institute. A new school building with capacity of 400 children from Primary to High School and new hostels have been built. In 1950 a training class for teachers for the Junior Vernacular standard was opened. Special courses were offered in building construction, irrigation, agriculture, animal husbandry, village improvement and health.[44]

STUNTZABAD

Large sections of the Punjab are crossed with irrigation canals and vast tracts made arable. Into these areas populations moved and villages were settled. Land was either sold to the highest bidder, given to Army grantees, or "on the five year half-returnable basis, under the terms of which land may be acquired by the poorest, and after five years . . . half must be paid or returned to Government."[45] On this basis land was secured in the Khanewal area of the Multan District. There the efforts of Butcher and Wilson to secure land for Christian colonies were brought to success by Stuntz. Grateful colonists have named the headquarters of the colony, Chak 135, Stuntzabad.[46] In half a dozen other Chaks Christians have settled in numbers. In these communities life could be controlled and directed; the land laid out for a civic centre with church, school, etc. With these developments the economic condition of the people showed improvement.

The primary school started in Stuntzabad was raised in 1953 to High School standard. Since all students live near by no Boarding Department is needed. This school, now a joint project of the W.D.C. S. and the D. W. M., is described as "the outstanding village school in the whole Conference". A Health Centre which is also sponsored by the two Divisions is rendering needed services and making an effective witness.[47]

Lucie F. Harrison High School

Reporting for their first year in Lahore Mrs. Thomas wrote: "At present my Girls' School is held in a carriage shed for which we have no carriage and is taught by the wife of our Pastor."[48] The next year there were thirty girls attending, but still no building. Heartsick that even after five years no building had been provided, Mrs. Butcher wrote: "There will of course be other girls this year and in all the years to come, but the girls of now are losing their chances."[49]

In 1912, after ten years, earnest pleas were answered when Miss L. D. Greene was appointed to Lahore to build and open a girls' school on land Butcher purchased adjoining the Mission headquarters. Named the Lucie Harrison Girls' School after the Branch Secretary who aroused interest for the project, it was opened in October with twenty-five girls. From Primary, through the Middle it grew to be a High School. When Provisional recognition as a High School was given in 1948 Miss Blackstock wrote "To the last child there has been a sense of pride in this achievement." The recognition was made permanent on February 3, 1953.[50] Miss Constance Blackstock completed fourteen years as Principal of "L.H." in July, 1953 and enhanced the tradition of good work which had characterized the school. Her father had reached Bombay in December, 1875 and one or more members of the family have been on the field since then unless on furlough.

Nur Niwas

A Lucie F. Harrison High School fits into a city like Lahore but when Miss E. M. Palmer was transferred to Hissar after five years in Lahore, two of them as Principal, she was among people who knew little of what "education" meant, and who needed to be persuaded to let children—especially girls go to school. Here she took a small school started by Miss Holman in 1928 and made it "a new school, into which she put all the fine resources of heart, mind and training."[51] It was only a primary school to start with but it became a middle (grade school) girls' boarding school, and welcomed little boys to the primary classes. Gardening and field work, sewing and cooking were all a part of the training each received.[52]

After Miss Palmer's death in 1938 Miss Coy and Miss Hakim continued the school which now served four districts. By 1936 seventeen girls had worked up to the middle classes. Five years later a boarding for the boys was built and dedicated. Nine girls appeared in the Government middle examinations in 1946 and all passed. Several went to high school and others took training.[53] Feel, if you can, the effect on village homes from which most of these girls came—*their girls* passing an examination; getting an education.

Ajmer

After the Misses Nelson left on furlough at the end of 1936 the Avery Girls' School was placed under the care of Miss McNaught of the Rajputana Scottish Church Mission.[54] The arrangement became permanent. Later Keislar wrote: "The handing over of the Girls' School was only the beginning of the withdrawal of our Church as such from Rajputana . . . . We do not close our work with a sense of regret but rather with the knowledge of a completed project."[55] For many years the boys' school had been closed but the Bowen Boys' Hostel was maintained "with the boys attending the Husband Memorial School of the Scottish Mission." The hostel was closed on May 1, 1938.[56]

"The Ajmer District expired December 31, 1940."[57] So starts the report for 1941. It has proved to be a lively corpse, for although the Methodist Church did not reopen boarding schools, it did not close its work in the city or district as the appointments for 1941 show when Ajmer was linked with Hissar. It is not a large District today—total membership 1,405 in 1954—but it sustains work in Rajputana, home of the Rajputs, where much of the land is waste or desert, but whose people have made their name famous in history.

Forman Christian College

This institution of the Presbyterian Church, U. S. A. had already established its reputation as the finest college in the Punjab, when in 1922, Robert E. Speer met in Conference with missionaries in the Punjab who were interested in Higher Education. The year before, a commission had found it advantageous for Missions to get together in work at College level, for in such union the problems of staff and equipment would be handled more easily. As a result the Methodists entered into cooperation with the Forman Christian College in 1924, thus making "for us a great place in the opportunities among the educational classes".[58] Dr. Paul W. Paustian a Missionary of the Board, and Mr. Thomas a local missionary "loaned to the college and supported by them," represented the Methodists in the College. Later B. C. Harrington joined Paustian.

Forman Christian College suffered severely from the partition of India and Pakistan. About twenty-five percent of the enrolment had been Muslim. Most of the India staff members were Hindus or Sikhs. "In

August, or before, there was a great exodus of both students and staff." When the College did reopen the enrolment was 150 against a normal 1,300.[59] The years since have shown the wisdom of the union. In 1953 the enrolment appeared to have "stabilized at a little over 600".[60] Methodist representatives now are W. C. Thoburn and S. L. Sheet.[61]

Kinnaird College

Sensing a need for a Christian College for women in the Punjab, representatives of the American Presbyterian Church, the Zenana Bible and Medical Mission, the United Presbyterian and Anglican churches made a small beginning in 1915 with a class of five girls. The institution was hampered by lack of funds and for some years occupied rented buildings. Long before Partition the Methodists were invited to join but presumably the Isabella Thoburn College met their needs. Real cooperation with the College began at the end of 1949 when Miss Nancy Kellogg joined the staff.[62] Full cooperation was commenced the next year when a grant of $1,000 annually and added members on the staff gave them representation on the Board of Governors of the only Christian Woman's College in all Pakistan. In 1956 the Woman's Division of Christian Service had four ladies on the staff. The enrolment in the College is limited to about three hundred.

The Kinnaird Training Centre

In 1949 Miss C. E. Blackstock reported: "We have been long associated with the Kinnaird Training Centre." It was a union institution in which nine Missions were affiliated at that time. The largest contributors were the Zenana Bible and Medical Mission and United Presbyterian Missions. The Centre had always been hampered by lack of adequate funds. Its enrolment at this time was forty-six just half of whom were Christians. In ten years it had graduated 161 Christians of whom eighteen were Methodists. This institution trains girls who have passed their High School for the Senior Vernacular Certificates. It also trains girls with the Intermediate Arts degree for the certificate of Certified teachers for work in high schools.[63]

The United Christian Hospital

In August, 1947 Muslims from India removed to Pakistan, Hindus and Sikhs from Pakistan to India, by the million. A Committee of Christians for Relief and Rehabilitation was organized in Lahore. During the period of migration eight mobile teams were put into the field which penetrated into India as far as Ambala and Karnal.

> They administered cholera vaccine to more than 350,000 people. They gave first aid and actually hospitalized in makeshift field hospitals about 25,000 who had been more or less seriously wounded in the fighting.

> They helped clean up the sanitation in camps that were hideously unsanitary. They met and virtually stopped an epidemic of small pox by mass vaccine inoculation of thousands.[64]

During this period of riots the Forman Christian College made two hostel blocks available as an emergency hospital, and the College recruited the medical personnel needed. The Government agreed to meet the running expenses. As the emergency drew to a close the Christian Council convened representatives of the several Missions to consider continuing the hospital as a united Christian Hospital. The College offered the buildings for a period of ten years. Largely through the efforts of Professor P. Carter Speers the hospital was opened on May 5, 1948, with six Missions cooperating in financial support and in provision of staff. Funds for purchasing equipment were found locally.[65]

After adapting the building to the need of a hospital the first emphasis was on the training of nurses—in 1953 there were forty-five in training—and preparing quarters for them. Other objectives were: beginning midwifery training and a public health-training program; reorganizing the out-patient clinic and extending evangelistic work in the hospital, and making wards out of small rooms.

The Methodist Church has been fortunate in having as its representatives, Drs. C. S. Trimmer and E. L. Rice. They report for 1953 a total of 30,000 out-patients and 2,366 in-patients. It could have been many more but for the lack of adequate medical and technical personnel.[66] A Medical Unit contributed by Overseas Relief, in 1955, toured in the villages around Lahore.

Gujranwala Theological Seminary

The Conference found itself cut off by Partition from its Theological Schools in Bareilly and Jabalpur. They were both in India! In Pakistan there was only one Theological Seminary—that of the United Presbyterians at Gujranwala. A study of the situation by several denominations with the help of the West Pakistan Christian Council, led to the Gujranwala Seminary becoming a Union institution, in which under a new constitution six churches were united: United Presbyterian, American Presbyterian, Church of Scotland, Methodist, Anglican and American Reformed Presbyterian. Students are recruited in three classes: over eighth class and less than matriculation—first class; Matriculation and First Arts pass—second class; Graduates in the third class.[67]

Sind and Baluchistan

J. N. Cutting, who went to Quetta in 1890, rose in position and honour with the Government, but never failed in faithfulness to the English church he had helped to start. He died in 1939, but some years earlier he had received ordination as an Elder and was regularly appointed to the Church as its pastor.[68] English services were continued for two years under Mr. and Mrs. Windsor, but were thereafter discontinued. G. B. Thompson wrote: "The Church . . . is really better organized and more promising than ever. Through the inspiration of his fine example other Europeans were united in one of the most efficient Official Boards in the Conference."[69] Hindustani services were continued regularly under Devji Karson, and more recently by V. E. Bhajjan and F. C. Peter.

In Karachi there has been an ebb and flow. In 1939 there was a proposal that the British Methodists "take over all our English work at Karachi and provide a suitable home for the Hindustani work elsewhere in the city".[70] This suggestion was only partially implemented. The rising importance of Karachi as the Capital of Pakistan and an international port, offers Methodism a present and a future field of service. Recognition of this is indicated in the recent opening of a new school in the suburbs of the city, the Drigh Road School, in the hope that it may become an outstanding coeducational High School.[71] Hindustani services have been regularly held and new appointments opened. The Drigh Road Christ Church, has become more important and its influence increases.

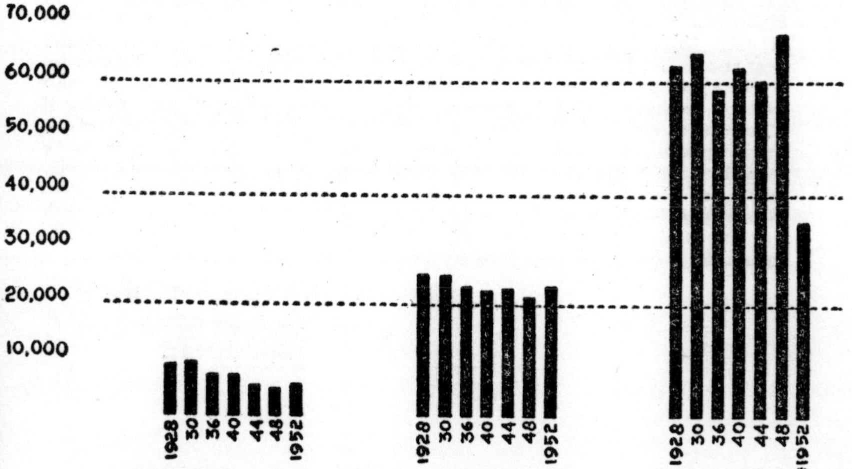

GROWTH OF THE CHRISTIAN COMMUNITY[76]

BENGAL CONF. LUCKNOW CONF. INDUS RIVER CONF.

* 4 Districts to Delhi Conf.

When I came to India as a missionary of the American Presbyterian Mission in Allahabad . . . the boundary between the Methodist and Presbyterian Missions was the River Ganges, and that continued to be the boundary until what is known as the Mass Movement set in, when the Methodist preachers began to cross the Ganges at Kasganj into the Etah, Farrukhabad and other districts, hitherto in the Presbyterian field, to follow up the work among the relatives of their converts. The result was that in a few years in the Etah, Farrukhabad, Mainpuri and Etawah districts, the Methodist converts were numbered by the hundreds—in Kasganj and the Etah district alone, over six thousand. . . . Then began friction between the preachers of the two Missions, which meant reproach to the name of Christ. To remove this a conference of representatives of the two Missions was called to meet in Cawnpore. So serious was the situation that the Presbyterians asked Dr. J. C. R. Ewing of Lahore to come down and strengthen us by his presence in the Conference . . . The representatives of the Presbyterian Mission met in Cawnpore the night before the Conference, and drew up a request to the effect that in the interests of peace and harmony the Methodist Mission should withdraw all their preachers and workers from Kasganj and the districts of Etah, Farrukhabad, Mainpuri and the greater part of Etawah, with the understanding that we would take over the care of the Christians belonging to the Methodist Church in those districts, and also purchase all the property of that Mission within those districts. That was a very drastic remedy, and it was with some fear and trembling that the Presbyterian members of the conference met the Methodists the next morning. We had no hesitation in asking Bishop Warne to preside over this joint meeting, and he did preside over the morning session with that blending of courtesy and gravity which won our heart. The reading of our request called forth questioning and discussions. I remember that one member of the conference pleaded with great earnestness that one or two tahsils of the Farrukhabad district, bordering on the Cawnpore district, should not be given up. After an hour or more of questioning and discussion, at Bishop Warne's suggestion, we took recess for several hours, that the members of each Mission might consider separately what had been proposed. At the next session Dr. J. C. R. Ewing took the chair at Bishop Warne's suggestion. I think we were prepared for a long discussion lasting a day or two, and perhaps ending in a compromise. At that tense moment Dr. Rockwell Clancy arose and said in substance: "We have considered the proposals of the Presbyterians, and not only accept them, but are ready to give up even more than they have asked".—and then, within an hour, the whole controversy, which had been growing for years, was settled. . . . I have always felt that Bishop Warne and Rockwell Clancy wrought together with the Head of the Church that day in Cawnpore, to save the name of Christ from reproach, and to restore the loving fellowship between the Methodists and the Presbyterians.

Dr. J. J. Lucas, A. P. Mission
The Indian Witness
April 21, 1932

XVI

The Delhi Area

When the Northwest India Annual Conference was organized in 1893 the name was appropriate. It included all that part of India west of the Ganges to the borders of Afghanistan on the west. The organizing of the Indus River Mission Conference in 1922 took this northwest corner from the older Conference thus making its name unsuitable. In 1944 the Central Conference approved the change of the name of the Northwest India Conference to Delhi Conference.[1]

In its session in 1949 the Delhi Conference accepted the report of a joint Commission of the Delhi and Indus River Conferences that the Districts of Ajmer-Hissar, Fazilka, Patiala and Batala, which were left in the India Union by the Partition, be included in the Delhi Conference.[2] The "Total Church Membership" in the Delhi Conference that year was 144,740. The new Districts brought in a further total of nearly 38,000.[3] The next General Conference authorized the Central Conference to increase the number of Annual Conferences by one during the quadrennium. It "recommended that Delhi and North India Annual Conferences be permitted to form a new Annual Conference within the boundaries of the said Conferences during the quadrennium".[4] The North India Conference in 1955 rejected the recommendation of the commission on boundaries which called for the transfer of some of its districts to the new Conference. It is expected that the new Conference will be formed by a division of the Delhi Conference before the Central Conference session in 1956.

Northwest India Conference

(Delhi Conference)

In the early Northwest India Conference Lahore was just a circuit of the Mussoorie District. Other circuits were Deoband, Mussoorie and Roorkee in the United Provinces, and Patiala in the Punjab, where there was some vernacular work. Lahore, opened by James Shaw, had continued as an appointment in spite of severe trials, under Gilder, Leonard, Tindale and others. In 1894 the appointment read "Lahore, John F. Deatker; one to be supplied". Multan was an outpost from Lahore, un-manned, although

J. W. McNair, a Local Preacher, had sustained regular services there and in 1894 told how he had been led to open vernacular work and had baptized sixteen men and women, and he believed that there was "every prospect of a great ingathering within a very short time".[5] By 1901 the statistics showed the numbers of Christians in some of the Punjab stations as: Lahore English, 22; Lahore Hindustani, 612; Multan, 519 and Delhi 996.[6] In 1902 the financial stringency upon the Conference was so severe as to lead it to decide to curtail its work in "the least productive field". This was the Punjab which in the previous year had been a part of the Aligarh District. J. E. Lawson, its P. E., pleaded against the decision:

> Delhi . . . is the key to the Punjab. Lahore . . . is its *heart.* Entrance, centre and circumference shall one day all throb and thrill with Gospel blesssedness and gladness.[7]
>
> The Indian pastors pleading for the continuance of the work asked: 'What will be done with our six hundred Christians?' They also stated that the field was unfruitful because it was not cultivated, but that given the same opportunity as others it would surpass them all. Their vision and pleading won over the Conference.[8]

Punjab District

Instead of closing the work in the Punjab, Lahore was made the headquarters of a Punjab District, with J. B. Thomas as P. E. which included Roorkee and Mussoorie as circuits, and Delhi. The same Conference, 1902, completed plans with the British Wesleyans for uniformity and harmony in all their work. An immediate result of this was that the Wesleyans took under their care Methodist English Churches in places where they held Garrison chaplaincies. The first such transfer was in Meerut. The English Church building was sold to the Wesleyans and the English work was made over to them. In 1905 J. C. Butcher sold the English Church in Lahore to the Wesleyans and in 1938 the chaplaincy of the troops in Karachi was given to them.[9]

Butcher lamented in 1914 that although the Roorkee and Delhi Districts and the Mussoorie circuit had been cut off, the Punjab District was still "too vast to be properly worked by one administration". After each division he had hoped for relief but there was none "because the pruned tree has given forth fresh branches so rapidly". Four of the circuit centres were 208, 187, 183 and 113 miles from Lahore and two or three others were more than fifty miles distant. The total number of Christians in October, 1913 was 18,099.[10]

Two major developments occurred in 1913-14: First, after the death of Mahbub Khan in 1912, Dr. Ashe held the Kasganj District until that work was transferred within the year to the Presbyterians; Second, the Punjab District was divided. To the new Southern Punjab District, which included Ambala, Bhatinda, Bikanir, Hissar, Sangrur and other circuits, Ashe was appointed as D. S. and he took the workers from the former Kasganj District. In 1916 F. M. Wilson became D. S. of the Punjab District and James Lyon of the South Punjab.[11] Batala District was formed in 1920 with I. U. Daniel as Superintendent, and in the same year the name Punjab District was changed to Lahore District.[12]

Delhi

For twenty-four years the Methodist Church had been working in Delhi and the adjacent territory, yet "aside from two small chapels" it owned no property in the city. The first resident missionaries, Rev. and Mrs. F. M. Wilson, came in 1910. At the next Conference he was made Superintendent and continued for three years. Before he left on furlough he announced that application had been made for a grant of land and that the Board had sanctioned its purchase and the erection of needed buildings, and also approved the idea of a "worthy monument . . . in commemoration of the heroic services of Dr. and Mrs. William Butler in India."[13]

Rockwell Clancy followed Wilson and in 1915 bought the land adjoining the Ridge. Here the bungalow for the D. S. was completed by J. C Butcher in 1918.[14] The next year he built some store rooms and a "temporary chapel . . . . It was the first pretense of a Church building which Methodism had in Delhi."

> The beginnings of the church were made in a courtyard of a humble home in Ganda Nala. After that services were held on the missionary's verandah at Rajpore Road. Later a temporary building was erected . . . at 4 Battery Lane. The congregation which now numbers about four hundred have outgrown this and hence the plans for the new church.[15]

A second plot adjoining the first was purchased in 1916, giving a total area of nine and a half acres. The site for the Butler Memorial Church and the Episcopal Residence, five and a half acres, was purchased in 1924. Bishop J.W. Robinson was appointed to the Delhi Area with residence in Delhi in May, 1924. On August 15, they entered their new home.[16]

Sir John Thomson, Chief Commissioner of Delhi, laid the corner stone of the Butler Memorial Church on Sunday, April 6, 1930. After service in the church on Battery Lane, "the congregation formed in a stately line and proceeded to the new site singing as they walked". The Pastor, Isaac Mann; the D. S., S.W. Clemes; the Church Treasurer, W. H. Sinclair; S. S. Superintendent, T. B. Franklyn; and Local Preacher, M. McGee, assisted in the service.[17] Miss Clementina Butler was present at the dedication. At the first session of the Central Conference in December,

1940, Mrs. J.R. Chitambar unveiled the corner stone on which the new name of the church, suggested by Miss Butler was inscribed, "Christ Church, a memorial to Dr. William Butler, Founder of the Methodist Mission in India, 1856-64. Dedicated to the Glory of God, December 20, 1931."[18]

It had been intended that the W. F. M. S. should have a part of the second plot near the Ridge, for a Girls' School—an approved share of the Memorial to the Butlers. The division of land depended in part on the securing of a site for the Bishop's residence and a church. Work on the school could not, therefore, move ahead until this land was assured. In the hope that the construction of the school might be commenced during the year Miss L. D. Greene was transferred to Delhi in 1923. Land difficulties and the deaths of Dr. and Mrs. Butcher in mid-summer of that year delayed matters, but in 1925 progress on the W. F. M. S. bungalow had reached the point that the school "became a reality".

> A Primary school with three teachers, a nurse and a matron, together with 23 pupils are now living in the Mission Compound. To be sure the school is held in a tent and the pupils with their teacher are occupying part of the W.F. M. S. bungalow which is still in the process of erection.[19]

Miss Greene served as Principal of the school for four years, followed by Miss Hermiston and then Miss Justin. In their first examinations in 1930 all seven girls passed.[20] The school building was not completed until 1932, and yet for seven years the school had flourished. There were then ninety-eight girls in the boarding and thirty-two day scholars. Regarding Mrs. A. Theophilus, the matron, and Miss D. Matthews, Head Mistress, the Principal paid this tribute: "By having before their eyes the finest of Indian womanhood, the girls may have exceptional development."[21]

The enrolment in 1949 passed the 300 mark. In the lower classes there is coeducation. It had originally been planned for the school to include the High School classes but in 1927 this was changed and Methodist girls have taken their advanced work in the Baptist High School.

The Holman Institute

There had been in Agra for several years, a Central Day School. It was for the children of *mohalla* families, primarily the sweepers, but for other depressed groups also. Attendance was very irregular for even the children's chores help in the family income and other groups would not relieve them to get to school. In 1924 Miss S. C. Holman turned her attention to this group, and invited these children to a better school, with better teachers, more systematic instruction and in a better environment. The recognized curriculum was followed and classes I–IV were started. When she reopened in July, 1926, 220 enrolled, and daily attendance reached eighty but it continued to climb.[22]

In 1927 a night school was opened and in connection with the Day School the weaving of rugs and towels was taught—"a real attempt to get our Christian community out of the scavenger class and to make them self-supporting".[23] On December 1, 1932 Bishop Robinson dedicated a fine new Holman Institute building with eight large class rooms and a big hall. A rug factory was also completed and rugs of good quality were produced. As early as 1935 the Holman sisters saw the sons from these depressed class homes as students in High Schools. It was indeed, "a great work paying large dividends in character building".[24]

Partition, in 1947, brought to Holman Institute a new challenge—to serve the Refugees. Miss C. L. Justin, Principal, opened the school to these needy people. It became affiliated with the United Mission Higher Secondary School, formerly the Baptist High School. With an enrolment of 670 students and a bee-hive activity, Holman Institute is now a project of both Divisions of the Board. It has

> more Christians than any other school in Agra, more Scheduled Caste students (formerly known as outcastes) and certainly more Refugees. Holman Branch schools do fine work, and extend our influence. Teachers and Bible Readers visit in the homes, and we are proud that a number of illiterate Christian women have begun to learn to read.[25]

Mathura

The Clancy High School is comparatively new, but a Boys' School in Mathura is almost as old as the oldest in the city. By 1894 "the boarding schools (had) outgrown their accommodation" in Flora Hall, in the heart of the city. The boys' hostel, provided by Blackstone, was situated across the road from the Mission. "Every Sunday 200 boys and girls and men and women, marched through the streets to Flora Hall for Sunday School."[26]

Mr. and Mrs. J.C. Pace lived in a rented bungalow for three years. In 1924 the bungalow with twelve acres of land adjoining was purchased. Science and manual training had been introduced in the Middle School, and gradually cottage industries were finding a place: rope making, rag carpet weaving and sewing. An approved class in Teacher's Training had been opened and there were more inquiries for trained teachers than could be met.[27]

Ralph Templin joined the school as principal, in 1927. In his first year he felt that "the original purpose" of the school could not be met by a school in the city. He set himself to establish a school on the newly purchased site. Six large rooms and a large verandah auditorium were completed in 1930. The first High School section was opened in July. This school is named for Rockwell Clancy, who died in 1929.

The Blackstone Missionary Institute with the Girls' Middle School, served not only the North India field, but for many years maintained an English Training department for zenana workers, Deaconesses and Evangelists, which was open to every India Conference. When the Leonard Theological College was established this department was transferred there. For twenty-nine years Miss Garnet Everley, who died in January, 1954, was in charge of the School and Institute. To them she dedicated her life, putting into them her vision and strength of leadership. The Mathura choir was her idea and developed through her gifts and efforts.

Dr. Martha Sheldon, who followed Dr. McDowell, opened a small dispensary in Vrindaban which she visited twice a week. This was the foundation for the work of Dr. Emma Scott who came in 1897.[28] The dispensary in Mathura was soon too small and had to be enlarged to meet the immediate need for more room while trying still to get a site for a hospital in Vrindaban.

Notwithstanding this resistance to the permeation of Christian influence in the city, Dr. Emma Scott's interest in the Church and Christian community enabled her to build a small church at a cost of Rs. 400 which Bishop Warne dedicated on August 8, 1901.[29] Then in 1906 the land for a hospital was purchased and building soon began. Miss Terrel, a trained nurse, was secured to help Dr. Scott, but the latter's health broke and Miss Cora Kipp had to accompany her to America, leaving Miss Terrel alone when work was on the increase, the number of Dispensary patients mounting to 20,000 in a year.[30]

The Sarah Creighton Memorial Hospital was dedicated in 1910. The appointments in Vrindaban for 1914 read: "Medical work, Miss Kipp, M. D.; Hospital, Miss Eunice Porter". In many steps in the development of a wider field of service, Miss Porter's has been the initiative. With her since 1928 has been Miss Elda Barry and from 1934 Miss, Dr. Burchard—a unique record, and a fine example of cooperation to achieve high purpose.

Main stages in its development have been: 1912, the Nurses' Training School opened; 1913, a day school for high caste girls started; 1928, a hospital ambulance received for work in villages; 1932, a laboratory technicians' course opened and continued for ten years; 1936, the Freeman wing of the hospital dedicated, since when the institution has been known as the Creighton-Freeman Hospital; 1940, a Westinghouse X-ray plant installed; 1949, the School of Midwifery started.

Some men had been admitted as in-patients from 1928. A men's building was dedicated on August 22, 1953. The first male doctor to serve in the hospital was Dr. J. S. Staley, in 1950. He was followed in 1954 by Dr. G. L. Downie, formerly of China. At the dedication of the men's building the people of Vrindaban showed the esteem in which they hold the hospital. Bishop Pickett writes:

> The famous temples of Vrindaban have no priests that are honoured or consulted by more people than are Miss Eunice Porter . . . Dr. Mary Burchard . . . and their colleagues, Indian and missionary. Many hundreds of residents of Vrindaban and the larger city of Mathura crowded into the hospital on the day of dedication.[31]

Institutions

In 1948 Miss E. Warner opened the High School classes in the Howard Plested Memorial Girls' School which had been opened in 1895 and had been a Middle or Junior High School for some years. In 1953 it became a Higher Secondary School with Miss Mildred Shepherd as Principal. These classes were open to girls of North India also. With the expansion of education under the present Government schools fill quickly. In 1954 Miss Shepherd wrote: "The largest part of the school is the high school".[32]

Under date of August 1, 1919 Dr. F. M. North wrote to Bishop Warne concerning the possibility of "developing a large centrally located institute in India to follow somewhat the lines which have been laid out so admirably by Hampton and Tuskegee and other centers in the South". The Board was feeling its way to help to establish in India an institution that would pioneer a way, and also train young people in lines that would lift the standards of living of people in the mass movement areas. The plans of the Board contemplated four such centers in India, at Pakaur, Nadiad, Kolar and a centre in the northern Hindi-Hindustani field.

Such a wide based program was not developed, but in the North and Northwest India Conference territory the Ingraham Institute was established at Ghaziabad, where forty acres of land were purchased. Here plans were made for a school with Teacher-training, a Preacher-training Department and a Dispensary to meet the needs of the community. Rev. and Mrs. Pace returned from furlough in July 1926, and at once began plans for opening the Ingraham Central Institute. Classes were begun in September. Bishop J. W. Robinson dedicated the buildings on October 27. A small primary school of day scholars was gathered.

> The Teacher Training School was moved from Muttra and boys for a small fifth class were transferred from Sonepat and Meerut. We now have classes V and VI in the middle school, Teacher Training School with classes for both men and women . . . and the Bible School which also has classes for both men and women all of these with an aggregate enrollment of about a hundred.[33]

Although all the boys worked on the farm and at some industry and in the gardens, it was not done as vocational training but because work and responsibility were necessary in the development of strong characters. Pace continued as Principal for two terms. Mr. and Mrs. Frank Williams of Korea joined them in 1941 and remained in charge after they left.

A gift from Mrs. Ingraham in memory of her husband made it possible to erect most of the Ingraham Institute plant. Some years later the will of his sister, Miss Frances T. Ingraham, created an endowment for the development of the extension program which was envisaged in the beginning. From 1946 the Board cooperated in gathering at the Institute a group of missionaries to plan and to develop the program at the centre, and to take it in an extension program to the villages beyond. The first of these was J. N. Hollister, with T. C. Badley who had been associated from the first with the planning that followed Dr. North's letter. With them was the Indian staff at the Institute, J. E. Titus, Headmaster, intimately familiar with the growth of the program; Comfort Shaw, one of the first students in the school; and Rafiq Masih, a teacher for many years.

The Teacher's Training class was enlarged. A small class of village teachers below Government standard was received and given the School's Rural Teacher Certificate. The Primary Department was integrated in the school under Mrs. Hollister; and coeducation, with the approval of the Conference Board of Education, beginning in the lower classes, was commenced, to give realistic and better facilities for practice teaching. Later, women were admitted to all Teacher Training classes.

In 1949 a Technical department was opened under J. W. Finney, an Independent Methodist from England who had been in India as their missionary and whom he still represents. H. Drewer Johns, in the same year, assumed direction of the Agricultural side of the program. In 1950 Miss Lois Biddle of the W. D. C. S. was appointed a Supervisor of the Primary Department, and associate in extension; and M. L. Sill, Sociologist, to develop extension. In 1953 the British Baptists increased their cooperation with the Ingraham Institute by providing a missionary tool-maker on the staff. Henry Lacy succeeded to the Principalship in the fall of 1953 and under his guidance the program has been "extending its services into new projects and rural centers".

Khatauli, a small town in the Muzaffarnagar district, was long an active center of work under the Church Missionary Society. Beside evangelistic work they had a school and a Theological Seminary. After partition they found it necessary to shorten their lines and to discontinue the Khatauli institutions. Bishop Pickett raised the funds necessary to purchase the property and a middle school was opened in 1950 which has been named n his honour. It has this year received recognition as a Higher Secondary School.

The United Christian Schools

The plan of such an institution originated in the thirties between the Methodists and the Presbyterians in the Punjab. They desired a new type of school, one which would permit creative contacts of teachers with students and present a new approach to some educational problems. A Board of Directors for the United Christian Schools was formed. They purchased 200 acres of land at Surra Nussi, five miles from Jullunder, where water and electricity were available. The school is an agriculture-bias High School, residential for both boys and girls. There were sixty boys in the hostel before the Matriculation examinations in 1946. Of fourteen who took this examination thirteen passed. Partition, with its aftermath, upset the school for the accepted boundary line between the two countries left Jullunder with Surra Nussi in India. The Directors in Pakistan turned to Raiwind for their school.

In India Methodists of the Delhi Conference and Presbyterians in East Punjab, got interested and continued the school, following the lines their comrades in Pakistan had planned to serve village children. In the two schools, one for boys and one for girls,

> Courses are given in agriculture, teacher-training, industrial training, home economics, art, handicrafts, commercial and pre-technical subjects. A dairy, fruit orchards, poultry farm and vegetable gardens give practical training.[34]

North India Conference

This is the only Conference in which our Centenary has made its full cycle. In that period the years of most rapid growth were the four decades at the centre, 1886–1926. The growth of the Christian community in these years shows as follows: 1886, 5,278; 1906, 49,798; and 1926, 83,946. In 1886 there were four districts with Zahur al Haqq as the only Indian Presiding Elder. In 1906 out of eight districts three were in charge of Indians—William Peters, Samuel Tupper and G. H. Frey. In 1926 again there were eight districts with Indian Superintendents in two, P.D. Phillips and D. M. Butler. In this last quadrennium all districts have been under Indian leadership.

The group movements that crowded forty years had taxed the efforts of under-manned and largely untrained staffs, when leaders and other resources were greatly depleted. The result goes deep and is clearly seen in a break down of the "total Church membership" in the N. I. Conference, 104,967, for 1954, as follows: Full members, 29,644(28%); Probationers,

44,705(43%); and Baptized, 30,618(29%). The proportions will vary in Conferences, but in any Conference where group movements have accelerated growth, the unfinished task is much the same. Although workers' classes were started in several districts it was not possible to keep up with the numbers asking for teaching. The accumulated weakness has never been overcome and constitutes today a major challenge to the Conference.

By request of the Central Conference and approval of the General Conference the Tirhut District from the Bengal Conference was transferred to the North India Conference in the sessions of 1913. The transfer was made because of the great difficulty experienced in getting Hindi and Hindustani workers in the Bengal Conference. This new territory reaching into Bihar made the Conference so large that it led to the formation of the Lucknow Conference in less than ten years.

ALMORA

The friendly relations in Kumaon between the Methodists and the representatives of the London Missionary Society in Almora go back to visits made by Butler and Humphrey to Mr. Budden from Naini Tal. When, in 1925, the L. M. S. felt it necessary to discontinue its Almora Mission in order to strengthen its work elsewhere in India, they offered the work to the Methodists. The transfer brought to the Conference established boys' and girls' High Schools, with hostels for Christian children; a splendid church building known as the Budden Memorial Church; residences for missionaries, etc., and a promising rural work in the district. The N. I. Conference sold the Boys' High School building in Naini Tal, our oldest school, on terms that assured it continuance, in part payment for the property. Almora has made a much better centre for district work than either Dwarahat or Naini Tal. A few years later the girls' school and hostel and the boys' hostel in Dwarahat were closed.

Two ministers of the L. M. S. were invited to join the Conference, Yunas Sinha and Ummed Singh Rawat.[35] Rawat was one of two Bhotiya brothers whose conversion in the High School created no little agitation in the community. Others from among the former L. M. S. workers later came into the Annual Conference.

In the transfer the Conference also assumed responsibility for the supervision of what is thought to be the oldest leper asylum in India. In 1840 Henry Ramsay, a Civil Officer in Almora, erected at his own expense a few simple rough stone huts for the shelter of twenty lepers at *Ganesh ki Gair*. Here, for several years, he and General Parsons maintained about twenty-five lepers. In 1848 a house was taken near the site of the present Sadr hospital, and a better organized effort was made to isolate lepers.

'here were then thirty-one inmates, one of them being blind. In 1851 the ıstitution then begun was put under the superintendency of J. H. Budden. 'he present site of the Asylum was secured in 1854; and twenty-five rooms vere erected for fifty inmates. In 1886 there were over 100 inmates.

> In 1869 the experiment was first tried of separating apparently healthy children from the parents and keeping them in an orphanage. This experiment has led to a common practice in Leper Asylums for saving untainted children.[36]

For nearly thirty years this Asylum has been under the supervision f Dr. Manohar Masih. At the time of the transfer of Almora work to the Methodists he was completing studies to qualify him to assume the Asylum esponsibilities. He has served without stint of time or strength in Almora, s adviser in Chandag and in stimulating an interest in the care of lepers hroughout the Almora civil district. In 1956 he was one of a small group hat represented the Mission to Lepers in answering a call from the Nepal overnment for help in opening leprosy work there. His father was a Hindu levotee moving about to encourage the worship of Hindu deities. In young nanhood he was converted and with all the zeal of a true convert—he chose he name Daulat Masih, the wealth of Christ—he wished to take the Gospel nessage to all who had known his earlier estate.

There was in Almora a Tuberculosis Sanatorium for women and girls stablished by the L. M. Society, but latterly under the control of the J. P. Christian Council. For a few years, 1945-1953, the North India Conference tried to maintain it as a Sanatorium, but the difficulty of having dequate medical supervision compelled the Conference to discontinue the ffort. Plans are now under consideration to use it as a convalescent home n connection with the chest-surgery-unit in Bareilly.

Theological Seminary

On the election of C. D. Rockey to the Episcopacy William Dye ecame Principal of the Bareilly Theological Seminary. Negotiations for naking the Seminary a union institution were consummated in July, 1948. 'oining us in this were the British Methodists and the British Baptists; the ourse continued to be vernacular, for three years. The Seminary has since een affiliated for the L. Th. Certificate (Licentiate in Theology) of Serampore College which is open to high school passed students. Gradually that tandard is being encouraged within the institution. With the rural hurch so desperately in need of Christian nurturing, and with the Leonard Theological College providing only for those who have passed high school, he provison of pastors for the village churches confronts the Church at this Centenary as an urgent need. With forty-three per cent of the community till on probation, and numerous others "under 12 years", who need a pastor's personal interest, and most of these in villages, men trained are neede in the villages today no less than in any earlier period. "L. Th." men a not happy to go to the villages where people want *Chhote padri*, little preacl ers, who will enter into their lives and problems.

It is not a new situation. T. J. Scott faced it. He quotes a fellow-mi sionary with evident approval.

> 'How can we educate our young men and yet keep them near tl heart of those among whom we pray they may become loved and efficie workers. Why this pathetic plea "send us little preachers"? Tl educating-away-from-the-people process is not only an intellectual on but of the heart also. . . . The tap root of the influence is direct financi help.'
>
> One would fane hope that such a baptism of the Spirit may com in times of refreshing that a little education will not deter our young me from the toil and privation of the ministry . . . and the joy of Him wh despised the cross and endured the shame.[37]

Dye brought to the Seminary an interest and an acquaintance wi Indian music that has revealed to many students its possible contribution evangelism. On November, 1955 Rev. Dan Singh Chowdhry, M. A., B. D was installed as Principal in succession to Dye who was soon to retire. A the same time Dr. Mani Dutt Patial became Vice Principal.

In 1951 Dr. Ram Dutt Joshi, then in the Bareilly Theological Semina instituted an annual short course in clinical training and pastoral counselli for pastors, hospital personnel and students. Dr. Dagmar Norell cooperat in the program.[38]

Schools

From the beginning the North India Conference took a special inte est in its schools. Every district had some schools and they were close related to others; primary to a middle, those to a high school and they turn to the colleges in Lucknow. Some twenty-five years ago the Board Education organized an Educational Service for the boys' schools of midd and high school grade. It included at first only Christian teachers, but soo was changed to include all men teachers. The Executive Committee this Service was recognized by the Provincial Educational Department the Managing Committee for its schools, with the right to employ, to pla and to transfer teachers who joined—the clause of transfer being included their agreements. Boys' schools of the Delhi Conference are now member

The Messmore High School Pauri was the first one to become a Intermediate College. The building, which owes its existence to the pr digious efforts of H. H. Weeks, was the best in Garhwal. The Governme selected the Messmore High School for its Intermediate College, it bei responsible for this section, and the Mission for the high school as befor

In 1950 the college classes with the equipment were turned over to the Management of the Messmore High School. When the Government reorganized its educational program, the Board of Education recommended that two other high schools should become Higher Secondary Schools, or Junior Colleges; Ramsey High School, Almora and Parker High School, Moradabad. The schools in Shahjahanpur, Budaun, Bareilly, Pithoragarh, Ranikhet and Dwarahat had become High Schools and the last two also became Higher Secondary Schools expecting to finance themselves without Conference responsibility,

The 'Boys' Orphanage' has for years ceased to be an orphanage, but has continued to be the school for children of the Shahjahanpur-Sitapur Districts, a too restricted field for best results. Its farm and tradition of work has distinguished it as different from other schools. Under H. A. Hanson it was named The Lodhipur Community School, the term denoting a measure of training in preparation for rural community life. Mr. and Mrs. Nave, in the last five years, have transformed the institution by erecting new dormitories and removing the last vestiges of the "boys' lines" built by T. S. Johnson; new staff quarters—much needed; and introducing the tractor on the farm. The name of the school has again been changed to Lodhipur Institute. The Naves hope to make Lodhipur a high school. More definitely they are seeking to make it a place for teaching industries and handicrafts. In this purpose they have just been joined by the Tunnie Martins.

Because the need for a Vernacular Normal School had been long felt where promising girls could be trained as teachers, the Woman's Conference chose Moradabad and in 1907 a class was opened under Miss Nora Waugh. There were seven girls in the first class; four in the second.[39]

In 1911 we read: "last year there were twelve girls in the normal school, three of these began their work as teachers in July. This year we have nineteen girls, nine in the senior and ten in the junior class." The girls had come from ten schools. The normal department was recognised by Government this year,

> one of three places in the United Provinces where middle passed girls may receive a teacher's training in the vernacular. . . . Cooking and sewing classes have been added, and the girls are having the responsibility of teachers, by caring for the school girls, being on duty at meals, for games and at bed time.[40]

The Managers of the girls' schools, with the approval of the Board of Education, about 1950 organized an Educational Service for their teachers, similar to that described for the boys' schools. While all girls' schools have been open for girls of all comunities, the Society has not left them under necessity of taking in enough students to be self-supporting as has been true of boys' schools. It has been possible, therefore, to maintain staffs with a larger proportion of Christian teachers; and to have schools where they are really needed for children of the Christian community. In the Delhi area, the first girls' High School, now Intermediate, was the Adams Girls' School in Almora. The next was the Plested Memorial in Meerut. For many years Budaun and Moradabad also had recognized teacher-training departments. That in Budaun was recently closed. Moradabad has just been recognized as a High School and for the Junior Teachers' certificate.

Clara Swain Hospital

This hospital has a position today of which its founder could not have dreamed. For nearly thirty-five years it continued on lines Dr. Swain had set—a zenana hospital. Conditions were still those of the first days. Dr. Margaret Lewis who arrived in 1901 describes the operating room:

> Many really serious operations have been performed, usually successfully although the condition of our operating room would seem to forbid any form of surgery, having a plaster and cement floor constantly throwing up dust; a tiled roof, with a ceiling cloth stretched below, which partially prevents the falling of dust from the roof, but is in itself a dirty thing. The only light for operating comes from a small window to the north.[41]

There were then few Nurses' Training Schools. "Only the most ignorant people were willing to help in the care of the sick."[42] It was the responsibility of the doctor! Dr. Lewis had wanted a training class for nurses but it could not be started until after 1905 when Dr. Esther Gimson had joined her. The first class of five girls finished in July 1909. They had passed in Elementary Anatomy, Hygiene, Materia Medica, Surgical Nursing, Anaesthesia, Compounding and Midwifery. Mrs. Bertha Shaw served as Superintendent of Nurses from 1912 to 1919. The standards of courses for Nurses' Training have since been raised both in requiring that applicants must have passed a High School examination and also in the prescribed studies.[43]

Dr. Mahler, a refugee from Vienna, joined the staff in 1939 and men began to be admitted as in-patients. At the end of 1940 Dr. Charles Perrill, son of the Fred Perrills, and his wife Dr. Wilma Conger Perrill, arrived and at the ensuing Conference they were appointed as Surgeon-in-charge and Medical Superintendent, respectively. The missionary staff had been increased so that there were two nurses, Misses Schlater and Landon, and the Business Manager, Miss Crawford.[44]

From 1941 the hospital has been under the joint support of both Divisions of the Board. Charles Perrill's interest in building techniques and his skill in improvising or making appliances, has greatly benefitted the hospital and aided its steady expansion. A course for Labortory Technicians was opened in 1948. A large, new out-patient Dispensary was erected with a gift of Rs. 90,000 from Sri Murli Manohar, the owner of a sugar factory in Bareilly, as a memorial to his father Sadhu Ram Narain. Later he also made possible a new children's ward, as a further memorial.[45] In 1951 a dental department was opened under Dr. Robert Peterson in a building whose cost was contributed by Sri Kapur, another citizen of Bareilly. Another addition was a surgical wing with three modern operating rooms as a gift of Charles' mother to her husband.

In the promotion of an anti-tuberculosis program a chest unit was opened in 1953 under Dr. J. Pomeroy, and a new building is under construction to give it ample accommodation. It will have its own X-ray facilities and other equipment.

The Woman's Conference of 1920 authorized the Clara Swain Hospital with Dr. Loal Huffman in charge, to open a Babies Home in a part of the hospital. Twenty-one babies were received during the year. The Home continued under the hospital until Miss Olive Kennard took it over in the fall of 1922. She held it for over two years. In the fall of 1924 Miss Edna Bacon assumed charge, and after her furlough in 1930, she was able to implement a conviction that had grown on her that the Baby Fold furnished a fine opportunity for a course in home making. "When in direct answer to prayer" Rs. 5000 was given for the building of a hostel for students, the school was opened in July, 1931. It was named the Lane School of Mothercraft in gratitude to Mrs. Lane of Lucknow. In addition to class work the students had practical training experience with the babies each day.

Inspired with the idea of Centenary objectives at the time of the Centenary of the Board of Missions in 1919 the Upper India Conferences accepted the "Baby Fold" as their project. Aside from a "small grant" from the W. D. C. S. they have maintained the Baby Fold which was named for Bishop Warne because of his great love for children.

Nepal

Before William Butler reached his chosen field, on October 27, 1856, he wrote to Durbin: "Oudh and Rohilkhund include the keys to Nepal, Tibet and Chinese Tartary. The door is open to us."[46] This hope was never lost. When Dr. Gray went to Pithoragarh in 1874 Johnson wrote: "This may open a way into Tibet, which together with Nepal, whose borders we have reached, should be occupied at no distant day."[47] Miss Sheldon and Harkua Wilson worked in this hope, and peeked in—then fell back, but from their outposts much literature reached the interior of both lands through traders.

In 1950, Robert Fleming, a Methodist missionary and an ornithologist who collected Himalayan birds for Chicago University, received permission to go into Nepal. With him was a young doctor, Carl Taylor. The great need for medical help appalled them. The small clinics Taylor set up were welcomed by the people. Two years later Fleming took Mrs. Fleming, M. D., with him and also Dr. Carl Friedericks. The Nepal Government learned of their medical help and invited Dr. Fleming to set up a medical mission in Nepal. In the fall of 1953 under a United Christian Mission affiliated with the National Christian Council work was opened, to be shared in by Methodists, Presbyterians and several Boards or Churches. The Flemings had furlough in 1954. Meantime Dr. Friedericks was able to open a small hospital at Tansen. On return from furlough the Flemings went to Kathmandu and are continuing their work in this newest Mission, which in ways Butler could not have guessed, has after almost a century, been opened.

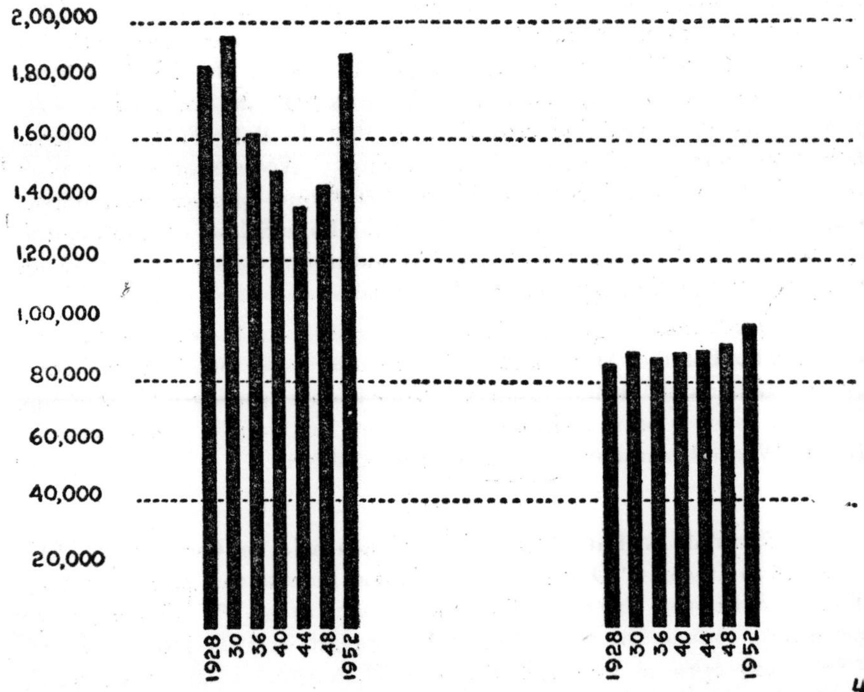

GROWTH OF THE CHRISTIAN COMMUNITY[4]

DELHI CONFERENCE NORTH INDIA CONFERENCE

Section V

THE INEVITABLE

IN PREPARATION

If my lips are stained,
Then the prayers they pray for you will be unclean
So I kneel and plead:
Oh! Hand of God, take Thou a burning coal
From off the altar on the holy mount
And lay it on my lips until their whole
Impurity goes up in clouds of smoke.

If my arm is weak,
Then 'twill fail to raise and lift you from the ground.
So I pray and plead:
Oh! Arm of God, reach down and take Thou hold
Of my weak arm, give it the living thrill
Of Thy great strength, as prophets felt when bold
They stretched theirs forth to lift the nations up.

If my life is dead,
Then before your face I'll be a stricken corpse.
With a cry I plead:
Oh! Life of God, breathe and make
Me live, that I within their midst may have
A full, rich being; so that they may take
Cognizance say—"Behold a life she lives."

Lois Buck.

In the poem the author addresses her field of labour as "you".

XVII

In A New Setting

How different is the India of today compared with the India to which Butler came in 1856! Only a century, but a world of change.

Nationalism has been defined as "Nothing more or less than the desire for independence."[1] That desire, expressed in Calcutta in 1883 culminated on August 15, 1947 in the independence of both India and Pakistan. In a remarkably short time thereafter more than five hundred separate states, some very strong, and each separately related to the British throne, were welded into a single Union of States. The Constituent Assembly framed a Constitution which was adopted on January 26, 1950. In the full import of these two dates, now National holidays, all Methodists, Indians and missionaries, rejoiced and do rejoice, for the progress of the nine years since reassure them that it is but a token of the great future that India will have in years to come.

The Church rejoices also in the high-minded principles enunciated in the Constitution, against any discrimination by the State on grounds of race, caste, sex or place of birth; against untouchability, and by granting the Right of Freedom of Religion under Article 25, which reads: "All persons are equally entitled to freedom of conscience and the right freely to profess, practice and propagate religion."[2] In addition "all minorities, whether based on religion or language, shall have the right to establish and administer educational institutions of their choice".[2]

Since such guarantees in a constitution are never anywhere adequate to secure all their rights to those concerned, the Government has already piloted legislation through both branches of Parliament, the Lok Sabha and the Rajya Sabha, to make them effective, and thus protecting those who used to be considered "untouchables" from discrimination, even to giving them the right to enter all Hindu temples; protecting widows in their right to inherit and to remarry; ensuring the rights of daughters to a proper share in an inheritance; and other social legislation.

The Christian churches are still strongly opposed by some political parties, by religious organizations and by an environment which has not kept pace with the great changes in the country. Indian Christians and missionaries have been described as anti-national, subversive, spies of foreign countries, proselyters. In the Rajasthan Vidhan Sabha (lower house), a resolution was introduced by a member of the Jan Sangh party asking the Central Government to prevent missionaries from receiving foreign aid. The Chief Minister paid a tribute to the work of missionaries and refused to undertake to appoint an inquiry commission as a condition for the mover to withdraw his resolution, which on vote was lost.[3]

In Madhya Pradesh such a commission was appointed. Its report was very critical of the work of Missions, the term being used collectively, many different Missions and many varieties of work brought under condemnation. On almost every occasion of scrutiny and criticism Missions have not lacked for support and appreciation from men in high office.

At another level there can be no doubt that Christians, particularly those from the Harijans ("untouchables") and lowly people elsewhere, are being discriminated against in securing employment, or in receiving scholarships for education, and in other ways. There have been reversions. This type of opposition, proselytism against Christians, will probably increase. It is a challenge to the Churches. As Dr. Jones says:

> We must set our own house in order. This we are endeavoring to do. If one-fourth of our endeavor is to share the gospel with others, three fourths of our endeavors are directed toward Christianizing un-Christian Christianity. We are more than aware of the problems within the Christian movement. We are burdened by them. . . . People have sometimes come into our faith with little or no change in character and life, and we are reaping the consequences of nominal Christianity.[4]

Church Union

Missions and Churches took a great step forward in cooperation when the Missionary Councils were formed. The continued growth of Nationalism brought about the next step in a change of name from Missionary Councils to Christian Councils, led by the National Christian Council whose headquarters are in Nagpur, M.P. Our own Bishop Mondol has recently served as its President for several years and rendered helpful service to the common cause. Through the *National Christian Council Review* Churches are informed of its work and policies, and in other articles of many matters touching Christian positions.

However good and helpful cooperation is it is not the end of the road. In 1920 the Bishops said:

> We hold ourselves ready to . . . entertain any proposals for a United Church in India . . . that is so Scriptural and spiritual, as would bring about such a vital union as that for which our Lord prayed.[5]

After an address by Dr. Yohan Masih, Fraternal delegate from the United Church of India, North, to the Central Conference in 1928, the Bishops were requested to appoint two Commissions, one "to consult but not negotiate" with the above Church, and the other with the South India United Church.[6] This move toward Union was the most significant development in the Methodist Church in the following quadrennium. Union in the South seemed impossible but there were "prospects of a happy and advantageous union in the North."[7] A Round Table Conference at Lucknow in 1929 achieved further understanding. A Joint Council was set up with representatives of the three groups. It was given "advisory powers in every realm of common interest".[8]

Other groups have joined in this quest for Union, notably the Church of India, Pakistan, Burma and Ceylon, and negotiations have continued. Each quadrennium has witnessed disappointment that the negotiating churches have not yet come to a final decision. Nevertheless, R. W. Scott says, "This is not a cause for discouragement." The entrance of new Churches into the quest for a basis of union has brought in new elements; the problems involved in uniting two episcopal churches with non-episcopal are complex; the necessity of having a final plan put into six languages besides English, so that a clear understanding may lead to a right decision—all of these make seeming long delays unavoidable. Since Central Conference cannot vote on a report in 1956 a further delay is necessary. Having shared often in the negotiations, Scott adds, "It is inconceivable that there is a lack of sincerity in the present stage of negotiations."[9]

Laymen

From the days of John Wesley Methodism has made wide use of Lay Preachers—Local Preachers and Exhorters—who are licensed by the Quarterly Conference in the local church, and by such status become members of the Quarterly Conference. In India many of these men are working under the Conference. Technically they are all laymen, even though the Local Preacher may be ordained. In the Quarterly Conference of a rural circuit they may by their numbers and influence dominate in any situation, and make impossible the election of any layman who is not of their number to the Annual Conference or to a committee for a creative program. In the cities where there are institutions, a similar situation may arise, for, in the words of Bishop Rockey,

> the custom of making honorary local preachers has grown up. Such honorary local preachers [may] never have taken any of the examinations required of Local Preachers, . . . [and] do not give most of their time to religious work under the appointment of a District Superintendent.[10]

This cleavage among laymen has greatly militated against successful cooperation in Laymen's organizations and the development of the local church. It tends to maintain the *status quo*. Non-mission employees disdain the other group as not "real laymen." Rev. O. Joshua describes the situation:

> The laymen outside the employment of the Church are free to make criticism (though not always of a constructive nature) and take a bold and independent stand on many issues as they are not under a missionary; nor look for their bread and butter from missionary sources. ... An independent layman ... after a few well intentioned attempts to attend an annual conference gave it up in utter disgust ... and let the work go on unchallenged, unquestioned and unremarked.[11]

Following the pattern set by the General Conference, the Central Conference in 1944 organized a Board of Lay Activities under the Chairmanship of Bishop S. K. Mondol and with Secretary, E. B. Paul. Besides two ministerial members the Lay Leaders of the several Conferences formed the membership. It had its first meeting in March, 1944. The Secretary reported that

> the lay leaders of the Church are seriously realizing the fact that the financial and evangelistic burden must gradually but steadily shift to the shoulders of the people in India; that the local churches have become not only self-supporting but other-supporting as well—missionary and evangelical in the fullest sense.[12]

To really boost that objective is a great goal and worthy of the fullest efforts of this important Board. Without the hearty lead and cooperation of the Laymen the goal can not be reached.

Pension—Provident Fund

It was not long after the India Mission Conference was formed that its attention was drawn to the need of providing for families of deceased ministers. Among Conference members the first to decease was Joseph Fieldbrave in 1867; the next, H. M. Daniel in 1868. Before the Conference in 1901 twenty-one members, including seven missionaries, had passed to their rewards, The minutes contain occasional references to collections for relief, but it would seem that no fixed method for pensions was in operation. In 1879 a special committee was appointed to make recommendations for A Fund for the Widows of Local Preachers.[13] The first reference to a Conference Claimants Fund in North India is in 1898 when Rs. 193 were raised; in 1899, Rs. 289. The first separate provision for Mission Claimants, Local Preachers and others than Conference members, was in 1908 when the collections under this head totaled Rs. 508.

By 1921 the number of deceased members had risen to sixty-six, including eighteen missionaries. There is no record of Local Preachers and Exhorters who had died. To meet the needs of Conference Claimants there was interest from an endowment that had been gathered, some generous gifts and a Book Concern contribution. With the number of Claimants increasing the Conference could not do what seemed to be needed in pensions. E. M. Moffatt took the lead in establishing a Provident Fund in North India in which two principles became fixed: Every member of the employed force was to be included, and no withdrawals were to be permitted before retirement. For those already retired, or soon to retire, pensions were continued. To this fund each member contributes, and the church, or W. D. C. S., an equal amount. Later when Moffatt became All India Treasurer he was able to establish the All India Provident Fund of the Methodist Church in Southern Asia, to which all Conferences belong. Its treasurer for several years has been H. R. Wilson of the North India Conference.

The Bombay Office And Finance

The Financial Boards established in four centers were very helpful in many ways. By loans which could be effected against property that was free of encumbrances, other fine properties were secured and good work made better. But it had also become easy for the Bishops or the several Conferences to borrow money for projects for which they hoped to raise funds in some near future. In the case of school buildings grants were promised on the understanding that the new buildings would be completed within the financial year. To secure the grant-in-aid a loan would be taken until the Mission share was received. In these, and other ways debts accumulated, until they exceeded $1,000,000[14] and in fact during the seventeen years that it took to pay all the debts with interest the total ran to $1,600,000. Large as was this total it represented only a tenth of the book valuation of over 2000 pieces of property in India and Burma. Toward this total the Conferences in India raised $1,000,000 through the sale of property and by savings. The Executive Board has replaced the several Financial Boards and the Property-holding bodies that had been created for property in certain Native States.

While serving as the Branch Treasurer of the Division of Foreign Missions in Bombay, E. M. Moffatt got the opportunity he had long wished for, to start an Office in India in which a few trained and experienced, business-minded missionaries could handle the accounts of a number of Missions together. The opportunity came when L. A. Blickenstaff of the Church of the Brethren Mission agreed with Moffatt to help each other in auditing their books. On his furlough in America in 1934 Moffatt discussed his plan with several Mission Boards in New York. It was also discussed in India. When the American Express Company heard of it they offered free office room and the funds to run it, if affiliated Missions would sell all their dollars, and do all their travel booking through them.

This offer was accepted and the Inter-Mission Business Office was opened. It does business for sixty-three Missions, but it does the Treasurer's work for less than a dozen of them, and a few Mission enterprises like the Hospital Supply Agency. Looking after travel facilities, finding accommodation in Bombay, meeting passengers at the boats and helping them through Customs—these and other services have been greatly appreciated. The Inter-Mission Business Office has proved to be a very successful effort in mission cooperation and service. W. W. Bell succeeded Moffatt as Branch Treasurer for several years. The Division of World Missions has recently appointed S. B. Tewarson, until then Principal of Parker Intermediate College, Moradabad, as Assistant Branch Treasurer, with C. P. Heins. He is the first National to be so appointed.

Until the early twenties of this century it was the practice of the Board to remit money for Mission workers and other estimates to their Treasurer who distributed it. If in addition to these sums a missionary received special gifts through correspondence he was in a position to do extras—put in more workers, build needed quarters, or otherwise boost his work. When, after the Centenary of the Board, funds dropped off, the missionary with special gifts could make ends meet, but one without such gifts had to reduce the work in his district. In 1924 the "cut"—for so the reduction came to be called, was forty-five *per cent*. Without some adjustment this would destroy work; only those with very special help could get along.

In the North India Conference this brought the first Budget Committee to plan adjustments. Those who had "specials" offered to share. Expenditures were also standardized to a pattern. Thereafter budgeting became a fixed procedure in North India. Not all Conferences have adopted the North India plan, but it is probable that every Conference has a form of budget for its annual financial planning. In more recent years when appropriations from the Board are few and most current work is supported by designated gifts, the budgeting has become even more necessary. Since the Nationals do not have the contacts in America to make the needed appeals for designated gifts, the burden of correspondence has become heavy for a few missionaries assigned to do it.

Budgeting led to a columnar system of book-keeping, which was followed in turn by more careful auditing. More funds in recent years, with more men handling funds, have revealed the need for an improved system of accounting and auditing. A plan was completed in 1951. Through seminars under the staff of this new Board led by O. Joshua, G. L. Terry and Miss M. Albertson, the new double-entry system of accounts has been introduced. Progress in establishing this system through the Conference has been made so that seventy-five per cent of districts and institutions are now operating on this new system.

The Executive Board

The Episcopal Address to the Central Conference of December, 1923 breathed a freshness not always found. It was written by Bishop H. Lester Smith "for the Bishops of Southern Asia": F. W. Warne, J. W. Robinson, F. B. Fisher and H. L. Smith. It was the first disappearing of Missionary Bishops and presents a perspective that those who grew up on the Mission Field perhaps had lost. Concerning the Executive Board it said:

> It seems desirable in this connection to point out that it has always been found to be a dangerous thing, a thing destructive of co-operation and productive of discord, to concentrate continuous and indefinite and rather arbitrary powers in the hands of a few. It is neither Methodistic nor democratic. The indications are that in India, we are drifting towards a centralization and an arbitrary control of All-India interests. Is this what you want?
>
> It seems wiser to us to recommend in place of this that we enlarge the powers of the Central Conference, and provide for a biennial meeting, if thought necessary, but that we decrease to a minimum the power and activity of the Executive Board. It is necessary—it has an important function—but, it seems to us that it would be wise not to increase its power or enlarge the scope of its administrative responsibility.[14a]

The Executive Board has continued. It is still "necessary" and it still has "an important function" in connection with all property and connectional funds of the Methodist Church of Southern Asia. It is now the Executive Committee of the Central Conference but in the last two quadrenniums no report is found in the Minutes of that body, and its published minutes reach only a select few. The members of the Executive Board include: eight ex-officio members—the four Bishops, the Secretary, the Treasurer, the Branch Treasurer and the Treasurer of the Woman's Division—four National Members of the Annual Conferences, four National Laymen (few of whom would be recognized by laymen as "independent"), four missionaries of the D. W. M., four members of the Woman's Conferences, and additional members, if from the above, any Conference has failed to receive at least one representative. In 1953 this provision added three members. The decisions of the Executive Board effect the Church throughout Southern Asia, and because it controls all connectional funds it is an important Committee. That it perpetuates the Mission mentality can hardly be gainsaid.

With the Executive Board a select committee has grown up, the Interim Committee. This was asked for by the Mission Board in New York that it might have a small, but authoritative and representative body to advise it on matters referred by the Board, such as applications for Crusade Scholarships, and requests for financial help on projects of the several Conferences. This Committee is the Agent of the Division of World Missions for distribution of relief or other funds from M. C. O. R., the Evangelistic Opportunity Fund, etc.

In 1944-45 the Central Conference recognized the Interim Committee as the "Executive Committee of the Executive Board" . . .

> to carry on routine or emergent work and to make adequate and periodical reviews of the financial and other interests of the Church during the interval between the sessions of the Executive Board

Besides the ex-officio members of the Executive Board, "two national laymen, two national ministers, two women (one of whom shall be a national), and two men missionaries", are elected to the Interim Committee by the Executive Board from its members.

Education

For thirty years the Central Conference manifested an almost personal interest in the several schools of all the Conferences. In the second session, 1887, for the first time a list of "our Conference schools, commended as worthy of patronage" was printed. There were thirteen:[15] schools for Indians as the Theological Seminary in Bareilly, the Goucher school in Moradabad and the Centennial and Girls' High School and Woman's College, Lucknow; English schools in Naini Tal, Calcutta, Rangoon, Poona and Mussoorie. There was an interest in the tuitional and financial condition of each. Session by session the Committee on Education noted the steady and substantial progress "of our Educational work in India."[16]

The many primary schools were considered a means of preparing people to read God's word and important in the progress of the growing Church. In 1894 twenty-five schools were listed as "under the jurisdiction of the Central Conference." As the schools increased in number the need for the educational work to be "unified and made thoroughly efficient" led to a request for the appointment of a General Secretary of Education, who "shall hold Teachers' Institutes and look after the vernacular schools where the work is spreading most rapidly."[17] L. A. Core was appointed to this position.[18]

The Central Conference instructed each Conference to appoint a Board of Education of five to nine members from the Annual and Woman's Conferences; then, mindful of the need to train teachers recommended the enlargement and improvement of the Normal Department of the Woman's

College at Lucknow as a Central Normal School for all the Conferences. This was effected in 1900.[19] Larger use of the Missionary Training School in Mathura was also urged.

It was not until 1915 that another Secretary was appointed. By cooperation of the Board and the W. F. M. S. it became possible then to appoint A. A. Parker as Director of Religious Education, a position he held until 1929.[20] The Constitution of the Board of Education, from 1931 called Council of Christian Education, was adopted in 1916.

When schools were listed for the last time in the Minutes of the Central Conference in 1916 they were grouped under the heads: Theological—Biblical Training Schools, European Education, Anglo Indian Orphanages, Anglo Vernacular and Vernacular Education and Industrial Education.

One of the earliest consequences of India's attainment of freedom was the effect on "English Schools". Anglo-Indian and European families in large numbers left India for their home land or emigrated to the Dominions. Wellesley closed at the end of the session of 1948; Philander Smith College had closed earlier. Others of the schools have adjusted to new constituencies and in the new circumstances are serving India in striving with good education, to build the best possible in Christian character.

In 1920 "the increasing complexity and importance of our educational work" had convinced the Bishops that

> several full-time educational secretaries . . . [were] essential to the effective articulation of our Board of Education organization and to ensuring of continuity of administrative policies. They would serve as the executive officers . . . coordinating the interests of the various areas . . . .
>
> The Board of Education, as at present constituted, is largely an advisory body, with little or no administrative authority, consequently its scope of usefulness is seriously restricted.[21]

In 1922 T. C. Badley, C. B. Hill and Miss U. Montgomery were appointed "to act as an Educational Commission to make a careful analysis and constructive study of our educational problems". In order that "each Secretary may be held responsible for the supervision of educational work" they were assigned to areas, and also to departments of education: Miss Montgomery, until 1928, Hostels, Domestic Economy, Middle Schools. Conferences: South India and Burma. T. C. Badley, until 1930, Higher Education, Agricultural Education, Buildings. Conferences: N. W. India, N. India, Lucknow and Bengal. C. B. Hill, until 1936, Teacher Training, European Education, Industrial and Vocational Education. Conferences: Indus River, Gujarat, Central Provinces, Bombay[22]. Miss M. F. Carpenter followed Miss Montogomery, 1928 to 1933.

E. L. King, son of W. L. King, South India Conference, became Secretary of the Epworth League in 1922. In that office, or as Secretary of the Council of Religious Education, and later Educational Secretary, he was active in promoting the cause of Youth and Education from 1922 to 1948. In this period he completed the Charter House Program for Religious Education in schools, in 1935. He has been prolific in the printing of material on Teachers and Teaching, much of it useful also for preachers; The *Charter House Teacher's Guide*, *By the Way*, *Christian Youth*, and *Christian Education*, which was started as *Methodist Education* by T.C. Badley and continued by King, through 1948. Mrs. E. B. King was Associate Secretary for Handicrafts, 1938-48, continued in a course at Leonard Theological College. Miss H. E. Fehr was also Associate Secretary for the same period, and R. S. Mandrelle for a short time. E. B. Paul has been in charge of the office of the Council of Religious Education almost from its inception.[23]

Gabriel Sundaram of the Hyderabad Conference has been Educational Secretary since 1948. *Christian Euducation* under his control has been improved and is widely appreciated. Institutes of varied types have been supported.

The Council of Christian Education, we read "shall be the Executive of the Executive Board in all matters of Christian Education and subject to its control and direction in exercising the following powers."[24] The Council has thus lost the intiative and administrative or executive authority which the Bishops in 1920 desired, and which gave it standing with other Councils. Control has shifted from a group selected for their educational experience and interest, to the Executive Board heavily *ex-officio*, and whose members have been chosen primarily for other reasons. The field of education is particularly vulnerable to legislation within the several States. Rejoicing as we do in our right to establish and administer our own educational institutions it would seem to be the part of wisdom to have a Council especially charged to watch the dikes, and maintain them intact throughout the range of "*our* Educational work".

Audio-Visual

From early days missionaries have used audio-visual aids to help arouse interest in their work, whether educational or evangelistic. We have seen how singing stimulated Sunday Schools. With or without instruments, singing has often been used to gather a group or a crowd for religious teaching. When gathered, the large Sunday School picture rolls have always proved helpful in holding attention. Picture cards have had drawing power for return visits. The magic lantern with glass slides giving the story of the life of Christ, or Bible and other stories, has held many an audience enthralled. Posters, flannel graphs, puppets have all been used. All are aids: none of these works itself; all have rendered excellent service.

The devices of earlier years have been recently outmoded by new aids, both audio and visual. Film strips and slides instead of glass slides; electric current in place of oil or carbide; recordings on wire, disc or tape instead of the voice may do better than any old device but they are still aids to an end.

Students of Leonard Theological College have produced religious films depicting The Prodigal Son, The Good Samaritan, The Transformed Life, which have been effective.

Less than ten years ago the Church, through the Central Conference, gave attention to these new devices when it added a paragraph to the India Discipline directing each Conference to form a Standing Committee on Audio-Visual Aids whose Chairman should be appointed by the Cabinet and serve as Director of Visual Aids, working in cooperation with the Board of Education. D. F. Ebright, who holds this position in the North India Conference, is also the Secretary of the Audio-Visual Committee of the National Christian Council, a new department in that national body.

As an aid in education and a very successful means of entertainment movies are extremely useful. J. E. McEldowney reports: "There is a lively debate in some centers as to whether still pictures are more effective teaching aids than moving pictures". The movies will draw a larger crowd but the still pictures "give more time and teaching opportunity" which in the villages is extremely important. For evangelism no machine can replace the evangelist and unless the evangelist is able to follow up the work of the trained audio-visual worker it has informational or recreational value chiefly. This may be considerable, however, in contributing to friendly attitudes.

Evangelism

This is the heart of Christian living, its very life, to experience and then to tell, to share. Before it had any missionary society the Methodist movement had a missionary spirit that took the message of the warmed heart across the Atlantic to America, then from its eastern States over the mountains to its prairies beyond. William Butler did not come to India because he was sent but because of his missionary spirit—his desire to share his Christian experience. So the work started from Naini Tal in Moradabad, in Lucknow, in Bareilly. The Methodist Church today, numbering close on to 600,000 has grown through evangelism, and continues to grow.

Yet in 1931, our Bishops said: "At no point in the total undertaking of our Church can we more clearly see the inadequacy of our efforts than in the matter of our Christian community."[25] That, because evangelism has another side, teaching and building up the hearers who are interested and want to grow. It is easy to attribute the failure to the Movement of large numbers. Other factors entered into the failure: Lack of funds to maintain the necessary teaching group and the inefficiency of that group; the inability of the W. F. M. S. to provide the District Evangelists to lead the work among the women without whom the women could not be reached. In 1921 Bishop Warne wrote that there were no lady evangelists in the Hissar, Bikanir, Delhi, Meerut, Bulandshahr and Aligarh districts. In North India, at the same time, there were over 28,000 women and girls, but "to train them into becoming real Christians there were . . . only five W. F. M.S. missionaries." Nor was this true only in the North. In Gulbarga there was a period of twenty years without a representative of the Society to promote work among women.[26] Missionaries of the Board were always fewer than were needed to give necessary supervision. Miss Lilavati Singh said to a friend:

> It has always been the weak side of Indian religions that they make a difference between religion and morals. The danger is now that Christianity may fall into the same line. To be religious, to pray, to preach, to witness, to be stirred up in a revival—nothing is easier for Indians.[27]

Many of our city, or *sadr*, churches in the northern conferences (and available reports do not indicate a different condition in other conferences) have for many years been well organized, supporting their pastors, providing regular services for medium to large congregations, made up in part of the students from the hostels of boys' and girls' schools, and Christian members of the staffs of those and other institutions. In Moradabad the first self-supporting church among Christians from the mass movement, was formed years ago. It still supports its pastor in full; its services are regularly held. At Christmas and Easter its membership unites with the congregation of the Central Church, but at other times they meet in their separate congregations. Many children of this group are attending both our boys' and girls' schools, a living promise of better days ahead.

Some of the strongest of the *sadr* churches are contributing liberally to the support of work in their respective districts, but very few are promoting any evangelistic program of their own in the cities in which they are located, to reach the non-Christian groups all around them. Baptisms and new members in most of these, are from Christian families or by transfers. A hopeful aspect of evangelism is found in reports from a few cities that individuals from educated classes are inquiring from preachers and missionaries concerning the Way. There can be little doubt that among many in these groups there is a desire for something deeper than the old faiths offer. T nany of these, denominational differences present difficulties. The situation :hallenges the Churches to come together.

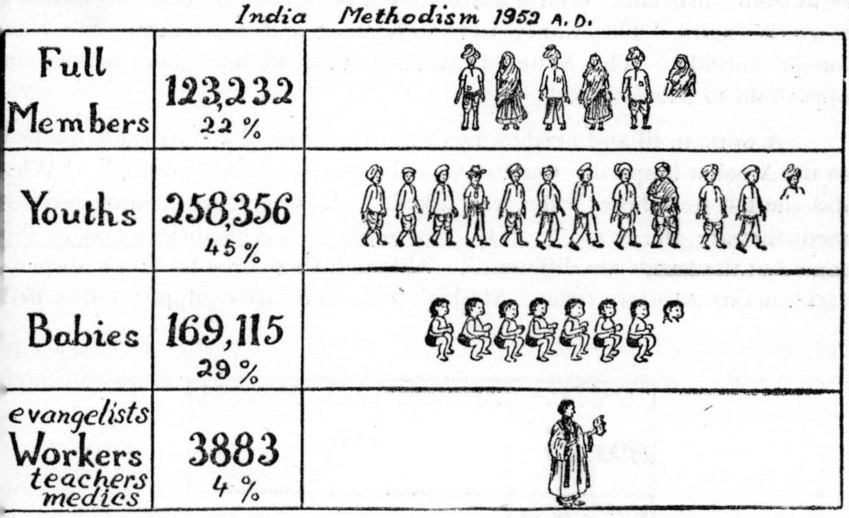

India Methodism 1952 A.D.
Full Members
123,232
22 %
Youths
258,356
45 %
Babies
169,115
29 %
evangelists
Workers
teachers
medics
3883
4 %

The people of India are religious. Through centuries they have hown themselves ready to sacrifice and to suffer for their beliefs. The ıssurance of evangelism is in the experience and promise that with the ›reacher there is Another Who draws to Himself. It remains the business of he Church to present Christ. It is an easy way for churches to support vorkers in their districts or Conferences, and a commendable thing to do, out it is imperative that every church be evangelistic in the community vhere it is. The Master himself described "salt" that had lost its flavour.

By and large the Churches are not using the Sunday school. In he cities where are boarding schools, Sunday Schools are held, composed ılmost entirely of the boys and girls who are in the hostels, with teachers rom those schools. Few children come from homes; adults seldom come. And yet the need for information and understanding of Christian truth is ınmet; and the fellowship that grows from meeting together and learning ogether, is lost. The Sunday Schools of the seventies to nineties were fruitul in arousing interest and in scattering truth. In the form they took they ould not be permanent. Methodist Churches in India need the acquainance with the Bible that only study together can produce. The Sunday School has proved its usefulness elsewhere, and yet India has not produced ıny alternative for that part in building the Church.

In God's providence India's constitution has given to "all persons" eligious freedom. We could not ask more. We reject the idea of proselytizing; we do not want nominal converts. We have the right "to propagate religion." There are today in India those who would be glad to take this right from Christians. Others frankly say it belongs to Indians only and not to any foreigner. They want it to be indigenous and spontaneous, free from foreign subsidy. The State of Madhya Pradesh has gone farthest in opposition to Mission work.

YEAR
TOTAL
INDIA METHODIST HOSPITALS
1900
6
(Peak)
1932
50
1952
41
NUMBER OF IN-PATIENTS
1900
15329
(Peak)
1928
32138
1952
36479
NUMBER OF OUT-PATIENTS
1900
27729
(Peak)
1924
689635
1952
339587

A woman, ill and needing medical care, entered a city and walked to the Mission hospital. On the way she passed another hospital. "Why did you not step there?" she was asked. "It was much nearer and the medicines are the same." "Oh," she replied, "the medicines may be the same but the hands are different." Although there may be fewer dispensaries in our Mission today, Methodist hospitals are equipped and staffed

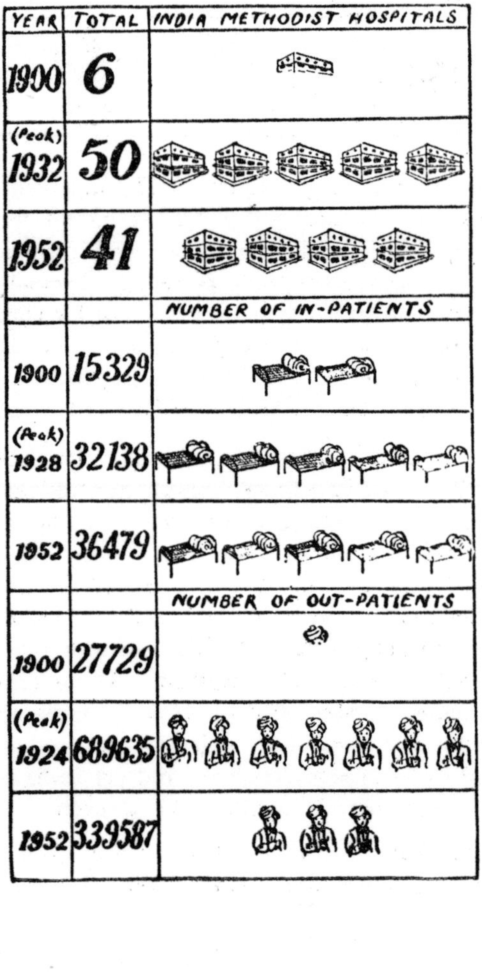

for better and wider service than ever before. They do bear a Christian witness in their ministry to all communities.

In connection with schools positions vary with the States. In some we are still as free as before freedom, if we wish to be, except that prescribed text-books have much teaching from another religion. However, some of our schools have grown so big in numbers, with so many non-Christian teachers that they cannot possibly provide Christian teachers for religious classes. They have barred themselves from what they were free to do, and rights surrendered are not easy to recover. Where there has been such loss there may well be the question, "Why then keep the school?" Early missionaries would certainly have replied, "Don't." Today there are some who say, "A Mission school still has influences." Perhaps the Central Conference will speak in answer for the Methodist Church.

A cut diamond on a piece of paper or in a pile with others, may not be beautiful. But when the jeweller sets it in a ring on prongs of gold, so that its every facet flashes light, it becomes a thing of beauty. How beautiful the Christian Church may become in the setting of Free India, one, lifted up with no chance for any to say "foreign", or "proselyte", "or any such thing . . . holy and without blemish." For the sceptical, Bishop Warne replied:

> One is often asked 'Do you believe that the mighty non-Christian nations will ever be evangelized?' Here is an answer. The Son of God has begun to build his Church among the Christless nations. Apply to himself his own statement about all that behold mocking 'the man who began to build and was not able to finish.'

The restless millions wait
The light whose dawning
Maketh all things new.
Christ also waits.
But men are late.
Have we done what we could?
Have I? Have you?[28]

I am no more able to tell how this problem [of reaching people] is to be solved than Peter was able to tell before he went up on the tanner's house to pray. There are 100,000 men among the non-Christians of India who are more or less prepared to repeat the part that Cornelius played, but there are very few Christians who are spiritually qualified to act the part of Peter . . . Every Christian should take comfort in the assurance that *somewhere* God is preparing a Cornelius for him. Peter's support in Caesarea was the least of all his cares. The real problem before us in this as in all good work is not how to get money, but men. A man 'thoroughly furnished' of God is as sure to get work, and food and clothing, as a flower is to receive color, or a sparrow to find a twig for its nest. But he must go where God sends him, when God sends him and do what God tells him . . . .

How shall we initiate a movement which will be self-propagating and which will speedily spread all over the country? I can conceive of only one answer to this question. Bring up every Church to the New Testament standard, especially the Antioch standard, develop the Barnabases and Sauls who shall be ready to go when the Spirit calls, and the question of support will settle itself as it did in ancient times. We should look for men and women of this stamp in every congregation. Paul picked them up wherever he went. A certain measure of spiritual power in a church will develop as sunshine brings out the buds and flowers in spring time. All the money, and methods, and machinery, in the world cannot produce one Peter, or one Paul; and till the men are forthcoming for the work it ill becomes any one to say that a self-supporting Gospel cannot be preached in India.

J. M. Thoburn,
Bombay Guardian, Nov. 8, 1879.

XVIII
Convictions Strong

The achievements of our Centenary have been wrought by men and women who have yielded their own choice, and accepted a different course under strong convictions. E. W. Parker would have stayed on a farm ; Thoburn wrestled with himself before he yielded ; Zahur al Haqq was willing for every difficulty when he was convinced that he had found the Truth. Under a sense of "call" missionaries left their homes and families for a strange country. Countless men and women in India, under like "call" and conviction have given themselves to building the Church.

We face a new century in a new India. The national climate, so to speak, demands adjustment, fortitude and initiative of Indian Methodists like unto that shown by the pioneers who opened work in the centennial now closing. It is still true, as Thoburn once said, that convictions "so strong and general" are an indication of God's beckoning.

Youth

From its early days the Methodist Church of Southern Asia has been solicitous for the training of children, particularly for those from Christian homes. That care has continued until today in what is probably the largest net work of schools of any Mission. To strengthen the development of character the E. W. Parkers organized the Oxford League. This gave place to the Epworth League, after which, in an effort to bring the children of all churches into one organization the Epworth League was merged with the Christian Endeavour Society.

The young people have been helped by another organization of the Church—the Sunday School. In fact the girls and boys of our hostels constitute the bulk of its membership. Of the work for young people the Bishops said in 1944 that it was receiving "very inadequate attention in our Church" as shown by statistics. The number of Sunday Schools, Scholars and Teachers, had shown a heavy drop to a point which "is certainly very low".

YEAR	TOTAL	INDIA METHODIST SUNDAY SCHOOL SCHOLARS
1876	8774	
(Peak) 1932	185906	
1952	56812	
		INDIA METHODIST SUNDAY SCHOOLS
1876	173	
(Peak) 1920	5913	
1952	1936	

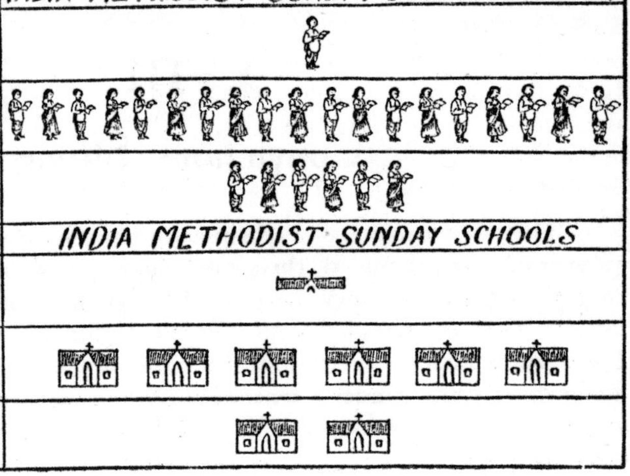

YEAR	TOTAL	INDIA METHODIST YOUTH SOCIETIES
1896	35	
(Peak) 1924	942	
1952	294	
		INDIA METHODIST YOUTH MEMBERS
1896	1800	
(Peak) 1924	43306	
1952	10857	

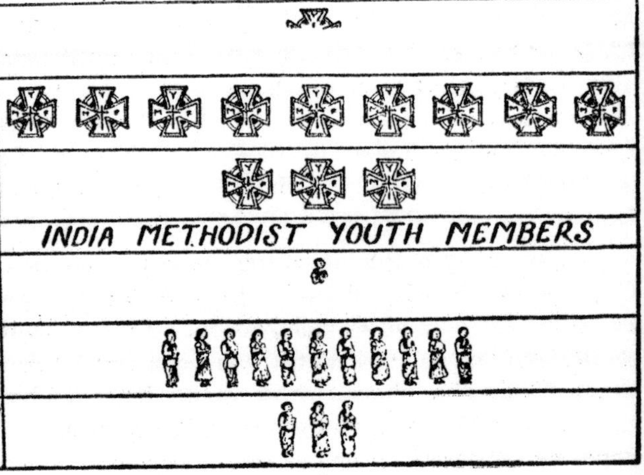

> Similarly the numbers in our Christian Endeavour work are appallingly low . . . [with] only 209 Christian Endeavour Societies of all grades in this vast area and only 6,870 members in all of these societies.[1]

Probably most of this number were connected with our hostels under teachers of the related schools and only indirectly with the churches. The sad fact is that very few pastors are connected with youth organizations. In the institutions, too, many do not want the boys and girls together, and if it should be approved for hostel children, the children of families in the city do not usually feel welcome. In this year, 1944, the Central Conference established a "Commission on Youth Work" and instructed "Annual Conferences to appoint or elect a Secretary of Youth Work . . . [to] become a corresponding member of the Commission, . . . [and] to organize a Conference Union of Christian Endeavour Societies."[2]

More recently the Methodist Youth Fellowship has been organized. The Central Conference adopted a full constitution for the M. Y. F. at the local Church, District and Annual Conference levels, with a program suggesting organizations in rural, urban and industrial areas.[3] It has not been very successful.

After Dr. Harold Ehrensperger had made a tour through India in 1946–47 he "stressed the necessity of developing a more effective program for the Youth of the Church," and urged the following steps :

> That the Church should concern itself with its youth as an age group which has both present and future contributions to the total religious community.
>
> That the youth organization should be church-centered so that young people will feel an integral part of the church itself. [4]

In his own inimitable way Bishop McDowell has shown the important place that youth should have with us. When Christ had told the disciples to feed the multitude and they knew not what to do:

> One man with a sure insight discovered one important fact: 'There is a lad here.' In the complexity of our church life, this safe fact out-ranks every other in significance—'there is a lad here,' in the church, in the Sunday School, in the city, in the world. He is a resource in himself, he has resources in his hands;
>
> 'It is a glorious thing to see a nation saved by its youth.' They are the 'trustees of posterity.' . . . Once more the Kingdom of Heaven is at hand, calling for adventure, for chivalry, for a sense of the future, for 'understanding and the gift of prophecy,' for the courage to set sail . . .
>
> This is our one greatest chance in the world. Perhaps we can hold one generation of childhood from getting away from Christ, train one entire generation of youth to be like Him and serve Him.[5]

It is possible that the conservation of our young people may be our major task in the years right ahead. In too many places our pastors are not wise to their needs. Through the schools and hostels much has been done for them. But how close is the local church to them? How close are they to it?

Industrial Schools And Economic Uplift

It was a truly Christian instinct, or conviction, that led Butler to plan for a Press in which boys could learn a trade. Others with similar conviction established associations to help the poor to attain better income and thereby to improve their standard of living. In some form or other, these convictions were manifested in almost every Conference. Efforts to implement them have been of two kinds, to help adults and to train boys.

The first was the more difficult for, however poor, the adults had established social roots and social habits, both on the side of the wife and of the husband, doubly strong. Unless an adult man, or a family is impelled by an inner urge to seek a new situation, success can only come if the benefactor is able somehow to assure it. Northern India has an expression, *ma-bap*, mother–father, and a second term, *parwarish*, which denotes the kind of care and nurture that parents give to small children. They are frequently on the lips of the depressed classes and of Christians from those groups. Too often missionaries are addressed in these terms and desired so to respond. The words are a symbol of poverty and discouragement. The Mission would be highly acclaimed if it would open factories to employ Christians who have no responsibility for its success. Again and again requests are made for Mission funds to settle Christians on land, or to back housing programs the income from which could be used "to support the Church". The history of our first centenary gives no hope for strengthening Christian character or the Christian community by such programs.

To teach the boys a trade start a Press; it was a thoroughly sound idea, but it came from above and was not the urgent desire of the boys. They did not learn enough to meet competition nor to open work on their own, and the Press could not run chiefly to maintain boys. As an outgrowth of the caste system there is a general idea that an educated man should not work with his hands—others do such work. By accepting the Government pattern in schools, the Missions have tacitly accepted the idea that those in the courses leading to the recognized examinations need not soil their hands. Thus the boys in Gujarat were divided between Nadiad and Baroda—the two types of education.

There were good reasons for this position: some of the orphans were "over age" for admission to regular schools; the Mission wanted its community educated so far as possible. This was the line of least resistance, the quickest way to get "workers", and the demand for "educated men" was in general large enough to absorb most of those who passed the examinations. The Government procedure brought grants and the Mission had no funds to operate more than one type of school system. And so the best of the Industrial Schools from which the Church had hoped so much were closed in the thirties; neither funds nor supervision were available.

In the India of today the old in education is giving place to a new pattern. The second five-years-plan now getting under way, is putting strong emphasis on industrialization. School programs are changing. In Uttar Pradesh mathematics has become a required subject in High School. Science classes have come to the saddle, many Intermediate Colleges having opened the new department in which science students outnumber those in the Arts classes. The training classes for teachers now prescribe work in villages where students share in improving drainage, making compost pits, planting trees. etc., while the ladies in the classes assist in cleaning homes and court yards, and in teaching sewing and handwork to the women. The work of the technical department at Ingraham Institute has received high approval. If our schools and our community are to keep pace with the country there will need be adjustments. The Christian community must have the opportunity to receive such technical preparation as will give it a share in the industrial development of the future.

PUBLISHING

It is worth remembering that three of the Presses established under the Central Conference of Southern Asia—Lucknow, Madras and Singapore—were started by practical printers who were otherwise busy, with small hand presses. Of these only the Lucknow Publishing House survives. After the "orphanages"—still continuing but very changed—it is the oldest institution of our Church, completing in this year of Jubilee ninety-five years of service. It has had its dark days as well as bright but it has rendered a magnificent service and at the threshold of our next centennial is better prepared and equipped to serve than it ever was before.

A record of its service in printed pages would run into fabulous figures. Its literature was written for the most part, on the side, by men with other appointments, as "a labour of love" to meet felt needs. At the close of thirty-nine years of service in India commencing in December, 1884, at Bishop Warne's request for a statement on his literary work, N. L. Rockey gave him a list of twelve items which he wrote or edited. Some of them are. *India Children's Friend*, a weekly, for twenty-eight years; Vernacular Sunday School Lessons for nine years and English for two years; a book, *John Wesley Mubashshir* (Evangelist) of 200 pages; and "thirty hymns translated which are used". In addition were many articles to Advocates in America and *Indian Witness* and *Kaukab* in India.

In the light of today's developments in India the Churches' program for Christian literature is entirely inadequate and needs to be greatly enlarged. Here are factors that high-light the opportunity: the efforts by Government and other groups to make India literate; the continuing increase in schools of all grades, most of which fill when they open; the need in our Christian community for literature, new, fresh and adapted to villagers and artisans, and to preachers and teachers. Today it is difficult to get Sunday School helps or good tracts for distribution. Beyond these is the increasing number of intellectual Indians who are eager for good religious literature. Much progress has been made toward these ends. In very recent years the Board of Missions has departed from its old practice of making no appropriation for Publishing and both the Division of World Missions and the Woman's Division of Christian Service have given grants to the Publishing House, and in support of the work of the Council of Literature and Publication, in which Miss Eunice Sluyter is the Director of Literature.

India has been for centuries a land of many languages. Its national language is now Hindi but the regional languages still prevail. This is a field in which Churches will find a large opportunity for agreement; where cooperation so supremely important has commenced in the National Christian Council, and where unity will serve the total cause.

Self-Support

In our earlier treatment of this subject we have defined self-support as the maintenance of its pastor by his church or circuit. We are not here dealing with institutions—schools, hostels and hospitals, which manifestly must be helped for an extended time. The plan suggested by Dr. Goucher and Bishop Foss in 1898 and approved by Annual and Central Conferences, was that each Finance Committee should fix an amount to be raised by each rural pastor, the balance of his salary to be paid by the Conference Treasurer, in proportion to the amount that he raised of his share. It carried tacit approval by the Board for scales of salary for preachers, and continued in operation into the thirties. With the depression and reduced appropriations many workers were discontinued and salary scales modified; a few churches became self-supporting. Meantime the Board dissociated itself from all salary scales and placed on the missionaries the responsibility for raising the portion of salaries not raised on the field.

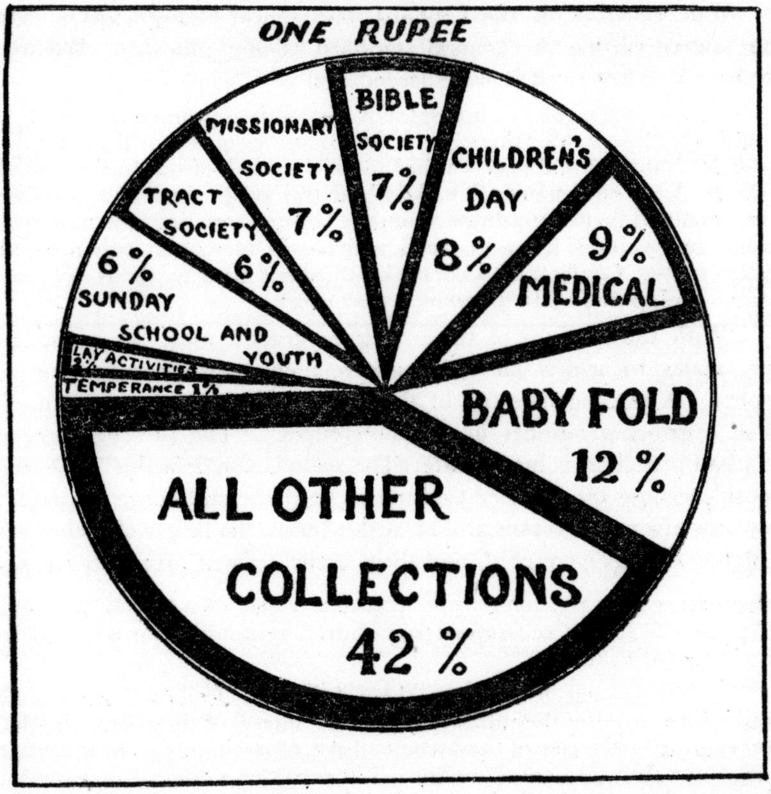

How India Methodism Divided its Benevolence giving in 1952.

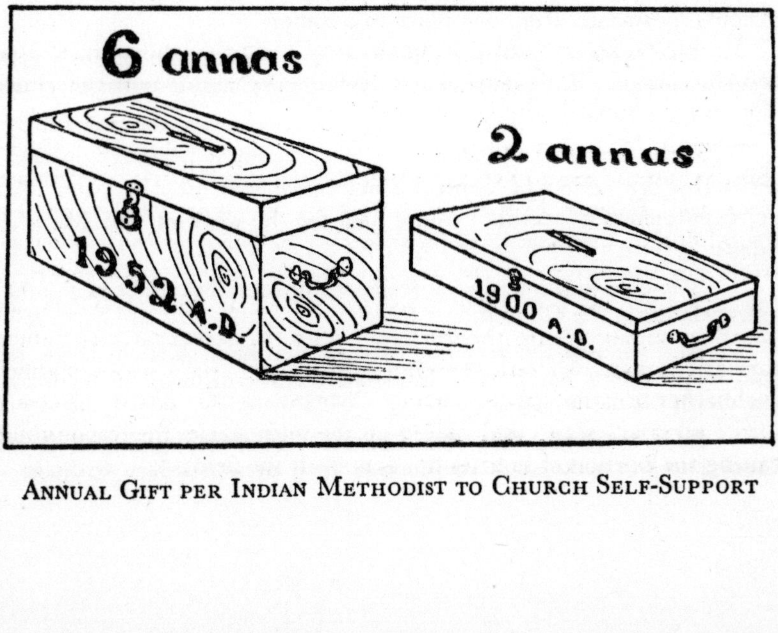

Annual Gift per Indian Methodist to Church Self-Support

The opening of the Leonard Theological College was a definit move toward raising the general standard of our ministry. Writing ir 1944 Ross tells how well it was succeeding:

> 20 years ago . . . among our Hyderabad group was one B. A. o equivalent, and all others were Matriculates or less. Then I take u our last minutes and observe that more than half of our Indian member are B. A. or equivalent [i. e. Jabalpur trained.] This year coming u for trial will be two graduates from art colleges, one intermediate trainec and one graduate from Leonard which will bring our Indian member ship in the Conference who rank as College men to about 65% of th total, compared to 16% twenty years ago.[6]

With the coming of these "higher grade" men, the questions o salary scales to which all workers were now accustomed became mor complex. A leading member of the Delhi Conference expressed the feel ings of a growing number in all Conferences. "The present salary scal for Indian preachers is inadequate. The scale is also defective". Defective forsooth, because the Finance Committee paid the difference between th collections of a rural worker and his scale; but in the larger churches wher the higher salaries were paid, and these better trained preachers went,

> the pastor is at the mercy and pleasure of the members of his church No one can hold a self-supporting church responsible for any deficienc in its pastor's salary.
>
> The young men know these facts very well and are naturall disinclined to enter the ministry . . . . The salary of the pastor should no depend upon the size of the income of the Church only, but other factor must be taken into consideration. The preacher's education, experience length of service should be considered . . . . There ought to be an equa adequate scale for ministers of equal education, experience and lengtl of service. Then appoint them [anywhere]. The salary must not b affected by transfer from one place to another.
>
> The present system of payment and raising the pastor's salar needs a change. It is detrimental both to the pastor and the church The pastor cannot be happy and carefree.[7]

That the writer of the above was not voicing a personal opinion i suggested by the action of Central Conference two months later. Afte urging Conferences to recruit "young men for the work of the Ministry" it added:

> The care and nurture of declared ministerial candidates should b a first claim on the Church.
>
> And whereas the very low salaries that have often hitherto beer paid to preachers has greatly hindered the recruitment of the finest o our youth for the ministry.
>
> Be it resolved, that this Central Conference urges all Annua Conferences to make such revisions in their present salary scales as wil

reduce the large disparity between the salaries of those in ministerial work and of those in educational work.[8]

The reference to salaries in educational work is to the mandatory ale fixed by Government for aided schools, which include our Mission hools. In the last twelve years the resolution has been very fully imple-ented in the Bareilly Seminary, the Leonard Theological College and in e whole range of workers' salaries, including Dearness Allowances which ame with and stayed after World War II.

Where is the policy taking the Methodist Church of Southern Asia? here may a policy take any Church when the Legislative body has no sponsibility for, nor any expectation to provide the "care and nurture" id the scales of pay it virtually enacts?

Ministerial support includes: Pastoral Support; Indigenous and nglish Churches; Episcopal Fund, District Superintendents' Fund, Con-rence and Mission Claimants' Funds. These last were replaced in time y the Provident Fund. Details of the other figures are given below for e years 1927–1952, a span of twenty-five years since the newest Conference as formed. The little attention given to the collections for District uperintendents and the great reduction resulting from the decline of nglish churches is noteworthy:

Conferences	Pastoral Support				Episcopal Fund		Dist. Supt.	
	Indigenous		English					
	1927	1952	1927	1952	1927	1952	1927	1952
ombay ...	39,744	26,125	52,009	9,640	885	407	...	126
ujarat ...	85,282	23,704	...	100	490	235	...	181
ladhya Pradesh ...	26,740	11,978	9,350	1,500	397	274	191	234
yderabad ...	21,434	31,963	6,763	1,680	266	230	...	...
outh India ...	66,210	30,718	33,468	6,984	976	498	...	488
engal ...	36,171	7,672	56,794	2,700	94	302	14	18
ucknow ...	66,300	14,352	19,509	2,800	890	380	1,110	3
dus River ...	67,382	15,364	13,572	...	372	325	25	...
elhi ...	143,036	54,856	4,971	...	1,834	534	...	52
orth India ...	110,459	31,872	6,316	...	910	615	109	548
Totals ...	662,758	248,604	202,752	25,404	7,114	3,800	1,449	1,650

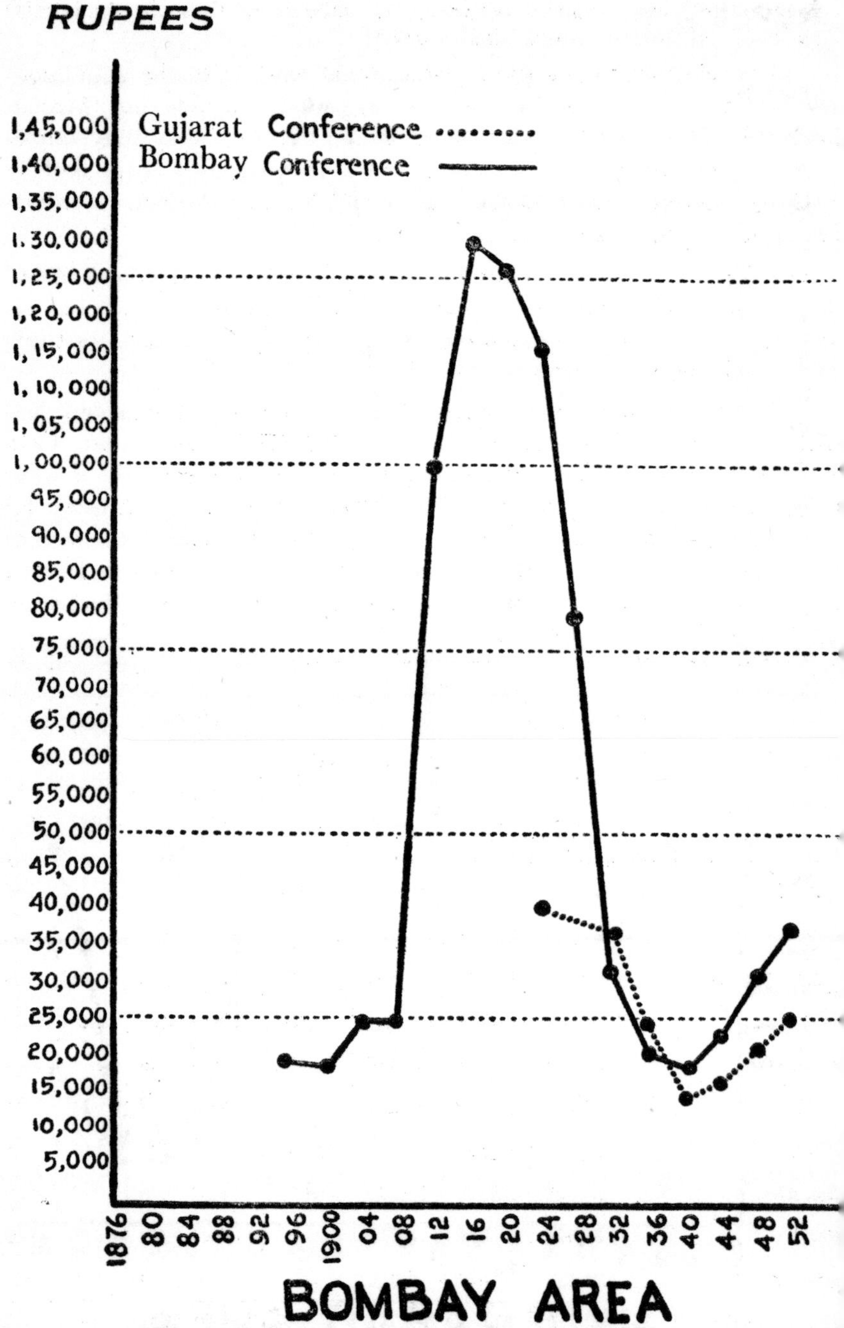

BOMBAY AREA

SHOWING TOTAL MINISTERIAL SUPPOR

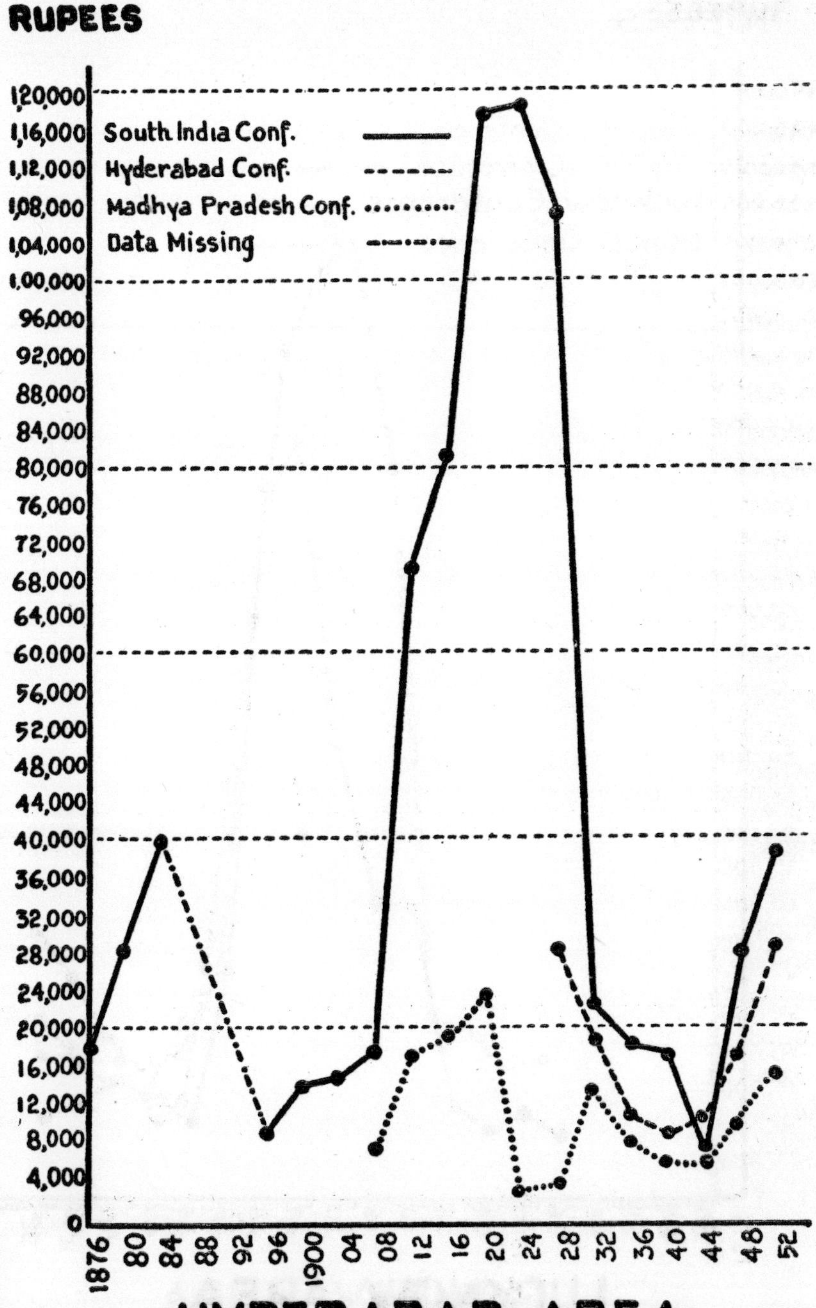

HYDERABAD AREA

SHOWING TOTAL MINISTERIAL SUPPORT

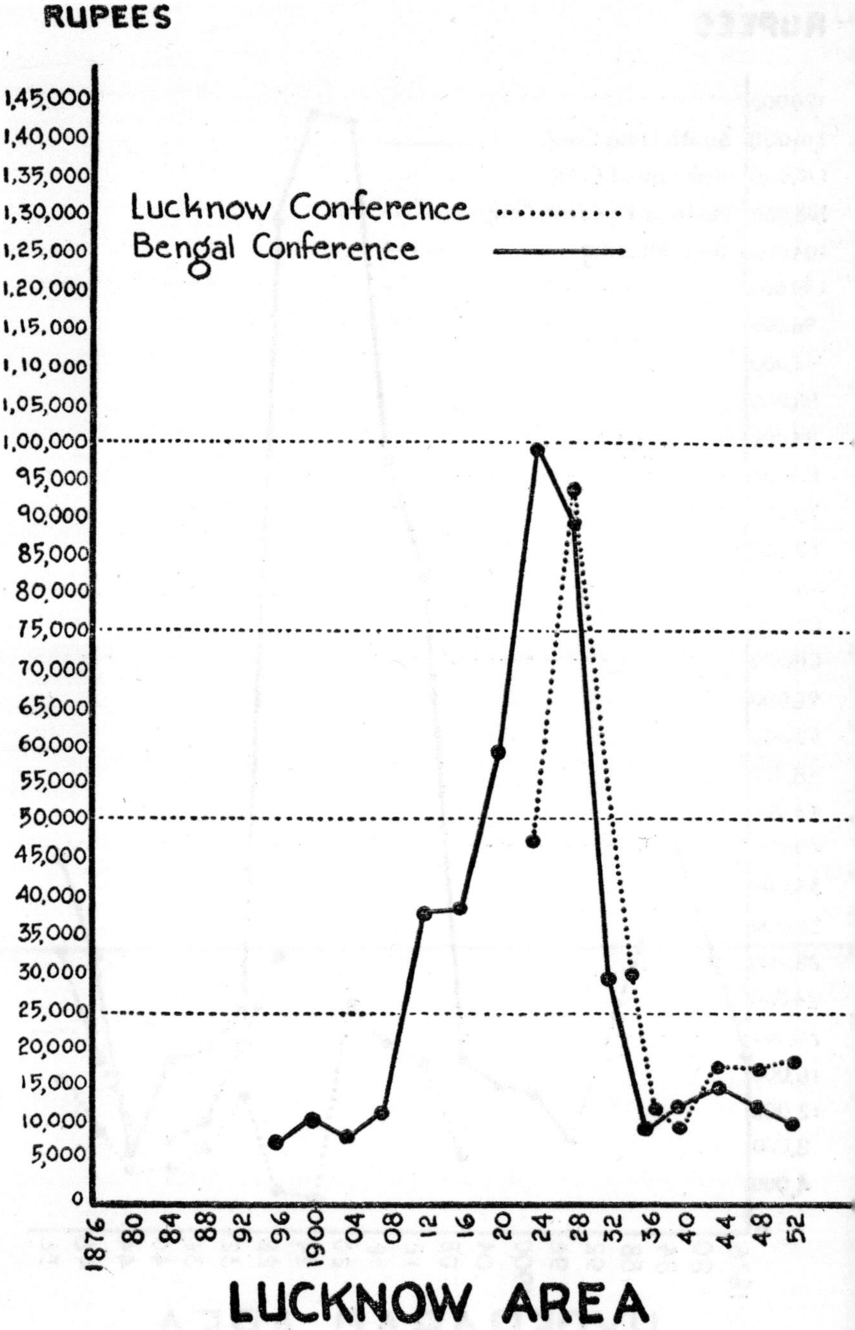

LUCKNOW AREA

SHOWING TOTAL MINISTERIAL SUPPORT

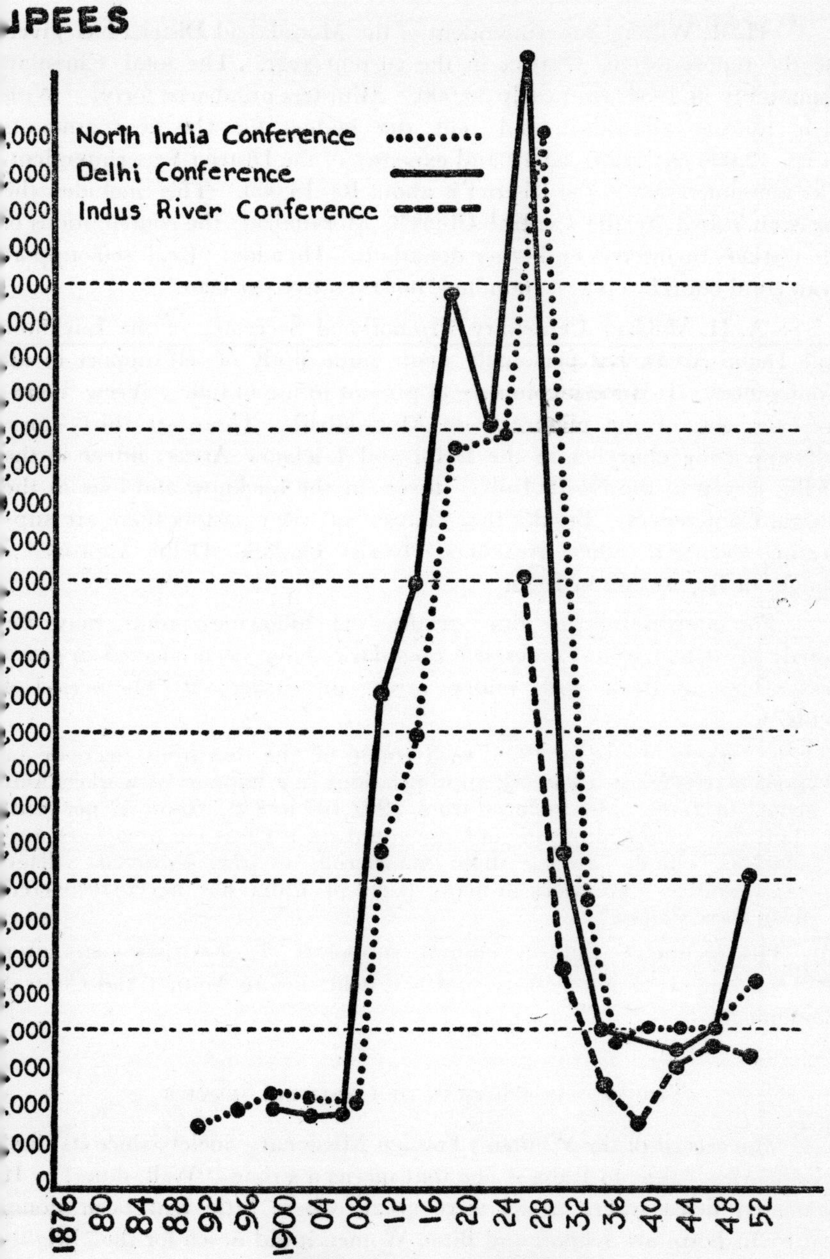

DELHI AREA

SHOWING TOTAL MINISTERIAL SUPPORT

H. R. Wilson, Superintendent of the Moradabad District has given me the report for his District in the current year. The total Christian community in 1954 was nearly 30,000. Ministers numbered forty. With their touring allowance and rent the budget for the year amounts to Rs. 42,000 excluding salary and expenses of the District Superintendent. The amount raised in the District is about Rs. 13,000. This includes the the sum raised by the Central Church, Moradabad, the contributions of the workers themselves and other donations. He adds: "Real self-support from rural churches is very nominal, not even five per cent."

A. H. McGee, Centenary Promotional Secretary of the Lucknow and Delhi Areas, has personally made some study of self-support in all Conferences. It is too incomplete at present to use in full. A few items, however, set off the picture from Moradabad: There are thirty-three self-supporting churches in the Delhi and Lucknow Areas: fifteen in the Delhi, eleven in the North India, three in the Lucknow and four in the Bengal Conferences. Besides the salaries of their pastors these are supporting seventeen other preachers. Christ Church, Delhi, approved a budget of Rs. 44,000 in 1956.

For interpreting the line graphs the following points may be noted: (1) Changes in Conference boundaries have been effected in every area, which are dealt with under areas, or earlier; (2) The period of "cuts";

> From 1926 to 1933, as a result of the disastrous decrease in missionary giving, the work appropriations [i. e. support of workers and boys] to India were reduced from $292,107 to $36,560, or 87 per cent. This led to the dropping of large numbers of Christian preachers and teachers, chiefly among those ministering to the scattered village communities. The work in many parts of India has never recovered from these shocks.[9]

(3) The decline of English church support; (4) For sixty years after 1873 self-support as a necessary goal was held before Annual and Central Conferences.

The Woman's Society of Christian Service

The record of the Woman's Foreign Missionary Society since its first missionaries came to India is one that merits a strong "Well done!" It pioneered fields where needs were great, where little had been done, and by its hospitals, schools and Bible Women it did much for the brightening and uplifting of India's womanhood. In the work of our Church in India the Society has been a "pervasive and powerful influence". Bishop Warne said facetiously that in "many phases of their work in India [they were] indeed our better half". Particularly in the roster of their educational nstitutions they have established a supremacy of which our Church is ·ightly proud.

"But," in village teaching, the Bishop added, they were behind the nen; "our earnest prayer is for more missionaries."[10] The number of nissionaries was never greatly increased. When we consider the great nfluence that women—even in villages—have in the direction of religious luties, and the extreme difficulty of their being reached by men, teachers ›r preachers, this "but" gains significance, a continued retarding of the ural church.

This, and other aspects of the work led Bishop H. L. Smith to onsider that "the outstanding need of the Woman's Foreign Missionary ›ociety throughout India . . . is coordination with the work of the Parent ›ociety.[11] At the session of the Executive Board in Baroda in 1921 dis-ussion was had as to "possible methods of increasing cooperation of effort etween the two Societies." In its report the joint committee recognized 'it as a fundamental principle" that the Board of Foreign Missions and he Woman's Foreign Missionary Society are but "joint agencies"; that in America

> the dual organization has its decided advantages in the collection of funds and in the recruiting of candidates for the field, but on the field itself the impact must be that of one Church, not of two Societies... on the field conditions make necessary a close correlation of work and a close cooperation of all missionaries.[12]

With the organization of the Methodist Church in 1939 the work of vomen was brought together in the Woman's Division of Christian Service. t includes three former organizations: The Ladies' Aid Society, the Voman's Foreign Missionary Society, and the Home Missionary Society. ts aim is to organize a Woman's Society of Christian Service, a counter-›art of the former Woman's Missionary Society in every local Church. The Woman's Conference continues as the unit of Women's Work in the Annual Conference.[13]

Of the three organizations which were merged in the Woman's ›ociety of Christian Service the Ladies' Aid was the oldest. It was in very Church, whether the other two were, or not. It concentrated on nything that would establish its Church, helping to raise the pastor's alary, annual repairs, or other ways. Many a small church was held ogether by the women who usually belonged also to one or both of the ther Societies.

In the work in India is the establishing of the small churches mphasized as it should be? Why is the salary of preachers an obligation n the Finance Committee of the Annual Conference if the impact is to e "of one Church, not of two Societies"? What is our major need? Is it to have strong rural Churches – preachers and buildings maintained by the people,—or a society with a purpose detached and to most of its members really unknown? Today some are, and in the tomorrows of the near future, many of our rural churches may be sorely tested by a new Nationalism. Should not both Conferences, the Woman's and the Annual, unite in an all-out effort to enable our churches—city and rural—to with-stand?

In order to help the more needy Christians of the group movements, the Central Conference over sixty years ago, approved the discontinuance of Zenana and City Schools. Thirty years later Mrs. M. T. Titus in a "North India Conference Survey" pleaded for "a new type of Bible Women, more Indian leaders...[as] outstanding needs of the Evangelistic work of the Conference."[14] Today an Indian District Superintendent in Madhya Pradesh, R. V. Nath, says:

> Our most urgent need is to work among the women. I think much can be done if we would change our method of work. The old methods were good once; but in this new day a change both in our objectives and the *modus operandi* are greatly desired. Can our Woman's Conference employ more women, and especially educated women for the Bible Readers' work?... We need consecrated women to work in place of the present type of zenana workers. The evangelistic program of the W. D. C. S. needs to be changed to suit the needs of the times. I would plead very strongly for revision of the policy before it is too late.[15]

Mission to Church

At the close of this first Centenary we cannot do other than look back and exclaim, "What hath God wrought!" Surely He has used men and women in a modern story of Missions no less real than the story of the first Apostles. These, too, had met the Christ of Galilee in their own home setting, and in obedience to His call they went forth to a land of which they knew little more than its name. But He had changed their whole outlook on life and made it their joy to do what they would never have chosen.

As a seed puts forth its stalk there was the small beginning in Bareilly, and that soon threatened with destruction; then the slow and steady growth of a community with its own leaders who had heard and with deep conviction knew that they had found the Truth for which they hungered. There followed a rapid development that threatened to swamp the growing Church in its hour of opportunity and challenge. Today, with ten Conferences and a community of nearly six hundred thousand we rejoice.

We have prided ourselves on our organization by which we have been a Church, and not a Mission in that the first Annual Conference brought foreign missionary and national leader into the same brotherhood, with the same rights, the same responsibilities; sharing the same challenge and the same work. That organization, however, has not protected us from weaknesses, nor can it save us. Only a few years since our Bishops reminded us that there are Quarterly Conferences

> totally unrepresentative of the indigenous church of the circuit, being composed entirely of men and women paid by Church or Mission funds and responsible to the District Superintendent.[16]

Bishop Thoburn wrote of "Hidden Resources." More recently his successors have stressed today's resources that are not tapped: our large community; our laymen who could do much more; the resources tied up by factions in local churches on account of which, "Spiritual power is lost.... The progress of the Church is crippled," the possibility of Central Funds in Conferences.[17]

Every Church might do well to listen at this Centenary hour to what the Spirit says to the Angel of the Methodist Church in Southern Asia. There will surely be an "I know thy works"—all that is good, all that is difficult; and "but this I have also". Early in his great career John R. Mott said:

> I believe in building for the future but am I not right in saying that the best way to build for the future is to serve our own generation by the will of God .... If we fail to do our duty in this generation we jeopardize our opportunities and prospects in the second and third generations.[18]

Miss Lilavati Singh used oft to ponder the words in Dr. Weir Mitchell's poem, "the patience of eternity"[19]—not the negative attitude of *karma* or *kismat* so prevalent in India, but the continued, active effort implied in Christ's word, "My Father worketh hitherto, and I work."

This word is enshrined in an incident in the Himalayas. Bishop Warne had visited Pithoragarh. When leaving there he passed near Chandag, home of Miss Reed, where he stopped for a short visit. Then as he went down the road, he turned and waved to her standing on a knoll and called, "Hitherto" came her reply, "Henceforth". It is a great partnership in which we may go forward. Recall Thoburn's words: "When Jesus said. 'Lo I am with you always', He meant what He said."

"If we, self-balked,
Stand still, a-strewing violets all the while,
These moved in vain, of whom we have vainly talked.
So rise up henceforth with a cheerful smile,
And, having strewn the violets, reap the corn,
And, having reaped and garnered, bring the plow
And draw new furrows 'neath the healthy morn,
And plant the great Hereafter in this Now."[20]

Bibliography

Key to References

BHB, Directory	Badley, Rev. B. H., M. A.	India Missionary Directory and Memorial Volume, 3rd. Edition 1886, Methodist Publishing House, Calcutta and Lucknow, India.
BHB, Biographies	,,	Unpublished Biographies of some Indian Preachers.
BTB, College	Badley, Rev. Brenton Thoburn, M. A.	The Making of a Christian College in India, Methodist Publishing House, Calcutta, India, 1906.
V and V	Badley, Bishop Brenton T.	Visions and Victories in Hindustan, Methodist Publishing House, Madras, India, 1931.
BTB, Warne	,,	Warne of India, Methodist Publishing House, Madras, India, 1932.
BTB, Chitambar	,,	The Making of a Bishop, The Life Story of Bishop Jashwant Rao Chitambar, Lucknow Publishing House, Lucknow, India, 1942.
TCB, Manual	Badley, Theodore C.	The Lucknow Christian College Manual of Urdu Shorthand, The Board of Trustees 1910.
Baker	Baker, Miss Frances J.	The Story of the W. F. M. S. of the M. E. Church, 1869-1895; Cincinnati, Cranston and Curtis, 1896.
Banerjea	Banerjea, Sir Surendranath	A Nation in Making, Humphrey Milford, Oxford University Press, London, 1925.
Barclay	Barclay, Wade Crawford	Early American Methodism, 1769-1844, The Board of Missions and Church Extension of the Methodist Church: New York, 1949.
Bardwell	Bardwell, Horatio	Memoir of Rev. Gordon Hall, A. M.; Flagg, Gould and Newman, New York, 1834.
Browne	Browne, Miss Eva C. M.	Life of Dr. Martha A. Sheldon, Missionary to Bhot.
Butler, C.	Butler, Miss Clementina	Mrs. William Butler, Two Empires and the Kingdom; The Methodist Book Concern, 1929.
Butler, W., Vedas	Butler, William	The Land of the Vedas. Hunt & Eaton. New York, 1895.
Butler, W., B to B	Butler, William	From Boston to Bareilly and Back; Phillips and Hunt, New York, 1886.
Butler, H.	Butler, Sir Harcourt, G.C.S.I. G.C.I.E., D.C.L.	India Insistent; William Herneman, Ltd., London, 1931.

Calkins	Calkins, Miss Ethel M.	The Sikh Religion and its Relatic to the Outcaste, Unpublishe Thesis, Kennedy School of Mission 1937.
Cartwright	Cartwright, Dr. Frank T.	Tuan Hoover of Borneo, The Abing don Press, New York, 1938.
Chew	Chew, Miss Flora	The Bareilly Orphanage an Boarding School for Girls, Methc dist Publishing House, Madras, 1903
Cook	Cook, Albert E.	The Bright Side and The Othe Side; Cincinnati, Jennings an Graham, 1907.
Crawford	Crawford, William Henry, Editor;	Thoburn and India, Eaton an Mains, New York, 1909.
De La Fosse	De La Fosse, C. F., M. A.	The History of India (Revised) Macmillan and Co., Ltd., 1913.
Discipline	Doctrines and Discipline of the Methodist Church	
Discipline, India	Doctrines and Discipline of the Methodist Church in Southern Asia. 1949	Lucknow Publishing House Lucknow, 1949.
Ernsberger	Ernsberger, Mrs. M. C.	India Calling - Unpublished Ms
Felt, Jabalpur	Felt, F. R.	Sketch of Methodist Work in Jabal pur, Typescript. 1899
Felt, Bastar	,,	The Story of our Work in Basta State. Typescript.
Ferrer	Ferrer, Cornelio M.	Unpublished Thesis, Drew Theo logical Seminary, 1948.
Foss, Equator	Foss, Bishop Cyrus D., D. D., LL.D.	From the Himalayas to the Equator Eaton and Mains, 1899.
Fraser	Fraser, Sir Andrew H. L., K. C. S. I., M. A., LL. D., Litt. D.	Among Indian Rajahs and Ryots Selly & Co., Ltd., London, 1911.
Gracey	Gracey, Mrs. J. T.	Woman's Medical Work in Foreig Lands. W. F. M. S. of M. E. Church Boston, Mass. 1888.
Haqq	Haqq, Rev. Zahur al	Autobiography of, Translated b Mrs. E. J. Humphrey, Printed fo the Missionary Society, New York, 1885.
Harper	Harper, Marvin Henry	The Methodist Episcopal Churcl in India, The Lucknow Publishin House, Lucknow, India, 1936.
Hewat	Hewat, Elizabeth G. K., M. A., Ph. D.	Christ and Western India, Missio Press, Surat, 1950.
Hodge	Hodge, J. Z., D. D.	Bishop Azariah of Dornakal, Th Christian Literature Society o India, Mysore, 1946.
Huizenga	Huizenga, Lee S., M. D., F. R. G. S.	Mary Reed of Chandag, Zonderva Publishing House, Grand Rapids Michigan, 1939.
Humphrey, Mrs.	Humphrey, Mrs. E. J.	Six years in India; Carlton and Porter, New York, 1866.
Humphrey, J. L.	Humphrey, Rev. J. L., M. D.	Twenty-one Years in India; Jenning and Graham, Cincinnati, 1905.

Hurst	Hurst, Bishop John Fletcher	Indika. The Country and People of India and Ceylon. (Title Page Missing-Foreword 1891)
Jackson	Jackson, John	Mary Reed, Missionary to the Lepers. Marshall Brothers, London, 1899.
Knowles	Knowles, Samuel	The Gospel in Gonda.
Knox	Knox, Rev. M. V. B., Ph. D., D. D.	A Winter in India and Malaysia Among the India Missions; Hunt and Eaton, N. Y., 1891.
Lacy	Lacy, Walter N.	A Hundred Years of China Methodism—Abingdon Cokesbury Press, N. Y., 1948.
Lapp	Lapp, George Jay, A. B., M. R. E.	The Christian Church and Rural India. Y. M. C. A. Publishng House, Calcutta, 1938.
Lee	Lee, Mrs. Ada	The Darjeeling Disaster, Its Bright Side. Fred Kelkar, Harrisburg, Pa. 1912.
Lovett	Lovett, Richard, M. A.	The History of the London Missionary Society, Vol. II, Henry Frowde, London, 1879.
Mayhew	Mayhew, Arthur, C. I. E.	The Education of India; Faber and Gwyer, London, 1926.
Messmore	Messmore, J. H.	The Life of Edwin Wallace Parker, D. D., Eaton and Mains, New York, 1903.
Mudge	Mudge, James	Historical Sketch of the Missions of the Methodist Episcopal Church; American Methodist Mission Press, Lucknow, Thomas Craven, 1877.
Nichols	Nichols, Florence L.	Lilavati Singh, A Sketch; The Tudor Press, Boston, Mass, 1909.
Norton	Norton, Albert	An Autobiographical Narrative; Anglo-vernacular Press, Bombay, 1884.
Nurullah	Nurullah, Syed B. A., M. Ed. and J. B. Naik, B. A.	A History of Education in India; Macmillan and Co., Ltd., Bombay, 1951.
Oldham, India	Oldham, W. F.	India, Malaysia and the Philippine Islands; Eaton and Mains, New York, 1914.
Oldham, Thoburn	„	Thoburn - Called of God; The Methodist Book Concern, N. Y., 1918.
Patterson	Patterson, John	Charles Edward Parker; Publisher, P. C. B. Balaram, Centenary Forward Movement.
Phillips	Phillips, Rev. Godfrey E.	The Outcastes' Hope. (The United Council for Missionary Education) Turnbull and Speare, Edinburgh.
Pickett, Mid India	Pickett, Bishop J. W., Rev. D. A. McGavran, Ph. D., and Rev. G. H. Singh, M. A.	Christian Missions in Mid-India. The Mission Press, Jubblupore, India, 1938.
Pickett, Mass Movements	Pickett, J. Waskom	Christian Mass Movement in India; The Abingdon Press, 1933.
Pickett, Christ's Way	„	Christ's Way to India's Heart—Lucknow Publishing House.

Price, Jubilee	Price, Frederick B.,	India Mission Jubilee, Methodi Publishing House, Calcutta. 1907.
R & G	Reid, J. M., D. D. Revised and extended by Gracey, J. T., D. D.	Missions & Missionary Society the Methodist Episcopal Churc Hunt and Eaton, N. Y., 189 Vols. II-III.
Richter	Richter, Julius,	A History of Missions in Indi Morrison and Gibb, Ltd., Edinburg
Robinson, J. E.	Robinson, J. E., D. D.	A Brief History of Methodis Methodist Publishing Hous Madras, 1921.
Robinson, Ruth	Robinson, Miss Ruth E.	A Girl of an Indian Garde Fleming H. Revell & Co., London Edinburgh, 1928.
Ross	Ross, Elsie	Unpublished typescript
Satthianadhan	Satthianadhan, S. M. A., LL. B.	Sketches of Indian Christian Christian Literature Societ for India, 1896.
Scott, Braj	Scott, J. E,. Ph. D., S. T. D.	Braj, The Vaishnava Holy Land Eaton and Mains, New York, 190
Scott, Observations	„	Observations of an Itinerant, Sco tish Mission Industries Co., Ltd Ajmer, 1905.
Scott, Famine Land	„	In Famine Land, Harper and Bro thers, N. Y. and London, 1904.
Scott, Fifty Years	„	History of Fifty Years, M. E. Pres Madras, 1906.
Scott, Missionary Life	Scott, T. J.	Missionary Life in India; Hitchcoc and Walden, Cincinnati, O.
Sherring	Sherring, Rev. M. A., LL. B.	The History of Protestant Missio in India, 1706-1871; Trubner an Co., London, 1875.
Smith, George	Smith, George, C.I.E., LL. D.	The Life of Dr. Duff, D. D., LL. D. William Briggs, Toronto.
Smith, Julius	Smith, Rev. Julius,	Ten Years in Burma; Eaton an Mains, New York, U. S. A., 1902.
Speer	Speer, Robert E.	George Bowen of Bombay. Printe 1938 privately.
Stephens	Stephens, Miss Grace	Triumphs of the Cross, Baltimor Branch of W. F. M. S., 1901.
Subhan	Subhan John A.	How a Sufi Found His Lord; Th Lucknow Publishing House Lucknow, India, 1943.
Swain	Swain, Dr. Clara A.	A Glimpse of India; James Po and Co., N. Y., 1909.
Taylor, Campaign	Taylor, William	Four Year's Campaign in India Hodder and Stoughton, London Nelson and Phillips, N. Y., 1875.
Taylor, Missions	„	Ten Years of Self-supporting Mis sions in India, Phillips and Hun N. Y., 1882.
Thoburn, I.	Thoburn, Isabella	Phoebe Rowe, Eaton and Mains N. Y., 1899.
J. M. T., Journal	Thoburn, James M.	Journal (at Allegheny College, Meadville, Pa.)

J. M. T., App.	Thoburn, James M.	My Missionary Apprenticeship, Phillips and Hunt, New York, 1884.
J. M. T., Ind. Mal.	Thoburn, Bishop, James M.	India and Malaysia, Cranston and Curts, Cincinnati, 1893.
J. M. T., Light	„	Light in the East, Thomas Craven, Evanston, Ill., 1894.
J. M. T., Life I. T.	„	Life of Isabella Thoburn, Eaton and Mains, N. Y., 1903.
Thomson,	Thomson, Bishop Edward, D. D., LL. D.	Our Oriental Missions, Vol, I, India and China, Hitchcock and Walden, Cincinnati, 1870.
Ward, Our Work	Ward, C. B.	Our Work; E. J. Decker Co., Chicago, 1894.
Ward, History	„	History of Twelve Years' Work in Nizam's Dominions, 1879-1891; A. V. Press and "Bombay Guardian," Printing Works.
Ward, W. T.	Ward, W. T.	Sunlight and Shadow of Missionary Life; J. Hallermann, Medan, Teb Tinggi, 1915.
Warne, Diary	Warne, Bishop Francis Wesley	Unpublished Diaries, (Leonard Theological College), Jabalpur, India.
Warne, Tribute	„ „ „	A Tribute to the Triumphant; The Methodist Book Concern, New York; 1926.
Warne, Ideals	„ „ „	Ideals That Have Helped Me; The Methodist Book Concern, 1928.
Weston, A-IR	Weston, C. N., M. A., M. R. S. T.	Anglo-Indian Revolutionaries. The Scripture Literature Press, Bangalore, India, 1938.
Weston, Retrospect	Weston, C. N., M.B.E., M.A., M. R. S. T.	Retrospect and Prospect, (Baldwin Boys' High School) C. L. S. Press, Bangalore, 1947.
Wilkie	Wilkie, Caroline Edna,	Philo Melvin Buck, Missionary to India; Rev. P. C. B. Balaram, Centenary Forward Movement; 1955.
Wilson	Wilson, J. Christy	Apostle to Islam, Baker Book House, Grand Rapids, Michigan, 1952.
Worley	Worley, Harry Wescott,	The Central Conference of the Methodist Episcopal Church; The Christian Herald Mission Press, Foochow, China, 1940.

BOOKLETS AND PAMPHLETS

Badley, Oldham	Badley, Bishop B. T.	Oldham, Beloved of Three Continents, Lucknow Publishing House 1937.
B. C. Man.		The Bengal Conference Manual (adopted at Pakaur, Feb. 1906) Methodist Publishing House Calcutta, 1906
Buck	Buck, P. M.	Corresponding Secretary's Book (Manuscript) Bengal and N. W. I. Conference 1889-1893.

Bullock	Bullock, Rev. G. Mc Callum	The Asylum for Lepers at Almora N.W.P., India, Almora, Nov. 1, 189
Butcher	Butcher, J. C.	The Beginning of the Mass Movement in the M. E. Mission.
Craven	Craven, Rev. Thomas, B. D.	Glimpses of India
Das, Jubilee	Das, Rev. Amar, compiler	From the Beginning or The Jubilee of the N. W. India Conference, 1892-1942. Station Press, Meerut
Foss, Through India	Foss, Bishop C. D.	Through India with Bishop Foss The Philadelphia Laymen's Association, Philadelphia, Pa., 1898
Gracey, Borderlands	Gracey, Lilly Ryder	Work in Borderlands, Martha Augusta Sheldon, M. D., in India Nepal, Tibet.
Griffiths	Griffiths, Walter G.	The Lee Memorial Mission
Harwood	Harwood, Harry J.	Methodism in Burma
Joyner	Joyner, Louise Halloway (Edited By)	The Opening Gate, Calcutta, India.
King	King, Earl L.	Mission Post, Jabalpur, 1922-1946, 1946.
Medics		Methodist Medics in India, Winter 1954. Division World Mission N. Y. 1954.
The Road		The Road as it Runs Through North-West India Conference
Robbins	Robbins, W. E.	The Methodist Episcopal Church in Western India. Unpublished Typescript Leonard Theological College
Strength		From Strength to Strength

PERIODICALS

BG	Bombay Guardian
CA	Christian Advocate
CCA	Central Christian Advocate
NWCA	Northwestern Christian Advocate
WCA	Western Christian Advocate
MME	Mass Movement Era
	MISSIONARY SOCIETY PUBLICATIONS
MA	Missionary Advocate
Gospel	The Gospel in All Lands
WWM	World Wide Missions
WO	World Outlook
HWF	The Heathen Woman's Friend
WMF	The Woman's Missionary Friend
MW	The Methodist Woman
CBC	Chand Bagh Chronicle
LBR	Lal Bagh Review

W	The Lucknow Witness
W	The Indian Witness
Ial. Mess.	The Malaysia Message

MINUTES AND REPORTS

For Woman's Conference Annual Conference Minutes W is inserted before C as MBWC]

IBC		Minutes Bengal Conference
IByC		„ Bombay „
IBMC		„ Burma Mission Conference
ICPMC		„ Central Provinces Mission Conference
ICPC		„ Central Provinces Conference
IMPC		„ Madhya Pradesh „
IGC		„ Gujarat „
IHC		„ Hyderabad „
IIRC		„ Indus River „
ILC		„ Lucknow „
IIMC		„ India Mission „
IIC		„ India „
INIC		„ North India „
INWIC		„ North-West India „
IDC		„ Delhi „
ISIC		„ South India „
ICC	Central Conference Minutes	„ Central Conference
ecennial	Decennial Conference Minutes	Report of the Second Decennial Missionary Conference, Calcutta, 1882-83, Baptist Mission Press, 1883 Report of the Third Decennial Missionary Conference, Bombay, 1892-93, Vol. I-II, Education Society's Press, Byculla, 1893. Report of the Fourth Decennial Conference, India Missionary Conference, Madras, December 11-18, 1902, Christian Literature Society, Madras.
elegated	Delegated Conference Minutes	Minutes of the Delegated Conference
ondon	London Missionary Conference	Report of, Edited by James Johnston, F. S. S., Vol. I, James Nisbet & Co., London, 1899
cumenical	Ecumenical Methodist Conference	Proceedings of the Ecumenical Methodist Conference, Sept. 1881, Walden and Stone, Cincinnati
CJ	General Conference Minutes	General Conference Journal
umaon	Kumaon Committee	First Report of the General Committee of the Kumaon Mission, Lucknow, 1872.
MS	Missionary Society	Annual Report of the Missionary Society

JAM		Journal of the Annual Meeting
Gaz		Gazetteer
WFMS	Woman's Foreign Missionary Society	Annual Report of the India Branch of the Woman's Foreign Missionary Society
		Annual Report of the Woman's Foreign Missionary Society.
NMC	National Missionary Council	Proceedings of the First Meeting of the National Missionary Council, Calcutta, Feb. 4-5, 1914. Office of the N. M. C., 48 Ripon St. and 86 College Street.

References

INTRODUCTION

1. IW, 1909, P. 308
2. HWF II No. 8, Feb. 1871, p. 85
3. De La Fosse, p. 252
4. Ibid., pp. 263-64
5. The Pioneer, Lucknow, Jan. 18, 1895
6. Richter, p. 128
7. Ibid., pp. 131-32
8. Lovett, p. 9
9. Richter, pp. 200-201
0. Nurullah, Chap. I
1. BG, Feb. 19, 1876, p. 401
2. Butler, C., p. 37
3. Messmore, p. 55
4. Humphrey, J. L., pp. 138-40
5. Butler, W., Vedas, pp. 221-22
6a. Butler, H., p. 44
6. CA May 10, 1855, p. 74
7. Butler, W., B to B
8. Ibid., p. 61
19. J M T, App., pp. 7-8
20. Ibid., pp. 7-14
21. CCA, April 21, 1909, pp. 11-15
22. Messmore, pp. 28-29
23. Ibid., p. 42
24. J M T Ind. Mal., p. 429
25. Speer, p. 64
26. BG Sept. 3, 1887, p. 564
27. Speer, p. 265
28. BG Feb. 11, 1888, p. 81
29. Speer, p. 277
30. Ibid., p. 275
31. R & G III, pp. 142-44
32. Butler, W., Vedas, p. 219, J. T. Janvier, Autograph, 1894
33. MNIC, 1901, pp. 41-42
34. Thomson, I
35. MNIC, 1880, p. 42
36. Butler, W., Vedas, pp. 256-57

CHAPTER I

1. Butler, W., B to B, p. 155
2. MA May 1857, p. 10
3. Butler, W., Vedas, p. 113, Butler, C., p. 61
4. Butler, W., Vedas, p. 214
5. MNIC 1939
6. Butler, C., p. 49
7. Harper, p. 20
8. Butler, C., pp. 44-45, 54
9. Butler, W., Vedas, p. 237
0. R & G II p. 361
1. Ibid., p. 364
2. Ibid., p. 367
3. Butler, W., Vedas, p. 246
4. MA Jan. 1858, p. 73; Nov. 1859
5. Knowles, p. 102
6. RMS 1860, p. 35
7. Butler, W., Vedas, pp. 410-13
8. Butler, C., p. 272
9. Ibid., pp. 243, 248
0. Humphrey, Mrs. pp. 70-71
1. IW, Aug. 16, 1953
2. Butler, W., Vedas, p. 434
3. Humphrey, Mrs. pp. 79-80
4. Humphrey, J. L., pp. 61-62
5. MNIC, 1884, p. 99
6. Butler, C., pp. 83-84
27. Humphrey, J. L., p. 76
28. Butler, W., Vedas, p. 457
29. J M T App., p. 70
30. MA, Dec. 1857
31. MNIC 1884, p. 89
32. MA Dec. 1859, p. 67
33. Butler, W., Vedas, p. 438
34. Ibid., pp. 442-52
35. J M T Ind. Mal., p. 229
    MA Nov. 1859, p. 58
36. MA Nov. 1859, p. 57 (Italics mine)
37. Ibid., Oct. 1859, p. 49
38. Humphrey, Mrs., pp. 114, 123
39. Humphrey, J. L., pp. 80-81
40. Sherring, pp. 225-26
41. J M T Ind. Mal., p. 266
42. Calkins
43. J M T Ind., Mal., p. 267
44. MIMC 1867, pp. 49-50
45. MA Nov. 1859, p. 59
46. Ibid., p. 49 (Italics mine)
47. Ibid., Sept. 1865, p. 44
48. Humphrey, Mrs., p. 132
49. MA Nov. 1859, p. 59
50. B H B Biographies (Italics mine)
51. Humphrey, J. L., p. 101
52. MA Nov. 1859, p. 57

53. Haqq, pp. 1-18
54. Humphrey, J. L., pp. 112-15
55. MNIC 1897, p. 35
56. MA 1875, p. 51 (Italics mine)
57. Humphrey, Mrs., pp. 133-37 (Italics mine)
58. B H B Biographies
59. Humphrey, J. L., pp. 146-50
60. B H B Directory, 1892, p. 241
61. Messmore, p. 56
62. J M T App., pp. 46-47
63. GCJ 1860, pp. 277-78
64. R & G II, p. 393
65. J M T Journal
66. MA Aug. 1861, pp. 33, 44, 45
R & G pp. 413-14
67. MA July 1863, pp. 25-26
68. Messmore, p. 84
69. MA Sept. 1863, pp. 41, 42
70. Thomson, pp. 69-70
71. J M T Journal, Sept. 1, 1863
72. R & G II 430
73. GCJ 1864, p. 219
74. J M T App., p. 108
75. R & G II pp. 404-405
76. Messmore, p. 80
77. R & G II p. 411
78. Butler, W., Vedas, p. 270
MA Oct. 1860 p. 50
79. Ibid., Dec. 1861, p. 73
80. Ibid., 1860, p. 68
81. Humphrey, J. L., pp. 132-33
R & G II p. 398
82. J M T App., pp. 60, 75

CHAPTER II

1. Butler, W., B to B. pp. 114-16
2. MA Jan. 1864, p. 74
3. Ibid., Nov. 1859, p. 59
4. Ibid.
5. Ibid., Feb. 1865, p. 81
6. Humphrey, Mrs., p. 204
7. Humphrey, J. L., pp. 106-107
8. MIMC 1869, p. 52
9. Ibid., 1868, pp. 78-79
10. Butler, W., B to B, pp. 253-54
11. MA Sept. 1865, p. 44
12. Humphrey, J. L., p. 141
13. Humphrey, Mrs., p. 205
14. HWF April 1871, p. 114
Baker, pp. 202-204
15. B H B Directory, 1892, p. 309
16. HWF July 1871 III pp. 151-52
17. MNIWC First Annual Report, p. 28
18. Humphrey, Mrs., p. 244
19. MIMC 1866, p. 40
20. Ibid. p. 19
21. Butler, C. p. 90
22. Unpublished letters from Waugh
23. MA Feb. 1862, p. 82
23a. Butler, C., p. 92
24. Humphrey, Mrs., p. 236
25. MIMC 1864, p. 42
26. Ibid.
27. Messmore, pp. 82-83
28. Butler, W., B to B, p. 114
29. Minutes of the Missionary Society, VI, p. 223
30. J M T App., p. 88
31. MA Dec. 1862, p. 65
32. R & G II p. 408
33. Knowles, pp. 2-3
34. MIMC 1872, p. 24
35. Ibid., 1868, p. 38
36. GCJ 1868, p. 390
37. Thomson, p. 90
38. MIMC 1864, p. 27
39. Ibid., pp. 26, 30
40. Lacy, p. 59
41. GCJ 1868, p. 392
42. J M T Journal, Sept. 5, 1859
43. Mudge, p. 164
44. Foss, Through India

CHAPTER III

1. MIMC 1867, p. 23
2. Ibid., 1872, p. 55
3. Ibid., 1873, p. 15
4. LW July 16, 1875, p. 186
5. Ibid., July 1877, p. 195
6. MNIC 1877, p. 30
7. Knowles, pp. 147-53
8. Ibid., pp. 12-13
9. Ibid., p. 6
10. Ibid., p. 151
11. MIMC 1866, p. 41
12. Ibid., 1870, p. 73
13. Ibid., 1869, p. 23
14. Wilkie, p. 8
15.
16. W. F. M. S. 7th Annual Report, p. 19
17. Ibid., 8th Annual Report, p. 25
18. MNIC 1876, p. 24
19. Ibid., p. 25
20. J M T Ind. Mal., p. 267
21. MIC 1873, p. 56
22. Ibid., p. 6
23. MNIC 1875, pp. 21-22
24. Ibid., 1876, P. 34
25. J M T App., p. 204
26. Ibid., p. 126
27. MIMC p. 47
28. Butcher, p. 2
29. MIMC 1869, pp. 40-41
30. Ibid., 1870, p. 38

31. Ibid., 1864, p. 14, (Italics mine)
32. Ibid. 1869, p. 62
33. MIMC 1867, p. 8
34. Ibid. 1870, pp. 4-5
35. MIMC 1866, p. 10
36. Ibid., p. 8
37. MIMC 1867, p. 24
38. Ibid., 1868, p. 70
39. Ibid., 1870, p. 64
-0. Ibid., 1873, p. 16
-1. HWF 1872, pp. 221-22
2. MIMC 1872, p. 13
3. Baker, p. 205
4. MIMC 1866, pp. 21, 23
5. Ibid., 1867, p. 19
6. MIC 1875, p. 74
7. MIMC 1870, p. 30
8. MIC 1873, p. 19
9. Ibid., p. 71
0. MIC 1874 (Italics mine)
1. MNIC 1878, p. 75
2. Ibid., 1879, p. 20
3. Ibid., 1882, p. 5; 1883, p. 21
Ibid., 1884, p. 24
4. MIMC 1866, p. 25
5. MIMC 1867, p. 20
6. Ibid., 1866, p. 41
7. MA Sept. 1865, p. 44
8. MA April 1869, p. 7; March, 1864
9. MIC 1875, p. 22
0. MIMC 1869, p. 63
1. Ibid. 1870, p. 61
2. MIC 1875, p. 12
2a. MIMC 1867, p. 7
3. Ibid., 1868, p. 6
4. Humphrey, Mrs., p. 221
5. Humphrey, J. L., p. 160
6. MNIC 1887, p. 46
7. MIMC 1872, p. 7
8. MIC 1876, p. 27
69. MNIC 1888, p. 45
70. J M T App., pp. 168-73
71. MIMC 1868, p. 70
72. Ibid. 1869, p. 56 (Italics mine)
73. Ibid. 1871, p. 15
74. MIC 1873, p. 10
75. V and V p. 196
76. MNIC 1878, pp. 26-27
WFMS 8th Annual Report, p. 25
77. V and V pp. 140-41
78. MNIC 1888, p. 41
79. Ibid. 1884, pp. 76, 93; 1885, p. 105
80. Baker, p. 211
81. Warne, Tribute, p. 62
82. MNIC 1887, p. 45
83. WFMS 6th Annual Report, pp. 13-14
85. Unpublished account by Mrs. Abbott.
86. MIMC 1866, pp. 13-14
87. MNIC 1893, p. 22
88. LW Dec. 6, 1872, p. 265
89. MIC 1875, pp. 86-87
90. J M T App., p. 304
91. MNIC 1893, p. 23
92. J M T App., pp. 222-23
93. MIMC 1869, p. 33
94. J M T App. p. 225
95. Ibid., p. 226
96. MIMC 1870, pp. 24, 26, 70
97. Ibid., 1871, p. 6
J M T Ind. Mal., p. 271
98. MIMC 1870, pp. 29, 40-41
99. Ibid., 1871, p. 37
100. MIC 1873, p. 21; MNIC 1876, p. 21
MNIC 1877, p. 16
101. Letter dated March 28, 1878 from Cunningham to Waugh.
102. MNIC 1880, p. 27
103. Ibid. 1883, p. 53
104. J M T Ind. Mal., p. 270
105. Messmore, p. 154

CHAPTER IV

. Butler, W., B to B, pp. 243, 248
. J M T App., p. 247
. Baker, pp. 9, 10
. MIMC 1866, pp. 31-32
. Baker, p. 11
. Ibid., p. 12
. Ibid., pp. 21-22
. J M T App., p. 247
. Ibid., p. 248
. Baker, p. 24
. Messmore, pp. 132-33
. Warne, Tribute, pp. 52, 53
. RMS VI, p. 506
. Humphrey, J. L., pp. 185-86
. MIMC 1869, pp. 62-64
. Humphrey, J. L., p. 186
. MA Oct. 19, 1869, p. 27
. MIMC 1870, p. 28
. HWF I Dec. 1869, p. 69
20. MA March 1870, p. 48
21. MIMC 1871, p. 38; 1872, p. 11
22. Humphrey, J. L., p. 187
23. Gracey, p. 37
24. HWF II Aug. 1870, p. 13
25. MIMC 1872, p. 11
26. Ibid., 1873, p. 8
27. Gracey, p. 69
28. MIMC 1873, p. 14
29. Gracey, p. 33
30. BG Nov. 15, 1879, p. 445
31. Gracey, p. 39; Calcutta Review, Vol. 85 Oct. 1887
32. Gracey, p. 40
33. MIC 1871, p. 6
34. Swain, p. 36
35. J M T Life I. T., p. 73
36. Swain, p. 40
37. Gracey, pp. 50-53

3

38. Ibid., pp. 78 ff.
39. Ibid., p. 46
40. IW Aug. 31, 1921, p. 657
41. Swain, p. 163
42. Calcutta Review, 1887, pp. 229-46
43. J M T Life I. T., pp. 75-76
44. Ibid., p. 32
45. Ibid., p. 91; LBR p. 28
46. J M T Life I. T., pp. 101-103
47. LBR p. 28
48. Ibid., pp. 31-32
49. J M T Life I. T., pp. 181-94
50. IW Nov. 19, 1936, p. 739
51. Price, Jubilee, p. 156
52. MIMC 1866, pp. 26, 27, 30
43. B T B College, p. 43
54. J M T Journal, May 16, 1870
55. B T B College, pp. 49-50
56. MNIC 1879, p. 36
57. B T B College, pp. 101, 117
58. Ibid., p. 108
59. Ibid., p. 120
60. Ibid., pp. 122, 161
61. T C B Manual, Preface
62. Taylor, Campaign, pp. 16-17
63. J M T App., p. 281
64. Taylor, Campaign, pp. 21-22
65. Ibid., pp. 64-65
66. Ibid., p. 75
67. Ibid., p. 69
68. J M T App., p. 284
69. Taylor, Campaign, p. 73
70. MIC 1875, p. 28 Italics (mine)
71. Taylor, Campaign, pp. 26-27
72. J M T Ind. Mal. p. 343
73. MIC 1873, p. 26
74. Ibid., 1875, p. 57; p. 7
75. Messmore, p. 166
76. MIC 1875, pp. 78-80
77. MIMC 1872, p. 48
78. IW Dec. 6, 1872, p. 265
79. J M T Journal, May 4, 1873
80. IW Feb. 3, 1882
81. Ibid., March 11, 1882, p. 59
82. MIMC 1864, p. 29
83. Ibid., 1866, p. 21
84. MA Sept. 1867, p. 41; MIMC 1869, p. 32
85. Messmore, pp. 157-58
86. MIMC 1872, pp. 35, 37, 44, 45
87. MIC 1873, p. 17
88. LW April 26, 1872, pp. 17-18
89. LW Dec. 28, 1877, p. 459
90. Catalogue and Report, 25th Year, p. 5
91. MNIC 1879, p. 17
92. Ibid., 1880, p. 12
93. Catalogue and Report, 1883, p. 24
94. Ibid., 1897
95. Foss, Equator, p. 30
96. J M T App., p. 191
97. Messmore, p. 81
98. MIMC 1868, p. 40
99. MA April 11, 1864; Messmore, p. 91
100. MIMC 1868, pp. 55, 83
101. Ibid., 1870, p. 60; J M T App., p. 192
102. J M T App., pp. 193, 242
103. LW Oct. 13, 1871
104. GCJ 1872, pp. 410, 411
105. Discipline, 1872, pp. 60-63
106. J M T Ind. Mal. p. 541
107. MNIC 1882, p. 27
108. MIMC 1871, p. 30
109. Ibid., 1872, p. 26
110. LW Sept. 5, 1873
111. Speer, p. 271; J M T App., p. 292; Taylor, Campaign, p. 343
112. J M T App., p. 293
113. MIC 1874, p. 53
114. WFMS 8th Annual Report, p. 52
115. WFMS 11th Annual Report, p. 19
116. MNIC 1882, p. 28
117. J M T Life I. T., pp. 200-203
118. Baker, pp. 216-17
119. MA 1875, p. 5 (Italics mine)
120. MA Aug. 15, 1871, p. 17
121. MIMC 1866, p. 32
122. R & G II, p. 431
123. Mudge, pp. 75-76
124. RMS 1873, p. 25
125. RMS 1883, p. 29
126. MA 1869, p. 15
127. MA 1873, p. 19
128. MA 1874, p. 59
129. MNIC 1880, pp. 58-59; 1879, p. 56
130. MIC 1873, p. 47
131. MNIC 1884, p. 34 (Italics mine)
132. Ibid., p. 39 (Italics mine)
133. Minutes of the Missionary Committee Nov. 12, 1874, p. 372
134. MIMC 1866, p. 24
135. MNIC 1883, p. 5
136. MIC 1876, p. 11
137. Ibid. p. 10
138. Ibid. p. 14
139. Ibid. p. 23
140. MNIC 1887 Statistics
141. Ibid. 1878, p. 35
142. Decennial, 1882, p. 269
143. MNIC 1885, pp. 92-93
144. LW Feb. 12, 1875, p. 378
145. MNIC 1882, p. 93; 1889, p. 41
146. RMS XLII 1862, p. 37
147. GCJ 1868, p. 282
148. Ibid. (Italics mine)
149. J M T App., p. 363
150. MIC 1876, p. 67
151. GCJ 1876, p. 106
152. GCJ 1864, p. 219
153. J M T Ind. Mal. p. 277
154. Ibid. p. 293
155. GCJ 1872, p. 421
156. Lovett, pp. 211, 219-20
157. Kumaon, p. 7
158. MIC 1875, p. 7; 1876, p. 9
159. MIC 1872, p. 56
160. MIC, 1876, p. 29

161. B H B Biographies
162. MNIC, 1884, p. 45
163. Ibid. 1885, p. 56
164. B H B Biographies
165. Ibid.
166. MNIC, 1904, p. 66
167. MA May 18, 1869
168. WFMS 4th Annual Report, p. 22

CHAPTER V

1. J M T App., p. 279
2. Taylor, Campaign, p. 101
3. Taylor, Missions, p. 118
4. Taylor, Campaign, pp. 209-210
Robbins, p. 6
5. Taylor, Missions, p. 122
6. Taylor, Campaign, p. 203
7. V and V, p. 226
8. Taylor, Campaign, pp. 219-24
9. Ibid., 234
10. Taylor, Campaign, p· 240
11. Joyner
12. Taylor, Campaign, pp. 270-72
13. BG Sept. 20, 1873, p. 233
14. Joyner
15. J M T Ind. Mal., Frontispiece, p. 208
16. LW, July 11, 1873, p. 106
17. Taylor, Campaign, pp. 286-87
18. BG Dec. 27, 1873, p. 345
19. Taylor, Missions, p. 142
20. MIC 1874, p. 41
21. Ibid., p. 43; 1875, pp. 50-51
22. MIC 1874, p. 44
23. MIC 1875, pp. 50-51
24. Taylor, Campaign, p. 300
25. BG March 9, 1878, p. 11
26. BG June 27, 1874, p. 129
27. Taylor, Campaign, pp. 318-19
28. BG July 11, 1874, p. 145
29. Stephens, Intro.
30. Taylor, Campaign, pp. 322-23
31. BG March 19, 1875, p. 11
32. LW July 18, 1879
33. BG Dec. 19, 1874 p. 329; Taylor, Campaign, pp. 325-26
34. Taylor, Campaign, pp. 361-64, 383
35. MIC 1875, pp. 56-57; 1876, p. 65
36. BG July 15, 1876, p. 153
37. MIC 1876, p. 69
38. BG Jan. 22, 1876, p. 369
39. GCJ 1904, pp. 597-600
40. BG May 23, 1874, p. 91
41. LW Nov. 24, 1876, p. 349
42. BG Nov. 18, 1876, p. 297
43. J M T App., p. 353
44. BG Jan. 13, 1883, pp. 19-20
45. BG Feb. 6, 1886, p. 84
46. Taylor, Campaign, pp. 396-97
47. Price, Jubilee, pp. 213-14
48. BG Feb. 13, 1886, p. 102
49. J M T Ind. and Mal., p. 301
50. J M T App. p. 358

CHAPTER VI

1. Robbins, pp. 7-8
2. BG Nov. 30, 1878, p. 313;
Dec. 18, 1880, p. 537
3. V and V, p. 230
4. MSIC 1887, p. 26
5. BG Feb. 6, 1886, p. 82; Feb. 13, 1886
6. V and V p. 229
7. MSIC 1887, p. 13
8. BG Aug. 28, 1880, p. 306
9. BG Feb. 4, 1888, p. 67
10. MA 1874, pp. 52-53
11. BG 1885, p. 581; 1886, p. 371
12. BG 1874, p. 322
13. V and V, p. 242
14. Taylor, Campaign, p. 235
15. Gospel, 1887, p. 59
16. BG Aug. 22, 1874, p.193;
June 17, 1876 p. 120
17. V and V, p. 361
18. BG March 14, 1885, p. 143
19. BG Feb. 7, 1874, p. 396;
Aug. 22, 1874, p. 193
20. BG June 17, 1876, p. 120
21. V and V, p. 361
22. MSIC 1887, p. 28
23. Ibid., 1883, p. 25
24. Gospel, 1887, p. 55
25. J M T App., p. 322
26. J M T Journal, Jan. 17, 1874
27. J M T App., pp. 332-33
28. LW Feb. 27, 1874, p. 370
29. Joyner, pp. 12-13
30. J M T App., pp. 337, 339 373
31. Warne, Ideals, pp. 60-61
32. LW April 28, 1876
33. LW Dec. 3, 1875, pp. 422-23
34. BG May 5, 1877, p. 73
35. WFMS 11th Annual Report, p. 10
36. IW Feb. 18, 1882, p. 562
37. Taylor, Campaign, p. 296
38. BG March 7, 1874
39. BG Dec. 19, 1874
40. BG Dec. 18, 1881, p. 786
41. BG Dec. 3, 1881, p. 621;
July 29, 1882
42. MSIC 1887, p. 39
43. Stephens, II; Baker, 425
44. MSIC 1882, pp. 16-17
45. Weston, Retrospect, p. 60
46. LW June 11, 1880, p. 121; June 18, p. 139; July 2, p. 157; July 9, p. 174
47. BG Feb. 1877, p. 386

48. MSIC 1883, p. 17
49. Ward, History, pp. 4-9
50. Gospel, Dec. 1900, pp. 534-37
51. R & G III pp. 137-38
52. MSIC 1887, p. 41
53. Gospel, Dec. 1900, pp. 534-37
54. MSIC 1893, p. 34
55. MSIC 1896, p. 31
56. MHC 1949, p. 124
57. MSIC 1902, p. 31
58. Taylor, Campaign, p. 275
59. MA 1874, pp. 52-53
60. BG Feb. 21, 1874, p. 409
61. BG Dec. 20, 1873, p. 334
62. BG July 21, 1877, p. 162
63. V and V p. 367
64. BG 1885, p. 339
65. LW March 8, 1878, p. 579
66. Price, Jubilee, p. 221
67. BG March 21, 1887, p. 326
68. Field Sketches, 1910, pp. 1-2
69. BG April 29, 1876, p. 66
70. BG May 27, 1887, p. 326
71. BG Oct. 27, 1888, p. 679
72. Gospel, 1887, p. 93
73. MSIC 1882, p. 21
74. BG Oct. 27, 1888, p. 679
75. Field Sketches, 1910, April
76. LW June 4, 1880, p. 14; V and V, p. 460
77. BG Aug. 8, 1885, p. 501
78. V and V, p. 461
82. MSIC 1881, p. 29
83. Ward, Our Work, pp. 73-75
84. Taylor, Campaign, p. 327; MIC 1875, p. 42
85. MSIC 1881, p. 33
86. BG June 12, 1886, p. 371; V and V, p. 535
87. BG Nov. 7, 1885, p. 711
88. BG Sept. 1, 1883, p. 550
89. MIC 1876, p. 55
90. BG Feb. 10, 1877, p. 393
91. V and V, p. 413
92. MSIC, 1882 p. 22
93. BG 1882, p. 499
94. V and V, pp. 475-76
95. MBC 1888
96. BG May 28, 1887, p. 447
97. BG July 30, 1887, p. 487
98. BG March 24, 1888
99. BG Feb. 26, 1881, p. 693
100. BG Jan. 8, 1881, p. 589
101. BG March 12, 1881, pp. 19-20
102. MSIC 1881, p. 23; 1883, p. 25

CHAPTER VII

1. Ward, Our Work, pp. 9-12
2. Ibid., pp. 20-21
3. MSIC 1891, p. 23
4. Ibid., 1890, p. 29
5. V and V, p. 764
6. MSIC 1891, pp. 21-22
7. V and V, pp. 670-71
8. MSIC 1913, pp. 69-70
9. V and V, pp. 622-23, 765-66
10. Ward, Our Work, pp. 62, 70-72, 83
11. V and V, p. 611
12. Ward, Our Work, pp. 136-37
13. V and V, p. 620
14. Ibid., pp. 612-14
15. Gospel, Feb. 1887, p. 55
16. WWM Jan. 1889, p. 5
17. V and V, p. 766
18. J. Jacob oral report; V and V, p. 624
19. MSIC 1904, p. 25
20. Ibid., 1905, p. 23
21. BG April 10, 1880, p. 66
22. V and V, p. 509
23. Report of Faith Mission, 1880
24. MSIC 1891, pp. 10, 30
25. B H B Directory, 1892, p. 286
26. MSIC 1893, p. 26
27. Ibid., p. 25
28. V and V, p. 514
29. Ward, Our Work, p. 204
30. Ibid., p. 233
31. MSIC 1893, p. 19
32. Ward, Our Work, pp. 265-66
33. V and V, pp. 743 ff.
34. Ward, Our Work, pp. 267-68
35. Ward, W. T., pp. 47-49

CHAPTER VIII

1. Messmore, p. 178
2. MNIC 1880, p. 60
3. MSIC 1879, p. 7
4. LW Jan. 23, 1880, p. 493
5. J M T Journal, Jan. 15, 1880
6. J M T Ind. and Mal., p. 140
7. MNIC 1882, Appendix
8. Delegated, 1881, p. 6
9. Worley, p. 138
10. GCJ, 1884, p. 349
11. GCJ 1884, p. 243
12. Ibid., pp. 349-50
13. Ibid., p. 285
14. Worley, p. 140
15. J M T Journal, July 11, 1884
16. Messmore, pp. 178-79
17. Delegated, 1881, p. 6; MCC, 1885, p. 9
18. Ibid., p. 5

J M T Journal, Jan. 17, 1885
MCC 1889, p. 6
GCJ 1856, pp. 144-66
MIMC 1868, p. 59
Minutes of the Missionary Committee, Nov. 9, 1887; NWCA 1912, p. 205
J M T Journal, June 21, 1884
BG Aug. 13, 1887, p. 513
26. BG Aug. 20, 1887, p. 534; Aug. 27, p. 552
27. Letter dated July 4, 1887 to J. W. Waugh
28. GCJ 1888, pp. 396-97
29. J M T Journal, May 29, 1888
30. BG June 2, 1888
31. BG Dec. 22, 1888, p. 803

CHAPTER IX

1. MCC 1887, pp. 8, 17, 18
2. MBC 1888, p. 7
3. Ibid., p. 15
4. B T B Warne, pp. 37-38
5. Joyner
6. MBC 1892, p. 25
7. Warne, Diary, Sept. 28, 1900
8. British Weekly, April 7, 1921
9. Warne, Diary, April 17, 18, 1895
10. MBC 1892, p. 25
11. Warne, Diary, Jan. 12-14, 1893
12. WCA July 26, 1911, p. 8
13. V and V pp. 424-26; Lee
14. J M T App., p. 333
15. J M T Journal, Oct. 7, 1878
16. BG June 2, 1883, p 333
17. MBC 1897
18. B. C. Man., pp. 5-7
19. Griffiths, pp. 2-5
20. MCC 1904, p. 40
21. MBC 1895
22. Griffiths, p. 6
23. V and V, p. 320
24. Ibid., pp. 524-25; WCA Dec. 20, 1911
25. B. C. Man.
26. Ibid., p. 7
27. V and V, pp. 676-78
28. MBC 1897
29. V and V, p. 679
30. Ibid., p. 322
31. B H B Directory, 1892, pp. 186, 192
32. NWCA March 27, 1912, p. 10
33. V and V, p. 687
34. MByC 1892, pp. 5-6
(1) From Bengal Conference
(2) From South India Conference
35. MByC 1892, pp. 28-30
36. V and V, pp. 655-62
37. MByC 1906, p. 25
38. Ross
39. MSIC 1891, p. 4
40. Ferrer
41. Knox, pp. 23-26
42. Robbins, pp. 29-30
43. WWM 1889, p. 7
44. MA 1874, pp. 52-53
45. Ross; MGC 1925, pp. 72-73
46. MSIC 1891, p. 20
47. MByC 1894, p. 26
48. MByC 1892, p. 28; 1893, p. 24
49. MSIC 1890, p. 21
50. MByC 1899, p. 48; 1901, pp. 2, ii
51. MByC 1896-97, p. 29
52. MByC 1897, p. 41
53. MByC 1900, p. 19, Statistics
54. MByC 1895, p. 20
55. MByWC 1900, p. 22; 1901, p. 20
56. MByC 1893, p. 26; 1892, p. 29
57. MByC 1897, p. 28
58. MByC 1901, pp. 44-45
59. Ibid., pp. 47-50
60. MByC 1892, p. 33
61. MByC 1893, p. 17
62. MByC 1892, p. 36
63. MByC 1893, p. 35
64. Ibid., p. 31; MByWC 1894, p. 25
65. MByWC 1901, pp. 37-38; 1894, p. 25
MByC 1901, p. 28; Field Sketches, Sept. 1908
66. MByC 1893, p. 31
67. MByWC 1896, pp. 34-35
68. Ibid., 1900, p. 27
69. Ibid., 1899, pp. 47-48; 1900, p. 27
70. Ibid., 1902, pp. 25-26
71. Gospel, 1887, p. 58
72. BG Nov. 20, 1886, p. 742; June 25, 1887, p. 406
73. MByWC 1892, p. 21
74. MByC 1900, p. 27
75. MByC 1895, p. 27
76. MByC, 1896 p. 39
77. MByC 1899, p. 35
78. V and V, pp. 433-434
79. V and V, p. 221
80. MCPMC 1905, p. 2
81. MCC 1904, p. 52
82. MCC 1892, p. 26
83. WWM Aug. 1892, pp. 1-2; Das, Jubilee, p. 24
84. MCC 1900, p. 21
85. MWCA March 27, 1912
86. Wilkie, p. 17
87. Price, Jubilee, pp. 199-200
88. Wilkie, p. 22
89. Ibid., p. 19
90. Thoburn I.
91. MCC 1900, p. 21
92. MCC 1896, pp. 34, 59; 1898, p. 53
93. The Road, pp. 9-10; MWIC 1894. p. 56
94. MCC 1900, pp. 33-34
95. MCC 1894, pp. 31, 56
96. Wilkie, p. 27
97. MNWIC 1894, p. 5
98. V and V, p. 648

99. Scott, Famine Land, p. 102
100. Ibid., pp. 124-25
101. V and V, p. 489; Scott, Famine Land, p. 244
102. V and V, p. 780
103. Ibid., p. 285
104. Scott, Famine Land, p. 165; Fifty Years p. 243
105. MNIC 1888, p. 57
106. Ibid., 1889, p. 43
107. BG March 24, 1888; MBC 1889, p. 2
108. V and V, pp. 643-44
109. Scott, Famine Land, p. 158
110. Price, Jubilee, p. 192
111. MNWIC 1893, Statistics and P. E. Report
112. MBC 1892, pp. 30, 35

CHAPTER X

1. LW Dec. 5, 1879
2. LW April 16, 1880, p. 30
3. BG April 17, 1880, p. 75
4. J M T App., pp. 392-393
5. Baker, pp. 217-18
6. V and V, pp. 437-39
7. MSIC 1882, p. 19
8. Knox, p. 263 ff.
9. Smith, Julius, p. 221
10. Boggess, Biographical Sketches
11. MSIC 1887, pp. 29-31
12. NWCA March 20, 1912, p. 12
13. Smith, Julius, pp. 240-41
14. MBMC 1901, p. 16
15. Smith, Julius, pp. 272-73
16. Ibid., pp. 286-87
17. J M T Ind. and Mal., p. 453
18. Letter to J. O. Peck from P. M. Buck, Cor. Sec., dated Aug. 24, 1899 (Microfilm, D. W. M.)
19. Price, Jubilee, pp. 229-30
20. MBMC 1913, p. 23
21. MBurmaC 1933, p. 28
22. Harwood, p. 18
23. J M T Ind. Mal., pp. 522-24
24. MNIC 1885, pp. 74,78
25. J M T Ind. and Mal., pp. 526-27
26. WWM July 1902, p. 4
27. MSIC 1887, pp. 32-33
28. WFMS 1887, pp. 23-24
29. MCC 1887, pp. 8-9
30. J M T Journal, Nov. 15, 1887
31. Gospel, 1887, p. 564
32. GCJ 1888, pp. 434-35
33. R & G III pp. 182-87
34. Letter from Bishop Thoburn to J. O. Peck, April 7, 1890 (Microfilm—D. W. M.)
35. WWM Nov. 1890, p.142
36. MCC 1892, p.13
37. Typed unpublished account on B.F. West's letterhead.
38. R & G III p. 195
39. Ferrer
40. GCJ 1900
41. Mal. Mess., March 1899
42. Ibid. Oct. 1899, p. 1
43. Price, Jubilee, p. 241
44. Gospel, June 1900, pp. 314-16
45. Mal. Mess., Oct. 1899. p. 1
46. GCJ 1900
47. Price, Jubilee, p. 243
48. Mal. Mess., Nov.1900, p .1
49. WWM Jan.1902, p.9
59. MCC 1904, p. 52
51. MCC 1908, pp. 88-89
52. MCC 1920, p. 47

CHAPTER XI

1. MCC 1885, p. 15; 1904, Statistics
2. MCC 1892, p. 43
3. MCC 1894, p. 17
4. Messmore, p. 239
5. MISC 1891, p. 29
6. MCC 1894, pp. 5, 59
7. MCC 1896, p. 65
8. MCC 1900, p. 46
9. MCC 1896, pp. 19, 46, 66
10. MCC 1892, p. 24 (Italics mine)
11. MCC 1894, p. 39
12. MCC 1896, pp. 42, 62-63
13. Foss, Equator, pp. 158-59
14. MCC 1904, p. 49
15. Manual of Woman's Conference, 1883, pp. 1-3
16. MCC 1887, p. 19
17. MCC 1892, p. 46
18. MCC 1896, p. 59
19. J M T Life I.T., p. 210 ff.
20. MCC 1899, p. 14
21. GCJ 1888, pp. 435-36
22. Baker, pp. 256-57
23. J M T Life I. T.,
24. Unpublished Log Book, Calcutta Girl School
25. MNIC 1891, p. 64
26. Joyner, pp. 1-3
27. MIC 1872, p. 33; 1874, p. 47
28. MIC 1873, pp. 54-55; 47
29. Unpublished Manuscript, Leonar Theological College, Jabalpur
30. MCC 1894, pp. 56-57
31. MCC 1904, p. 68
32. MCC 1894, p. 65
33. MCC 1896, pp. 67-68

34. MCC 1898, p. 63
35. Letter to J. F. Goucher from Bishop Thoburn, dated July 9, 1890 (Microfilm, D. W. M.)
36. MCC 1900, p. 31
37. MCC 1898, p. 43
38. MCC 1896, p. 36
39. IW Reprint
40. Landor, The Forbidden Land
41. Bhot Typescript
42. Typed account by Miss Sheldon
43. Jackson, p. 13
44. JMT Light
45. Jackson, pp. 10-12
46. MNIC 1886, p. 51
47. MNIC 1887, p. 56
48. WWM March 1899, p. 5
49. BMMS March 21, 1899, p. 387
50. Ibid., 1899 p. 478, p. 57, p. 88
51. CA August 3, 1899, p. 1230; Mal. Mess., September 1899
52. BMMS June 19, 1900, p. 256
53. Ibid. September 18, 1900
54. Ibid., April 23, 1901, p. 52
55. WWM March 4, 1901, p. 4.
56. MCC 1896, pp. 44-45
57. MCC 1900, p. 23
58. MCC 1898, p. 28
59. MCC 1900, p. 25
60. GCJ 1908, p. 433
61. Messmore, pp. 273, 298

CHAPTER XII

1. Banerjea, p. 88
2. Ibid., pp. 98-101
3. GCJ 1908, p. 844
4. Wasson, The Influence of Missionary Expansion, p. 13
5. MCC 1904, p. 36
6. MCC 1920, p. 112
7. NWCA April 22, 1903
8. GCJ 1936, p. 1271
9. Warne, Diary, May 20, 1916
10. GCJ 1920, p. 455
11. Warne, Diary, October 1921
12. CA July 17, 1930
13. Zion's Herald, February 1, 1928, p. 138
14. IW May 22, 1930, pp. 321-22
15. B T B Chitambar
16. MCC 1940 p. ii
17. Pickett, Mass Movements, p. 5
18. Subhan
19. Ecumenical, 1881, p. 484
20. Ibid., p. 487
21. MNWIC 1902, p. 13
22. Decennial, 1882, p. ix
23. Ibid., 1902, pp. 6-11
24. MNIC 1920, p. 72
25. MNIC 1912, p. xxiii
26. GCJ 1928, pp. 420, 431
27. V and V, p. 593
28. MNIWC 1938 (Dec.) p. 57
29. Ibid., 1941 (Jan.) p. 61
30. Ibid., 1950 (Jan.) p. 55
31. Gaz., 1953, p. 142
32. V and V, p. 572
33. MNIC 1921, p. 81
34. MLC 1934, p. 39
35. MLC 1940, p. 30
36. Gaz., 1953, p. 142
37. MNIC 1916, p. 111
38. MNIC 1919, p. 87 (Italics Mine)
39. Ibid.
40. Leonard Theological Statement by A. A. Parker
41. MNIWC 1906, pp. 112-13
42. V and V, p. 494
43. MIRC 1922, p. 41; 1923, p. 105
44. MIRC 1926, p. 32
45. Report of Ex. Sec. D. W. M., 1941, p. 31
46. IW November 4, 1954
47. Ibid., p. 346
48. Report of Ex. Sec., D. W. M., 1941, p. 63; IW September 2, 1943, p. 275
49. Report of Ex. Sec. D. W. M., 1943, p. 214; Ibid., 1944, p. 65
50. Gaz., 1953, p. 142
51. Quoted by Bishop Pickett to Ex. Sec. of Vellore Board, January 8, 1954
52. MNWIWC 1906, pp. 95, 110-111
53. WFMS 1905-1906, p. 134
54. IW November 4, 1954, p. 352
55. The Sunday Statesman, March 21, 1954, p. 4
56. MLC 1954, pp. 42-43
57. IW November 4, 1954, p. 353
58. Wilson, pp. 149, 176
59. MCC 1898, p. 32
60. MNIC 1898, p. 23
61. MCC 1898, p. 62
62. MCC 1908, p. 34
63. B T B Chitambar, p. 29
64. MCC 1904, p. 48
65. MCC 1908, p. 64
66. MCC 1920, pp. 12, 20, 31
67. MCC 1923, pp. 146-48
68. GCJ 1924, p. 539
69. MCC 1936, pp. 16, 78
70. MCC 1944, pp. 33, 97

CHAPTER XIII

1. MCC 1923, pp. 102, 103
2. MByC 1906, pp. 70-77
3. V and V, p. 243
4. MByC 1907, pp. 19,62
5. MByC 1909, pp. 25, 37
6. MByC 1925 (Jan:), pp. 55-56; (Dec.) pp.126-27
7. MByC 1925 (Jan.) pp. 126-27
8. MByC 1926, p. 212; 1929, p. 123
9. MByC 1930, p. 200
10. Gaz., 1953, p. 119; MByC 1954, p. 33
11. MByC 1926, p. 213
12. MByC 1954 p. 33
13. IW Nov. 4, 1954, p. 352
14. MByC 1940, pp. 39-40; 1954, p. 30
15. MByC 1925 (Jan.) p. 43
16. MByC 1926, p. 202
17. V and V, p. 372
18. MByC 1896 (Dec.) p. 27
19. MByC 1898, p. 31
20. MByC 1906 p. 77
21. MByC 1929, p. 125
22. MByC 1954, pp. 32, 35
23. MByC 1906, p. 54
24. MByC 1906 (Dec.) p. 52
25. MGC 1924-25, p. 29
26. Ibid., pp. 72-73
27. MByC 1906, pp. 61-62
28. MByC 1909, p. 12
29. MByC 1913, pp. 80-81
30. Gaz., 1953
31. MByC 1906, p. 57
32. MByC 1907, p. 28
33. MByC 1913, p. 79
34. MGC 1929, pp. 120, 133
35. MGC 1954, 1955
36. MByC 1909 (Jan.) p. 36
37. MByC 1906, p. 59
38. Report Godhra Normal School, Reminiscences
39. Christian Education, 1940, First Quarter; Aug. 17, 1943
40. MGC 1940, p. 45
41. MGC 1954, p. 48
42. Baker, pp. 143-146
43. MByC 1817, pp. 17, 40; 1898, p. 47
44. MByC 1906 (Dec.) p. 21
45. MByC 1909, pp. 13, 37
46. Ibid., p. 13
47. MByC 1910 (Dec.) p. 60; V and V, p. 721
48. Gaz., 1953
49. MByC 1909 (Jan.) p. 37
50. MByC 1913, pp. 86-87
51. MCC 1925, p. 24
52. IW Nov. 4, 1954, p. 351
53. MGC 1954, p. 40
54. MCC Statistics

CHAPTER XIV

1. GCJ 1908, p. 456
2. GCJ 1920, p. 408
3. MCC 1908
4. Lovett, pp. 126-28
5. MSIC 1905, pp. 35-38
6. MSIC 1910 (Jan.) p. 44
7. MSIC 1910, (Dec.) pp. 43-45; V and V, p. 813
8. Ibid., p. 814
9. Ibid., 813
10. Typescript—E. C. Reddy
11. MSIC 1900, p. 31,
12. MSIC 1892, p. 19
13. MSIC 1895, p. 22
14. V and V, p. 606; MSIC 1910 (Dec.) 61
15. MSIC 1893, p. 18
16. MSIC 1901, p. 31
17. MSIC 1925, p. 326
18. MSIC 1911, p. 45
19. MSIC 1911, p. 46
20. MSIC 1906, p. 35
21. MSIC 1911, p. 45
22. MSIC 1907, p. 52; MSIWC 1924, p. 33
23. MSIC 1925, p. 255; MSIWC 1924, p. 33
24. MSIC 1925, p. 255
25. Gaz., 1953, p. 144
26. MSIC 1893, p. 18
27. MSIC 1895 (Jan.) p. 22
28. MSIC 1895 (Dec.) p. 21
29. MSIC 1907, p. 52
30. Gaz. 1953, p. 144
31. MSIC 1954, p. 118
32. MSIC 1900, p. 30
33. MSIC 1910, p. 67
34. Gaz., 1953, p. 44
35. MSIC 1954; IW Nov. 4, 1954, p. 350
36. MSIC 1909, p. 41
37. IW Aug. 2, 1934, p. 484
38. WFMS 1909, p. 119
39. V and V, pp. 515-16
40. Ibid.
41. IW Nov. 4, 1954, p. 350
42. Ibid.
43. MSIC 1919 p. 367
44. MSIC 1892, p. 17
45. MSIC 1904 (Jan.) p. 32
46. MSIC 1905, p. 28; 1910, p. 59
47. MSIC 1910 (Jan.), p. 59
48. MSIC (Dec.) p. 58
49. MSIC 1913, p. 43, Statistics
50. MSIC 1926 p. 395, Statistics

51. GCJ 1924, p. 540
52. MSIC 1925, pp. 199, 209
53. MHC 1926, p. 7
54. MSIC 1895, p. 21
55. MSIC 1906, p. 28
56. Ibid., 1907, p. 39; 1909, p. 46
57. MSIC 1896 (Dec.) p. 31; 1920, p. 58
58. MSIC 1921, p. 176
59. MSIC 1922, p. 86
60. MME pp. 27-30
61. MSIC 1910, p. 51
62. Strength (Mrs. Parker); Narrative (R Partridge)
63. MSIC 1909, p. 65
64. V and V, p. 671; MSIC 1906, p. 28
65. MSIC 1907, p. 52
66. MHC 1949, p. 33
67. MSIC 1905, p. 23
68. MSIC 1909, p. 65
69. MHC 1949, p. 32
70. MSIC 1906, p. 28
71. MSIC 1904, p. 45; 1905 (Jan.) p. 45; (Dec.) p. 22; 1909, p. 46
72. MSIC 1910, p. 26
73. V and V, p. 673; MSIC 1913, p. 51
74. MSIC 1923
75. MSIC 1927, p. 21
76. IW Nov. 4, 1954, p 344
77. V and V, p. 747 ff.
79. MCPWC 1905, p. 5
79. Ibid., 1909, p. 10
80. Ibid., 1910, p. 27
81. Ibid., 1913, p. 38
82. V and V p. 750 ff.
83. Ibid., p. 754
84. MCPC 1918, pp. 242-43
85. MCPC 1945, pp. 28-30
86. V and V, p. 758 ff.
87. MCPC 1913, p. 13
88. MCPC 1929, p. 118
89. MCC 1912, p. 73 ff.
90. Gaz., 1953, p. 120 ff.
91. MCPC 1954, p. 37
92. MCPWC 1905, p. 12
93. MCPC 1929, p. 118
94. MCPWC 1908
95. MCPC 1915
96. MCPWC 1905, p. 24
97. MCPWC 1907 (Jan.) p. 37
98. MCPMC 1905, pp. 39, 40, 42
99. MCPWC 1908, p. 8
100. MCPMC 1905, p. 42
101. MCPC 1914, p. 62 ff.
102. MCPC 1915
103. MCPC 1921, pp. 192 ff.
104. MCPC 1930, p. 184
105. Gaz., 1953, p. 121
106. V and V, p. 819-20
107. MCPWC 1909, p. 19
108. MCPC 1930, p. 179
109. MCPC 1940, p. 21
110. MCPC 1954, p. 38
111. MCPWC 1908, pp. 13.14; 1909 (Dec.) p. 15
112. MCPWC 1909, pp. 15-16; 1912 p. 27
113. MCPWC 1909 (Dec.) pp. 11-12; 1912, p. 26; 1913, p. 28
114. V and V, p. 351
115. Typescript, Miss Soule
116. V and V, p. 347
117. MCC Statistics

CHAPTER XV

1. MBC 1926, p. 225
2. MBWC 1938, p. 15
3. V and V, pp. 677 ff.
4. MBWC 1929, p. 37; Gaz., 1953, p. 117
5. MBWC 1929, p. 37
6. MBC Appointments
7. Typescript, Miss Soule
8. MBC 1941, p. 35
9. V and V, p. 681
10. MBWC 1913, p. 40
11. MBWC 1919, (Dec.)
12. MBWC 1921, (Jan.)
13. MBWC 1924
14. MBC 1922, p. 144
15. MBC 1927, p. 233
16. MBC 1951, p. 36
17. Lee Memorial Superintendent's File.
18. MBC 1951, p. 35
19. MBC 1954, p. 32
20. MBC 1926, p. 225
21. MBC 1947, p. 23; 1948, p. 22
22. GCJ 1920, p. 546
23. MNIC 1921, p. 35
24. MLC 1921, p. 16
25. Warne, Diary, Feb. 2, 1921
26. V and V, p. 693
27. MBC 1908, p. 41
28. V and V, p. 698
29. Ibid., p. 703
30. MLC 1921, p. 36; 1922, p. 33
31. MLC 1926, p. 34
32. Ibid.
33. MCC 1948, p. 45
34. V and V, p. 188
35. Ibid., p. 215
36. Ibid., pp. 594-95
37. MNIWC 1948, p. 42
38. MNIWC 1951, pp. 43-44
39. Report of Ex. Sec. D.W.M. 1944, p. 66
40. MIRMC 1922, p. 23
41. MIRMC 1924, p. 6
42. MNWIC 1908, xiii
43. Typescript, C. B. Stuntz
44. MIRMC 1922, pp. 51-52; MIRC 1934, p. 29; MIRC 1935, p. 74
45. MIRMC I923, p. 124

46. MIRC 1936, p. 40
47. Gaz., 1953, p. 148
48. MIRMC 1922, p. 6
49. MIRC 1939, pp. 210, 211
50. Gaz., 1953, p. 148
51. MNWIWC 1902, p. 70
52. Ibid., 1907, p. 54
53. MIRC 1953, p. 54
54. MIRC 1938, p. 163; 1939, p. 211
55. MIRC 1934, p. 27
56. MIRC 1941, p. 31; 1946, p. 79
57. MIRC 1936, pp. 34, 35; 1938, p. 153
58. MIRC 1940, p. 21
59. MIRC 1933 (Jan.) p. 28; 1936, p. 35; 1938, p. 153
60. MIRC 1941 (Oct.) p. 28
61. MIRC 1925, p. 37
62. MIRC 1948, p. 22
63. MIRC 1953, p. 50
64. MIRC 1939, p. 24
65. MIRC 1949 (Jan.) p. 29
66. Ibid., p. 44; 1949 (Nov.) pp. 32-33
67. MIRC 1949 (Jan.) p. 33
68. Typescript, C. B. Stuntz
69. MIRC 1951, pp. 39-40
70. MIRC 1953, pp. 62-63
71. Typescript, C. B. Stuntz; Gaz., 1953; p. 147
72. MIRC 1939, pp. 200, 205
73. Ibid., p. 205
74. Ibid., p. 200
75. Gaz., 1953, p. 148
76. MCC Statistics

CHAPTER XVI

1. MCC 1944, p. 91
2. MDC 1949, p. 14
3. MDC 1951, Statistics
4. MCC 1952, p. 79
5. MNWIC 1894, p. 14
6. MNWIC 1902 Statistics
7. Ibid., p. vi
8. V and V, p. 518; MNWIC 1924; p. 27
9. MNWIC 1902, pp. 13, 16, 23; V and V, p. 519; MIRC 1938, p. 158
10. MNWIC 1914, pp. 95 ff.
11. MIRC 1939, pp. 209 ff.
12. Ibid.
13. MNWIC 1914, pp. 79-80
14. V and V, p. 728
15. MNWIC 1931 (Feb.) p. 221-22
16. MNWIC 1924, p. 41; 1925, p. 45
17. MNWIC 1931 (Feb.) p. 221
18. MNWIC 1941, p. 32; MCC 1940, p. 22
19. MNWIC 1925 (Dec.) p. 47
20. MNWIC 1931, p. 222
21. MNWIC 1933 (Jan.) p. 35
22. MNWIC 1926, p. 46
23. MNWIC 1927, p. 62
24. MNWIC 1935, p. 126
25. MDC 1949, p. 50
26. MNWIC 1913, p. 89
27. MNWIC 1924, p. 45
28. Price, Jubilee, p. 105
29. MNWIC 1902, p. xvii
30. WFMS 1909, p. xvii
31. Bishop Pickett's News Letter, Nov. 1953
32. MDC 1954, p. 9
32a. MNWIC 1927, pp. 60-61
33. Gaz., 1953, p. 127
34. MNIC 1926 (Nov.) p. 9
35. Bulloch, 1892; MNIC 1926, p. 36
36. Catalogue and Report, 1900, pp. 6-7
37. Report of Ex. Sec. D.W.M., 1951, p. 54
38. WFMS 1909, p. 109
39. WFMS 1911, p. 102
41. WFMS 1905-1906, p. 128
42. IW Aug. 2, 1934, p. 484
43. V and V, p. 28; WFMS 1909, p. 103
44. MNIC 1941, p. 4
45. Medics, p. 7 ff; IW Nov. 4, 1954, p. 347
46. Butler, C., p. 41
47. MNIC 1875, p. 8
48. MCC Statistics

CHAPTER XVII

1. Christian Century, June 20, 1956, p. 742
2. MCC 1952, p. 45
3. Hindustan Times, Dec. 1955
4. Christian Century, Nov. 10, 1954, p. 1363
5. MCC 1920, p. 47
6. MCC 1928, pp. 23-24
7. MCC 1931, p. 93
8. Ibid., p. 73
9. Christian Century, Nov. 16, 1955, p. 1340
10. MLC 1954, pp. 52-53
11. IW Dec. 16, 1943
12. IW May 4, 1944, p. 140
13. MNIC 1880, p. 62
14. MCC 1935, p. 87; Letters, E. M. Moffatt
14a. MCC 1944, p. 90
15. MCC 1887, p. 14

16. MCC 1892, p. 32
17. MCC 1898, pp. 46-47
18. MCC 1900, pp. 12, 32
19. Ibid.
20. King
21. MCC 1920, pp. 54-55
22. MCC 1923, pp. vi, 57, 86, 87
23. King
24. MCC 1935, p. 112
25. MCC 1931, p. 86
26. IW Aug. 1921, pp. 12-13
27. Nichols
28, GCJ 1904, p. 660

CHAPTER XVIII

1. MCC 1944, p. 124
2. Ibid., p. 46
3. MCC 1953, pp. 68-71
4. Report of Ex. Sec., D.W.M., 1947, p. 213
5. GCJ, 1920, pp. 158, 160-163
6. IW Nov. 23, 1944, p. 294
7. Ibid.
8. MCC 1944, p. 83
9. Report of Ex. Sec., D.W.M., 1943, p. 59
10. NWIWC, 1904, p. 52
11. IW Aug. 31, 1921, p. 665
12. Cooperation, A Tentative Report, Typescript
13. MCC 1940, pp. 73-75
14. IW Aug. 31, 1921, p. 679
15. MMPWC, 1954, p. 128
16. MCC 1940, p. xxx
17. MCC 1948, pp. 48-49
18. WWM 1902, p. 6
19. J M T Life I T, p. 365
20. Selected, Author unknown

Index

PRINTED AND PUBLISHED FOR THE EXECUTIVE BOARD OF THE METHODIST CHURCH IN SOUTHERN ASIA, BY REV. W. W. BELL AT THE LUCKNOW PUBLISHING HOUSE OF THE METHODIST CHURCH, LUCKNOW, INDIA.